Artificial Cognition Systems

Angelo Loula, State University of Campinas
and State University of Feira de Santana, Brazil

Ricardo Gudwin, State University of Campinas, Brazil

João Queiroz, State University of Campinas
and Federal University of Bahia, Brazil

IDEA GROUP PUBLISHING

Hershey • London • Melbourne • Singapore

Acquisitions Editor: Michelle Potter
Development Editor: Kristin Roth
Senior Managing Editor: Jennifer Neidig
Managing Editor: Sara Reed
Copy Editor: Mike Goldberg
Typesetter: Marko Primorac
Cover Design: Lisa Tosheff
Printed at: Integrated Book Technology

Published in the United States of America by
          Idea Group Publishing (an imprint of Idea Group Inc.)
          701 E. Chocolate Avenue
          Hershey PA 17033
          Tel: 717-533-8845
          Fax: 717-533-8661
          E-mail: cust@idea-group.com
          Web site: http://www.idea-group.com

and in the United Kingdom by
          Idea Group Publishing (an imprint of Idea Group Inc.)
          3 Henrietta Street
          Covent Garden
          London WC2E 8LU
          Tel: 44 20 7240 0856
          Fax: 44 20 7379 0609
          Web site: http://www.eurospanonline.com

Library of Congress Cataloging-in-Publication Data

Artificial cognition systems / Angelo Loula, Ricardo Gudwin and Joao Queiroz, editors.
     p. cm.
  Summary: "This book presents recent research efforts in Artificial Intelligence about building artificial systems capable of performing cognitive tasks. A fundamental issue addressed in this book is if these cognitive processes can have any meaningfulness to the artificial system being built"--Provided by publisher.
  ISBN 1-59904-111-1 (hardcover) -- ISBN 1-59904-112-X (softcover) -- ISBN 1-59904-113-8 (ebook)
  1. Artificial intelligence--Research. 2. Cognitive science--Research. I. Loula, Angelo, 1977- II. Gudwin, Ricardo, 1967- III. Queiroz, Joao, 1963-
  Q335.7A76 2007
  006.3--dc22
                              2006010096

British Cataloguing in Publication Data
A Cataloguing in Publication record for this book is available from the British Library.

Artificial Cognition Systems

Table of Contents

Section II: Methodological Issues

Section III: Cognition and Robotics

Section IV: Cognition in Virtual Agents

Section V: Theoretical and Philosophical Isues

Foreword

The central questions confronting artificial intelligence and cognitive science revolve around the nature of meaning and of mind. Minds are presumed to be the processors of mental content, where that content has the capacity to influence our speech and other behavior. The hard part is figuring out how that is done. Mental states must exercise causal powers that sometimes have the effect of bringing about other mental states (which take the form of shifts from one mental state to another as forms of thought transition) and sometimes have the effect of bringing about physical actions (which occur within a context that includes our beliefs, motives, ethics, abilities, and capabilities). Whether our actions are successful tends to depend upon whether things are as we take them to be (whether our beliefs are true) and the extent to which we have been successful in thinking things through (whether our actions are appropriate).

This volume brings together a collection of interesting studies that address the kinds of questions raised by this general conception and attempt to answer them. One of the underlying issues is how mental states themselves can stand for other things, such as objects and their properties in the world. This has sometimes been called 'the symbol grounding problem," because it concerns the "ground," or basis, that connects mental states to objects and properties in the world. But it is better viewed as "the sign grounding problem," insofar as Charles Peirce explained the distinction between icons (as signs that resemble what they stand for), indices (as signs that are causes or effects of what they stand for) and symbols (as signs that are merely habitually associated with what they stand for). The grounding problem applies across the board for different kinds of signs, but Peirce pointed to the general direction in which its solution lies.

If some signs resemble what they stand for, others are their causes or effects, and others are merely habitually associated with that for which they stand, then the kinds of things that have minds of the most elementary kind must have the capacity to detect and utilize resemblance relations between signs and things; those of an intermediate kind must have the capacity not only to detect and utilize resemblance relations between signs and things but also cause and effect relations between things, while those of a yet higher kind must have not only the capacity to detect and utilize resemblance relations between signs and things as well as cause and effect relations between things, but also have the capacity to acquire and exercise relations between signs and things that are merely habitual. This higher grade of mentality appears to exist in species other than human beings, but has its most extensive expression in our species.

If this approach appears promising for the purpose of illuminating the nature of mind and of meaning, it does not resolve the question of whether, under suitable conditions, it might be possible to create an inanimate machine with at least some of the mental powers of human beings. The lowest level of mentality would do for a start, where iconic minds have the capacity to utilize icons. On first consideration, it seems almost irresistible to infer that digital machines which process data on the basis of its shape, size and relative location must have at least iconic capacity, which in turn implies that they have at least iconic mentality. But for that to be true, it must not only be the case that digital machines process data not as a purely causal process (in the fashion of sieves sorting gains of sand) but that they do so because those shapes, sizes and relative locations resemble that for which they stand. And what is that?

Absent "stand for" relations, processes can be causal without being mental. In terminology derivative of Peirce's theory of signs (or "semiotic"), the question is whether inanimate systems are causal systems that process signs (as "semiotic systems"). That digital machines can become more and more complex with greater and greater capacity (through ingenious design and clever programming) to mimic thought and behavior is not the question. Without any doubt, they can do this with increasing sophistication, as generations past have amply displayed. The question is whether they can overcome the gap between mere causal systems and thinking things, as causal systems of a distinctive kind. If it is possible to establish that inanimate machines can process signs (where those signs stand for something for those machines and not simply for the users of those machines), it will be the occasion to agree that artificial intelligence has been attained.

Of course, the creation of inanimate thinking things is not the only function that digital machines can perform. Throughout human history, after all, there have been three great revolutions: the agricultural revolution (in putting nature to work for us growing food), the industrial revolution (in putting machines to work for us performing physical labor) and the computer revolution (in putting machines to work for us performing tasks that in the past required human minds). The computer revolution continues to make a permanent difference in our lives. The question that remains, which these studies address, concerns the gap that remains between digital machines and thinking things. Whether or not the studies succeed in closing that gap, readers of this book are bound to agree that they provide important analyses and stimulating suggestions that assist us in assessing how close we are coming to creating artificial thinking things.

James H. Fetzer

Preface

Synthetic methodologies (as opposed to analytical ones — cf. Braitenberg, 1984) are characterized by a "reverse" methodology, which allows one to build systems capable of performing cognitive tasks to test and evaluate hypotheses and theories. They have been used to model and simulate cognitive processes (e.g., perception, planning, navigation, inference, communication and language) from many different perspectives. Evolutionary robotics, cognitive robotics, artificial life, animat research, adaptive behavior, computational neuroethology and computational semiotics are some of the interdisciplinary areas of research dedicated to the synthetic design of **artificial cognition systems**. These areas have been designing environments that work as experimental labs, where it is possible to test the predictions derived from theoretical models. They are based on different computational tools and have various ambitions, being heavily influenced by formal theoretical constraints and empirical constraints in the design of the environment, the morphological definitions of sensors and effectors and the implementation of cognitive architecture and processes of the conceived systems.

In their turn, simulations offer the opportunity to quantify and formalize ideas, concepts and propositions constituting a theory in terms of programming (Parisi, 2001). Importantly, artificial cognition systems provide scientists the means to perform "mental experiments" about the necessary and sufficient conditions to observe processes of interest (Bedau, 1998; Dennett, 1998) — How would a certain system change, given different initial conditions and/or developmental path? What set of conditions is sufficient for the emergence of specific traits of the system?

Moreover, research into modeling cognition in artificial systems provides a new generation of ever more flexible and robust systems able to interact with an unpredictable dynamical world. It is almost a consensus among researchers that when building such systems, one fundamental issue, among others, needs to be faced sooner or later in models and experiments — *meaning*. How could cognitive processes be meaningful to the artificial systems? An early concern regarding meaning was the statement of the symbol grounding problem (Harnad, 1990). Thus, new approaches to artificial cognition systems either implicitly or explicitly try to address problems and critics to the symbolic approach and overcome them presenting new learning, adaptation and evolving autonomous agents. There is, however, a tendency to focus on low-level cognitive processes, like sensorial and motor abilities. Much of this restriction is due to epistemological questions not being clearly answered yet, especially the question about how these processes could be meaningful to the intelligent agents. While going through this book, the watchful reader will notice the problem of *meaning* in artificial cognition systems, even centrally addressed in all the chapters presented here. It appears related to diverse issues — embodiment, situatedness, learning, spatial cognition, language and communication, intentionality and emotion — thus providing contributions to the understanding of meaning in a magnitude of cognitive levels.

Organization and Overview of This Book

Section I: Modeling Cognition

This section focuses on the proposal of original models for cognition based on different computational approaches but aiming at describing how general cognitive processes can be modeled in artificial systems.

Chapter I: *The Goose, the Fly, and the Submarine Navigator: Interdisciplinarity in Artificial Cognition Research,* is by Alexander Riegler.

In this chapter, the importance of interdisciplinary research for an alternative path to artificial cognition systems is argued. The author starts by describing four problems in the new approaches to model artificial cognition: the anthropomorphical definition of simulated entities, the use of behaviorist stateless models, the application of crisp symbolic production systems rules and the poor explanatory power of connectionist.

In order to build an alternative road, accounts from ethology, evolutionary theory and epistemology of constructivism are brought forth and condensed into four boundary conditions. They lead to the outline of an architecture for genuine cognitive systems, which seeks to overcome traditional problems known from artificial intelligence research paragraphs and to avoid the pitfalls pointed out in the new approaches. Two major points in the architecture are stressed: the maintenance of explanatory power by favoring an advanced rule-based system rather than neuronal systems and the organizational closure of the cognitive apparatus, with far-reaching implications for the creation of meaningful agents. The proposed model framework is evaluated and compared with other, mainly neural network-related, approaches. The chapter concludes with a description of future trends and problems that still need to be addressed.

Chapter II: *An Embodied Logical Model for Cognition in Artificial Cognition Systems*, is by Guilherme Bittencourt and Jerusa Marchi. An original logic-based generic model for a cognitive agent is described in this chapter. This model found inspiration in several sources: systemic approach, autopoiesis theory, theory of evolution and memetics theory, neurobiology, Piaget's genetic epistemology, logicist school, cognitive robotics and Wittgenstein's work. The syntactical definition of the model consists of logical propositions, but the semantic definition includes, besides the usual truth value assignments, what is called emotional flavors, which correspond to the state of the agent's body translated into cognitive terms. The combination between logical propositions and emotional flavors allows the agent to learn and memorize relevant propositions that can be used for reasoning. These propositions are represented in a specific format — prime implicants/implicates — which is enriched with annotations that explicitly store the internal relations among the propositions' literals. Based on this representation, a memory mechanism is described and algorithms are presented that learn a proposition from the agent's experiences in the environment and that are able to determine the degree of robustness of the propositions, given a partial assignment representing the environment state. The logic-based approach to model cognition in behavior-based artificial creatures situated in the world constitutes a quite original contribution in this chapter and brings back this formal computational approach into a new perspective for artificial cognition systems.

Chapter III: *Modeling Field Theory of Higher Cognitive Functions*, is by Leonid Perlovsky. This chapter presents a mathematical theory of higher cognitive functions, the modeling field theory (MFT) and also dynamic logic, which would govern their temporal evolution. It discusses specific difficulties encountered by previous attempts at mathematical modeling of the mind and how the new theory overcomes these difficulties.

An example of problem solving, which was unsolvable in the past, is shown. The author argues that the theory is related to an important mechanism behind workings of the mind, which is called "the knowledge instinct" as well as to other cognitive functions. The mathematical descriptions are complemented with detailed conceptual discussions so the content of the chapter can be understood without necessarily following mathematical details. The author relates mathematical results and computational examples to cognitive and philosophical discussions of the mind. Also discussed are neurobiological foundations, cognitive, psychological and philosophical connections, experimental verifications and an outline of emerging trends and future directions. This chapter provides an original view of how mathematical principles can be used to understand and model different cognitive functions, including concepts, emotions, instincts, understanding, imagination and intuition.

Section II: Methodological Issues

In this section, methodological discussions about modeling and experimenting with artificial cognition systems are presented that concern how interdisciplinary sources can or should be taken together to model such systems.

Chapter IV: *Reconstructing Human Intelligence within Computational Sciences: An Introductory Essay*, is by Gerd Doeben-Henisch. This chapter outlines a possible research program for computational systems representing human-like intelligence. After a short historical introduction, a possible theoretical framework is described showing how it is possible to integrate heterogeneous disciplines like neurobiology, psychology and phenomenology within the same computational framework. Concrete examples are given by reconstructing behavioural (Morris) and phenomenal semiotics (Peirce) with the aid of formal theories. The author contributes to the interdisciplinary discussion about adaptive computational models of human-like intelligence through a unified theoretical framework.

Chapter V: *Stratified Constraint Satisfaction Networks in Synergetic Multi-Agent Simulations of Language Evolution*, is by Alexander Mehler. In this chapter, a simulation model of language evolution that integrates synergetic linguistics with multi-agent modeling is described. This model permits the use of knowledge about the distribution of parameter values of system variables to constrain the model itself and to establish a criterion of simulation validity. It also accounts for synergetic interdependencies of microscopic system variables and macroscopic order parameters. The relevant levels of linguistic dynamics to be modeled are identified as those of single information processing agents, communication processes, social system and language system. The chapter also identifies reliable sources of evaluating these simulation models, discussing several starting points of falsification on the level of single agents, of interpersonal learning and of the speech community as a whole. Important semiotic constraints of sign processing in multi-agent systems are described in terms of system variables and order parameters that describe and control the unfolding of language acquisition in multi-agent systems. The paper concentrates on conceptual modeling, leaving its implementation for future work.

Section III: Cognition and Robotics

The use of robotic agents as a platform for experiments in artificial cognition are discussed in this section, which presents their use to model language evolution and spatial cognition, in addition to a describing the limitations of current robotic systems.

Chapter VI: *Language Evolution and Robotics: Issues on Symbol Grounding and Language Acquisition*, is by Paul Vogt. This chapter focuses on recent studies of the origins and evolution of language that have used multiple robot systems as their primary platform. The aim is to present why robotics is a fruitful approach to study language origins and evolution, identify the main topics, report the major achievements and problems and provide a roadmap for future studies. The chapter starts by providing some theoretical background on language evolution and discussing an alternative view on the symbol-grounding problem. Next, some foundations toward studying language evolution using robots are presented, together with a number of themes within the evolutionary linguistics that have been the subject of robotic studies thus far. These themes include categorisation, the formation of vocabularies, the evolution of grammar and the emergence of meaningful communication. Following this review, future avenues for research are discussed. Finally, it is pointed out that robotics is, indeed, a very promising methodology to study language evolution and that, although many insights have been gained, research is still closer to the starting point than to the endpoint.

Chapter VII: *Evolutionary Robotics as a Tool to Investigate Spatial Cognition in Artificial and Natural Systems*, is by Michela Ponticorvo, Richard Walker, and Orazio Miglino. Chapter VII presents evolutionary robotics as a means of studying spatial cognition in artificial and natural systems. This approach is used to replicate quantitative observations of spatial behavior in laboratory animals, and it is argued that it offers a powerful tool to understand the general mechanisms underlying animal orientation. In particular, the authors show that "artificial organisms," with controller architecture that precludes the presence of "cognitive maps," can accurately replicate the observed behavior of animals in classical experimental set-ups, thus suggesting that spatial orientation may not require abstract spatial representations and that sensory-motor coordination, in the presence of environment constraints, may be enough on its own to generate complex spatial behavior. The chapter starts by describing examples of spatial behavior in animals, briefly outlining the debate between "cognitivist" versus "action-based" explanations and introducing a number of methodological issues. Next, evolutionary robotics (ER) and its potential role in cognitive research are discussed. Four ER simulations of animal spatial behavior (environmental shape recognition, detour behavior, landmark navigation and spatial learning) are described. The chapter concludes by summarizing what has been achieved and outlining the advantages and limitations of ER as a tool in cognitive research.

Chapter VIII: *The Meaningful Body: On the Differences Between Artificial and Organic Creatures*, is by Willem Haselager and Maria Eunice Q. Gonzalez. This chapter, directly related with what is called situated and embodied cognition, discusses how cognitive processes can be meaningful to artificial agents in the light of recent developments in AI robotics, specifically, in the area of reactive and evolutionary approaches. The authors argue that the embodied and embedded nature of these systems and the interactions between these robots and their environment do not guarantee the emergence of meaningful cognitive processes. Robots seem to lack any sensitivity to the significance of these processes. The authors suggest that the artificiality of the body of current robots precludes the emergence of meaning. Moreover, they question whether the label "embodied" genuinely applies to current robots. Such robots should be seen as "physicalized," given that the types of matter used in creating robots bear more similarity to machines like cars or airplanes than to organisms. Thus, the chapter investigates how body and meaning relate. It is suggest that meaning is closely related to the strengths and weaknesses of organic bodies of cognitive systems in relation to their struggle for survival. Specifically, four essential characteristics of organic bodies (autopoiesis, metabolism, centrifugal development and self-organization) are said to be lacking in artificial systems, therefore there will be little possibility of the emergence of meaningful processes.

Section IV: Cognition in Virtual Agents

Experiments with virtual agents, which are embedded in simulated environments, are presented in this section. Such systems of artificial cognition are discussed in the light of a biologically- inspired methodology called synthetic ethology and used in experiments concerning the emergence of meaning and signaling influenced by environmental variability.

Chapter IX: *Making Meaning in Computers: Synthetic Ethology Revisited*, is by Bruce MacLennan. This chapter describes synthetic ethology, a scientific methodology in which is constructed synthetic worlds wherein synthetic agents evolve and become coupled to their environment. First, the motivations for synthetic ethology as an experimental methodology are reviewed and its use to investigate intentionality and meaning; then the mechanisms from which the motivations emerge is explained. Second, several examples of such experiments are presented in which genuine (i.e., not simulated), meaningful communication evolved in a population of simple agents. The author explains that in these experiments the communications were meaningful to the artificial agents themselves, but they were only secondarily and partly meaningful to the experimenters. Finally, the chapter discusses the extension of the synthetic ethology paradigm to the problems of structured communications and mental states, complex environments and embodied intelligence, and one way is suggested in which this extension could be accomplished. Synthetic ethology would offer a new tool in a comprehensive research program investigating the neuro-evolutionary basis of cognitive processes.

Chapter X: *Environmental Variability and the Emergence of Meaning: Simulational Studies Across Imitation, Genetic Algorithms, and Neural Networks*, is by Patrick Grim and Trina Kokalis. In Chapter X, a development of earlier work in which we study the emergence of simple signaling in simulations involving communities of interacting individuals is presented. The model involves an environment of wandering food sources and predators, with agents "embodied" in this artificial environment and subject to its spatial and temporal contingencies. Individuals develop coordinated behavioral strategies in which they make and respond to "sounds" in their immediate neighborhoods using any of a variety of mechanisms: imitation of successful neighbors, localized genetic algorithms and partial neural net training on successful neighbors. Crucial to variations of the model explored are different updating mechanisms of strategy change, all of which are key to the behavior of the most successful neighbors. The models are biologically inspired in emphasizing strategy changes across a community of individuals embodied in a common environment. The authors introduce a further characteristic of environments: variability. The essential question posed is what role environmental variability — and environmental variability of what type — may play in the emergence of simple communication. Inspiration comes from the role that environmental variability seems to play in a range of apparently disparate phenomena, from species diversity to individual learning. Results for environments with (a) constant resources, (b) random resources and (c) cycles of "boom and bust" are compared. In the models presented, across all mechanisms for strategy change applied by individuals, the emergence of communication is strongly favored by cycles of "boom and bust," where resources vary cyclically, increasing and decreasing throughout time. These results are particularly intriguing given the importance of environmental variability in fields as diverse as psychology, ecology and cultural anthropology.

Section V: Theoretical and Philosophical Issues

In this section, the Central-European phenomenological tradition and Peircean pragmatic semeiotic provide theoretical and philosophical support in speculations on the structure of the psyche and approaches to the problem of meaning formation.

Chapter XI: *Mimetic Minds: Meaning Formation through Epistemic Mediators and External Representations*, is by Lorenzo Magnani. The chapter maintains that we can overcome many of the difficulties of creativity and meaning formation studies by developing a theory of abduction, in the light of Charles Sanders Peirce's first insights. According to the author, the "computational turn" and the creation of "artificial cognition systems" provide a new way to understand cognitive processes. The creation of new meanings through creative processes is no longer seen as a mysterious process but as a complex relationship among different inferential steps that can be clearly analyzed and identified.

Artificial intelligence and cognitive science tools allow us to test concepts and ideas previously conceived in abstract terms. It is in the perspective of these *actual models* that we find the central role of *abduction* in the explanation of meaning formation.

Chapter XII: *First Steps in Experimental Phenomenology*, is by Roberto Poli. The chapter uses some of the ideas developed by early phenomenologists in order to sketch fragments of a new architecture for artificial minds. The main objective is to show that at least some of the ideas developed by Central-European thinkers can still be fruitfully exploited for the scientific advancement of our understanding of the world and our experience of it. This work has mixed experimental data on the structure of the specious present with categorical analyses conducted within the framework of the theory of levels of reality and some bold speculation on the general structure of the psyche.

References

Braitenberg, V. (1984). *Vehicles: Experiments in synthetic psychology.* Cambridge, MA: MIT Press.

Bedau, M. (1998). Philosophical content and method of artificial life. In T. Bynum & J.H. Moor (Eds.), *The digital phoenix: How computers are changing philosophy* (pp. 135-152). Oxford, UK: Blackwell Publishers.

Dennet, D. (1998). *Brainchildren: Essays on the designing minds.* Cambridge, MA: MIT Press.

Harnad, S. (1990) The symbol grounding problem. *Physica D: Nonlinear Phenomena, 42,* 335-346.

Parisi, D. (2001). *Simulazioni: La realtà rifatta nel computer.* Il Mulino: Bologna.

Acknowledgments

The editors would like to acknowledge the help of all involved in the collation and review process of the book, without whose support the project could not have been satisfactorily completed.

Most of the authors of chapters included in this also served as referees for articles written by other authors. Thanks go to all those who provided constructive and comprehensive reviews.

Special thanks also go to the publishing team at Idea Group Inc.

The editors would like to thank the Brazilian National Research Council (CNPQ), the Graduate Personnel Improvement Coordination (CAPES) and the State of São Paulo Research Foundation (FAPESP) for research financial support.

In closing, we wish to thank all of the authors for their insights and excellent contributions to this book. We also want to thank all of the people who assisted us in the reviewing process.

Angelo Loula
Ricardo Gudwin
João Queiroz
Campinas, São Paulo, Brazil
January 2006

Section I

Modeling Cognition

Chapter I

The Goose, the Fly, and the Submarine Navigator:
Interdisciplinarity in Artificial Cognition Research

Alexander Riegler, Center Leo Apostel for Interdisciplinary Studies, Belgium

Abstract

Interdisciplinary research provides inspirations and insights into how a variety of disciplines can contribute to the formulation of an alternative path to artificial cognition systems. The chapter suggests that results from ethology, evolutionary theory and epistemology can be condensed into four boundary conditions. They lead to the outline of an architecture for genuine cognitive systems, which seeks to overcome traditional problems known from artificial intelligence research. Two major points are stressed: (a) the maintenance of explanatory power by favoring an advanced rule-based system rather than neuronal systems, and (b) the organizational closure of the cognitive apparatus, which has far-reaching implications for the creation of meaningful agents.

Introduction

Old Problems with Designing a Mind

The history of artificial intelligence and cognitive science shows that the *complexity* of the structures and dynamics of cognition have often been underestimated. Typical examples include the scaling problem of microworlds, which become NP-complete as soon as they are populated by a nontrivial amount of objects, and the difficulties in formalizing the enormous complexity of human expertise in knowledge-based systems. This matter of fact can be attributed to: (1) the naive-realistic approach (Riegler, 1992), which is mainly based on Cartesian dualism, which distinguishes between subjective and objective levels of description, and (2) the objectification of "information." These aspects created problems that have been hampering research in artificial intelligence (AI) ever since. Among them are the *Symbol Grounding Problem* (Harnad, 1990), which demands an account for meanings, and the *Frame Problem* (Dennett, 1984; Pylyshyn, 1987), which asks for the appropriate form of representation of sensory input in real-world environments, where the number of possible propositions and their mutual relationships are practically infinite.

Dissatisfaction with traditional methods of research has led to the search for alternatives, such as artificial life (Langton, 1989, 1992). It focuses on the *behavioral and evolutionary foundations* of life in general and cognition in particular (Wilson, 1991). Autonomous agents are studied in terms of (cognitive) systems that interact with each other and with their respective environments. These approaches press for an understanding of mechanisms responsible for the generation of behavior rather than for the specification and implementation of isolated cognitive functions. In recent years this has resulted in the formulation of the "embodiment" paradigm, i.e., the concept that cognition is intimately connected with the functioning of the body (Lakoff, 1987; Riegler, 2002; Ziemke, 2003) such that sensory and motor functions as well as information-processing and memory components are no longer considered independent and sequentially working parts of the cognitive apparatus.[1]

In general, work on artificial cognition systems can be viewed as the creation and investigation of self-organizing cognitive creatures and meaningful systems made by humans. These systems are an attempt to find the fundamental dynamical principles underlying biological phenomena, which in turn can be used to recreate these phenomena in other physical media (Langton, 1992). Since this research includes animats (Wilson, 1991), mobile robots (Brooks, 1991) and software agents inhabiting virtual realities and operation systems (Etzioni, 1993), any theory rooted in this alternative movement must reside on a *functional-abstract level* in order to be applicable in as many domains as possible. In this context, "functional" refers to the concept that we can abstract from the material structure of living entities. For example, it is obvious that the behavior of animals per se is not directly encoded in their respective genotype. Rather, the morphological structure of an organism serves as a predisposition for its behavioral repertoire. In other words, the physics of the body provides the basis for cognitive behavior in humans but it does not determine it. Other predispositional structures could serve the same purpose such that the issue of embodiment does not relate to the physical instantiation but rather to how the system relates in its entirety to the structure out of which it has emerged.

Given the problems traditional approaches face, the objective of this chapter is to show how interdisciplinary considerations can provide inspirations and insights into how a variety of disciplines can contribute to the formulation of an alternative path to artificial cognition systems. This demonstration is twofold: (1) I shed light on four potential problems that may also affect those new approaches. In particular, I argue that syntactical "PacMan"-models are unlikely candidates for genuine cognitive systems. Furthermore, such systems should not be based on situational-behaviorist designs that forgo internal states, nor should they rely on crisp symbolic production systems. And finally from a complexity-based perspective, I argue against the use of neural networks. (2) In order to build an alternative road to ACS, I suggest condensing observations in ethology, evolutionary theory and epistemology into four boundary conditions. They lead to the outline of a cognitive architecture that seeks: (1) to overcome traditional problems discussed in the introductory paragraphs, and (2) to avoid the pitfalls pointed out in the following section. The proposed model framework will be evaluated and compared with other, mainly neural network-related approaches. The chapter concludes with a description of future trends and problems that still need to be addressed.

New Problems for Creating Meaningful Agents

In the introduction, I argued in favor of new approaches to artificial cognitive systems. While these new approaches to building artificial cognitive systems are considered promising competitors for more conservative artificial intelligence models, they are by no means immune to flaws, as the following list illustrates.

1. In what I called *PacMan systems* (Riegler, 1995; 1997; Peschl & Riegler, 1999), simulated organisms interact with anthropomorphically defined entities, such as "food" and "enemy." Well-known examples are the models used in Dave Ackley and Michael Littman's study of the Baldwin effect (Ackley & Littman, 1992), Toby Tyrell's action-selection research (Tyrell, 1993) and Joshua Axtell and Robert Epstein's simulations related to social processes (Axtell & Epstein, 1996). The goal of this type of model is mere optimization of certain parameters such as energy gain, hunting success, etc. However, the crucial question regarding the emergence of meanings for the organisms is completely neglected. There is no account of why this icon on the computer screen represents food for another icon that is supposed to be a cognitive agent because, as Stan Franklin (1995) points out, "things don't come labeled". Rather, the programmer imposes meanings onto the modeled creature.

In a broader context, Richard Feynman (1985) describes the adverse implications of this approach. He came up with an intriguing analogy by introducing the notion of "cargo cult science." Inhabitants of a fictional island in the South Sea had witnessed the support of goods by airplanes during World War II. As they wished this to happen again, they started to create runways with fires along their sides; they set up a wooden hut for a man to sit in, with two wooden plates on his head as headphones and bars of bamboo sticks which looked like antennae. The form was perfect and everything *looked* the way it had before. But, not surprising to us, it didn't work; no plane ever landed. Of course, the lack of understanding resulted from a lack of being embodied in the world of Western science and technology. Similarly, predefining the interactional patterns of pixels in computer simulations may save the *exogenous* form but it says little about the *endogenous* cognitive mechanisms of the animals the simulation allegedly portrays.

2. The cognitive apparatuses used in *situational systems* are behaviorist stimulus-response systems with no, or only a few, internal states. These systems are used in research on autonomous robots dealing with navigational or similar tasks that appear trivial to the layman but intractable in mathematical terms. In the extreme case, cognitive capabilities are accounted for in terms of exploiting the physical structure of robots and self-organizing properties of group processes. For example, Rene te Boekhorst and Marinus Maris (1996) describe a collective heap building process by a group of robots. The sensor input of the robots is restricted such that they can only detect obstacles that are diagonally to the left or right but not in front of them. Since they cannot perceive and consequently avoid objects exactly in front of them, the robots push them in the direction of their movement. As soon as they perceive another block on the left or right, they change direction in order to avoid collision. Therefore, the block pushed so far remains in the vicinity of the perceived block. Ultimately, this leads to the formation of clusters. In general, one may argue that collecting objects into clusters *must* be the result of deliberate cognition, but this scenario rather suggests that the goal was accidentally accomplished.

The situational behavior-based approach can be compared with lower animals that are only capable of processing "instantaneous information" (Lorenz, 1978). Such stimulus-response strategies include kinesis, phobia and taxes. In biology, kinesis is the response to changes in the intensity of a particular stimulus by altered movement activity or by changes in direction, which are not necessarily related to the direction of the stimulus itself. For example, ciliata leave disadvantageous environments by acceleration of vibratile movements. As soon as they reach a more advantageous environment, the vibratile movements are decelerated. Phobic reactions are a kind of fleeing-behavior and are more complex than kinesis. For example, if the front-end of a paramecium hits an obstacle it will reverse its vibratile movements and therefore its direction. After a slight turn it continues its movement. This appears to be an evolutionary sufficiently reliable strategy to avoid obstacles, and has been copied by many roboticists, e.g., in the experiment of te Boekhorst and Maris. A genuine orientation behavior related to an obstacle or a target is called a "taxis." There are a great number of taxes, ranging from tropotaxis to geotaxis and phototaxis, depending on which modality the respective organism senses.

In the heyday of cybernetics, these simple behavioral strategies already attracted the interest of researchers. The experiments of Walter Grey Walter (1951) with three-wheeled tortoises left the observer with the impression that the artifacts carry out purposeful, and hence meaningful, cognitive acts by exploring simple stimulus-response conditions similar to the biological behavioral patterns described earlier. Since then, numerous artificial life models have dealt with such primitive forms of behavior. Many of them were triggered by Braitenberg's (1984) thought experiment whose often-cited vehicles became representative of this approach. Braitenberg investigates the relationship between simple structures (interpreted as the creature's genotype) and behavior (the phenotype). He argues that simple structures can cause an enormous variety of behavioral patterns. In some sense, Braitenberg's "synthetic psychology" claims to have solved the problem of inferring from behavior to structure and was therefore considered paradigmatic for the artificial life movement (cf. Langton, 1989). Consequently, a branch of "new" artificial intelligence emerged populated by ideas such as "the world is its own best model" (Brooks, 1991), which abandon the concept of cognitive representation altogether. No doubt the results of situational and embedded systems are impressive (e.g., Pfeifer & Scheier, 1999) given their bias for simple structures. Technologically, Mark Tilden even went a step back to the times of Grey Walter and demonstrated that systems based on the situational principle do not necessarily need to follow the computational paradigm. Instead, he built tiny analogically-working robots (Hasslacher & Tilden, 1995).

However, as with behaviorism in psychology, which refrained from using internal states in their explicatory models of the human mind, there are severe limitations with situational stimulus-response cognition, such as not being able to cope with delayed effects and ignoring biological plausibility in the case of higher animals, including cardinal cognitive capacities such as learning. The failure of educational methods based on the behaviorist paradigm, as well as the all-too-mechanistic worldview of behaviorism, make behaviorist approaches inappropriate for cognitive research. Another criticism that applies to the behaviorist program refers to its exclusive reliance on observational data, and will be discussed later in this chapter.

3. In *symbolic production systems* rules perform crisp binary classifications that neglect the continuous nature of "real-world" contexts where the appearance of things is somewhat fuzzy. For example, even though a very light red object of four centimeters in size is less likely to be an apple than another object with glaring red color and a height of eight centimeters, this is by no means a binary yes-no decision. A symbolically working system can only attribute the label "apple" or "non-apple." However, the advantage of crisp categorization is that it can easily be translated into propositions, which are used predominately in analytic philosophy and in logic-oriented programming languages such as Prolog. Even today, epistemologically sophisticated and ambitious systems such as closed-loop discovery use propositional representations. In particular, the dynamical approach to cognition (e.g., van Gelder, 1998) emphasizes the difference between classical digital computation of representational entities and dynamical processes among quantitative variables. It has been argued that the classical propositional approach copes badly with both temporal issues *and* aspects of context and embeddedness. For example, King, et al. (2004) have developed a "robot scientist," a system that "automatically originates hypotheses to explain observations, devises experiments to test these hypotheses, physically runs the experiments using a laboratory

robot, interprets the results to falsify hypotheses inconsistent with the data, and then repeats the cycle." The specific goal of the robot scientist — to determine the function of genes from the performance of knockout mutants — was implemented as the interplay of abduction and deduction; the former infers missing chemical reactions that could explain observed phenotypes, the latter checks the consistency of hypotheses. The authors emphasize that the "key point is that there was no human intellectual input in the design of experiments or the interpretation of data." However, looking closely at how the system represents prior biological knowledge reveals a rather anthropomorphic picture: Nodes in a directed graph denote metabolites and its arcs are interpreted as enzymes. This results in a set of logical propositions, which are used by the programming language Prolog to compute predictions. So, while the actual processing cycle might indeed be "human-free," the algorithm itself is disembodied and symbolic. The problem with such disembodied propositions is a twofold arbitrariness: (1) the arbitrariness of grounding propositions in the world as mentioned in the introduction, and (2) the arbitrariness of linking propositions in a sensible way. Assume that in an astronomical discovery system, a proposition such as P1: "perceive (Mars, x, y)" leads to another proposition, say P2: "move (telescope, x', y')." How can P2 be contingent on P1, or how can P2 be a logically necessary consequence of P1? The transition appears arbitrary; it is as "semantically blind" as the scientific device in Jonathan Swift's *Gulliver's Travels, A Voyage To Laputa.* This scientific machine could make "a complete body of all arts and sciences" through mechanical combination of all words in a language. It was the task of the human user to pick out the meaningful sentences — the machine could not do that. In other words, the crisp symbolic approach inevitably gets stuck in the complexity trap since in real-world environments the number of possible propositions and their mutual relationships are *practically infinite* (referred to as the frame problem (Dennett, 1984)) such that picking the *meaningful* propositions is rendered impossible (the symbol grounding problem of Harnad, 1990).

4. While connectionist models, i.e., *massively distributed systems* and *neural networks,* exhibit a vast variety of "natural" behavior, they have a rather poor explanatory performance, which obfuscates the causal details of observed cognitive behavior. The experimenter is in the situation of an ethologist who can analyze only the behavior of the observed biological creature rather than its internal cognitive dynamics. Ethologists put emphasis on observing behavioral patterns, i.e., they are interested in the exogenous view. They observe behavior, describe it in terms of rules and consequently postulate a link between rule-like behavior and a cognitive structure that allegedly generates the behavior. The focus of attention is necessarily on the output of the observed system, which ethologists map onto their own experiential network. In this sense, behaviors are anthropomorphically attributed (Sjölander, 1997). Foerster (1970) referred to it as "anthropomorphizations," i.e., "projecting the image of ourselves into things or functions of things in the outside world." However, a human observer is *not embodied* in the world of the observed animal (Nagel, 1974; Riegler, 2002). Rather, she interprets its behavior within her own referential system of understanding. In general, there are a huge number of possible inferences from the appearance to the inner working, from observational data onto any model. The sheer astronomical number of ways to explain data points (McAllister, 2003) requires an intellectual capacity beyond that of humans. Facing this

intellectual problem, all we can do is trivialize complex systems. In other words, we reduce the degrees of freedom of a given complex entity to behave like a "trivial" machine (Foerster, 1972), i.e., an automaton that maps input directly on output without referring to internal states. Neural networks, too, are usually described in simplified terms such as input-output mapping, as no human is capable of tracing their inner concurrent mode of working.

So what have we gained using neural networks? Their degree of complexity corresponds to what Warren Weaver (1948) has called "organized complexity." It appears in systems of a sufficiently high number of variables such that they are not tractable, either by equations used in classical physics or by statistical mathematics. Both living cognitive systems and artificial neural networks belong to this class. A considerable amount of entities interact with each other in countless non-negligible ways such that it is impossible to reconstruct and comprehend the working of either class of systems. This renders the use of neural networks as explanatory tools for ACS research impracticable despite their performance potential. From the scientific perspective that tries to formulate comprehensible explanations for phenomena, we cannot ignore this fundamental flaw. The researcher using neural networks is little more than a cargo cult scientist in Feynman's sense who is guided by superficial resemblances. Or to paraphrase Tim Smithers (1991), just examining the firing patterns of neurons inside a brain does not explain the behavior of that particular person. Dynamical systems (van Gelder, 1998) may run into this problem too since their behavior can only be described on a global "emerging" level through attractors, bifurcations and other concepts drawn from chaos theory.

As an alternative to neural network models, I would like to provide arguments for an advanced rule-based approach. Note that using rules does not mean employing a typical machine learning approach in which rules are explicitly and *a priori* specified by a knowledge engineer (e.g., Maes, 1994). Rather, I want to stress the fact that rule-based systems comply with one of the primary tasks of science, i.e., to explain phenomena. This coincides with the intention of maintaining the explanatory power of artificial cognitive systems. The advantage over neural networks is obvious: It is much easier to track the interlocked chain of rules in order to explain why a particular behavioral pattern has ultimately emerged. In neural nets, one can only try to relate clusters of activity with the behavior of the system, which, as I argued earlier, may hide crucial details from the researcher.

John Holland et al. (1986) pointed out that there are far more advantages of the rule-based approach: (1) it is a well understood methodology based on many years of research; (2) rules lend themselves into building modular architectures; and (3) rules come close to the way we think, the way our language describes transitions in the environment. Additionally, from a psychological perspective, rules may serve as appropriate vehicles for implementing psychological models, including Piaget's schema mechanism (cf. Drescher, 1991), as their data structures are quite similar to schemes.

A crucial aspect, however, is to substitute the main feature of neural networks, inherent parallelism, with another powerful and biologically plausible aspect. Therefore, rule-based systems need to take the following issues into consideration: (1) Condition parts of rules should feature smoothly varying, nonlinear, interpolable classification boundaries known from fuzzy logic. In other words, the output of conditions is defined over a probability distribution such as a Gaussian curve or a triangular approximation as used in fuzzy logic; (2) Action parts should perform more sophisticated computations than single neurons in a neural network, i.e., they should perform numeric computations rather than simple accumulation of activations towards a threshold. This measure counterbalances the fact that rules may be outnumbered by neurons in large networks; and (3) Rules should allow for implementing anticipatory behavior. That is, rules and their components are able to self-organize into chains of conditioned executions, which represent expectations about future states. A detailed biologically motivated justification for the important role of anticipation is provided in the following section (cf. also Riegler, 2001b, 2003).

Respecting the four problem areas discussed in this section and complying with the requirements of an advanced rule-based approach, I will now turn to insights from other disciplines and then address the question of how an artificial cognitive system must be designed in order to avoid these pitfalls. This endeavor is guided by the goal of ACS to build autonomous systems that are capable of creating their own independent system of meaning generation and maintenance.

Interdisciplinary Inspirations

As pointed out by many authors (e.g., Klein, 1990; Weingart & Stehr, 2000) the interdisciplinary approach is believed to be fruitful for advances in science. In what follows, I present insights and accounts from ethology, evolutionary theory and the epistemology of constructivism which counteract the obstinate problems described earlier in this chapter and contribute to the development of an artificial cognition architecture.

The Goose

Lorenz and Tinbergen (1939) made the following classical ethological observation: If an egg falls out of the nest, the incubating graylag tries to roll it back into the nest with its bill. In ethological terms, this implements a releasing mechanism where a certain perceptual context triggers a sequence of actions. In the literature, releasing mechanisms are characterized as neurosensory filter mechanisms related to certain behavior patterns. They specify the response to sign stimuli by filtering out ineffective stimuli. One of the goals in this chapter is to show that the concept of "filtering environmental stimuli" can be turned upside down in that individuals do not filter out irrelevant information from the huge amount of "incoming data." Rather, they only check the presence or absence of certain stimuli when the currently running rule requires it.

This and related observations give rise to the assumption that cognition is rule-based. Each time a certain condition is met, the execution of the associated behavior is begun. The animal is rather skilful though and compensates for any sideward rolling of the egg caused by the uneven ground. In other words, its behavior sequence allows for contingent corrections; it is a flexible *action pattern* rather than a stereotype motor program.

However, the goose neglects environmental events while retrieving the egg. When Lorenz and Tinbergen removed the egg midway through this action pattern, the bird nevertheless continued its behavior until its bill reached the border of the nest. So, once an action pattern has been triggered, the processing of sensor information is reduced and stays focused on the current behavior until it terminates.

Both the condition and the action parts can be rather complex, as revealed by the goose's behavior to compensate for any deviations of the egg's path. This compensating behavior can be described algorithmically by a repeated checking of *decision points* to ensure that the egg is still on track. In its entirety, the behavior is expectation-driven, reinforced by the evolutionary robustness of egg retrieval. Since statistically it makes sense to anticipate that egg retrieval will return any egg back into the nest, it is not worth checking whether the egg has been removed during the retrieval action and thus interrupt the behavioral pattern.

These observations teach us that it is neither necessary to search the problem space entirely nor is it desirable to look for absolute solutions. In other words, the species of geese had solved the frame problem long before it arose in artificial intelligence by foregoing logically exhaustive representations (Riegler, 2000).

The behavior of the goose hints at the general importance of anticipation for cognition. Although ridiculously simpleminded at first sight, the behavior of the goose is evolutionarily successful, as it integrates the anticipation that the egg will eventually reach the nest again. Rudolfo Llinás (2001) claims that the "capacity to predict the outcome of future events — critical to successful movement — is, most likely, the ultimate and most common of all global brain functions." This becomes obvious in studies regarding the difference between expert and amateur players. Skilled players read their opponent's game: They look at the right cues and make the proper anticipations from these cues. As in the case of egg retrieving, anticipating is not a conscious process (Riegler, 2002b). The perception of motion of a human body is constrained by its anatomical and biochemical properties (Kourtzi & Shiffrar, 1999). The skilled player takes advantage of the unconscious knowledge of these constraints and uses them to anticipate sequences of the opponent's actions (Verfaillie & Daems, 2002). For example, in tennis, the ball's trajectory is anticipated from the opponent's body posture and its dynamical aspect before the opponent even hits the ball. Such cognitive sophistication is the result of training and exercise, or "habit learning" (Graybiel, 1998). It can be accomplished by chunking perception and action sequences, which can be recalled and replayed without an interfering consciousness. A human tennis champion would appear quite inept when playing against a Martian player with a different, and therefore unpredictable, physiology (Riegler, 2002b).

The Fly

One of the most spectacular mutations is the so-called *homeotic* mutation. It represents inherited genetic errors, which become visible, for example, in the bithorax mutation of *Drosophila*. It emerges through a mutation of a distinctive gene so that the whole complex subsystem of a thorax is developed twice. The pet fly of geneticists can also mutate to become *Drosophila antennapedia*, which has legs instead of antennae. Apparently, various gene locations are linked with each other in such a way that entire body parts can develop at completely wrong locations. This gives rise to the assumption that there is a sort of switch genome which connects all these corresponding genes and which is able to retrieve all information necessary for building whole subsystems. Rupert Riedl (1977), partly building on Conrad Waddington's (1942) concept of epigenetic landscapes (cf. Riegler, 1994a), was the first evolutionary theoretician to explain this matter of fact in terms of *functional coupling* among genes. It leads to a parallel development of phenotype features that share a functional relationship. On a genetic level, *homeoboxes* are responsible for such couplings: By orchestrating structural genes, homeotic genes control the formation of the body structure of a creature. A single mutation of a homeotic gene suffices to cause the development of a leg at the site where an antenna would normally be. Consequently, the mechanism of functional coupling introduces a system of interdependences and hierarchies whose primary advantage is a dramatic increase of both developmental robustness (Simon, 1969) and evolutionary speed (Riegler, 2001a) as it enhances the chances of adaptation by several orders of magnitude.

From an algorithmic point of view, we can implement the effect of functional couplings by combining primitive procedural and structural elements into groups, which are under the control of rules on a higher level. Instead of modifying single structural elements, only the metaelement is subject to change, which makes the complexity problem manageable.[2] For example, Koza's (1992) "automatically defined functions" (ADF) and Angeline's (1994) "module acquisition" approach draw partly on this insight. The idea is to encapsulate segments of the representational and dynamical structure of a program such that it cannot be modified through learning or mutation, while the runtime performance remains unchanged. Consequently, these encapsulations become building blocks that can be reused by other programs which, in turn, can be encapsulated (Cf. also "Learning component" section).

The Submarine Navigator

In order to deal with the symbol-grounding problem, I will discuss Maturana and Varela's (1980) paradigmatic analogy at the crossing point between philosophy and biology. The authors posit a submarine gracefully surfacing near a shore, and an observer who congratulates the navigator on his skill at avoiding reefs and handling the submarine in a beautiful manner. However, this leaves the navigator perplexed, "What's this about reefs and surfacing? All I did was push some levers and turn knobs and make certain relationships between indicators as I operated the levers and knobs. It was all done in a prescribed sequence, which I'm used to. I didn't do any special maneuver, and on top of that, you talk to me about a submarine."

What the authors are implying at is the fact that the cognitive apparatus is in a similar situation. In living cognitive beings, all the nervous system does is to maintain a certain dynamical relationship among its states of activity rather than between input and output states. Only the observing psychologist or ethologist is able to assign the label "input" and "output" to a subset of these states because the nervous signals themselves do not carry any information about the physical nature of the agents that triggered the signal (Foerster, 1973). It is up to the cognitive brain to make sense of the vast amount of incoming signals, which differ only with respect to their intensity. Based on this insight, the epistemology of radical constructivism (Glasersfeld, 1995; Riegler, 2001c) formulated the concept of *organizational closure* of the cognitive system (Maturana & Varela, 1980; Winograd & Flores, 1987), that is, from the perspective of the cognitive system, the activity of any set of its states is only affected by the activity of the set of other (or the same) states. Since states can only refer to each other, the cognitive system cannot distinguish between internal states and states referring to the "external world." Therefore, it is futile to claim a representational correspondence between reality structures and cognitive structures (Peschl & Riegler, 1999). This entails that meaning can no longer be considered passively received and processed as if it was a quality external to the system. Rather, it is actively built up by the cognizing subject as the "function of cognition is adaptive and serves the organization of the experiential world, not the discovery of ontological reality" (Glasersfeld, 1988). Since "meaning" and "information" are constructed, they do not reside in the "reality out there" and are not independent of the cognitive system that generates them.

The conclusion here is that perceptual stimuli can only perturb the interaction among internal states. Perturbations may influence, but cannot determine the operation of the cognitive apparatus. This viewpoint opposes the traditional information-processing paradigm, which describes cognitive behavior as a sensing-thinking-acting chain. Only within this paradigm the symbol-grounding problem appears as a threat to artificial cognition, since it treats meaning and information as mind-independent qualities whose respective translations must remain mysterious in thought-experiments such as Searle's Chinese room argument (Searle, 1980). A mechanism that just shuffles (human interpreted) "information" from A to B is as intelligent as a CD player, which "understands" the music it plays in the confines of transforming bits on the CD to the loudspeaker.

A methodological consequence of this constructivist approach is that the perspective of the autonomous system is independent of that of the designer in the following sense: While the designer is interested in the *output* of the system they build, an autonomous system focuses on its *input*. It executes certain actions in order to change its input state, such as avoiding the perception of an obstacle or no longer feeling hungry. It is only the observer-designer who, lacking the ability to sense the system's input state ("first-person experience"), focuses on the system's output. Consequently, the designer-programmer defines systems over the range of their behaviors, and constructs them accordingly. The results are *anthropomorphic* rather than autonomous artifacts.

In a philosophical perspective, Maturana emphasizes that what occurs within a composed entity (e.g., living systems) is different from what happens to this entity. This is particularly obvious in the case of living systems, which exist in the domains of physiology and behavior. These two phenomenal domains do not intersect, since the description of a composite unity takes place in a metadomain with respect to the description of the components that constitute that unity. An observer may simultaneously look at both. They might state that changes in physiology cause changes in the behavior of an observed creature, but that is not a logical necessity. Instead, "[I]n order to explain a given behavior of a living system, the observer must explain the generation and establishment of the particular structures of the organism and of the environment that make such behavior possible at the moment it occurs" (Maturana, 1974).

The Boundary Conditions

Considering the problem areas of the introduction, and condensing the insights gained in the previous section, we can outline an alternative way of implementing cognition in artifacts based on the following requirements:

C1.   The notion of *cognition* refers to aspects of the organization and evolution of increasingly complex patterns of behavior, which help creatures to cope with their environment and to maintain themselves. In this sense, it equates cognition with life (Maturana & Varela, 1980; Stewart, 1991, 1996; Heschl, 1990). (Intelligence, by contrast, is the capacity of rational problem solving.)

C2.   Cognitive development is an incremental bottom-up process (Piaget, 1937/1954; Drescher, 1991), which starts at the sensorimotor level. Each advanced level builds on the previous levels. Therefore, *cognitive structures* are organized in a hierarchical manner, where higher cognitive functions and structures build on lower ones. However, this split does not divide the cognitive system into independently working modules (e.g., Fodor, 1983). Rather, the hierarchical structure lends developmental robustness and evolutionary speed to cognitive systems (Simon, 1969).

C3.   The aspect of organizational closure requires that the operation of the cognitive apparatus must not be defined in terms of the semantics of the environment. There should be a clear separation between both.

C4.   Since cognitive processes must remain explicable on an abstract, functional level, massively distributed approaches cannot be taken into consideration. Not only neural networks, but also *flat* rule-based systems equipped with a learning component, may grow so complex that it will be rather difficult, if not impossible, to interpret their dynamics. However, the proposed model in this chapter is *hierarchically* organized. This means that the cognitive scientist seeking an explanation for the system's behavior can gradually explore deeper levels of encapsulation because the system is linearly decomposable.

Outline of an Artificial Cognition Model

The boundary conditions described earlier can be used to formulate an artificial cognitive apparatus as follows (for an earlier version, cf. Riegler, 1994ab, 1995, 1997). This outline is intended to *encourage* implementations that comply with the boundary conditions and to *motivate* further conceptual-philosophical discussions.

Performance Component

In order to satisfy C4, the apparatus is based on a production system. As pointed out earlier, this decision does not only agree with comparable models (such as Holland's (1992) classifier systems), it also concurs with the fact that rules have an inherent familiarity with the sequential nature of human thinking. This has been exploited in various knowledge-based systems that require an explanatory component. However, since the apparatus does not start with an *a priori*-defined knowledge base but relies on various learning mechanisms as described later, it does not import the problems associated with the impossibility of making expert knowledge explicit (e.g., Dreyfus & Dreyfus, 1990). In fact, due to the learning component, the initial set of rules in an individual can either be empty or inherited from ancestral individuals. Alternatively, an individual may also start with a small set of human-defined short rules (cf. "reflex" rules, as explained later) to cover some basic cognitive competences.

In contrast to most artificial neural networks, which work with several layers of discrete nodes, the apparatus uses only one layer that consists of a set S of states s, which are defined over a numeric range between the global constants min and max, i.e., min $d \le |s| \le d \le$ max. These states (or *cells*) can be written (implemented as "set" action), read and compared with each other (both implemented as "call" actions). The single-layer approach reduces the structural complexity in favor of a procedural hierarchy, which is required to satisfy condition C2, as explained next.

Furthermore, since nervous impulses have a continuous range, the condition parts of rules are to inherit the smoothly varying, nonlinear, interpolable classification boundaries available in connectionist models. Fuzzy rule systems feature conditions that comply with this requirement. They merge crisp rule systems with the idea of partial membership in a set, as formally described by fuzzy set theory (Zadeh, 1965). Similarly, in this artificial cognition model, the query response of conditions is defined over a continuous Gaussian curve rather than a discrete interval. Consequently, a single query $q(c, s)$ determines the extent to which the value of the addressed state s falls within the Gaussian interval defined by c.

Each fuzzy production rule (or *schema*) r consists of an independent condition part and an action part. Both components obey the building block principle. For the condition part there are single "primitive" queries c_p and collections of queries c_c, so-called *concepts* which combine primitive conditions to represent composed entities. For the observer of the system, who can only access the system's output, such composed entities can be multimodal perceptions, complex representations, composed hypotheses, etc.

As with primitive conditions, primitive actions a_p, too, can be chained to form action sequences a_c. Both condition and action chains can contain primitive and combined elements.

The separation between cognitive apparatus and environment required by C3 entails that all schemata deal with semantic-free states rather than with propositional representations of "real" entities and their features. To bridge the gap, a "transduction shell" is introduced, that is, a sensorimotor sur-face which maps perceptive stimuli from the outside onto internal states S and vice versa. Not only does this "anonymity" implement

C3, it also keeps the number of primitive actions as low as possible. Two action types are sufficient. The *set* action modifies the state of a particular cell, and the *call* action can insert any arbitrary building block (i.e., primitive condition or action, concept or action sequence or an entire schema) into the action part of a schema. A primitive action may contain various flags, such as stopping the current schema, or moving the execution of the current schema into the background such that the apparatus can start the concurrent execution of another schema.

In summary, the apparatus P is defined as follows. $P = <R, S>$, with $r \in R$, $r = <c_c, a_c>$, $c_c = \{c_p | c_c\}^+$, $a_c = \{a_p | a_c\}^+$ and $s \in S$, min d $\leq |s|$ d $\leq$ max. The indices p and c refer to "primitive" and "combined," respectively. From this description it follows that both condition and action part form nested hierarchies in which encapsulations are reused as building blocks. Elements can be functionally coupled as they make use of encapsulations and/ or are part of encapsulations themselves. Therefore, the cognitive apparatus is a hierarchical system, which complies with C3 (cf. Figure 1).

Procedurally, the apparatus works as follows. The algorithm uses the current context, i.e., the internal states S, which have partly been set by the transduction shell, to find a match among the condition parts of the existing rules. The matching is biased by the *priority* of the rules, which is inversely proportional to the length of the respective rule's condition part. These rules are at the lower end of the behavioral spectrum and could be anthropomorphically called "reflexes." The priority measure is motivated by the fact that reflexes are rather unspecific rules with low computational costs. It is also in alignment with the default hierarchy concept of Holland et al. (1986) where the most general elements have the shortest access path. Generally speaking, these reflex rules enable the apparatus to respond to critical events that endanger the existence of the cognitive system. Another conflict resolution criterion is the *generality* of competing rules (as defined in the next section). The algorithm prefers rules with low generality.

At the other end of the behavioral spectrum are rules with long action parts and embedded conditions, which in the extreme case could make initial rule triggering superfluous as they keep on branching to other action sequences and rules. The rules implement cognitive flexibility and dynamical continuity. However, an action sequence can come to a halt after the last action element is executed or if an embedded condition explicitly stops the execution of the current rule. In this case, the algorithm again matches the current state against the condition parts to determine which rule may fire.

Given the perpetual interplay of actions and conditions, which is rarely interrupted by initial rule firing, the system does not *compute* cognitive functions. Rather, it is a dynamical system that unfolds cognitive competence in time, as characterized by the dynamical approach to cognition (van Gelder, 1998).

Learning Component

The following two parameters are at the core of the system's learning capabilities:

1.   The *generality* of a condition part is the (weighted) sum of the widths of the Gaussian intervals over all included conditions. The generality may either become

Figure 1.

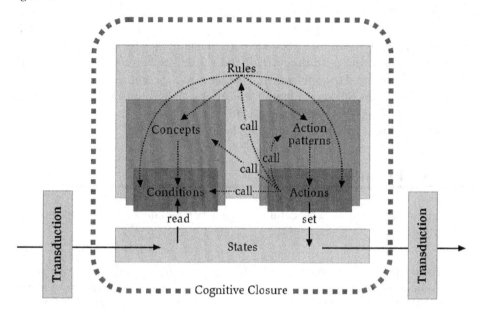

smaller, so that the rule is more specialized to a particular context, or become bigger, so that the rule covers more similar situations. In other words, specific condition parts are more "spiked" than general ones.

2.   The *importance* of a schema is the (weighted) sum of maximal degrees of member-ship over all included conditions. Rules with a higher importance are more likely to be executed.

These *ontogenetic* parameters enable the cognitive system to accommodate its schemata without explicit reference to external entities and rewarding schemes. Rather, the system follows the general idea that the more often a schema has been executed in the past, the higher its probability of being executed in the future. This evaluation measure is sufficient to implement C1, which defines cognition in terms of success in the process of life: It is unlikely that the agent would have survived so far if frequently calling a particular schemata had a negative impact on its survival (cf. the egg retrieval of the goose).

Beside development during the lifespan of a single cognitive system, the set of cognitive schemata can also evolve on a larger timescale. These *phylogenetic* learning strategies include the application of genetic operators, such as mutation and recombination known from genetic algorithms (Goldberg, 1989). They can alter the composition of non-primitive conditions and actions by adding, removing or permuting their components.

To implement condition C2, the apparatus draws from Angeline's (1994) "module acquisition" approach. The author used compression and expansion operators to reduce the length of genotypes such that these genotypes have a de-fining length of 0 and order of 1. Therefore, they are perfect candidates for quick distribution among other genotypes according to Holland's (1992) schema theorem. Unfortunately, Angeline failed to apply genetic operators to the compressed genotypes as he did to genotypes of normal length. But this is exactly the key advantage of functional couplings between control and structural genes as they implement homeotic mutations, which accelerate phylogenetic learning.

Distinct Features

In the following, I will outline the defining characteristics of the ACS model specified in this section.

1.   The model starts at the lowest possible level and thus avoids as many *a priori* assumptions by the designer of the system as possible. Since the aim of ACS is to investigate how cognitive capacities emerge, this means starting below the cognitive level, i.e., at a level that is free of anthropomorphic ascriptions regarding the *content* of the cognitive apparatus. By favoring a rule-based approach, which forgoes specifying both content of rules and linking among rules, the model maintains sufficient explanatory power. To circumvent problems in production systems used in decision support systems and other industrial applications, the model promotes fuzzy schemata consisting of fuzzy interval conditions. Grouping such conditions allows for data fusion and the implementation of intermodal concepts. It has been argued that in the animal kingdom the transition from monomodal to intermodal cognition was a major step in increasing cognitive capacities (Sjölander, 1995). Animals such as snakes only perceive through one channel at a time. Mammals, however, are capable of multimodal perception that does not degrade objects in the environment to mere data sensations. Intermodality allows for integration of qualitatively different sensor data among individual objects in order to predict their behavior. While a constrictor snake sometimes may even lose track of a prey that it has already struck (because it does not use its tactile senses to locate the prey around which it is wrapped), a cat knows that it is worth waiting in front of the hole into which a mouse has disappeared simply because the cat's cognition does not depend on "processing instantaneous information", as discussed earlier.

2.   Since the *semantics* of the cells that the cognitive apparatus works on is not projected from the outside into the system, the apparatus develops its own referential framework. It produces actively predictive hypotheses whose validity is tested against internal rather than external states. This makes it possible for the cognitive apparatus to be separated from the physiology of the sensor and motor functions. The operational closure eases the portability of the cognitive apparatus

to different problem tasks. Actions do not need to be tailored for specific environments as is the case of propositional production systems. The latter are based on the semantics of objects and events. Representations that work on propositions such as "pullout (wagon, room)" or "perceive (Mars, x, y)" require (a), the definition of a large set of propositions and elements the meaning of which cannot be specified, i.e., grounded, and (b), the redefinition of the elements in case the situational context changes. In contrast, the cognitive apparatus defined in this chapter features only two actions: One to modify the content of its cells ("set") and the other to establish hierarchical connections between structural elements of the cognitive architecture ("call").

3. Computational costs are reduced due to the expectation-driven hierarchically organized algorithm. Functional coupling establishes a hierarchical and recurrent organization in the cognitive apparatus. Couplings enable coordinated development between structural elements of the cognitive apparatus in the sense that a *regulatory* element at a higher hierarchical level concurrently modifies elements at lower levels. Any mutation in a regulatory element simultaneously changes all connected elements as well. As a result, adaptability is increased because regulatory elements make synchronization possible among those dynamical elements which have to develop congruently since their proper functioning depends on each other.

Comparison with Neuronal Approaches

In the beginning of this chapter I argued against the use of neural networks in ACS research. In this section, I review the arguments again by comparing the outlined model with neural networks and related approaches.

Comparison with Neuronal Networks

Like neural networks, and neuro-fuzzy systems, the cognitive architecture presented in this chapter is an approach to abstract regularities from data.

At their core, neural networks are systems in which values (typically Boolean) are propagated along vertices. These connections are weighted and lead to nodes in which the values are summed. Depending on whether the sum transcends a given threshold, outgoing vertices carry a value or not. This results in a temporarily changing pattern of activity. A subset of nodes is defined as input layer, which receives values from the environment. Another subset of nodes is interpreted as the output of the network whose pattern of activity affects the environment.

From a certain perspective, the cognitive architecture in this chapter can be seen as a neural network approach in the sense that numeric values (in contrast to semantic entities in the case of typical programming languages) are passed from one schema to the next (appropriate) one, and that in the condition part of a schema incoming values are numerically computed and compared against a threshold. However, the range of *output* values is based on integer, thus permitting a finer grading. Also, the emphasis shifts from computing many simple nodes in parallel (which eventually results in a single output) to a technique which carefully selects the serial chain of rules that yield the output behavior.

Since serial processing comes closer to the way humans think, the advantage of the present cognitive architecture over neural networks is that it maintains explanatory power. For example, in the context of providing active recommendation services for Web browsing, this feature is indispensable, as the output of such a system will be used by humans later on. Like ordinary street maps, a "semantic Web topology" generated by the system must remain interpretable in order to find one's way from A to B.

Comparison with Neuro-Fuzzy Systems

Traditionally, neuro-fuzzy models are targeted at the domain of controlling tasks. As such they are mainly supervised techniques in the sense that they need a reference to which they have to adapt. Unfortunately, neither in a biological-evolutionary context (Maturana & Mpodozis, 2000) nor in certain application contexts, such as building a semantic topology of WWW-like environments, can such references be given. Thus, many neuro-fuzzy approaches that make use of supervised learning strategies cannot be employed in ACS. However, some neuro-fuzzy systems are considered useful for knowledge acquisition and data analysis, such as *fuzzy clustering* (Bezdek & Pal, 1992; Nauck et al., 1997) which requires unsupervised clustering of data. In the following, I will discuss different types of neuro-fuzzy systems based on the proposal of Detlef Nauck et al. (1997) who points out that neuronal networks and fuzzy systems can be combined in either of four ways:

1. Fuzzy methods can be used to enhance the performance and learning capabilities of neural networks (*fuzzy neural networks*). Here, the same arguments hold true which have already been used for neuronal networks and their black-box/cargo-cult behavior. It is difficult to figure out how they work and how to integrate existing knowledge.

2. Neural networks preprocess the input of a fuzzy system, or post-process its output (*concurrent approach*). Such processing is useful in cases where data are either incomplete or mixed with noise, such as in real-world environments. In such environments, the claim for semantic transparency, the idea that propositions represent the environment in a linguistically transparent way, can no longer be justified (Peschl & Riegler, 1999). This is in contrast to artificial Web-like environments, which serve a certain (technical) purpose and which consist of fully and unambiguously accessible and discrete data. Thus, there is no need to employ a concurrent neuro-fuzzy model in which the input is preprocessed or whose output is "interpreted" by a neural network. In some respects, the cognitive architecture presented in this chapter can be considered as a fuzzy system. The inclusion of a neural network component would destroy the explanatory power of the architecture.

3. Since the parameters of a fuzzy system, such as appropriate membership functions and fuzzy rules, are hard to determine in advance, neural learning algorithms are employed to accomplish this task during the learning period (*cooperative neuro-fuzzy*), e.g., using self-organizing feature maps to find fuzzy rules. However, semantic problems may arise as the neural network may transcend the typical numerical range of parameters of the fuzzy sets and/or weighting of fuzzy rules like FAMs (fuzzy associative memory) (Kosko, 1992). In contrast to cooperative neuro-fuzzy systems, the cognitive architecture uses statistical information such as the generality of condition parts and the importance of schemata for self-adaptation.

4. In "hybrid" models, both fuzzy and neuronal systems are combined into a homo-geneous architecture (e.g., Nauck et al., 1997). The core is that of a neural perceptron in which weights are substituted by fuzzy sets. Ideally, it should always be possible to interpret it as a system of fuzzy rules in order to keep semantics transparent, which is necessary to check the system for plausibility and to maintain it. While this variant is the most advanced neuro-fuzzy approach it should be rejected as a methodology in cognitive systems for the following reasons. Cognitive systems [human] acquire knowledge about a certain domain by being exposed to that domain for a long period of time. For example, getting to know the World-Wide Web requires surfing it for many hours. Obviously, it is easier to formulate a semantic Web topology based on serial surfing behavior rather than on raw data mining methods. The serial presentation of pages on the Web is a crucial component of a semantic understanding. Therefore, a serial approach comes closer to the under-lying browsing behavior than a parallel neural network and the hybrid approach discussed earlier. For example, finding shortcut solutions for traveling from A to B involves combining action sequences in higher-level entities, i.e., schemata in terms of the cognitive architecture. In general, a serial model enables canalized and therefore accelerated cognitive development while it is difficult to directly imple-ment canalization in neuronal-inspired architectures.

Future Research

The main tenet in this chapter is based on the idea that genuine cognitive capabilities cannot arise in systems that have been fed with propositions about the environment in which they are situated. Rather, such abilities can only emerge in systems equipped with a cognitive apparatus whose content is the result of learning and evolution. In order to avoid *tabula rasa* situations for individual cognitive systems, it is insufficient to apply ontogenetic learning mechanisms only, which require each individual in a population to learn even the most basic capabilities from scratch. This is unattainable for artificial cognitive systems working in complex environments. In the case of natural cognitive systems, each individual starts with a set of predispositions accumulated by generations of ancestors of its species. Philosophically, this has been condensed into Konrad Lorenz's (1941/1982) *evolutionary epistemology*. It naturalized Immanuel Kant's (1781) *a priori*s of space and time, which Kant regarded indispensible for understanding raw sensory experience, and reinterpreted them as phylogenetically acquired categories

(Riegler, 2005). These aspects should be of great concern for future research endeavors and appear to be fruitful fields for further investigations concerning ACS and its mutual feedback with natural systems. Some of them are sketched in the following:

1.   How is the releasing mechanism genetically determined and how does this genetic disposition evolve into the phenotype? These questions address the aspect of *functionalism*: It is obvious that behavior per se is not directly encoded in the genotype. Rather, the morphological structure of an organism serves as a basis for its behavioral patterns. But how is this correlation between matter and behavior realized?

2.   Can the evolutionary system be described as a rule system within which the inputs are certain internal and external states and whose outputs are instructions for building up the phenotype? If so, how are these inputs and building instructions formulated on a functional level (in contrast to the molecular level in genetic research)? And what appearance do such inputs and outputs have in the case of behavioral structures? Current biology and genetics are unable to answer such *epigenetic* questions. The reason is that development is a multi-scale process which runs on different levels of organization and space, e.g., gene regulation within cells, interaction between cells and tissue mechanics.

3.   Why is the number of regulatory genes in higher animals far greater than the number of structural genes? In unicellular organisms one can find the inverse proportion. This question can be partially solved by the observation that during evolution old structures remain in a system. They form the basis for newer structures and must not be removed.

4.   What exactly is the difference between external and internal constraints and selective pressures? This question refers to the old dichotomy between organism and environment, between subject and object. Theoretical insights such as Stuart Kauffman's (1993) theory of *Random Boolean Networks* show that in the absence of any external force, a complex system of nontrivial dimensions can reach high degrees of reliable dynamical order. Kauffman himself aligned his model to the genetic system that develops the few hundred different cell types in organisms out of about 10^5 genes.

My suggestion is that answers to many of these questions can be found by carefully crafting artificial cognitive systems that not only comply with the boundary conditions listed earlier in this chapter but which may also implement the cognitive architecture outlined here.

Conclusion

Based on interdisciplinary results from ethology, evolution theory and epistemology, I formulated a set of boundary conditions for the design of artificial cognition systems. Complying with the conditions helps to avoid the pitfalls of comparable systems such as the symbol grounding problem, the frame problem and the complexity problem. These conditions require: (1) equating cognition with life-maintaining processes; (2) the implementation of a procedural rather than structural hierarchy; (3) the organizational closure of the cognitive apparatus; and (4) using a fuzzy production system.

Based on these conditions, I outlined a cognitive architecture which tries to refrain from anthropocentric assumptions as much as possible. Due to the semantic-free working of the architecture, both its performance and learning component are independent of the actual set of sensors and effectors, which are attached to the system via a transduction shell. Furthermore, the expectation-driven character of the model and its hierarchical composition lead to increased adaptability.

These features open up new possibilities of how to build meaningful artificial cognition systems used in both industrial applications, e.g., to cope with the challenges of our knowledge-based society, and as objects of scientific and philosophical research. However, the model not only provides a new approach in ACS but also promotes the general idea that in disciplines of "organized complexity," which don't enjoy the descriptive and mathematical simplicity of classical physics, combining the results from various scientific disciplines launches new paths of exploration.

References

Ackley, D. H., & Littman, M. L. (1992). Interactions between learning and evolution. In C. G. Langton, C. Taylor, J. D. Farmer, & S. Rasmussen (Eds.), *Artificial life II* (pp. 487-509). Reading, MA: Addison-Wesley.

Angeline, P. J. (1994). Genetic programming and the emergence of intelligence. In K. E. Kinnear, Jr. (Ed.), *Advances in genetic programming*. Cambridge, MA: MIT Press.

Bezdek, J. C., & Pal, S. K. (Eds.). (1992). *Fuzzy models for pattern recognition*. New York: IEEE Press.

Braitenberg, V. (1984). *Vehicles: Experiments in synthetic psychology*. Cambridge, MA: MIT Press.

Brooks, R. (1991). Intelligence without reason. In J. Myopoulos & R. Reiter (Eds.), *Proceedings of the 12th International Joint Conference on Artificial Intelligence (IJCAI-91)* (pp. 569-595). San Mateo, CA: Morgan Kaufmann.

Dennett, D. C. (1984). Cognitive wheels: The frame problem of AI. In C. Hookway (Ed.), *Minds, machines, and evolution: Philosophical studies*. London: Cambridge University Press.

Drescher, G. (1991). *Made-up minds*. Cambridge: MIT Press.

Dreyfus, H. L., & Dreyfus, S. E. (1990). Making a mind versus modelling the brain: Artificial intelligence back at a branch-point. In M. Boden (Ed.), *The philosophy of artificial intelligence*. New York: Oxford University Press.

Epstein, J. M., & Axtell, R. L. (1996). *Growing artificial societies: Social science from the bottom up*. Cambridge: MIT Press.

Etzioni, O. (1993). Intelligence without robots: A reply to Brooks. *AI Magazine, 14*(4), 7-13.

Feynman, R. (1985). *Surely you're joking, Mr. Feynman!* New York: W. W. Norton.

Fodor, J. A. (1983). *The modularity of mind*. Cambridge: MIT Press.

Foerster, H. v. (1970). Molecular ethology, an immodest proposal for semantic clarification. In G. Ungar (Ed.), *Molecular mechanisms in memory and learning* (pp. 213-248). New York: Plenum Press. (Reprinted from Foerster, H. von [2003]. *Understanding understanding* [pp. 133-168]. New York: Springer.)

Foerster, H. v. (1972). Perception of the future and the future of perception. *Instructional Science, 1*(1), 31-43. (Reprinted from Foerster, H. von [2003]. *Understanding understanding*. New York: Springer.)

Foerster, H. v. (1973). On constructing a reality. In F. E. Preiser (Ed.), *Environmental design research* (Vol. 2, pp. 35-46), Stroudberg: Dowden, Hutchinson & Ross. (Reprinted from Foerster, H. von [2003]. *Understanding understanding* [pp. 211-228]. New York: Springer.)

Franklin, S. (1995). *Artificial minds*. Cambridge: MIT Press.

Glasersfeld. (1988). The reluctance to change a way of thinking. *The Irish Journal of Psychology, 9*, 83-90.

Glasersfeld, E. v. (1995). *Radical constructivism: A way of knowing and learning*. London: Falmer Press.

Goldberg, D. E. (1989). *Genetic algorithms in search, optimization and machine learning*. Reading: Addison Wesely.

Graybiel, A. (1998). The basal ganglia and chunking of action repertoires. *Neurobiology of Learning and Memory, 70*(1/2), 119-136.

Grey Walter, W. (1951). A machine that learns. *Scientific American, 185*(2), 60-63.

Haken, H. (1978). *Synergetics*. Berlin: Springer-Verlag.

Harnad, S. (1990). The symbol grounding problem. *Physica D, 42*, 335-346.

Hasslacher, B., & Tilden, M. W. (1995). Living machines. In L. Steels (Ed.), *Robotics and autonomous systems: The biology and technology of intelligent autonomous agents*. New York: Elsivier Publishers.

Heschl, A. (1990). L = C: A simple equation with astonishing consequences. *Journal of Theoretical Biology, 145*, 13-40.

Holland, J. H. (1992). *Adaption in natural and artificial systems*. Cambridge: MIT Press.

Holland, J. H., Holyoak, K. J., Nisbet, R. E., & Thagard, P. R. (1986). *Induction: Processes of inference, learning, and discovery*. Cambridge, MA: MIT Press.

Kant, I. (1781). Vorrede zur zweiten Ausgabe. In *Kritik der reinen Vernunft* (pp. 21-25). Leipzig, Germany: Reclam jun.

Kauffman, S. A. (1993). *The origins of order.* New York; Oxford: Oxford University Press.

King, R. D., Whelan, K. E., Jones, F. M., Reiser, P. G. K., Bryant, C. H., Muggleton, S. H., et al. (2004). Functional genomic hypothesis generation and experimentation by a robot scientist. *Nature, 427,* 247-252.

Klein, T. J. (1990). *Interdisciplinarity: History, theory and practice.* Detroit, MI: Wayne State University Press.

Kosko, B. (1992). *Neural networks and fuzzy systems: A dynamical systems approach to machine intelligence.* Englewood Cliffs, NJ: Prentice-Hall.

Kourtzi, Z., & Shiffrar, M. (1999). Dynamic representation of human body movement. *Perception, 28,* 49-62.

Koza, J. R. (1992). *Genetic programming.* Cambridge, MA: The MIT Press.

Lakoff, G. (1987). *Women, fire and dangerous things.* Chicago: Chicago University Press.

Langton, C. G. (1989). Artificial life. In C. G. Langton (Ed.), *Artificial life* (pp. 1-48). Redwood City, CA: Addison Wesley.

Langton, C. G. (1992). Introduction. In C. G. Langton et al. (Eds.), *Artificial life II.* Redwood City, CA: Addison Wesley.

Llinás, R. R. (2001). *I of the vortex.* Cambridge MA: MIT Press.

Lorenz, K. (1978). *Vergleichende Verhaltensforschung: Grundlagen der Ethologie.* Vienna: Springer.

Lorenz, K. Z. (1941). Kants Lehre vom Apriorischen im Lichte gegenwärtiger Biologie. *Blätter fur Deutsche Philosophie, 15,* 94-125. K.Z. Lorenz, Trans. (1982). Kant's doctrine of the a priori in the light of contemporary biology. In H. C. Plotkin (Ed.), *Learning, development and culture* (pp. 1121-1143), Chichester, UK: John Wiley.

Lorenz, K. Z., & Tinbergen, N. (1939). Taxis und Instinkthandlung in der Eirollbewegung der Graugans. *Zeitschrift fur Tierpsychologie, 1/2.*

Maes, P. (1994). Agents that reduce work and information overload. *Communications of the ACM, 37*(7), 31-40.

Maris, M., & te Boekhorst, R. (1996). Exploiting physical constraints: Heap formation through behavioral error in a group of robots. In M. Asada (Ed.), *Proceedings of IRO'96: IEEE / RSJ international conference on intelligent robots and systems* (pp. 1655-1660).

Maturana, H. R. (1974). Cognitive strategies. In H. v. Foerster (Ed.), *Cybernetics of cybernetics* (pp. 457-469). Biological Computer Laboratory, University of Illinois.

Maturana, H. R., & Mpodozis, J. (2000). The origin of species by means of natural drift. *Revista chilena de historia natural, 73*(2), 261-310.

Maturana, H. R., & Varela, F. J. (1980). *Autopoiesis and cognition: The realization of the living.* Dordrecht: Reidel.

McAllister, J. W. (2003). Algorithmic randomness in empirical data. *Studies in the History and Philosophy of Science, 34,* 633-646.

Nagel, T. (1974). What is it like to be a bat? *Philosophical Review, 83*, 435-450.

Nauck, D., Klawonn, F., & Kruse, R. (1997). *Foundations of neuro-fuzzy systems*. Chichester, UK: Wiley.

Peschl, M., & Riegler, A. (1999). Does representation need reality? In A. Riegler, M. Peschl, & A. v. Stein (Eds.), *Understanding representation in the cognitive sciences* (pp. 9-17). New York: Kluwer Academic & Plenum Publishers.

Pfeifer, R., & Scheier, C. (1999). *Understanding intelligence*. Cambridge, MA: MIT Press.

Piaget, J. (1937). *La construction du réel chez l'enfant*. Neuchâtel: Délachaux & Niestlé. English translation: J. Piaget (1954). *The construction of reality in the child*. New York: Ballantine.

Pylyshyn, Z. (Ed.). (1987). *The robot's dilemma*. Norwood: Ablex.

Riedl, R. (1977). A systems analytical approach to macro-evolutionary phenomena. *Quarterly Review of Biology, 52*, 351-370.

Riegler, A. (1992). Constructivist artificial life, and beyond. In B. McMullin (Ed.), *Proceedings of the workshop on autopoiesis and perception* (pp. 121-136). Dublin: Dublin City University.

Riegler, A. (1994a). Constructivist artificial life: The constructivist-anticipatory principle and functional coupling. In J. Hopf (Ed.), *Proceedings of the Workshop on Genetic Algorithms within the Framework of Evolutionary Computation at the 18th German Conference on Artificial Intelligence* (pp. 73-83). Saaarbrücken, Germany.

Riegler, A. (1994b). Fuzzy interval stack schemata for sensorimotor beings. In P. Gaussier, & J. D. Nicoud (Eds.), *Proceedings of the Perception to Action Conference* (pp. 392-395). Los Alamitos: IEEE Computer Society Press.

Riegler, A. (1995). CALM — Eine konstruktivistische Kognitionsarchitektur für Artificial Life. In K. Dautenhahn, et al. (Eds.), *Proceedings of the Workshop "Artificial Life"* (pp. 73-82). Sankt Augustin: GMD Studien No. 271.

Riegler, A. (1997). Ein kybernetisch-konstruktivistisches Modell der Kognition. In A. M. K. H. Müller, & F. Stadler (Eds.), *Konstruktivismus und Kognitionswissenschaft: Kulturelle Wurzeln und Ergebnisse* (pp. 75-88). Wien; New York: Springer.

Riegler, A. (2000). Können wir das Problem der Echtzeitkognition lösen? In K. Edlinger, G. Fleck, & W. Feigl (Eds.), *Reduktion, Spiel, Kreation: Zur Problematik von Reduktionismus und Artificial Life* (pp. 48-59). Frankfurt, Germany: Peter Lang.

Riegler, A. (2001a). The cognitive ratchet: The ratchet effect as a fundamental principle in evolution and cognition. *Cybernetics and Systems, 32*, 411-427.

Riegler, A. (2001b). The role of anticipation in cognition. In D. M. Dubois (Ed.), *Computing anticipatory systems. Proceedings of the American Institute of Physics 573* (pp. 534-541). Melville, New York: American Institute of Physics.

Riegler, A. (2001c). Towards a radical constructivist understanding of science. *Foundations of Science, 6*, 1-30.

Riegler, A. (2002). When is a cognitive system embodied? *Cognitive Systems Research*, Special issue on "Situated and embodied cognition," *3*, 339-348.

Riegler, A. (2003). Whose anticipations? In M. Butz, O. Sigaud, & P. Gerard (Eds.), *Anticipatory behavior in adaptive learning systems: Foundations, theories, and systems* (pp. 11-22). New York: Springer-Verlag.

Riegler, A. (2005). Like cats and dogs: Radical constructivism and evolutionary epistemology. In *Evolutionary epistemology, language and culture: A non-adaptationist, systems theoretical approach* (pp.47-65). Dordrecht: Springer.

Searle, J. R. (1980). Minds, brains, and programs. *Behavioral and Brain Sciences, 1*, 417-424.

Simon, H. A. (1969). *The sciences of the artificial.* Cambridge: MIT Press.

Sjölander, S. (1995). Some cognitive breakthroughs in the evolution of cognition and consciousness, and their impact on the biology of language. *Evolution & Cognition, 1*, 3-11.

Sjölander, S. (1997). On the evolution of reality: Some biological prerequisites and evolutionary stages. *Journal of Theoretical Biology, 187*, 595-600.

Smithers, T. (1991). The pretender's new clothes: BBS target article commentary on *The emperor's new mind* by Roger Penrose. *Behavioral and Brain Sciences, 13*, 683-684.

Stewart, J. (1991). Life = cognition: The epistemological and ontological significance of artificial life. In F. J. Varela & P. Bourgine (Eds.), *Toward a practice of autonomous systems* (pp. 475-483). Cambridge, MA: MIT Press.

Stewart, J. (1996). Cognition = life: Implications for higher-level cognition. *Behavioural Processes, 35*, 311-326.

Tyrrell, T. (1993). The use of hierarchies for action selection. *Journal of Adaptive Behavior, 1*, 387-420.

van Gelder, T. J. (1998). The dynamical hypothesis in cognitive science. *Behavioral and Brain Sciences, 21*, 1-14.

Verfaillie, K., & Daems, A. (2002). Representing and anticipating human actions in vision. *Visual Cognition, 9*, 217-232.

Waddington, C. H. (1942). Canalization of development and the inheritance of acquired characters. *Nature, 150*, 563-565.

Weaver, W. (1948). Science and complexity. *American Scientist, 36*, 536-544.

Weingart, P., & Stehr, N. (Eds.). (2000). *Practising interdisciplinarity.* Toronto: University of Toronto Press.

Wilson, S. W. (1991). The animat path to AI. In J. A. Meyer & S. W. Wilson (Eds.), *From animals to animats. Proceedings of the First International Conference on Simulation of Adaptive Behavior* (pp. 15-21). Cambridge, MA: MIT Press.

Winograd, T., & Flores, F. (1986). *Understanding computers and cognition: A new foundation for design.* Norwood: Ablex.

Zadeh, L. (1965). Fuzzy sets. *Journal of Information and Control, 8*, 338-353.

Ziemke, T. (2003). What's that thing called embodiment? In *Proceedings of the 25th Annual Meeting of the Cognitive Science Society* (pp.1305-1310). Hillsdale: Lawrence Erlbaum.

Endotes

[1]   Although it has gained popularity in recent years, the idea of embodiment was formulated much earlier. Already in 1970, Heinz von Foerster claimed that "Memory contemplated in isolation is reduced to 'recording,' learning to 'change,' perception to 'input,' and so on. In other words, in separating these functions from the totality of cognitive processes, one has abandoned the original problem and is now searching for mechanisms that implement entirely different functions which may or may not have any semblance to some processes that are subservient to the maintenance of the integrity of the organism as a functioning unit" (Foerster, 1970, pp. 135-136).

[2]   In physics, a related idea can be found in Haken's (1978) synergetics approach to complex phenomena.

Chapter II

An Embodied Logical Model for Cognition in Artificial Cognition Systems

Guilherme Bittencourt, Universidade Federal de Santa Catarina, Brazil

Jerusa Marchi, Universidade Federal de Santa Catarina, Brazil

Abstract

In this chapter we describe a cognitive model based on the systemic approach and on the Autopoiesis theory. The syntactical definition of the model consists of logical propositions but the semantic definition includes, besides the usual truth value assignments, what we call emotional flavors, which correspond to the state of the agent's body translated into cognitive terms. The combination between logical propositions and emotional flavors allows the agent to learn and memorize relevant propositions that can be used for reasoning. These propositions are represented in a specific format — prime implicants/implicates — which is enriched with annotations that explicitly store the internal relations among their literals. Based on this representation, a memory mechanism is described and algorithms are presented that learn a proposition from the agent's experiences in the environment and that are able to determine the degree of robustness of the propositions, given a partial assignment representing the environment state.

Introduction

In recent years the interest in logical models applied to practical problems such as planning (Bibel, 1997) and robotics (Scherl et al., 2003) has been increasing. Although the limitations of the *sense-model-plan-act* approach have been greatly overcome (Giacomo et al., 2002), the gap between the practical *ad hoc* path to "behavior-based artificial creatures situated in the world" (Brooks, 1991) and the logical approach is yet to be filled.

In this chapter we define a logic-based generic model for a cognitive agent. This model found inspiration in several sources. From the systemic approach (Morin, 1991) and from the Autopoiesis theory (Varela, 1989) came the hypothesis that cognition is an emergent property of a cyclic dynamic self-organizing process. From the theory of evolution (Darwin, 1998) and from the memetics theory (Dawkins, 1976) came the belief that variability and selection is the base of both life and cognition. From (dilettante) neurobiology (Changeux, 1983, 2002; Damasio, 1994, 2000) came the guidelines for pursuing psychological plausibility. From Piaget's *genetic epistemology* (Piaget, 1963; Piaget, 2001) came the requirement that learning and cognition should be closely related and, therefore, that the cognitive modeling process should strongly depend on the cognitive agent's particular history. From the logicist school (Newell, 1980, 1982; Brachman et al., 1985) and the work on *cognitive robotics* (Levesque et al., 1998; Shanahan, 1993) came the focus on computational logical models. From Wittgenstein (Wittgenstein, 1933) came the intended epistemological status of logic.

Assuming that cognition can be captured by a computational model (Scheutz, 2002) and that this model is somehow based on evolutionary computation (Baum, 2004), in order to model cognition it is necessary to define the elements of an evolutionary environment where such evolutionary computation can take place. In natural evolution, the DNA codes for proteins, but the protein behavior depends on its three-dimensional structure that is not coded in the DNA. The match between code and "good" behavior is computed by selection; staying alive (and reproducing) is the positive feedback to the significant matching. To model cognition using an evolutionary algorithm, we need to define, on the one hand, the code (we propose to adopt a specific logical representation — prime implicants/implicates) and, on the other hand, the necessary feedback modeled in a minimalist approach, only by "good" or "bad" *emotions*. Finally, we need variability and selection, and time to let them work. Although no particular evolutionary algorithm is described, the chapter formally defines a possible computational framework that supports these necessary features.

The model to be defined is a first approximation. Several aspects of the model could and should be extended to include more complex mechanisms, but this presentation remains as simple as possible in order to stress the solution schema proposed by the model to a specific conceptual problem: *how a cognitive agent is to learn and explore meaning in its environment*. This problem has wide philosophical, biological, computational and physical implications. This first approximation is restricted to a simple computational context defined through an artificial environment, but the ultimate ambition of the proposed model is to meet Brian Smith's criteria for a *theory of computing* (Smith, 1996):

- *Empirical:* to explain the full range of computational practice
- *Conceptual:* to be independent of an external semantics
- *Cognitive:* to provide an intelligible foundation for the computational theory of mind

The model characteristics are mainly presented through examples: a more formal presentation of the mathematical details is done elsewhere (Marchi et al., 2004). The proposed model can be viewed from two perspectives: an external one that consists of the model's desiderata and includes the description of *what* it would be interesting for a cognitive mechanism to do, given the restrictions imposed by the environment definition, and an internal one that describes *how* the interesting features of the cognitive mechanism — learning, reasoning and remembering — are in fact implemented. In the sequel, *italic* expressions should be understood as technically defined terms in the model and "quoted" expressions are intended to evoke a certain "meaning" whose precise definition is out of the scope of the model.

The chapter is organized as follows: In the Background section, some aspects of theories that directly inspired the proposed model are presented. In the External View section, the general framework of the proposed cognitive model is defined. In Section Representation, the main logical concepts and notations adopted in the chapter are introduced and the central hypothesis of the proposed model is presented. In the Internal View section, the internal organization, structure and functioning of the cognitive agent is described. Finally, in the Conclusion, conclusions and future work are presented.

Background

Among all the inspirational sources above, the theories briefly commented on in this section cover, in a complementary way, the most general aspects of the proposed model. Wittgenstein's *Tractatus Logico-Philosophicus* (Wittgenstein, 1933) defines the intended epistemological interpretation of the model, and the Autopoiesis theory has indicated how to deal with the practical aspects of the model functioning.

Tractatus Logico-Philosophicus

The Austrian thinker Ludwig Wittgenstein (1889-1951) is one the greatest philosophers in history. The relevance of the "young" Wittgenstein to the proposed model is that his approach to philosophy is characterized by an emphasis on language and how it can be used to express thoughts. According to Wittgenstein, philosophical problems arise because of misuse of language, and it is only when we understand everyday language that these questions may be dealt with.

We do not intend to present any interpretation of Wittgenstein's *Tractatus Logico-Philosophicus;* we limit ourselves to quoting some passages from the preface and some of the aphorisms of the book that, we think, quite precisely define the epistemological status of the proposed model, in the sense that it is intended to model *thoughts*. When relevant, these aphorisms are recalled during the presentation of the model through the notation (TLP *n.m*), where *n.m* is the aphorism number.

Preface

... The whole sense of the book might be summed up the following words: what can be said at all can be said clearly, and what we cannot talk about we must pass over in silence. Thus the aim of the book is to draw a limit to thought, or rather — not to thought, but to the expression of thoughts: for in order to be able to draw a limit to thought, we should have to find both sides of the limit thinkable (i.e. we should have to be able to think what cannot be thought). It will therefore only be in language that the limit can be drawn, and what lies on the other side of the limit will simply be nonsense... If this work has any value, it consists in two things: the first is that thoughts are expressed in it, and on this score the better the thoughts are expressed — the more the nail has been hit on the head — the greater will be its value... On the other hand the truth of the thoughts that are here communicated seems to me unassailable and definitive. I therefore believe myself to have found, on all essential points, the final solution of the problems. And if I am not mistaken in this belief, then the second thing in which this work consists is that it shows how little is achieved when these problems are solved.

Selected Aphorisms

1. The world is everything that is the case.

    1.1 The world is the totality of facts, not of things.

    1.2 The world divides into facts.

2. What is the case, the fact, is the existence of atomic facts.

3. The logical picture of the facts is the thought.

    3.4 The proposition determines a place in logical space: the existence of this logical place is guaranteed by the existence of the constituent parts alone, by the existence of the significant proposition.

    3.41 The propositional sign and the logical co-ordinates: that is the logical place.

4. The thought is the significant proposition.

    4.022 The proposition shows its sense. The proposition shows how things stand, if it is true. And it says, that they do so stand.

    4.1 A proposition presents the existence and non-existence of atomic facts.

    4.2 The sense of a proposition is its agreement and disagreement with the possibilities of the existence and non-existence of the atomic facts.

    4.461 The proposition shows what it says, the tautology and the contradiction that they say nothing.

    The tautology has no truth-conditions, for it is unconditionally true; and the contradiction is on no condition true. Tautology and contradiction are without sense.

(Like the point from which two arrows go out in opposite directions.)

(I know, e.g. , nothing about the weather, when I know that it rains or does not rain.)

5.   Propositions are truth-functions of elementary propositions. (An elementary proposition is a truth-function of itself.)

6.   The general form of truth-function is: $[\bar{p}, \bar{\xi}, N(\bar{\xi})]$. This is the general form of proposition.

7.   Whereof one cannot speak, thereof one must be silent.

Autopoiesis

The autopoiesis and enaction theory of Humberto Maturana and Francisco Varela (Maturana et al., 1980) connects cognition and action stating that "all knowing is doing and all doing is knowing." Although some computational models of the biological aspects of the theory have been developed, in the context of artificial life research (McMullin et al., 1997), Autopoiesis in the cognitive domain has not yet been the subject of computational experiments to the authors knowledge.

The following definitions clarify the notion of autopoietic system (Maturana et al., 1980):

- A *domain* is a description for the "world brought forth" — a circumscription of experiential flux via reference to current states and possible trajectories.

- A *unity* is that which is distinguishable from a background, the sole condition necessary for existence in a given domain. The nature of a unity and the domain in which the unity exists are specified by the process of its distinction and determination; this is so regardless of whether this process is conceptual or physical.

- A *space* is the domain of all the possible interactions of a collection of unities that the properties of these unities establish by specifying its dimensions.

- A *composite unity* exists in the space that its components, seen as unities, specify, because it interacts through the properties of its components. On the other hand, a composite unity is realized as a unity in the space that its properties, as a simple unity, specify.

- The *organization* of a composite unity is the relations that define it as a machine, and determine the dynamics of interactions and transformations which it may undergo as such a unity.

- The *structure* of a composite unity is the actual components plus the actual relations that take place between them while realizing it as a particular composite unity characterized by a particular organization.

In these terms, it is possible to define an autopoietic cognitive system:

A cognitive system is a system whose organization defines a domain of interactions in which it can act with relevance to the maintenance of itself, and the process of cognition is the actual (inductive) acting or behaving in this domain.

During the presentation of the model, the adopted instantiations of the concepts above are defined.

External View

"Everything should be made as simple as possible, but not simpler."

Albert Einstein

The proposed *cognitive agent* is immersed in an unknown environment and is going through an "experiencial flux" (TLP 1). This flux, its *domain* according to the Autopoiesis theory nomenclature, is represented as a set of *primitive* propositional symbols: $-P = \{p_1, \cdots, p_n\}-$, the *simple unities* that compose the cognitive agent (TLP 2). In a first approximation, the only property of each propositional symbol is its *truth value*.[1] Therefore, the *space* is defined as the set of all possible truth assignments to this set of propositional symbols $- A_p$. We also suppose that the environment drifts along the possible states through flips of the primitive propositional symbols truth values (TLP 1.1 and 1.2).

Therefore, from the agent point of view, the environment, including the agent itself, is "conceived" as an unbound sequence of assignments ..., $\varepsilon_{t-1}, \varepsilon_t, \varepsilon_{t+1}$ ... where $\varepsilon_i \in A_p$, $\varepsilon_i : P \to \{true, false\}$ are semantic functions that map propositional symbols into truth values. The transition from a state t to a state $t + 1$ is defined by the set of flipping propositional symbols $F_t \subseteq P$, such that if $p_i \in F_t$ then $\varepsilon_t(p_i) \neq \varepsilon_{t+1}(p_i)$ (see Figure 1). At each state, the agent is only *aware* of a partial assignment, i.e., although the agent may know which are the relevant propositional symbols, their truth values are only partially known.

Based on a Kripke structure (Kripke, 1963), the semantics of the evolving environment could be formalized using a modal (Halpern et al., 1985) or temporal logic (Shoham et al., 1988). To keep the logical framework of the model as simple as possible, we prefer, instead of considering a sequence of assignments, to attach a state label to the propositional symbols and to consider a single classical logic assignment ε. More formally, the set of propositional symbols is redefined as $P = ...P^{t-1} \cup P^t \cup P^{t+1} \cup ...$ where $P^t = \{p_1^t, ..., p_n^t\}$, and $\varepsilon : P \to \{true, false\}$. In principle, the agent could store an arbitrary number of past states and it could consider an equally arbitrary number of possible future sequences of states (TLP 6).

The primitive propositional symbols can be of two kinds: *controllable* and *uncontrollable*. Roughly, uncontrollable symbols correspond to *perceptions* and controllable ones to *actions*. Perceptions may include *internal perceptions*, i.e., internal properties

Figure 1. The space evolution

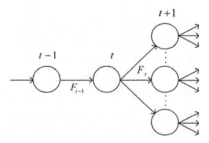

of the agent that are "felt," such as proprioception information (Berthoz, 1997), and actions may include orders to the agent body. Both controllable and uncontrollable symbols are "neutral," in the sense that *a priori* the agent is indifferent to which semantic values (true or false) they assume (TLP 4.1 and 4.2).

Primitive propositional symbols can be combined into *propositions* that correspond to the *composite unities*, according to the Autopoiesis theory nomenclature. The *organization* that defines these propositions is simply the rules of propositional logic syntax, i.e., a proposition is simply a well-formed formula of propositional logic and its semantics is derived from the truth values of its components as usual (TLP 5). The *structure* associated with a specific proposition is the actual syntactical expression by which it is represented. It should be noted that a proposition can change its structure through any logically valid transformation, e.g., the application of an inference rule. Because the proposed cognitive agent is a computational one, the particular adopted syntactical representation can have an important impact on the computational properties of the cognitive mechanism, such as efficiency, modularity and reuse potential. The composite unities can be used as components of other composite unities, i.e., it is possible to associate an *abstract propositional symbol* with a proposition and to use it as an ordinary proposition symbol in another proposition. Let $Q = \{q_1, q_2, ...\}$ be the set of all abstract propositional symbols. Propositions that contain abstract propositional symbols are called *abstract propositions*.

In order to "embody" the agent, we assume that the state of the agent's "body" can be perceived through *emotional flavors*.[2] An emotional flavor has two complementary aspects: from the cognitive point of view it can be true or false and from the agent's body point of view it can be, in a first approximation, either "good" or "bad," in the sense that the agent has the *motivation* that good emotional flavors be true and bad ones false.[3]

These emotional flavors correspond to what Damasio call "emotions" (Damasio, 2003) and define the raison d'être of the agent's cognitive mechanism: to control the truth values of emotional flavors using controllable symbol manipulations. Damasio has suggested that while the senses of vision, hearing, touch, taste and smell (the primitive propositional symbols of the proposed model) function by nerve activation patterns that correspond to the state of the external world, emotions are nerve activation patterns that correspond to the state of the internal world. If we experience a state of fear, then our brains will record this body state in nerve cell activation patterns obtained from neural and hormonal feedback, and this information (the emotional flavors of the proposed model) may then be used to adapt behavior appropriately.

Clearly, the binary nature of the adopted emotional flavors is a coarse approximation of the concept intended by Damasio. Based on the notion of *somatic markers*, he describes a range of qualitatively different phenomena, from genetically determined emotions to socially learned feelings.

From the cognitive point of view, any motivation is directly or indirectly derived from the desire to control the truth values of emotional flavors and therefore, beyond their truth values, propositions only have "meaning" with respect to the emotional flavors to which they are associated.

To satisfy this motivation, the cognitive agent should be able to learn the relevant relations between specific emotional flavors and propositions built up from primitive propositional symbols. Once a proposition is known to be true whenever a given "good" emotional flavor is true, this proposition can be associated with an abstract propositional symbol that becomes the *cognitive* counterpart of the emotional flavor (TLP 3). Using this proposition, the agent can "rationally" act on the truth values of the proposition's controllable symbols in such a way that the proposition truth status is preserved when the values of the uncontrollable symbols change. This relation between an emotional flavor and an abstract propositional symbol (and its learned proposition) is called a *thought* (TLP 4).

Example 1. To apply the proposed cognitive model to an experimental situation, the first step would be to define the emotional flavors and build the non-cognitive part of the agent in such a way that the adopted emotional flavors suitably represent the internal functioning of the agent and its articulation with the external environment. Consider the simple agent-environment setting shown in Figure 2. The environment consists of floor and walls. The agent is a robot that interacts with the environment through six uncontrollable and two controllable primitive propositional symbols. The uncontrollable symbols are associated with left, front and right short distance sensors (s_l, s_f and s_r) and long distance sensors (v_l, v_f and v_r). The controllable ones are associated with left and right motors (m_l and m_r).

A possible "good" emotional flavor would be Move, that is, true when the robot is moving. Another possible class of emotional symbols would be "target detectors"[4] that can be "good" if the target is a "friend" (e.g., some specific fellow robot identified by the emotional flavor Track Mom), or "bad," if the target is an "enemy." For the sake of simplicity, the emotional flavors of the example were chosen, according to Damasio's concepts, much closer to primitive emotions (i.e., general goals of an artificial agent) than to sentiments.

Figure 2. A simple robot

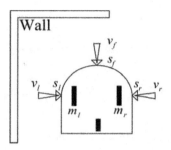

A logical proposition built up of propositional symbols becomes associated, after learning, with each emotional flavor. These logical propositions are associated with abstract propositional symbols (e.g., q_{move}, q_{tmom}). The relation between logical propositions and emotional flavors is what we call thoughts.

A thought combines an emotional flavor and a logical proposition. Such a proposition, because of its logical properties, can possibly be factored into simpler sub-propositions, and these sub-propositions can be associated with abstract propositional symbols. This factoring mechanism can give rise to new derived thoughts, composed by the sub-propositions and "refined" versions of the original emotional flavor. These new emotional flavors are refined in the sense that, although they share the same motivating character of the original emotional flavor, they are restricted by their associated sub-propositions and, therefore, they can be recognized as "different" from one another with respect to the environment. The new derived thoughts "entangle"[5] the "meaning" of the original emotional flavor with the environment properties captured by their associated sub-propositions, whose truth values ultimately depend on the primitive propositional symbols (TLP 3.4).

The formalism that supports this entanglement is the central point of the proposed solution to the problem of extracting meaning from the environment. On the one hand, its syntactical abstraction mechanism allows for the construction of complex control mechanisms, articulated with the environment properties through the progressive automatizing of the lower level abstract propositions. On the other hand, semantically it allows that general emotional flavors, such as *hunger* and *sexual attraction*, be refined in principle into complex thought structures able to control behaviors such as *search for eatable fruits* and *build a nest to show you are a good sexual partner*; or even *go to a French restaurant* and *buy a red Ferrari*.

Example 2. Considering the scenario in Example 1, after learning the logical proposition q_{move}, the agent could factor it into three sub-propositions that differ in the patterns of sensors and motor activation they allow — q_f, q_l, q_r. This factoring can lead to new *refined emotional flavors — Move forward, Move left and Move right — that share the same "moving" motivation of the original emotional flavor Move, but differ with respect to their associated sub-propositions. Analogously, logical proposition q_{tmom} can be factored, according to the sensor patterns, into sub-propositions represented by abstract propositional symbols q_{tmf}, q_{tml}, q_{tmr} that refine the emotional flavor Track Mom into Track Mom forward, Track Mom at left and Track Mom at right. The relation between the refined emotional flavors and the abstract propositional symbols (and their associated sub-propositions) gives rise to new derived thoughts.*

The intended scenario can be described as a modified Chinese room "gedankenexperiment" (Searle, 1980): A cognitive agent lies in an isolated room where a set of light spots correspond to the uncontrollable propositional symbols and a set of buttons to the controllable ones. In the modified experiment, there is also a communication window through which objects from the outside world can be introduced into the room. These objects correspond to the emotional flavors and are inherently "good" (e.g., water or food) or "bad" (e.g., garbage or mosquitoes) from the agent point of view, in which "inherently" is to be understood as determined by the evolutionary history of both the agent and the environment that provides the objects. In the case of artificial agents, the lack of an evolutionary history implies that the good/bad discrimination capacity should be defined by design. This capacity should reflect the agent "intentions" and should be based on a measure of the "quality" of the agent's present (or expected future) state with respect to these intentions.

The goal of the agent's cognitive mechanism is to discover the relation between light spots and button pressing and the objects introduced into the room in such a way that the bad ones are avoided and the good ones encouraged. Clearly, the agent's success depends, on the one hand, on the existence of an external relation between the light spots and buttons patterns and the objects introduced into the room, and on the other hand, on the possibility of modeling this relation using the agent's cognitive mechanism. Another consequence is that the only meaningful relations are exactly those that associate introduced objects and light spots and button patterns. Although the agent can build arbitrary propositions about the light spot patterns and verify their validity, these propositions will only have "meaning" if they predict in a sensible way the relation between buttons and the introduced objects.

A natural metaphor of this situation is the honeybee hive. The social cognitive mechanism is localized inside the hive and its only access to the world is the incoming bees. They bring in a quality, distance and angular pattern that refers to a honey possibility. This pattern is processed in the form of a dance that results in an action — sending out other bees having the same pattern — and eventually, the action results in more honey inside the hive. The hive cognitive mechanism does not know anything about flowers, it only knows about the honeybee dance and honey. In other words, cognition is like a honeybee dance, but instead of modeling flower location it models the "world" or "alles, was der Fall ist" (Wittgenstein, 1933).

Representation

The essence of the agent's cognitive mechanism consists of *thoughts*, i.e., relations between propositions and emotional flavors. The use and maintenance of this structure can be seen as the *autopoietic activity* of the agent's cognitive mechanism, its self construction mechanism. The syntactical character of the model led to the hypothesis that it is interesting to restrict the organization and structure of the logical propositions that compose the agent's thoughts in order to define learning, reasoning and remembering mechanisms that can be seen as cyclic dynamic self-organizing processes (Varela, 1979). In this section, we introduce some notation, formally define the adopted restrictions and discuss their advantages.

Preliminaries

As above, let $P = \{p_1, ..., p_n\}$ be a set of propositional symbols and $LIT = \{L_1, ..., L_{2n}\}$ the set of their associated literals, where $L_i = p_j$ or $L_i = \neg p_j$. A *clause* C is a *disjunction* (Fitting, 1990) of literals: $C = L_1 \vee \cdots \vee L_{k_C}$ and a *dual clause*, or *term*, is a *conjunction* of literals: $D = L_1 \wedge \cdots \wedge L_{k_D}$. Given a propositional logic language $L(P)$ and an *ordinary formula* $\psi \in L(P)$, there are algorithms for converting it into a *conjunctive normal form (CNF)* and into a *disjunctive normal form (DNF)*, e.g., (Quine, 1959; Slagle et al., 1970; Socher, 1991). The CNF is defined as a conjunction of clauses, $CNF_\psi = C_1 \wedge \cdots \wedge C_m$, and the DNF as a disjunction of terms, $DNF_\psi = D_1 \vee \cdots \vee D_w$, such that $\psi \Leftrightarrow CNF_\psi \Leftrightarrow DNF_\psi$.

A clause C is an *implicate* (Herzig et al., 1999; Jackson, 1990; Kean et al., 1990) of a formula ψ if $\psi \vDash C$, and it is a *prime implicate* if for all implicates C' of ψ such that $C' \vDash C$, we have $C \vDash C'$, or syntactically (Ramesh et al., 1997), for all literals $L \in C$, $L \in C$, $\psi \nvDash (C - \{L\})$. We define PI_ψ as the conjunction of all prime implicates of ψ, clearly $\psi \Leftrightarrow PI_\psi$.

A term D is an *implicant* of a formula ψ if $D \vDash \psi$, and it is a *prime implicant* if for all implicants D' of ψ such that $D \vDash D'$, we have $D' \vDash D$, or syntactically, for all literals $L \in D$, $(D - \{L\}) \nvDash \psi$. We define IP_ψ as the disjunction of all prime implicants of ψ, again $\psi \Leftrightarrow IP_\psi$. This normal form is also known as *Blake canonical form*.

In propositional logic, implicates and implicants are dual notions. In particular, an algorithm that calculates one of them can also be used to calculate the other (Socher, 1991; Bittencourt et al., 2001).

Alternatively, prime implicates and implicants can be defined as special cases of CNF (or DNF) formulas that consist of the smallest sets of clauses (or terms) closed for inference, without any subsumed clauses (or terms) and not containing a literal and its negation. In the sequel, conjunctions and disjunctions of literals, clauses and terms are treated as sets. The symbols [] are used as delimiters for disjunctions and the symbols ⟨⟩ are used as delimiters for conjunctions.

Quantum Notation

Given a formula ψ, represented by a conjunctive normal form CNF_ψ and by a disjunctive normal form DNF_ψ, we introduce the concept of a *conjunctive quantum*, defined as a pair (L, F_c), where L is a literal that occurs in ψ and $F_c \subseteq CNF_\psi$ is its set of *conjunctive coordinates* that contains the subset of clauses in CNF_ψ to which literal L belongs. A quantum is noted L^F. Dually, we define a *disjunctive quantum* as a pair (L, F_d), where L is a literal that occurs in ψ and $F_d \subseteq DNF_\psi$ is its set of *disjunctive coordinates* that contains the subset of terms in DNF_ψ to which literal L belongs. The rationale behind the choice of the name *quantum* is to emphasize that we are not interested in an isolated literal, but that our *minimal* unit of interest is the literal and its situation with respect to the proposition in which it occurs (TLP 3.41).

The quantum notation can be used to characterize PI_ψ and IP_ψ of a formula ψ, given, respectively, by one CNF_ψ and one DNF_ψ. Let $D = L_1 \wedge ... \wedge L_k$ be a term represented by a set of conjunctive quanta, $L_1^{F_c^1} \wedge ... \wedge L_k^{F_c^k}$. D is an implicant of ψ if $\cup_{i=1}^k F_c^i = CNF_\psi$ and $L_i \not\Leftrightarrow \neg L_j, i, j \in \{1, ..., k\}$, i.e., D contains at least one literal that belongs to each clause in CNF_ψ, spanning a path through CNF_ψ, and no pair of contradictory literals. To be a prime implicant, a term D must satisfy a *non-redundancy* condition, i.e., each of its literals should represent *alone* at least one clause in CNF_ψ. To define this condition, we introduce the notion of *exclusive coordinates*. Given a term D and a literal $L_i \in D$, the exclusive conjunctive coordinates of L in D, defined by $\widehat{F}_c^i = F_c^i - \cup_{j=1, j \neq i}^k F_c^j$, are the clauses in the set F_c^i, to which no other literal of D belongs. Using this notion, the non-redundancy condition can be written as: $\forall i \in \{1, ..., k\}, \widehat{F}_c^i \neq \varnothing$.

Dually, a clause $C = L_1 \vee ... \vee L_k$ represented by a set of disjunctive quanta, $L_1^{F_d^1} \vee ... \vee L_k^{F_d^k}$, such that $\cup_{i=1}^k F_d^i = DNF_\psi$, with no pair of tautological literals allowed, is an implicate. Again C is a prime implicate if it satisfies the non-redundancy condition, expressed by $\forall i \in \{1, ..., k\}$, $\widehat{F}_d^i \neq \varnothing$, where $\widehat{F}_d^i = F_d^i - \cup_{j=1, j \neq i}^k F_d^j$ is the set of exclusive disjunctive coordinates of L_i in C.

Given a proposition ψ, it is possible to determine the sets of conjunctive and disjunctive quanta that define IP_ψ with respect to PI_ψ and PI_ψ with respect to IP_ψ, respectively. This prime quantum notation is an enriched representation for prime implicate and implicant sets, in the sense that it explicitly contains the relation between literals in one form and the clauses (or terms) in which they occur in the other form. We call PIP the set of all such pairs of prime representations:

$$PIP = \{(PI_\psi, IP_\psi) \mid \psi \in L(P)\}$$

It is interesting to note that tautologies and contradictions have trivial representations as PIP pairs — $(\top \top)$ and $(\bot \bot)$, respectively, where $\top$ and $\bot$ are the syntactical counterparts of the truth values *true* and *false* — and therefore "mean" nothing (TLP 4.461).

Example 3. The prime forms of possible abstract propositional symbols q_{move} and q_{tmom}, associated with the emotional flavors Move and Track Mom, that use the propositional symbols introduced in Example 1 can be represented by the following PIP pairs:

$$\left(\begin{array}{l} 0:[-m_l^{\{0\},\{0\}}, -s_f^{\{2,3,4\},\{2,3\}}, -s_r^{\{1,4\},\{1\}}] \\ 1:[-m_l^{\{0\},\{0\}}, -m_r^{\{1\},\{2\}}, -s_f^{\{2,3,4\},\{2,3,4\}}] \quad 0:\langle -m_l^{\{0,1\},\{0,1\}}, m_r^{\{4,6\},\{4,6\}}, -s_l^{\{2,3,5\},\{2,3,5\}}\rangle \\ 2:[-m_l^{\{1\},\{1\}}, -s_f^{\{2,3,4\},\{3,4\}}, -s_l^{\{0,2\},\{0\}}] \quad 1:\langle m_l^{\{5,6\},\{5,6\}}, -m_r^{\{1,2\},\{1,2\}}, -s_r^{\{0,3,4\},\{0,3,4\}}\rangle \\ 3:[-s_f^{\{2,3,4\},\{3\}}, -s_l^{\{0,2\},\{0\}}, -s_r^{\{1,4\},\{1\}}] \quad 2:\langle m_r^{\{4,6\},\{4,6\}}, -s_f^{\{0,1,2,3\},\{0,1\}}, -s_r^{\{2,3,5\},\{5\}}\rangle \\ \quad 4:[m_r^{\{0,2,3\},\{0,2,3\}}, -s_r^{\{1,4\},\{1,4\}}] \quad 3:\langle m_l^{\{5,6\},\{5\}}, m_r^{\{4,6\},\{4\}}, -s_f^{\{0,1,2,3\},\{0,1,2,3\}}\rangle \\ \quad 5:[m_l^{\{1,3,4\},\{1,3,4\}}, -s_r^{\{0,2\},\{0,2\}}] \quad 4:\langle m_l^{\{5,6\},\{5,6\}}, -s_f^{\{0,1,2,3\},\{1,2\}}, -s_r^{\{0,3,4\},\{4\}}\rangle \\ \quad 6:[m_l^{\{1,3,4\},\{1,4\}}, m_r^{\{0,2,3\},\{0,2\}}] \end{array}\right)$$

$$\left(\begin{array}{l} 0:[v_f^{\{1\},\{1\}}, v_l^{\{2\},\{2\}}, v_r^{\{0\},\{0\}}] \\ 1:[-v_f^{\{0,2\},\{0\}}, -v_r^{\{1,2\},\{1\}}] \quad 0:\langle -v_f^{\{1,3\},\{1\}}, -v_l^{\{2,3\},\{2\}}, v_r^{\{0\},\{0\}}\rangle \\ 2:[-v_l^{\{0,1\},\{0\}}, -v_r^{\{1,2\},\{2\}}] \quad 1:\langle v_f^{\{0\},\{0\}}, -v_l^{\{2,3\},\{3\}}, -v_r^{\{1,2\},\{1\}}\rangle \\ 3:[-v_f^{\{0,2\},\{2\}}, -v_l^{\{0,1\},\{1\}}] \quad 2:\langle -v_f^{\{1,3\},\{3\}}, v_l^{\{0\},\{0\}}, -v_r^{\{1,2\},\{2\}}\rangle \end{array}\right)$$

where both coordinate (F) and exclusive coordinate $(\hat{F})$ sets, are shown for each quantum in the form: $L^{F,\hat{F}}$.

Working Hypothesis

The main hypothesis underlying the proposed cognitive model consists in restricting the organization and structure of the propositions that participate in thoughts in such a way that these propositions are always represented using *prime normal forms*. This choice is due to the following properties of these normal forms:

1.   The prime form representations are unique (up to the order of literals, clauses and terms that occur in them). The only other unique representation for propositions is complete DNF[6], which is usually much larger than prime forms.

2.   Given both prime representations of a given formula ψ, the prime representations of its negation can be obtained directly[7]: $PI_{\neg\psi} = \overline{IP_\psi}, IP_{\neg\psi} = \overline{PI_\psi}$.

3.   The prime implicates and implicants of a proposition can be queried in polynomial time for consistency, validity, clause entailment, implicants, equivalence, sentential entailment and model enumeration (Darwiche et al., 2001).

4.   Prime implicates and implicants of a proposition present a holographic relation, where each literal in a clause is associated with a dual clause and, conversely, each literal in a dual clause is associated with a clause. This allows the identification of which dual clauses are "critically" affected by a given clause (TLP 4.022).

The first and most important property — the uniqueness of the prime representations — deserves more comment. The prime representations in *PIP* are unique in the sense that, given a set P of propositional symbols, any proposition build up with symbols of P has one and only one representation in *PIP*, but the structure of any pair in *PIP* depends only on the *relations* between the propositional symbols and not on their identity with respect to the set P. Therefore, each pair represents a whole *family* of structurally identical propositions that only differ in the *names* that are attributed to its variable symbols. Propositions that belong to the same family can be transformed among them simply by renaming their propositional symbols, possibly by a negated value. Such transformations can be formalized as sequences of applications of two syntactical transformation functions:

- *Exchange* ($X : PIP \times P \times P \to PIP$): Given a prime pair and two propositional symbols, exchange the identity of the symbols in the given prime pair.
- *Flip* ($F : PIP \times P \to PIP$): Given a prime pair and one propositional symbol, negate all literals in the prime pair where the symbol occurs.

Any proposition build up with n propositional symbols will be true in some subset of the 2^n possible models, therefore the total number of non trivial propositions is given by:[8]

$$\sum_{i=1}^{2^{n-1}} C_i^{2^n}$$

But the number of families in a given n-dimensional *PIP* set grows much slower than this total number as n increases. Therefore, this extended uniqueness property of the set *PIP* can be very useful to organize the thoughts that compose the agent's cognitive mechanism.

The problem of determining the number of families for a given n has been studied in the more general context of *boolean functions* (Harrison, 1965) for a long time. George Polya (1940) proposed a method based on a representation of the complete disjunctive normal form of a proposition as a set of vertexes in an n-dimensional hypercube, where each dimension is associated with one propositional symbol. In this representation, the *Exchange* function can be represented by a rigid rotation. He also calculated the number of families up to four propositional symbols. Table 1 shows the total number of propositions and the corresponding number of *PIP*-pair families for up to 5 propositional symbols.

Table 1. Number of propositions

n		$C_1^{2^n}$	$C_2^{2^n}$	$C_3^{2^n}$	$C_4^{2^n}$	$C_5^{2^n}$	$C_6^{2^n}$	$C_7^{2^n}$	$C_8^{2^n}$	⋮	$\sum$
2	all	4	6							⋮	10
	pip	1	2							⋮	3
3	all	8	28	56	70					⋮	162
	pip	1	3	3	6					⋮	13
4	all	16	120	560	1820	4368	8008	11440	12870	⋮	39202
	pip	1	4	6	19	27	50	56	58	⋮	221
5	all	32	496	4960	35960	...	...	...	...	⋮	2448023842
	pip	1	5	10	47	...	...	...	...	⋮	...

The psychological properties of these proposition families, such as the ease with which they are learned from examples, were studied since the 1950s. In Feldman (2003), a review of this research and a complete catalog of the propositions with up to four propositional symbols are presented. The propositions are shown in complete DNF, in Polya's hypercube-based notation and in a (heuristically determined) minimal form. To our knowledge, the prime forms were not yet considered either in the boolean functions or in the psychological research contexts.

Internal View

"What's in a name? that which we call a rose
By any other word would smell as sweet."

Romeo and Juliet, Act II, Scene I,
William Shakespeare

Applying the adopted hypothesis to the proposed cognitive model leads to a more precise definition of the organization and structure of the agent's cognitive mechanism. A *thought* τ is (re)defined as a relation between an abstract propositional symbol (associated with a logical proposition represented by a pair) and an emotional flavor. This relation consists of three elements:[9]

- A generic pair $\pi_\tau \in PIP$ with *variable* propositional symbols $V(\pi_\tau) = \{x_1,...,x_k\}$.
- A set of propositional symbols $P_\tau = \{p_1,...,p_k\}$ associated with an emotional flavor[10] and with its cognitive counterpart, the abstract propositional symbol q_τ.

- A mapping $\mu_\tau : P_\tau \rightarrow V(\pi_\tau)$ that associates with each p_i a x_i that occur in the *PIP* pair.

It should be noted that: (i) every thought is an operational recipe to control the truth value of an emotional flavor; (ii) each emotional flavor can be associated with different *PIP* pairs (different ways to control its value) and thus can participate in different thoughts; and (iii) the *PIP* pairs are independent of the thought contents and can also participate in different thoughts.

This last property shows that, beside the semantic relation that associates thoughts that share the same emotional flavors, thoughts can also be associated through a syntactical relation, when they share the same *PIP* pair. Because the syntactical relation occurs at the proposition level and not at the propositional symbol level, it can lead to significant *metaphorical* relations across different domains (Johnson, 1987). These metaphorical relations can be used, for instance, to guide the decomposition of new learned propositions into significant sub-propositions (see Section Horizontal Optimization).

These two dimensions can be compared with Jerry Fodor's basic methodological principle (Fodor, 1983) that considers two fundamentally different types of mental processing: vertical processing, taking place in specialized systems that carry out a restricted set of operations on a limited type of input, and horizontal processing, that is neither domain-specific nor informationally encapsulated. Thoughts that share the same emotional flavors are similar to the specialized Fodor's vertical modules, and thoughts that share the same PIP pairs are similar to the general horizontal modules, but in the proposed model both types share the same representational structure.

The cognitive agent performs two types of activities: the actual interaction with the environment, its "daylight" activities, and the reorganization of its internal structure in order to optimize storage space and reasoning efficiency, its "dreaming" activities.

During its interaction with the environment, at each moment there are several active emotional flavors. Each emotional flavor evokes a set of memorized thoughts in which it participates (a thought may "entangle" more than one emotional flavor). To say that the agent is *aware* of a given thought means that the agent wants to control the emotional flavor entanglement associated with the thought and has available an instance of the *PIP* pair that represents the abstract propositional symbol associated with that thought. Let the present thought be τ. To attain the goal of controlling the truth value of the associated emotional flavor entanglement, the agent executes the following actions:

- Instantiate the *PIP* pair π_τ using the propositional symbols in P_τ and the mapping μ_τ.
- Apply the appropriate reasoning method (see Section Reasoning) on the *PIP* pair.
- Decide to act according to the deduced controllable propositional symbols or continue to analyze new thoughts. These new thoughts may have three sources: (i) if one or more of the propositional symbols in P_τ are abstract then their associated thoughts can become new thoughts; (ii) other thoughts that share the same *PIP* pair π_τ can become new thoughts; and (iii) another emotional flavor may become active and invoke new thoughts.

During the reorganization period, the agent does not interact with the environment. It executes an internal activity that can be defined as a search for the "most suitable" definitions of abstract propositional symbols with respect to storage space and reasoning efficiency. According to the principles adopted in Bittencourt (1997), we assume that this optimization mechanism is implemented through an internal evolutionary algorithm that evolves the best representations.

The interaction activity uses the environment semantics compressed into memorized thoughts, together with all its relations with similar thoughts that share either the same emotional goals or the same operational patterns, to learn and generate behavior intended to control the truth values of active emotional flavors. The reorganization activity builds and refines these relations.

To implement these two types of activities it is necessary to define a mechanism that acquires the agent propositions: a *learning* method, a mechanism that uses the acquired propositions in order to recognize and predict states of the environment, a *reasoning* method and, finally, a maintenance mechanism that optimizes, according to some given criteria, the proposition representation, a *memory* management method. The following two sections — learning and reasoning — present how the proposed representation supports acquisition and reasoning with respect to a single significant proposition. The third — memory — proposes a structure in which these propositions can be stored and a mechanism that allows for the discovery and exploration of the relations among them. These three sections contain the proposed solution to the problem of extracting meaning from the environment.

Learning

Learning methods in artificial intelligence usually adopt a "tabula rasa" hypothesis, assuming that the learning agent does not know anything and that the environment provides it with true statements that should be generalized into internal knowledge representations that capture the environment structure (Alpaydin, 2004).

In the proposed model, the agent already knows what to learn — how to control emotional flavors — and the environment provides it with information about the characteristics of the situations in which the emotional flavors assume the intended truth values (or not), through the uncontrollable symbols.

The learning mechanism should initially learn, for each emotional flavor, which are the situations, i.e., the patterns of perceptions (uncontrollable symbol values) and actions (controllable symbol values), as described by primitive propositional symbols that result in the intended truth value for the emotional flavor. These learned propositions are associated with abstract propositional symbols and are stored in the memory as thoughts.

The relation between propositions and emotional flavors can be learned either directly from the situations that occur in the environment, *practical* learning, or from being told by another trustful agent, *intellectual* learning. Both learning forms, to be effective, need an incremental algorithm that updates a pair, given either a new clause or a new term. This incremental algorithm should also include some *belief revision* (Alchourrón et al., 1985) or *belief update* (Herzig et al., 1999) mechanism in the case the new information contradicts the already learned proposition (Bittencourt et al., 2004).

Practical Learning

The domain definition introduces a semantic asymmetry among PI and IP: The "real things" are the assignments that describe the possible environment states and the assignments are associated with the IP. Therefore, to directly learn from experience, the agent should consider the sequence of assignments as examples or counter-examples of terms in the IP. In this way, propositions can be learned by perceiving and acting in the environment, while keeping track of the truth value of the relevant emotional flavor entanglement to which the resulting proposition is to be associated. The relation between emotional flavors and situations can also be obtained through communication with another agent that can be trustfully used as an oracle to identify a hypothetical situation as an instance of a given emotional flavor.

The proposed learning mechanism has some analogy with the reinforcement learning method (Kaelbling et al., 1996), where the agent acts in the environment monitoring a given utility function.

Example 4. Consider the robot of Example 1. To learn the relation between the emotional flavor Move and the controllable (m_1, m_r) and uncontrollable (s_l, s_f, s_r) symbols, it may randomly act in the world, memorizing the situations in which the Move emotional flavor is true. After trying all $2^5 = 32$ possible truth assignments, it concludes that the emotional flavor Move is satisfied only by the 12 assignments[11] in Table 2.

The dual transformation, applied to the dual clauses associated with the good assignments, returns the clauses of the PI. A further application of the dual transformation returns the IP. The resulting PIP pair (shown in Example 3) is then associated with the abstract propositional symbol q_{move}, that is true whenever the emotional flavor Move is true.

It should be noted that contains less dual clauses than the original number of assignments, nevertheless each assignment satisfies at least one of this dual clauses.

Intellectual Learning

There is nothing in the environment that directly corresponds to the CNF, i.e., it is a purely cognitive representation and it has only an internal meaning. Nevertheless, its conjunctive nature makes it interesting to communicate knowledge: If the proposition is valid, then each clause in the CNF is independently valid due only to its local propositional symbols, i.e., each clause can be seen as a local rule that can be transmitted and effectively applied to the situations it describes without any concern with the global proposition.

Table 2. Learning a proposition

$$\langle s_l, s_f, \neg s_r, m_l, \neg m_r \rangle$$
$$\langle s_l, \neg s_f, s_r, m_l, m_r \rangle$$
$$\langle s_l, \neg s_f, \neg s_r, m_l, m_r \rangle$$
$$\langle s_l, \neg s_f, \neg s_r, m_l, \neg m_r \rangle$$
$$\langle \neg s_l, s_f, s_r, \neg m_l, m_r \rangle$$
$$\langle \neg s_l, s_f, \neg s_r, m_l, \neg m_r \rangle$$
$$\langle \neg s_l, s_f, \neg s_r, \neg m_l, m_r \rangle$$
$$\langle \neg s_l, \neg s_f, s_r, m_l, m_r \rangle$$
$$\langle \neg s_l, \neg s_f, s_r, \neg m_l, m_r \rangle$$
$$\langle \neg s_l, \neg s_f, \neg s_r, m_l, m_r \rangle$$
$$\langle \neg s_l, \neg s_f, \neg s_r, m_l, \neg m_r \rangle$$
$$\langle \neg s_l, \neg s_f, \neg s_r, \neg m_l, m_r \rangle$$

In this case, to teach a proposition, the trusted oracle would communicate all the relevant rules (i.e., clauses) that define the proposition's PI. This transmission of rules is called intellectual, because it does not involve any direct experience in the environment.

By hypothesis, all learning must be accompanied by a motivating emotional flavor. In the case of intellectual learning, the source of the emotional flavor is the relationship between teacher and student, i.e., in how much the student "believes" that the teacher's lessons are relevant and "true" with respect to the environment.

It is interesting to note that most descriptive texts written in occidental natural languages are indeed stated in a form analogous to a CNF, i.e., as a set of possibly conditional sentences that should be considered independently true. From this point of view, finding the smallest CNF[12] that represents a given proposition is a relevant problem, because this would be the fastest way to communicate the proposition.

Example 5. Considering that all available outlets to recharge robots are on the walls, then it is safer to stay near the walls. A fellow robot can teach its pupil the Follow left wall emotional symbol transmitting the abstract propositional symbols q_{flw}, given by the following PIP pair:

$$\begin{pmatrix} 0 : [\neg m_l^{\{1\}}, \neg s_f^{\{0\}}] \\ 1 : [\neg s_f^{\{0\}}, \neg s_l^{\{1\}}] \\ 2 : [\neg m_l^{\{1\}}, s_l^{\{0\}}] \\ 3 : [m_l^{\{0\}}, \neg s_l^{\{1\}}] \\ 4 : [m_r^{\{0,1\}}] \end{pmatrix} \quad \begin{matrix} 0 : \langle m_l^{\{3\}}, m_r^{\{4\}}, \neg s_f^{\{0,1\}}, s_l^{\{2\}} \rangle \\ 1 : \langle \neg m_l^{\{0,2\}}, m_r^{\{4\}}, \neg s_l^{\{1,3\}} \rangle \end{matrix}$$

This can be done either by "giving the example," i.e., by "encouraging" the pupil to restrict its behavior to the models covered to $IP_{q_{ftw}}$, a practical learning, or by "symbolically communicating" some set of clauses equivalent to $PI_{q_{ftw}}$, a pure intellectual learning.

Reasoning

Given a thought and a partial assignment describing the domain state, to reason means to take into account the effect of the assignment on the *PIP* pair associated with the thought and to calculate a new resulting *PIP* pair. According to property 4 in section Working Hypothesis, this new pair can be seen as a complex action rule, specific to the situation described by the partial assignment: The disjunctive part indicates which are the closest situations in which the proposition is true and the conjunctive part can be used as local rules to choose an appropriate action. In the case that the proposition has a small *PI* with respect to the size of the *IP*, then a conjunctive reasoning is more efficient, otherwise a disjunctive one is more adequate. Property 3 in section Working Hypothesis guarantees that these operations can be done in polynomial time.

It should be noted that, although the results obtained by the proposed reasoning method are compatible with the usual propositional logic deduction, the method itself is in some sense "holistic" because it refers to complete PIP pairs that simultaneously describe, through a distributed representation, the possible situations and the rules that state that those are properly the possible situations. The proposed reasoning process is also cyclic, each change in the partial assignment that describes the environment begins a new reasoning cycle that can lead (or not) to an action.

Conjunctive Reasoning

Using the *PI*, the agent can verify whether a partial assignment satisfies a proposition using the following method. Given a partial assignment concerning the uncontrollable propositional symbols $-\langle \psi_1,...,\psi_k \rangle-$, the agent, using the *IP* coordinates of the quanta (that specify in which clauses of the *PI* each literal occurs), constructs the following set of quanta:

$$\langle \psi_1^{F_1},...,\psi_k^{F_k} \rangle$$

If $\cup_{i=1}^{n} F_i = PI$ then the assignment satisfies the proposition and no change is necessary in controllable symbol values. If $PI - \cup_{i=1}^{n} F_i$ is not empty, then the clauses in it should be made true by appropriately flipping controllable symbol values.

The number of times a given coordinate appears in the associated set of quanta informs how robust the assignment is with respect to changes in the truth value of the propositional symbol associated with it. The smaller this number, the more *critical* is the clause denoted by the coordinate. If a given coordinate appears only once, then flipping the truth value of the propositional symbol associated with it will cause the assignment not to satisfy the proposition any more. In this case, the other literals in the critical rule represent additional changes in the assignment that could lead to a new satisfying assignment.

The critical clauses are analogous to the active rules in an expert system, in the sense that if a clause is not critical then either its conclusion is already in the assignment or its conditions are not satisfied, or both. This is a step beyond the Rete algorithm (Forgy, 1982), because not only the literals in the assignment are associated with the conditions of the relevant rules, but the conclusions of the rules are also taken into account.

Example 6. Consider the proposition in Example 3 and the following partial assignment — $\langle \neg s_l, \neg s_f, \neg s_r \rangle$ — *that corresponds to a possible situation for the sensor values. The IP coordinates (that refer to the PI) of the literals in the assignment are:*

$$\langle \neg s_l^{\{2,3,5\}}, \neg s_f^{\{0,1,2,3\}}, \neg s_r^{\{0,3,4\}} \rangle$$

The union of all coordinates — $\{0, 1, 2, 3, 4, 5\}$ — is not equal to the complete clause set and, therefore, the assignment does not satisfy the proposition. The only coordinate that does not appear in the clause set corresponds to Clause 6:

$$6 : [m_l^{\{1,3,4\}}, m_r^{\{0,2,3\}}]$$

and therefore something should be done to make it true. The clause states that in this situation, activating either one or both of the motors will make the emotional flavor Move true. The critical clauses, whose coordinates appear only once in the literals of the assignment, are:

$$1 : [\neg m_l^{\{0\}}, \neg m_r^{\{1\}}, \neg s_f^{\{2,3,4\}}]$$
$$4 : [m_r^{\{0,2,3\}}, \neg s_r^{\{1,4\}}]$$
$$5 : [m_l^{\{1,3,4\}}, \neg s_l^{\{0,2\}}]$$

These clauses indicate the possible actions to be taken if one of the sensors is activated: s_f, turn off at least one motor; s_r, turn on only the right motor; and s_l, turn on the left motor.

If the assignment is $\langle s_l, \neg s_f, \neg s_r \rangle$, then the coordinates of the literals are:

$$\langle s_l^{\{\}}, \neg s_f^{\{0,1,2,3\}}, \neg s_r^{\{0,3,4\}} \rangle$$

and the union of all coordinates is $\{0,1,2,3,4\}$. Again the assignment does not satisfy the proposition and the missing clauses, already simplified by the assignment, are:

$$5:[m_l^{\{1,3,4\}}]$$
$$6:[m_l^{\{1,3,4\}},m_r^{\{0,2,3\}}]$$

They state that in order to move when the left sensor is on it is necessary to turn on either the left motor alone (and go right) or both motors (and go ahead).

The critical clauses, also simplified by the assignment (Clause 1 becomes subsumed by Clause 2), are:

$$2:[\neg m_r^{\{1\}},\neg s_f^{\{2,3,4\}}]$$
$$4:[m_r^{\{0,2,3\}},\neg s_r^{\{1,4\}}]$$

They indicate that when the left sensor is already on, if the frontal sensor activates, then the right motor should be turned off (to go necessarily right) and, when the right sensor activates, then the right motor should be turned on (to go necessarily ahead).

Disjunctive Reasoning

Using the IP, the agent can verify whether a partial assignment satisfies a proposition using the following method. Given a partial assignment, $\langle \psi_1,...,\psi_k \rangle$, the agent should determine whether one of the dual clauses in the IP is included in the assignment. To facilitate the search for such a dual clause, the following set of quanta is constructed:

$$\langle \psi_1^{F_1},...,\psi_k^{F_k} \rangle$$

where the F_i are the PI coordinates (that specify in which dual clauses of the IP each literal occurs). The number of times a given coordinate appears in this set of quanta informs how many literals the dual clauses denoted by the coordinate shares with the assignment. If this number is equal to the number of literals in the dual clause then it is satisfied by the assignment. Dual clauses that do not appear in $\cup_{i=1}^n F_i$ need not be checked for inclusion. If a dual clause is not satisfied by the assignment, it is possible to determine the set of literals that should be flipped in the assignment to satisfy it.

The interpretation of the critical clauses associated with an assignment as the active rules in an expert system, is analogous to our interpretation of the set of reachable dual clauses associated with an assignment in the framework of case-based reasoning (CBR) systems (Allen, 1994). Let the CBR knowledge base be represented by a proposition and a given case by an assignment over the propositional symbols of this proposition. The procedure above shows how to find the compatible dual clauses associated with the assignment and how to minimally modify them, according to possible changes.

Example 7. Consider the proposition in Example 3 and the first assignment of Example 6: $\langle \neg s_l, \neg s_f, \neg s_r \rangle$. *The coordinates of the quanta in the PI (that refer to the IP) associated with the literals in the assignment are:*

$$\langle \neg s_l^{\{0,2\}}, \neg s_f^{\{2,3,4\}}, \neg s_r^{\{1,4\}} \rangle$$

The coordinates indicate which terms in *IP* share which literals with *PI* the assignment (see Table 3). Compared to Example 6, where the available information on the *PI* is interpreted as a set of rules that predict possible good truth assignment flips, in this case the available information on the *IP* gives a measure of how different (or how similar) each possible dual clause is from the current assignment. This can be used to determine how "easy" it is to satisfy the proposition for which the indicated actions are shown in the column Need in Table 3. Again, the easier actions to keep moving are turning on either motor or both.

The column Don't care in Table 3 indicates which propositional symbols are not relevant for keeping the proposition true, e.g., considering the last line in Table 3, if the frontal sensor in off and both motors are on (and the agent is going ahead) then the activation of either lateral sensor is not relevant.

Consider now the proposition in Example 3 and the second assignment of Example 6: $\langle s_l, \neg s_f, \neg s_r \rangle$. The *PI* coordinates of the literals are:

$$\langle s_l^{\{\}}, \neg s_f^{\{2,3,4\}}, \neg s_r^{\{1,4\}} \rangle$$

The coordinates determine which dual clauses share which literals with the assignment (see Table 4).

Table 3. Literal sharing

Dual clause	Share	Need	Don't care
2	$\{\neg s_l, \neg s_f\}$	$\{m_r\}$	$\{\neg s_r\}$
4	$\{\neg s_r, \neg s_f\}$	$\{m_l\}$	$\{\neg s_l\}$
0	$\{\neg s_l\}$	$\{\neg m_l, m_r\}$	$\{\neg s_r, \neg s_f\}$
1	$\{\neg s_r\}$	$\{m_l, \neg m_r\}$	$\{\neg s_l, \neg s_f\}$
3	$\{\neg s_f\}$	$\{m_l, m_r\}$	$\{\neg s_l, \neg s_r\}$

Table 4. Literal sharing

Dual clause	Share	Need	Don't care
4	$\{\neg s_r, \neg s_f\}$	$\{m_l\}$	$\{s_l, m_r\}$
1	$\{\neg s_r\}$	$\{m_l, \neg m_r\}$	$\{s_l, s_f\}$
3	$\{\neg s_f\}$	$\{m_l, m_r\}$	$\{s_l, s_r\}$
2	$\{\neg s_f\}$	$\{\neg s_l, m_r\}$	$\{s_r, m_l\}$

Memory

The agent's memory contains thoughts. These thoughts are "indexed" according to two different dimensions: a semantic one that associates thoughts that share the same emotional flavor, and a syntactical one that associates thoughts that share the same *PIP* pair (see Figure 3).

Modeling the emotional flavors is out of the scope of the proposed model; to keep it simple each emotional flavor was just given a truth value and, indirectly, a degree of activity that makes a thought that is evoked by an emotional flavor one of which the agent is *aware*. Nevertheless, emotional flavors are what the model is all about: the thoughts that are (best) learned are those that were (successfully, or dramatically unsuccessfully) associated with (very) active emotional flavors. On the other hand, each learned thought refines its associated emotional flavors, providing an extra way of controlling them and simultaneously imposing conditions on their satisfaction (some are thirsty, others long for Pinot noir wine).

Although the memory contains thoughts, it does not need to contain the logical structure of the propositions associated with the thoughts, only their "indexes." The fact that the structure of the thoughts' propositions, the *PIP* pairs, can be shared by several thoughts reduces significantly the storage requirements, especially if abstract propositional symbols are defined in such a way that preferentially low dimension *PIP* pairs are used. Besides reducing the storage requirements, using low dimension *PIP* pairs increases the probability that different thoughts share the same *PIP* pair.

Because of this two dimensional character of memory, abstract propositional symbols plays a crucial role: Without them the number and size of the necessary *PIP* pairs would grow without limit and, more importantly, the emotional flavors would not be refined into specialized versions. The definition of abstract propositional symbols is in principle arbitrary. But, on the one hand, in an agent society these definitions should be consensual to allow learning by being told; on the other hand, these definitions have an important impact on the efficiency of the reasoning methods because they directly affect the size of the associated prime forms.

Figure 3. Memory structure

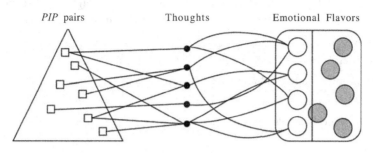

Example 8. If we replace the long distance sensors (v_l, v_f and v_r) by the short distance sensors (s_l, s_f and s_r) in the PIP q_{move} presented in Example 3, we obtain a new proposition that could be associated with an emotional flavor such as Stay away from the walls: a new thought with no additional representation cost.

The "daylight" activity of the memory is to provide relevant thoughts to be used to control active emotional flavors. As stated above, this "remembering" mechanism is based on the two indexing dimensions. The "dreaming" activity consists of organizing the structure of memorized thoughts in such a way that the "remembering" mechanism works effectively. The goal of the organizing mechanism is to find (or better, to evolve) sensible abstract propositional symbol definitions that facilitate the storage, inference and communication of thoughts. The search for these definitions is done by some evolutionary algorithm. The detailed description of this algorithm is also out of the scope of the proposed model; we just describe the necessary framework for such an algorithm.

A central element in any evolutionary algorithm is the *fitness function* that, in our case, should take into account the number of propositional symbols that occur in each abstracted proposition. The smaller this number, the better is the abstraction policy. The idea would be to choose abstraction policies that define abstract propositional symbols that in turn reduce the number of symbols in the original proposition and that, at the same time, contain in their definitions the smallest number of symbols possible. Besides these syntactical properties, the fitness function should also take into account the emotional flavors of the involved thoughts. How this could be done is not treated here.

The fitness function allows selection, but it needs variability. In our case, this can be achieved through transformations of the involved logical propositions. These transformations are of two complementary kinds: to abstract part of its structure in the form of abstract propositional symbols, and to obtain an "exploded" version of it where the abstract propositional symbol is replaced by its definition, if the *PIP* pair contains an abstract propositional symbol.

The latter is simple. Consider a proposition, expressed by a *PIP* pair (*P I IP*), that contains an abstract propositional symbol *q* among its propositional symbols. This abstract propositional symbol is also associated with a *PIP* pair : (PI_q, IP_q). To incorporate this definition into the *PIP* pair of the original proposition, it is enough to substitute the literals associated with the abstract propositional symbol q by the following expressions:

- Positive literals in a clause of *PI* by PI_q
- Positive literals in a term of *IP* by IP_q
- Negative literals in a clause of *PI* by PI_{-q}
- Negative literals in a term of *IP* by IP_{-q}

Property 2 in the section Working Hypothesis allows for an easy calculation of PI_{-q} and IP_{-q} given PI_q and IP_q. After the substitution, it is necessary to apply the distributive property of the $\wedge$ and $\vee$ operators in the resulting expressions and possibly some simplification rules to obtain the *PIP* representation of the "exploded" proposition.

The former kind of transformation, to find sensible abstractions, can be further divided into two types: to find good decompositions of a given proposition into a set of abstract propositions (a *vertical* optimization), and to find relations between propositions that share either the logical structure or some emotional flavor — a *horizontal* optimization. These types correspond to the "remembering" dimensions: the vertical optimization is concerned with efficient syntactical retrieval and the horizontal optimization with efficient semantic retrieval.

Vertical Optimization

As is usual in evolutionary computation, sensible abstractions of a given *PIP* pair can be found by trial and error, but some heuristics can help to improve the efficiency of the process. We present below two heuristics for finding sensible abstractions of a given *PIP* pair; other heuristics are of course possible. The first heuristic is to search for repeated patterns of propositional symbols that appear in the pair's *IP*. Each such pattern is always a good candidate for an abstract propositional symbol with a single term in its *IP*. A second heuristic takes into account the fact that there are controllable and uncontrollable symbols and analyzes repeated configurations of symbols of the same type that appear in the pair's *IP*. If the number of configurations is less than would be possible, given the involved propositional symbols, then to abstract these configurations into abstract propositional symbols may simplify the original proposition.

Example 9. Consider the PIP pair q_{move} in Example 3, associated with the emotional flavor Move. Analyzing the possible controllable symbol configurations that belong to terms in $IP_{q_{move}}$, we conclude that $\langle \neg m_i, \neg m_i \rangle$ is the only configuration, among the four possible, that does not appear in any term. A possible abstraction policy would be to define as abstract propositional symbols each one of the other three configurations.

This results in the following abstract propositional symbols which correspond to the refined emotional flavors introduced in Example 2:

$$q_f = \begin{pmatrix} 0:[\neg s_f^{\{0\}}] \\ 1:[m_r^{\{0\}}] & 0:\langle m_l^{\{2\}}, m_r^{\{1\}}, \neg s_f^{\{0\}} \rangle \\ 2:[m_l^{\{0\}}] \end{pmatrix}$$

$$q_l = \begin{pmatrix} 0:[\neg s_l^{\{0\}}] \\ 1:[m_r^{\{0\}}] & 0:\langle \neg m_l^{\{2\}}, m_r^{\{1\}}, \neg s_l^{\{0\}} \rangle \\ 2:[\neg m_l^{\{0\}}] \end{pmatrix}$$

$$q_r = \begin{pmatrix} 0:[\neg s_r^{\{0\}}] \\ 1:[\neg m_r^{\{0\}}] & 0:\langle m_l^{\{2\}}, \neg m_r^{\{1\}}, \neg s_r^{\{0\}} \rangle \\ 2:[m_l^{\{0\}}] \end{pmatrix}$$

and we can write:

$$q_{move} = \begin{pmatrix} & & 0:\langle q_f^{\{0\}} \rangle \\ 0:[q_f^{\{0\}}, q_l^{\{1\}}, q_r^{\{2\}}] & 1:\langle q_l^{\{0\}} \rangle \\ & & 2:\langle q_r^{\{0\}} \rangle \end{pmatrix}.$$

Note that the same kind of decomposition can be done with abstract propositional symbol q_{mom} and its sub-propositions q_{tmf}, q_{tml} and q_{tmr} (see Example 2).

The analysis of the uncontrollable symbols in this case does not lead to interesting results, because the satisfying configurations do not occur in isolation in the terms that belong to $IP_{q_{move}}$.

Using the original proposition, the agent would reason using a proposition with five propositional symbols, seven prime implicates and five prime implicants. The abstraction mechanism allows the agent to split the reasoning process into two levels: At the bottom level, it uses three sub-propositions, each one with three propositional symbols, three prime implicates and one prime implicant. At the top level, it uses one proposition with three propositional symbols, one prime implicate and three prime implicants. It is interesting to note that the three low level propositions share the same *PIP* pair and that its negation is the *PIP* pair associated with the top level proposition.

The second heuristic to abstract propositions can be obtained by exploring the structure of the prime implicants of a proposition ψ. Let $IP_\psi = \{D_1,...,D_k\}$ be the set of prime implicants of the proposition. We define the relation $Resol(Di, Dj, D_{ij})$ as the set of ntuples of terms such that D_{ij} is the the resolvent of D_i and D_j. A good candidate for a new abstract propositional symbol would be a proposition with the following set of prime implicants: $IP_{p_{new}} = [D_i - (D_i \cap D_j), D_j - (D_i \cap D_j)]$. If $D_i \cap D_j$ contains more than one literal, it can also be defined as a new abstract propositional symbol: $p_\cap = [D_i \cap D_j]$. These definitions would reduce the original set of terms $\{D_i, D_j, D_{ij}\}$ to a single term given by: $\langle p_\cap, p_{new} \rangle$.

Example 10. Some of the prime implicants of the proposition in Example 3 can be obtained as resolvents of other prime implicants: Term 2 is the resolvent between terms 1 and 3, and Term 4 is the resolvent between terms 0 and 3.

The set of literals $\{m_l\}$ is shared by terms 1, 2 and 3, and the set of literals $\{m_r\}$ is shared by terms 0, 3 and 4. According to the proposed abstraction mechanism, we can define the following abstract propositional symbols, given by their PIP pairs:

$$q_{rf} = \begin{pmatrix} 0:[\neg m_r, \neg s_f] & 0:\langle \neg m_r, \neg s_r \rangle \\ 1:[m_r, \neg s_r] & 1:\langle m_r, \neg s_f \rangle \\ 2:[\neg s_f, \neg s_r] & \end{pmatrix}$$

$$q_{lf} = \begin{pmatrix} 0:[\neg m_l, \neg s_f] & 0:\langle \neg m_l, \neg s_l \rangle \\ 1:[m_l, \neg s_l] & 1:\langle m_l, \neg s_f \rangle \\ 2:[\neg s_f, \neg s_l] & \end{pmatrix}.$$

The original proposition is reduced to the following PIP pair:

$$\begin{pmatrix} 0:[q_{lf}^{\{1\}}, m_l^{\{0\}}] & \\ 1:[q_{lf}^{\{1\}}, q_{rf}^{\{0\}}] & 0:\langle m_l^{\{0,2\}}, q_{rf}^{\{1,3\}} \rangle \\ 2:[m_l^{\{0\}}, m_r^{\{1\}}] & 1:\langle m_r^{\{2,3\}}, q_{lf}^{\{0,1\}} \rangle \\ 3:[m_r^{\{1\}}, q_{rf}^{\{0\}}] & \end{pmatrix}.$$

In this case, the abstraction mechanism allows the agent to reason initially using two propositions with two propositional symbols, three prime implicates and two prime implicants, and then a high level proposition with four propositional symbols, four prime implicates and two prime implicants.

Horizontal Optimization

Up to this point, we have discussed the operations necessary to abstract and explode thoughts. These operations are used to optimize the vertical structure of the memory contents: how thoughts are related to sub- and superthoughts. Once these best definitions are found for several different thoughts, the semantic "meaning" of these thoughts can be increased by exploring the *horizontal* structure of memory: how thoughts that belong to different emotional flavor domains but share analogous structural decompositions are related. The goal of the horizontal optimization is to find and reuse common "properties" that are shared by propositions. These common properties may lead to sensible metaphors (Lakof et al., 1980).

Example 11. Consider three propositions — ψ_1, ψ_2, ψ_3 — that are mutually exclusive. If they are represented by three abstract propositional symbols — q_1, q_2, q_3 —, their disjunction can be represented by the following generic PIP pair:

$$\left(0:[x_1^{\{0\}},x_2^{\{1\}},x_3^{\{2\}}] \quad \begin{matrix} 0:\langle x_1^{\{0\}}\rangle \\ 1:\langle x_2^{\{0\}}\rangle \\ 2:\langle x_3^{\{0\}}\rangle \end{matrix} \right)$$

to which the following substitution is applied $\{x_1/q_1,\ x_2/q_2,\ x_3/q_3\}$, provided that an auxiliary property is taken into account:

$$\psi_{excl} = \left(\begin{matrix} 0:[\neg x_0^{\{0,2\}},\neg x_1^{\{1,2\}}] & 0:\langle \neg x_0^{\{1,2\}},\neg x_2^{\{0,2\}}\rangle \\ 1.[\neg x_0^{\{0,?\}},\neg x_2^{\{0,1\}}] & 1:\langle \neg x_1^{\{0,1\}},\neg x_2^{\{0,?\}}\rangle \\ 2:[\neg x_1^{\{1,2\}},\neg x_2^{\{0,1\}}] & 2:\langle \neg x_0^{\{1,2\}},\neg x_1^{\{0,1\}}\rangle \end{matrix} \right).$$

To see how this could be useful, let's enrich our example with a further emotional flavor: Be with Mom, which is true when the agent is near enough to a fellow robot. This emotional flavor is represented by the abstract propositional symbol q_{mom}. Suppose also that the agent has originally learned the following proposition to maintain the Be with Mom emotional flavor true:

$$\left(\begin{matrix} 0:[q_{move}^{\{0\}}] \\ 1:[q_{tmom}^{\{0\}}] \end{matrix} \quad 0:\langle q_{move}^{\{0\}},q_{tmom}^{\{1\}}\rangle \right)$$

that is, if the agent is tracking mom, then move, otherwise do not move. This proposition is not very effective, but the fact that both q_{move} and q_{mom} (see Example 9) share the mutual exclusion generic PIP pair can lead to refined propositions q_{momf}, q_{moml}, and q_{momr} with the same mutual exclusion property:

$$q_{momf} = \begin{pmatrix} 0:[q_f^{\{0\}}] & \\ 1:[q_{tmf}^{\{0\}}] & 0:\langle q_f^{\{0\}}, q_{tmf}^{\{1\}}\rangle \end{pmatrix}.$$

Using these refined propositions, we can write: $q_{mom} = q_{momf} \lor q_{moml} \lor q_{momr}$, that has the same generic *PIP* pair. The "exploded" q_{mom} proposition has an *IP* with three terms but its *PI* has 35 clauses, necessary to guarantee the mutual exclusion.

We claim that horizontal optimization is especially important in human intelligence because it allows the production of thoughts that entangle originally unrelated emotional flavors and therefore can lead to the transference of expertise between totally different domains that is so characteristic of human intelligence.[13]

Conclusion

The chapter has described a logical cognitive model that allows an agent to learn, reason and remember using "significant propositions." The main hypothesis underlying the model is that prime implicants/implicates are good candidates for "cognitive building blocks." The algorithms presented in the chapter have been implemented in Common Lisp and tested with the theories in the SATLIB (http://www.satlib.org/) benchmark. The most critical algorithm, because of its complexity — NP-complete (Zhang et al., 2002) — is the dual transformation (Bittencourt et al., 2003). It was tested with several groups of theories in the SATLIB benchmark and showed promising results in spite of its proof-of-concept implementation, in which efficiency was not the first priority. The model also assumes that the agent is "embodied" and that its "body" state is reported to the cognitive mechanism through *emotional symbols*, whose exact nature is not specified. Using these assumptions, the concept of *thought* is formally defined and its properties explored.

Future work includes implementing experiments where the whole model, including emotional flavors and evolutionary optimization, could be tested. Some possible application domains that are being investigated are robot soccer (Costa et al., 2000) and Internet search (Freitas et al., 2003). We also intend to refine the logical part of the model introducing modal and first-order formalisms (Bittencourt et al., 2001).

The proposed model is the highest of the three-level cognitive architecture presented in Bittencourt (1997). Each of the three levels models a complete operational nervous system and the higher levels are intended to have evolved after and upon the lower ones. Figure 4 sketches this evolutionary process. The first versions of nervous systems would be *reactive* systems, with genetically determined neuron configurations whose excel-

Figure 4. The nervous system evolution

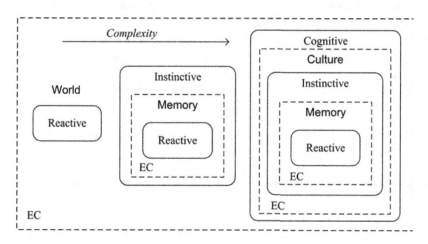

lence was directly guaranteed by the natural selection of individuals acting in the real world. In terms of the proposed model, they would be represented by fixed propositions that connect perception and action to fixed emotional flavors that represented the fixed individual goals. There are not yet thoughts, only an automatic decision mechanism. The second level, called *instinctive*, adds a *memory* to the system and with the memory, the possibility of "internalizing" the evolutionary mechanism in order to internally "test" reactive behaviors, instead of directly applying them in the world. In terms of the proposed model, adding a memory as defined means adding thoughts and all the logical machinery that they allow, but the relevant emotional flavor entanglements remain genetically fixed, i.e., the range of possible thoughts is fixed. The individuals can have any degree of "logical intelligence," i.e., the vertical optimization mechanism is almost fully operational, but it will be applied to solve fixed problems in fixed ways. Because of the shared (fixed) thoughts, complex learning and even communication languages may evolve, but the range of possible "meanings" that are captured and transmitted is bounded. The third level, properly called *cognitive*, frees the emotional flavor entanglements from the genetic determinacy and uses a further "internalized" evolutionary mechanism to work out the best entanglements. This is only possible by reifying thoughts, giving them "names" and sharing these "names" in a cultural environment where this last "internalized" evolutionary mechanism takes place (it would perhaps be better to say that this last mechanism was "externalized" into the cultural world). In terms of the proposed model, the third level adds the abstract propositional symbols and the horizontal optimization mechanism, allowing metaphors, and, with them, the possibility of assigning "meaning," i.e., particular emotional flavor entanglements, to new, possibly abstract thoughts.

The fact that the third level involves the reuse of the already available internalized evolutionary mechanism with different purposes could explain how the small difference between chimpanzee and human DNA, only about 1%, is enough to code for the huge functional difference of their intelligence.

Therefore, according to the proposed model, the difference between humans and other animals could lie in the human capacity of giving "names" to emotional flavor entanglements, and to use the logical machinery not (only) to devise means of satiating their urge, but to reason about the "convenience" of doing so.

References

Alchourrón, C., Gärdenfors, P., & Makinson, D. (1985). On the logic of theory change: Partial meet functions for contaction and revision. *Journal of Symbolic Logic, 50*, 510-530.

Allen, B. (1994). Case-based reasoning: Business applications. *Communications of ACM, 37*(3), 40-42.

Alpaydin, E. (2004). *Introduction to machine learning*. Cambridge, MA: MIT Press.

Baum, E. B. (2004). *What is thought?* (p. 478). Cambridge, MA:The MIT Press.

Belnap, N. D. (1977). A useful four-valued logic. In J. M. Dunn & G. Epstein (Eds.), *Modern uses of multiple-valued logics* (pp. 8-37). Dordrecht, Holland: D. Reidel Publishing Company.

Berthoz, A. (1997). *Le sens du mouvement*. Paris: Editions Odile Jacob.

Bibel, W. (1997). Let's plan it deductively. In *Proceedings of IJCAI 15,* Nagoya, Japan (pp. 1549-1562). San Francisco: Morgan Kaufmann.

Bittencourt, G. (1997). In the quest of the missing link. In *Proceedings of IJCAI 15,* Nagoya, Japan (pp. 310-315). San Francisco: Morgan Kaufmann.

Bittencourt, G., Marchi, J., & Padilha, R. S. (2003). A syntactic approach to satisfaction. In B. Konev & R. Schmidt (Eds.), *Proceedings of the 4ᵗʰ International Workshop on the Implementation of Logics, International Conference on Logic for Programming Artificial Intelligence and Reasoning (LPAR'03)* (pp. 18-32). University of Liverpool and University of Manchester, UK.

Bittencourt, G., Perrussel, L., & Marchi, J. (2004, August 22-27). A syntactical approach to revision. In Ramon López de Mántaras and Lorenza Saitta (Eds.), *Proceedings of the 16ᵗʰ European Conference on Artificial Intelligence (ECAI'04)* (pp. 788-792). Valencia, Spain.

Bittencourt, G., & Tonin, I. (2001). An algorithm for dual transformation in first-order logic. *Journal of Automated Reasoning, 27*(4), 353-389.

Brachman, R., & Levesque, H., (Eds.). (1985). *Readings in knowledge representation*. Los Altos, CA: Morgan Kaufmann Publishers.

Brooks, R. A. (1991). Intelligence without representation. *Artificial Intelligence (Special Volume: Foundations of Artificial Intelligence)*, *47*(1-3), 139-159.

Bryson, J. J., Tanguy, E. A. R., & Willis, P. J. (2004). The role of emotions in modular intelligent control. *AISB Quarterly The Newsletter of the Society for the Study of Artificial Intelligence and Simulation of Behaviour*, 117.

Changeux, J.-P. (1983). *L'homme neuronal*. Collection Pluriel, Librairie Arthème Fayard.

Changeux, J.-P. (2002). *L'homme de vérité*. Harvard University Press.

Costa, A. C. P. L., & Bittencourt, G. (2000, November 19-22). Dynamic social knowledge: A comparative evaluation. In *Proceedings of the International Joint Conference IBERAMIA2000 (Ibero-American Artificial Intelligence Conference) SBIA'2000 (Brazilian Artificial Intelligence Symposium): Vol. 1952. Lecture notes in artificial intelligence* (pp. 176-185). São Paulo, Brazil: Springer Verlag.

Damasio, A. R. (1994). *Descartes'error: Emotion, reason, and the human brain*. New York, NY: G.P. Putnam's Sons.

Damasio, A. R. (2000). *The feeling of what happens: Body and emotion in the making of consciousness*. Harvest Books.

Damasio, A. R. (2003). *Looking for Spinoza, joy, sorrow, and the feeling brain*. Orlando, FL: Harcourt Books.

Darwiche, A., & Marquis, P. (2001, August 4-10). A perspective on knowledge compilation. In *Proceedings of the 17th International Joint Conference on Artificial Intelligence (IJCAI'01)* (pp. 175-182). Seattle, Washington.

Darwin, C. (1998). *The origin of species*. New York: Modern Library.

Dawkins, R. (1976). *The selfish gene*. Oxford: Oxford University Press.

Feldman, J. (2003). A catalog of boolean concepts. *Journal of Mathematical Psychology*, *47*, 75-89.

Fitting, M. (1990). *First-order logic and automated theorem proving*. New York: Springer Verlag.

Fodor, J. A. (1983). *The modularity of mind*. A Bradford Book: Cambridge, MA: The MIT Press.

Forgy, C. (1982). Rete, a fast algorithm for pattern match problem. *Artificial Intelligence*, *19*, 17-37.

Freitas, F. L. G., & Bittencourt, G. (2003, August 9-15). An ontology-based architecture for cooperative information agents. In *Proceedings of IJCAI 18*, Acapulco, Mexico (pp. 37-42). Denver, CO: Professional Book Center.

Giacomo, G. D., Lespérance, Y., Levesque, H., & Sardina, S. (2002). On the semantics of deliberation in indigolog — From theory to implementation. In D. Fensel, F. Giunchiglia, D. McGuiness, & M. A. Williams (Eds.), *Principles of knowledge representation and reasoning (KR2002)* (pp. 603-614). Toulouse, France: Morgan Kaufmann.

Halpern, J., & Moses, Y. (1985). A guide to the modal logics of knowledge and belief. In *Proceedings of IJCAI 9* (pp. 480-490).

Harrison, M. A. (1965). *Introduction to switching and automata theory*. McGraw Hill.

Herzig, A., & Rifi, O. (1999). Propositional belief base update and minimal change. *Artificial Intelligence, 115*(1), 107-138.

Jackson, P. (1990). Computing prime implicants. In *Proceedings of the 10 International Conference on Automatic Deduction, LNAI No. 449* (pp. 543-557). Kaiserslautern, Germany: Springer Verlag.

Johnson, M. (1987). *The body in the mind: The bodily basis of meaning, imagination, and reason*. Chicago: The University of Chicago Press.

Kaelbling, L. P., Littman, M. L., & Moore, A. (1996). Reinforcement learning: A survey. *Journal of Artificial Intelligence Research, 4*, 237-285.

Kean, A., & Tsiknis, G. (1990). An incremental method for generating prime implicants/ implicates. *Journal of Symbolic Computation, 9*, 185-206.

Kripke, S. (1963). Semantical considerations on modal logic. *Acta Philosophica Fennica, 16*, 83-94.

Lakoff, G., & Johnson, M. (1980). *Metaphors we live by*. Chicago: The University of Chicago Press.

Levesque, H., Pirri, F., & Reiter, R. (1998). Foundations for the situation calculus. *Electronic Transactions on Artificial Intelligence, 2, 159-178*

Marchi, J., & Bittencourt, G. (2004, September 29 - October 1). Propositional reasoning for an embodied cognitive model. In *Proceedings of the XVII Brazilian Symposium on Artificial Intelligence (SBIA '04), Lecture Notes in Artificial Intelligence*. São Luís, Maranhão, Brazil: Springer Verlag.

Maturana, H. R., & Varela, F. J. (1980). Autopoiesis and cognition: The realization of the living. In R. S. Cohen & M.W. Wartofsky (Eds.), *Boston studies in the philosophy of science* (Vol. 42). Dordecht, The Netherlands: D. Reidel Publishing Co.

McMullin, B., & Varela, F. J. (1997). Rediscovering computational autopoiesis. In P. Husbands & I. Harvey (Eds.), *Proceedings of the Fourth European Conference on Artificial Life*. Cambridge, MA: MIT Press.

Morin, E. (1991). *La méthode 4, Les idées*. Paris: Editions du Seuil.

Newell, A. (1980). Physical symbol systems. *Cognitive Science, 4*, 135-183.

Newell, A. (1982). The knowledge level. *Artificial Intelligence, 18*, 87-127.

Peirce, C. (1974). *The collected papers of C.S. Peirce*. Cambridge, MA: Harvard University Press.

Piaget, J. (1963). *The origins of intelligence in children*. New York: Norton.

Piaget, J. (2001). *The psychology of intelligence*. M. Piercy & D. E. Berlyne (Trans.). Routledge Classics.

Polya, G. (1940). Sur les types des propositions composées. *The Journal of Symbolic Logic, 5*(3), 98-103.

Quine, W. (1959). On cores and prime implicants of truth functions. *American Mathematics Monthly, 66*, 755-760.

Ramesh, A., Becker, G., & Murray, N. V. (1997). CNF and DNF considered harmful for computing prime implicants/implicates. *Journal of Automated Reasoning, 18*(3), 337-356.

Rao, A. S., & Georgeff, M. P. (1995). BDI-agents: From theory to practice. In *Proceedings of the 1st International Conference on Multiagent Systems* (pp. 312, 319). San Francisco: MIT Press.

Scherl, R., & Levesque, H. J. (2003). Knowledge, action, and the frame problem. *Artificial Intelligence, 1*(144), 1-39.

Scheutz, M. (Ed.). (2002). *Computationalism new directions.* A Bradford Book The MIT Press.

Searle, J. (1980). Minds, brains and programs. *The Behavioral and Brain Sciences, 3*(7), 585-642.

Shanahan, M. (1993). Explanation in the situation calculus. In R. Bajcsy (Ed.), *Proceedings of the Thirteenth International Joint Conference on Artificial Intelligence* (pp. 160-165). San Mateo, CA: Morgan Kaufmann.

Shoham, Y., & McDermott, D. (1988). Problems in formal temporal reasoning. *Journal of Artificial Intelligence, 36*(1), 49-61.

Slagle, J., Chang, C., & Lee, R. (1970). A new algorithm for generating prime implicants. *IEEE Transactions on Computing, 19*(4), 304-310.

Smith, B. C. (1996). *On the origin of objects.* A Bradford Book The MIT Press.

Socher, R. (1991). Optimizing the clausal normal form transformation. *Journal of Automated Reasoning, 7*(3), 325-336.

Thangarajah, J., Padgham, L., & Harland, J. (2002, January). Representation and reasoning for goals in BDI agents. In *Proceedings of the 25th Australasian Conference on Computer Science.* Melbourne, Australia: Australian Computer Society.

Varela, F. J. (1979). *Principles of biological autonomy.* New York: Elsevier (North Holland).

Varela, F. J. (1989). *Autonomie et connaissance: Essai sur le vivant.* Paris: Editions du Seuil.

Wittgenstein, L. (1922, 1933). *Tractatus logico-philosophicus.* London: Routledge & K. Paul.

Yager, R., & Filev, D. (Eds). (1994). *Essentials of fuzzy modeling and control.* New York: John Wiley.

Zhang, L., & Malik, S. (2002). The quest for efficient boolean satisfiability solvers (Invited Paper). In *Proceedings of 8th International Conference on Computer Aided Deduction (CADE 2002)* (pp. 295-313). London: Springer-Verlag.

Endnotes

[1]   This property could be generalized to allow fuzzy (Yager et al., 1994) or multiple values (Belnap, 1977). The adopted logic could also be first-order or even a higher-order, instead of propositional logic.

[2]   It should be noted that the proposed cognitive model is intended as the highest level of a multi-level architecture (Bittencourt, 1997). The emotional flavors should be seen as the result of lower level processes associated with the internal functioning of the agent and with its interaction with the external environment, e.g., Bryson et al. (2004). These processes are out of the scope of the present cognitive model.

[3]   The representation and use of motivation have been intensively studied in the multi-agent community. A popular approach is the so-called beliefs, desires and intentions (BDI) (Thangarajah et al., 2002; Rao et al., 1995).

[4]   Target detectors are common perceptive features in many species.

[5]   Although "entangle" is not a technically defined term of the model, it would be if the model is extended to emotional flavors, because it represents the necessary combination operation that would have to be defined in any emotional flavor theory.

[6]   The disjunction of all the models of the proposition represented as conjunctions of literals.

[7]   We note as $\overline{A}$ the formula A with the truth values of all its literals flipped.

[8]   The propositions with more than $\frac{2^n}{2} = 2^{n-1}$ models are equivalent to the negations of the propositions with less than 2^{n-1} models.

[9]   These three elements are analogous to the three "subjects" in the semiosis definition: "... an action, or influence, which is, or involves, a cooperation of three subjects, such as a sign, its object, and its interpretant, this tri-relative influence not being in any way resolvable into actions between pairs" (Peirce, 1974).

[10]   We explicitly avoid representing the emotional flavor in the formalism because only its syntactical counterpart actually belongs to the proposed cognitive model.

[11]   To simplify the notation, an assignment is noted as a set of n literals, where n is the number of propositional symbols that appear in the proposition, such that $\langle \psi_1,...,\psi_i,...,\psi_n \rangle$ represents the assignment $\varepsilon(p_i) = true$ if $\psi_i = p_i$ or $\varepsilon(p_i) = false$ if $\psi_i = \neg p_i$, and $\varepsilon(p) \to \{true, false\}$ is the semantic function that maps propositional symbols into truth values.

[12]   Usually the PI, as defined above, is not the smallest CNF representation of the proposition.

[13] The presentation of Wittgenstein's Tractatus and of the Autopoiesis theory, in Sections Tractatus Logico-Philosophicus and Autopoiesis, followed by the definition of the proposed model, in Section Internal View, in which pointers are provided to highlight similar concepts, can be seen as an example of the kind of relation we would like the horizontal optimization to construct.

Chapter III

Modeling Field Theory of Higher Cognitive Functions

Leonid Perlovsky, Air Force Research Center, USA

Abstract

The chapter discusses a mathematical theory of higher cognitive functions, including concepts, emotions, instincts, understanding, imagination and intuition. Mechanisms of the knowledge instinct are proposed, driving our understanding of the world. Aesthetic emotions and perception of beauty are related to "everyday" functioning of the mind. We briefly discuss neurobiological grounds as well as difficulties encountered by previous attempts at mathematical modeling of the mind encountered since the 1950s. The mathematical descriptions below are complemented with detailed conceptual discussions so the content of the chapter can be understood without necessarily following mathematical details. We relate mathematical results and computational examples to cognitive and philosophical discussions of the mind. Relating a mathematical theory to psychology, neurobiology and philosophy will improve our understanding of how the mind works.

Working of the Mind

How the mind works has been a subject of discussions for millennia; from Ancient Greek philosophers to mathematicians, to modern cognitive scientists. Words like *mind, thought, imagination, emotion and concept* present a challenge: People use these words in many ways colloquially, but in cognitive science and in mathematics of intelligence they have not been uniquely defined and their meaning is a subject of active research and ongoing debates (for the discussions and further references see: Grossberg (1988); Albus, and Meystel (2001); Perlovsky (2001). Standardized definitions come after completion of a theoretical development (for instance "force" was defined by Newton's laws, following centuries of less precise usage). Whereas the mind theory is a developing science, this chapter adheres to the following guidelines regarding our proposals: (1) they must correspond to current discussions in the scientific and mathematical community, (2) they must correspond to philosophical discussions and general cultural usage, (3) they must be clear and mathematically tractable, and finally (4) deviations or discrepancies must be noted and discussed. A dictionary definition of the mind, which we take as a starting point, includes conscious and unconscious processes, thought, perception, emotion, will, memory and imagination, and it originates in brain (*The American Heritage College Dictionary*, 2000). These constituent notions will be discussed throughout the chapter. Specific neural mechanisms in the brain "implementing" various mind functions constitute the relationship between the mind and brain. We will discuss possible relationships of the proposed mathematical descriptions to neural structures in the brain.

The problem addressed in this chapter is developing a mathematical technique suitable to describe higher cognitive functions. Such a technique could serve two purposes. First, it would lead to the development of smart computers and intelligent robots. Second, it would help to unify and clarify complex issues in philosophy, psychology, neurobiology and cognitive science. I rely on an underlying methodological assumption that "the minds" are actually existing physical entities, and in various disciplines I am interested in contents related to this assumption of "physics of the mind." Achieving the two purposes of intelligent computers and mind theory will require the collaboration of many people. Developing intelligent computers based partially on ideas described in this chapter is being pursued by several dozens of companies. Similarly, several university groups pursue research relating these ideas to specific disciplines (philosophy, psychology, neurobiology, evolution of languages, psycholinguistics and even musical theory). In this chapter the purpose is limited to describing the mathematical technique and to making a step toward relating it to a vast field of philosophy, psychology, neurobiology and cognitive science. Needless to say, not every point of view can be addressed, and not every reader can be satisfied. The aim of the chapter will be achieved if the reader gets a taste for and an interest in the unifying approach to this vast and fascinating field.

A broad range of opinions exists about the mathematical methods suitable for the description of the mind. Founders of artificial intelligence, including Allan Newell (1983) and Marvin Minsky (1988), thought that formal logic was sufficient and no specific mathematical techniques would be needed to describe the mind. An opposite view was advocated by Brian Josephson (1997) and Roger Penrose (1994), suggesting that the mind cannot be understood within the current knowledge of physics; new unknown yet physical phenomena will have to be accounted for explaining the working of the mind. Some authors considered quantum computational processes that might take place in the brain (Penrose, 1994; Josephson, 1997; Hameroff, 1994). This chapter develops a point of view that there are few specific mathematical constructs, or "first principles" of the mind. Several researchers advocated this view. Grossberg (1988) suggested that the first principles include a resonant matching between bottom-up signals and top-down representations, as well as an emotional evaluation of conceptual contents (Grossberg & Levine, 1987). Zadeh (1997) developed the theory of granularity; Meystel (1995) developed the hierarchical multi-scale organization; Edelman suggested neuronal group selection (see Edelman & Tononi, 1995); and the author suggested the knowledge instinct, aesthetic emotions and dynamic logic among the first principles of the mind (Perlovsky, 2001; Perlovsky & McManus, 1991; Perlovsky, 1996).

This chapter presents modeling field theory (MFT), a mathematical "structure" that we propose is intrinsic to operations of the mind, and dynamic logic, governing its temporal evolution. It discusses specific difficulties encountered by previous attempts at mathematical modeling of the mind and how the new theory overcomes these difficulties. I show an example of solving a problem that was unsolvable in the past. We argue that the theory is related to an important mechanism behind workings of the mind, which we call "the knowledge instinct" as well as to other cognitive functions. I discuss neurobiological foundations, cognitive, psychological and philosophical connections, experimental verifications and outline emerging trends and future directions.

Logic and the Mind

For long time, people believed that intelligence was equivalent to conceptual understanding and reasoning. A part of this belief was that the mind works according to logic. Although it is obvious that the mind is not logical, over the course of two millennia since Aristotle, many people came to identify the power of intelligence with logic. Founders of artificial intelligence in the 1950s and 60s believed that by relying on rules of logic they would soon develop computers with intelligence far exceeding the human mind.

The beginning of this story is usually attributed to Aristotle, the inventor of logic. He was proud of this invention and emphasized, "nothing in this area existed before us" (Aristotle, IV BCE, a). However, Aristotle did not think that the mind works logically; he invented logic as a supreme way of argument, not as a theory of the mind. This is clear from many Aristotelian writings, for example in "Rhetoric for Alexander" (Aristotle, IV BCE, b), he lists dozens of topics on which Alexander had to speak publicly. For each topic, Aristotle identified two opposing positions (e.g., making peace or declaring war; using or not using torture for extracting the truth, etc.). Aristotle gives logical arguments to support each of the opposing positions. Clearly, Aristotle saw logic as a tool to express decisions that were already made; he did not consider logic as the mechanism of the mind. Logic, if you wish, is a tool for politicians. (I would add that scientists should use logic to present their results, but not to arrive at these results). To explain the mind, Aristotle developed a theory of Forms, which will be discussed later. During the centuries following Aristotle, the subtleties of his thoughts were not always understood. With the advent of science, the idea that intelligence is equivalent to logic was gaining ground. In the nineteenth century, mathematicians turned their attention to logic. George Boole noted what he thought was not completed in Aristotle's theory. The foundation of logic, since Aristotle (Aristotle, IV BCE, c), was the law of excluded middle (or excluded third): Every statement is either true or false, any middle alternative is excluded. But Aristotle also emphasized that logical statements should not be formulated too precisely (say, a measure of wheat should not be defined with an accuracy of a single grain), that language implies the adequate accuracy and everyone has his mind to decide what is reasonable.

Boole thought that the contradiction between exactness of the law of excluded middle and vagueness of language should be corrected, and a new branch of mathematics, formal logic, was born. Prominent mathematicians contributed to the development of formal logic in addition to Boole, including Gottlob Frege, Georg Cantor, Bertrand Russell, David Hilbert and Kurt Gödel. Logicians "threw away" uncertainty of language and founded formal mathematical logic based on the law of excluded middle. Hilbert developed an approach named Formalism, which rejected intuition as a part of scientific investigation and thought to define scientific objects formally in terms of axioms or rules. Hilbert was sure that his logical theory also described mechanisms of the mind, "The fundamental idea of my proof theory is none other than to describe the activity of our understanding, to make a protocol of the rules according to which our thinking actually proceeds" (see Hilbert, 1928). In 1900, he formulated the famous Entscheidungsproblem: to define a set of logical rules sufficient to prove all past and future mathematical theorems. This entailed formalization of scientific creativity and the entire human thinking.

Almost as soon as Hilbert formulated his formalization program, the first hole appeared. In 1902 Russell exposed an inconsistency of formal procedures by introducing a set R as follows: *R is a set of all sets which are not members of themselves.* Is R a member of R? If it is not, then it should belong to R according to the definition; but if R is a member of R, this contradicts the definition. Thus either way we get a contradiction. This became known as Russell's paradox. Its jovial formulation is as follows: A barber shaves everybody who does not shave himself. Does the barber shave himself? Either answer to this question (yes or no) leads to a contradiction. This barber, like Russell's set, can be logically defined, but cannot exist. For the next 25 years, mathematicians were trying to develop a self-consistent mathematical logic, free from paradoxes of this type. But in 1931, Gödel (see in Gödel, 1986) proved that it is not possible, formal logic was inexorably inconsistent and self-contradictory.

Belief in logic has deep psychological roots related to functioning of the human mind. A major part of any perception and cognition process is not accessible to consciousness directly. We are conscious about the "final states" of these processes, which are perceived by our minds as "concepts," approximately obeying formal logic. For this reason prominent mathematicians believed in logic. Even after the Gödelian proof, founders of artificial intelligence still insisted that logic is sufficient to explain how the mind works. This is examined in the next section; for now let us simply state that logic is not a mechanism of the mind, but rather the result of the mind's operation (in Section 5 we discuss mathematics of dynamic logic, which suggest a mathematical explanation of how logic appears from illogical states).

Perception, Complexity, and Logic

Simple object perception involves signals from sensory organs and internal representations of objects. During perception, the mind associates subsets of signals corresponding to objects with object representations. This recognition activates brain signals leading to mental and behavioral responses, which are important for the phenomenon of understanding.

Developing mathematical descriptions of the very first *recognition* step in this seemingly simple association-recognition-understanding process has not been easy; a number of difficulties have been encountered over the last 50 years. These difficulties were summarized under the notion of combinatorial complexity CC (Perlovsky, 1998). "CC" refers to multiple combinations of various elements in a complex system; for example, recognition of a scene often requires concurrent recognition of its multiple elements that could be encountered in various combinations. CC is prohibitive because the number of combinations is very large. For example, consider 100 elements (not too large a number); the number of combinations of 100 elements is 100^{100}, exceeding the number of all elementary particle events in life of the Universe. No computer would ever be able to compute that many combinations.

The problem was first identified in pattern recognition and classification research in the 1960s and was named "the curse of dimensionality" (Bellman, 1961). It seemed that adaptive self-learning algorithms and neural networks could learn solutions to any problem "on their own" if provided with a sufficient number of training examples. The following thirty years of developing adaptive statistical pattern recognition and neural network algorithms led to a conclusion that the required number of combinations often was combinatorially large. Self-learning approaches encountered *CC of learning requirements*. Rule-based systems were proposed to solve the problem of learning complexity. An initial idea was that rules would capture the required knowledge and eliminate a need for learning. However, in the presence of variability, the number of rules grew; rules depended on other rules, combinations of rules had to be considered and rule systems encountered *CC of rules*. Beginning in the 1980s, model-based systems were proposed. They used models that depended on adaptive parameters. The idea was to combine advantages of learning-adaptivity and rules by using adaptive models. The knowledge was encapsulated in models, whereas unknown aspects of particular situations were to be learned by fitting model parameters (see discussions in [1], and in Perlovsky, Webb, Bradley, & Hansen, 1998). Fitting models to data required selecting data subsets corresponding to various models. The number of subsets, however, was combinatorially large. A general popular algorithm for fitting models to data, multiple hypotheses testing (Singer, Sea, & Housewright, 1974) is known to face CC of computations. Model-based approaches encountered *computational CC* (N and NP complete algorithms).

CC is related to the type of logic underlying various algorithms and neural networks (Perlovsky, 1998). Formal logic is based on the "law of excluded middle," according to which every statement is either true or false and nothing in between. Therefore, algorithms based on formal logic have to evaluate every variation in data or models as a separate logical statement (hypothesis). A large number of combinations of these variations result in combinatorial complexity. In fact, combinatorial complexity of algorithms based on logic was related to Gödel theory: It is a manifestation of the inconsistency of logic in finite systems (Perlovsky, 1996). Multivalued logic and fuzzy logic were proposed to overcome limitations related to the law of excluded middle (Kecman, 2001). Yet the mathematics of multivalued logic is no different in principle from formal logic; "excluded middle" is substituted by "excluded n+1." Fuzzy logic encountered a difficulty related to the degree of fuzziness. If too much fuzziness is specified, the solution does not achieve the required accuracy, if too little, it becomes similar to formal logic. Complex systems require different degrees of fuzziness in various elements of system operations; searching for the appropriate degrees of fuzziness among combinations of elements again would lead to CC. Is logic still possible after Gödel? Bruno Marchal (2005) recently reviewed the contemporary state of this field; logic after Gödel is much more complicated and much less logical than was assumed by the founders of artificial intelligence. The problem of CC remains unresolved within logic.

Various manifestations of CC are all related to formal logic and Gödel theory. Rule systems relied on formal logic in a most direct way. Self-learning algorithms and neural networks relied on logic in their training or learning procedures, every training example was treated as a separate logical statement. Furthermore, fuzzy logic systems relied on logic for setting degrees of fuzziness. CC of mathematical approaches to theories of the mind are related to the fundamental inconsistency of logic.

Structure of the Mind

In the 1950s and 60s, developers of artificial intelligence naïvely believed that they would soon create computers exceeding human intelligence, and that mathematics of logic was sufficient for this purpose. As we discussed, logic does not work, but the mind does. So let us turn to the mechanisms of the mind. Possibly, we will find inspiration for developing the mathematics needed for intelligent computers and decipher mechanisms of higher cognitive functions. Mechanisms of the mind, essential for the development of a mathematical theory of intelligence in this chapter include: instincts, concepts, emotions and behavior. Let us look briefly at their current definitions in cognitive science and psychology.

The definitions of instincts, concepts and emotions, as mentioned, are the subject of research and debate, while theories of life and intelligence are in development. Let me summarize few related definitions (*The American Heritage College Dictionary*, 2000; *Catholic Encyclopedia*, 2005; Wikipedia, 2005) as a starting point for further elaboration. Instincts are innate capabilities, aptitudes or behavior, which are not learned, complex and normally adaptive. Instincts are different from reflexes, a word used for more simple immediate mechanisms. In humans and higher animals, instincts are related to emotions. Psychoanalysts equated instincts with human motivational forces (such as sex and aggression); today these are referred to as instinctual drives. Motivation is based on emotions, on the search for positive emotional experiences and the avoidance of negative ones.

We will use a word "concept" to designate a common thread among words like concept, idea, understanding, thought or notion. Different authors use these words with subtle differences. A common thread among these words is an abstract, universal psychical entity that serves to designate a category or class of entities, events or relations. A concept is the element of a proposition rather in the way that a word is the element of a sentence. Concepts are abstract in that they omit the differences of the things in their extension, treating them as if they were identical. Concepts are universal in that they apply equally to everything in their extension. Plato and Aristotle called them ideas, or forms, and considered them the basis for how the mind understands the world. Similarly, Kant considered them a foundation for the ability to understand, the contents of pure reason. According to Jung, conscious concepts of the mind are learned on the basis of inborn unconscious psychic structures, archetypes. Contemporary science often equates the mechanism of concepts with internal representations of objects, their relationships, situations, etc.

Ray Jackendoff (2002) considers the term *representation* or *symbol* as too loaded with the "thorny philosophical problem of intentionality," and uses the word *model*. I do not think we should be afraid of intentionality; John Searle's (1980, 1983) emphasis on intentionality as "aboutness" is too narrow.[2] All brain mechanisms and mental functions are intentional; in fact everything within a living being is a result of long evolution and has evolved with a certain intent, or better put, a purpose. We are purposeful beings, and I will return to this discussion later. But I agree with Jackendoff, that the word model is most appropriate for concept or representation.

Emotions refer to both expressive communications and to internal states related to feelings. Love, hate, courage, fear, joy, sadness, pleasure and disgust can all be described in both psychological and physiological terms. Emotion is the realm where thought and physiology are inextricably entwined, and where the self is inseparable from individual perceptions of value and judgment. Emotions are sometimes regarded as the antithesis of reason, as suggested by phrases such as "appeal to emotion" or "don't let your emotions take over." A distinctive and challenging fact about human beings is a potential for both opposition and entanglement between will, emotion and reason. It has also been suggested that there is no empirical support for any generalization suggesting the antithesis between reason and emotion, indeed, anger or fear can often be thought of as a systematic response to observed facts. What should be noted, however, is that the human psyche possesses many possible reactions and perspectives in regard to the internal and external world — often lying on a continuum — some of which may involve the extreme of pure intellectual logic (often called "cold"), other the extreme of pure emotion unresponsive to logical argument ("the heat of passion"). In any case, it should be clear that the relation between logic and argument on the one hand, and emotion on the other, merits careful study. Many have noted that passion, emotion or feeling can add backing to an argument, even one based primarily on reason — particularly in regard to religion or ideology, areas of human thought which frequently demand an all-or-nothing rejection or acceptance, that is, the adoption of a comprehensive worldview partly backed by empirical argument and partly by feeling and passion. Moreover, several researchers have suggested that typically there is no "pure" decision or thought, that is, no thought based "purely" on intellectual logic or "purely" on emotion — most decisions and cognitions arc founded on a mixture of both.

An essential role of emotions in the working of the mind was analyzed by many researchers, from various perspectives: philosophical — Rene Descartes (1646)[3], Immanuel Kant (1790) and Jean Paul Sartre (1948); analytical psychology — Carl Jung (1921); psychological and neural — Stephen Grossberg and Daniel Levine (1987), Andrew Ortony (1990) and Joseph Ledoux (1998); philosophical-linguistic — P. Griffiths (1998); neuro-physiological — Antonio Damasio (1995); and from the learning and cognition perspective by the author (Perlovsky, 1999). Descartes attempted a scientific explanation of passions. He rationalized emotions, explained them as objects and related them to physiological processes. According to Kant, emotions are closely related to judgments, about which individual experiences and perceptions correspond to which general concepts and vice versa. The ability for judgment is a foundation of all higher spiritual abilities, including the beautiful and sublime. Kant's aesthetics has been a foundation of aesthetic theories to this very day (we will continue this discussion later). Sartre equated emotions, to a significant extent, with unconscious contents of psyche; today this does not seem to be adequate. Jung analyzed conscious and unconscious aspects of emotions. He emphasized undifferentiated status of primitive, fused emotion-concept-behavior psychic states in everyday functioning and their role in psychoses. He also emphasized the rational aspect of conscious, differentiated emotions. Ortony explains emotions in terms of knowledge representations and emphasizes abductive logic as a mechanism of inferring other people's emotions. Ledoux analyses neural structures and pathways involved in emotional processing, especially fear. Griffiths considers basic emotions and their evolutionary development within social interactions. According to Damasio, emotions are primarily bodily perceptions, and feelings of emotions in the brain invoke "bodily markers." Grossberg and Levine consider emotions as neural signals that relate instinctual and conceptual brain centers. In processes of perception and cognition, emotions evaluate concept-models of objects and situations for satisfaction or dissatisfaction of instinctual needs. In Section 6, I discuss relationships of these various theories of emotions to mathematical descriptions; here I will just mention that this mathematical description closely corresponds to ideas of Kant, Jung, Grossberg and Levine. Ideas of Sartre and Damasio I did not find detailed enough for mathematical elaboration.

Behavior is comprised of many mechanisms. It is controlled by the endocrine and nervous systems. The complexity of an organism's behavior is related to the complexity of its nervous system. In this chapter I refer only to neurally controlled behavior; it involves mechanisms of negative feedback (e.g., when reaching an object with a hand) and positive feedback (e.g., when making a decision). The first does not reach consciousness, a second, is potentially available to consciousness (Grossberg, 1988).

Even this cursory review of basic notions used for describing the mind illustrates that they are far from being crystal clear; some notions may seem to contradict others. Below I summarize and simplify this discussion of basic mechanisms of the mind and relate them to a mathematical discussion in the next section. Some readers may question my way of summarization and simplification of the huge body of ongoing discussions; therefore, let me repeat that I draw my inspiration in trying to find unifying themes in commonsense understanding and technical discussions from ancient philosophers to today's research in multiple disciplines. The volume of this chapter does not allow for detailed discussions of all points of views. Presented here are summaries and references with few discussions, and the reader will judge to what extent I succeeded in unifying and simplifying this complex and diverse field.

Explaining basic mind mechanisms, let me repeat, requires no mysterious assumptions, and mathematical descriptions can be developed. Among the mind cognitive mechanisms, the most directly accessible to consciousness are concepts. Concepts are like internal models of the objects and situations in the world. This analogy is quite literal, e.g., during visual perception of an object, a concept-model in our memory projects an image onto the visual cortex, where it is matched to an image projected from the retina (this simplified description will be refined later).

Concepts serve for satisfaction of the basic instincts, which emerged as survival mechanisms long before concepts. We have briefly mentioned current debates on the roles of instincts, reflexes, motivational forces and drives. Inborn, unconscious, less adaptive and more automatic functioning often is referred to as instinctual. This lumping together of various mechanisms is inappropriate for the development of a mathematical description of the mind's mechanisms. I follow proposals (see Grossberg & Levine, 1987, for further references and discussions) to separate instincts as internal sensor mechanisms indicating the basic needs, from "instinctual behavior," which should be described by appropriate mechanisms. Accordingly, I use the word "instincts" to describe mechanisms of internal sensors: For example, when the sugar level in blood goes below a certain level an instinct "tells us" to eat. Such separation of instinct as "internal sensor" from "instinctual behavior" is only a step toward identifying all the details of relevant biological mechanisms.

How do we know about instinctual needs? We do not hear instinctual pronouncements or read dials of instinctual sensors. Instincts are connected to cognition and behavior by emotions. Whereas, in colloquial usage emotions are often understood as facial expressions, higher voice pitch and exaggerated gesticulation, these are outward signs of emotions, serving for communication. A more fundamental role of emotions within the mind's system is that emotional signals evaluate concepts for the purpose of instinct satisfaction. This evaluation is not according to rules or concepts (like rule-systems of artificial intelligence), but according to a different instinctual-emotional mechanism, described first by Grossberg and Levine (1987), and described below for higher cognitive functions. The emotional mechanism is crucial for breaking out of the "vicious circle" of combinatorial complexity.

A mathematical theory described in the next section leads to an inevitable conclusion: Humans and higher animals have a special instinct responsible for cognition. Let me emphasize, this is not an abstract mathematical theorem, but a conclusion from the basic knowledge of the mind's operations as described in thousands of publications. Clearly, humans and animals engage in exploratory behavior, even when basic bodily needs, like eating, are satisfied. Biologists and psychologists discuss curiosity in this regard (Berlyne, 1960, 1973). However, it is not mentioned among "basic instincts" on a par with those for food and procreation. The reasons were that it was difficult to define, and that its fundamental nature was not obvious. The fundamental nature of this mechanism is related to the fact that our knowledge always has to be modified to fit the current situation. One rarely sees exactly the same object: Illumination, angles and surrounding objects are usually different; therefore, adaptation-learning is required. A mathematical formulation of the mind's mechanisms makes obvious the fundamental nature of our desire for knowledge. In fact, virtually all learning and adaptive algorithms (tens of thousands of publications) maximize correspondence between the algorithm's internal structure (knowledge in a wide sense) and objects of recognition. As discussed in the next section, concept-models that our mind uses for understanding the world are in constant need of adaptation. Knowledge is not just a static state; it involves a process of adaptation and learning. Without adaptation of concept-models, we will not be able to understand the ever-changing surrounding world. We will not be able to orient ourselves or satisfy any of the bodily needs. Therefore, we have an inborn need, a drive, an instinct to improve our knowledge. I call it *the knowledge instinct*. Mathematically, it is described as a maximization of a similarity measure between concept-models and the world (as it is sensed by sensory organs; but I would add that the very sensing is usually adapted and shaped by the knowledge instinct).

Emotions evaluating satisfaction or dissatisfaction of the knowledge instinct are not directly related to bodily needs. Therefore, they are "spiritual," or aesthetic emotions. I would like to emphasize that aesthetic emotions are not peculiar to the perception of art, they are inseparable from every act of perception and cognition. Conceptual-emotional understanding of the world results in actions in the outside world or within the mind. In this chapter we only discuss an internal behavior within the mind, the behavior of learning and understanding the world. In the next section we describe a mathematical theory of conceptual-emotional recognition and understanding. In addition to concepts and emotions, the theory involves mechanisms of intuition, imagination, the conscious and unconscious. This process is intimately connected to an ability of the mind to think and to operate with symbols and signs. The mind involves a hierarchy of multiple layers of concept-models, from simple perceptual elements (like edges or moving dots), to concept-models of objects, to relationships among objects, to complex scenes and upwards along a hierarchy toward the concept-models of the meaning of life and purpose of our existence. Hence, the tremendous complexity of the mind; still, relatively few basic principles go a long way in explaining this system.

I would like to mention that Ortony and Turner (1990) summarized views of fourteen authors on basic emotions; three authors mentioned emotions that I consider aesthetic (Frijda, Izard, and McDougall mentioned interest and wonder). One reason for scientific community being slow in adopting these results is the already mentioned cultural bias against emotions as a part of thinking processes. Plato and Aristotle thought that emotions are "bad" for intelligence, and this is a part of our cultural heritage ("you have to be cool to be smart"), and the founders of artificial intelligence repeated this truism (Newell, 1983). Yet, as discussed in the next section, combining conceptual understanding with emotional evaluations is crucial for overcoming the combinatorial complexity and to understanding how the mind works.

I'd like to add a side comment. In neural, cognitive and psychological literature about the mind and brain, one often encounters a statement that the brain is a "kludge," a non-elegant, non-optimal design, a concoction of modules that appeared in evolution first for one purpose, and were then used for a different purpose, etc. (Clark, 1987; Minsky, 1995; Pinker, 1995; Chomsky, 2000). These statements are made usually by non-mathematicians, whose ideas about mathematical optimality and elegance are at best naive (we mentioned that in this line of research, many considered formal logic as the peak of optimality and elegance, even after Gödel proved its mathematical inconsistency).

Mathematical analysis of evolution demonstrates just the opposite (Perlovsky, 2002); there was more than enough information for evolution to attain optimality. The mind is often optimal (Charness & Levin, 2003). Among those preaching non-optimality of the brain and mind, no one produced a computer program working better or more optimal than the mind. Therefore, it is reasonable to consider mathematically optimal methods for modeling the mind.

Modeling Field Theory (MFT)

Modeling field theory is a multi-layer, hetero-hierarchical system (Perlovsky, 2001). The mind is not a strict hierarchy; there are multiple feedback connections among several adjacent layers, hence the term hetero-hierarchy. MFT mathematically implements mechanisms of the mind discussed above. At each layer there are concept-models encapsulating the mind's knowledge; they generate top-down signals, interacting with input, or bottom-up signals. These interactions are governed by the knowledge instinct, which drives concept-model learning, adaptation and formation of new concept-models for better correspondence to the input signals.

This section describes a basic mechanism of interaction between two adjacent hierarchical layers of bottom-up and top-down signals (fields of neural activation); sometimes, it will be more convenient to talk about these two signal-layers as an input to and output from a (single) processing-layer. At each layer, input signals are associated with (or recognized as, or grouped into) concepts according to the models and the knowledge instinct at this layer. These recognized concepts become output signals for the next layer. This general structure of MFT corresponds to our knowledge of neural structures in the brain. This is true about mathematical description in the following sub-sections; however, it is not mapped to specific neurons or synaptic connections. How actual brain neurons "implement" models and the knowledge instinct is a subject for future research. The knowledge instinct is described mathematically as maximization of a similarity measure. In the process of learning and understanding input signals, models are adapted for better representation of the input signals so that similarity between the models and signals increases. This increase in similarity satisfies the knowledge instinct and is felt as aesthetic emotions.

The Knowledge Instinct

At a particular hierarchical layer, we index neurons by $n = 1,... N$. These neurons receive bottom-up input signals, $\mathbf{X}(n)$, from lower layers in the processing hierarchy. $\mathbf{X}(n)$ is a field of bottom-up neuronal synapse activations, coming from neurons at a lower layer. Each neuron has a number of synapses. For generality, we describe each neuron activation as a set of numbers, $\mathbf{X}(n) = \{X_d(n), d = 1,... D\}$. Top-down, or priming, signals to these neurons are sent by concept-models, $\mathbf{M}_h(\mathbf{S}_h,n)$, indexed by $h = 1,... H$. Each model is characterized by its parameters, $\mathbf{S}_h$; in the neuron structure of the brain they are encoded by strength of synaptic connections; mathematically, we describe them as a set of numbers, $S_h = \{S^a_h, a = 1, \ldots A\}$. Models *represent* signals in the following way. Consider signal $X(n)$ coming from sensory neurons activated by object h, characterized by parameters S_h. These parameters may include position, orientation or lighting of an object h. Model $M_h(S_h, n)$ predicts a value $X(n)$ of a signal at neuron n. For example, during visual perception, a neuron n in the visual cortex receives a signal $X(n)$ from the retina and a priming signal $M_h(S_h, n)$ from an object-concept-model h. A neuron n is activated if both the bottom-up signal from lower-layer-input and the top-down priming signal are strong. Various models compete for evidence in the bottom-up signals, while adapting their parameters for a better match as described below. This is a simplified description of perception. The most benign everyday visual perception uses many layers from retina to object perception. The MFT premise is that the same laws describe the basic interaction dynamics at each layer. Perception of minute features, or everyday objects, or cognition of complex abstract concepts is due to the same mechanism described below. Perception and cognition involve models and learning. In perception, models correspond to objects; in cognition, models correspond to relationships and situations. Input signals, models and other parts of the learning mechanisms at a single processing layer described below are illustrated in Figure 1.

Learning is an essential part of perception and cognition, and is driven by the knowledge instinct. It increases a similarity measure between the sets of models and signals, $L(\{X\}, \{M\})$. The similarity measure is a function of model parameters and associations between the input bottom-up signals and top-down, concept-model signals. For concreteness, I refer here to an object perception using a simplified terminology, as if perception of objects in retinal signals occurs in a single layer.

In constructing a mathematical description of the similarity measure, it is important to acknowledge two principles. First, the exact content of the visual field is unknown before perception occurred. Important information could be contained in any bottom-up signal; therefore, the similarity measure is constructed so that it accounts for all input information, $X(n)$,

$$L(\{X\}, \{M\}) = \prod_{n \in N} l(X(n)). \tag{1}$$

This expression contains a product of partial similarities, $l(X(n))$, over all bottom-up signals; therefore it forces the mind to account for every signal (even if only one term in the product is zero, the product is zero, and thus the knowledge instinct is not satisfied). This is a reflection of the first principle. Second, before perception occurs, the mind does not know which retinal neuron corresponds to which object. Therefore, a partial similarity measure is constructed so that it treats each model as an alternative (a sum over models) for each input neuron signal. Its constituent elements are conditional partial similarities between signal $X(n)$ and model M_h, $l(X(n)|h)$. This measure is "conditional" on object h being present,[4] therefore, when combining these quantities into the overall similarity measure, L, they are multiplied by r(h), which represents the measure of object h actually being present. Combining these elements with the two principles noted above, a similarity measure is constructed as follows[5]:

$$L(\{\mathbf{X}\},\{\mathbf{M}\}) = \prod_{n \in N} \sum_{h \in H} r(h)\, l(\mathbf{X}(n)\,|\,h). \qquad (2)$$

The structure of (2) follows standard principles of the probability theory: A summation is taken over alternatives h and various pieces of evidence n are multiplied. This expression is not necessarily a probability, but it has a probabilistic structure. If learning is successful, it approximates probabilistic description and leads to near-optimal Bayesian decisions. The name "conditional partial similarity" for $l(\mathbf{X}(n)|h)$, or simply $l(n|h)$, follows the probabilistic terminology. If learning is successful, $l(n|h)$ becomes a conditional probability density function, a probabilistic measure that signals in neuron n originated from object h. Then L is the total likelihood of observing signals $\{\mathbf{X}(n)\}$ coming from objects described by models $\{\mathbf{M}_h\}$. Coefficients $r(h)$, called priors in probability theory, contain preliminary biases or expectations, expected objects h have relatively high $r(h)$ values; their true values are usually unknown and should be learned, like other parameters $\mathbf{S}_h$.

Note. In the probability theory, a product of probabilities usually assumes that evidence is independent. Expression (2) contains a product over n, but it does not assume independence among various signals $\mathbf{X}(n)$. There is a dependence among signals due to models: Each model $\mathbf{M}_h(\mathbf{S}_h, n)$ predicts expected signal values in many neurons n.

During the learning process, concept-models are constantly modified. From time to time a system forms a new concept while retaining an old one as well; alternatively, old

Figure 1. Learning mechanisms of a single processing layer

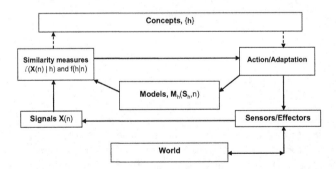

For a single layer of MFT, bottom-up input signals are unstructured data $\{X(n)\}$ and output signals are recognized or formed concepts $\{h\}$ with high values of similarity measures. Top-down, "priming" signals are models, $M_h(S_h, n)$. Conditional similarity measures $l(X(n)|h)$ and association variables $f(n|h)$ (Equation (3)), associate data and models. They initiate adaptation, Equations (4) and (5)), and concept recognition (see Equation 14 and discussion there). The adaptation-learning cycle defined by this structure and Equations (3), (4) and (5) maximizes similarity measure (1). Psychologically, it satisfies the knowledge instinct; changes in similarity (1) correspond to aesthetic emotions. New data coming from sensors, if they do not match exactly existing models, reduce similarity value, do not satisfy the knowledge instinct and produce negative aesthetic emotions. This stimulates the constant renewal of adaptation-learning cycles.

concepts are sometimes merged or eliminated. This mechanism works as follows. In this chapter we consider a case when functional forms of models $M_h(S_h, n)$ are all fixed, and learning-adaptation involves only model parameters S_h. More complicated structural learning of models is considered in Perlovsky (2004; 2006). Formation of new concepts and merging or elimination-forgetting of old ones require a modification of the similarity measure (2); the reason is that more models always result in a better fit between the models and data. This is a well known problem; it can be addressed by reducing similarity (2) using a "penalty function," $p(N,M)$, that grows with the number of models M, and this growth is steeper for a smaller amount of data N. For example, an asymptotically unbiased maximum likelihood estimation leads to multiplicative $p(N,M) = \exp(-N_{par}/2)$, where N_{par} is a total number of adaptive parameters in all models (this penalty function is known as Akaike Information Criterion, see Perlovsky (1996) for further discussion and references).

Dynamic Logic

The learning process consists in estimating model parameters S and associating signals with concepts by maximizing the similarity (2). Note, all possible combinations of signals and models are accounted for in expression (2). This can be seen by expanding a sum in (2) and multiplying all the terms; it would result in H^N items, a huge number. This is the number of combinations between all signals (N) and all models (H). Here is the source of CC of many algorithms used in the past. For example, multiple hypothesis testing algorithms attempt to maximize similarity L over model parameters and associations between signals and models in two steps. First they take one of the H^N items, that is one particular association between signals and models, and maximize it over model parameters. Second, the largest item is selected (that is, the best association for the best set of parameters). Such a program inevitably faces a wall of CC, the number of computations on the order of H^N.

Modeling field theory solves this problem by using dynamic logic (Perlovsky, 1996, 2001). An important aspect of dynamic logic is matching vagueness or fuzziness of similarity measures to the uncertainty of models. Initially, parameter values are not known and uncertainty of models is high; so is the fuzziness of the similarity measures. In the process of learning, models become more accurate and the similarity measure more crisp; the value of the similarity increases. This is the mechanism of dynamic logic.

Mathematically it is described as follows. First, assign any values to unknown parameters, $\{S_h\}$. Then, compute association variables f(h|n):

$$f(h|n) = r(h) \, l(\mathbf{X}(n)|h) / \sum_{h' \in H} r(h') \, l(\mathbf{X}(n)|h'). \tag{3}$$

Equation (3) looks like the Bayes formula for *a posteriori* probabilities; if l(n|h) in the result of learning become conditional likelihoods, f(h|n) become Bayesian probabilities for signal *n* originating from object *h*. The dynamic logic of the Modeling Fields (MF) is defined as follows:

$$df(h|n)/dt = f(h|n) \sum_{h' \in H} \{[\delta_{hh'} - f(h'|n)] \cdot$$

$$[\partial \ln l(n|h')/\partial \mathbf{M}_{h'}] \partial \mathbf{M}_{h'}/\partial \mathbf{S}_h \cdot d\mathbf{S}_h/dt, \tag{4}$$

$$d\mathbf{S}_h/dt = \sum_{n \in N} f(h|n)[\partial \ln l(n|h)/\partial \mathbf{M}_h]\partial \mathbf{M}_h/\partial \mathbf{S}_h, \tag{5}$$

here

$$\delta_{hh'} \text{ is 1 if h=h', 0 otherwise.} \tag{6}$$

Parameter *t* is the time of the internal dynamics of the MF system (like a number of internal iterations). A more specific form of (5) can be written when Gaussian-shape functions are used for conditional partial similarities:

$$l(n|h) = G(\mathbf{X}(n) | \mathbf{M}_h(\mathbf{S}_h, n), \mathbf{C}_h). \tag{7}$$

Here G is a Gaussian function with mean $\mathbf{M}_h$ and covariance matrix $\mathbf{C}_h$. Note, a "Gaussian assumption" is often used in statistics; it assumes that signal distribution is Gaussian. This is not the case in (7): Here signal is not assumed to be Gaussian. Equation (7) is valid if *deviations* between the model $\mathbf{M}$ and signal $\mathbf{X}$ are Gaussian; these deviations usually are Gaussian. If they are not Gaussian, (7) is still not a limiting assumption: A weighted sum of Gaussians in (2) can approximate any positive function, like similarity. Now the dynamic logic of the MF can be defined as follows:

$$dS_h^a/dt = [Y_h^{-1}]^{ab} Z_h^b, \tag{8}$$

$$Y_h^{ab} = \sum_{n \in N} f(h|n)[\mathbf{M}_h^{:a}\mathbf{C}_h^{-1}\mathbf{M}_h^{:b}], \tag{9}$$

$$Z_h^b = \sum_{n \in N} f(h|n)[\mathbf{M}_h^{:b}\mathbf{C}_h^{-1}\mathbf{D}_{nh}], \tag{10}$$

$$dC_h/dt = -0.5C_h^{-2} \sum_{n \in N} f(h|n)[\mathbf{C}_h - \mathbf{D}_{nh}\mathbf{D}_{nh}^T]; \tag{11}$$

$$\mathbf{D}_{nh} = (\,\mathbf{X}(n) - \mathbf{M}_h\,). \tag{12}$$

Here, superscript T denotes a transposed row-vector; summation is assumed over repeated indexes a, b; and (;) denotes partial derivatives with respect to parameters S with corresponding indexes:

$$\mathbf{M}^{;b}_{\,h} = \partial \mathbf{M}_h / \partial S^b_{\,h}. \tag{13}$$

The following theorem was proven (Perlovsky, 2001):

Theorem. Equations (3) through (6) (or (3) and (8 through 12)) define a convergent dynamic MF system with stationary states defined by $\max_{\{Sh\}} L$.

It follows that the stationary states of an MF system are the maximum similarity states satisfying the knowledge instinct. When partial similarities are specified as probability density functions (pdf), or likelihoods, the stationary values of parameters $\{S_h\}$ are asymptotically unbiased and efficient estimates of these parameters (Cramer, 1946). A computational complexity of the MF method is linear in N.

In plain English, this means that dynamic logic is a convergent process. It converges to the maximum of similarity, and therefore satisfies the knowledge instinct. Several aspects of MFT convergence are discussed below (in sections "Example of Dynamic Logic Operations," "MFT Hierarchical Organization" and "MFT Dynamics"). If likelihood is used as similarity, parameter values are estimated efficiently (that is, in most cases, parameters cannot be better learned using any other procedure). Moreover, as a part of the above theorem, it is proven that the similarity measure increases at each iteration. The psychological interpretation is that the knowledge instinct is satisfied at each step: A modeling field system with dynamic logic *enjoys* learning.

Example of Dynamic Logic Operations

Finding patterns below noise could be an exceedingly complex problem. If an exact pattern shape is not known and depends on unknown parameters, these parameters should be found by fitting the pattern model to the data. However, when location and orientation of patterns are not known, it is not clear which subset of the data points should be selected for fitting. A standard approach for solving these kinds of problems as discussed, multiple hypothesis testing (Singer, Sea, & Housewright, 1974), tries all combinations of subsets and models, faces combinatorial complexity. In this example, we are looking for "smile" and "frown" patterns in noise shown in Figure 2a without noise, and in Figure 2b with noise, as actually measured. Each pattern is characterized by a three-parameter parabolic shape. The image size in this example is 100×100 points, and the true number of patterns is three, which is not known. Therefore, at least four patterns should be fit to the data, to decide that three patterns fit best. Fitting 4×3=12 parameters to a

100x100 grid by brute-force testing would take about 10^{32} to 10^{40} operations, a prohibitive computational complexity.

To apply MFT and dynamic logic to this problem, we need to develop parametric adaptive models of expected patterns. We use a uniform model for noise, Gaussian blobs for highly-fuzzy, poorly resolved patterns and parabolic models for "smiles" and "frowns." The parabolic models and conditional partial similarities for this case are described in detail in Linnehan et al. (2003). The number of computer operations in this example (without optimization) was about 10^{10}. Thus, a problem that was not solvable due to CC becomes solvable using dynamic logic.

During an adaptation process, initial fuzzy and uncertain models are associated with structures in the input signals, making the fuzzy models more definite and crisp. The type, shape and number of models are selected so that the internal representation within the system is similar to input signals: The MF concept-models represent structure-objects in the signals. The figure below illustrates operations of dynamic logic. In Figure 2 (a) true "smile" and "frown" patterns are shown without noise; (b) actual image available for recognition (signal is below noise, signal-to-noise ratio is between –2dB and –0.7dB); (c) an initial fuzzy model, a large fuzziness corresponds to uncertainty of knowledge; (d) through (h) show improved models at various iteration stages (a total of 22 iterations). Every five iterations the algorithm tried to increase or decrease the number of pattern-models. Between iterations (d) and (e), the algorithm decided that it needed three Gaussian models for the "best" fit. There are several types of models: One uniform model describing noise (it is not shown) and a variable number of blob models and parabolic models, in which number, location and curvature are estimated from the data. Until about stage (g), the algorithm used simple blob models; at (g) and beyond, the algorithm decided that it needed more complex parabolic models to describe the data. Iterations stopped at (h), when similarity stopped increasing.

MFT Hierarchical Organization

The previous sub-sections described a single processing layer in a hierarchical MFT system. At each layer of a hierarchy there are input signals from lower layers, models, similarity measures (2), emotions, which are changes in similarity (2), and actions; actions include adaptation, behavior satisfying the knowledge instinct — maximization of similarity, Equations (3) through (6) (or (3) and (8 through 12)). An input to each layer is a set of signals $\mathbf{X}(n)$, or in neural terminology, an input field of neuronal activations. The result of signal processing at a given layer is activated models, or concepts h recognized in the input signals n; these models, along with the corresponding instinctual signals and emotions, may activate behavioral models and generate behavior at this layer.

The activated models initiate other actions. They serve as input signals to the next processing layer, where more general concept-models are recognized or created. Output signals from a given layer, serving as input to the next layer, could be model activation signals, a_h, defined as:

Figure 2. Finding "smile" and "frown" patterns in noise, an example of dynamic logic operation

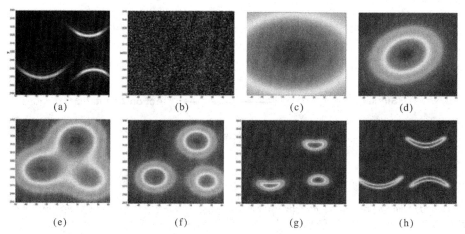

(a)   (b)   (c)   (d)

(e)   (f)   (g)   (h)

(a) True "smile" and "frown" patterns are shown without noise; (b) actual image available for recognition (signal is below noise, signal-to-noise ratio is between −2dB and −0.7dB); (c) an initial fuzzy blob-model, the fuzziness corresponds to uncertainty of knowledge; (d) through (h) show improved models at various iteration stages (total of 22 iterations). Between stages (d) and (e) the algorithm tried to fit the data with more than one model and decided that it needed three blob-models to "understand" the content of the data. There are several types of models: One uniform model describing noise (it is not shown) and a variable number of blob-models and parabolic models, which number, location and curvature are estimated from the data. Until about stage (g), the algorithm "thought" in terms of simple blob models; at (g) and beyond, the algorithm decided that it needed more complex parabolic models to describe the data. Iterations stopped at (h), when similarity (2) stopped increasing. This example is discussed in more detail in Linnehan, Mutz, Perlovsky, Weijers, Schindler, and Brockett (2003).

$$a_h = \sum_{n \in N} f(h|n). \tag{14}$$

Alternatively, output signals may include model parameters. The Hierarchical MF system is illustrated in Figure 3. Within the hierarchy of the mind, each concept-model finds its "mental" meaning and purpose at a higher layer (in addition to other purposes). For example, consider a concept-model "chair." It has a "behavioral" purpose of initiating sitting behavior (if sitting is required by the body), this is the "bodily" purpose at the same hierarchical layer. In addition, it has a "purely mental" purpose at a higher layer in the hierarchy, a purpose of helping to recognize a more general concept, say, of a "concert hall," which model contains rows of chairs.

Models at higher layers in the hierarchy are more general than models at lower layers. For example, at the very bottom of the hierarchy, if we consider vision system, models correspond (roughly speaking) to retinal ganglion cells and perform similar functions;

Figure 3. Hierarchical MF system

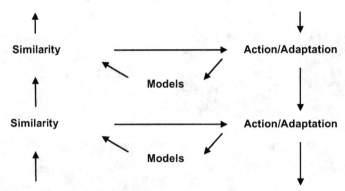

At each layer of a hierarchy there are models, similarity measures and actions (including adaptation, i.e., maximizing the knowledge instinct-similarity); high levels of partial similarity measures correspond to concepts recognized at a given layer; concept activations are output signals at this layer and they become input signals to the next layer, propagating knowledge up the hierarchy.

they detect simple features in the visual field; at higher layers, models correspond to functions performed at V1 and higher in the visual cortex, that is, detection of more complex features, such as contrast edges, their directions, elementary moves, etc. Visual hierarchical structure and models are studied in detail (Grossberg, 1988; Zeki, 1993); these models can be used in MFT. At still higher cognitive layers, models correspond to objects, to relationships among objects, to situations and relationships among situations, etc. (Perlovsky, 2001). Still higher are even more general models of complex cultural notions and relationships, like family, love, friendship and abstract concepts, like law, rationality, etc. Contents of these models correspond to a cultural wealth of knowledge, including the writings of Shakespeare and Tolstoy; detailed mechanisms of the development of these models are beyond the scope of this chapter (they are addressed in Perlovsky (2004, 2006). At the top of the hierarchy of the mind, according to Kantian analysis[6], are models of the meaning and purpose of our existence, unifying our knowledge, and the corresponding behavioral models aimed at achieving this meaning.

From time to time, as discussed, a system forms a new concept or eliminates an old one. This mechanism works as follows. At every layer, the system always keeps a reserve of fuzzy inactive concept-models (with large covariance, C, Equation (7)). They are inactive in that their parameters are not adapted to the data; therefore their similarities to signals are low. Yet, because of a large fuzziness (covariance) the similarities are not exactly zero. When a new signal does not fit well into any of the active models, its similarities to inactive models automatically increase (because first, every piece of data is accounted for [see endnote 4 for further discussion], and second, inactive models are vague-fuzzy and potentially can "grab" every signal that does not fit into more specific, less fuzzy, active models). As activation signal a_h, Equation (14), for an inactive model exceeds a certain threshold, the model is activated. Similarly, when an activation signal for a particular model falls below a threshold, the model is deactivated. Thresholds for activation and deactivation are set usually by mechanisms at a higher hierarchical layer based on prior information, system resources, numbers of activated models of various types, etc. Activation signals for active models at a particular layer { a_h } form a "neuronal field," which provides input signals to the next layer, where more abstract and more general concepts are formed, and so on along the hierarchy toward higher models of meaning and purpose.

Higher Cognitive Functions

This section relates in more detail the above mathematical descriptions to higher cognitive functions, illustrating that MF theory is rich enough to describe the mind on one hand without mysticism, and on the other hand, without reductionism, in general agreement with cognitive science, psychology and philosophy. A fundamental role in our higher cognitive functions is played by the knowledge instinct, which we described mathematically as maximization of similarity between concept-models and the world. The mathematical description of higher cognitive functions opens perspectives to better understanding of the mind functioning, and to solving previously unsolved problems associated with higher mind functions, including consciousness, feelings of the sublime, and beauty.

MFT Dynamics

Dynamical equations (3) and (4-6), or (7-12), describe an elementary process of perception or cognition maximizing similarity between models and the world, in which a large number of model-concepts compete for incoming signals; model-concepts are modified and new ones are formed, and eventually, connections are established among signal subsets on the one hand, and model-concepts on the other. Perception refers to processes in which the input signals come from sensory organs and model-concepts correspond to objects in the surrounding world. Cognition refers to higher layers in the hierarchy where the input signals are activation signals from concepts activated at lower layers, whereas model-concepts are more complex, abstract and correspond to situations and relationships among lower-layer concepts.

This process is described by dynamic logic. Its salient mathematical property is a correspondence between uncertainty in models and fuzziness in associations f(h|n). During perception, as long as model parameters do not correspond to actual objects, there is no match between models and signals; many models poorly match many objects, and associations remain fuzzy. This can be described more specifically, if Gaussian functions are used for l($\mathbf{X}$|h): For poorly matched models, the covariances, $\mathbf{C}_h$, are large (that is, model uncertainties are large). Uncertainty in models prevents f(h|n) from attaining definite (0,1) values. Eventually, one model (h') wins the competition for a subset {n'} of input signals $\mathbf{X}$(n), when parameter values match object properties. $\mathbf{C}_{h'}$, becomes smaller than other C_h, and f(h'|n) values become close to 1 for n∈ {n'} and 0 for n∉ {n'}. Upon the convergence, the entire set of input signals {n} is approximately divided into subsets, each associated with one model-object; C_h becomes small, and fuzzy *a priori* concepts become crisp concepts. Cognition is different from perception in that models are more general, more abstract and input signals are the activation signals from concepts identified (cognized) at a lower hierarchical layer. The general mathematical laws of cognition and perception are similar in MFT. Let us discuss relationships between the MFT theory and concepts of the mind originated in psychology, philosophy, linguistics, aesthetics, neuro-physiology, neural networks, artificial intelligence, pattern recognition and intelligent systems.

Elementary Thought-Process

Thought-process, or thinking, involves a number of sub-processes and attributes, including internal representations and their manipulation, attention, memory, concept formation, knowledge, generalization, recognition, understanding, meaning, prediction, imagination, intuition, emotion, decisions, reasoning, goals and behavior, conscious and unconscious (Perlovsky, 2001; Grossberg, 1988; Meystel, 1995). A "minimal" subset of these processes has to involve mechanisms for afferent and efferent signals (Grossberg, 1988), in other words, bottom-up and top-down signals coming from outside (external sensor signals) and from inside (internal representation signals). According to Carpenter and Grossberg (1987), every recognition and concept formation process involves a "resonance" between these two types of signals. In MFT, at every layer in a hierarchy, the afferent signals are represented by the input signal field X, and the efferent signals are represented by the modeling field signals M_h; resonances correspond to high similarity measures l(n|h) for some subsets of {n} that are "recognized" as concepts (or objects) *h*. The mechanism leading to the resonances is given by (3-6), or (7-12), and we call it an elementary thought-process. In this process, subsets of signals corresponding to objects or situations are understood as concepts and signals acquire meaning.

Kant's three volumes on the theory of the mind, Critique of Pure Reason, Critique of Judgment and Critique of Practical Reason (Kant, 1781, 1790,; 1788) describe the structure of the mind similar to MFT. Pure reason, or the faculty of understanding, contains concept-models. The faculty of judgment, or emotions, establishes correspondences between models and data about the world acquired by sensory organs (in Kant's terminology, between general concepts and individual events). Practical reason contains models of behavior. Kant was first to recognize that emotions are an inseparable part of cognition. The only missing link in Kantian theory is the knowledge instinct. Kant underappreciated a pervading need for concept adaptation; he considered concepts as given *a priori*.

A dynamic aspect of the working of the mind, as given by MFT and dynamic logic, was first given by Aristotle (IV BCE). He described thinking as a learning process in which an *a priori* form-as-potentiality (fuzzy model) meets matter (sensory signals) and becomes a form-as-actuality (a concept). He pointed out an important aspect of dynamic logic: reduction of fuzziness during learning; forms-potentialities are fuzzy (do not obey logic), whereas forms-actualities are logical.

History preserved for us evidence of Aristotle's foresight. When Alexander the Great, an Aristotelian pupil, was fighting in Persia, he wrote to his teacher: "Aristotle, I heard you are writing books now. Are you going to make our secret knowledge public?" In a reply letter Aristotle wrote: "Alexander, do not worry: nobody will understand" (Plutarch, II AD).

Understanding

In the elementary thought process, subsets in the incoming signals are associated with recognized model-objects, creating *phenomena* (in the MFT-mind) which are *understood* as objects. In other words, *signal subsets* acquire *meaning*; for example, a subset of retinal signals acquires the meaning of a chair. There are several aspects to understanding and meaning. First, object-models are connected by emotional signals (Perlovsky, 2001; Grossberg & Levine, 1987) to instincts that they might satisfy, and also to behavioral models that can make use of them for instinct satisfaction. Second, an object is understood in the context of a more general situation in the next hierarchical layer, consisting of more general concept-models, which accepts as input-signals the results of object recognition. That is, each recognized object-model (phenomenon) sends (in neural terminology, "activates") an output signal; a set of these signals comprises input signals for the next layer models, which "cognize" more general concept-models, like relations and situations. This process continues up the hierarchy of the mind toward the most general models a system could come up with, such as models of the universe (scientific theories), models of self (psychological concepts), models of the meaning of existence (philosophical concepts) and models of *a priori* transcendent intelligent subject (theological concepts).

Conscious and Unconscious

Why is there consciousness? Why would a feature like consciousness appear in the process of evolution? The answer to this question seems clear: Consciousness directs the will and results in a better adaptation for survival. In simple situations, when only minimal adaptation is required, instinct alone is sufficient, and unconscious processes can efficiently allocate resources and will. However, in complex situations, when adaptation is complicated, various instincts might contradict one another. Undifferentiated unconscious psychic functions result in ambivalence and ambitendency; every position entails its own negation, leading to an inhibition. This inhibition cannot be resolved by an unconscious that does not differentiate among alternatives. Direction is impossible without differentiation. Consciousness is needed to resolve an instinctual impasse by suppressing some processes and allocating power to others. By differentiating alternatives, consciousness can direct a psychological function to a goal.

Totality and undividedness of consciousness are the most important adaptive properties needed to concentrate power on the most important goal at every moment. This is illustrated, for example, by clinical cases of divided consciousness and multiple personalities, resulting in maladaptation up to a complete loss of functionality. Simple consciousness needs only to operate with relatively few concepts. One needs more and more differentiation for selecting more and more specific goals. The scientific quest is to explain the emergence of consciousness from the unconscious in the process of evolution. Consciousness has emerged, driven by unconscious urges for improved adaptation, by the knowledge instinct. And, among goals of consciousness is improvement of understanding of what is not conscious, inside and outside of the psyche. Thus, the cause and the end of consciousness are unconscious; hence, the limitations of consciousness, its causal mechanisms and goals are in the unconscious.

Most of our organismic functioning, like breathing, digestion, etc., are unconscious. In the process of evolution, only gradually have psychic processes separated from other organismic functions. In psychic functioning, our evolutionary and personal goals are to increase consciousness. But, this is largely unconscious, because our direct knowledge of ourselves is limited to consciousness. This fact creates a lot of confusion about consciousness. So, what is consciousness?

Consciousness is an awareness or perception of inward psychological facts, a subjective experience of sensing, feelings or thoughts. This definition is taken from the Webster's *Dictionary*. But a more detailed, scientific analysis of consciousness has proven to be difficult. For a long time it seemed obvious that consciousness completely pervades our entire mental life, or at least its main aspects. Now, we know that this idea is wrong, and the main reason for this misconception has been analyzed and understood: We are conscious only about what we are conscious of, and it is extremely difficult to notice anything else.

Popular misconceptions about consciousness noted by Jaynes (1976) include: Consciousness is nothing but a property of matter, or a property of living things or a property of neural systems. These three "explanations" attempted to dismiss consciousness as an epiphenomenon, an unimportant quality of something else. They are useless because the problem is in *explaining* the relationships of consciousness to matter, to life and to neural systems. These dismissals of consciousness are not very different from saying that there is no consciousness; but, of course, this statement refutes itself (if somebody makes such a statement unconsciously, there is no point of discussing it). A dualistic position is that consciousness belongs to the world of ideas and has nothing to do with the world of matter. But the scientific problem *is* in explaining the consciousness as a natural-science phenomenon; that is, to relate consciousness and the material world. Searle (1992) suggested that any explanation of consciousness has to account for it being real and based on physical mechanisms in the brain. Among properties of consciousness requiring explanation, he listed unity and intentionality (we perceive our consciousness as being *unified* in the space of our perceptions and in the time of our life; consciousness is about something; this "about" points to its *intentionality*).

Searle (1997) reviews recent attempts to explain consciousness, and comes to a conclusion that little progress was made during the 1990s. Penrose (1994) suggested that consciousness cannot be explained by known physical laws of matter. His arguments descend from the Gödel's proofs of inconsistency and incompleteness of logic. This, however, only proves (Perlovsky, 1996) that the mind is not a system of logical rules, which we have already discussed in previous sections.

Knowledge of consciousness is primarily of introspective origin. Understanding of consciousness requires differentiating conscious and unconscious psychic processes, so we need to understand what is psychic, what is unconscious and what is conscious-ness. Our experiences can be divided into somatic and psychic. A will modifying instinctual reflexes indicates a presence of psyche, but not necessarily consciousness. Often, we associate consciousness with a subjective perception of free will. Conscious-ness about somatic experiences is limited by the unknown in the outer world. Similarly, consciousness about psychic experiences is limited by *the unknown in the psyche, or unconscious.* Roughly speaking, there are three conscious/unconscious levels of psychic contents: (1) contents that can be recalled and made conscious voluntarily (memories); (2) contents that are not under voluntary control; we know about them because they spontaneously irrupt into consciousness; and (3) contents inaccessible to consciousness. We know about the latter through scientific deductions.

Consciousness is not a simple phenomenon, but a complicated differentiated process. Jung (1921) differentiated four types of consciousness related to experiences of feelings, thoughts, sensations and intuitions. In addition to these four psychic functions, consciousness is characterized by attitude: introverted, concentrated mainly on the inner experience, or extroverted, concentrated mainly on the outer experience. Interplay of various conscious and unconscious levels of psychic functions and attitudes results in a number of types of consciousness; interactions of these types with individual memories and experiences make consciousness dependent on the entire individual experience producing variability among individuals.

Intentionality is a property of referring to something else, and consciousness is about something. This "aboutness" many philosophers refer to as intentionality. In everyday life, when we hear an opinion, we do not just collate it in our memory and relate to other opinions (like a pseudo-scientist in a comedy), this would not lead very far. We wish to know what are the aims and intentions associated with this opinion. Often, we perceive the intent of what is said better then specific words, even if the words are chosen to disguise the intent behind causal reasoning. The desire to know and the ability to perceive the goal indicate that in psyche, *final standpoint or purpose* is more important than the *causal* one. This intentionality of psyche was already emphasized by Aristotle (VI DCE) in his discussions of the end cause of forms of the mind. Intentionality of consciousness is more fundamental than "aboutness," it is *purposiveness.*[7]

The intentional property of consciousness led many philosophers during the last decades to believe that intentionality is a unique and most important characteristic of consciousness: According to Searle, only conscious beings could be intentional. But, we feel that this view is not adequate. Intentionality is a fundamental property of life; even the simplest living being is a result of long evolution, and its every component, say a gene or a protein, has a purpose and intent. In particular, every model-concept has evolved with an intent or purpose to recognize a particular type of signal (event, message or concept) and to act accordingly (e.g., send recognition messages to other parts of the brain and to behavioral models). Aristotle was the first to explain the intentionality of the mind this way; he argued that intentionality should be explained through the *a priori* contents of the mind.[8]

Even in an artificial intelligent systems, every part is intentional;they were designed and built with intent to accomplish something. Every concept-model is intentional; the intent is to recognize an object or a situation. As discussed previously, objects that we see around us belong not to the outer world of matter, but to the world of concepts, the realm of interaction between the mind and matter. Thus, every object is an intentional concept. It is important to differentiate this statement from a philosophical position of *pan-psychism,* which assumes that matter itself, in all its forms, has a degree of psyche or spirit as its fundamental property. Pan-psychism does not really explain matter or psyche. This is why Descartes "exorcised" spirit from the world of matter. To a significant degree, pan-psychism is a result of a failure to differentiate between the world of matter and the world of concepts.

This analysis of intentionality works for cultural concepts as well. Every cultural concept and every man-made object are intentional because they emerged, or were created (consciously or otherwise), with a specific intent (or purpose). The intentionality, I repeat, is therefore the same property that Kant called purposiveness.[9] There are two aspects of purposiveness or intentionality: Higher intellectual intention of a concept is to correspond to the world and thus to satisfy the knowledge instinct; and lower bodily intention is to be used for appropriate utilitarian or bodily-instinctive purposes. (For example, a table in my kitchen is not just a thing-in-itself, but an intentional concept-object; its higher intellectual intention is to recognize the table-as-a-part-of-material-world and use it for building a coherent picture of the world in my mind, and its lower bodily intention is to use the table-object appropriately for sitting and eating, etc. In this regard, some philosophers (Freeman, 2000) talk about the table as an *external represen-tation* of the concept "table").

Is there any specific relationship between consciousness and intentionality? If so, it is just the opposite of Searle's hypothesis of intentionality implying consciousness. Affective, subconscious lower-bodily-level emotional responses are concerned with immediate survival, utilitarian goals, and therefore are *intentional in the most* straight-forward way. A higher-intellectual-level consciousness is not concerned with immediate survival, but with the overall understanding of the world, with knowledge and beauty; it can afford to be impartial, abstract and less immediately-intentional than the rest of the psyche. Its intentions might be directed toward meanings and purposes of life. The highest creative aspect of individual consciousness and the abilities of perceiving the beautiful and sublime are intentional without any specific, lower-level utilitarian goal. They are intentional toward self-realization, toward future-self beyond current-self.

Unity of consciousness refers to conscious mental states being parts of a unified sequence, and simultaneous conscious events are perceived as unified into a coherent picture. Searle's unity is close to what Kant called "the transcendental unity of apperception." In MFT, this internal perception is explained, as all perceptions, due to a property of the special model involved in consciousness, called Ego by psychologists. The properties of the Ego-model explain the properties of consciousness. When certain properties of consciousness seems difficult to explain, we should follow the example of Kant; we should turn the question around and ask: Which properties of Ego model would explain the phenomenological properties of consciousness?

Let us begin the analysis of the structures of the Ego-model and the process of its adaptation to the constantly changing world, from evolutionary-preceding simpler forms. What is the initial state of consciousness? Is it an undifferentiated unity or a "booming, buzzing confusion"? Or, let us take a step back in the evolutionary develop-ment and ask, What is the initial state of pre-conscious psyche? Or, let us move back even farther toward evolution of sensory systems and perception. When building a robot for a factory floor, why provide it with a sensor? Obviously, such an expensive thing as a sensor is needed to achieve specific goals: to sense the environment with the purpose to accomplish specific tasks. Providing a robot with a sensor goes together with an ability to utilize sensory data. (Why have sensors otherwise?)

Similarly, in the process of evolution, sensory abilities emerge together with perception abilities. A natural evolution of sensory abilities can not result in a "booming, buzzing confusion," but must result in evolutionary advantageous abilities to avoid danger, attain food, etc. Initial perception abilities are *limited* to a few types of concept-objects (light-dark, warm-cold, edible-nonedible, dangerous-attractive, etc.) and are directly "wired" to proper actions. When perception functions evolve further, beyond immediate actions, it is through the development of complex internal model-concepts, which unify simpler object-models into a unified and flexible model of the world. Only at this point of possessing relatively complicated differentiated concept-models composed of a large number of sub-models, can an intelligent system experience a "booming, buzzing confusion," if it faces a new type of environment. A primitive system is simply incapable of perceiving confusion: It perceives only those "things" for which it has concept-models, and if its perceptions do not correspond to reality, it just does not survive without experiencing confusion. When a baby is born, it undergoes a tremendous change of environment, most likely without much conscious confusion. The original state of consciousness is undifferentiated unity. It possesses a single modality of primordial undifferentiated Self-World.

The initial unity of psyche limited abilities of the mind, and further development proceeded through differentiation of psychic functions or modalities (concepts, emotions and behavior); they were further differentiated into multiple concept-models, etc. This accelerated adaptation. Differentiation of consciousness is a relatively recent process (Jaynes, 1976; Jung, 1921).

Consciousness is about aspects of concept-models (of the environment, self, past, present, future plans and alternatives) and emotions (evaluative feelings)[10] to which we can direct our attention. As already mentioned, MFT explains consciousness as a specialized Ego-model. Within this model, consciousness can direct attention at will. This conscious control of will is called the free will. A subjective feeling of free will is a most cherished property of our psyche. Most of us feel that this is what makes us different from inanimate objects and simple forms of life. And this property is a most difficult one to explain rationally or to describe mathematically. But, let us see how far we can go towards understanding this phenomenon. We know that raw percepts are often not conscious. For example, in the visual system, we are conscious about the final processing stage and the integrated crisp model but unconscious about intermediate processing. We are unconscious about eye receptive fields: about details of visual perception of motion and color as far as it takes place in our brain separately from the main visual cortex, etc. These unconscious perceptions are illustrated in blindsight: A visual perception occurs, but a person is not conscious of it (Zeki, 1993). In most cases, we are conscious only about the integrated scene, crisp objects, etc.

These properties of consciousness follow from properties of concept-models; they have conscious (crisp) and unconscious (fuzzy) parts, which are accessible and inaccessible to consciousness, that is to the Ego-model. In pre-scientific literature about mechanisms of the mind, there was a popular idea of homunculus, a little mind inside our mind, which perceived our perceptions and made them available to our mind. This naive view is amazingly close to actual scientific explanation. The fundamental difference is that the scientific explanation does not need an infinite chain of homunculi inside homunculi. Instead, there are hierarchy of the mind models with their conscious and unconscious aspects. The higher in the hierarchy, the less is the conscious differentiated aspect of the models, until at the top of the hierarchy there are mostly unconscious models of the meaning of our existence (which we discuss later).

Our internal perceptions of consciousness, let me repeat, are due to the Ego-model "perceiving" crisp conscious parts of other models similar to models of perception "perceiving" objects in the world. The properties of consciousness as we perceive them, such as continuity and identity of consciousness, are due to properties of the Ego-model. What is known about this "consciousness" model? Since Freud, a certain complex of psychological functions was called Ego. Jung considered Ego to be based on a more general model or archetype of Self. Jungian archetypes are psychic structures (models) of a primordial origin, which are mostly inaccessible to consciousness, but determine the structure of our psyche. In this way, archetypes are similar to other models, e.g., receptive fields of the retina are not consciously perceived, but determine the structure of visual perception. The Self archetype determines our phenomenological subjective perception of ourselves and, in addition, structures our psyche in many different ways which are far from being completely understood. An important phenomenological property of Self is the perception of uniqueness and indivisibility (hence, the word *individual*).

Consciousness, to a significant extent, coincides with the conscious part of the archetype-model of Self. A conscious part of Self belongs to Ego. Not everything within Ego (as defined by Freud) is conscious. Individuality, as a total character distinguishing an individual from others, is a main characteristic of Ego. Not all aspects of individuality are conscious, so the relationships among the discussed models can be summarized to some extent, as:

$$\text{Consciousness} \in \text{Individuality} \in \text{Ego} \in \text{Self} \in \text{Psyche}.$$

The sign "$\in$" here means "is a part of." Consciousness-model is a subject of free will; it possesses, controls and directs free will. Free will is limited by laws of nature in the outer world and in the inner world by the unconscious aspects of Self. Free will belongs to consciousness, but not to the conscious and unconscious totality of the psyche.

Many contemporary philosophers consider subjective nature of consciousness to be an impenetrable barrier to scientific investigation. Chalmers differentiated hard and easy questions about consciousness as follows. Easy questions, that will be answered better and better, are concerned with brain mechanisms: Which brain structures are responsible for consciousness? Hard questions, that no progress can be expected for, are concerned with the subjective nature of consciousness and *qualia*, subjective feelings associated with every conscious perception. Nagel (1974) described it dramatically with a question: "What is it like to be a bat?" But I disagree. I don't think these questions are hard. These questions are not mysteries; they are just wrong questions for a scientific theory. Newton, while describing the laws of planet motion, did not ask: "What is it like to be a planet?" (even so, something like this feeling *is* a part of scientific intuition). The subjective nature of consciousness is not a mystery. It is explained due to the subjective nature of the concept-models that we are conscious of. The subjectivity is the result of combined apriority and adaptivity of the consciousness-model, the unique genetic *a priori* structures of psyche together with our unique individual experiences. I consider the only hard questions about consciousness to be *free will and the nature of creativity*.

Let us summarize. Most of the mind's operations are not accessible to consciousness. We definitely know that neural firings and connections cannot be perceived consciously. In the foundations of the mind there are material processes in the brain inaccessible to consciousness. Jung suggested that conscious concepts are developed by the mind based on genetically inherited structures or archetypes, which are inaccessible to consciousness (Jung, 1921, 1934). Grossberg (1988) suggested that only signals and models attaining a resonant state (that is signals matching models) can reach consciousness. This was further detailed by Taylor (2005); he related consciousness to the mind being a control mechanism of the mind and body. A part of this mechanism is a prediction model. When this model's predictions differ from sensory observations, the difference may reach a resonant state, which we are consciousness about. To summarize the above analyses, the mind mechanisms, described in MFT by dynamic logic and fuzzy models, are not accessible to consciousness. Final results of dynamic logic processes, resonant states characterized by crisp models and corresponding signals are accessible to consciousness.

Imagination

Imagination involves excitation of a neural pattern in a sensory cortex in the absence of an actual sensory stimulation. For example, visual imagination involves excitation of visual cortex, say with closed eyes (Grossberg, 1988; Zeki, 1993). Imagination was long considered a part of thinking processes; Kant (1790) emphasized the role of imagination in the thought process; he called thinking "a play of cognitive functions of imagination and understanding." Whereas pattern recognition and artificial intelligence algorithms of the recent past would not know how to relate to this (Newell, 1983; Minsky, 1988), Carpenter and Grossberg (1987) resonance model and the MFT dynamics, both describe imagination as an inseparable part of thinking. Imagined patterns are top-down signals that *prime* the perception cortex areas (*priming* is a neural terminology for making neurons more readily excited). In MFT, the imagined neural patterns are given by models M_h.

Visual imagination, as mentioned, can be "internally perceived" with closed eyes. The same process can be mathematically modeled at higher cognitive layers, where it involves models of complex situations or plans. Similarly, models of behavior at higher layers of the hierarchy can be activated without actually propagating their output signals down to actual muscle movements and actual acts in the world. In other words, behavior can be imagined. Along with its consequences, it can be evaluated, and this is the essence of plans. Such a mathematical procedure based on MFT and dynamic logic was implemented for several applications (some of them were described in Perlovsky, 2001; other applications for Internet search engines, military applications and financial predictions remain unpublished). It is our suggestion that this mathematical description corresponds to actual workings of the mind. At this point, I would only say that this suggestion does not contradict known facts from psychology and neuro-biology. Current research relating this mathematical description to psychology of high cognitive behavior, to its evolution, and to brain regions supporting this functioning is going on in collaboration with other researchers (D. Levine and F. Fontanari). Sometimes, imagination involves detailed alternative courses of actions considered and evaluated consciously. Sometimes, imagination may involve fuzzy or vague, barely conscious models, which reach consciousness only after they converge to a "reasonable" course of action, which can be consciously evaluated. From a mathematical standpoint, this latter mechanism is the only one possible; conscious evaluation cannot involve all possible courses of action, it would lead to combinatorial complexity and impasse. It remains to be proven in brain studies, which will identify the exact brain regions and neural mechanisms involved.

MFT (in agreement with neural data) just adds details to Kantian description: Thinking is a play of top-down *higher-hierarchical-layer* imagination and bottom-up *lower-layer* understanding. Kant identified this "play" [described by (3-6) or (7-12)] as a source of aesthetic emotion. Kant used the word "play," when he was uncertain about the exact mechanism; this mechanism, according to our suggestion, is the knowledge instinct and dynamic logic.

Instincts and Emotions

Functioning of the mind and brain cannot be understood in isolation from the system's "bodily needs." For example, a biological system (and any autonomous system) needs to replenish its energy resources (eat). This and other fundamental unconditional needs are indicated to the system by instincts. As we discussed, scientific terminology in this area is still evolving; for our purpose of making a step toward uncovering neural mechanisms of the mind, we describe instincts mathematically as internal sensors indicating unconditional needs of an organism. Emotional signals, generated, say, by instinct for food are perceived by psyche as "hunger," and they activate behavioral models related to food searching and eating. In this chapter we are concerned primarily with the behavior of understanding the surrounding world, with acquiring knowledge. The knowledge instinct demands that we improve our knowledge; the corresponding "internal sensor" is a measure of similarity between the knowledge (internal models of the mind) and the world around us (that we sense through sensory organs). Bodily instinctual influences on understanding modify the object-perception process (3) - (6) in such a way that desired objects get enhanced recognition. This is the reason a hungry person "sees food all around." In MFT it can be accomplished by modifying priors, $r(h)$ in Equations (2) and (3), according to the degree to which an object of type h can satisfy a particular instinct. Details of these mechanisms are not considered here.

Aesthetic Emotions and the Instinct for Knowledge

Recognizing objects in the environment and understanding their meaning is so important for survival that a special instinct evolved for this purpose. This instinct for learning and improving concept-models I call the instinct for knowledge. In MFT it is described by maximization of similarity between the models and the world, Equation (2). Emotions related to satisfaction-dissatisfaction of this instinct are perceived by us as harmony-disharmony (between our understanding of how things ought to be and how they actually are in the surrounding world). According to Kant (1790), these are aesthetic emotions (emotions that are not related directly to satisfaction or dissatisfaction of bodily needs).

The instinct for knowledge makes little kids, cubs and piglets jump around and play fight; their inborn models of behavior must adapt to their body weights, objects and animals around them long before the instincts of hunger and fear will use the models for direct aims of survival. Kiddy behavior just makes the work of the knowledge instinct more observable; to varying degrees, this instinct continues acting all of our life. All the time we are bringing our internal models into correspondence with the world; in adult life, when our perception and understanding of the surrounding world is adequate, aesthetic emotions are barely perceptible: The mind just does its job. Similarly, we do not usually notice adequate performance of our breathing muscles and satisfaction of the breathing instinct. However, if breathing is difficult, negative emotions immediately reach consciousness. The same is true about the knowledge instinct and aesthetic emotions: If we do not understand the surroundings, if objects around do not correspond to our expectations, negative emotions immediately reach consciousness. We perceive these emotions as disharmony between our knowledge and the world. Thriller movies exploit the instinct for knowledge: They are mainly based on violating our expectations; their personages are shown in situations where knowledge of the world is inadequate for survival.

Let me emphasize again, aesthetic emotions are not peculiar to art and artists, they are inseparable from every act of perception and cognition. In everyday life we usually do not notice them. Aesthetic emotions become noticeable at higher cognitive layers in the mind's hierarchy, when cognition is not automatic, but requires conscious effort. Damasio's (1995) view of emotions defined by visceral mechanisms, as far as discussing higher cognitive functions, seems erroneous in taking secondary effects for the primary mechanisms. People often devote their spare time to increasing their knowledge, even if it is not related to their job and a possibility of promotion. Pragmatic interests could be involved: Knowledge makes us more attractive to friends and could help find sexual partners. Still, there is a remainder, a pure joy of knowledge: aesthetic emotions satisfying the knowledge instinct.

Beautiful and Sublime

Contemporary cognitive science is at a complete loss when trying to explain the highest human abilities, the most important and cherished abilities to create and perceive beautiful and sublime experiences. Their role in the working of the mind is not understood. MFT explains that simple harmony is an elementary aesthetic emotion related to improvement of object-models. Higher aesthetic emotions are related to the development and improvement of more complex models at "higher" levels of the mind hierarchy. The highest forms of aesthetic emotion are related to the most general and most important models near the top of the hierarchy. According to Kantian analysis (1790, 1798), among the highest models are those of the meaning of our existence, of our purposiveness or intentionality; beauty is related to improving these models.

Models of our purposiveness are largely fuzzy and unconscious. Some people, at some points in their life, may believe that their life purpose to be finite and concrete. Say, make a lot of money or build a loving family and bring up good children. These models are aimed at satisfying powerful instincts, but not the knowledge instinct, and they do not reflect the highest human aspirations. Everyone who achieved a finite goal of making money or raising good children knows that this is not the end of his or her aspirations. The reason is that everyone has an ineffable feeling of partaking in the infinite, while at the same time knowing that our material existence is finite. This contradiction cannot be resolved. For this reason, models of our purpose and meaning cannot be made crisp and conscious, they will forever remain fuzzy and partly unconscious.

Everyday life gives us little evidence to develop models of meaning and purposiveness of our existence. People are dying every day and often from random causes. Nevertheless, life itself demands belief in one's purpose; without such a belief it is easier to get drunk or take drugs than to read this book. These issues are not new; philosophers and theologists have expounded upon them from time immemorial. The knowledge instinct theory gives us a scientific approach to the eternal quest for the meaning. We perceive an object or a situation as beautiful, when it stimulates improvement of the highest models of meaning. Beautiful is what "reminds" us of our purposiveness. This is true about perception of beauty in a flower or in an art object. The MFT explanation of the nature of beautiful resolves a number of mysteries and contradictions in contemporary aesthetics (Perlovsky, 2002, 2006).

The feeling of spiritual sublimity is similar and different from the beautiful. Whereas the beautiful is related to improvement of the models of *cognition*, the sublime is related to improvement of the models of *behavior* realizing the highest meaning in our life. The beautiful and sublime are not finite. MFT tells us that, mathematically, improvement of complex models is related to choices from an infinite number of possibilities. A mathematician may consider 100^{100}, or million power million as a finite number. But for a physicist, a number that exceeds all elementary events in the life of the Universe is infinite. A choice from infinity is infinitely complex and contains infinite information. Therefore, choices of the beautiful and sublime contain infinite information. This is not a metaphor, but exact mathematical fact. Beauty is at once objective and subjective. It really exists; cultures and individuals cannot exist without an ability to appreciate beauty, and still, it cannot be described by any finite algorithm or a set of rules.

Beauty of a physical theory, discussed sometimes by physicists, is similar in its infinity to beauty in an artwork. For a physicist, beauty of a physical theory is related to a need to improve the models of the meaning in our understanding of the universe. This satisfies a scientist's quest for purpose, which he identifies with purpose in the world.

Intuition

Intuitions include inner perceptions of object-models, imaginations produced by them, and their relationships with objects in the world. They include also higher-level models of relationships among simpler models. Intuitions involve fuzzy unconscious concept-models, which are in a state of being formed, learned and adapted toward crisp and conscious models (say, a theory). Conceptual contents of fuzzy models are undifferentiated and partly unconscious. Similarly, conceptual and emotional contents of these fuzzy mind states are undifferentiated; concepts and emotions are mixed up. Fuzzy mind states may satisfy or dissatisfy the knowledge instinct in varying degrees before they become differentiated and accessible to consciousness, hence the vague and complex emotional-cognitive feel of an intuition. Contents of intuitive states differ among people, but the main mechanism of intuition is the same among artists and scientists. Composer's intuitions are mostly about sounds and their relationships to psyche. Painter's intuitions are mostly about colors and shapes and their relationships to psyche. Writer's intuitions are about words, or more generally, about language and its relationships to psyche. Mathematical intuition is about structure and consistency within a theory, and about relationships between the theory and *a priori* content of psyche. Physical intuition is about the real world, first principles of its organization and mathematics describing it.

Creativity, Differentiation and Synthesis

Creativity is an ability to improve and create new model-concepts. In a small degree it is present in everyday perception and cognition. Usually the words "creativity," "creative" or "discovery" are applied to improving or creating new model-concepts at higher cognitive levels, concepts that are important for the entire society or culture. Making one's discoveries well-known to the entire society, recognized and available to the entire culture is a separate process. We know, for example, that skillful and expensive advertising could be important, but this is not a part of the original discovery or creation. Certain discoveries and works of art became famous centuries after their creation.

MFT explains that a completely crisp model could only match a very specific content; therefore, it cannot lead to the creation of new contents. Creativity and discovery, according to MFT, involve vague, fuzzy models, which are made more crisp and clear. It occurs, therefore, at the border between consciousness and unconscious. A similar nature of creative process, involving consciousness and unconscious, was discussed by Jung (1921). Creativity usually involves intuition, as discussed above: fuzzy undifferentiated feelings-concepts.

Two main mechanisms of creativity are differentiation and synthesis. Differentiation is a process of creating new, more specific and more detailed concept-models from simpler, less differentiated and less conscious models. Mathematical mechanisms of differentiation were discussed earlier.

Synthesis is a process of connecting detailed, crisp concept-models to unconscious instincts and emotions. The need for synthesis comes from the fact that most of our concept-models are acquired from language. The entire conceptual content of the culture is transmitted from generation to generation through language; cognitive concept-models can not be transmitted directly from brain to brain. Therefore, concepts acquired from language have to be transformed by individual minds into cognitive concepts. Mathematical mechanisms of integrating cognition and language require the extension of MFT considered in Perlovsky (2004). It explains that purely-language concepts could be detailed and conscious, but not necessarily connected to cognitive concept-models, emotions and to the knowledge instinct. Every child acquires language between one and seven years, but it takes the rest of their life to connect abstract language models to their life's needs, to cognitive concept-models, to emotions and instincts. This is the process of synthesis; it integrates language and cognition, concepts and emotions, conscious and unconscious, instinctual and learned into a unified whole.

Differentiated concepts acquire meaning in connections with instinctual and unconscious. In the evolution of the mind, differentiation speeds up the development of consciousness, but may bring about a split between conscious and unconscious and between emotional and conceptual. If the split affects collective psyche, it leads to a loss of the creative potential of a nation. This was the mechanism of death of great ancient civilizations. The development of culture, the very interest of life, requires *combining differentiation and synthesis*. Evolution of the mind and cultures is determined by this complex, non-linear interaction: One factor prevails, then another. Evolution of cultures as determined by the interaction of mechanisms of differentiation and synthesis is considered in more detail in Perlovsky (2006).

Mind, Brain and MFT Testing

Historically, the mind is described in psychological and philosophical terms, whereas the brain is described in terms of neurobiology and medicine. Within scientific exploration, the mind and brain are different description levels of the same system. Establishing relationships between these descriptions is of great scientific interest. Today we approach solutions to this challenge (Grossberg, 2000), which eluded Newton in his attempt to establish a physics of "spiritual substance" (Westfall, 1983). Detailed discussion of established relationships between the mind and brain is beyond the scope of this chapter, as well as relating in detail MFT to brain mechanisms is a subject of ongoing and future research. In this section we briefly mention the main known and unknown facts and give references for future reading. General neural mechanisms of the elementary thought process which are similar in MFT and ART (Carpenter & Grossberg, 1987), have been confirmed by neural and psychological experiments. These include neural mechanisms for bottom-up (sensory) signals, top-down imagination model-signals and the resonant matching between the two (Grossberg, 1975). Adaptive modeling abilities are well studied with adaptive parameters identified with synaptic connections (Koch & Segev, 1998; Hebb, 1949); instinctual learning mechanisms have been studied in psychology and linguistics (Piaget, 2000; Chomsky, 1981; Jackendoff, 2002; Deacon, 1998).

Ongoing and future research will confirm, disprove or suggest modifications to specific mechanisms considered: model parameterization and parameter adaptation, reduction of fuzziness during learning, similarity measure (2) as a foundation of the knowledge instinct and aesthetic emotion, relationships between psychological and neural mechanisms of learning on the one hand and, on the other, aesthetic feelings of harmony and emotion of beautiful. Specific neural systems will have to be related to mathematical descriptions on the one hand, and on the other, to psychological descriptions in terms of subjective experiences and observable behavior. Ongoing joint research with Fontanari addresses the evolution of models jointly with that of language (Fontanari & Perlovsky, 2005a, b, 2004); joint research with Levine addresses relationships of MFT and the knowledge instinct to issues of behavioral psychology and to specific brain areas involved in emotional reward and punishment during learning. We will have to develop differentiated forms of the knowledge instinct, which are the mechanisms of synthesis, and of the infinite variety of emotions perceived in music (Perlovsky, 2006). Future experimental research needs to study in detail the nature of hierarchical interactions: To what extent is the hierarchy "hardwired" versus adaptively emerging? What is a hierarchy of learning instinct? We will have to develop further interactions between cognitive hierarchy and language hierarchy (Perlovsky, 2004).

Teleology, Causality and the Knowledge Instinct

Teleology explains the universe in terms of purposes. In many religious teachings it is a basic argument for the existence of God: If there is purpose, an ultimate designer must exist. Therefore, teleology is a hot point of debates between creationists and evolutionists: Is there a purpose in the world? Evolutionists assume that the only explanation is causal. Newton's laws gave a perfect causal explanation for the motion of planets: A planet moves from moment to moment under the influence of a gravitational force. Similarly, today's science explains motions of all particles and fields according to causal laws, and there are exact mathematical expressions for fields, forces and their motions. Causality explains what happens in the next moment as a result of forces acting in the previous moment. Scientists accept this causal explanation and oppose teleological explanations in terms of purposes. The very basis of science, it seems, is on the side of causality, and religion is on the side of teleology.

This assumption, however, is wrong. The contradiction between causality and teleology does not exist at the very basic level of fundamental physics. The laws of physics, from classical Newtonian laws to quantum superstrings, can be formulated equally as causal or as teleological. An example of teleological principle in physics is energy minimization, i.e., particles moving so that energy is minimized. It is as if particles in each moment know their purpose: to minimize the energy. The most general physical laws are formulated as minimization of action. Action is a more general physical entity than energy; it is an intuitive name for a mathematical expression called Lagrangian. Causal dynamics, motions of particles, quantum strings and superstrings are determined by minimizing Lagrangian-action (Feynman & Hibbs, 1965). A particle under force moves from point to point as if it knows its final purpose, to minimize Lagrangian-action. Causal dynamics and teleology are two sides of the same coin.

The knowledge instinct is similar to these most general physical laws: Evolution of the mind is guided by maximization of knowledge. A mathematical structure of similarity (2), or its continuous version, is similar to Lagrangian and plays a similar role: It bridges causal dynamic logic of cognition and teleological principle of maximum knowledge. Similar to fundamental physics, dynamics and teleology are equivalent. Dynamic logic follows from maximization of knowledge and vice versa. Ideas and concept-models change under the "force" of dynamic logic, as if they know the purpose: maximum knowledge. One does not have to choose between scientific explanation and teleological purpose: Causal dynamics and teleology are equivalent.

Acknowledgments

It is my pleasure to thank people whose thoughts, ideas, encouragement and support shaped this chapter: R. Brockett, G. Carpenter, A. Chernyakov, R. Deming, V. Dmitriev, W. Freeman, K. Fukunaga, L. Garvin, I. Ginzburg, R. Gudwin, S. Greineder, S. Grossberg, M. Karpovsky, S. Kashin, L. Levitin, R. Linnehan, T. Luginbuhl, A. Meystel, S. Middleton, K. Moore, C. Mutz, A. Ovsich, R. Payne, N. Pechersky, I. Perlovsky, V. Petrov, C. Plum, J. Rumer, E. Schakhnovich, W. Schoendorf, N. Shokhirev, J. Sjogren, D. Skatrud, R. Streit, E. Taborsky, I. Ternovsky, T. Ternovsky, E. Tichovolsky, B. Weijers, D. Vinkovetsky, Y. Vinkovetsky, P. Werbos, M. Xiarhos, L. Zadeh and G. Zainiev. Anonymous reviewers made many valuable suggestions.

References

Albus, J.S., & Meystel, A.M. (2001). *Engineering of mind: An introduction to the science of intelligent systems*. New York: Wiley.

The American Heritage College Dictionary (3rd ed.). (2000). Boston: Houghton Mifflin. I would emphasize, these general dictionary formulations could only be taken as a starting point.

Aristotle. (1995). *Complete Works of Aristotle* (IV BCE, a). J. Barnes (Ed.). Princeton, NJ: Princeton University Press.

Aristotle. (1995). Rhetoric for Alexander, in *Complete Works of Aristotle* (IV BCE, b), J. Barnes (Ed.), Princeton, NJ: Princeton University Press.

Aristotle. (1995). Organon, in *Complete Works of Aristotle* (IV BCE, c). J. Barnes (Ed.), 18a28-19b4; 1011b24-1012a28. Princeton, NJ: Princeton University Press..

Aristotle. (1995). Metaphysics, in *Complete Works of Aristotle* (IV BCE). J. Barnes (Ed.), W.D. Ross (Trans.). Princeton, NJ: Princeton University Press.

Bellman, R.E. (1961). *Adaptive control processes*. Princeton, NJ: Princeton University Press.

Berlyne, D.E. (1960). *Conflict, arousal, and curiosity*. New York: McGraw-Hill.

Berlyne, D.E. (1973). *Pleasure, reward, preference: Their nature, determinants, and role in behavior*. New York: Academic Press.

Carpenter, G.A., & Grossberg, S. (1987). A massively parallel architecture for a self-organizing neural pattern recognition machine. *Computer Vision, Graphics and Image Processing, 37*, 54-115.

Catholic Encyclopedia. Retrieved from http://www.newadvent.org/cathen/08050b.htm

Chalmers, D.J. (1997). *The conscious mind: In search of a fundamental theory*. Oxford University Press.

Charness, G., & Levin, D. (2003). *When optimal choices feel wrong: A laboratory study of Bayesian updating, complexity, and affect* (Paper 9-03, http://repositories.cdlib.org/ucsbecon/dwp/9-03). Departmental Working Papers, Department of Economics, UCSB.

Chomsky, N. (1981). *Principles and parameters in syntactic theory*. In N. Hornstein & D. Lightfoot (Eds.), *Explanation in linguistics: The logical problem of language acquisition*. London: Longman.

Chomsky, N. (2000). *New horizons in the study of language and mind*. Cambridge, UK: Cambridge University Press.

Clark, A. (1987). The kludge in the machine. *Mind and Language*, *2*, 277-300.

Cramer, H. (1946). *Mathematical methods of statistics*. Princeton, NJ: Princeton University Press.

Damasio, A.R. (1995). *Descartes' error: Emotion, reason, and the human brain*. New York: Avon.

Deacon, T.W. (1998). *The symbolic species: The co-evolution of language and the brain*. New York: W.W. Norton & Company.

Descartes, R. (1646/1989). *The passions of the soul: Les passions de lame*. Indianapolis IN: Hackett Publishing Company.

Edelman, G. M., & Tononi, G. (1995). *A universe of consciousness: How matter becomes imagination*. New York: Basic Books.

Feynman, R.P., & Hibbs, A. R. (1965). *Quantum mechanics and path integrals*. New York: McGraw-Hill.

Fontanari, J. F., & Perlovsky, L.I. (2004). Solvable null model for the distribution of word frequencies. *IE, 70*(04290), 1 4.

Fontanari, J. F., & Perlovsky, L.I. (2005). Evolution of communication in a community of simple-minded agents. In *IEEE International Conference On Integration of Knowledge Intensive Multi-Agent Systems* (pp. 285-290). Waltham, MA.

Fontanari, J. F., & Perlovsky, L.I. (2005). Meaning creation and modeling field theory. In *IEEE International Conference On Integration of Knowledge Intensive Multi-Agent Systems* (pp. 405-410). Waltham, MA.

Freeman, W. J. (2000). *Neurodynamics: An exploration in mesoscopic brain dynamic*. New York: Springer.

Freeman, W.J. (n.d.). *Mass action in the nervous system*. New York: Academic Press.

Gödel, K. (1986). *Kurt Gödel collected works, I*. In S. Feferman et al. (Eds.). Oxford: Oxford University Press.

Griffiths, P. E. (1998*). What emotions really are: The problem of psychological categories*. Chicago: University of Chicago Press.

Grossberg, S. (1975). *Neural networks and natural intelligence*. Cambridge, MA: MIT Press.

Grossberg, S. (2000). Linking mind to brain: The mathematics of biological intelligence. *Notices of the American Mathematical Society*, *47*, 1361-1372.

Grossberg, S., & Levine, D.S. (1987). Neural dynamics of attentionally modulated Pavlovian conditioning: Blocking, inter-stimulus interval, and secondary reinforcement. *Psychobiology*, *15*(3), 195-240.

Hameroff, S. (1994). *Toward a scientific basis for consciousness*. Cambridge, MA: MIT Press.

Hebb, D. (1949). *Organization of behavior*. New York: J.Wiley & Sons.

Hilbert, D. (1928/1967). The foundations of mathematics. In J. van Heijenoort (Ed.), *From Frege to Gödel* (p. 475). Cambridge, MA: Harvard University Press.

Jackendoff, R. (2002). *Foundations of language: Brain, meaning, grammar, evolution*. New York: Oxford University Press.

James, W. (1890). *The principles of psychology*. New York: Dover Books,

Jaynes, J. (1976). *The origin of consciousness in the breakdown of the bicameral mind* (2nd ed.). Boston: Houghton Mifflin Co.

Josephson, B. (1997). *An integrated theory of nervous system functioning embracing nativism and constructivism*. Nashua, NH: International Complex Systems Conference.

Jung, C.G. (1921/1971). Psychological types. In *Collected Works* (v.6, Bollingen Series XX). Princeton, NJ: Princeton University Press.

Jung, C.G. (1934/1969). Archetypes of the collective unconscious. In *Collected Works* (v.9, II, Bollingen Series XX). Princeton, NJ: Princeton University Press.

Kant, I. (1781/1943)). *Critique of pure reason*. J.M.D. Meiklejohn (Trans.). New York: John Wiley.

Kant, I. (1788/1986). *Critique of practical reason*. J.H Bernard (Trans.) 1986. Hafner.

Kant, I. (1790/1914). *Critique of judgment*. J.H.Bernard (Trans.). London: Macmillan & Co.

Kant, I. (1798/1974). *Anthropology from a pragmatic point of view*. M.J. Gregor (Trans.). Boston: Kluwer Academic Pub.

Kecman, V. (2001). *Learning and soft computing: Support vector machines, neural networks, and fuzzy logic models (complex adaptive systems)*. Cambridge, MA: The MIT Press.

Koch, C., & Segev, I. (Eds.). (1998). *Methods in neuronal modeling: From ions to networks*. Cambridge, MA: MIT Press.

Ledoux, J. (1998) *The emotional brain: The mysterious underpinnings of emotional life*. New York: Simon & Schuster.

Linnehan, R., Mutz, Perlovsky, L.I., Weijers, B., Schindler, J., & Brockett, R. (2003, October 1-3). Detection of patterns below clutter in images. In *Proceedings of the*

International Conference on Integration of Knowledge Intensive Multi-Agent Systems (pp. 385-390). Cambridge, MA.

Marchal, B. (2005). Theoretical computer science & the natural sciences. *Physics of Life Reviews*, *2*(3), 1-38.

Meystel, A. (1995). *Semiotic modeling and situational analysis*. Bala Cynwyd, PA: AdRem.

Meystel, A.M., & Albus, J.S. (2001). *Intelligent systems: Architecture, design, and control*. New York: Wiley.

Minsky, M. (1988). *The society of mind*. Cambridge, MA: MIT Press.

Minsky, M. (1995). Smart Machines. In Brockman (Ed.), *The third culture* (pp. 152-166). New York: Simon & Shuster.

Nagel, T. (1974). What is it like to be a bat? *The Philosophical Review*, *11*, 207-212.

Newell, A. (1983). Intellectual issues in the history of artificial intelligence. In *The Study of Information*. F. Machlup & U. Mansfield (Eds.). New York: John Wiley.

Ortony, A., Clore, G.L., & Collins, A. (1990). *The cognitive structure of emotions*. UK: Cambridge University Press.

Ortony, A., & Turner, T.J. (1990). What's basic about basic emotions? *Psychological Review*, *97*, 315-331.

Penrose, R. (1994). *Shadows of the mind*. Oxford, UK: Oxford University Press.

Perlovsky, L.I. (1996). Gödel theorem and semiotics. In *Proceedings of the Conference on Intelligent Systems and Semiotics '96,* Gaithersburg, MD (Vol. 2, pp. 14-18).

Perlovsky, L.I. (1996). Mathematical concepts of intellect. In *Proceedings, World Congress on Neural Networks* (pp. 1013-16). San Diego, CA: L. Erlbaum.

Perlovsky, L.I. (1997). Physical concepts of intellect. *Proceedings of the Russian Academy of Sciences*, *354*(3), 320-323.

Perlovsky, L.I. (1998). Conundrum of combinatorial complexity. *IEEE Trans. PAMI*, *20*(6), 666-70.

Perlovsky, L.I. (1998). Cyberaesthetics: aesthetics, learning, and control. *STIS '98*, Gaithersberg, MD.

Perlovsky, L.I. (1999). Emotions, learning, and control. *Proceedings of the International Symposium on Intelligent Control, Intelligent Systems & Semiotics*, Cambridge MA (pp. 131-137).

Perlovsky, L.I. (2001). *Neural networks and intellect: Using model based concepts*. New York: Oxford University Press.

Perlovsky, L.I. (2002). Aesthetics and mathematical theories of intellect. (Russian.) *Iskusstvoznanie*, *2*(02), 558-594.

Perlovsky, L.I. (2002). Statistical limitations on molecular evolution. *Journal of Biomolecular Structure & Dynamics*, *19*(6), 1031-43.

Perlovsky, L.I. (2004). Integrating language and cognition. *IEEE Connections*, Feature Article, *2*(2), 8-12.

Perlovsky, L.I. (2006a). Symbols: Integrated cognition and language. In A. Loula & R. Gudwin (Eds.), *Computational semiotics.*

Perlovsky, L.I. (2006b). *The knowledge instinct.* New York: Basic Books.

Perlovsky, L.I., & McManus, M.M. (1991). Maximum likelihood neural networks for sensor fusion and adaptive classification. *Neural Networks, 4*(1), 89-102.

Perlovsky, L.I., Webb, V.H., Bradley, S.R., & Hansen, C.A. (1998). Improved ROTHR detection and tracking using MLANS. *AGU Radio Science, 33*(4),1034-44.

Piaget, J. (1981/2000). *The psychology of the child.* H.Weaver (Trans.). Basic Books.

Pinker, S. (1995). Smart machines. In *The third culture* (pp. 223-238). J. Brockman (Ed.). New York: Simon & Shuster.

Plutarch. (2 AD/2001). *Lives.* Modern Library.

Sartre, J.P. (1948/1984). *Emotions.* See also J. P. Sartre, *Existentialism and human emotions.* Sacramento, CA: Citadel Press.

Searle, J.R. (1980). Minds, brains, and programs. *The Behavioral and Brain Sciences, 3,* Cambridge University Press.

Searle, J.R. (1983). *Intentionality: An essay in the philosophy of mind.* Cambridge, UK: Cambridge University Press.

Searle, J.R. (1992).*The rediscovery of the mind.* Cambridge, MA: MIT Press.

Searle, J.R. (1997). *The mystery of consciousness.* New York: New York Review of Books.

Singer, R.A., Sea, R.G. & Housewright, R.B. (1974). Derivation and evaluation of improved tracking filters for use in dense multitarget environments. *IEEE Transactions on Information Theory,* IT-20, 423-432.

Taylor, J. G. (2005). Mind and consciousness: Towards a final answer? *Physics of Life Reviews, 2*(1), 57.

Westfall, R.S. (1983). *Never at rest: A biography of Isaac Newton.* Cambridge: Cambridge University Press.

Wikipedia. Retrieved from http://en.wikipedia.org/wiki/Instinct

Zadeh, L.A. (1997). Information granulation and its centrality in human and machine intelligence. *Proceedings of the Conference on Intelligent Systems and Semiotics '97,* Gaithersburg, MD (pp. 26-30).

Zeki, A. (1993). *A vision of the brain.* Oxford, UK: Blackwell.

Endnotes

[1]   A simple example of an adaptive model is linear regression: The knowledge is encapsulated in the choice of variables, the uncertainty and adaptivity is in the unknown parameters, fitted to the data. Whereas linear regression uses one model, model-based systems used a large number of models. For example, a scene is described using geometric models of many objects. Parameters may include: size,

orientation angles, color, illumination conditions, etc. A simple, still nontrivial, problem causing difficulties in applications till today is tracking multiple objects in the presence of clutter (Singer, Sea, & Housewright, 1974; Perlovsky, Webb, Bradley, & Hansen, 1998).

[2]   Searle's views of intentionality are seen by many researchers as too narrow. (For example, see Workshop on Neurodynamics and Dynamics of Intentional Systems, 2005, International Joint Conference on Neural Networks, Montreal, Canada). It is not possible to give a complete treatment of such issues as intentionality and purposiveness in this chapter, which differ in cognitive science, artificial intelligence, classical philosophy and theory of action (D. Davidson, Essays on Actions and Events in Philosophical Essays of Donald Davidson, Oxford University Press, 2002; M. Bratman, Faces of Intention: Selected Essays on Intention and Agency, Cambridge University Press, 1999). Nevertheless, it is impossible to avoid these issues, because intentionality and purposiveness, as discussed later, are fundamental to living beings and to higher brain functions. Therefore, my approach in this chapter here and below is to use commonsense understanding of terms whenever possible, while noticing discrepancies among various understandings and to give corresponding references for further reading. I would like to emphasize again that the choice among various understandings of many philosophical, psychological and cognitive terms used in this chapter is driven by four principles specified in the first section and is consistent with the mathematical theory presented next. Never was a single narrow technical definition selected to fit the mathematical structure. On the other hand, the mathematical structure turned out to be compatible with general understanding of these terms gradually developed since time of Socrates. The mutual compatibility of knowledge among Socrates, Plato, Aristotle, Kant, Jung and contemporary research is emphasized and discrepancies are noticed, whenever relevant.

[3]   Descartes, Rene (1646). Passions of the Soul. Descartes deeply penetrated into the interaction between emotions and consciousness: "those who are the most excited by their passions are not those who know them best and their passions are... confused and obscure." He did not differentiate between thoughts and emotions consistently: "of all the various kinds of thoughts... these passions,..." "...the action and the passion are thus always one and the same thing." Descartes showed a bias toward unconscious and fused perception of emotions charateristic of a thinking psychological type.

[4]   Mathematically, the condition that the object h is present with absolute certainty, is expressed by normalization condition: $\int l(X|h) \, dX = 1$. We should also mention another normalization condition: $\int l(X(n)) \, dX(n) = 1$, which expresses the fact that, if a signal is received, some object or objects are present with 100% certainty.

[5]   This construction is not unique. Expression (2) is inspired by the notion of likelihood between models and signals. Another general type of similarity measure suitable for the knowledge instinct (Perlovsky, 2001) is inspired by the notion of mutual information in the models about the signals. Here we would like to mention a modification of (2) for a specific case. Sometimes a set of observations, N, is more convenient to describe mathematically as a continuous flow of signals, for example,

a flow of visual stimuli in time and space; then, it is convenient instead of Equation (1) to consider its continuous version:

$$L = \exp + \int_N \ln \left(\sum_{h \in H} r(h) \, l(X(n) \mid h) \right),$$

where N is a continuum of bottom-up signals, such as in time-space.

[6]   See (Kant, 1790). Some of my colleagues think that these are all Kantian ideas, other think that it is all my invention and Kant never said anything that specific. I agree with both. I learned these ideas from Kant, but it is also true that other Kant readers did not understand Kant the same way. Every year there are dozens of papers published interpreting Kantian views, so clearly, the matter cannot be definitely settled within this chapter. I would just repeat that my inspiration for understanding Kant, Aristotle and many other philosophers and scientists is driven by a desire for a unified view of the mechanisms of the mind. I would emphasize that I am skeptical about the value of critical approaches to understanding old texts: When I read that Kant or Aristotle did not understand this or that, usually I feel that the authors of these statements do not understand Kant or Aristotle. Similarly, I wonder what Freud or Jung would think about their contemporary followers. In one movie comedy, Kurt Vonnegut wrote an essay for a college course about his own writing; this essay received "C-." This joke reminds us to be modest about how well we can understand other people. I maintain that the only proof of correct understanding of any idea comes when it is positively integrated within the development of science.

[7]   Let me repeat, it is not possible to review all relevant points of view here[2].

[8]   I'll repeat that Aristotle called intentionality the "end causes of Forms" and he called the a priori contents of the mind the "Formal causes" that are the mechanisms of Forms (Metaphysics).

[9]   According to Kant, purposiveness is the a priori principle of the ability for judgment (Kant, 1790). It was mathematically described as the knowledge instinct: It drives us to find the best reason (knowledge) for any judgment or action in this chapter.

[10]   Consciousness of emotions and mechanisms of this type of consciousness is a separate, important and interesting topic considered elsewhere (L. Perlovsky, 2006, The Knowledge Instinct, Basic Books); it is beyond the scope of this chapter.

Section II

Methodological Issues

Chapter IV

Reconstructing Human Intelligence within Computational Sciences:
An Introductory Essay

Gerd Doeben-Henisch
University of Applied Sciences Frankfurt am Main, Germany

Abstract

This chapter outlines a possible research program for computational systems representing humanlike intelligence. After a short historical introduction, a possible theoretical framework is described showing how it is possible to integrate heterogeneous disciplines like neurobiology, psychology and phenomenology within one and the same computational framework. Concrete examples are given by reconstructing behavioural (Morris) and phenomenal semiotics (Peirce) with the aid of formal theories. The author hopes to improve the interdisciplinary discussion about adaptive computational models of humanlike intelligence through a unified theoretical framework.

The Problem

The term "intelligence" and especially "human intelligence" (HI), is used in many different disciplines, especially in psychology, but is still more fuzzy than clear. The rise of modern computational sciences induces still more terminological fuzziness. But for scientists, it is an interesting question whether and how it is possible to reconstruct and model the fuzzy phenomenon of "human intelligence" within computational sciences. In this essay I try to establish a unified formal framework based on modern Science Theory to relate all the known theoretical aspects of human intelligence within one unified view, not as a final answer, but as a research program. The format of an essay is due to the fact that the nature of the problem does not allow a complete answer, but deserves, nevertheless, an embracing, unifying framework.

Historical Introduction

At the time of this writing, the term *intelligence* is highly loaded with different associated meanings which are deeply rooted in history and spread over a multitude of disciplines. As the ethologist Marc D. Hauser states it, "… no one has managed to delineate the key symptoms of intelligence in humans, let alone operationalize the concept for cross-species comparisons …." (Hauser, 1996, 112). This judgement is shared by other researchers in the field of intelligence, such as the authors of the book, *Die Entdeckung der Intelligenz — oder Können Ameisen denken?* (The Discovery of Intelligence — Can Ants Think?). The authors stress the point that all the factors that are involved in the multifaceted phenomenon of intelligence are still not really known, and, therefore, one should not start with a too narrow definition in the beginning (Cruse, Dean, & Ritter, 1998, 21). Very similar is the statement of Rolf Pfeifer and Christian Scheier in *Understanding Intelligence* (Pfeifer & Scheier, 1999, 6ff). But, how can we start then? Historically, philosophy was first in trying to understand intelligence as part of human behaviour and self-experience. Although these philosophical works have been highly influential to many new developments in modern sciences, I will discuss this only occasionally when I am describing some of the modern scientific contributions later on. From the point of view of science, a good starting point can be the rise of *modern experimental psychology.* This happened in 1879 when Wundt founded his famous psychological laboratory in Leipzig (Germany) with forerunners like Herbart and Fechner. This beginning was very influential; it led, along with others, to the movement of *behaviouristic psychology,* mainly in the USA (e.g., J.B.Watson, E.L.Thorndike, I.P.Pawlow, E.R.Guthrie, C.L.Hull and B.F.Skinner; see Bower &Hilgard, 1981) during the first half of the 20th century. By restricting allowed facts to observable behaviour and observable properties of the environment, behaviourism tried to reconstruct biological systems by the interplay of stimuli and responses. As more results became available, the limits of this approach were exposed. The method to explain behaviour constrained to stimuli and responses was on account of the inherent complexity of the observed behaviour not really feasible (e.g. , Chomsky, 1959). During that time the knowledge was increasing that overtly observable behaviour is rooted in the physiological, and especially neurological, machinery. When the movement of behaviourism was slowly declining, a new, more differentiated movement began to rise from the midst of the twentieth century: *Modern Ethology* (*ethos* — Greek: behaviour). Tinbergen and K. Lorenz are known as the founders of this new movement, which is based on the work of several forerunners. They used the concept of behaviour like the behaviourists but they tried to look at the whole picture of an organism: the observable behaviour, the underlying neuronal mechanisms, the growth process, endogenous and learned behaviour, structural similarities between individuals, species, etc. (Eibl-Eibesfeldt, 1980; Immelmann, Barlow, Petrinovich, & Main, 1982). Human ethology was part of the general ethology thus demonstrating the continuity of the phenomenon of human behaviour with non-human behaviour as well as the individual characteristics of human behaviour different from all other species. This whole behavioural approach is framed by a general developmental view stemming from sciences like geology, palaeontology, physics, cosmology, chemistry and biology (Bowler, 1989). Often underestimated in this context is the driving role of *modern mathematics*. With the rise of modern empirical sciences, beginning in the sixteenth century with Galilei, there was a growing demand on representational mechanisms to represent the dynamic character of many of the phenomena under investigation with their inherent complexity. These representational mechanisms are provided by modern logic and mathematics which have developed very strongly during these centuries (e.g., Bourbaki, 1984; Cohen, 1980; Dieudonne, 1985; Dijksterhuis, 1986). The rise of *modern logic*, which is deeply rooted in Aristotelian Logic for centuries, started only at the end of the 19th century with Boole, Frege, Whitehead and Russell and was closely related to the fundamental discussions in *meta mathematics* about the foundations and limits of mathematics as such (Cantor, Hilbert, Bouwer, Fraenkel, Gödel et al.)(Kneale & Kneale, 1986). And it was this lengthy and heated discussion about the decidability of formal theories which not only led to the limiting results of Gödel in 1931 (see Gödel, 1931), but also to the birth of the modern concept of computation by Turing (Turing, 1936/7), later labelled as Turing machine. With the availability of a commonly accepted concept of *computation* it was possible to define other important concepts like *decidability* and *complexity* (Garey & Johnson, 1979) based on *computing processes* or to relate other concepts like *formal language* and *formal grammar* to computation (Rozenberg & Salomaa, 1997). Although Turing himself was connected to the development of the earliest computing machines in Great Britain (Hodges, 1983), it was only the advent of the transistor in 1947 and then the first integrated microprocessors in 1971 when the practical usage of modern affordable universal programmable machines started (Brey, 2003). These machines are one kind of possible instance of the formal concept of computation, biological neuronal structures can be another.

Already by the 1950s, Booth, Weaver and Bar-Hillel had launched the usage of computers for an *automatic translation* of texts (the historical introduction by Bruderer, 1982). This first approach was not very successful. The early protagonists didn't have enough knowledge in the realm of linguistics and psycholinguistics. But these first failures led afterwards to the new discipline of computational linguistics. Broadening the scope from machine translation to automatic indexing of documents, as well as dialogue systems, the discipline moved away from a purely *descriptive* paradigm to an approach which included more and more aspects of the *simulation* of the understanding and production of language (Batori, Lenders, & Puschke, 1989, Chapter 1). The main lesson from this development was the insight that true success in the field of computational linguistics was not possible within the limits of computation alone. The advent of practically usable computing machines also introduced a new strong spirit in the field of psychology, especially *cognitive psychology*. For half a century, captured within the methodological boundaries of the stimulus-response paradigm of behaviouristic psychology, cognitive psychology received a new momentum, emerging from the fields of *mathematical communication theory* (Shannon, Weaver, Broadbent, Hoveland & Miller) as well as from linguistics. During the 1950s it became apparent that a string of words acting as stimuli has to be distinguished from the *content* which can be communicated by such words; although a person usually can remember the *content*, they can not, in most of the times, remember the individual words used within the communications. Thus, to deal with such facts one needs a new conceptual framework. And it was the *computer-simulation model* which gained the status of a new technique for theory-construction within psychology (Estes, 1975). But this strong extension of the conceptual power of cognitive psychology by using algorithms raised a lot of methodological questions: How can the paradigm of an organism as a computer-based information-processing system be a valuable basis for an empirically sound theory about human cognition? How can this approach account for the fact that human cognition is embedded in a body, which is part of a biological process generating biological structures of a certain shape? Isn't it fallacious to use psychological terms taken from everyday human experience as synonymous with theoretical terms of formal cognitive theories, being part of information processing structures which are different from the biological structures of human bodies? The modelling potential of the computational paradigm did not only inspire linguistics and cognitive psychology, it also inspired computer science itself as well as related fields like formal logic. This gave raise to a special movement within Computer Science called *Artificial Intelligence*. Starting in the 1960s with research in automated reasoning leading to computational logic (Siekmann &Wrightson, 1983), the paradigm of expert systems was gaining attention during the *1980*s, mostly based on concepts of computational logic (Davis & Lenat, 1982; Nilsson, 1998; Rich, 1983); that kind of *artificial intelligence (AI)*, which later on had been labelled as *symbolic AI*. The inherent problems of the symbolic approach at that time (e.g., difficulties with fuzzy concept adaptation as well as robustness) lead to an alternative paradigm called *parallel distributed processing* (Grossberg, 1982; Haykin, 1999, 38-44; Rumelhart & McClelland, 1986). This approach tried to set up models, which copied to some extend the structure of *biological neuronal networks*. Already in the 1990s, the concept of artificial intelligence was exploding with applications and the mixing of methods and paradigms, that makes it more and more difficult to give a systematic account of all the developments now in action (Winston & Shellard, 1990). Another important discipline which has gained momentum during the last 100 years, and which is highly influential in field of intelligence, is neurobiology (Changeux, 1983; Roth, 1995; Shepherd, 1994) accompanied by neuropsychology (Gale & Edwards, 1983; Gazzaniga, 1995; Kolb & Wishaw, 1993), neurolinguistics (Obler & Gjerblow, 1999; Pulvermüller, 1996) and molecular biology as well as *genetics* (Lewin, 1998). With these disciplines, for the first time in history it is possible to make empirically based guesses about the interrelationships between subjective experiences (phenomena) and observable behaviour at one hand, and the underlying physiological machinery at the other. Now one can see that the overall phenomenon of intelligence is a collection of distinguishable properties of different kinds and related to different structures of varying complexity. Moreover one can now also investigate the evolution of the biological structures in time and see the interplay of certain types of environments and dedicated biological structures in service to sustain and improve life as such. More and more this reveals a chain of presuppositions leading from forms of intelligence to changing bodies belonging to populations in environments; bodies can be understood as phenotypes caused by genotypes during a dynamic process of *ontogenesis*. The genotype is subject of a complex copying-process which allows changes in the course of time; evolution and co-evolution. In this wider framework, the phenomenon of intelligence is no longer an isolated property; intelligence is becoming part of the wider context of adaptation of life such as which happens over the course of time and simultaneously at different levels of the system. In all these divergent aspects, it has to do with some improvement of the system. Furthermore, the evidence is growing that one of the greatest achievements during the evolution of life is the unfolding of the species *homo sapiens* with regard to those physiological structures which allow symbolic communication and thinking (Deacon, 1997; Hauser, 1996; Mackintosh, 1994, 1995; Schnelle, 1994). Inspired by the deficits of the *classical symbolic AI-approach* as well as by the new concepts of connectionism and technological developments in the area of robotics there was some first reaction against the *classical AI* approach as well as against the information processing Cognitive psychology approach.

This new approach can be identified with the so-called new AI or with the *embodied cognitive science* approach, which started in the end of the 1980s (Pfeifer & Scheier, 1999). This movement identified the root of intelligence in the interaction of the body with the real world. The ability to *adapt* in a changing environment is understood as the manifestation of this kind of intelligence (Pfeifer & Scheier, 1999, 20ff). Here the *autonomous agent*, with a *body interacting* with the *environment*, has to be the main target of research, of experiments, of artifacts and of simulations. Closely related to the embodied intelligence movement is the epigenetic robotics movement (Epigenetic Robotics, 2001-2005). The idea of embodiment is combined with the idea of development and emergence and is very closely tied to, for example, neurobiology, developmental psychology and linguistics. Still, one of the weakpoints in these new movements is the topic of *communication*, especially symbolic communication with languages. But first steps can be observed, e.g., in the work of de Boer (de Boer, 2001) and in the team around Luc Steels (Steels, 1997a; Steels, 1997b; Steels, 1998).

Inroads:
Some Hypotheses to Bank On

Confronted with such a diversity of disciplines implying difficult methodological problems, one could be tempted to remove oneself from this disturbing multidisciplinarity.

But a removal from that multidisciplinarity cannot be a solution any more. As Estes (1975) stated it clearly:

The basic reason why we not only should but must be multidisciplinary is that the evolution of the human organism has presented us with a fantastically multi layered system with old and new portions of the brain, more primitive and more sophisticated learning and behavioural mechanisms all existing and functioning side by side — sometimes in almost total independence, sometimes in intricate interactions. (p. 21)

Adhering to the vision of a unified science, I try to relate in the following sections all the disciplines associated with the phenomenon of intelligence to a certain concept of structure which shall serve as a general framework for possible scientific theories.

What is the Right Methodological Framework?

The vision of unified sciences is rooted in the modern theory of science movement. Although there are some prominent forerunners of a Theory of Science, like Bacon, Whewell, Duhem and Mach, it is common opinion that the modern theory of sciences starts rather with the so-called *Wiener Kreis (Vienna Circle)* during the 1920s (most prominent: Carnap, von Neurath, Schlick) (Schilpp, 1963). In the time following, these ideas have been discussed, enriched and modified by several scholars (see, e.g., Hempel, Bridgman, Dingler, Popper, Hanson, Kuhn, van Fraassen, Giere, P.Suppes, Salmon, Kitcher, Lakatos, Glymour, de Finetti, Howson and Urbach). What makes the great distinction to classical philosophy is the focus on explicating the nature of the knowledge as it is involved in the explication of empirical phenomena using *experiments*, *measurement, formal languages, formal logic* and formal *mathematics* connected to communities of researchers. Theory of sciences is also investigating the *meta communications*, which enables the participants to establish ("bootstrapping") their scientific communications (for an overview of modern theory of science; see, e.g., Balzer et al., 1987; Kuhn, 1957, 1962, 1978; Mittelstrass, 1995-1996, & Suppe, 1979).

From theory of science I take the following general view which I will call here the *Scientific Framework*. The root of every scientific explanation is given by a community of scientists (here also including the *engineers* for completeness). The community of scientists has to clarify what they will understand as their *domain of investigation*. There is no domain of investigation independent of a community! To come to a common understanding of the domain of investigation, the community has to *communicate*. This communication includes inevitably some portion of *meta communication*, i.e., those kinds of communications, which are necessary to establish *ordinary communication*. Only if the communication is successful, can some domain of investigation come into existence for the community. For the *scientific* investigation of some domain of interest, one needs some *method of measurement*. Additionally, the community has to accept some *language for the representation of measured items*, a *language for data* $[L_{DATA}]$. Using measurement and a data representation language, the community can produce *data.* Because data are by nature *individual/ concrete/ local,* the community's need is for general statements regarding some more general structures. For this, the community has to agree about some *language for theoretical statements* [L_{THEORY}], *which can include the data language as a subset.* Then the community can establish general structures or models to express general laws. One can distinguish in the realm of theoretical models between the *potential models (P-Models)* and the *axiomatized models (A-Models).* The A-Models differ from the P-Models only by some *axioms* which are included. P-Models — which are represented in a set theoretical language — contain only sets and relations (for an example see the section about Peirce). To operate with general structures and single statements, the community has also to agree about some kind of *logic,* which allows *deductions* leading to *proofs.* Equipped with all this, the community can prove theorems, which can be compared to the measured data. If the set of possibly proved statements is not in direct *contradiction* to sets of measured data (including error measures) the general model has some validity; otherwise the general structure has to be modified (it is a problem on its own to define clearly when there a point will be reached which tells that the general structure is no longer valid).

Based on available general structures, the engineers can try to construct *concrete instances* of these general structures within the real world. This happens within a *process of engineering,* which is today highly regulated by so-called *standards* or even certain *laws.* The engineering and the usage of those concrete instances produces knowledge, which to a great extent will usually not be explicitly included in the founding models.

Rethinking the Domain for Computational Intelligence

To work within a scientific framework one has to agree about a common domain of investigation. It is desirable to rethink the domain for the research of the phenomenon of intelligence in a way that the phenomenon of intelligence can be reconstructed in its full richness without any substantial reductions. What we know is this: all the different kinds of natural phenomena which we associate with intelligence are bound to bodies. Every body "hosting" intelligence is produced during a process called *onto genesis,* leading from a *genotype* to a the body as a *phenotype.* But the genes of a genotype are making sense only if they are part of a *population.* It's not the individual body that has to survive in the long run, it is the population as such! And talking about the *adaptation* of populations leads to biological life as a whole (the term adaptation itself is not without problems, e.g., Mayr, 1988; Rosenberg, 1985; Shettleworth, 1994), *but it would be more difficult to give this term up instead of using it.* The only kind of biological life which is known today is DNA-based life here on Earth. Thus, if intelligence should be linked with adaptation of bodies in the world, then one should investigate the phenomenon of intelligence in this dynamic context of emerging life at all levels of complexity.

The term "intelligence" is not to be misunderstood in the sense that intelligence "is" adaptation, but intelligence — as whatever it will show up in the long run of future scientific investigations — is manifesting itself in these different phenomena. Thus, to investigate intelligence one has to investigate all these different phenomena of adaptation as possible inroads to the presupposed underlying structure of intelligence.

A Structure for Biological Theories

After this short outline of the theory of the scientific point-of-view, we have to pose the question whether we can set up the case of biological systems within this framework. We have to look for the main properties of the domain under investigation and whether and how these can be expressed in some theory language L_T. There are many books which deal with the question of the general theoretical outlook of possible biological theories (e.g., Küppers, 1990; Mayr, 1988; Rosenberg, 1985; Weingarten, 1993), but besides deep reflections on many of the aspects of the field of biology, they do not provide formal structures which can finally be used for theoretical modelling. I myself cannot here provide a complete formal theory of biological systems either. I can only describe some coordinates of such possible formal theories, and I will give later on some more elaborated examples in the case of human systems as examples of biological systems.

So far, it seems that the tentative *domain of intelligence* as manifested within the timebound phenomenon of adaptation can at least be partitioned in the following substructures: (i) molecules, (ii) cells, (iii) cell-assemblies, (iv) bodies, (v) populations and (vi) species. From this one could propose as a general structure a layered network of *input-output-systems (IO-systems)* (see below) where systems of layer i can use systems of layer i-1. *Furthermore does this assumption imply* that human persons have to be seen as part of the overall DNA-based type of life, as biological systems with outstanding capabilities. Within the scientific framework would this allow only four fundamental kinds of data to be used as possible fundamental domains of investigations in the case of biological systems: observable stimuli (S), observable responses (R), observable internal physiological states, like neurons (N) as well as the experience of phenomenological states called phenomena (P). The domains S,R, and N belong — in a usual classification (which later will be revised) — to "the outside," to the third person view; the domain P belongs to the "inside," to the first person view (Nagel, 1986). Some of these domains — or combinations of these — are historically associated with certain disciplines (see Table 1).

Phenomenology, for example, is based onto the P-domain and can produce P-Models. Behavioural psychology is based on the SR-domain and produces SR-Models. In the case of Neurobiology, the domain is restricted to the brain inside the body, which can include other internal states of the body too. Possible theoretical models are called N-models. A combination of the SR+N-domains to SNR-domains with SNR-Models as theoretical output should be labelled Behavioural Neuropsychology. And a combination of all domains SNPR could be labelled Neuropsychology. Classical Psychology can be attached to the SR+P-domains producing SPR-Models. But one has to mention that this terminology is not stable in the literature. Only the labels Phenomenology, Behavioural Psychology and Neurobiology are used more or less consistently. The case of SNR-based and P-based human systems will later be analysed a bit more in discussing the main paradigms of semiotics of Morris and Peirce.

In the following paragraphs I introduce some theoretical terms which seem to be fundamental for all biological systems, and I give a short outline on how these terms can be placed within an overall theoretical structure for a dynamic biological theory.

One basic building block is the term *input-output systems* (IO-Systems) with a structure like <<I,IS,O>,<f>>, where f is the system-function f: I x IS x O → O mapping the input states I, the internal states IS and the output states O into output states. If one assumes the sets I and R to be subsets of IS because every kind of external state has to be mapped into internal states to be able to be processed, then one could lay out the system function also as f*: IS → IS allowing IS = f*(IS). In this case, the system is a *dynamic* system in the sense that every new state is based on the preceding state. This includes, for example, the phenomena of *memory* and *learning*. As long as the involved function f is a fixed function, then we have the case of systems with *weak learning* (WL) depending only on a dynamic memory. To realize *strong learning* (SL), one has to assume that there is a set of *possible system functions* F as part of the structure together with a special learning function *sl*, which can select different actual system functions f: <<I,IS,O,F>,<sl, f>>, where f is the actual system-function f: IS → IS and *sl* is the strong learning function mapping potential functions into the real system function: *sl*: F x {f} x IS→ F. One has to take into account that the strong learning function *sl* operates on another language level than f.

The process of onto genesis, which includes *growing*, extends the description still further. Here we need *systems as objects* and a growth-function operating upon these system-objects. One has to assume a minimal structure like <<PROP, PSYS, SYS, GEO>,<pos, fenv, birth, death, stim, resp, growth>> which could be interpreted as a structure having sets of environmental properties PROP, a set of potential systems PSYS, a set of actual systems SYS and some kind of a geometry GEOM. The position-function *pos maps* properties and systems into the geometry. The environmental function *fenv* maps the environment onto itself. The birth-function *birth* creates a new actual system out of potential systems, the death-function *death* deletes actual systems. The stimulus-

Table 1. Possible domains of investigations

Possible Domains of Investigations					
S	N	P	R	Combined Domain	Label
		+		P	Phenomenology
+			+	SR	Behavioral Psychology
+		+	+	SPR	Psychology
	+			N	Neurobiology
+	+		+	SNR	Behavioral Neuropsychology
+	+	+	+	SNPR	Neuropsychology

function *stim* maps environmental properties onto systems and the response function *resp* maps system-properties onto the environment. Finally, a *partially indeterministic* growth-function *growth* maps potential and actual systems into actual system thereby eventually also changing the geometry.

The process of *heredity,* including *mutation,* would be a minimal extension of the foregoing structure. Such a minimal structure could look like <<PROP, PSYS, SYS, GEO, GENOM>, <pos, fenv, birth, death, stim, resp, growth, heredity >> where GENOM is a set of possible genomes which can be attached to a system and the function *heredity* can map from the set GENOM into the set GENOM and thereby induce some mutations. The function *growth* will translate a genome into a new system.

Whether this conceptual framework is *in principle* strong enough to represent all necessary properties of a dynamic process of biological populations showing intelligence has to be seen in the future. In the next section I will investigate whether, and how, it would be possible to reframe the subject matter of biological systems within a computational framework.

Computable Models of Biological Systems?

In this section it shall be clarified whether it is possible to reframe the general structure of a biological system as it has been outlined in the preceding one within a computational framework. One of the most popular measures for the property of being computable is the possibility to map a problem onto a *universal turing machine (UTM)*.

The formal concept of the universal turing machine is a *mathematical concept* characterizing the concept of *computability,* which has been proven during the last 50 years to be a point of reference for all other concepts in this domain (e.g., Davis, 1958; Davis, 1965; Minsky, 1967). Constructing *technical devices* which are able to simulate computable functions, like those described by the mathematical concept of a universal turing machine, allows the judgement that these technical devices are *concrete instances* of the general mathematical concept. But none of these technical devices can be *complete* instances because the mathematical concept of the universal turing machine includes the concept of *infinite storage* for information, whereas every concrete technical device only includes *finite* storage. Besides limitations of building a concrete instance of a universal turing machine, one has to keep in mind that the mathematical concept of the universal turing machine does *not say anything about the concrete structure* of possible instances of the concept! The fact that the mathematical concept of the universal turing machine as described by Turing himself has a structure which is similar to most of the micro controllers and PCs used today is irrelevant to the meaning of the mathematical concept. The concrete layout of the concept is unimportant as one can see from the fact that there are numerous different formal structures which have been detected which are *formally equivalent* to the concept of the universal turing machine; also they are *completely different* in the way they are constructed. Examples for such formally equivalent but concretely different structures are, the recursive functions (Goedel, Herbrand), the lambda calculus (Church), the post production systems (Post), the

Markov chains (Markov) and much more. Thus, if some day in the future someone would present a concrete machine constructed out of some new material arranged in a new structure which is able to simulate all the defined computable functions, then this clearly also would be an instance of the concept of a universal turing machine. The point here is that the universal turing machine is functioning like a *representative of an equivalence class called computational functions*. Thus, to say that a concrete device *d* is an instance of the concept of a universal turing machine is synonymous with the statement that the device *d* is an instance of the general concept of the *class of computable functions*.

What about *parallel distributed networks* of neurons as instances of the *connectionist* paradigm? How are they related to the concept of the universal turing machine? The answer is straightforward: Insofar the class of functions which can be simulated by a connectionist device is a subset of the set of computable functions, then clearly a connectionist device is such an instance of the class of structures whereof the universal turing machine is representative. To say that the connectionist paradigm is radically different is wrong on a general mathematical level; it can be true with regard to the way the computation is realized. A special problem is that there exist definitions of neuronal networks whose mathematics includes concepts which are not computable. In that case, one has to state that these models are generally outside of the class of computable functions. But then one has to ask whether these mathematical models are   adequate models of the *biological brain* as a *concrete device,* which is clearly a finite machine based on finite processes.

To answer the question of this section, whether there exists computable models for biological structures, I will show how one can construct a mapping between the theoretical concept of a biological structure and a turing machine.

The basic idea of the mapping is to distinguish between descriptions and executions. *Descriptions* are structures representing some domain written in a certain language. *Executions* are parts of the machine table of an UTM which can translate a certain description into a sequence of turing machine operations. Thus, executions can be understood as a kind of *operational semantics* for the descriptions. On the tape of the UTM you can find all necessary descriptions, and in the machine table you will find all the executions.

One part of the tape is dedicated to the input-output data of a system, which represents the environment ENV for the system. Then, in the case of *input-output systems (IO-Systems)* with the assumed structure $<<I,IS,O>,<f>>$, you can find the description of the system as a turing machine TM including the system function f. Possible additional internal states IS are written on the tape close to the machine description. The execution labelled $exec_{TM,IS}$ will interpret these descriptions and will simulate the behavior of the system "as it is."

In the case of IO-systems with strong learning $<<I,IS,O,F>,<sl, f>>$ there is the additional meta-function sl: $F \times \{f\} \times I \times IS \times O \rightarrow F$. One has to extend the description on the tape with a description of the function sl combined with a description of the set of possible functions F. The execution of the additional strong learning function sl needs a special execution block called $exec_{SL,F}$ which can read the description of sl and F and which can change the description of TM and f.

In a next step, you can extend the description by the growth function *growth,* which is combined with the genetic information in the genome *GENOM: growth: TM x IS x {f} x {sl} x F x GEO → TM x IS x F x GEO.* If one would assume that the strong learning function as such can also change during the growth process — which is somehow likely — then one should assume an additional set of possible strong learning functions *SL.* Analogously, as in the case of the strong learning function *sl,* one has to assume an special execution block *exec$_{growth}$ GENOM* which can read the growth description and can transform the descriptions of *TM, IS, f, SL* and *F* accordingly.

Finally, one can add the description of the heredity function *heredity: GENOM x growth → GENOM x growth.* The related execution block *execheredity can* read this description and can make a copy of the GENOM-description together with the growth-description. This copy can include *mutations.* When the copy has been finished, the growth-function can start to build up the descriptions of *TM, f, SL* and *F* out of the *GENOM.*

As one can see from these considerations, one needs at least nine *different levels of languages* which are interacting in a complex manner.

One can conclude from these considerations that the modeling of biological systems as computable systems within the formal framework of an UTM could be done in principle. Whether a concrete biological system will be "computable" in the sense of being "decidable," will depend on the concrete system in question; not every theory is decidable and biological systems usually are not.

Can Semiotics be Part of Computational Sciences?

If one places human persons in the wider framework of biological systems, then not only do human biological systems have a lot in common with other biological systems, but also they have differences. One of the exiting differences is the ability to think and to communicate symbolically (Deacon, 1997). In the following I will examine the discipline of semiotics from the point of view of a possible computational theory of semiotics. As "prototypes" of semiotic theories, I will use those of Charles W. Morris (1901-1979) and Charles S. Peirce (1839-1914). These prototypes of semiotic modelling are examples of the two main formats of scientific theories as described before: the SNR-Paradigm and the P-Paradigm.

The paradigm of Morris covers the SR- and the SNR-data. The sign-theory of Peirce is based on P-Data. Traditionally this is understood as the "opposite" side of the behaviouristic approach. But, if the working hypothesis is true that the subjective states (P-domain) are functions of neuronal states (N-domain), then it should — in principle — be possible to map (not as a reduction) any kind of model which is based on the first person view onto a model based on the third person view (P-Model → N-Model, or SPR → SNR). *Therefore, if* the model of a semiotic agent according to Morris is based on a third person view, then it should be possible to map a phenomenological model onto it. This will be discussed later on.

The Case of Charles W. Morris: A Behaviouristic Framework

In this section I am starting the exploration with the writings of Charles W. Morris (1901-1979) to discuss the connection between semiotics and computation. This does not mean that I exclude the works of the other "great fathers" of modern semiotics (e.g., Peirce, de Saussure, von Uexküll, Cassirer, Bühler and Hjelmslev, to mention only the most prominent). But Morris seems to be the best starting point for the discussion because his proximity to the modern concept of science makes him a sort of bridge between modern science and the field of semiotics. The case of Charles S. Peirce I will discuss in the next section.

At the time of the *Foundations* in 1938, his first major work after his dissertation of 1925, Morris was already strongly linked to the new movement of a "science-of-the-sciences" (the theory of science topic mentioned before), which was the focus of several groups connected to the Vienna Circle, to the Society of the History of the Sciences, to several journals and conferences and congresses on the theme and especially to the project of an Encyclopedia of the Unified Sciences (e.g., Morris, 1936).

In the *Foundations,* he states clearly that semiotics should be a science, distinguishable as pure and descriptive semiotics, and that semiotics could be presented as a deductive system (Morris, 1971, 23, 24). The same statement appears in his other major book about semiotics, in which he specifically declares that the main purpose of the book is to establish semiotics as a scientific theory (Morris, 1946, 28). He makes many other statements in the same vein.

To reconstruct the contribution of Charles W. Morris within the theory concept is not as straightforward as one might think. Despite his very active involvement in the new science-of-the-sciences movement, and despite his repeated claims to handle semiotics scientifically, Morris did not provide any formal account of his semiotic theory. He never left the level of ordinary English as the language of representation. Moreover, he published several versions of a theory of signs which overlap extensively but which are not, in fact, entirely consistent with each other.

Thus, to speak about "the" Morris theory would require an exhaustive process of *reconstruction*, the outcome of which might be a theory that would claim to represent the "essentials" of Morris's position. Such a reconstruction is beyond our scope here. Instead, I will rely on my reconstruction of Morris's *Foundations* of 1938 (Döben-Henisch, 1998) and on his basic methodological considerations in the first chapter of his *Signs, Language, and Behaviour* of 1946.

As the *group of researchers,* we assume Morris and the people he is communicating with. As the *domain of investigation,* Morris names all those processes in which "signs" are involved. And in his *pre-scientific view* of what must be understood as a sign, he introduces several basic terms simultaneously. The primary objects are distinguishable organisms which can act as *interpreters [I]*. An organism can act as an interpreter if it has internal states called *dispositions[IS]* which can be changed in reaction to certain stimuli. A *stimulus [S]* is any kind of physical energy which can influence the inner states of an organism. A *preparatory-stimulus [PS]* influences a response to some other stimulus. The source of a stimulus is the *stimulus* object [*SO*]. The *response [R]* of an organism is any kind of observable muscular or glandular action. Responses can form a *response* sequence [$<r_1, ..., r_n>$], whereby every singly intervening response r_i is triggered by its specific *supporting* stimulus. The stimulus-object of the first response in a chain of responses is the *start object,* and the stimulus-object of the last response in a chain of responses is the *goal object.* All *response* sequences with similar *start object* and similar *goal objects* constitute a behaviour-family [SR-FAM].

Based on these preliminary terms he then defines the characteristics of a *sign* [*SGN*] as follows: "If anything, A, is a preparatory-stimulus which in the absence of stimulus-objects initiating response-sequences of a certain behaviour-family causes a disposition in some organism to respond under certain conditions by response-sequences of this behaviour-family, then A is a sign" (Morris, 1946, 10,17). Morris stresses that this characterization describes only the necessary conditions for the classification of something as a sign (Morris, 1946, 12).

This entire group of terms constitutes the *subject matter* of the intended science of signs (= semiotics) as viewed by Morris (1946, 17). And based on this, he introduces certain additional terms for discussing this subject.

Already at this fundamental stage in the formation of the new science of signs, Morris has chosen "behavioristics," as he calls it, in line with von Neurath, as the point of view that he wishes to adopt in the case of semiotics. In the *Foundations* of 1938, he stresses that this decision is not necessary (Morris, 1971, p. 21) and also in his "Signs, Language, and Behavior" of 1946, he explicitly discusses several methodological alternatives ("mentalism" AND "phenomenology"), which he thought not to be in contradiction to a behaviouistic approach. But at that time he considered a behavioristic approach more promising with regard to the intended scientific character of semiotics (Morris, 1946, p. 30 and Appendix).

Morris did not mention the problem of *measurement* explicitly. Thus, the modes of measurement are restricted to normal perception, i.e., the subjective (= phenomenologi-cal) experience of an inter-subjective situation was restricted to observable stimuli and responses and the symbolic representation has been done in ordinary English (=L_1) without any attempt at formalization. Moreover, he did not limit himself to characterize the subject matter of his "science of signs" in basic terms but introduced a number of additional terms. These terms establish a *structure* which is intended to shed some theoretical light on "chaotic reality." In a "real" theory, Morris would have to "trans-form" his basic characterizations into a formal representation, which could then be formally expanded by means of additional terms if necessary. But he didn't.

Morris used the term *interpretant[INT]* for all interpreter dispositions (= inner states) causing some response-sequence due to a "sign = preparatory-stimulus." The goal-object of a response-sequence "fulfilling" the sequence and in that sense *completing* the response-sequence Morris termed the *denotatum* of the sign causing this sequence. In this sense one can also say that a sign *denotes* something. Morris assumes further that the "properties" of a denotatum which are connected to a certain interpretant can be "formulated" as a set of conditions which must be "fulfilled" to reach a denotatum. This set of conditions constitutes the *significatum* of a denotatum. A sign can trigger a significatum, and these conditions control a response-sequence that *can* lead to a denotatum, but must *not necessarily* do so: A denotatum is not *necessary*. In this sense, a sign *signs* at least the conditions which are *necessary* for a denotatum but not *sufficient* (Morris, 1946, p. 17). A *formulated significatum* is then to be understood as a formulation of conditions in terms of other signs (Morris, 1946, p.20). A formulated significatum can be *designative* if it describes the significatum of an existing sign, and *prescriptive* otherwise. A *sign* vehicle [*SV*] can be any particular physical event which is a sign (Morris, 1946, p. 20). A set of similar sign-vehicles with the same significate for a given interpreter is called a *sign* family.

In what follows I will restrict the discussion of Morris to the terms introduced so far and I will formalize the concept of Morris to such an extent that we can map it onto the concept of a turing machine, and vice versa. This will be done with the intention to show that a computational form of semiotics is possible without being a reduction.

First, one must decide how to handle the "dispositions" or "inner states" (IS) of the interpreter I. From a radical behaviouristic point of view, the interpreter has no inner states (my discussion in Döben-Henisch ,1998). Any assumptions about the system's possible internal states would be related to "theoretical terms" within the theory which have no direct counterpart in reality (this is a very common situation in theories of physics). If one were to enhance behavioural psychology with physiology (including neurobiology and neuropsychology), then one could identify internal states of the system with (neuro-) physiological states (whatever this would mean in detail). In the following, we shall assume that Morris would accept this latter approach. We shall label such an approach an SNR-theory or SNR-approach (the opposite concept with phenomenological states is discussed in following sections, e.g., in the section about Peirce).

Within an SNR-approach, it is, in principle, possible to correlate an "external" stimulus event S with a physiological ("internal") event S' as Morris intended: A stimulus S can exert an influence on some disposition D' of the interpreter I, or, conversely, a disposition D' of the interpreter can cause some external event R.

To work this out, one must assume that the interpreter is a structure with at least the following elements: $I(x)$ iff $x = <IS, <f_1, ..., f_n>, Ax>$; i.e., an x is an Interpreter I if it has some internal states IS as objects (whatever these might be), some functions fi operating on these internal states like fi: $2^{IS} \rightarrow 2^{IS}$ and some axioms stating certain general dynamic features. These functions we will call "type I functions" and they are represented by the symbol "f."

By the same token, one must assume a structure for the whole environment E in which those interpreters may occur: $E(x)$ iff $x = <<I,S,R,O>, <p_1, ..., p_m>, Ax>$. An environment E has as objects O, at least some interpreters $I \subseteq O$, and something which can be identified as stimuli S or responses R (with $\{S,R\} \subseteq O$) without any further assumptions about the "nature" of these different sets of objects. Furthermore, there must be different kinds of functions p_i:

- (Type E Functions [f_E]:) p_i: $2^{\{I,S,R,O\}} \rightarrow 2^{\{I,S,R,O\}}$, stating that there are functions which operate on the "level" of the assumed environmental objects. A special instance of these functions would be functions of the type p_i^*: $2^S \rightarrow 2^R$;

- (Type E u I Functions [$f_{E \cup I}$]:) p_j: $2^S \rightarrow 2^{IS}$, stating that there are functions which map environmental stimuli events into internal states of interpreters (a kind of "stimulation" function);

- (Type I Functions [f_I]:) pj: $2^{IS} \rightarrow 2^{IS}$, stating that there are functions which map internal states of the interpreter into themselves (a dynamic function, which can include mechanisms like memory and planning); and

- (Type I u E Functions [$f_{I \cup E}$]:) p_j: $2^{IS} \rightarrow 2^R$, stating that there are functions which map the internal states of interpreters into environmental response events (a kind of "activation" or "response" function).

The concatenation of all partial functions results in the function $f_E = f_{E \cup I} \circ fI \circ f_{I \cup E}$, i.e., the mapping f_E of environmental stimuli S into environmental responses R should yield the same result as the concatenation of $f_{E \cup I}$ (mapping environmental stimuli S into internal states IS of an interpreter I), followed by f_I (mapping internal states IS of the interpreter I onto themselves) followed by $f_{I \cup E}$ (mapping internal states IS of the interpreter I into environmental responses R). It has to be noticed that the Type E functions f_E as well as the type IS functions f_I can be understood as *dynamical* functions in the sense that the next state is always determined by the preceding one. Even these very rough assumptions make the functioning of the sign more precise. A sign as a preparatory stimulus S2 "stands for" some other stimulus S1 and this shall especially work in the *absence* of S1. This means that if S2 occurs, then the interpreter takes S2 "as if" S1 occurs. How can this work?

We make the assumption that S2 can only work because S2 has some "additional property" which encodes this aspect. We assume that the *introduction* of *S2* for *S1* occurs in a situation in which S1 and S2 occur "at the same time." This *"correlation by time"* yields some representation "(S1', S2')' " in the system which can be "reactivated" each time one of the triggering components S1' or S2' occurs again. If S2 occurs again and triggers the internal state S2', this will then trigger the component S2", which yields the activation of S1" which in turn yields the internal event S1'. Thus S2 → S2' → (S2", S1") → S1' has the same effect as S1 → S1', and vice versa. The *encoding property* is here assumed, then, to be a representational mechanism which can somehow be reactivated.

Readers who are familiar with the Peircean classification of signs may be tempted to identify this reconstruction of a sign with the *indexicals* of Peirce and may furthermore conclude that the model of Morris is so simple as to produce more advanced types of signs. But this is misleading. The preceding analysis shows only a general structure and how this structure can be embedded within such a type of a system. All other types of signs from the Peircean classification can also be reconstructed in this model of Morris, at least as long the definitions of Peirce are clear enough to be able to interpreted with regard to some definable process. But — more generally — a comparison of Morris and Peirce is not as simple as it often is assumed. Both models are methodologically completely different and I try to show in the final sections how one can set up a unified model in which the models of Morris and Peirce are both integrated as two corresponding models explaining each other!

After this rough reconstruction of Morris's possible theory of a sign agent as an interpreter we shall compare Morris's interpreter with Turing's computing device, the Turing machine, to show, that between this concept of a sign agent and the concept of a universal computing machine can be establish a direct mapping.

In the case of the *turing machine,* we have a tape with symbols [SYMB] which are arguments for the machine table [MT] of a Turing machine as well as values resulting from computations; i.e., we have MT: $2^{SYMB} \rightarrow 2^{SYMB}$.

In the case of the interpreter [I], we have an environment with stimuli [S] which are "arguments" for the interpreter function fE that yields responses [R] as values, i.e., f_E: $2^R \rightarrow 2^R$. The interpreter function fE can be "refined" by replacing it by three other functions: f_{EI}: $2^S \rightarrow 2^{IS}$, fI: $2^{IS} \rightarrow 2^{IS}$ and f_{IE}: $2^{IS} \rightarrow 2^R$ so that:

$$f_E = f_{EuI} \mathbf{o} \, f_I \, \mathbf{o} \, f_{IuE}.$$

Now, because one can subsume stimuli S and responses R under the common class "environmental events EV," and one can represent any kind of environmental event with appropriate symbols $SYMB_{ev}$, with $SYMB_{ev}$ as a subset of SYMB, one can then establish a mapping of the kind:

$$SYMB \leftarrow SYMBev <-\!\!-\!> EV <-\!\!-\; S \, \mathbf{u} \, R.$$

What then remains is the task of relating the machine table MT to the interpreter function f_E. If the interpreter function f_E is taken in the "direct mode" (the case of pure behaviorism), without the specializing functions f_{EuI} etc., we can directly establish a mapping:

$$MT \leftrightarrow f_E.$$

The argument for this mapping is straightforward: Any version of f_E can be directly mapped into the possible machine table MT of a turing machine, and vice versa. In the case of an interpreted theory, the set of "interpreted interpreter functions" will be a true subset of the set of possible functions. If one replaces f_E by $f_E = f_{EuI} \mathbf{o} \, f_I \, \mathbf{o} \, f_{IuE}$, then we must establish a mapping of the kind:

$$MT \leftrightarrow f_E = f_{EuI} \mathbf{o} \, f_I \, \mathbf{o} \, f_{IuE}.$$

The compound function fE $= f_{EuI} \mathbf{o} \, f_I \, \mathbf{o} \, f_{IuE}$ operates on environmental states EV — in the case of the TM the symbols on the tape — and on the internal states IS of the interpreter. The internal states are, in case of the TM, those symbols on the tape which the TM can "write" on its own independently of externally provided symbols.

But what about the function $f_{EuI} \mathbf{o} \, f_I \, \mathbf{o} \, f_{IuE}$ as such? The machine table MT of the Turing machine is "open" to any interpretation of what "kind of states" can be used to "interpret" the general formula. The same holds true for Morris. He explicitly left open which concrete states should be subsumed under the concept of an internal state. The "normal" attitude (at least today) would be to subsume "physiological states." But Morris pointed out (Morris, 1946) that this might not be so; for him it was imaginable to subsume also "mental" or "phenomenal" states. With the interpretation as physiological states it follows that we can establish a mapping of the kind:

SYMB ← IS.

Because the tape — but not the initial argument and the computed value — of a turing machine can be infinite, one has to assume that the number of distinguishable internal states IS of the interpreter that are not functions can also be "infinite." In the case of the interpretation of the IS as physiological states, the cardinality of IS would be only finite and in this sense would a semiotic agent be, at most, as powerful than a turing machine, but in no case "stronger."

What remains then is the mapping between MT and the compound interpreter function $f_{EuI} \mathbf{o} f_I \mathbf{o} f_{IuE}$. In the case of the compound interpreter function $f_{EuI} \mathbf{o} f_I \mathbf{o} f_{IuE}$, it also makes sense to assume that the number is finite, because the number of physiological states bound to neurons in a biological system is finite. It is thus fairly straightforward to map any machine table into a function $f_{EuI} \mathbf{o} f_I \mathbf{o} f_{IuE}$ and vice versa.

Thus, we have reached the conclusion that an exhaustive mapping between Turing's machine and Morris's interpreter is possible (although a concrete interpreter as an instance of the abstract concept will normally be more restricted). This is a far-reaching result. It enables every semiotician working within Morris's semiotic concept to use the turing machine to introduce all of the terms and functions needed to describe semiotic entities and processes. As a by-product of this direct relationship between semiotics à la Morris and the Turing machine, the semiotician has the additional advantage that any of his/her theoretical constructs can be used directly as a computer program on any computational machine. Thus "semiotics" and "computational semiotics" need no longer be separately interpreted, because what they both signify and designate is the same. Thus, one can (and should) claim that

semiotics = computational semiotics.

I like to mention — especially for those readers who are interested in semiotics but are not so experienced with the computational terms — that one should keep in mind that the theoretical result that some structure is *in principle* computable is *not necessarily* of great help to *construct a concrete function* which is fulfilling a certain task. In other words, knowing that a description of a semiotic agent can be done as a computable function does not give any hint how this can be done as a concrete function. And, in the light of the preceding discussion, one can imagine that a more elaborated formal account of sign processes within a population of sign agents is far from trivial.

The Case of Charles S. Peirce: A Phenomenological Framework

Those who are working with the semiotic model of Peirce usually have problems with the semiotic model of Morris (at least with the early versions of his concept of a sign user). From the point of view of phenomenology, it is difficult — if not impossible — to come to an agreement with a behaviouristic terminology (see for some critics, e.g., Nöth, 2000, 88 and Sebeok, 1976, 17. This is no surprise because the unsolved conflict between these two views is as "mind-body" conflict or as "naturalizing phenomenology" program a real "hot spot" in the philosophical discussions from the times of Greek philosophy until today. Before I will discuss this problem in the following sections, I will in this section show that it is possible to formalize a phenomenological theory in the like manner as any kind of empirical theory without any reductions of the phenomena! If this conceptual experiment will survive the future discussions, then we have a new situation in which it will be possible to discuss details of phenomenalistic models in a rigour which is necessary for far more advanced theoretical endeavours.

In the following, I try to model a semiotic agent according to Peirce which is methodologically a phenomenological model.

For this modeling I will take a certain interpretation of Peirce without giving arguments for its completeness and correctness. Even more than in the case of Morris, it is difficult, if not impossible, to give "the exhaustive and final" interpretation based on all the texts of Peirce. Because what I want to do here is a "conceptual experiment," this procedure is sufficient for the beginning. I will take as point of reference for the Peircean Position the presentation which is given by Nöth (2000, p. 59) extended with some direct links to the collected papers of Peirce.

According to Nöth, the triadic sign of Peirce is a phenomenon of the third of the three perception-based categories. The *sign* is seen as a triadic phenomenon where the constituents of the relation are the *representamen* (S) (that perceptional entity which can stand for something else in some respect or quality, the immediate object), the *object* (O) (that which is signified), and the *interpretant* (I) (the cognition produced in the mind on account of the object restricted to the immediate object). Only if these three constituents are cooperating then we have the process of *semiosis* realized by triadic signs (CP, 5.484). The object O can be a *real* object or an *imagined* one ("real" and "imagined" are within the phenomenological view of different qualifications of phenomena! A phenomenon, which is qualified as "real" is something which is connected to the idea of "external space," "reality," the "hereness and nowness" and "the shock of the non-ego upon us"(CP, 8.266). The representamen can only be introduced on occasion of an object; it presupposes an object. Enabled by the introduction on occasion of an object the representamen is correlated with the potential object through the immediate object. The interpretant I can be *immediate* (as revealed in the right understanding of the sign itself), *dynamical* (the actual effect which the sign as a sign really determines) and *final* (the manner in which the sign tends to represent itself to be related to its object)(CP, 5.536).

How can we construct a model based on this first simple phenomenological description? What are the entities to model? What are the relationships?

The entities are those phanerons (phenomena) which are "in any sense present to the mind" (CP 1.284). For those, we have as starting points S, O and I. But the entities in an actual consciousness can be distinguished one from another; not every element o from O is correlated with a certain representamen s of S but only that one, which corresponds in some respect to o. If this "respect" can not be considered by our mind as "something" which can be distinguished from another "something," then such a distinction would be impossible. Therefore we have to assume for our modelling that there exist some qualities (Q) (or features (F)) as part of the S and O (and I; see below) which enable some distinctness. These qualities are indecomposable elements (CP, 1.288). Because an element s of S or o of O consists of some finite set of qualities q from Q, we assume S and O are subsets of the power set of Q, written 2^Q. The immediate Object which relates some s to some o can therefore be understood as some finite set of qualities q which are common to s and o:

$$immediate\_object(s,o) = s \ \underline{cut} \ o = q.$$

So far some first entities. But what are possible relations which can be modelled? Generally it can be assumed that according to Peirce signs occur within a process of semiosis (CP, 5.484), i.e., there must be some sequence of states which are distinguishable one from another. Every state in this sequence represents the content of the actual consciousness. For each state following another state in such a process it holds that it can only appear either to be unchanged or changed with regard to some qualities. And because qualities are bound to entities, there must entities disappearing or showing up. Thus we could assume that we have as basic the relation between states of consciousness. Let us call it *flow*: $flow: 2^{2Q} \longrightarrow 2^{2Q}$ going from one actual state c to the "next" state c* (With the term 2^{2Q}, I encode the fact that the content of the state of a consciousness is assumed to be a set of entities where each entity is again a set of qualities). Thus, if c, c* would be two states then $\underline{flow}(c) = c*$ would mean that c* has occurred after c. But although the same state can repeat (by content) we would not say that flow is reflexive in the sense that if $\underline{flow}(c) = c*$ then $\underline{flow}(c*) = c$. In our feeling (CP, 1.344ff) c* does occur after c and c does precede c*. This results in the assumption that the flow-relation is irreflexive (if $\underline{flow}(c) = c*$ then $\sim\underline{flow}(c*) = c$). In this sense a mind can state that c precedes c* if there is a flow from c to c* (if $\underline{flow}(c) = c*$ then PRECEDES(c,c*) or c < c*). The other question is whether the mind would state that c** follows c if we have $\underline{flow}(c) = c*$ and $\underline{flow}(c*) = c**$? Even though a mind probably would state that c < c** if we have $\underline{flow}(c) = c*$ and $\underline{flow}(c*) = c**$, under these conditions it is unlikely to state that $\underline{flow}(c) = c**$. Thus it seems that the flow is restricted to the actual presence of states whereas the judgements of preceding somehow transcends the actual presence and is setting up relations taken from the actual states and thereby representing some kind of implicit memory. This yields the characterization that the flow-relation is not transitive whereas the precedes-relation is.

Additionally, because the mind is able to detect whether c^* is different in the flow to the preceding c, we can assume functions indicating all those elements which have changed, either as disappeared or as showing up: disappeared(c,c*) = {elements which disappeared} and showing_up(c,c*) = {elements which have shown up}. Thus, if c would be the conscious state at some point in the flow of the consciousness, and for the mind an object o would suddenly disappear as well as an object o* would suddenly showing up as new, then we would have a flow with flow(c) = c* with disappeared(c,c*) = {o} and showing_up(c,c*) = {o*}.

Now we can ask two questions: (i) how can we define a triadic sign relation? (ii) how is it possible to establish a triadic sign?

A definition could be constructed as follows: First we have to remember that there is some flow between states within which an introduction of a sign must happen. Because we want to introduce a sign constituted by some elements o,s and I, and s presupposes the o with regard to some respect r (r is a subset of Q), we have to assume some flow flow(c) = c* with s and o showing up in c* showing_up(c,c*) = {s,o}. Then one could assume that o and s have the qualities r in common with the immediate object immediate_object(s,o) = r. But because not every co-occurrence of some o and some s must necessarily be "understood" as a relation within a sign, one has to assume that there must be an additional condition which has to trigger the introduction of a sign relevant relation or not. Without such an additional trigger would this co-occurrence as such not install a sign-relevant relationship between o and s. This triggering condition can be reconstructed in several ways. One way is explicitly to assume a sequence of flows where the relations have been fixed according to this "intuition." Thus, we could say: The entities o,s and i are forming a sign with regard to the set of qualities r if and only if there exist some states c, c*, c** which have occurred in flows flow(c) = c* and flow(c*) = c** with the ordering c < c* < c** and where the entities o and s have shown up in c* and then the entity i has shown in c** and no entity disappeared in c** and the qualities r of the entity o are common to i as well to s.

This definition would allow to state, when some entities are forming a triadic sign. But it would not be possible to introduce a sign actively. To do so an operator is needed whose application would generate those circumstances which establish a triadic sign. It is conceivable here to introduce an operator (functor, function) grounding in the sense that this operator exactly generates those conditions which according to Peirce have to be met that one can speak of a triadic sign. If we assume as type for the grounding operator O x S x Q → I then we can postulate for a grounding operator that it will generate an interpretant i which is through a respect r connected to an occurring potential object o and an occurring potential representamen s. Thus, if we have some flow flow(c) = c* between two states c,c* with the ordering c < c* and in the state c* holds that the entities {s,o} are new with r as a subset of o, then the grounding operator has to generate a new flow flow(c*) = c** with the additional ordering c* < c** and a new element i. The entities s and o from the preceding state are not allowed to disappear and the new element i has the respect r in common with o and s.

With these assumptions it is possible in this model to (i) state when a triadic sign relation within the flow of conscious states is given and (ii) to generate a triadic sign within the flow of conscious states. The complete formal model looks like this:

PEIRCEAN_SEMIOTIC_AGENT(a) iff a = <<Q, S, O, I>,<$\underline{flow}$, PRECEDES, $\underline{immediate\_object}$, $\underline{disappear}$, $\underline{show\_up}$, SIGN, $\underline{grounding}$ >>

with

BASIC SETS

Q := set of qualities &
S := set of representamen &
O := set of objects &
I := set of interpretants &

TYPIFICATION

$\{I,S,O\} \underline{c} \, 2^Q$ &
$\underline{flow}: 2^{2^Q} ---> 2^{2^Q}$ &
PRECEDES $\underline{c} \, 2^{2^Q} \times 2^{2^Q}$ &
$\underline{immediate\_object}: 2^Q \times 2^Q ---> 2^Q$ &
$\underline{disappear}: 2^{2^Q} \times 2^{2^Q} ---> 2^{2^Q}$ &
$\underline{show\_up}: 2^{2^Q} \times 2^{2^Q} ---> 2^{2^Q}$ &
SIGN$\underline{c} \, O \times S \times I \times Q$ &
$\underline{grounding}: O \times S \times Q ---> I$ &

AXIOMS

Ax1: (Irreflexive) $\underline{flow}(c) = c^* ==> \sim\underline{flow}(c^*) = c$
Ax2: (Intransitive) $\underline{flow}(c) = c^*$ & $\underline{flow}(c^*) = c^{**} ==> \sim\underline{flow}(c) = c^{**}$
Ax3: // PRECEDES(c,c*) can also be written c < c* //
$c < c^* <==> \underline{flow}(c) = c^*$
Ax4: (Transitivity) if $c < c^*$ & $c^* < c^{**} ==> c < c^{**}$

Ax5: $\underline{immediate\_object}(x,y) = \{z \mid z \underline{in} \, x \, \underline{cut} \, y \, \& \, x,y \, \underline{in} \, 2^Q \}$
Ax6: $\underline{disappear}(c,c^*) = \{z \mid z \underline{in} \, c\backslash c^* \, \& \, \underline{flow}(c) = c^* \}$
Ax6: $\underline{show\_up}(c,c^*) = \{z \mid z \underline{in} \, c^*\backslash c \, \& \, \underline{flow}(c) = c^* \}$
Ax7: SIGN(o,s,i,r) $<==>$ (E:c,c*,c**)($\underline{flow}(c) = c^*$ &
$\underline{flow}(c^*) = c^{**}$ & $c < c^* < c^{**}$ & $\underline{showing\_up}(c,c^*) = \{s,o\}$ & $\underline{showing\_up}(c^*,c^{**}) = \{i\}$ &
$\underline{disappearing}(c^*,c^{**}) = \{\}$ & $r \underline{c} \, o$ & $\underline{immediate\_object}(o,i) = r = \underline{immediate\_object}(s,o)$)
Ax8: $\underline{grounding}(o,s,r) = i ==> (A:c,c^*,c^{**})(\underline{flow}(c) = c^*$ &
$c < c^*$ & $\underline{showing\_up}(c,c^*) = \{s,o\}$ & $r \underline{c} \, o ==> \underline{flow}(c^*,c^{**})$ & $c^* < c^{**}$ &
$\underline{showing\_up}(c^*,c^{**}) = \{i\}$ &
$\underline{disappearing}(c^*,c^{**}) = \{\}$ & $\underline{immediate\_object}(o,i) = r = \underline{immediate\_object}(s,o) = \underline{immediate\_object}(s,i)$)
Ax9: (E:c,c*) (flow(c) = c* & $\sim$(E:x) x < c)

Example

From Axiom 9 it follows that there is at least one flow of conscious states c to c* with no preceding states, and from Axiom 3 it follows that in this case c precedes c*

F0: (E:c,c*) (flow(c) = c* & ~(E:x) x < c)

F0: flow(c) = c* & ~(E:x) x < c

F0: c < c*

We assume that in the state c* the entities s and are showing up as new with a subject r of o

A1: <u>showing_up</u>(c,c*) = {s,o} & r <u>c</u> o

We assume further that the mind is doing some grounding by using o and s with r to establish an interpretant i with the immediate object r

A2: <u>grounding</u>(o,s,r) = i

Because the primary condition of Axiom 8 is fulfilled we can deduce the conditioned part

F1,2: (A:c,c*,c**)*(<u>(flow</u>(c) = c* & c < c* & <u>showing_up</u>(c,c*) = {s,o} & r c o ==> <u>flow</u>(c*,c**) & c* < c** & <u>showing_up</u>(c*,c**) = {i} & <u>disappearing</u>(c*,c**) = {} & <u>immediate_object</u>(o,i) = r = <u>immediate_object</u>(s,o) = <u>immediate_object</u>(s,i))*

Because the further condition is also given we can deduce the final part. Now we can state that through the grounding operator a new flow has been induced with the new entity i and the immediate object r between o,s and i

F,1,2: <u>flow</u>(c*,c**) & c* < c** & <u>showing_up</u>(c*,c**) = {i} & <u>disappearing</u>(c*,c**) = {} & <u>immediate_object</u>(o,i) = r = <u>immediate_object</u>(s,o) = <u>immediate_object</u>(s,i)

With these new facts we can generate an existential expression fitting the conditions for the SIGN-Predicate

F1,2: (E:c,c*,c**)*(<u>flow</u>(c) = c* & flow(c*) = c** & c < c* < c** & <u>showing_up</u>(c,c*) = {s,o} & <u>showing_up</u>(c*,c**) = {i} & <u>disappearing</u>(c*,c**) = {} & r c o & <u>immediate_object</u>(o,i) = r = <u>immediate_object</u>(s,o))*

This shows how the model can generate a semiosis process and within this process a triadic sign-relation

F1,2: SIGN(o,s,i,r)

<u>End of Example</u>

This formalization is only one possibility; many alternatives are possible. Furthermore this model is, by far, not a complete formalization of the mentalistic case. But it shows at least with regard to the Peircean triadic sign relation as such that a given sign SIGN(o,s,i,r) can be the starting point for new sign relations in at least twofold ways: (i) with <u>grounding</u>(i,s*,r*) it could generate a new i* with the old interpretant i as new object; (ii) with <u>grounding</u>(s,s*,r*) it could be generated a new interpretant i* with the old representamen s as object. Both cases show the recursiveness of the sign relation according to Peirce. If one takes into account that the arguments of the grounding operator are completely general with regard to entities of 2^{2Q} then one can also form operations like <u>grounding</u> (o **u** o*,s*,r*) with r* <u>c</u> o **u** o* or even <u>grounding</u> (i **u** o*,s*,r*) with r* <u>c</u> i **u** o*. This means that the grounding operator can take any combination of entities as input to establish a sign relation.

Body and Mind / Brain and Consciousness

After the preceding modelling experiments with the semiotic approaches of Morris and Peirce, one can ask: Which one is more important? The behaviouristically shaped approach of Morris (third person view or S(N)R-Model) or the phenomenalistic approach of Peirce (first person view or P-Model)?

I like to embed the answer to this question within the ongoing debate about the relationship of the brain and consciousness. This debate can be rooted back until the times of Greek philosophy. Over the last 50 years, the philosophical arguments been sharpened a bit more, perhaps due to the influence of modern sciences (e.g., Bunge, 1980; Metzinger, 2000; Shear, 1995, 1997). But a final solution seems still be pending. My intention is not to examine the full discussion here. I will only show how the computational semiotics approach fits in this overall discussion and why computational semiotics perhaps can contribute to this discussion.

For this I will start with an extreme position which has been introduced by Revonsuo (Revonsuo, 2000). Revonsuo is dealing with the unsolved question of how the relationship between brain and consciousness has to be explained. He postulates first a systematic scientific research program within which different competing theories should be possible. He then formulates informally several postulates, which I like to summarize as follows: (P1) Subjective phenomenal consciousness is a real, natural, biological phenomenon that literally resides in the brain. (P2) The science of consciousness is a biological science of consciousness. (P3) Consciousness is the phenomenal level of organization in the brain. (P4) There must be something in the brain, that literally resembles or is similar to consciousness — that is to say, consciousness itself. (P5) There must be an isomorphism between one specific level of organization in the brain and phenomenal consciousness, because brain and consciousness are one and the same thing. (P6) A science of conciousness must first treat the phenomenal level of organization as a proper level of description. The lower levels of explanatory mechanisms can be invoked only after we have a clear conception of the phenomenon that these mechanisms are supposed to explain.

This position raises several questions. In short, I would accept in the case of (P1) to say that the consciousness is a natural phenomenon because it is part of the known nature, but by methodological reasons I would not classify consciousness as a biological phenomenon, as it is usually understood within the empirical discipline of biology. In this critique I make also use of the fact that until today the only source of direct knowledge about the consciousness is the first-person view. Only by our subjective experience we have a primary understanding of consciousness; outside of this view there is no other primary knowledge available. From this follows that from the point of view of sources of knowledge, there are at least two different kinds: (i) the normal first-person view and (ii) the third-person view. The latter is, strictly speaking, a subset of the former. Thus, the data of the third-person view are those phenomena of the first person view which are methodologically restricted by the postulate, that only those phenomena are interpreted as empirical data which can be gained by inter subjectively valid methods of measurement. This distinction is the cornerstone of modern empirical science!

Such a distinction of different sources of knowledge must not necessarily imply an ontological dualism. There can be different points of view denoting the *same* subject, i.e., to assume that consciousness is identical with parts of the brain and assume at the same time that we have at least two different modes of understanding of this aspect of the brain is methodologically compatible (for such a dual-aspect-view see Bunge, 1980; Nagel, 1986). It is just a speciality of our brain that it offers us the possibility to have some kind of an "inner view" of the brain and also some kind of view "from the outside."

When Revonsuo in (P5) claims that there must be an isomorphism between one specific level of organization — say A — in the brain and phenomenal consciousness — another level of organization, say B, then this raises some questions. The concept of an isomorphism presupposes usually two structures with sets, relations and/or functions which can be mapped onto each other. Between "lower" and "higher" structures this doesn't work. If — on the contrary — the neuronal structures, which — according to Revonsuo — shall explain that the level of conscious organisation in the brain would be identical, then one can ask why Revonsuo talks about an isomorphism at all?

There is another possibility — possibly simpler — to bypass these problems. If one takes into account that we have at least two sources of knowledge, first person and third person view, then it would be straightforward to take the data of each view and construct structures accordingly, i.e., one can set up an SNR-Model based on the third-person view and one can set up an P-Model based on the first-person view. Both models can be constructed as formal (algebraic) structures representing entities, relations and operations. In this case it would be very clear whether there exists an isomorphism or not. It would also be clear from the beginning what the level of phenomenal organization looks like; this kind of organization is given directly within the first person view. Here one can use an idea of Revonsuo, who interprets the phenomenal level of organization as the brain's natural virtual reality system, which is creating an "out-of-the-brain-experience" (Revonsuo, 2000,65). Thus, in this interpretation would consciousness be an effect which is generated by our brain and it is *this effect as such* which is the *phenomenon under investigation*. In other words, if one would not take this effect as the phenomenon under investigation but the machinery behind it, which is presupposed to produce this effect, then one would probably miss the interesting point. Therefore, it could be that we either take this effect as it is within the first-person view or we probably will not have the phenomenon at all.

I prefer to assume that consciousness, as it appears in the firt-person view, is that special effect of our brain. As consequence, I would not look in the brain for a structure which is this consciousness, but I would propose — as before — to construct a P-Model based on the first-person data and with the aid of such a P-Model it would be possible to look for SNR-structures which can be correlated with the P-Model.

Within such a methodological approach it is conceivable that — in the long run — enough data can be gained and models can be constructed which could eventually explain how the brain generates this special effect called consciousness. Thus, there is some order in the steps to do: First clarify the structure of the consciousness and then start a search for correlated SNR-Structures. Otherwise, without a clear understanding of the structure of the consciousness, it is methodologically not possible to "understand" the SNR-Structures in their possible contributions for the special effect called consciousness. Here I am in agreement with (P6) of Revonsuo. The relationship from an SNR-Model to a P-Model then could be understood as SNR-explanation of the P-Model, and vice versa is an P-Model the basis for a P-interpretation of the SNR-Model.

Naturalizing Phenomenology

Close to the mind-body discussion, but somehow also different, is the discussion within phenomenology of, whether and how one can or should naturalize phenomenology, as it has been developed from Edmund Husserl (1859-1938). To introduce Husserl in this context makes sense because one of the most accepted semiotic models, that of Peirce, is rooted in phenomenology. But Peirce himself did not develop phenomenology in such a broad and distinguished way as Husserl did. As Roy, Petitot, Pachoud and Varela state it, "Husserlian Phenomenology is by and large the most thorough of modern times, if not of the whole history of though" (Roy et al., 2000, 24). Thus, using phenomenology today in connection with semiotics forces the semioticians to apply to the modern development of phenomenology, i.e., dealing with Husserl and the phenomenological movement after Husserl.

In a lengthy and thorough paper with an extensive and detailed account of most of the relevant philosophical positions Roy, Petitot, Pachoud and Varela discuss the possibility and necessity of what they are calling the naturalization of phenomenology. Although Husserl himself holds the view that phenomenology is anti-naturalist because there is a dimension of the mental that escapes the natural sciences (Roy et al., 2000, 36), Roy, Petitot, Pachoud and Varela are investigating whether this position of Husserl can or must today be re-interpreted because arguments of the past have changed, which have hindered Husserl from bridging the gap with the natural sciences. And because Roy, Petitot, Pachoud and Varela identify behavioural (SR-Data) and especially neural data (N-Data) as the most important kinds of data which should have been integrated with conscious data (P-Data), they are searching for conceptual strategies of how to bridge this gap.

After long arguments, they present four different kinds of strategies which seem to them conceivable as possible contributions: (i) Linking Propositions between SNR- and P-statements; (ii) Isomorphism between SNR- and P-Models; (iii) Operational generativity; and (iv) Phenomenalization of physical objectivity (Roy et al., 2000, 67).

Because (i) seems to be only a weak form of (ii) and therefore an implicit subcase, I will not discuss (i) explicitly. (iii) is a further and much more demanding specification of (ii), therefore (iii) presupposes (ii); (iv) is different from (i) - (iii) and it is not quite clear how to evaluate it. I will start the discussion with (ii) and (iii).

Roy, Petitot, Pachoud and Varela are describing the conceptual strategy (ii) with the isomorphism as follows: "...the job of phenomenology is to provide descriptions relevant to first person phenomena. The job of natural science is to provide explanatory accounts in the third person. Both approaches are joined by a shred logical and epistemic accountability" (Roy et al., 2000, 68). This description fits well with the Morris-Peirce case which I have described above. Having set up a formal SNR-structure (the Morris-Model) and a formal P-structure (the Peirce-Model) it is possible to investigate the kinds of formal relations between these structures. This kind of conceptual structure to naturalize phenomenology can work; it is really possible; examples exist.

What about the conceptual strategy (iii) extending (ii)? Here Roy et al., have claimed that the mutual constraints "are further required to be operationally generative, that is to say, to be in a position to generate in a principled manner eidetic descriptions that can directly link to explicit processes of biological emergence." And Roy, Petitot, Pachoud and Varela remark that the "neurobiological and the phenomenological accounts have to achieve a level of formal and mathematical precision to make this passage possible" (Roy et al., 2000, 68). With regard to the formal SNR-P-Structures used in the case of computational semiotics, this claim is of the right formal and mathematical precision naturally fulfilled; these structures are, from the beginning, complete formal theories in the modern sense. And to demand a generative character of the structures in the sense that the dynamic flux of phenomena in the P-Model is accompanied by the appropriate accompanying processes in the SNR-Model is not a principle deviation of the SNR-P-Structure. It is "only" a question of the ingenuity of the model builder as well as the availability of empirical and phenomenological data to supply the SNR-P-Model with such generating functions. Therefore, the generative conceptual strategy (iii) can also be classified as in principle possible; concrete examples have to be worked out.

To evaluate conceptual strategy (iv) requiring the phenomenalization of physical objectivity deserves some additional arguments. To understand the following argument, one has to keep in mind that usual practice of discussing nature and empirical data on the same epistemological level as phenomenal data is a "sloppy" way of speaking, which in many cases suffices, but in the actual case it is misleading.

From the point of view of phenomenology, empirical data are not different to phenomena nor are they "outside" of the realm of phenomena. The so-called empirical data — SR or N or SNR-Data — are those phenomena which are inter subjective and additionally correlated with empirical methods of measurement. In this sense are SNR-Data a subset of the overall set of phenomena P (SNR $\subseteq$ P). From this point of view it is clearly no problem to phenomenalize nature; not conceivable is how the converse relation should be understood. Thus, the endless discussions and proposals to naturalize the consciousness by trying to eliminate P first and then trying to generate it "somehow" out of SNR-structures is logical nonsense. In every formal system one can only infer facts which are already "in" the system. A SNR-Theory without a "proper" content of P-structures will never generate P-Structures.

When we therefore take as a starting point the phenomenological point of view with the subset of those phenomena which are empirical, we can deduce some more interesting properties and consequences. Seen from a phenomenological point of view, one can — as we have discussed before — set up an empirical SNR-theory with correlations to a phenomenological P-Theory. To the extent to which a P-Theory is elaborated, one can try to construct a SNR-Theory which is generative in the sense that the actual content of a modelled Consciousness in the P-Theory will be generated according to processes in the body-brain modelled in the SNR-Theory. Both theories are texts whose meaning is mediated by the complex interactions of sign and their mediating interpretents. Thus, to set up theories one needs not only a general P-Theory but additionally a semiotic P-Theory. The only known model of a phenomenological semiotic theory so far is the model of Peirce. Worked out as a formal semiotic theory and moreover as a computational theory, it could be a substantial part of the intended overall P-Theory. The corresponding SNR-Theory has to be constructed accordingly including the semiotic processes.

What about the computability of formalized phenomenological models? Analogous to the argumentation in the context of the SNR-Model of Morris, one can state that a formalized P-Model is clearly computable if one assumes that the described consciousness is an effect of the underlying neuronal machinery. If one postulates some unknown factor X as part of the phenomenon of consciousness not caused by the neuronal machinery, then the question is open and a serious discussion is impossible as long as one cannot characterize this factor X sufficiently well within an acceptable scientific discourse.

Conclusion:
Outline of a Research Program

After these "visits" in some fields of science and philosophy, one can see that the phenomenon of intelligence is indeed correlated with a diversity of phenomena and methods, and it is hard to imagine how it would be possible to squash this manifold view into only one, unified picture. In a more pragmatic fashion one could perhaps give up such an idea of a unified view as long as one can find some partial models which work for dedicated problems. But there are contexts in which an understanding of the "whole" subject is necessary, otherwise one is missing the target. Facing the diversity of the phenomenon of intelligence, it is my impression that the most adequate picture of this phenomenon is given within a temporal perspective where the actual behaviour is seen as a property of a dynamic system whose internal structure and "logic" is encoded within a process called evolution of DNA-based life. And it is an outstanding characteristic of the human species that its members are viewing the world and themselves in a mode called consciousness whereby this conscious mode seems to be a special effect generated by the brain. Consciousness is the cognitive format under which a human individual gains his or her primary knowledge about their environment though the environmental machinery itself and seems to be quite different from the shapes within the consciousness. Thus, to gain "real" knowledge means to "transcend" the phenomenological knowledge with the aid of formal models and measurements which look "beyond" the primary phenomenological worldview. The main tool in building up knowledge seems to be symbolic communication, or language. This is the most recent and most complex kind of behaviour which has emerged on Earth, located within the human species. Without language there is no shared knowledge (Deacon, 1997; Hauser, 1996). If we are seriously interested in an understanding of the "whole" phenomenon as well as in a "reconstruction" in the manner of working simulations, we have to take it as it is: a dynamic phenomenon including many levels of organization. In the following I will sketch the outline of a research program which follows from all the preceding considerations and one which I will try to realize in the future. Perhaps there is no real "fixed point" ahead where one can say that now "everything" is explained, but I am convinced that this program — or some modified version of it — can help to coordinate the activities between working groups all around the world.

To describe the whole program in detail is beyond the scope of this chapter. But what I want to do is to give an outline of a hierarchy of interacting formal theories which are good candidates to play a central role in the upcoming multi-layered computational theory of evolutionary intelligence.

One can divide the whole domain of intelligence into certain organizational layers. The top layer is understood as the layer of the environment E of acting bodies B. The central idea is that the next state of an environment E will be determined by a transfer function T_E, which computes the next state of the environment based on the actual given state E; written as $E = T_E(E)$. Part of the transfer function T_E is also a description of possible interactions between acting bodies. If one wants to describe the participating bodies in more detail, one has to model also the structure of these bodies with a special transfer function T_B for the bodies with $B = T_B(B)$. The body-transfer function computes the next state of a body with the given states of the body. The body B contains, besides other structures, a matrix M of neurons as well as a consciousness C which is a special effect of the matrix M. Here I will assume two transfer functions: one for the matrix M of neurons $M = T_M(M,C)$ and one for the consciousness $C = T_C(M,C)$. In both transfer functions, the interplay of M and C will be described. Because the matrix M of neurons consists of neurons N and their properties, one has to provide some theory to describe a neuron and its behaviour. There can be different kinds of neurons, as in the real brain (for an example of a structural description of neurons with post synaptic membranes and end bulbs, see Erasmus, Döben-Henisch, & Bodenstein, 2004; Erasmus & Bodenstein, 2004) $N = T_N(N)$. For many interesting phenomena — especially with regard to the ability to adapt and to learn — it has been found that the post synaptic membranes P as well as the end bulbs U are important. Therefore, one has to provide also some theories for P and U. Thus we have $P = T_P(P)$ and $U = T_U(U)$. The interplay of end bulbs with post synaptic membranes is described by the transfer function TM which is looking onto the whole matrix and their connections.

The overall structure of all participating theories is always the same: there are the main sets of the structure — the X-Sets with X in { P, U, N, M, C, B, E } — onto which several relations or operations are defined. The main operator in all these partial theories is the transfer function T_X. Every layer i can be related with a partial theory. The elements of the set { P,U,N,M,C,B,E } can be numbered as follows: { P=U=-4, N=-3, M=C=-2, B=-1, E=0 }. If more than one layer of theories is used, then layer i presupposes layer i-1. With regard to the transfer functions, we have the concatenation $T_E \circ T_B \circ T_C \circ T_M \circ T_N \circ T_P \circ T_U$ with a right to left order of computation.

What is still missing is a description of the dynamical aspects which are induced by the phenomenon of ontogenesis and phylogenesis. As I have shown in a preceding section is the inclusion of these dimensions into the theory in principle possible. For practical reasons it would be very convenient to have a brain-developing function. This should be done in another paper.

References

Balzer, W. (1982). *Empirische Theorien: Modelle, Strukturen, Beispiele.* Wiesbaden, Germany: Friedr. Vieweg & Sohn.

Balzer, W., Moulines, C. U., & Sneed, J. D. (1987). An architectonic for science. Dordrecht, Germany: D. Reidel Publishing Company.

Batori, I.S., Lenders, W., & Puschke, W. (Eds.). (1989). *Computational linguistics.* An International Handbook on Computer Oriented Language Research and Applications. Berlin: Walter de Gruyter & Co.

Benacerraf, P., & Putnam, H. (Eds.). (1983). *Philosophy of mathematics: Selected readings* (2nd ed.). London: Cambridge University Press.

Bernays, P. (1976). *Abhandlungen zur Philosophie der Mathematik.* Darmstadt, Germany: Wissenschaftliche Buchgesellschaft.

Bourbaki, N. (1970). *Theorie des ensembles.* Paris: Hermann.

Bourbaki, N. (1984). *Elements d'histoire des mathematiques.* Paris; New York: Masson.

Bower, G. H, & Hilgard, E.R. (1983). *Theorien des Lernens I+II* (5th rev.ed.). *H. Aebli, & U. Aechenbacher (Trans.).* Stuttgart: Klett-Cotta.

Bowler, B. J. (1989). *Evolution — The history of an idea* (rev. ed.). Berkeley: University of California Press.

Brey, B. B. (2003). *The Intel microprocessors: Architecture, programming, and interface* (6th ed.). Prentice Hall: Pearson Education International.

Bruderer, H. A. (Ed.). (1982). *Automatische Sprachübersetzung.* Darmstadt, Germany: Wissenschaftliche Buchgesellschaft.

Bunge, M. (1980). *The mind-body problem: A psychobiological approach.* Oxford: Pergamon Press.

Casti, J. L. (1992). *Reality rules: I. Picturing the world in mathematics. The fundamentals.* New York: John Wiley & Sons.

Changeux, J. P. (1983). *Der neuronale Mensch. Wie die Seele funktioniert — die Entdeckung der neuen Gehirnforschung* (trans. from the French edition 1983). Reinbeck bei Hamburg, Germany: Rowohlt Verlag.

Chomsky, N. (1959). *A review of Skinner's verbal behaviour.* Language, *35,* 26-58.

Cohen, I. B. (1980/1985). *The Newtonian revolution with illustrations of the transformations of scientific ideas.* Cambridge (London & New York): Cambridge University Press.

Cruse, H., Dean, J., & Ritter, H. (1998). Die Entdeckung der Intelligenz — oder Können Ameisen denken? München: Verlag C.H.Beck.

Davis, M. (1958). *Computability and unsolvability.* New York: McGraw-Hill Book Company.

Davis, M. (Ed.). (1965). *The undecidable.* Basic Papers On Undecidable Propositions, Unsolvable Problems And Computable Functions. New York: Raven Press.

Davis, R., & Lenat, D.B. (1982). *Knowledge-based systems in artificial intelligence.* New York: McGraw-Hill.

Deacon, T. W. (1997). *The symbolic species: The co-evolution of language and brain.* New York: W.W.Norton.

de Boer, B. (2001) *The origins of vowel systems.* Oxford: Oxford University Press.

de Boer, B. (2000). Emergence of sound systems through self-organisation. In Chr. Knight, J. R. Hurford, & M. Studdert-Kennedy (Eds.), *The evolutionary emergence of language: Social function and the origins of linguistic form.* Cambridge: Cambridge University Press.

Dieudonne, J. (1985). *Geschichte der Mathematik 1700-1900: Ein Abriß.* Braunschweig-Wiesbaden, Germany: Friedr, Vieweg & Sohn.

Dijksterhuis, E. J. (1986). *The mechanization of the world picture: Pythagoras to Newton.* Princeton, NJ: Princeton University Press.

Döben-Henisch, G. (1998). Semiotic machines — An introduction. In E. W. Hess-Lüttich & J. E. Müller (Eds.), *Zeichen und Raum* [Signs and Space] (pp. 313-327). Tübingen: Gunter Narr Verlag.

Eibl-Eibesfeldt, I. (1980). *Grundriss der Vergleichenden Verhaltensforschung* (6th rev. ed.). München: Piper & Co Verlag.

Elman, J. L., Bates, E. A., Johnson, M. H., Karmiloff-Smith, A., Parisi, D., & Plunkett, K. (1996). *Rethinking innateness: A connectionist perspective on development.* Cambridge, MA: The MIT Press.

Epigenetic Robotics. (2001-2005). *Epigenetic robotics.* Retrieved November 21, 2005, from http://www.lucs.lu.se/epigenetic-robotics/

Erasmus, L. D., & Bodenstein, C. P. (2004). Real neurons, artificial intelligence based on the mechanisms of biological intelligence. In *IEEE Africon 2004, 1,* 423-428.

Erasmus, L. D., & Döben-Henisch, G., & Bodenstein, C. P. (2004). A model of the real neuron. In *IEEE Africon 2004, 2,* 1071-1078.

Estes, W. K. (Ed.). (1975/1976). *Handbook of learning and cognitive processes* (vols. 1-4). New York: John Wiley & Sons.

Gale, A., & Edwards, J. A. (Eds.). (1983). *Physiological correlates of human behaviour* (vols. 1-3). London: Academic Press.

Garey, M. R., & Johnson, D. S. (1979). *Computers and intractability: A guide to the theory of NP-completeness.* San Francisco: W.H.Freeman and Company.

Gazzaniga, M. S. (Ed.). (1995). *The cognitive neurosciences.* Cambridge, MA: The MIT Press.

Gödel, K. (1931). Über formal unentscheidbare Sätze der Principia Mathematica und verwandter Systeme I. *Mh. Math. Phys., 38,* 175-198.

Grossberg, S. (1982). *Studies of mind and brain: Neural principles of learning, perception, development, cognition and motor-control.* Dordrecht (Holland): D. Reidel Publishing Company.

Hauser, M. D. (1996). *The evolution of communication.* Cambridge, MA: MIT Press.

Haykin, S. (1999). *Neural networks: A comprehensive foundation* (2nd ed.). Upper Saddle River, NJ: Prentice Hall.

Hintikka, J. (Ed.). (1975). *Rudolf Carnap, logical empiricist*. Dordrecht - Boston: D. Reidel Publishing Company.

Hodges, A. (1983). *Alan Turing, enigma* (2nd ed. 1994). New York: Springer Verlag.

Immelmann, K., Barlow, G., Petrinovich, L., & Main, M. (Eds.). (1982). *Verhaltensentwicklung bei Mensch und Tier*. Berlin: Verlag Paul Parey.

Kitcher, P. (1984). *The nature of mathematical knowledge*. New York; Oxford: Oxford University Press.

Kneale, W. & Kneale, M. (1986). *The development of logic*. Oxford: Clarendon Press.

Körner, S. (1968). *Philosophie der Mathematik. Eine Einführung*. München: Nymphenburger Verlagshandlung GmbH. [The Philosophy of Mathematics. An Introductory Essay]. London: Hutchinson & Co.

Kolb, B., & Wishaw, I. Q. (1993). *Neuropsychologie. Heidelberg-Berlin-Oxford: Spektrum Akademischer Verlag*. [transl. from the engl. edition (1990)]. Fundamentals of Human Neuropsychology (3rd ed.). W.H. Freeman & Company.

Küppers, B. O. (1990). *Der Ursprung biologischer Information. Zur Naturphilosophie der Lebensentstehung* (2nd ed.). München-Zürich: Piper Verlag.

Kuhn, T. S. (1957). *The Copernican revolution: Planetary astronomy in the development of western thought*. Cambridge, MA: Harvard University Press.

Kuhn, T. S. (1962). *The structure of scientific revolution*. Chicago: University of Chicago Press.

Kuhn, T. S. (1978). *Die Entstehung des Neuen. Studien zur Struktur der Wissenschaftsgeschichte* (Krüger, L. Ed.). Frankfurt am Main, Germany: Suhrkamp Verlag.

Lewin, B. (1998). *Molekularbiologie der Gene. Heidelberg — Berlin: Spektrum Akademischer Verlag GmbH* (transl. from the engl. version 1997). Genes. Oxford University Press.

Ludwig, G. (1978a). *Die Grundstrukturen einer physikalischen Theorie*. Berlin; Heidelberg; New York: Springer.

Mackintosh, N. J. (Ed.). (1994). *Animal learning and cognition*. Academic Press.

Mayr, E. (1988). *Eine neue Philosophie der Biologie* [Toward a New Philosphy of Biology]. Darmstadt:Wissenschaftl. Buchgesellschaft.

Metzinger, T. (Ed.). (2000). *Neural correlates of consciousness: Empirical and conceptual questions*. Cambridge; London: The MIT Press.

Minsky, M. L. (1967). *Computation: Finite and infinite machines*. Englewood Cliffs, NJ: Prentice Hall.

Mittelstrass, J. (Ed.). (1995-1996). *Enzyklopädie Philosophie und Wissenschaftstheorie* (vols. 1-4). Stuttgart — Weimar, Germany: J.B.Metzler.

Morris, C.W. (1925). *Symbolik und Realität* (German translation 1981 of the unpublished dissertation of Morris by Achim Eschbach). Frankfurt: Suhrkamp Verlag.

Morris, C.W. (1936). *Die Einheit der Wissenschaft* (German translation of an unpublished lecture by Achim Eschbach). In Morris, 1981 (pp.323-341).

Morris, C.W. (1938). *Foundations of the theory of signs.* Chicago: University of Chicago Press (repr. in Morris, 1971).

Morris, C.W. (1946). *Signs, language and behavior.* New York: Prentice-Hall Inc.

Morris, C.W. (1971). *Writings on the general theory of signs.* Paris: Mouton Publishers.

Morris, C.W. (1977). *Pragmatische Semiotik und Handlungstheorie: Mit einer Einleitung von Achim Eschbach.* Frankfurt: Suhrkamp Verlag.

Nagel, T. (1986). *The view from nowhere.* New York: Oxford University Press.

Nilsson, N. J. (1998). *Artificial intelligence: A new synthesis.* San Francisco: Morgan Kaufmann Publishers.

Nöth, W. (2000). *Handbuch der Semiotik* (2nd rev. ed.). Stuttgart-Weimar: Verlag J.B.Metzler.

Nöth, W. (Ed.). (1994). *The origins of semiosis: Sign evolution in nature and culture.* Berlin; New York: Mouton de Gruyter.

Obler, L. K., & Gjerblow, K. (1999). *Language and the brain.* Cambridge: Cambridge University Press.

Peirce, C. S. (1931-58). Collected Papers of Charles Sanders Peirce. Vols. 1-6. ed. by Charles Hartshorne, &Pauls Weiss. (vols. 7-8). Arthur W.Burks (Ed.). Cambridge, MA: Harvard University Press.

Petitot, J., & Varela, F. J., Pachoud, B., & Roy, J. M. (Eds.). (1999). *Naturalizing phenomenology: Issues in contemporary phenomenology and cognitive science.* Stanford, CA: Stanford University Press.

Pfeifer, R., & Scheier, Ch. (Eds.). (1999). *Understanding intelligence.* Cambridge, MA: The MIT Press.

Pulvermüller, F. (1996). *Neurobiologie der Sprache.* Düsseldorf: Pabst Science Publishers.

Revonsuo, A. (2000). Prospect for a scientific research program for consciousness. In T. Metzinger (Ed.), *Neural correlates of consciousness. Empirical and conceptual questions* (pp. 57-75). London: The MIT Press.

Rich, E. (1983). *Artificial intelligence.* New York: McGraw-Hill.

Rosenberg, A. (1985). *The structure of biological science.* Cambridge: Cambridge University Press.

Roth, G. (1995). *Das Gehirn und seine Wirklichkeit* (2nd ed.). Frankfurt am Main: Suhrkamp Verlag.

Roy, J. M., Petitot, J., Pachoud, B., & Varela, F. J. (1999). Beyond the gap: An introduction to naturalizing phenomenology. In J. M. Roy, J. Petitot, B. Pachoud, & F.J. Varela (Eds.). (1999). *Naturalizing phenomenology: Issues in contemporary phenomenology and cognitive science* (pp. 1-80). Stanford, CA: Stanford University Press.

Rozenberg, R., & Salomaa, A. (Eds.). (1997). *Handbook of formal languages* (Vol. 1-3). Berlin; Heidelberg; New York: Springer.

Rumelhart, D. E., McClelland, J. L., et al. (1986). *Parallel distributed processing: Explorations in the microstructure of cognition* (vols.1 - 2). Cambridge, MA: The MIT Press.

Schilpp, P. A. (Ed.). (1963). *The philosophy of Rudolf Carnap*. London: Cambridge University Press.

Schnelle, H. (1994). *Language and brain*. In W. Nöth. (pp. 339-363).

Sebeok, T. A. (1976). *Contributions to the doctrine of signs*. Bloomington, IN: Indiana University Press.

Shear, J. (Ed.).(1995/1997). *Explaining consciousness:The 'hard problem.'* London; Cambridge: The MIT Press.

Shepherd, G. M. (1994). *Neurobiology* (3rd ed.). Oxford; New York: Oxford University Press.

Shettleworth, S. J. (1994). Biological approaches to the study of learning. In N.J.Mackintosh (Ed.), *Animal learning and cognition* (pp. 185-219). London: Academic Press.

Siekmann, J., & Wrightson, G. (Eds.). (1983). *Automation of reasoning* (pp. Vols.1 &2). *Classical papers on computational logic 1957-1970*. Berlin: Springer-Verlag.

Sneed, J. D. (1979). *The logical structure of mathematical physics* (2nd rev.ed.). Dordrecht; Boston; London: D.Reidel Publishing Company.

Steels, L. (1997a). The synthetic modelling of language origins. *Evolution of Communication, 1*(1), 1-34.

Steels, L. (1997b). The origins of syntax in visually grounded robotic agents. In M. Pollack (Ed.), *Proceedings of the IJCAI-97 Conference*. Los Angelos: Morgan Kaufmann.

Steels, L. (1998). The origins of syntax in visually grounded robotic agents. *Artificial Intelligence, 103*(1, 2), 133-156.

Suppe, F. (Ed.). (1979). *The structure of scientific theories* (2nd ed.). Urbana: University of Illinois Press.

Thiel, Ch. (1995). *Philosophie und Mathematik: Eine Einführung in ihre Wechselwirkung und in die Philosophie der Mathematik*. Darmstadt: Wissenschaftliche Buchgesellschaft.

Turing, A. M. (1936). On computable numbers with an application to the entscheidungsproblem. In *Proceedings of the London Math. Soc.*, Ser.2, *42*, 230-265. (Reprinted in M.Davis, 1965, pp. 116-151).

Weingarten, M. (1993). *Organismen: Objekte oder Subjekte der Evolution*. Darmstadt: Wissenschaftliche Buchgesellschaft.

Winston, P. H., & Shellard, S. A. (Eds.). (1990). *Artificial intelligence at MIT expanding frontiers* (vols.1-2). Cambridge, MA; London: MIT Press.

Chapter V

Stratified Constraint Satisfaction Networks in Synergetic Multi-Agent Simulations of Language Evolution

Alexander Mehler
Bielefeld University, Germany

Abstract

We describe a simulation model of language evolution which integrates synergetic linguistics with multi-agent modelling. On the one hand, this enables the utilization of knowledge about the distribution of the parameter values of system variables as a touch stone of simulation validity. On the other hand, it accounts for synergetic interdependencies of microscopic system variables and macroscopic order parameters. This approach goes beyond the classical setting of synergetic linguistics by grounding processes of self-regulation and self-organization in mechanisms of (dialogically aligned) language learning. Consequently, the simulation model includes four layers, (i) the level of single information processing agents which are (ii) dialogically aligned in communication processes enslaved (iii) by the social system in which the agents participate and whose countless communication events shape (iv) the corresponding language system. In summary, the present chapter is basically conceptual. It outlines a simulation model which bridges between different levels of language modelling kept apart in contemporary simulation models. This model relates to artificial cognition systems in the sense that it may be implemented to endow an artificial agent community in order to perform distributed processes of meaning constitution.

Introduction

Computer-based simulation of sign processes is a much considered topic in cognitive linguistics, computer science and related disciplines. Starting from the insight that a biological agent's capacity to survive correlates with its ability to process linguistic signs, a lot of simulation models of the evolution of sign systems have been elaborated (Batali, 1998; Cangelosi & Parisi, 2002b; Kirby, 2002; Steels, 1996, 1998, 2000; Turner, 2002). According to these approaches, neither rule-based nor statistical models alone account for the dynamics of sign systems as an outcome of countless events in which agents make use of signs to serve their communication needs (Andersen, 2000). Rather, the evolution of sign systems — which natural agents use in order to collectively survive — is simulated by means of computer-based *multi-agent systems* (Christiansen & Kirby, 2003).

The paradigm of multi-agent modelling opposes any approach to the simulation of intelligent behaviour by means of *single* artificial agents operating (and thus processing language) in isolation. Rather, intelligent behaviour is seen to emerge from the cooperation of many cognitive systems without being reducible to any single one of them. This is what Hollan et al. (2000) call *distributed cognition* — cf. Maturana and Varela (1980) for a more philosophical grounding of this approach. According to this view, a full *semiotic* (i.e., sign processing) *agent* is seen to be definable only against the background of a community of structurally coupled agents. That is, a single agent is not supposed to re-use a pre-established language, but to cooperatively acquire a sign system as a means of representing and mastering his or her environment (Maturana & Varela, 1980; Rieger, 2002). This is tantamount to a reconstruction of the *grounding problem* (Ziemke, 1999; Riegler et al., 1999) in terms of distributed, social intelligence (Hollan et al., 2000; Steels, 2002). In methodological terms, this means to abandon the approach of strong *artificial intelligence* (Searle, 1980) and artificial life (Pattee, 1988) — insofar as they aim at *realizing* intelligent behaviour by means of artificial agents — in favour of computer-based *simulations* of language evolution.[1]

Approaches to simulation models of language evolution are well documented in the volume of Cangelosi and Parisi (2002b) — see also Kirby (2002) for a comprehensive overview of this field of research.[2] These approaches have in common that they utilize *multi-agent* computer-simulations (Cangelosi & Parisi, 2002a; Gilbert & Troitzsch, 1999) in order to model aspects of phylo, onto or glossogenetic evolution of language (Christiansen & Kirby, 2003).[3] The *iterated learning model* (Kirby, 2002) can be referred to as an architectural simulation model which addresses the bottleneck problem, according to which a language is transmitted from generation to generation via agents who evidently do not have access to the totality of knowledge characterizing the language to be learned. Consequently, language change — subject to the pressure of varying speaker and hearer needs — is inescapable. Generally speaking, in this and related models language learning is tackled with respect to referential semantics and symbolic grounding in a multi-agent setting (Cangelosi et al., 2002; Steels, 1996, 2002), the learning of lexical knowledge (regarding the articulation of content and expression plane) (Hashimoto, 2002; Hutchins & Hazlehurst, 2002; Kirby & Hurford, 2002), the learning of syntax formation (Hashimoto, 2002; Kirby & Hurford, 2002) and the interrelation of lexico-grammar and semantics (as regards, for example, the emergence of compositionality) (Kirby & Hurford, 2002). All these approaches apply machine learning techniques (e.g., classification, grammar induction, etc.) in order to model language learning of individual agents and thus relate — from a methodological point of view — to *computational linguistics*. Moreover, Kirby and Hurford (2002) demonstrate the usability of frequency distributions as they are studied in quantitative linguistics. Generally speaking, knowledge about the validity of such distributions can be utilized in two respects: First, this knowledge can be used to constrain the model itself. That is, simulations can be endowed by the experimenter with probability distributions restricting the actualization of meanings as represented in semantic space.[4] The semantic space model is a reference model for mapping a certain meaning aspect in cognitive linguistics.

Second, they can be seen as specifying necessary conditions for the validity of the outcome of simulation experiments. In this chapter, we will refer to both of these readings, thereby describing a layered synergetic network of such constraints.

The chapter is organized around four questions:

- *What are relevant levels of linguistic dynamics to be mapped?*

  One of the central claims of simulation approaches is that they better account for the manifold dynamics of sign processing and thus allow tackling the grounding problem and related issues without the need to pre-establish artificial agents with sign knowledge. Although this chapter does not deal with grounding of meaning representations, it nevertheless identifies various levels of the dynamics of language evolution. This starts with the most elementary level of single sign processing systems and goes up to the level of the language as a whole.

- *What kind of machine learning can be applied in order to implement language learning by the simulation model under consideration?*

  Simulation models of language evolution necessarily realize a sort of unsupervised learning (though there are also approaches to utilizing the paradigm of supervised learning in language evolution simulation (cf. Turner, 2002)). Amongst other things, this relates to grounding developmental stages of the simulation in terms of corresponding stages (classes) of the socialsemiotic system(s) being modelled. This holds especially for agent learning as a model of learning as performed by real speakers. In order to shed light on this question, the apparatus of inductive learning is referred to with respect to lexical and schematic knowledge.

- *What are reliable sources of evaluating these simulation models?*

  As simulation models perform a kind of *unsupervised, distributed learning*, an answer to this question is even harder to determine. However, there are several starting points of falsification: on the level of single agents, of interpersonal learning and of the speech community as a whole. The chapter contributes to this question too.

*   *What are semiotic constraints of sign processing in multi-agent systems?*

    A central aim of the chapter is to describe *system variables* and *order parameters* which describe and control the unfolding of language acquisition in multi-agent systems, respectively. This is done regarding three operative levels: the level of *individual* sign processing systems, the level of dialogically communicating agents and the system of social networking structuring and stratifying the corresponding speech community. According to cognitive science (Rickheit & Strohner, 1992), any of these levels can be described in terms of its structural/ functional integrity, its stability and its creativity to invent new systems. We will likewise outline constraints regarding the evolvement of sign system on these levels.

The chapter is organized as follows: we first integrate several paradigms of machine learning and language modelling utilizing the paradigms of synergetic linguistics and multi-agent simulation. Synergetic linguistics is not left unaffected by this integration. Rather, we reconstruct macroscopic order parameters and microscopic system variables in terms of social networks and agent communication, respectively, and thus dissolve the synergetic abstraction of system needs and speakers/hearers which, in synergetic linguistics, are conceived as, so to speak, idealized interlocutors. Next the four layer-model of language simulation is presented in more detail. That is, the simulated (class of) language system(s) is identified as an epiphenomenal system which is aggregated on grounds of countless communication events performed by information processing agents whose communication is enslaved by the encompassing social system (of social groups, social norms, etc.). We then take up this four-level model and sheds light on constraints interlinking these levels in more detail. Finally, we give a conclusion and prospective on future work. In summary, the chapter concentrates on conceptual modelling, leaving out its implementation to future work.

Stratification in Language Simulations

The model to be presented in the following sections is based on five paradigms of language modelling and machine learning: *constraint satisfaction, synergetic linguistics, inductive learning, distributed cognition* and *alignment in communication*. We refer to these paradigms as offering building blocks to be integrated into a simulation of language evolution which models processes of inductive learning on the level of single agents, groups of agents and social networks. A main contribution of the present chapter is an outline of how these strata interact, where their interaction is mainly specified in terms of synergetic constraint satisfaction of order parameters enslaving system variables on the level of individual text processing and dialogical communication.

Constraint Satisfaction

Communication in general, and language comprehension/production in particular, can be described in terms of *constraint satisfaction processes* providing or preventing *coherence* of the focal system (Smolensky, 1995a,b).[5] Thagard (2000) gives a general account of *parallel* constraint satisfaction in the context of optimizing a system's coherence. In this model, coherence maximization is understood as maximizing the degree to which the operative positive/negative constraints are met. More specifically, coherence relations are described as *soft constraints* (Zadeh, 1997). That is, optimizing coherence does not necessarily mean satisfying all, but as many of the most prioritized constraints as possible. The paradigm of constraint satisfaction is related to specifying fitness functions in agent-based simulations of language evolution in terms of genetic algorithms (Turner, 2002), where — instead of directly defining a target function of the system to be simulated — constraints are specified which any candidate solution has to satisfy. The general architecture of Thagard's model looks as follows:

1. *Constituents:* Let E be a finite set of elements $\{e_i \mid i \in I\}$ and $C \subseteq E \times E$ a set of binary constraints, e.g., $(e_i, e_j) \in C$, where C is divided into the set of positive and negative constraints C^+ and C^-, respectively.[6] Further, each constraint is assigned a number w representing its weight.

2. *Optimization:* The coherence problem defined by C on E is solved by partitioning E into two sets A and R (of accepted and refused elements, respectively) so that compliance with the following conditions is maximized:

    (i) $\forall (e_i, e_j) \in C^+ : e_i \in A \Leftrightarrow e_j \in A$ (a positive constraint is satisfied, if both its elements belong to A).

    (ii) $\forall (e_i, e_j) \in C^- : e_i \in A \Leftrightarrow e_j \in R$ (a negative constraint is satisfied, if its elements are distributed among A and R).

3. *Quantification:* Against this background, "coherence maximization" means that E is partitioned into A and R so that the sum W of weights of positive and negative constraints satisfied by A and R, respectively, is maximized.

In order to instantiate this type of model, several parameters have to be set: "To show that a given problem is a coherence problem ... it is necessary to specify the elements and constraints, provide an interpretation of acceptance and rejection and show that solutions to the given problem do in fact involve satisfaction of the specified constraints" (Thagard, 2000, 20). Following the general idea of Thagard's approach of indirect, pattern-based specifications of fitness functions, we depart from his focus on *parallel* constraint satisfaction by describing constraint satisfaction as evolving in a *stratified* network of synergetic order parameters. Moreover, we do not concentrate on integration processes, but also account for construction in actual, onto-, and glossogenetic learning.

Synergetic Linguistics

A second methodological, but also epistemological, basis of the model to be presented is given by *synergetic linguistics* (Köhler, 1987). It is based on *synergetics* as the theory of spontaneous emergence and development of structures by means of self-organization and regulation (Haken, 1998). Synergetic linguistics describes languages as self-organizing systems whose evolvement is controlled by *order parameters* which constrain or "enslave" the dynamics of the focal system components. As macroscopic units, order parameters (e.g., system needs or groups of interlocutors) do not belong to the level of microscopic units they enslave. The idea is that their dynamics destabilize the language system and thus produce an adaptation pressure which the system answers by evoking mechanisms of self-organization and regulation in order to restore an equilibrium meeting the constraints induced by the operative order parameters. Because of permanently changing order parameters, languages do not reach stable states of equilibrium, but are in a constant state of flux on their own.

According to Köhler (1987), this process evolves by analogy with evolutionary processes based on selection and mutation. Regarding mutation, this can be outlined as follows: Random variants of system properties emerging according to countless fluctuating communication events are subject to a competition in which only those variants survive which best meet the prevalent system needs. These mechanisms are manifested by microscopic processes (i.e., by processes internal to the system being enslaved) which adapt the affected language units in order to meet the operative system needs. The systematization of macroscopic needs and the clarification of their functional impact on various microscopic variables is an invaluable contribution of synergetic linguistics (Köhler, 1993). This holds, amongst others, for the *need of encoding* (Cod), i.e., the need for linguistic means of encoding meanings and its relation to functional equivalents meeting it (e.g., morphological, lexical, syntactical and prosodical means) (Köhler, 1999).

As will be shown, it is the synergetic perspective on the cooperation and competition of order parameters which allows for an understanding of system variables to span a *constraint network* which Köhler (1993) models, for example, as a system of equations. This conception of a macroscopic constraint network restricting a corresponding microscopic network of constraints enables one to go beyond any simple integration of Zipfian constraints[7] into the framework of simulating language evolution, since it necessarily focuses on the interrelation of order parameters and system variables to be integrated.

The synergetic conception of order parameters allows for the integration of Thagard's constraint satisfaction model: Elements are defined as order parameters or as system variables, whereas acceptance and rejection occur to the degree that the parameter value (or distribution) of a system variable meets the needs restricting it. As far as this integration is alternatively done in the framework of multi-agent-based simulations of language evolution, the level of abstraction of synergetic linguistics has to be replaced in favour of a model of finer resolution. This relates to the structures as well as processes involved. For the time being, synergetic linguistics accounts for the functional relation of order parameters (e.g., minimization of production effort or minimization of memory effort and inventory size) and enslaved variables of the language system (e.g., word length, frequency and lexicon size) on a rather abstract level. This leaves unspecified the learning and acquisition of *specific* linguistic units and their *specific* relations (e.g., of words and their sense relations) as a result of communication between *specific* agents in a multi-agent simulation setting. But from the point of view of agent-based simulations, these learning processes have to be made an object of modelling on their own. This also demands extending the class of models of linguistic dynamics which, for the time being, is modelled — beyond synergetic systems of equations — by means of steady state models and stochastic processes (Altmann & Köhler, 1996):

- *Steady state* models start from assumptions about boundary conditions of the focal language processes in equilibrium in order to derive, for example, probability distributions whose validity is the object of subsequent empirical studies. This kind of modelling does not deny the process view of language, but abstracts from the operative processes by focusing on their summary outputs.

- *Process models* incorporate discrete or continuous time variables in order to describe stochastic processes proceeding from state to state, where each state is described as a system of qualitative/quantitative variables (e.g., construction length, vocabulary size, etc.). Other than steady state models, this allows direct observation of changes of the focal system variables dependent on state alternation (Brainerd, 1976).

The present chapter complements these classes by a (type of) model which is based on a reconstruction of multi-agent-based language simulations in the framework of synergetic linguistics. This approach goes beyond any simple intersection of both modelling paradigms which can be explained as follows:

- *Other than in classical approaches to multi-agent-based simulations*, constraints regarding the values and distributions of the focal system variables are seen to be *systematically interrelated as constituents of a stratified constraint network*.

- *Other than in classical approaches to synergetic modelling*, processes of agent-based language learning are not abstracted away, but modelled with a resolution down to their input/output in the form of *concrete linguistic units, their relations and cognitive processes operating on them*.

It is the latter extension which demands specifying processes of language learning as they are actually performed by social networks and their constitutive agents. In order to do this, single agent learning has to be distinguished from distributed learning performed by groups of agents. We first consider inductive learning of single agents, leaving out deductive and abductive learning in order to keep the model simple.

Inductive Learning and Routinization

Dealing with learning lexico-grammatical knowledge of single agents, at least three questions have to be dealt with:

- How does an agent acquire knowledge about lexical items, their denotations and interrelating sense relations as they are relevant for him to successfully communicate with other agents of the same speech community?

- How does an agent learn references of utterances, that is, how is their interpretation in concrete communication situations finally grounded in sensory perceptions, collaboration with other agents and other kinds of (distributional) cognition?

- How does an agent acquire syntactical and textual knowledge which allows him to produce/comprehend an infinite number of complex expressions on the basis of finite inventories of linguistic units and encoding means?

These questions refer to learning aspects of structural and referential meaning as well as to the semantic compositionality of complex signs. The following subsections outline first answers in the framework of machine learning and computational linguistics.

Structural Meaning

Latent semantic analysis (LSA) has been proposed as an approach to automatically learning unsystematic sense relations (i.e., contiguity and similarity associations) of lexical units. In the area of lexical ontology learning, this model (or some variant of it) is adapted to derive systematic sense relations (e.g., hyperonymy, synonymy, etc.). Thus, LSA can be seen as a partial answer to the first question. Based on single value decomposition, it proposes a formal mathematical framework for simulating the acquisition of lexical knowledge. More concretely, Landauer and Dumais (1997) propose it as a solution to the knowledge acquisition problem which they describe as follows:

One of the deepest, most persistent mysteries of cognition is how people acquire as much knowledge as they do on the basis of as little information as they get. (Landauer & Dumais, 1997, 212)

The solution Landauer and Dumais (1997) propose is based on the hypothesis that similarity relations of cognitive units result from a *two-level process of inductive learning* starting from the units' contiguity relations. In case of lexical items, these contiguity relations are equated with co-occurrence relations. More specifically, the learning of similarity relations of signs is described as a process of dimensionality reduction, as a result of which similarities of items can be detected even if they do not, or only rarely, co-occur. That is, similarity associations of linguistic items are described as functions of their contiguity associations. According to this model, inductive learning of similarity relations of linguistic items results from exploiting the similarities of their usage contexts.

This and related approaches follow (some variant of) the so-called *weak contextual hypothesis* (Miller & Charles, 1991). It says that the similarity of the contextual representations of words contributes to their semantic similarity. The weak contextual hypothesis can be traced back to Harris' (1954, 156) distributional hypothesis which states that "... difference in meaning correlates with difference of distribution." Likewise following this line of argumentation is Rieger (2002). But instead of conceptualizing the two-stage process of learning in terms of associationism, he refers to the structuralist opposition of syntagmatic and paradigmatic relations. As these relations can be traced back to a cognitive reinterpretation of contiguity and similarity relations (cf. Jakobson, 1971), Rieger's approach coincides with LSA. Nevertheless, there are two differences which support its preference over LSA: First, his model does not amalgamate contiguity and similarity learning in a single step, but rather keeps both steps apart. Second, he endows a single artificial agent with his two-stage induction algorithm in order to let him learn reference relations. Thus, he tackles the first two questions, even if his model leaves out the collaborative learning of reference relations as claimed by answering the second question.

Referential Meaning

An answer to this second question would serve as a solution of the grounding problem (Ziemke, 1999) which is tackled, for example, in the work of Steels (2002, 2004). It will be disregarded in the present chapter; hence we abstract from the referential meaning of linguistic units. Furthermore, we do not model the agents' environments in terms of a model of physical environment. Rather, we restrict the notion of environment to communication systems and social networking, that is, the environment of an agent at a certain space-time location is seen to include those agents with which it participates in the same communication event at this location. In more general terms, environment is seen to be restricted by a social network which thereby also restricts agent interaction and thus communication. Whether it is possible to disregard grounding (as it is tackled in Steels' approach) and to still speak of a valuable simulation is an open question — for a related discussion in the area of artificial life, compare Pattee (1988). The present model also leaves unspecified social behaviour beyond communication and more elaborate cognitive processes as, for example, strategic planning and cooperative interaction in a simulated environment. How to grasp the dynamics of communication as based on environmental dynamics and the latter kind of processes is an open question too, which will need to be answered in order to make simulation models more realistic.[8]

Compositionality

A general contribution to the third question is given by the *principle of compositionality* (CP). It says that the meaning of a complex expression is a function of the meanings of its parts and the way they are combined (Janssen, 1997). In more general terms, a *compositionality theory* is a formal approach describing a family of properties $\{P_i \mid i \in I\}$ belonging to entities of the focal object area as a function of the same or related properties of these entities' constituents and the way they are combined (Kamp & Partee, 1995). The importance of the CP for simulating the acquisition of linguistic knowledge can be justified on grounds of its *empirical* interpretation in cognitive science. More specifically, Fodor and Pylyshyn (1988) ascribe to compositionality the role of a precondition of three fundamental properties of cognitive representations as part of a "language of thought." According to the supposed homomorphism of the language of thought and natural languages (Fodor & McLaughlin, 1995), these properties can be reformulated in terms of natural language sentences:

- *Productivity:* Natural languages allow producing/comprehending an infinite number of complex expressions on the basis of finite inventories of elementary morphological, lexical, syntactical and prosodical inventories.

- *Systematicity:* (The meanings of) natural language sentences are systematically related (on the basis of their constituents and their systematic meanings).[9]

- *Inferrability:* Certain sentences are systematically related with certain systematically reproducible inferences.

According to Fodor and Pylyshyn (1988), these properties presuppose compositionality of the language of thought. Davidson (1994) and Partee (1995) likewise view compositionality as a precondition of the learnability of natural languages, an argumentation which can be traced back to Frege (1966). Hintikka and Kulas (1983) contradict these and related argumentations. They state that compositionality can play the role demanded only in conjunction with context-freeness of sign meaning — a demand which is obviously in contradiction to empirical observations. This contradiction is cleared when reformulating the CP in terms of situation semantics (Barwise & Perry, 1983). In order to do this, the principle's parameters need to be generalized accordingly. Replacing, amongst others, *function* by *relation,* one gets the following reformulation of it, henceforth called CP2 (cf. Mehler, 2005):

The meaning of a linguistic item x is a relation over:

- *its usage-regularities;*
- *its usage contexts as systems of (syntactic dependency and) cohesion and coherence relations to which it participates;*
- *the meanings of its components, the way they are combined; and*
- *described situations.*[10]

The interpretation of x in a given context is the situation it describes subject to concrete values of the latter parameters.

Starting from the relational concept of meaning as defined in situation semantics (Barwise & Perry, 1983), this informal specification introduces two extensions: First, *coherence relations* are additionally referred to as determinants of interpretation. Second, it refers to *usage regularities* according to which the interpretation of lexical items can change their usage conditions and thus their interpretation in subsequent communication situations. In this sense, the CP2 introduces a kind of dynamics which relates to *learning* linguistic knowledge (e.g., routinization, schematization, etc.) and which is left out in the classical reading of the CP.

The present version of the CP2 is underspecified in the sense that it contains several innumerable parameters. Usage regularities, for example, are dynamic entities which cannot be enumerated as lexicon entries. In order to tackle their dynamics, the CP2 needs to be redefined by including *procedural models of cognitive processes* which allow computing parameter values subject to the operative contexts:

The meaning of a linguistic item x is a procedure P generating its interpretation based on its usage regularities, the contexts of its usage, the meanings of its components and the way they are combined.

In order to guarantee interpretability of the measurement operation performed by P, it is required that not only its input and output have modelling function with respect to cognitive entities, but also P with respect to cognitive processes.

In Mehler (2005) the criterion of procedural interpretability is met on grounds of the *constructions-integration* (CI) *theory* of Kintsch (1998). In this model, construction leads to the rather (though not completely) unconstrained generation of possibly incoherent candidate interpretations which are selected in subsequent integration processes in order to derive the most coherent interpretation. Thus, text interpretation is conceived as a process of alternating construction and integration processes, starting with elementary text components and finally integrating — if successful — the input text as a whole.

Comparable to its classical predecessor, the CP2 contains several parameters. This relates to the notion of *context, meaning, linguistic items,* their *components*, the way they are *combined* and the *usage regularities* of elementary items. In Mehler (2005), an instantiation of the CP2 is proposed in terms of a numerical semantics which extends the weak contextual hypothesis of Miller and Charles (1991) to discourse units and thus takes inductive learning of the structural meanings of lexical units into consideration. More-over, it integrates usage regularities of elementary constituents as an additional param-eter and thus accounts for the context-sensitive acquisition of lexical knowledge. Finally, it reconstructs — other than Thagard (2000) — compositionality in the framework of constraint satisfaction by taking integration *and* construction processes into account. This is done by means of operations on semantic spaces, resulting from the two-stage process of inductive learning described above (for details, see Mehler, 2005).

Syntactic Patterns

What is missed in this approach so far is an account of learning syntagmatic patterns (Stubbs, 2001), syntactic patterns and even more complex textual schemata (van Dijk & Kintsch, 1983) which constrain production and comprehension of complex expressions up to whole texts. Although Landauer and Dumais apply their model to learning lexical associations and text similarities only, it is evident how to extend it for learning higher level syntactic patterns. Examples of how this is done are given by Schütze (1997) and Ruge (1995) who apply LSA and related models of similarity associations in order to learn, for example, predicate argument structures and to disambiguate prepositional phrase (PP) attachment. In the present chapter we utilize the framework of Solan et al. (2003). The reason is that it directly builds on Harris's distributional hypothesis in order to develop an algorithm of grammar induction. This algorithm recursively applies the distributional hypothesis that units occurring in the same (or alike) contexts belong to the same category. The algorithm of Solan et al., automatically learns distributional categories and their relations on the basis of a stream of input sentences. Because of its general nature, it is directly applicable to higher level units and thus allows looking forward at learning other than by only syntactical relations (e.g., sentence, text and discourse schemata). This generality makes it suitable for the kind of grammar induction needed in the framework of language learning.

An approach which likewise integrates learning of lexical semantics and grammatical patterns is described by Hashimoto (2002). It can be seen as a reference approach which allows comparative evaluations of newly developed approaches using, for example, different procedural models of learning lexical semantics.

Synthesis

Endowing a single agent with these learning mechanisms, a foundation is laid for his or her solipsistic text comprehension and production. This raises the question of how inductive learning is interrelated with compositional text interpretation. In other words: How are processes of construction and integration interrelated with processes of knowledge activation and expectation-driven information filtering, and how do these processes together interact with learning lexical, syntactical and textual knowledge by a single text processing system? In order to outline an answer, we utilize the text comprehension model of Schmotz (1994) (cf., Figure 1) who distinguishes the text base, the previous knowledge and the mental model (integrating the latter) as subsystems of text comprehension.[11] According to this approach, bottom-up operating processes of knowledge activation have two functions:

- They serve to transfer information (e.g., about previously unknown and unexpected linguistic/thematic/schematic units) from the stream of text comprehension into the long term memory. This transfer results in a modification of memory composition.

- Second, they concern modifications of the memory structure as a result of activation processes which, in the present model, are seen to be implemented by priming processes.[12] This relates to the priming of linguistic knowledge (as induced by the focal text base) and thematic/schematic knowledge (as induced by the active mental model).

Figure 1. The modified diagram of Schnotz (1994) added by pictograms of short and long-term cognitive processes

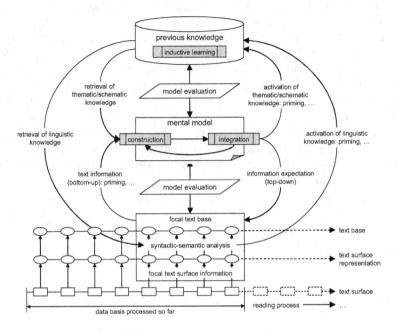

These processes of information transfer and knowledge (pre)activation destabilize the system of previous knowledge which compensates perturbations by means of processes of inductive learning which finally result in modifications of this knowledge base. This affects lexical knowledge as well as syntactical and textual patterns. Beyond that, priming also affects the build-up of mental models. That is, text bases do not only provide informational input for the integration of mental models, but also prime *cotext* (i.e., *linguistic context*) adequate components of them.

Top-down operating processes of knowledge retrieval have equally two functions:

- They provide linguistic, thematic and schematic knowledge as input for the generation of text bases and mental models, respectively.
- Beyond that, knowledge retrieval also provides expectation-driven constraints of text interpretation on both levels.

Following this line of argumentation, *construction* and *integration* occur on the level of the actual-genetic generation of text bases and mental models: Top-down operating retrieval processes provide, together with bottom-up operating priming processes, construction alternatives, where the former also retrieve integration constraints. Successfully integrated units are themselves the starting point of activation and information transfer (from the text base level to the level of mental models, and from there to the knowledge level). On the other hand, inductive learning occurs on the level of onto-genetic knowledge acquisition and maintenance. A central idea of the chapter is that the cooperation/competition of priming, construction and integration is described in summary by the CP2, whereas inductive learning evolves according to the two-stage process of syntagmatic and paradigmatic learning — *on all levels of linguistic resolution.* Of course, this is a simplification regarding the variety of learning. It is indispensable in order to have, firstly, a sufficiently complex learning system which, secondly, allows simulating language learning *without the need to presuppose knowledge on any of these levels and thus without the need to supervise learning.*

Distributed Cognition and Alignment in Communication

The inductive learning model presented so far focuses on single learning agents which produce/process a stream of monological texts, thereby building-up a linguistic knowledge system (including, for example, lexical units, sense relations, syntactic patterns and textual schemata). What is missed in this approach is an account of collaborative, distributive learning, that is, an account of inductive learning distributed over several agents which is both the very condition and the result of their structural, cognitive coupling. To put it in other words: An approach to *organizational, glossogenetic learning* of linguistic structures is needed in addition to a model of ontogenetic learning of a single system as outlined above. Learning linguistic knowledge is now object to the acquisition of a shared lexicon and a shared grammar (Hutchins & Hazlehurst, 2002). In cognitive linguistics, this kind of *distributed learning* can be studied, as far as it is based on dialogical communication in terms of *alignment in communication* (Pickering & Garrod, 2004; Rickheit 2005).

Pickering and Garrod's alignment model describes dialogical communication as a process of mutual structural coupling of interlocutors on various levels of cognitive-linguistic representation. Other than approaches to coordination-by-negotiation, this approach to coordination-by-alignment hypothesizes a great part of structural coupling to be done automatically by means of short-term priming and long-term routinization mechanisms. More specifically, "data transmissions" of interlocutors via a restricted multi-model channel are seen to evoke, maintain and stabilize (if successful) a process of increasing structural coupling, possibly leading to a recurrent coupling of situation models and the generation of dialogue routines. A central advantage of this model is that it does not rely on a notion of strategically, intentionally controlled alignment, but focuses on the emergence of aligned (though not necessarily shared) representations and processing/production routines of different interlocutors.

The alignment model can be utilized as an elementary *interaction model* (Hutchins & Hazlehurst, 2002, 281) which accounts for *collaborative* language production and comprehension. More specifically, it *couples* production and comprehension processes in the sense that, as Pickering and Garrod (2004, 176) put it, the "... interlocutors build up utterances as a joint activity ..., with interlocutors often interleaving production and comprehension tightly." This is the starting point for integrating the dialogical alignment model with the monological model of compositional text comprehension and inductive learning. It has to be accounted for that the input text in Figure (1) is in part generated

Figure 2. Dialogical alignment of two interlocutors

by the processing agent on his own and that his text production/processing is dialogically coupled with at least one other agent so that inter-agent priming occurs according
to Pickering and Garrod's model. If successful, this inter-agent priming invokes an actual-
genetic coupling of the interlocutors' mental models, which may result in an ontogenetic
coupling of their knowledge bases as it is confirmed by subsequent interactions. Figure
2 demonstrates this situation by example of two agents. The interlocking of their text
productions simplifies the interleaving of production and comprehension processes.
This asks for a quantitative, distributional model of turn-taking as an order parameter of
dialogical alignment (see below) which obviously needs to be embedded into a model of

group formation and social networking, allowing the derivation a respective turn-taking distribution for any group of interlocutors.

So far, the interaction model only describes immediate, dialogical communication of agents, which is seen to be further constrained by synergetic order parameters (see Figure 5). These constraints result from its embedding into a model of *distributed interaction* of possibly nested, overlapping groups of agents (see Figure 6). This embedding of the elementary dialogical model of linguistic interaction allows accounting for two related processes (left out in many other approaches to computer-based simulation of language evolution):

- *Mediate learning:* Speech communities with a literary language to allow for the dispensing of the spatiotemporal continuity of text production and reception (Rieger, 2002). That is, interlocutors have the opportunity to learn *mediately* from other agents of the same community, even if they are not physically present in the communication situation, by reading their textual output, whether the writers are still alive or not. In the present framework, this situation is easily integrated by processes of inductive learning embodied by single agents. But in order to do this, we have to know which agents get which textual input by which other agents and with which probability. Generalizing this question, we need to know both: the probability of immediate and of mediate communication. This gives rise finally to the question of social networking.

- *Social networking:* Speech communities do not just consist of randomly chosen pairs of interlocutors. Rather, agents join — in varying roles — different social groups of varying size which are themselves recursively organized into more and more complex, interlinked networks. It is evident that an agent's membership in such groups constrains the probability of his communication with (groups of) other agents. Thus, a model of social networking allows for the deriving of order parameters with the probability of immediate and mediate communication. A candidate model comes from social network theory. It relates to the well known phenomenon of *small worlds*, which have shorter paths than regular graphs and higher cluster coefficients than random graphs (for details cf. Watts & Strogatz, 1998; Watts, 1999).

In the present chapter, we propose utilizing the small world theory as the starting point for deriving order parameters of the probability distribution of groupwise agent communication (see Figure 6). That is, a model of the small world of social networking is seen to allow for specifying the probability by which agents communicate with each other in certain roles.

So far, the synergetic multi-agent model accounts for language learning on three different strata: on the level of single agents, on the level of dialogical systems and on the level of social networks as a whole. The basic idea of the synergetic multi-agent model is to integrate learning processes on these three levels of distributed cognition: as enslaved system variables, as mechanisms of self-regulation/organization or as order parameters in a synergetic network of constraint satisfaction. Thus, an instantiation of this model specifies which input/output units of which cognitive processes of self-regulation/

organization actually serve as microscopic system variables which enslave order parameters.[13] The following section outlines such a separation into explaining and explained variables in detail.

Spanning and Stratifying the Constraint Network

So far, three strata of language learning have been distinguished, on the level of single text processing systems, of systems of dialogical alignment and on the level of the corresponding social network as a whole. This vertical stratification is accompanied by a horizontal stratification distinguishing three perspectives on systems (Rickheit & Strohner, 1992):

1. From the point of view of *tectonics*, the focal system's structural integrity is dealt with. This relates to its composition, i.e., its components, their relations and the system's functional embedding into its environment.

2. From the point of view of *dynamics*, a system's (actual and ontogenetic) self-regulation is dealt with. This relates, more specifically, to processes of compensating perturbations from the system environment, which evoke destabilizing changes of system state. This perspective necessarily concerns the actual-genetic *process view* on a system's information processing.[14]

3. From the point of view of *genetics*, systems are described in terms of (onto- and phylogenetic) self-organization. This also includes the generation of new (sub) systems which are describable regarding their tectonics, dynamics and genetics on their own.[15]

As Rickheit and Strohner (1992) demonstrate, text processing, communication and language systems as a whole can be described along these perspectives. This gives a 3×3 matrix of views on language simulation. We extend this matrix in two respects (see Table 1):

Table 1.Representation levels of simulation models of language evolution

	TECTONICS	DYNAMICS	GENETICS
TEXT SYSTEM	table (4)	table (4)	table (4)
DIALOGUE SYSTEM	table (5)	table (5)	table (5)
Text Network	table (6)	table (6)	table (6)
Social Network	table (6)	table (6)	table (6)
LANGUAGE SYSTEM	table (7)	table (7)	table (7)

- First, a layer of text and social networking is introduced. The reason is twofold: First, dialogically manifested immediate learning operates as a process of self-organization on system variables whose dynamics are partly controlled by the small world of the encompassing social network which constrains, for example, the probability of verbal interaction. This dependence is reflected by introducing the layer of social networking in Table 1. Secondly, textually manifested mediate learning likewise affects system variables, whose dynamics are partly controlled by the small world of the encompassing text network which constrains, for example, the probability of text linkage (e.g., by means of citation relations). This dependence is reflected by introducing the layer of text networking in matrix (1). Consequently, these two types of networks are likewise specified with respect to their tectonics, dynamics and genetics (see Table 4).

- The second further development concerns the specification of each cell of Table 1, not only with respect to its support system (e.g., text, dialogue or language system), but in particular with respect to system variables (modelled, for example, as summary indices or distributions) and cognitive processes operating on them, which serve as candidate order parameters and enslaved system variables, respectively.

These preliminaries allow specifying a stratified synergetic constraint satisfaction process as the procedural kernel of simulations of language evolution: As far as language evolution is concerned, variables of the focal language system (e.g., the composition of its lexicon, the system of its text types, etc. — cf. Table 5) serve as "enslaved" units, whose parameter values are controlled by the dynamics of environmental order parameters. In accordance with Altmann (1985), this environment is seen to be spanned by the speakers/hearers of the corresponding speech community. But other than Altmann, we view it being stratified in the sense of Table 1. That is, we consider it to consist of a system of interlocutors whose (dialogical) text production is controlled by the social network to which they belong. In this sense, the language environment is seen to consist of agents and their mono- and dialogical output, whose environment is, in turn, spanned by the corresponding social network and its textual manifestation in the form of a text network. This has important consequences regarding the status of the language system to be simulated: Other than Köhler (1987, 1993), we do not consider it to be directly affected by environmental system needs whose procedural organization is — just as their corresponding language internal mechanisms of self-organization — abstracted away. Rather, the social network is (together with its textual manifestation) seen as enslaving the distributed system of speakers/hearers of the corresponding speech community. Consequently, parameter values of the focal language system are seen to be epiphenomenal with respect to these dynamics. At the same time, this conception allows specifying all processes of self-regulation and organization in terms of concrete cognitive processes which the enslaved systems invoke in order to compensate perturbations from their environment.[16] In other words: In the present framework, models of self-regulation and organization are introduced as models of agent internal cognitive processes (of language processing and learning), whereas social network internal processes are conceived as procedural order parameters. Finally, language internal processes, as described for example by Ricœur (1976), are seen as epiphenomenal abstractions of these latter processes.

Table 2 .Views on single text processing systems and their textual input/output

SYSTEM LEVEL	TECTONICS	DYNAMICS	GENETICS
Support System	a mental model resulting / underlying text processing / production	a text comprehension or production process of a single agent	the cognitive learning apparatus of a single agent
Microscopic System Variables:			
Attributes and Indices	**expression plane:** • text vocabulary size • segment length • text length and Zipfian number • Markov order of text structuring • … **content plane:** • genre and register affiliation (w.r.t field, tenor and mode) • number of topics • readability, activity… • …	• short term memory size • balance between compositionality and contextuality • processing time • cognitive capacity / cognitive load • Markov order of text processing / production • …	• long term memory size (lexicon size, etc.) • balance between analytic / synthetic and idiomatic means of encoding • learner age / learning capacity / duration / transfer rate / etc. • learning periodicity • learnable "grammar" type • …
Distributions	• frequency structure or spectrum of text units • length distribution of text units • preference ordering of topics … • …	• Markov processes on various language levels • vocabulary growth • periodicity (repetition / clustering / aggregation of identical / alike elements) • …	• parameterization and transition between distributions • …
Mechanisms of Self-Regulation (Dynamics) and -Organization (Genetics):			
Processes	• procedural organization of the operative mechanisms • …	• construction and integration • evaluation and reparation • lexical, syntactic, semantical and textual priming • information percolation between different processing levels • …	• memorization, inventarization, superization, idiomatization, routinization (as the long-term correspondent of priming) and schematization • (two-level) inductive learning of lexico-grammatical patterns (e.g., grammar and text schema induction) • synergetic balancing between functional equivalents of encoding • diversification, unification • …

But how do co-enslaving constraints interact in this model? And how do we know whether the simulation is valid? It is now that synergetic linguistics comes into play again. According to its terminology, we have to distinguish (i) system internal processes adapting (ii) system variables according to the dynamics of (iii) certain order parameters which may be given by system variables or processes on their own.[17] In this scenario,

Figure 3. Comparison of the agent-abstracting model of synergetic linguistics and the agent-including model of synergetic simulation of language evolution

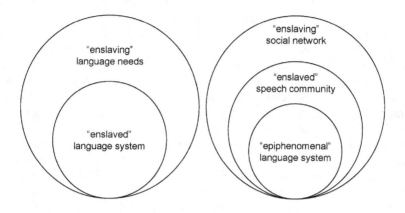

the role of synergetic constraints can be explained as follows: System variables span constraint networks restricting each other's parameter values. The smaller the inventory of phonemes of a language, for example, the longer the average length of its words. Interrelations of this kind can be seen to be mediated by the impact of system needs. In the present example, the need for minimizing the effort of language production and of memorizing signs ask for shorter words (Köhler, 1986). A central insight of synergetic linguistics is that such interrelationships are common and thus span dense networks of constraints on the values of system variables (e.g., lexicon size, polylexy or polytexty). From the point of view of evaluation, this has important consequences:

- If a system variable *is not included* into the simulation, that is, if there is no order parameter included into the simulator, whose (im)mediate impact on this variable is simulated (or if its values are not pre-established by the modeller), the value taken by this variable as a result of simulation runs can be compared with the observed/ expected value of the corresponding variable in the simulated (class of) system(s), provided that the initial conditions of the simulator and its simulation time measure a certain state of the (class of) simulated system(s) and a certain period of its lifetime, respectively. In this case, a correspondence, but not necessarily a similarity as claimed by Gilbert and Troitzsch (1999), between the *uncontrolled* and the *simulated* variable is a touchstone of simulation validity. That is, knowledge about a language subsystem behaving in a certain way and a simulation of this behaviour in which certain parameter values *emerge* as valuable measurements of certain simulated variables can be used as an indicator of simulation quality: If the correspondence is missed, the simulation is *falsified*, otherwise it is *not falsified*, but nothing more. According to synergetics, emergence means, amongst other things, that the parameter value of the corresponding system variable is neither predetermined by the modeller, nor determined by the operative order parameters.

A prominent example is the emergence of compositionality in the experiments of Kirby and Hurford (2002).

- If instead, the impact of competing/cooperating order parameters on the focal variable is part of the simulation, that is, if the modeller specifies the way they (in)directly affect its parameter values, three constellations of constraint satisfaction can be distinguished: on the level of interrelations of microscopic system variables, on the level of macroscopic order parameters and on the level of interrelations of these two levels. Köhler (1987) models these interrelations as functions in order to derive the controlled variables' values by means of value insertions. Grounding instead models of self-regulation and organization in models of cognitive processes of short-term priming and of long-term routinization, of text comprehension/production and of alignment, we propose to run simulations of the competition/cooperation of order parameters which derive *simulated data* regarding the composition of the lexico-grammatical system of the simulated (class of) language, which finally allows deriving summary indices as, for example, "lexicon size" and "polylexy." In this case, the pre-established parameter values and distributions serve as constraints on simulation runs.

In both scenarios, an evaluation of a simulation model also means an evaluation of the implementations of the cognitive processes included. But, as synergetic linguistics teaches, observing system variables in isolation does not suffice to evaluate a system. Consequently, the next modelling step concerns the specification of system variables, order parameters *and their interrelations*.[18] Quantitative linguistics and soft computing offer a great variety of choices for modelling them as univariate, bivariate or multivariate indices, as distributions and feature spaces or as systems of fuzzy rules and related systems of structure modelling (Mehler, 2004). If, for example, word length is considered as a system variable, it may be modelled by means of a statistical moment of a certain distribution or by the distribution itself. The Tables 2-5 make these distinctions on the levels of indices, distributions and multidimensional feature spaces, and map them onto the respective strata and system perspectives as distinguished in Table 1.

These considerations allow us to finally specify: A *synergetic multi-agent simulation model* is a four level multi-agent simulation model whose runs produce simulated data fitting a system of indices, distributions, etc. which independently characterizes the class of natural languages. Independently means that the validity of this system is confirmed by independent linguistic investigations on the synergetic nature of natural languages. A synergetic multi-agent simulation model thus includes (i) the microscopic level of single information processing (i.e., text and dialogue processing/producing) agents (Table 2) which are (ii) dialogically aligned in communication processes (Table 3) enslaved (iii) by the macroscopic social system in which the agents participate (Table 4) and whose countless communication acts shape (iv) their language as an epiphenomenal system whose attributes aggregate the corresponding attributes of the single agents (Table 5).

Table 3. Views on alignment systems and their dialogical manifestations

SYSTEM LEVEL	TECTONICS	DYNAMICS	GENETICS
Support System	an alignment model of a conversation of at least two interlocutors	an alignment process implemented by at least two interlocutors	a distributed cognitive system of at least two interlocutors
Microscopic System Variables			
Attributes and Indices	**field:** • number of topics communicated • ... **tenor:** • number, roles and relations of interlocutors • number of turns • ... **mode:** • modes and media • direct / indirect communication • ...	• Markov order of turn taking • inter-interlocutor latency, duration of priming • duration of communication • ...	• long term memory size (latency of models of interlocutors) • ...
Distributions	**field:** • topic distribution • ... **tenor:** • distribution of roles • distribution of turns • length distribution of turns • ... **mode:** • distribution of modes and media • ...	• Markov process of turn taking • periodicity (repetition, clustering and aggregation of like elements) across turn taking • ...	• parameterization and transition between distributions • ...
Mechanisms of Self-Regulation (Dynamics) and -Organization (Genetics):			
Processes	• procedural organization of the operative mechanisms • ...	• interpersonal alignment • cooperative evaluation and reparation • interpersonal lexical, syntactic and semantic priming between interlocutors • information percolation between alignment levels • ...	• cooperative memorization, inventarization, superization, idiomatization, routinization (as the long-term correspondent of priming) and schematization • interpersonal learning of dialogue routines, ... • synergetic balancing between functional equivalent modes in a multi-modal setting • ...

Table 4. Views on social networks and their textual/dialogical manifestations

SYSTEM LEVEL	TECTONICS	DYNAMICS	GENETICS
Support System	a cognitively distributed model of a text network	a short-term networking process of a speech community	the long-term learning apparatus of a speech community
Macroscopic Order Parameters			
Attributes and Indices	**expression plane (text network):** • number of nodes, hubs, edges, components, … • cluster coefficient, compactness • average path length, diameter • … **content plane (genre and register level):** • number of genres, registers, text types • …	• network latency • flow rate and velocity of topical, thematic propagation • Markov order of text chain and cluster formation • growth rate of text chains (of registers (thematic fields) and genres) • social permeability, openness, • …	• size of long-term cultural memory (capacity to invent different genres, registers and their relations) • birth- and mortality rate of registers (thematic fields) and genres • …
Distributions	**expression plane:** • distribution of component size, text chain length, node connectivity, clustering, centrality and prestige, of path length, … • distribution of main- and borderlines, branch points, … • … **content plane:** • preference order of genres / registers, • stratification, nesting of genres / registers • …	• Markov processes on text chain continuation, … • temporal organization of text chains • distribution of the growth rate • periodicity of thematization / topicalization (repetition, clustering, aggregation of alike text network components) • …	• distribution of birth, growth maturity, decay of genres, registers, text types, … • …
Mechanisms of Self-Regulation (Dynamics) and -Organization (Genetics):			
Processes	• procedural organization of the operative mechanisms • …	• initiation, continuation, combination, parallelization, …, termination of text chains • inserting, replacing, deleting, rewiring, linking, clustering, … of textual/dialogical units … • …	• conventionalization • inductive learning of types of single texts, of text chains, clusters, of (sub-) network types, … • synergetic balancing of the system of genres, registers and text types • …

Table 5. Views on language systems

SYSTEM LEVEL	TECTONICS	DYNAMICS	GENETICS
Support System	language system	language use	language change
Simulated, Epiphenomenal Microscopic System Variables			
Indices	• lexicon size • average unit (word, phrase, sentence, text …) and length • average polylexy • average polytexty • rate of neologisms • rate of idiomatization • degree of compositionality • number of genres, registers and text types • …	• polytexty rate of change • order of Markov processes of the genre- / register-sensitive usage of linguistic items • …	• Polylexy rate of change invention / durability / shrinking rate of linguistic items, attributes and categories … • velocity of propagation and propagation rate of new linguistic items, attributes and categories … • rate of change of the fractions of morphological, lexical, syntactical and prosodical encoding means • …
Distributions	• Zipf's laws • length distributions • semantic and formal diversification / unification • distribution of the fractions of morphological, lexical, syntactical and prosodical encoding means • distribution of linguistic units and pattern units over special languages • …	• distribution of general and genre-/register-specific lexical units • Markov processes of the genre-/register-sensitive usage of linguistic items • distribution of the changes of polytexty • …	• age distribution of linguistic units • distribution of the polytexty changes • word formation and loaning (Piotrowski's law) • time distribution of the fractions of morphological, lexical, syntactical and prosodical encoding means • …
Structures and Processes	• kernel vocabulary, technical terminologies and special languages and lexical fields • lexico-grammar • text types • …	• percolation of items between different word fields • …	• invention of new lexico-grammatical and textual categories, patterns and schemata • invention, termination, fusion and splitting of lexical fields • …

Constraint Networking in a Zipfian Perspective

In the last section, social networks were described as providing order parameters with respect to the strata of monological and dialogical text processing. It was further argued that constraint networks operate on these three strata. Polytexty, for example, interrelates with polylexy which, on its part, interrelates with lexicon size (Köhler, 1986). This section sheds more light on this kind of constraint networking on the level of order parameters and microscopic system variables. This is done by focusing on lexical meaning, that is, on lexical relations of the content and expression plane.

According to Tuldava (1998), distributions of semiotic units tend to follow a preference ordering along decreasing importance. He refers to Zipf's first law (Zipf, 1972) as an example of this more general law of *semiotic preference order*. It describes a topological invariant which seems to play a comparative role in quantitative descriptions of social systems as the Gaussian distribution with respect to natural systems. Zipf-like distributions also play an invaluable role in constraining and evaluating simulations of language systems. Consequently, Table 5 mentions Zipf's law (on the relationship of rank and frequency) and (the law of) semantic diversification on a certain relation of expression and content plane. As Zipf's consideration on linguistic frequency distributions have already been utilized for constraining the initial conditions of simulations of language evolution (Kirby & Hurford, 2002), we now place emphasis on the integration of preference orderings into the framework of synergetic constraint satisfaction. This is done with respect to *semantic diversification* (Altmann, 1991) on the level of single linguistic items and on the level of the lexical system as a whole.

Altmann (1996) explains the process of semantic diversification as follows: At the time of their emergence, lexical items are in a state of semantic unification, that is, they have only one meaning. As their frequency of usage in ever-changing communication situations increases, they tend to adopt additional meanings in order to meet the speakers' need for minimizing encoding effort. If this process evolved without restraint, it would result in a system-wide semantic diversification in which as few lexical items as possible manifest as many meanings as are needed to encode. In this case, the polysemy of lexical items would increase on average. But diversification is opposed by unification processes which tend to decrease polysemy in order to meet the hearers' need for minimizing decoding effort. As a consequence of an unrestricted evolvement of unification, more and more items would carry less and less meanings. It is assumed that the competition of these opposing needs results in a dynamic equilibrium which is characterized by rank frequency distributions where — from the point of view of a single item — the empirically most frequent (theoretically most probable) meaning has the first rank, and the most infrequent meanings take up the lowest ranks. Distributions of this sort model a characteristic decrease in probability which guarantees that in cases of a decoding error (if the first option of highest rank fails) the proximate choice still has the same degree of differentiability compared to the remaining options. In other words, probability distributions are assumed which keep constant a high "recall rate" in case of successive decoding errors along the ranked meanings. From the point of view of the hearer, such distributions decrease the effort of decoding compared to rectangular distributions characterizing highly polysemous units. From the point of view of the speaker, such distributions decrease the effort of encoding compared to unambiguous items.

As theses processes are distributed over all communication situations in which speakers/hearers of the corresponding speech community participate, they distinguish two perspectives: Whereas Altmann (1991) focuses on the semantic diversification of single units in isolation, it is the distribution of meanings over all lexical units which is studied by Krylov's *law of polysemy*. According to Krylov (1982), the distribution of the number f_x of lexical items with exactly x meanings, $x = 1, 2, \ldots$, shows concentration and dispersion effects as they are characteristic of diversification processes. Krylov hypothesizes that the number of polysemous words decreases according to a geometric progression with their number of meanings so that the set of unambiguous items covers 50 percent of the lexicon, the set of items with exactly two meanings 25 percent and so on till the set of most polysemous words is reached covering only a tiny fraction of the lexicon. This relationship is described by the formula:

$$P_x = 2^{-x} \tag{1}$$

where P_x is the probability of randomly choosing a lexical item with exactly x meanings from the lexicon of the focal language. According to this model, Krylov hypothesizes that natural language words have on average two meanings.

Semantic diversification of single units and of the lexical system as a whole is complemented by inverse processes of synonym formation — on the level of single meanings and the meaning system as a whole (Altmann, 1996).[19] Whereas hypotheses on semantic diversification have already been confirmed in many empirical studies, their counterparts regarding formal diversification have not.

Now the question arises how polysemy and synonymy on a system level interact with semantic and formal diversification on the level of system components. That is, we ask how regularities on these different levels *constrain each other*. In order to keep things simple, we abstract away from the stratification of the lexicon according to common and genre/register specific vocabularies. This allows reformulating the latter question by means of Table 6 which opposes lexical units $x_1, \ldots, x_m$ by meanings $M_1, \ldots, M_n$, abstracting from any concrete definition of what meaning is as well as from meaning relations as they are demanded by the purpose of getting a simplified picture of the whole landscape.

Next, we hypothesize that x_i is the ith most frequently used lexical item and M_j the jth most frequently coded meaning of the focal language L. Consequently, x_1 is the most frequently used item and M_1 the most frequently encoded meaning in L. In other words, it is hypothesized that — as predicted by the impact of diversification and unification

Table 6. A two-dimensional distribution of units of content and expression plane

	M_1	M_2	M_3	...	M_n
x_1	f_{11}	...			f_{1n}
x_2	$\vdots$	$\ddots$			
x_3					
$\vdots$					
x_m	f_{m1}				f_{mn}

on the expression and content plane of L — the most "important" meaning of a language is encoded by its most frequent word which, according to Köhler (1987), is also supposed to be (one of) the shortest items in the lexicon. Moreover, following the considerations on semantic diversification of single lexical units, it is implied that rows of matrix (2) tend by the majority to manifest a monotonously falling rank frequency distribution (supposing that those cells are disregarded for which $f_{ij} = 0, i \in \{1,...,m\}, j \in \{1,...,n\}$).[20] The same kind of consideration also relates to the content plane, and thus to the expectation of monotonously decreasing frequency distributions manifested by the columns of matrix (2). Further, we can assume that the marginal distribution of lexical items $x_1, ..., x_m$ follows a variant of Zipf's law and that the marginal distribution of meaning units $M_1, ..., M_n$ analogously follows a frequency distribution. Moreover, if we apply a function to any cell of matrix (2) which decides for any frequency f_{ij} whether item x_i should count as having meaning M_j, it is evident that this matrix also derives a distribution whose fitting with formula (1) can be tested. As far as all these assumed distributions are valid, an interrelation of semantic diversification on the level of single units and the law of polysemy can be stated too. These considerations finally raise the question for the kind of two-dimensional distribution of the total system of lexical units and lexically coded meanings of L. That is, we can ask whether interdependencies of all diversification and unification processes are integrated by a single two-dimensional distribution. In order to make this model more realistic, the stratification of both planes according to the operative system of genres and registers (and their linguistic manifestations in the form of text types) has to be considered too. That is, we expect not a single two-dimensional distribution, but a system of them according to the distribution of language over these genres and registers, respectively. Nevertheless, each of these subsystem-specific distributions is expected to show the same kind of regularities and interdependencies as described so far. Thus, the evolvement of the genre/register system has to be considered a further level of synergetic constraint networking.[21]

These considerations show a remarkable interweaving of constraints regarding the distribution of lexical units and their meanings, which have to be reproduced by language simulations as far as these distributional hypotheses are empirically and sufficiently confirmed. As explained above, this includes semantic and formal diversification of single lexical items and meaning units as well as diversification on the level of the lexicon as a whole. This also includes the Zipfian gestalt of the frequency distribution of lexical units, its analogue on content plane and Krylov's considerations on the distribution of polysemy. It additionally includes Köhler's study on the relation of item frequency and item length and thus indirectly relates formal and semantic attributes. Following the line of argumentation of the last section, any specific simulation experiment has to decide *ex ante* which of these variables is controlled by which order parameters and which of them are left out as touchstones for a subsequent evaluation. The key point now is that whatever decision is made, synergetic linguistics places emphasis on a further level of evaluation: Although a simulation may result in simulated data which obey these distributions separately, it may nevertheless be the case that their interdependencies are not met — in contradiction to what is known about these interdependencies. In other words, obeying a distributional constraint is only a necessary, but not a sufficient, condition as long as their synergetic interdependencies are not taken into consideration.

These considerations motivate a sequence of stages of evaluation:

1. In this sequence, the lowest level of validity is reached if the simulated data only fit a single (probability) distribution in the sense that the differences of the simulated distribution and the one derived from theoretical and confirmed by empirical investigations (independently from the simulation) are statistically insignificant.[22]

2. This validity is augmented to the rate that more and more distribution models of the latter kind are fitted.

3. As long as the distributions are met independently form each other, a further level of validity is still missed which relates to the synergetic interdependencies of the distributions restricting their specific parameters.[23]

According to the varying numbers of distributions and their possible synergetic constraints, which are included as variables into the second and third stage of this sequence, this coarse-grained graduation can be further subdivided. Evidently, the system of indices and distributions characterizing the epiphenomenal language system layer is a valuable candidate for such evaluations.

Conclusion

This chapter presented a first attempt in systematizing the strata, order parameters and system variables of a simulation model of language evolution which finally grounds mechanisms of self-organization and regulation in cognitive processes of inductive learning — *on the level of single agents and on the level of alignment in communication.* Following this line of argumentation, Section (4) exemplified a network of lexical-semantic system variables. It shows that the values they take by simulation runs cannot serve as a touchstone for the validity of the simulation model *as long as they are analyzed in isolation,* nor can they — for the very same reason — constrain the simulation separately if they are included as order parameters. Rather, system variables are synergetically interlinked and thus need to be observed in accordance with this network. This can be seen as making a speech for a cooperation of research in synergetic linguistics and machine learning in order to implement this new kind of simulation model of language evolution. As such, simulations indispensably include models of inductive learning of linguistic knowledge; they do not need to presuppose this knowledge and thus can perform without supervised learning. Such a simulation model prospectively integrates synergetic and fuzzy linguistics in order to reconstruct synergetic order parameters and their impact on system variables by means of fuzzy constraints.

Acknowledgment

Many thanks go to Reinhard Köhler and Burghard Rieger for their support on thinking about opening synergetic linguistics and fuzzy linguistics to computer-based simulations in the framework of *multi*-agent modelling and to the anonymous reviewers for their useful hints and comments to the present work.

References

Altmann, G. (1985). On the dynamic approach to language. In T.T. Ballmer (Ed.), *Linguistic dynamics. Discourses, procedures and evolution* (pp. 181-189). Berlin-New York: de Gruyter.

Altmann, G. (1991). Modelling diversification phenomena in language. In U. Rothe (Ed.), *Diversification processes in language: Grammar* (pp. 33-46). Medienverlag, Hagen, The Netherlands: Margit Rottmann.

Altmann, G. (1996). Diversification processes of the word. In *Glottometrika 15* (pp. 102-111). WVT: Trier.

Altmann, G., & Köhler, R. (1996). "Language forces" and synergetic modelling of language phenomena. In *Glottometrika 15* (pp. 62-76). Bochum: Brockmeyer,.

Andersen, P. B. (2000). Genres as self-organising systems. In P.B. Andersen, C. Emmeche, N.O. Finnemann, & P.V. Christiansen (Eds.), *Downward causation: Minds, bodies and matter* (pp. 214-260). Aarhus: Aarhus University Press.

Barwise, J., & Perry, J. (1983). *Situations and attitudes.* Cambridge, MA: MIT Press.

Batali, J. (1998). Computational simulations of the emergence of grammar. In J. R. Hurford, M. Studdert-Kennedy, & C. Knight (Eds.), *Approaches to the evolution of language* (pp. 405-426). Cambridge: Cambridge University Press.

Brainerd, B. (1976). On the Markov nature of the text. *Linguistics, 176,* 5-30.

Cangelosi, A., Greco, A., & Harnad, S. (2002). Symbol grounding and the symbolic theft hypothesis. In A. Cangelosi & D. Parisi (Eds.), *Simulating the evolution of language* (pp. 191-210). London: Springer Verlag.

Cangelosi, A., & Parisi, D. (2002a). Computer simulation: A new scientific approach to the study of language evolution. In A. Cangelosi & D. Parisi (Eds.), *Simulating the evolution of language* (pp. 3-28). London: Springer.

Cangelosi, A., & Parisi, D. (Eds.). (2002b). *Simulating the evolution of language.* London: Springer.

Christiansen, M. H., & Kirby, S. (2003). Language evolution: Consensus and controversies. *Trends in Cognitive Sciences, 7(7),* 300-307.

Davidson, D. (1994). *Wahrheit und Interpretation.* Frankfurt am Main, Germany: Suhrkamp.

Ferrer i Chancho, R., Riordan, O., & Bollobas, B. (2005). The consequences of Zipf's law for syntax and symbolic reference. *Proceedings of the Royal Society, 272*, 561-565.

Fodor, J. A., & McLaughlin, B. P. (1995). Connectionism and the problem of systematicity: Smolensky's solution doesn't work. In C. MacDonald & G. MacDonald (Eds.), *Connectionism: Debates on psychological explanation* (pp. 199-222). Blackwell.

Fodor, J. A., & Pylyshyn, Z.W. (1988). Connectionism and cognitive architecture: A critical analysis. *Cognition, 28*(1-2), 3-71.

Frege, G. (1966). *Logische Untersuchungen*. Göttingen: Vandenhoeck & Ruprecht.

Gilbert, N., & Troitzsch, K. G. (1999). *Simulation for the social scientist*. Buckingham: Open University Press.

Haken, H. (1998). Can we apply synergetics to the human sciences? In G. Altmann & W.A. Koch (Eds.), *Systems: New paradigms for human sciences*. Berlin; New York: de Gruyter.

Harris, Z. S. (1954). Distributional structure. *Word, 10*, 146-162.

Hashimoto, T. (2002). The constructive approach to the dynamical view of language. In A. Cangelosi & D. Parisi, D. (Eds.), *Simulating the evolution of language* (pp. 307-324). London: Springer Verlag.

Hintikka, J., & Kulas, J. (1983). *The game of language*. Dordrecht: Reidel.

Hollan, J., Hutchins, E., & Kirsh, D. (2000). Distributed cognition: Toward a new foundation for human-computer interaction research. *ACM Transaction on Computer-Human Interaction, 7*(2), 174-196.

Hutchins, E., & Hazlehurst, B. (2002). Auto-organization and emergence of shared language structure. In A. Cangelosi & D. Parisi (Eds.), *Simulating the evolution of language* (pp. 279-306). London: Springer Verlag.

Jakobson, R. (1971). *Selected writings II: Word and language*. The Hague: Mouton.

Janssen, T. M. V. (1997). Compositionality (with an appendix by Barbara H. Partee). In J. van Benthem & A. ter Meulen (Eds.), *Handbook of logic and language* (pp. 417-473). Amsterdam: Elsevier.

Kamp, H., & Partee, B. (1995). Prototype theory and compositionality. *Cognition, 57*(2), 129-191.

Kintsch, W. (1998). *Comprehension: A paradigm for cognition*. Cambridge: Cambridge University Press.

Kintsch, W. (2001). Predication. *Cognitive Science, 25*, 173-202.

Kirby, S. (2002). Natural language from artificial life. *Artificial Life, 8*(2), 185-215.

Kirby, S., & Hurford, J. R. (2002). The emergence of linguistic structure: An overview of the iterated learning model. In A. Cangelosi & D. Parisi (Eds.), *Simulating the evolution of language* (pp. 121-148). London: Springer Verlag.

Köhler, R. (1986). *Zur linguistischen synergetik: Struktur und Dynamik der Lexik*. Bochum: Brockmeyer.

Köhler, R. (1987). Systems theoretical linguistics. *Theoretical Linguistics, 14*(2, 3), 241-257.

Köhler, R. (1993). Synergetic linguistics. In R. Köhler & B.B. Rieger (Eds.), *Contributions to quantitative linguistics* (pp. 41-51). Dordrecht: Kluwer.

Köhler, R. (1999). Syntactic structures: Properties and interrelations. *Journal of Quantitative Linguistics, 6,* 46-57.

Krylov, J. K. (1982). Eine Untersuchung statistischer Gesetzmäßigkeiten auf der paradigmatischen Ebene der Lexik natürlicher Sprachen. In H. Guiter & M.V. Arapov (Eds.), *Studies on Zipf's law* (pp. 234-262). Bochum: Brockmeyer.

Landauer, T. K., & Dumais, S. T. (1997). A solution to Plato's problem: The latent semantic analysis theory of acquisition, induction, and representation of knowledge. *Psychological Review, 104*(2), 211-240.

Maturana, H. R., & Varela, F. J. (1980). *Autopoiesis and Cognition: The realization of the living.* Dordrecht: Reidel.

Mehler, A. (2004). Quantitative methoden. In H. Lobin & L. Lemnitzer (Eds.), *Texttechnologie: Perspektiven und Anwendungen* (pp. 83-107). Tübingen: Stauffenburg.

Mehler, A. (2005). Compositionality in numerical text semantics. In A. Mehler & R. Köhler (Eds.), *Aspects of automatic text analysis: Studies in fuzziness and soft computing.* Berlin: Springer.

Miller, G. A., & Charles, W. G. (1991). Contextual correlates of semantic similarity. *Language and Cognitive Processes, 6*(1),1-28.

Partee, B. H. (1995). Lexical semantics and compositionality. In L.R. Gleitman & M. Liberman (Eds.), *Language: An invitation to cognitive science* (vol. 1, pp. 311-360). Cambridge: MIT Press.

Pattee, H. H. (1988). Simulations, realizations, and theories of life. In C.G. Langton (Ed.), *Artificial life: SFI studies in the sciences of complexity* (pp. 63-77). Redwood: Addison-Wesley.

Pickering, M. J., & Garrod, S. (2004). Toward a mechanistic psychology of dialogue. *Behavioral and Brain Sciences, 27,* 169-226.

Rickheit, G. (2005). Alignment und Aushandlung im Dialog. *Zeitschrift für Psychologie, 213*(3), 159-166.

Rickheit, G., & Strohner, H. (1992). Towards a cognitive theory of linguistic coherence. *Theoretical Linguistics, 18,* 209-237.

Ricœur, P. (1976*). Interpretation theory: Discourse and the surplus of meaning.* Fort Worth: The Texas Christian University Press.

Rieger, B. B. (1989). *Unscharfe Semantik: Die empirische Analyse, quantitative Beschreibung, formale Repräsentation und prozedurale Modellierung vager Wortbedeutungen in Texten.* Frankfurt am Main: Peter Lang.

Rieger, B. B. (2001). Computing granular word meanings: A fuzzy linguistic approach in computational semiotics. In P. Wang (Ed.), *Computing with words* (pp. 147-208). New York: John Wiley & Sons.

Rieger, B. B. (2002). Semiotic cognitive information processing: Learning to understand discourse. A systemic model of meaning constitution. In R. Kühn, R. Menzel, W.

Menzel, U. Ratsch, M.M. Richter, & I.O. Stamatescu (Eds.), *Perspectives on adaptivity and learning* (pp. 47-403). Berlin: Springer.

Riegler, A., Peschl, M., & von Stein, A. (Eds.). (1999). *Understanding representation in the cognitive sciences: Does representation need reality?* New York; Boston; Dordrecht: Kluwer-Plenum.

Ruge, G. (1995). *Wortbedeutung und Termassoziation: Methoden zur automatischen semantischen Klassifikation.* Hildesheim: Olms.

Schnotz, W. (1994). *Aufbau von Wissensstrukturen: Untersuchungen zur Kohärenzbildung beim Wissenserwerb mit Texten.* Weinheim, Germany: Beltz.

Schütze, H. (1997). *Ambiguity resolution in language learning: Computational and cognitive models, Vol. 71, CSLI Lecture Notes.* Stanford: CSLI Publications.

Searle, J. R. (1980). Minds, brains, and programs. *The Behavioral and Brain Sciences, 3,* 417-457.

Smolensky, P. (1995a). On the proper treatment of connectionism. In M. Donald & G. MacDonald (Eds.), *Connectionism: Debates on psychological explanation* (vol. 2, pp. 28-89). Oxford: Blackwell.

Smolensky, P. (1995b). Connectionism, constituency and the language of thought. In M. Donald & G. MacDonald (Eds.), *Connectionism: Debates on psychological explanation* (vol. 2, pp. 164-198). Oxford: Blackwell.

Solan, Z., Ruppin, E., Horn, D., & Edelman, S. (2003). Automatic acquisition and efficient representation of syntactic structures. In S. Thrun (Ed.), *Advances in neural information processing* (vol. 15). Cambridge: MIT Press.

Steels, L. (1996). Self-organising vocabularies. In C. Langton & T. Shimohara (Eds.), *Proceedings of Artificial Life V.* Japan: Nara.

Steels, L. (1998). Synthesizing the origins of language and meaning using coevolution, self-organization and level formation. In J.R. Hurford, M. Studdert-Kennedy, & C. Knight (Eds.), *Approaches to the evolution of language* (pp. 384-404). Cambridge: Cambridge University Press.

Steels, L. (2000). The puzzle of language evolution. *Kognitionswissenschaft, 8,* 143-150.

Steels, L. (2002). Grounding symbols through evolutionary language games. In A. Cangelosi & D. Parisi (Eds.), *Simulating the evolution of language* (pp. 211-226). London: Springer Verlag.

Steels, L. (2004, July 21-26). Constructivist development of grounded construction grammars. In W. Daelemans (Ed.), *Proceedings of the 42nd Annual Meeting of the Association for Computational Linguistics* (pp. 9-16). Barcelona, Spain.

Stubbs, M. (2001). On inference theories and code theories: Corpus evidence for semantic schemas. *Text, 21*(3), 437-465.

Thagard, P. (2000). *Coherence in thought and action.* Cambridge, MA: MIT Press.

Tuldava, J. (1998). *Probleme und Methoden der quantitativ-systemischen Lexikologie.* Trier: WVT.

Turner, H. (2002). An introduction to methods for simulating the evolution of language. In A. Cangelosi & D. Parisi (Eds.), *Simulating the evolution of language* (pp. 29-50). London; Berlin: Springer.

van Dijk, T. A., & Kintsch, W. (1983). *Strategies of discourse comprehension.* New York: Academic Press.

Vogt, P. (2004). Minimum cost and the emergence of the Zipf-Mandelbrot law. In J. Pollack, M. Bedau, P. Husbands, T. Ikegami, & R.A. Watson (Eds.), *Artificial life IX: Proceedings of the ninth international conference on the simulation and synthesis of living systems.* Cambridge, MA: MIT Press.

Watts, D. J. (1999). *Small worlds: The dynamics of networks between order and randomness.* Princeton: Princeton University Press.

Watts, D. J., & Strogatz, S. H. (1998). Collective dynamics of "small-world" networks. *Nature, 393,* 440-442.

Zadeh, L. A. (1997). Toward a theory of fuzzy information granulation and its centrality in human reasoning and fuzzy logic. *Fuzzy Sets and Systems, 90,* 111-127.

Ziemke, T. (1999). Rethinking grounding. In A. Riegler, M. Peschl, & A. von Stein (Eds.), *Understanding representation in the cognitive sciences: Does representation need reality?* (pp. 177-190). New York; Boston; Dordrecht: Kluwer-Plenum.

Zipf, G. K. (1972). *Human behavior and the principle of least effort: An introduction to human ecology.* New York: Hafner Publishing Company.

Endnotes

[1]   The present chapter argues the possibility of computer-based realizations of natural language evolution. This means to refuse the view that the simulating system has essentially the same properties as the simulated one (instead of only having modelling function with respect to the latter). To put it in other terms: As a computer simulation of weather systems does not realize, but only simulates weather, we do not assume to realize natural languages.

[2]   See also the "Language Evolution and Computation Bibliography" (http://www.isrl.uiuc.edu/~amag/langev/index.html) which collects relevant papers.

[3]   That is, language evolution is described on at least three different time-scales (Kirby, 2002) so that simulation models face the problem of interrelating these different scales.

[4]   The semantic space model is a refence model for mapping a certain meaning aspect in cognitive linguistics (Kintsch, 2001) and computational linguistics (Rieger, 2001, 2002). It will be explained in more detail next.

[5]   Generally speaking, coherence means being connected. In cognitive linguistics (Kintsch, 1998) it is a well established term which is referred to, for example, in order to distinguish a random sequence of sentences from natural language texts.

[6]   Since Thagard presupposes the order of elements in a constraint to be irrelevant, we represent these constraints as sets.

[7]   By the latter phrase we refer to ranked (e.g., frequency) distributions of linguistic units which are highly skewed and thus depart, for example, from normal distributions.

[8]   A method to integrate a sort of dynamics, which is otherwise left out, is to include, for example, probability functions introducing noise into the model according to the expected dynamics (Gilbert &Troitzsch, 1999).

[9]   This systematicity relates, for example, to logical relations and implicatures.

[10] The notion of described situation (Barwise & Perry, 1983) denotes situations (modelled as systems of relations of varying arity) described by the focal sentence or text from the point of view of its content. It was proposed as an alternative to model theory in possible world semantics.

[11] The terms text comprehension and interpretation stem from cognitive linguistics where they are well established — theoretically and empirically. For reference definitions see Kintsch (1998) and Schnotz (1994). In the present approach, they are not used metaphorically — as one may assume because we disregard referential semantics — but only dealt with in terms of a structural-cognitive semantics whose meaning units are purely conceptual. As proposed by LSA, these meaning units are derived on grounds of a learning model operating on linguistic units only. How this can be enlarged in order to model the meanings and interpretations of complex units was initially described by Kintsch (2001) and is extended in Mehler (2005).

[12] Priming is a cognitive process in which a so-called prime systematically pre-activates certain (linguistic) knowledge from long-term memory in a way which increases the probability of primed (e.g., lexical) units to be produced or recognized, for example. In cognitive linguistics, there is much research on the sort of units having this priming function as, for example, isolated lexical units in contrast to the preceding text of a certain text position to be processed. See Kintsch (1998) for a prominent priming theory in cognitive linguistics.

[13] In this chapter we refer to mechanisms of self-regulation if they result in changes of the focal system's structure (e.g., invention of lexical units). In contrast to this we speak of self-organization when changes of the system's organization, and thus of its function, are concerned (e.g., invention of a lexicon). In the following section, we will speak alternatively of a system's dynamics (self-regulation) and genetics (self-organization) in order to maintain this distinction.

[14] In case of single cognitive information processing systems, this relates, more specifically, to short scale, reading/speaking time or position-dependent learning.

[15] In case of cognitive information processing systems, this relates to learning (e.g., routinization and memorization) in long term memory.

[16] This also prevents one from speaking of abstract mechanisms as, for example, the process of language internal "extension of the size of the lexicon" or the "invention of lexical coding means," etc.

17   It is common in synergetics to view the distinction of micro and macroscopic variables as a matter of modelling perspective in the sense that what is viewed as a microscopic variable in one experiment may be investigated as a macroscopic order parameter of certain enslaved system variables in another experiment.

18   Vogt (2004), for example, considers a Zipfian-ranked frequency distribution of category usage emerging from a multi-agent language game on grounds of the iterated learning model (ILM) (cf. Kirby, 2002). In this experiment, the assumed frequency distribution emerging in the simulation without being "directly" pre-established (e.g., by an appropriate signal-meaning mapping) serves as a criterion of simulation validity, that is, of the validity of the simulation model. In Vogt's model this relates, amongst others, to the n-level multidimensional, though "hierarchicalized," category system. To what extent this "hierarchicalization" and the assumed procedure of category invention determine the resulting distribution in the framework of the ILM is an open question. This is a possible starting point for the present model as far as it proposes, for example, to restrict the build-up and maintenance of the category system by means of further "language laws" of the Zipfian nature. How such laws may interrelate is outlined in Section (4).

19   These considerations presuppose countability of (forms and) meanings, a hypothesis which is disputed by fuzzy linguistics (Rieger, 2001). It gives rise to the introduction of fuzzy granules and distributed meaning representations and thus proposes to combine the apparatus of probability and fuzzy theory (Zadeh, 1997). Although this is a more realistic approach which coincides with models of inductive learning of lexical meanings, we will nevertheless retain Altmann's and Krylov's simplification.

20   One may think that such a monotonously falling rank frequency distribution only arises if cells are appropriately re-ordered. But this is not expected to be necessary if this two-dimensional system is (almost) Zipfian as induced by the form and content-related Zipfian distributions supported on grounds of empirical investigations in quantitative linguistics.

21   Another starting point for Zipf-like regularities of matrix (2) is proposed by Ferrer i Chancho et al. (2005) who describe a Zipfian law of node degree in a derived signal-signal matrix based on an analogue to (2). The idea of their approach is that the validity of such a distribution allows deriving (almost) connectedness (i.e., a large connected subgraph induced by the signal-signal matrix) as a precondition of syntax. Anyhow, this argumentation leaves out several prerequisites of syntactic structure. Amongst others, this relates to recursive structure.

22   As the object being modelled by the simulations under consideration is not a specific language, this fitting does not relate to the factual values the fitted distribution takes for different values of the independent variable in any specific language.

23   As an example, consider the parameters of models describing the vocabulary growth in texts which partly reflect the influence of genres, registers and their linguistic manifestations as text types (Altmann, 1991) whose evolvement can be described as a synergetic process on its own.

Section III

Cognition and Robotics

Chapter VI

Language Evolution and Robotics:
Issues on Symbol Grounding and Language Acquisition

Paul Vogt,
University of Edinburgh, UK and Tilburg University, The Netherlands

Abstract

This chapter focuses on recent studies on the origins and evolution of language which have used multiple robot systems as their primary platform. After presenting some theoretical background regarding language evolution and the symbol grounding problem, the chapter discusses a number of themes within evolutionary linguistics that have been subject of robotic studies this far. These themes include categorisation, the formation of vocabularies, the evolution of grammar and the emergence of meaningful communication. Following this review, future avenues for research are discussed. The objective of the chapter is to present why robotics is a fruitful approach to study language origins and evolution, identify the main topics, report the major achievements and problems and provide a roadmap to future studies. The chapter concludes that robotics is, indeed, a very promising methodology to study language evolution and that, although many insights have been gained, we are still closer to the starting point than to the endpoint.

Introduction

One of the key aspects that distinguishes humans from other species is that humans use a complex communication system that is — among other things — symbolic, learned, compositional and recursive, whereas all other species' communication systems typically lack these properties. It is often thought that this unique human feature is the key to understanding the nature (and nurture!) of human cognition. In order to understand the foundations of this distinction between humans and other species, scientists study the *origins and evolution of language.*

Traditionally, the origins and evolution of language has been studied by biologists, anthropologists, psychologists, palaeontologists, philosophers and linguists — although the Linguistic Society of Paris had strangely enough banned any studies on this issue between 1866 and 1974, because too many theories were proposed that were hard to verify at the time. With the recent advancements in computational resources, an increasing number of simulations studying various aspects of language origins and evolution have emerged (see, e.g., Briscoe, 2002; Cangelosi & Parisi, 2002; Kirby, 2002; Steels, 1997, for overviews).

Mostly, these computational studies incorporate a multi-agent system that can learn, or evolve, a communication system of varying complexity that allows the system to communicate about a predefined set of meanings. However, as human communication is about the real world, understanding the underlying principles of language requires an understanding of the mechanisms with which a language's meanings are rooted in reality. Models based on predefined meanings therefore face what is often referred to as the *symbol grounding problem* (Harnad, 1990). A few studies have tried to tackle this problem using robotic models of language origins and evolution, most notably Marocco, Cangelosi, and Nolfi (2003), Steels, Kaplan, McIntyre, and van Looveren (2002), Steels and Vogt (1997), and Vogt (2000a).

In this chapter, I will present an overview of robotic (and other related) studies on the evolution of language. The aim is to present why robotics is a fruitful approach to study language origins and evolution, identify the main topics, report the major achievements and problems and provide a roadmap to future studies. Although I will cover most robotic studies on the evolution of language, the overview is not exhaustive and will, for instance, not cover studies on language learning robots, such as Oates, Eyler-Walker, and Cohen (2000), Roy (2000), Steels and Kaplan (2000), and Sugita and Tani (2005), since these deal with human-robot interaction rather than with multi-robot communication.

In the next section, I will provide some theoretical background on language evolution, discuss an alternative view on the symbol grounding problem and present some foundations toward studying language evolution using robots. Then I will present an overview of topics that have been studied in language evolution robotics. These topics will be illustrated with case studies and a critical review of the approaches taken. Following this, an outlook to future endeavours is presented, after which the chapter concludes.

Background

The question of why humans have evolved the ability to use natural language is one of the most intriguing in contemporary cognitive science, and possibly one of the hardest problems in science (Christiansen & Kirby, 2003). Looking at recent collections on the evolution of language (e.g., Hurford, Knight, & Studdert-Kennedy, 1998; Wray, 2002; Christiansen & Kirby, 2003), we can find that most prominent questions include: For what purpose has human languages evolved? How have human sound systems evolved? How have we become a symbolic species? How have we established a shared signalling system of symbols? How has syntax emerged? How has linguistic diversity emerged? How do languages change through time? Among these questions, the emergence of syntax is considered by many to be the most important question (Kirby, 2002).

One of the most prominent debates regarding language evolution concerns the nature versus nurture paradigm. On the one side, many scholars adhere to the nativist approach, which aims at explaining language universals in terms of biological adaptations (Chomsky, 1980; Pinker & Bloom, 1990). Only a few modellers take up this approach by developing models that try to evolve an innate Universal Grammar (e.g., Briscoe, 2000; Nowak, Plotkin, & Jansen, 2000; Yamauchi, 2004). On the other side of the debate are those who believe language is an empirically learnt system (Elman, Bates, Johnson, Karmiloff-Smith, Parisi, & Plunkett, 1996; MacWhinney, 1999) or a culturally evolved system (Tomasello, 1999). Most computer modellers follow the cultural evolution paradigm and assume that language is a *complex adaptive dynamical system* (Steels, 1997).

A complex dynamical system is a system of which the total behaviour is an indirect, non-hierarchical consequence of a set of interacting elements. A complex adaptive dynamical system is a complex system where "the behaviour of individual elements and the nature of the interactions may change thus giving rise to a higher-order dynamics" (Steels, 1997, p. 3). If we view individuals of a language community as interacting elements who change their linguistic behaviour in order to conform to other individuals, we can regard the language community as a complex adaptive dynamical system. When individuals interact culturally, they try to form conventions in order to communicate successfully. To this aim, they may invent new elements in the language, adopt elements from other individuals and strengthen or weaken elements that are effective or ineffective. If we further assume that individuals tend to reuse strong elements, these elements will give further rise to other individuals adopting and strengthening these elements. As a result, these strong elements will become shared among larger groups of individuals; in a similar way ant paths are formed. The process by which this is achieved is called *self-organisation*. So, according to this paradigm, language is assumed to have evolved through self-organisation resulting from cultural interactions and individual learning.

Related to this paradigm, Kirby and Hurford (2002) extended this view by regarding language evolution as an interplay "between three complex adaptive systems:

*   *Learning:* During *ontogeny* children adapt their knowledge of language in response to the environment in such a way that they optimise their ability to comprehend others and to produce comprehensible utterances.

- *Cultural evolution:* On a historic (or *glossogenetic*) time scale, languages change. Words enter and leave the language, meanings shift and phonological and syntactic rules adjust.

- *Biological evolution:* The learning (and processing) mechanisms with which our species has been equipped for language, adapt in response to selection pressures from the environment, for survival and reproduction." (Kirby & Hurford, 2002, p. 122)

Figure 1 illustrates the interaction between these three complex adaptive systems. The remainder of this chapter will primarily focus on studies involving the complex adaptive dynamical system approach, as this is — up to now — the most studied paradigm in robotic studies.

Although, as mentioned, questions relating to the emergence of syntax are generally considered the most important questions, it has been argued that the first important questions should relate to the emergence of *symbolic* communication (Deacon, 1997; Jackendoff, 1999). Traditional cognitivist approaches in artificial intelligence have assumed that human cognition can be seen as a *physical symbol system* (Newell & Simon, 1976). Physical symbol systems are systems that can store, manipulate and interpret symbolic structures according to some specified rules. Assuming this is a correct characterisation, we need to define symbols. Cognitivists have treated symbols as internal structures that — following De Saussure (1974) — relate representations of meanings with arbitrary signals or labels. In AI, both these internal structures and labels are symbols. In these approaches, it is left unspecified how the meaning relates to reality, which has caused famous fundamental problems such as the *frame problem* (McCarthy & Hayes, 1969), the *Chinese Room problem* (Searle, 1980) and the *symbol grounding problem* (Harnad, 1990). The main issue with these problems is that in the cognitivist approach, symbols are neither situated — i.e., they are not acquired in interaction with an environment, nor embodied — i.e., they are not based on bodily experiences (Clancey, 1997; Pfeifer & Scheier, 1999).

Figure 1. Illustration of how the three adaptive systems interact to explain the emergence of language (Adapted from Kirby & Hurford, 2002)

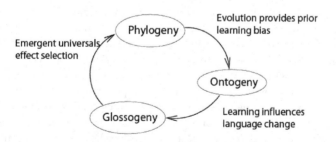

Figure 2. The semiotic triangle illustrates the relations that constitute a sign. When the relation between form and meaning is either arbitrary or conventionalized, the sign can be interpreted as a symbol. (Adapted from Ogden & Richards, 1923)

To deal with these problems of cognitivism, Brooks (1990) proposed the *physical grounding hypothesis*, which states that intelligence should be grounded in the interaction between a physical agent and its environment. In the physical grounding hypothesis, Brooks has argued that symbols are no longer necessary; intelligent behaviour can be established by parallel operating sensorimotor couplings. Although physically grounded systems are both situated and embodied, from the point of linguistics, Brooks' hypothesis is problematic, since human language is indeed considered to be symbolic.

It has been argued that the true problem of the cognitivist approach lies in the definition of symbols. If we were to accept there must be symbols, they should be defined as structural couplings connecting objects to their categories based on their sensorimotor projections (Clancey, 1997; Maturana & Varela, 1992). I have argued (Vogt, 2002b), however, that such a definition is already present from the semiotic theorist Charles Sanders Peirce (1931-1958). Peirce has defined symbols as a triadic relation between a referent, a meaning and a form[1] as illustrated in the semiotic triangle (Figure 2), where the relation between meaning and form is either arbitrary or conventionalised such that the relation must be learnt. Similar definitions are very common among linguists and other cognitive scientists (e.g., Barsalou, 1999; Deacon, 1997; Lakoff, 1987). To distinguish between the cognitivist and Peircean definitions of symbols, I have coined Peirce's definition *semiotic symbols* (Vogt, 2002b).

In this definition, the term *meaning* requires extra care. According to Peirce, the meaning of a symbol arises from the process of *semiosis*, which is the interaction between form, meaning and referent. This means that the meaning is the mental effect determined or caused by the symbol. This way, I have argued that the meaning depends on how the symbol is constructed and with what function. As such, the meaning of a symbol can be regarded as a functional relation between its form and referent based on an agent's bodily experience and interaction with the referent. The experience is based on the agent's history of interactions with the referent and/or form. The ways these bodily experiences are represented and memorized form the internal representation of the meaning. The actual interaction between an agent and a referent "defines" the functional relation (note that I will use the term *category* to denote the internal representation of meaning). (In addition, as is common in linguistics I will sometimes use the term *meaning* interchangeably with the term category when discussing the robotic models.)

I have argued that when the semiotic definition of symbols is adopted, the symbol grounding problem no longer exists as a fundamental problem (Vogt, 2002b). This is primarily because semiotic symbols are *per definition* meaningful and grounded. The problem, however shifts into a hard technical problem, which I have called the *physical symbol grounding problem*, and which relates to the *construction* of the triadic relation between referent, meaning and form (Vogt, 2002b).[2] (In the remainder of this chapter, I will use the term *symbol* to denote a *semiotic symbol*. When I refer to the cognitivist sense of a symbol, this will be made explicit.)

So, when studying the origins of symbolic communication, the symbols should arise from an interaction of an agent with its environment; this justifies the use of robotic models. Preferably physical robots are used, but simulated robots can offer a suitable platform too (see Pfeifer & Scheier, 1999), since experiments with real robots may be very time consuming and costly. Ideally, the experiments have an ecological validity in that the robots have a "life task" to solve (Ziemke & Sharkey, 2001), but — as will become clear — most robotic models so far have little or no ecological validity.

During the course of language evolution, symbols have become culturally shared in a population, i.e., the members of a language society have learnt more or less similar meanings and referents of signals. Learning the meanings of words is — in principle — a notoriously hard problem. In a seminal work, Quine (1960) has shown that when you hear a novel word, this word can — logically — have an infinite number of meanings. He illustrates this point by considering a linguist studying a language that he or she does not know. The linguist observes a native speaker exclaiming "gavagai!" when a rabbit scurries by. It would be natural for the linguist to note that gavagai means rabbit, but logically, gavagai could mean an infinite number of different things, such as undetached rabbit parts, a running rabbit or even it is going to rain today. Deciding which meaning to associate with a signal is an extremely hard problem for robotic models, but humans solve this task seemingly very easily. Researchers in child language acquisition have proposed a number of constraints and means to reduce the number of possible inferences as to the meanings and referents of words. Examples include *representational constraints*, such as a *whole object bias* (Macnamara, 1982) or a *shape bias* (Landau, Smith, & Jones, 1988); *interpretational constraints*, such as *mutual exclusivity* (Markman, 1989) and the *principle of contrast* (Clark, 1993); and *social constraints,* such as *joint attention* (Tomasello, 1999), *corrective feedback* (Chouinard & Clark, 2003) and *Theory of Mind* (Premack & Woodruff, 1978) that allow individuals to understand that others have intentions similar to themselves. For an overview, consult, e.g., Smith (2005b).

Once a shared symbolic communication system was in place, humans are thought to have developed a *protolanguage* (Jackendoff, 1999). Some have argued that the protolanguage was formed from unstructured expressions of multiple words (Bickerton, 1984), others have argued that expressions of the protolanguage were mainly single holistic utterances (Wray, 1998). It is widely assumed that from the protolanguage, grammatical structures have emerged that resemble modern languages (Bickerton, 1984; Jackendoff, 1999; Wray, 1998). Some scientists believe this transition was due to a biological adaptation in the brain (Bickerton, 1984; Pinker & Bloom, 1990); others think that the language itself has adapted to become learnable (Deacon, 1997). Although there have emerged many ungrounded computational models that simulate this transition (Batali, 2002; Brighton, 2002; Kirby, 2001), this area is still largely unexplored in robotics (but see Steels, 2004;

Vogt, 2005b). One idea in which robotics can contribute to the study of grammar evolution is that robots can exploit structures that occur in the interaction between robots and their environment. Both the world and our interaction with the world contain combinatorial structures that could serve as the basis of the semantic structures, which — in turn — form the basis of the syntactic structures in languages. For instance, objects such as apples can have different colours, sizes or other properties, which could serve as the basis of what could be called *adjective noun phrases*, such as "the red apple." Another structure that could be exploited is that actions are typically performed by a subject on an object, which could have resulted in the universal tendency of languages to have expressions combining subjects, objects and verbs.

Philosophically, the physical symbol grounding problem has provided sufficient ground to favour robotic models over what I call *ungrounded* models (i.e., models that have predefined meanings or no meanings at all); but what about more pragmatic reasons? Here I mention two reasons: First, ungrounded models may be built on false assumptions. For instance, in most ungrounded models, all agents have the same meanings. This is clearly not a realistic assumption, because in real life meanings arise from interactions of an individual with his or her environment and with other individuals, and therefore each individual will have different experiences. In addition, when the model uses a population turnover, in realistic models the older experienced agents should have a matured set of meanings, while the new agents have not developed any meanings at all. Ungrounded models are completely ignorant about this. Ungrounded models also tend to assume that hearers can observe both the communicated signal and its meaning. Clearly, humans do not observe the meaning of a word that resides in a speaker's brain, because that would make the signal redundant (Smith, 2003). In an idealised world, humans can observe a word's referent, though — as mentioned — logically each word can have an infinite number of meanings (Quine, 1960) and a learner has to infer the word's meaning. In robotic models, the meanings typically develop during an agent's lifetime. As a result, meanings are private and may differ substantially from agent to agent. Moreover, as a matter of principle, robots cannot observe other agents' internal representations, unless the experimenter "cheats," which can be useful if, for instance, joint attention is hard to achieve, as in Vogt (2000a).

Second, robotic models can actually exploit the nature of the interaction with the environment. I have already mentioned exploiting structures for constructing semantic structures. In addition, interactions and feedback mechanisms could be exploited to reduce the number of possible meanings of an expression. If the response of an action induced by a communication act is positive, the agents participating in the communication could use the positive reward to reinforce the used association between expression and meaning, thus allowing the agent to learn a word's meaning more easily.

Topics and Case Studies

This section presents an overview of some robotic studies on the evolution of language. The overview is not exhaustive; for instance, I will not discuss the very interesting study on the evolution of communication channels by Quinn (2001), nor will I discuss language learning models based on human-robot interaction, such as Oates et al. (2000), Roy (2000),and Sugita and Tani (2005). Instead, the focus will be on language development in multi-robot systems, providing a clear review of the topics studied showing the state-of-the-art. The topics in this section are — more or less — increasingly complex. First, I present how semiotic symbols can be constructed. The learning of conventions is explained subsequently. Then I will present studies on the emergence of grammar. In all these presentations, meaning formation is only treated as forming an internal represen-tation of meaning (or *category*), rather than in a functional manner. The functional development of meaning is discussed at the end of this section.[3]

Constructing Semiotic Symbols

The first problem that needs to be solved is the physical symbol grounding problem (i.e., creating the semiotic triangle). The problem can be decomposed into three parts: (1) Sensing and pre-processing of raw sensorimotor images, (2) categorisation or meaning construction and (3) labelling. The labelling problem is either trivial (in case of using arbitrary forms) or it is based on learning conventions through language. In this section, I will assume the trivial solution and focus on the sensing, pre-processing and meaning formation. Learning conventions will be discussed later.

The discussion of how semiotic symbols can be constructed is presented for individual robots. Constructing a semiotic symbol usually starts with a sensori (motor) stimulation based on the robot's interaction with the real world (when embedded in communication, construction can also start upon "hearing" an expression). Sensorimotor stimulation can be based on a scene acquired by a camera, which may be static as in the Talking Heads experiment (Steels et al., 2002), or dynamic, as in more recent experiments of Luc Steels (Steels, 2004; Steels & Baillie, 2003); the activation of infrared, sonar or simple light sensors (Vogt, 2003a); the flow of sensorimotor activity (Billard & Dautenhahn, 1999; Vogt, 2000b) or the activation of a sensorimotor coupling (Vogt, 2002a). Often, the raw data is pre-processed to reduce the huge amount of data. Typically, regions of interest are identified and some feature extraction algorithm is used to describe such regions in terms of feature vectors. How this is done can be quite complex and is not discussed further in this chapter; for details consult the individual papers. When the sensing is based on the activation of sensorimotor couplings, pre-processing may not be required (Vogt, 2002a). Furthermore, in simulations the image is often more abstract, such as a bitstring representing mushrooms (Cangelosi & Harnad, 2000) or just random vectors (Smith, 2003), which do not require any more pre-processing.

At the heart of creating semiotic symbols lies — technically — an agent's ability to categorise the (pre-processed) perceptual data. Once these categories are in place, the agent can simply associate a label (or form) to this category, thus constructing the symbol. (Whether this symbol is useful or functional is another question, which will be dealt with at the end of this part.) A number of techniques have been developed that allow a robot to construct categories from scratch with which it is able to recognise or discriminate one experience from another. These techniques usually rely on techniques that have been present in AI for quite some time, such as pattern recognition and neural

Figure 3. Illustration of three subsequent discrimination games using a protoype representation

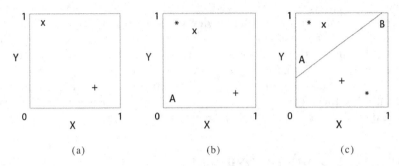

(a)   (b)   (c)

*The figure shows three instances of a combined feature space and conceptual space. The x and + are feature vectors of observed objects (e.g., the location of an object in a 2D plane), the * denotes a prototype, while A and B are categories. Each individual plot represents one discrimination game. In game (a), the robot observed 2 objects (x and +), but has not yet formed any categories. Consequently, the game fails and a new category A is added to the conceptual space of which the feature vector of the target object serves as an exemplar for its prototype — the * in figure (b). In the second situation (b), again two objects are observed, which are now both categorised with category A. In this case, no distinction can be made. Suppose the + was the target (a.k.a. the topic) of the discrimination game, then a new category is formed by adding the feature vector + to the conceptual space as the prototype of category B in figure (c). Not that this alters the initial category A. In the third game (c), both objects can be categorised distinctively. Irrespective of which one is the topic, the discrimination game succeeds. Typically, when a discrimination game succeeds, the prototype is moved slightly in the direction of the topic's feature vector.*

networks. Some researchers use neural networks to associate (pre-processed) sensorimotor images with forms (e.g., Billard & Dautenhahn, 1999; Cangelosi & Harnad, 2000; Marocco et al., 2003), which — although they work well — makes it hard to analyse how the meanings are represented. Moreover, these techniques are often inflexible with respect to the *openness* of the system, because, typically, the number of nodes in a neural network are fixed. Another technique that is frequently used in grounded models of language evolution is the *discrimination game* (Steels, 1996b).

The aim of the discrimination game is to categorise a sensorimotor experience such that this category distinguishes this experience from other experiences. If such a *distinctive category* (or meaning) is found, the game is considered a success. If it fails, a new category is formed based on the experience that is categorised, such that discrimination can succeed in a future situation. This allows the agent to construct a repertoire of categories from scratch, as illustrated in Figure 3.

The discrimination game, illustrated in Figure 3, has successfully been implemented in the Talking Heads simulation THSim (Vogt, 2003c).[4] Experiments have shown that the discrimination game is typically a fast learning mechanism and is very robust in using different representations for categories. The original implementation used *binary trees* (Steels, 1996b), which were used in various robotic experiments (Steels et al., 2002; Steels & Vogt, 1997) and simulations (Smith, 2003). Other representations that were used include *binary subspaces* (de Jong, 2000), *radial basis function networks* (Steels &

Belpaeme, 2005), *neural networks* (Berthouze & Tijsseling, 2002), *predicate logic* (De Beule, 2004; Sierra-Santibáñez, 2001) and different variants of the prototype representation (Vogt, 2003a, 2004, 2005b).

The discrimination game is context dependent; the robot always contrasts the topic with respect to other objects in the context. This has the consequence that the game may succeed, even if the observed feature vector has a relatively large distance to the category's prototype, leading to an overextension of symbols. However, after a while, the categories become finer grained, thus allowing the agents to resolve overextensions. It is a well known fact, however, that young children also tend to overextend during early word-learning (Bloom, 2000).

One way of organising the space of categories is by using a hierarchical layering where the top layer has only one category (or a few), while the lower layers have increasingly more categories allowed. This way, the top layer has the most general category and the bottom layer the most specific category. One way of implementing such a hierarchy is by using a binary tree (cf., Steels, 1996b) or binary subspaces (cf. de Jong, 2000). Although most implementations of the prototype representations have only one layer, Vogt (2004) presents a hierarchically layered version of prototypical categories. It was shown that when agents using such a layered version and had a built in preference for selecting the most general categories to communicate about, the emerging lexicons revealed a Zipf distribution of the frequency with which word-meaning pairs were used. This is interesting, since such a distribution is a very sound universal observed across the world's languages (Zipf, 1949). Similar to Zipf's *principle of least effort* explanation for the emergence of this distribution, Mandelbrot (1965) has explained the emergence of such a distribution based on the *principle of minimal cost*. These explanations always focused on the minimising the cost for producing and interpreting speech sounds. However, given that in Vogt's (2004) simulations agents also minimise cost for categorising objects, this may provide an alternative or additional explanation for the emergence of Zipf's law.

When the sensing typically yields only one region of interest (i.e., there is only one object or action), the discrimination game can only be applied in contrast to some sensorimotor images that are in the robot's memory. In such cases different models can be used as well. The *classification game* was used in experiments with Sony's AIBO where whole (segmented) images of the camera were stored as exemplars (Steels & Kaplan, 2000). The *identification game* was used to categorise the motor flow of robots following each other (Vogt, 2000b). The latter used a pre-processing of the raw sensorimotor flow based on constructing delay vectors from time series (Rosenstein & Cohen, 1998). The identification game is very similar to the discrimination game in that the delay vector (or feature vector) is categorised with the nearest prototype, provided its distance was within a certain threshold. If not, the delay vector is added to the ontology as an exemplar.

As mentioned, once a category, which is a representation of the meaning in a semiotic symbol, is in place, the category can be associated with a form. This form may be arbitrary, but in language forms need to be conventionalised. In language evolution models, this is often modelled by interactions called *language games* (Steels, 1996a) which will be explained hereafter.

Sharing Semiotic Symbols

Among the biggest problems in modelling language evolution using robots is the development of a shared communication system, which is related to Quine's problem of the *indeterminacy of meaning*. The models will have to include some mechanism to establish shared or joint attention to some object or event. Since human children face the same problems when they grow up, it is important that robotic models are based on what is known about how children learn language.

Another important aspect relates to the *openness* of human languages. Unlike the communication systems of other animals, human languages are open systems (i.e., new words, meanings, objects, agents and grammatical structures appear, disappear and change rapidly). Many models assume that language is a closed system, for instance, by fixing the number of signals and meanings. Although this occurs in some grounded models (Billard & Dautenhahn, 1999; Cangelosi & Parisi, 1998; Marocco et al., 2003), it most frequently occurs in ungrounded models (e.g., Smith, 2002; Oliphant, 1999). Furthermore, in order to maintain efficiency in an open language system, humans must learn these changes; they cannot be innate, as is, for instance, the case with Vervet monkeys (Seyfarth & Cheney, 1986).[5] Most models of language evolution (both grounded and ungrounded) acknowledge this principle and allow agents to learn language (Smith, 2002; Cangelosi & Harnad, 2000; Oliphant, 1999). However, there are some models that violate the idea of language acquisition by using genetic algorithms to evolve the communication system (e.g., Marocco et al., 2003; Cangelosi & Parisi, 1998). One widely used open system is the language game model, which has successfully been implemented on physical robots to study the emergence of lexicons (Steels et al., 2002; Steels & Vogt, 1997).

The Language Game

The language game, which is illustrated in Figure 4, typically involves two agents — one speaker and one hearer — and a context of objects and/or actions. Both agents perceive (p) the context and extract feature vectors (f) and categorise these with meanings (m), e.g., by using the discrimination game. The speaker selects one object as the topic and tries to produce an utterance (u) based on its lexicon. The lexicon is typically an associative memory between meaning representations (or meanings for short) and forms, see Figure 5(a). Each association has a score σ_{ij} that indicates the effectiveness (or occurrence frequency) of the association based on past interactions. These lexicons, like the ontologies, are private and thus can differ from one agent to another. The speaker searches his or her lexicon for an association that corresponds to the meaning of the topic and that has the highest score. If such an association is found, the corresponding form is uttered. When hearing a form, the hearer searches for this form, the association that has the highest score ($\sigma_{ij}>0$) for those meanings that are in the context or that relate to the topic, if this is known.

Figure 4. The semiotic square illustrates the working of a language game (See the text for details)

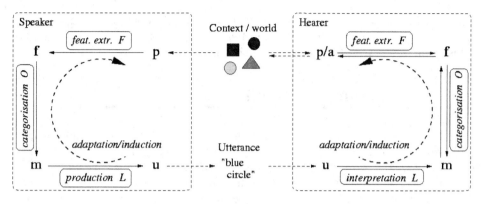

Figure 5. Typical open association matrix

	m_1	m_2	...	m_M
w_1	0.5	0.2	...	σ_{1M}
w_2	0.6	0.8	...	σ_{2M}
⋮	⋮	⋮	⋮	⋮
w_N	σ_{N1}	σ_{N2}	...	σ_{NM}

	m_1	m_2	...	m_M
w_1		-		
w_2	-	+	...	-
⋮		⋮		
w_N		-		

(a)   (b)

Figure (a) shows a typical open association matrix where forms w_i are associated with meanings m_j with some strength (or score) σ_{ij}. Due to the openness of the system, N and M may grow — in principle — indefinitely and need not have the same values. However, since the memories are limited in size, N and M are bounded. When the speaker of a language game tries to produce an utterance about meaning m_j, he or she searches the corresponding column for the highest score σ_{ij} and finds its utterance w_i in that row. When the hearer tries to interpret a word w_i, it searches the corresponding row for the meaning m_j with the highest score σ_{ij}, provided this meaning is pragmatically possible (i.e., it should fit the context). Figure (b) illustrates the update of scores in case of a successful language game. Suppose that the association between word w_2 and m_2 was used successfully, the strength of σ_{22} is increased, while all competing associations σ_{i2} and σ_{2j} are laterally inhibited (i.e., those associations that are in the same row or column as the successful association: $i=1,3,4,...,N$ and $j=1,3,4,...,M$).

Typically, the success of the game is evaluated and if the game succeeds, the used associations are reinforced, while competing associations are laterally inhibited as illustrated in Figure 5(b). If the game fails, the scores of the used associations are decreased. These adaptations ensure that successfully used elements tend to be reused again and again, while unsuccessful ones tend to get weaker. This serves a self-organisation of the lexicon shared at the global population. At the start of an agent's lifetime, its lexicon is empty, so initially, most language games fail. When they do, the lexicon needs to be expanded. When the speaker encounters a meaning that has no association in its lexicon, the speaker can invent a new form. When the hearer receives a form that has no association in his or her lexicon, they will adopt the form associated with the meaning of the topic or with the meanings of all objects in the context if the topic is unknown. In this way, the language is an open system.

Lexicon Grounding on Mobile Robots

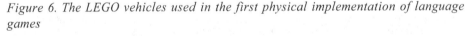

The first implementation of the language game on a physical system was done using LEGO robots, such as shown in Figure 6 (Steels & Vogt, 1997). In this experiment, the robots evolved a lexicon to name the different types of light sources in their environment, which they could detect using very simple light sensors mounted on the front of the robots. In order to acquire a sensory image of their environment, the two robots participating in the game first approached each other to stand facing each other at a close distance, after which each robot rotated 360 degrees. The raw image was then pre-processed to identify the different light sources, which were then described in feature vectors. The speaker selected a topic and "pointed" at this object, so that the hearer could identify the topic as well. Then both robots played a discrimination game to categorise the topic's feature vector. When the discrimination game succeeded, the remainder of the language game was played as explained above. Note that the type of language game in which the speaker points at the topic, thus establishing joint attention, has become known as the *observational game* (Vogt, 2000c, 2002b).

Although the experiments were very successful, many problems have arisen during the development of the model (for more up-to-date details, consult Vogt, 2000a, 2000c, 2002b, 2003a). Most problems had to do with the inconsistencies between what the two robots

Figure 6. The LEGO vehicles used in the first physical implementation of language games

had seen during a language game, thus leading to different contexts, and with the difficulty in achieving joint attention by means of pointing. Importantly, these problems have helped in realising the effect that the false assumptions in ungrounded models have on the soundness and realism of their results.

The inconsistencies between the robots' sensory images were due to the fact that when two physical bodies were standing opposite of each other, then each individual sensed something different, for instance, because one robot obscured the visibility of an object, or the distance from a light source was too large for one of the robots to detect it. Also differences in the sensitivity to noise of the sensors and different lighting conditions played a significant role. So, although the robots were designed to talk about the "here and now" (something what young children also tend to do), the hearer may not have seen what the speaker was talking about. Moreover, even if the hearer saw the speaker's topic, it could have detected a completely different sensory image of this object. Interestingly, the self-organisation and adaptiveness of the language game model partly solved this problem. By allowing an agent to acquire many categories, which they could employ in different situations for the same referent while maintaining only one or two forms associated with a referent, the robots could communicate about the referents consistently and reliably. So, the robots acquired (near) one-to-one mappings between referent and form, and one-to-many mappings between referent and meaning and between form and meaning (Figure 7). One consequence of this result is that the model thus might help us explain how we deal with notions such as *family resemblance* (Wittgenstein, 1958) and *object constancy*. It is beyond the scope of this paper to repeat this argumentation, for details consult Vogt (2000c, 2003a).

Problems with respect to the unreliability of pointing made us look at other ways to solve the mapping problem. While trying to model how the robots could estimate the reliability of pointing, based on Steels and Kaplan (1998), it was found that the speaker's pointing was not necessary, provided the agents could verify the success of the game in order to provide rewards to the learning mechanism. This has lead to the development of what has become known as the *guessing game*, which has also been applied in the Talking Heads experiment (Steels et al., 2002). In the guessing game, the hearer guesses the speaker's referent and then the success of the game is evaluated by the speaker who can — in the case of failure — provide corrective feedback on the word's meaning. In the LEGO robots (and the Talking Heads) this was done by the hearer "pointing" (unreliably) at the object it guessed the speaker referred to, thus allowing the speaker to verify success, which was then signalled back to the hearer. In case of failure, the speaker could then point at his or her topic to provide the hearer with feedback in order for the hearer to acquire the proper meaning. But since this was adding another source of noise and the world only contained four light sources, associating the form with a randomly chosen meaning appeared just as effective (Vogt, 2000c).

Experiments comparing the guessing game with the *observational game* (the game where the speaker points at the topic prior to the verbal communication) have shown that both methods can achieve high levels of communicative success. Although the high levels are reached faster by playing observational games, the lexicons that emerge from the guessing games contain more information, meaning that a form is used more specifically and consistently in naming a referent. This latter result is explained by realising that when hearers have to guess the referent of an utterance, the words have to be informative.

Figure 7. This semiotic landscape shows the associations between referents (L$_j$), meanings (m$_i$) and word-forms evolved for two robots in one of the robotic experiments on lexicon grounding

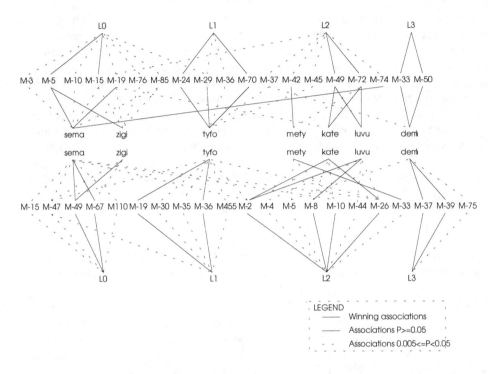

As this figure shows, each referent was categorised using different meanings in different situations, but only a few forms were used to name the referents, the thickness and type of the line indicate the frequency with which associations were used.

When the hearer already knows the topic, this is not required. It has been argued that in both games a strong competition between associations exists, and that the guessing game provides more pressure to disambiguate the language (Vogt, 2000a; Vogt & Coumans, 2003), an effect that has recently been confirmed in a simple ungrounded model (Wedel, 2004).

Although many researchers in child language acquisition believe there is ample evidence of caregivers providing corrective feedback with respect to the meaning of words (Chouinard & Clark, 2003; Brown & Hanlon, 1970), its availability is controversial (Bloom, 2000). Since corrective feedback may be unrealistic and joint attention — in principle — cannot be assumed to be precise, a third game was developed. This *selfish game[6]* is based on the principle of cross-situational learning (Hurford, 1999; Siskind, 1996), or more precisely, *cross-situational statistical learning* (Vogt & Smith, 2005). The idea is that the robots learn the meaning of a word solely based on co-variances that occur across different situations. Unfortunately, cross-situational statistical learning (CSSL) did not work on the in the LEGO robot experiments because the environment was very minimal and few variations could be detected across situations — even when variation was imposed by the experimenter (Vogt, 2000a, 2000c). Work by Andrew Smith (2003) and recent simulations of the Talking Heads (Vogt, 2004, 2003b) have proved that CSSL may become a viable learning strategy. Although the learning mechanism is much slower than the observational and guessing game models, and coherence between the agents in the population is hard to achieve (Vogt & Coumans, 2003), results can improve if additional constraints on acquiring the meaning of new words, such as *mutual exclusivity* (Markman, 1989), are added (Smith, 2005a).

Talking Heads and Other Related Work

Probably the best known robotic experiment regarding language evolution is the Talking Heads experiment (Belpaeme, Steels, & van Looveren, 1998; Steels et al., 2002). This large scale experiment consisted of several installations distributed across the world and connected with each other through the Internet.[7] Each installation contained two physical robots embodied as pan-tilt cameras connected to a computational unit. Each camera (or Talking Head) was oriented toward a white board on which geometrical coloured figures were pasted. The population contained a large number of agents that could migrate from one site to another through the Internet; at each site, each agent then played a given number of guessing games. If an agent participated in a game, it first embodied itself inside a Talking Head. The speaker would select an arbitrary object from a randomly selected region of interest (a subset of the white board) as topic. The speaker then indicated (or "pointed") to the hearer what the region of interest was, thus establishing the context, and the guessing game (explained above) started. Feedback was evaluated by the hearer "pointing" at his or her guessed topic.

Human users could interact with the experiment by launching agents, which they could send around the different installations, and by changing the words agents had acquired with words given by the human user. So, new agents entered the population and others left regularly. Furthermore, at the physical sites, people were allowed to alter the geometrical world, thus introducing new objects and removing others. Although this made the experiment largely uncontrolled, it added to the openness of the system. Two experiments were launched; the second and longest experiment had lasted for about seven months in which a total of approximately 6,000 agents had played roughly 400,000 guessing games. The average communicative success was around 60% during this period (see van Looveren, 2001; Steels et al., 2002 for detailed results). Although many agents had participated, one must realise that not all agents were present during the entire experiment; most were probably only present for short periods. Furthermore, although there was no central control of the language, some agents were present almost the entire experiment and were thus likely to have a large impact on the lexicon that evolved. Nevertheless, the Talking Heads experiment was a significant contribution in showing that a large open system of robotic agents was able to evolve a stable, though dynamic, set of shared semiotic symbols in a world that had many different and varying conditions, especially with respect to the illumination.

Another related set of experiments on mobile LEGO robots and in simulations was carried out by Billard and colleagues (Billard & Dautenhahn, 1999; Billard & Hayes, 1999). In these experiments, a (group of) learner robot(s) learnt a lexicon through interacting with a teacher robot that had its lexicon predefined. Although these experiments did not explicitly study the origins and evolution of language, the experiments are related, since the experiments involved autonomous robot-robot communication and imitation learning. The robots were designed using a dynamical recurrent associative neural network architecture (DRAMA) that fully connected three sensorimotor modules: a communication input/output module, a sensor input module and an actuator output module. In essence, the learner robots were to follow the teacher in an environment that contained different patches on the surface (objects or places of interest) that the robots could communicate about. In addition, the robots could communicate about proprioceptive states and events, such as orientation, inclination and action. Interestingly, although the design was set up such that the robots avoided problems involved with pointing in, e.g., Steels and Vogt (1997), they were faced with other problems concerning the establishment of joint attention. These were mainly caused by the delay with which learners observed the objects or events the teacher talked about. The model was a closed system in the sense that the lexicon for the teacher was predefined with a fixed number of words. This disallowed the introduction of completely new objects without altering the teacher's lexicon. Although different numbers of learners were allowed in the system, it might have proved difficult to allow a fully open system in terms of population dynamics, where agents continuously enter and leave the society.

An alternative approach of evolving a shared vocabulary in a robotic model was issued by Marocco et al. (2003), in which a genetic algorithm (GA) was used to evolve a lexicon to coordinate interactions of a robot arm with two different objects: a sphere and a cube. The arm was a configuration of three segments with a total of six degrees of freedom. The controller was an artificial neural network, of which the weights were evolved using a GA. Fitness was not calculated based on communication, but was assessed by counting the number of appropriate interactions of the robots with the objects: the arm had to touch the sphere and avoid the cube. It was shown that a reasonably well shared lexicon evolved that improved the fitness. The problem with this approach is that Marocco et al. used a GA as a model of evolution, but the system lacked a learning episode of each individual. This is therefore not a realistic model of language evolution; rather these simulations use a GA as a machine learning technique to optimise the robot controller, which makes use of the evolved lexicon. A more realistic approach using a GA is to let the GA evolve the connections of the controller and/or the initial values of the weights in the neural network and then use a learning mechanism to adjust the weights of individuals while they interact with each other. An example of such an approach is in Cangelosi and Harnad (2000), which will be discussed later.

The Emergence of Grammar

As mentioned, one of the most distinctive features of human languages is the high degree of compositionality they contain. This means that the utterances of human languages are highly structured in that parts of the utterances map onto parts of the whole meaning of these utterances. For instance, in the phrase "orange square," the word "orange" refers to the colour orange and the word "square" to a square. In contrast, in a holistic phrase such as "kick the bucket" (referring to dying), no part of the utterance refers to a part of its meaning. One influential hypothesis suggests that during the course of evolution, human languages have changed into compositional languages from initially holistic *protolanguages* (Wray, 1998). Many ungrounded models have been developed, which provide support to this idea (Brighton, 2002; Kirby, 2001; Smith, Brighton, & Kirby, 2003).

What Brighton, Kirby, K. Smith and others (BKS for short) have shown is that when learners learn the language of an adult population while observing only a part of the language (i.e., there is a transmission *bottleneck*), holistic languages are not sufficient to allow for stable learnable communication systems. This can be understood by realising that when the learners become adults and start communicating to the next generation of learners, they have no means to produce expressions about objects/meanings they have not encountered before. Compositional languages, however, could allow a learner to produce utterances for previously unseen meanings when the learnt structures can be combined. For instance, if an agent has learnt the proper structures from the phrases "orange square," "orange triangle" and "red square," it would be able to produce the phrase "red triangle," even though it would never have encountered a red triangle before. BKS have shown that — given a predefined structured semantics and a learning mechanism that can discover such compositional structures — a compositional language can emerge from an initially holistic language, *provided* the language is transmitted through a bottleneck. In a way, the language changes to become more learnable for future generations.

This approach has recently been implemented in a simulation of the Talking Heads experiment, in which the semantics was not predefined, but co-developed with the language (Vogt, 2005a, b, c, d). The agents could detect four perceptual features of objects: the three components of the RGB colour space and one feature indicating the shape of an object. The semantic structures developed from a combination of the discrimination game to construct categorical features (elements in one dimension) and an inducer to discover conceptual spaces[8] of one or more dimensions that could serve to represent linguistic categories, such as colours or shapes (note that there was no restriction on which dimensions would constitute a conceptual space — all possible combinations were allowed). On the other hand, syntactic structures could be discovered by looking for coinciding substrings at the utterance level, in a very similar way to the approach taken in Kirby (2001). The model thus investigated the following twofold hypothesis:

1. The emergence of compositional linguistic structures is based on exploiting regularities in (possibly random and holistic) expressions, though constrained by semantic structures.

2. The emergence of combinatorial semantic structures is based on exploiting regularities found in the (interaction with the) world, though constrained by compositional linguistic structures.

The model combines the two most familiar approaches taken in modelling language evolution: the *iterated learning model* (ILM) of BKS and the language game model. The iterated learning model typically implements a vertical transmission of language, in which the population contains adults and learners; the learners learn from utterances produced by adults. At some given moment, the adults are replaced by the learners and new learners enter the population and the process repeats, thus providing a generational turnover. Typically (a part of) the language is transmitted from one generation to the next in one pass, without competition (but see Kirby (2000) for a model with competition) and in a population of size two, i.e., with one adult and one learner. The integration of the ILM with the language game allows for competition between different rules and structures, but it requires more passes through the language in order for the language to be learnt sufficiently well.

The experiments reported in Vogt (2005b) have revealed that learners from the first generation already develop a compositional structure, even in the absence of a transmission bottleneck. The reason for this rapid development of compositionality is to be sought in the statistically high level of reoccurring structures in both the feature spaces (thus speeding up the development of semantic structures) and in the signal space (thus increasing the likelihood of finding structures at the syntactic level), see Vogt (2005a) for a detailed analysis. In the case that the population was of size two, this compositionality was rather stable, but when the population increased to a size of six, a transmission bottleneck was required to provide stability in compositionality. (Instability of compositionality means that the compositional languages collapse and holistic ones take over.) This difference can be understood by realising that when a learner learns from only one adult, the input received by the learner is consistent, allowing them to adopt the compositional structures reliably. When multiple learners learn from multiple adults who do not speak to each other, then the input to each learner is highly inconsistent, making it harder to learn the language and to converge on the language.

With the "larger" population size of six agents, compositionality was only stable over multiple generations when the guessing game model was used. When the observational game was used, the transmission bottleneck caused compositional structures to remain longer in the population, but they eventually died out (Figure 8). Like for the experiments on lexicon development, the differences between the guessing game and observational game could be explained by the pressure to disambiguate competing structures. Where in the guessing game this pressure is high, because the hearer has to guess the speaker's topic based on the received expression, this pressure is absent in the observational game, because the hearer already knows the topic and the information of the expression is redundant. It appears that the lack of this pressure allows the meanings to drift through the conceptual spaces. If the meanings are part of a whole meaning, i.e., they are part of a compositional structure, a meaning shift affects a larger part of the language. However, when the meaning is associated holistically, a shift has little effect on the rest of the language. Consequently, the shift of meanings makes the language less stable and thus harder to learn than holistic structures.

Another interesting result that was found is that when learners are allowed to speak as well, which is typically not the case in the BKS models, no experimentally imposed transmission bottleneck is required for populations of six agents (Vogt, 2005c). Instead

Figure 8. The results of an experiment comparing the guessing game (a) with the observational game (b)

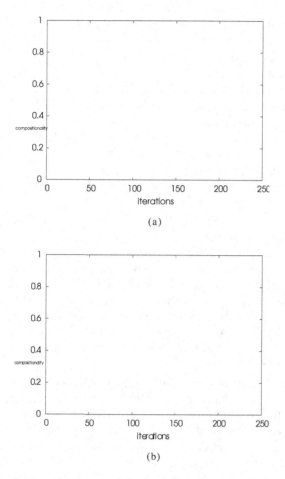

(a)

(b)

In the experiment, the language is transmitted from one generation to another during an iteration (x-axis). The graphs show the evolution of compositionality, which measures the degree with which produced or interpreted expression has a compositional structure. Each line shows the evolution in one run of the experiment. The experiment was done with a population of size six and with a transmission bottleneck of 50% (Vogt, 2005b).

of starting to speak when they are adults, the learners now speak during their development. In this way, the learners face the bottleneck earlier in life, because they have to produce utterance about previously unseen objects. This may be an important result, because it may help to explain why children are so good at learning grammar early in life. Moreover, this property may even explain why children are thought to be the driving force for the development of grammar in Nicaraguan sign language (Senghas, Kita, & Özyürek, 2004).

A recent study in which the population size was varied from two to 100 revealed that this model can lead to compositional structures in larger populations (Vogt, 2005d). Interestingly, at first when the population becomes larger (up to 40 agents), the less frequent compositionality is stable, but when the population becomes even larger, compositionality emerges even more frequently at a high stable level.

A more complex model implemented in an extended physical version of the Talking Heads experiment is being developed by Steels and his co-workers (Steels, 2004; Steels & Baillie, 2003). In this experiment, the cameras do not look at a static scene pasted on the white board but observe a dynamic scene played in front of them, such as "pick up red ball." The events are processed through a visual processing system, which — although advanced — is still very limited. Only slow movements can be captured and only a few objects can be recognised, but only *after* training the visual module. The pre-processed events are then matched with top-down generated world knowledge, which is represented in the form of a predicate calculus of which the basic building blocks are predefined (Steels & Baillie, 2003).

Using these event descriptions, the guessing game (or *description game*) proceeds. Where possible, the agents use the knowledge (lexicon, syntax and semantics) they already acquired, but when events or semantics cannot be described with the given knowledge, new parts of the language are invented, abducted or induced. New words, semantic categories, syntactic categories and hierarchical structures can be constructed using some complex techniques, which are largely based on existing techniques from computational linguistics. This way *grounded construction grammars* (Lakoff, 1987) can develop, as some preliminary experiments have shown (Steels, 2004). The experiments reported so far were carried out with two robots of one generation, which took turns in taking the role of speaker.

Although using such small populations without a population turnover is not uncommon in robotic models (see, e.g., Steels & Vogt, 1997; Vogt, 2003a), the results achieved may not be stable in larger populations with a generational turnover as shown in Vogt (2005b,d). However, given that the model also incorporates the guessing game, which is in favour for a strong selective pressure on the competition between different structures in the language, the model is likely to scale up in terms of population size and population dynamics. Apart from the higher complexity in experimental set up and learning mechanisms, one of the main differences between Steels' model and my own is that in Steels' model the speaker can invent new grammatical structures, whereas in my model, this can only be achieved by the hearer. Although it is unclear what the implications are for this distinction, experiments with my model have confirmed that the productive power of speakers — even though they do not invent new compositional structures — has a positive effect on the stability of the evolved grammars (Vogt, 2005c).

Ecological Models

All models discussed so far have completely ignored the ecological value of language and thus fail to investigate the functional meanings of semiotic symbols. In human societies, language is clearly used to exchange information that can be used to enhance some aspect of behaviour. For instance, language can be used to indicate the whereabouts of food sources, the presence of predators or other dangers. So far, no physical robot study has been carried out in which the evolved language is used to achieve something. There exist, however, a few grounded simulations in which the language is used to coordinate activity that improves the viability of the artificial organism.

Well known are the studies on the emergence of symbolic communication in a world of edible and non-edible mushrooms (Cangelosi & Harnad, 2000; Cangelosi & Parisi, 1998). In these studies, the task of the agents was to approach the edible mushrooms and avoid the poisonous ones. The mushrooms were perceptually distinguishable through the encoding of a bitstring. The controller of the agents was implemented as a multilayered feedforward network. In Cangelosi and Parisi (1998), the weights of the network were trained using a GA, where the fitness was based on the organisms' energy levels (the profit of eating edible mushrooms was smaller than the cost of eating non-edible ones). As mentioned before, training a neural network using only a GA is far from realistic for modelling language evolution, since it lacks a model of language acquisition.

In Cangelosi and Harnad (2000), the agents do have a learning cycle in which the neural network is adapted using backpropagation and the initial weights evolve using the GA. Although this model is more realistic, backpropagation uses the output vector of the target behaviour to update the weights. Cangelosi and Harnad (2000) investigated two conditions: (I) one in which no communication was used to classify edible and non-edible mushrooms, and (II) one in which communication was used. They have shown that using communication achieved higher performance on categorisation than in the condition without communication, *provided* the population in condition II first evolved the ability to categorise the mushroom world using the method of condition I. This is in contrast with the language game model, in which the ability to categorise the world co-develops with the language. Given the rapid changing nature of natural language, co-development of meaning and forms seems more realistic.

Interestingly, the analysis of the evolved neural networks has shown how the networks had emerged with different internal representations in both conditions. Condition II yielded a more structured representation of the categories, allowing Cangelosi and Harnad (2000) to conclude that language influences the way in which the individuals observe the world. A similar Whorfian effect (Whorf, 1956) has also been observed with the language games (Steels & Belpaeme, 2005). A nice property of the Cangelosi et al. experiments is that they show how language can emerge to improve the population's fitness, which was not defined in terms of communicative accuracy.

A related ecological experiment, where the categories co-developed with the language was carried out by de Jong (2000). This simulation, which was inspired by the alarm call system of Vervet monkeys, contained a number of agents, which were placed on a two-dimensional grid of size $N \times 3$.[9] At given times, a predator was present in one of the three rows; the row in which it was present resembled the type of predator. In order to avoid the predator, the agents that were in that row had to move to another row. The agents had a vision system with which they could see the predator, but this system was subject to noise so the presence was not always detected. The agents were also equipped with a language game model, in which they could develop categories that represented their own position, location of the predator and the appropriate action to take. The categorisation was modelled using the discrimination game with an adaptive subspace representation that allowed the emergence of *situation concepts* (de Jong, 2000). Situation concepts relate — based on past experiences — perceptual categories with actions that need to be performed in order to remain viable. De Jong showed that the agents could successfully evolve a lexicon to avoid predators. Moreover, de Jong successfully showed that the lexicon development can be classified as attractor dynamics, thus providing support for considering the language game as a complex adaptive dynamical system.

Inspired by earlier work of Steels (1994) on ecological robot models, Vogt (2002a) reported an experiment in which two simulated mobile robots developed a lexicon to improve on their ability to remain viable over longer periods of time. The robots operated

Figure 9. This figure illustrates the principles of the Braitenberg vehicles used in the experiments of Vogt (2002a).

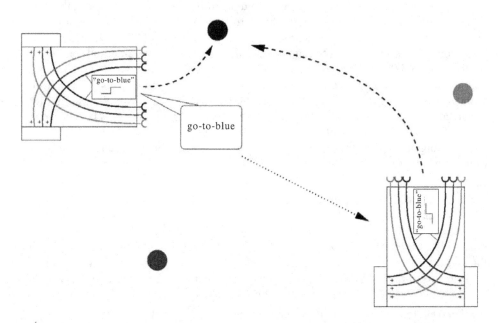

Different sensorimotor modules connect the sensors that are sensitive to a particular colour directly to the motors of the two wheels of the robot. These reactive systems make sure that when one module is activated, the robot will move towards the light source of the corresponding colour. Activation of a coupling could be regulated by the need of some energy source, or by the interpretation of a received signal. When a coupling was activated due to the need of some energy source, this robot would try to produce an utterance that is associated with this coupling (e.g., the "go-to-blue" signal in the figure), using the standard guessing game. In turn, the hearer would interpret the signal, which could activate its associated sensorimotor coupling. If both robots then ended up visiting the same energy source, they received energy which then served as a positive feedback mechanism for updating the association scores in the lexicon.

in an environment that contained four different charging stations at which they could increase their energy levels. The only way to get access to the energy was to arrive at a charging station simultaneously. Each charging station had a different colour and at some randomly selected moment[10], one robot initiated a game and selected a charging station that was in its visual field. The robots played a guessing game and the hearer would guess where the initiator was going to and activated the corresponding sensorimotor coupling. When both robots arrived at the same charging station, their energy levels would be refilled, thus providing a positive feedback loop for updating the scores in their lexicons. The robots' control mechanisms were based on a simple Braitenberg vehicle (Braitenberg, 1984) and had four excitatory sensorimotor connections sensitive to the four different light colours, which they used to navigate towards the corresponding light source (Figure 9).

Each connection served as a category, and when activated, they could activate an associated form. This way, the semiotic symbols could be viewed as symbols that had as referent the action of moving towards a charging station in order to refill their energy supplies; the form is obviously the signal, which they conventionalised using the guessing game, and the meaning was represented by the activation level (0 or 1) of the sensorimotor connection that functioned as the "life-task" of the robots to maintain their energy levels. This, then, could be an interesting step toward the development of a robotic model in which the meanings of the symbols are truly meaningful according to Ziemke and Sharkey (2001). A nice aspect with respect to the implementation is that the meaning of the actions are not represented in terms of the temporal (sensori)motor flow, as was the case in Vogt (2000b), but more directly in the activation of a reactive mechanism. This is much more in line with Brooks' (1990) remark that "once the essence of being and reacting are available" (p. 5), the development of higher order functions, such as using language, would be rather simple.

Future Trends

Up to the present, a lot has been achieved by using robots to study the origins and evolution of language. However, it is clear from the overview in this chapter that we are still far from understanding the entire picture. Can we ever design a group of robots that can evolve languages similar to human languages? Personally, I think that the human brain and body is so complex that we may never be able to unravel all its secrets — as we may never unravel the complete working of our universe, which is similarly complex. Nevertheless, I think that we can use robotics profitably to answer some of the questions that are posed in our effort to understand language evolution. Much future research will need to focus on ecological models, models of grammar, categorisation of more human-like concepts and on models of the Theory of Mind. Furthermore, the models will have to be scaled up at many levels, such as population size, sensorimotor complexity and complexity of the world in which the robots operate.

A recently started European project called New Ties[11] aims at developing a simulation in which a large community of robots (over 1,000 agents) evolve a cultural society, including language. The society "lives" in an environment where they have to cooperate in order to survive (Gilbert, Schuster, den Besten, & Yang, 2005). The agents will evolve and learn techniques to deal with the constraints set by the environment in order to improve their viability (Griffioen, Schut, Eiben, Bontovics, Hévízi, & Lõrincz, 2005). In addition, the agents will be designed to evolve language as the motor for evolving the cultural society (Vogt & Divina, 2005). The techniques these agents will use are heavily based on the language game techniques that have been developed so far. One of the major innovations — apart from its complexity and ecological setting — will be a design on the Theory of Mind, which at a later stage is intended to become subject of the evolution.

Given that many problems in modelling language evolution on robots relate to the difficulties in establishing joint or shared attention to the referent of the communication, studies into the nature of this ability are extremely important. Only few studies are known that investigate how joint attention can emerge (e.g., Kaplan & Hafner, 2004). One of the key aspects with respect to joint attention and related issues is that agents need to infer the intentions of other agents. This ability can loosely be characterised by the Theory of Mind (Premack & Woordruff, 1978). It may well be that the Theory of Mind is one of the major innovations of the human species with respect to language origins, and therefore its origins deserve more attention in models of language evolution.

On the physical side of the implementation, research is starting to focus on the development of more humanoid-like platforms. Such implementations have more complex sensorimotor systems, which inevitably will provide more complex data from which a more complex language — in terms of grammar and vocabulary size — can develop.

With respect to the origins and evolution of grammar and compositionality, research needs to be done regarding the way learning mechanisms could have evolved that allow individuals to construct grammatical and compositional structures. Up to now, all studies on grammaticalisation have assumed that such learning mechanisms exist and therefore only investigate how grammar can emerge given these mechanisms.

Another important direction that needs to be tackled is in relation to the grounding of more abstract and higher level symbols, such as, for instance, number systems, arithmetic, planning and "feelings" (internal states). Up to now, all research has focused on the emergence of language about events or objects that are directly observable to the robots. We humans often use language to communicate about events that happened in the past or that may happen in the future. Some work on the development of time concepts has been done (De Beule, 2004), but it would be good if a robot could communicate, for instance, the presence of an interesting object at a distant location, which the robot has visited before.

Most techniques used so far are based on simple language games where some aspect of a visible entity is communicated in one direction to investigate learning techniques. However, human language use is based much more on dialogues. Future robotic models should investigate how dialogues can aid in evolving language. This could be particularly interesting for applications where robots develop their own language in order to cooperate in environments we don't know, such as planets, or using sensors that we find difficult to read, such as infrared, sonar or other exotic sensors.

Conclusion

In this chapter, an overview of robotic (and other grounded) models of language evolution is presented. There are many reasons for using robotic models to study the evolution of language. The most fundamental one is that robots — necessarily — have to solve the *symbol grounding problem* (Harnad, 1990). It is argued that by using the Peircean definition of symbols (or *semiotic symbols*), the symbol grounding problem is solved, because these symbols are *per definition* grounded in the real world. This, however, shifts the problem in the *physical symbol grounding problem* (Vogt, 2002b), which deals with constructing these semiotic symbols. More pragmatic reasons for using robots to study language origins and evolution are:

1. robotic models can reveal false assumptions that are typically incorporated in ungrounded models, e.g., the assumption that all agents have the same meanings and are given the meaning of a signal during communication and

2. robots can actually exploit the nature of the interaction with the environment to develop certain structures in language.

The overview shows that in many areas, robots can successfully be used to study certain aspects of language evolution, though the state of the art is still extremely limited, especially when compared to human languages. The design of robotic models is extremely hard and time consuming, for many difficult problems need to be solved. One of the most difficult problems that was identified in most models deals with the robots' ability to infer the referent of a heard utterance. If we assume that this ability is the key aspect of a Theory of Mind (Bloom, 2000; Premack & Woodruff, 1978), then the studies indicate that the evolution of a ToM is perhaps the most important transition in human evolution with respect to language evolution.

Robotics has successfully been applied to study the emergence of small lexicons and simple grammatical structures, and to study how language evolution can aid in operating cooperatively in an ecological environment. Most of the models presented started from the assumption that language is a complex adaptive dynamical system in which language evolves through self-organisation as a result of cultural interactions and individual learning. The studies reported have shown that the language game in general provides a robust model in which robots can develop a culturally shared symbol system despite (1) the difficulties they face in establishing joint attention and (2) the differences in their perception and meaning development. The studies have also revealed how agents can exploit structures they find in their interaction with their environment to construct simple grammars that resemble this structure. Furthermore, the studies reveal some of the effects that the nature of social interactions and the co-development of language and meaning have on the emergence of language. In addition, ecological models on the evolution of language indicate how the functional use of language can provide feedback on the effectiveness of communication, which individuals can use to learn the language.

Concluding, robotics provides a fruitful platform to study the origins and evolution of language, thus allowing us to gain more insights about the nature and nurture of human language.

Acknowledgments

The writing of this chapter was sponsored by an European Commission Marie Curie Fellowship at the University of Edinburgh and a VENI grant awarded by the Netherlands Organisation for Scientific Research at Tilburg University. The author thanks Tony Belpaeme, Andrew Smith and the anonymous reviewers for their invaluable comments on earlier versions of this manuscript.

References

Barsalou, L. W. (1999). Perceptual symbol systems. *Behavioral and Brain Sciences, 22,* 577-609.

Batali, J. (2002). The negotiation and acquisition of recursive grammars as a result of competition among exemplars. In T. Briscoe (Ed.), *Linguistic evolution through language acquisition: Formal and computational models.* Cambridge: Cambridge University Press.

Belpaeme, T., Steels, L., & van Looveren, J. (1998). The construction and acquisition of visual categories. In A. Birk & J. Demiris (Eds.), *Learning robots, proceedings of the EWLR-6* (LNAI 1545). Berlin: Springer.

Berthouze, L., & Tijsseling, A. (2002). Acquiring ontological categories through interaction. *The Journal of Three Dimensional Images, 16*(4), 141-147.

Bickerton, D. (1984). The language bioprogram hypothesis. *Behavioral and Brain Sciences, 7,* 173-212.

Billard, A., & Dautenhahn, K. (1999). Experiments in social robotics: Grounding and use of communication in autonomous agents. *Adaptive Behavior, 7*(3-4), 415-438.

Billard, A., & Hayes, G. (1999). Drama, a connectionist architecture for control and learning in autonomous robots. *Adaptive Behaviour, 7*(1), 35-64.

Bloom, P. (2000). *How children learn the meanings of words.* Cambridge, MA: The MIT Press.

Braitenberg, V. (1984). *Vehicles, experiments in synthetic psychology.* Cambridge MA: The MIT Press.

Brighton, H. (2002). Compositional syntax from cultural transmission. *Artificial Life, 8*(1), 25-54.

Briscoe, E. J. (2000). Grammatical acquisition: Inductive bias and coevolution of language and the language acquisition device. *Language, 76*(2), 245-296.

Briscoe, E. J. (Ed.). (2002). *Linguistic evolution through language acquisition: Formal and computational models*. Cambridge: Cambridge University Press.

Brooks, R. A. (1990). Elephants don't play chess. *Robotics and Autonomous Systems, 6*, 3-15.

Brown, R., & Hanlon, C. (1970). Derivational complexity and order of acquisition in child speech. In *Cognition and the development of language*. New York: Wiley.

Cangelosi, A., & Harnad, S. (2000). The adaptive advantage of symbolic theft over sensorimotor toil: Grounding language in perceptual categories. *Evolution of Communication, 4*(1), 117-142

Cangelosi, A., & Parisi, D. (1998). The emergence of "language" in an evolving population of neural networks. *Connection Science, 10*, 83-93.

Cangelosi, A., & Parisi, D. (Eds.). (2002). *Simulating the evolution of language*. London: Springer.

Chomsky, N. (1980). Rules and representations. *Behavioral and brain sciences, 3*, 1-61.

Chouinard, M. M., & Clark, E. V. (2003). Adult reformulations of child errors as negative evidence. *Journal of Child Language, 30*(3), 637-669.

Christiansen, M. H., & Kirby, S. (Eds.). (2003). *Language evolution*. Oxford: Oxford University Press.

Clancey, W. J. (1997). *Situated cognition*. Cambridge: Cambridge University Press.

Clark, E. V. (1993). *The lexicon in acquisition*. Cambridge: Cambridge University Press.

Coradeschi, S., & Saffiotti, A. (2000). Anchoring symbols to sensor data: Preliminary report. In *Proceedings of the Seventeenth National Conference on Artificial Intelligence (AAAI-2000)* (pp. 129-135). Austin, TX: AAAI press.

De Beule, J. (2004). Creating temporal categories for an ontology of time. In R. Verbrugge, N. Taatgen, & L. Schomaker (Eds.), *Proceedings of the 16th Belgian-Dutch Conference on Artificial Intelligence (BNAIC '04)* (pp.107-114). Groningen, The Netherlands.

de Jong, E. D. (2000). *The development of communication*. PhD thesis, Vrije Universiteit Brussel.

De Saussure, F. (1974). *Course in general linguistics*. New York: Fontana.

Deacon, T. (1997). *The symbolic species*. New York: W. Norton and Co.

Elman, J. L., Bates, E. A., Johnson, M. H., Karmiloff-Smith, A., Parisi, D., & Plunkett, K. (1996). *Rethinking innateness: A connectionist perspective on development*. Cambridge, MA: MIT Press.

Gärdenfors, P. (2000). *Conceptual spaces*. Cambridge, MA: MIT Press.

Gilbert, N., Schuster, S., den Besten, M., & Yang, L. (2005). Environment design for emerging artificial societies. In *Proceedings of AISB 2005: Socially inspired computing joint symposium* (pp. 57-63). Hatfield, UK: Society for the Study of Artificial Intelligence and the Simulation of Behaviour.

Griffioen, A., Schut, M., Eiben, A., Bontovics, A., Hévízi, Gy., & Lőrincz, A. (2005). New Ties agent. In *Proceedings of AISB 2005: Socially Inspired Computing Joint Symposium* (pp. 72-79). Hatfield, UK: Society for the Study of Artificial Intelligence and the Simulation of Behaviour.

Harnad, S. (1990). The symbol grounding problem. *Physica D, 42*, 335-346.

Hurford, J. R. (1999). Language learning from fragmentary input. In K. Dautenhahn & C. Nehaniv (Eds.), *Proceedings of the AISB '99 Symposium on Imitation in Animals and Artifacts* (pp. 121-129). Society for the Study of Artificial Intelligence and the Simulation of Behaviour.

Hurford, J. R., Knight, C., & Studdert-Kennedy, M. (Eds.). (1998) *Approaches to the evolution of language*. Cambridge: Cambridge University Press.

Jackendoff, R. (1999). Possible stages in the evolution of the language capacity. *Trends in Cognitive Science, 3*(7), 272-279.

Kaplan, F., & Hafner, V. (2004). The challenges of joint attention. In L. Berthouze, H. Kozima, C. Prince, G. Sandini, G. Stojanov, G. Metta, et al. (Eds.), *Proceedings of the 4th International Workshop on Epigenetic Robotics: Modeling Cognitive Development in Robotic System, 117* (pp. 67-74). Lund: Lund University Cognitive Studies.

Kirby, S. (2000). Syntax without natural selection: How compositionality emerges from vocabulary in a population of learners. In C. Knight, M. Studdert-Kennedy, & J. R. Hurford (Eds.), *The evolutionary emergence of language: Social function and the origins of linguistic form* (pp. 303-323). Cambridge: Cambridge University Press.

Kirby, S. (2001). Spontaneous evolution of linguistic structure: An iterated learning model of the emergence of regularity and irregularity. *IEEE Transactions on Evolutionary Computation, 5*(2), 102-110.

Kirby, S. (2002). Natural language from artificial life. *Artificial Life, 8*(3), 185-215.

Kirby, S., & Hurford, J. R. (2002). The emergence of linguistic structure: An overview of the iterated learning model. In A. Cangelosi & D. Parisi (Eds.), *Simulating the evolution of language* (pp. 121-148). London: Springer.

Lakoff, G. (1987). *Women, fire and dangerous things*. Chicago: The University of Chicago Press.

Landau, B., Smith, L. B., & Jones, S. S. (1988). The importance of shape in early lexical learning. *Cognitive Development, 3*, 299-321.

Loula, A., Gudwin, R., & Queiroz, J. (2003). Synthetic approach of symbolic creatures. *S.E.E.D. Journal — Semiotics, Evolution, Energy, and Development, 3*(3), 125-133

Macnamara, J. (1982). *Names for things: A study of human learning*. Cambridge, MA: MIT Press.

MacWhinney, B. (1999) *Emergence of language*. Mahwah, NJ: Lawrence Erlbaum Associates.

Mandelbrot, B. B. (1965) Information theory and psycholinguistics. In B. B. Wolman & E. Nagel (Eds.), *Scientific psychology* (pp. 550-562). New York: Basic Books.

Markman, E. (1989). *Categorization and naming in children*. Cambridge, MA: The MIT Press.

Marocco, D., Cangelosi, A., & Nolfi, S. (2003). The emergence of communication in evolutionary robots. *Philosophical Transactions: Mathematical, Physical and Engineering Sciences, 361*(1811), 2397-2421.

Maturana, H. R., & Varela, F. R. (1992). *The tree of knowledge: Yhe biological roots of human understanding*. Boston: Shambhala.

McCarthy, J., & Hayes, P. J. (1969). Some philosophical problems from the standpoint of artificial intelligence. *Machine Intelligence, 4*, 463-502.

Newell, A., & Simon, H. A. (1976). Computer science as empirical inquiry: Symbols and search. *Communications of the ACM, 19*, 113-126.

Nowak, M. A., Plotkin, J. B., & Jansen, V. A. A. (2000) The evolution of syntactic communication. *Nature, 404*, 495-498.

Oates, T., Eyler-Walker, Z., & Cohen, P. R. (2000). Toward natural language interfaces for robotic agents: Grounding linguistic meaning in sensors. In *Proceedings of the 4th International Conference on Autonomous Agents* (pp. 227-228).

Ogden, C. K., & Richards, I. A. (1923). *The meaning of meaning: A study of the influence of language upon thought and of the science of symbolism*. London: Routledge & Kegan Paul.

Oliphant, M. (1999). The learning barrier: Moving from innate to learned systems of communication. *Adaptive Behavior, 7*(3-4), 371-384.

Peirce, C. S. (1931-1958). *Collected papers (Volume I-VIII)*. Cambridge, MA: Harvard University Press.

Pfeifer, R., & Scheier, C. (1999). *Understanding intelligence*. Cambridge, MA.: MIT Press.

Pinker, S., & Bloom, P. (1990). Natural language and natural selection. *Behavioral and Brain Sciences, 13*, 707-789,

Premack, D., & Woodruff, G. (1978). Does the chimpanzee have a theory of mind? *Behavioral and Brain Sciences, 1*(4), 515-526.

Quine, W. V. O. (1960). *Word and object*. Cambridge: Cambridge University Press.

Quinn, M. (2001). Evolving communication without dedicated communication channels. In J. Kelemen & P. Sosík (Eds.), *Proceedings of the 6th European Conference on Artificial Life (ECAL 2001)* (LNAI 2159, pp. 357-366). Berlin; Heidelberg, Germany: Springer-Verlag.

Rosenstein, M., & Cohen, P. R. (1998). Symbol grounding with delay coordinates. In *Working notes of the AAAI-98 Workshop on the Grounding of Word Meaning* (pp. 20-21). Menlo Park, CA: AAAI Press.

Roy, D. (2000). A computational model of word learning from multimodal sensory input. In *International Conference of Cognitive Modeling*, Groningen, The Netherlands.

Searle, J. R. (1980). Minds, brains and programs. *Behavioral and Brain Sciences, 3*, 417-457.

Senghas, A., Kita, S., & Özyürek, A. (2004). Children creating core properties of language: Evidence from an emerging sign language in Nicaragua. *Science, 305*(5691), 1779-1782.

Seyfarth, R., & Cheney, D. (1986). Vocal development in vervet monkeys. *Animal Behavior, 34*, 1640-1658.

Sierra-Santibáñez, J. (2001). Grounded models as a basis for intuitive reasoning. In *Proceedings of the International Joint Conference on Artificial Intelligence 2001* (pp. 401-406).

Siskind, J. M. (1996). A computational study of cross-situational techniques for learning word-to-meaning mappings. *Cognition, 61*, 39-91.

Smith, A. D. M. (2003). Intelligent meaning creation in a clumpy world helps communication. *Artificial Life, 9*(2), 559-574.

Smith, A. D. M. (2005a). Mutual exclusivity: Communicative success despite conceptual divergence. In M. Tallerman (Ed.), *Language origins: Perspectives on evolution* (pp. 372-388). Oxford: Oxford University Press.

Smith, A. D. M. (2005b). The inferential transmission of language. *Adaptive Behavior, 13*(4).

Smith, K. (2002). The cultural evolution of communication in a population of neural networks. *Connection Science, 14*(1), 65-84.

Smith, K., Brighton, H., & Kirby S. (2003). Complex systems in language evolution: The cultural emergence of compositional structure. *Advances in Complex Systems, 6*(4), 537-558.

Steels, L. (1994). A case study in the behavior-oriented design of autonomous agents. In D. Cliff, P. Husbands, J. A. Meyer, & S. W. Wilson (Eds.), *From Animals to Animats 3. Proceedings of the Third International Conference on Simulation of Adaptive Behavior, SAB'94* (pp. 445-452). Cambridge, MA: MIT Press.

Steels, L. (1996a). Emergent adaptive lexicons. In P. Maes (Ed.), *From Animals to Animats 4: Proceedings of the Fourth International Conference On Simulating Adaptive Behavior*. Cambridge MA: MIT Press.

Steels, L. (1996b). Perceptually grounded meaning creation. In M. Tokoro (Ed.), *Proceedings of the International Conference on Multi-Agent Systems*. Menlo Park, CA.: AAAI Press.

Steels, L. (1997). Language learning and language contact. In W. Daelemans, A. Van den Bosch, & A. Weijters (Eds.), *Workshop Notes of the ECML/MLnet Familiarization Workshop on Empirical Learning of Natural Language Processing Tasks* (pp. 11-24). Prague.

Steels, L. (2004). Constructivist development of grounded construction grammars. In W. Daelemans (Ed.), *Proceedings Annual Meeting of Association for Computational Linguistics*.

Steels, L., & Baillie, J.C. (2003). Shared grounding of event descriptions by autonomous robots. *Robotics and Autonomous Systems 43*(2-3), 163-173.

Steels, L., & Belpaeme, T. (2005). Coordinating perceptually grounded categories through language: A case study for colour. *Behavioral and Brain Sciences, 28,* 469-489.

Steels, L., & Kaplan, F. (1998). Stochasticity as a source of innovation in language games. In C. Adami, R. Belew, H. Kitano, & C. Taylor (Eds.), *Proceedings of Alive VI* (pp. 368-376). Cambridge, MA: MIT Press.

Steels, L., & Kaplan, F. (2000). Aibo's first words: The social learning of language and meaning. *Evolution of Communication, 4*(1), 3-32.

Steels, L., Kaplan, F., McIntyre, A., & van Looveren, J. (2002). Crucial factors in the origins of word-meaning. In A. Wray (Ed.), *The transition to language.* Oxford: Oxford University Press.

Steels, L., & Vogt, P. (1997). Grounding adaptive language games in robotic agents. In C. Husbands & I. Harvey (Eds.), *Proceedings of the 4th European Conference on Artificial Life.* Cambridge, MA: MIT Press.

Sugita, Y., & Tani, J. (2005). Learning semantic combinatoriality from the interaction between linguistic and behavioral processes. *Adaptive Behavior, 13*(1), 33-52.

Tomasello, M. (1999). *The cultural origins of human cognition.* Cambridge, MA: Harvard University Press.

van Looveren, J. (2001). Robotic experiments on the emergence of a lexicon. In B. Kröse, M. de Rijke, G. Schreiber, & M. van Someren (Eds.), *Proceedings of the 13th Belgian/Netherlands Artificial Intelligence Conference (BNAIC'01)* (pp. 175-182).

Vogt, P. (2000a). Bootstrapping grounded symbols by minimal autonomous robots. *Evolution of Communication, 4*(1), 89-118.

Vogt, P. (2000b). Grounding language about actions: Mobile robots playing follow me games. In J.-A. Meyer, A. Bertholz, D. Floreano, H. Roitblat, & S. W. Wilson (Eds.), *SAB2000 Proceedings Supplement Book.* Honolulu, HI: International Society for Adaptive Behavior.

Vogt, P. (2000c). *Lexicon grounding on mobile robots.* PhD thesis, Vrije Universiteit Brussel.

Vogt, P. (2002a). Anchoring symbols to sensorimotor control. In *Proceedings of the 14th Belgian/Netherlands Artificial Intelligence Conference (BNAIC '02)* (pp. 331-338).

Vogt, P. (2002b). The physical symbol grounding problem. *Cognitive Systems Research, 3*(3), 429-457.

Vogt, P. (2003a). Anchoring of semiotic symbols. *Robotics and Autonomous Systems, 43*(2), 109-120.

Vogt, P. (2003b). Grounded lexicon formation without explicit meaning transfer: Who's talking to who? In W. Banzhaf, T. Christaller, P. Dittrich, J. T. Kim, & J. Ziegler (Eds.), *Advances in Artificial Life — Proceedings of the 7th European Conference on Artificial Life (ECAL)* (pp. 545-552). Berlin; Heidelberg, Germany: Springer Verlag.

Vogt, P. (2003c). THSim v3.2: The talking heads simulation tool. In W. Banzhaf, T. Christaller, P. Dittrich, J. T. Kim, & J. Ziegler (Eds.), *Advances in Artificial Life — Proceedings of the 7th European Conference on Artificial Life (ECAL)* (pp. 535-544). Berlin; Heidelberg, Germany: Springer Verlag.

Vogt, P. (2004). Minimum cost and the emergence of the Zipf-Mandelbrot law. In J. Pollack, M. Bedau, P. Husbands, T. Ikegami, & R. A. Watson (Eds.), *Artificial Life IX Proceedings of the Ninth International Conference on the Simulation and Synthesis of Living Systems* (pp. 214-219). Cambridge, MA: MIT Press.

Vogt, P. (2005a). Meaning development versus predefined meanings in language evolution models. In L. Pack-Kaelbling & A. Saffiotti (Eds.), *Proceedings of IJCAI-05* (pp. 1154-1159).

Vogt, P. (2005b). The emergence of compositional structures in perceptually grounded language games. *Artificial Intelligence, 167*(1-2), 206-242.

Vogt, P. (2005c). On the acquisition and evolution of compositional languages: Sparse input and the productive creativity of children. *Adaptive Behavior, 13*(4).

Vogt, P. (2005d). Stability conditions in the evolution of compositional languages: Issues in scaling population sizes [Computer software]. In *Proceedings of the European Conference on Complex Systems*.

Vogt, P., & Coumans, H. (2003). Investigating social interaction strategies for bootstrapping lexicon development. *Journal for Artificial Societies and Social Simulation, 6*(1). Retrieved from http://jasss.soc.surrey.ac.uk

Vogt, P., & Divina, F. (2005). Language evolution in large populations of autonomous agents: Issues in scaling. In *Proceedings of AISB 2005: Socially Inspired Computing Joint Symposium* (pp. 80-87). Society for the Study of Artificial Intelligence and the Simulation of Behaviour.

Vogt, P., & Smith, A. D. M. (2005). Learning colour words is slow: A cross-situational learning account. *Behavioral and Brain Sciences, 28,* 509-510.

Wedel, A. (2004). Self-organization and categorical behavior in phonology. In *Proceedings of hte Berkley Linguistics Society (Vol. 29)*

Whorf, B. L. (1956). *Language, thought, and reality*. Cambridge, MA: MIT Press.

Wittgenstein, L. (1958). *Philosophical investigations*. Oxford: Basil Blackwell.

Wray, A. (1998). Protolanguage as a holistic system for social interaction. *Language and Communication, 18,* 47-67.

Wray, A. (Ed.). (2002). *The transition to language*. Oxford: Oxford University Press.

Yamauchi, H. (2004). *Baldwinian accounts of language evolution*. PhD thesis, University of Edinburgh.

Ziemke, T., & Sharkey, N. E. (2001). A stroll through the worlds of robots and animals: Applying Jakob von Uexküll's theory of meaning to adaptive robots and artificial life. *Semiotica, 134*(1-4), 701-746.

Zipf, G. K. (1949). *Human behaviour and the principle of least effort: An introduction to human ecology*. Cambridge, MA: Addison-Wesley.

Endnotes

[1] Peirce actually used the terms object, interpretant and representamen to denote what I call referent, meaning and form respectively. Throughout the text I will also use the terms label, word and signal interchangebly to denote a form.

[2] This problem is similar to the anchoring problem (Coradeschi & Saffiotti, 2000), which deals with the technical problem of connecting traditionally defined symbols to the real world, see Vogt (2003a) for a discussion.

[3] Although this is not necessarily more complex than the evolution grammar, it is treated at the end of this section because it is helpful to have the background provided in the first three sections.

[4] THSim is freely downloadable from http://www.ling.ed.ac.uk/~paulv/thsim.html.

[5] Note that although it is believed that Vervet monkeys learn the meaning of their alarm calls, the calls themselves are believed to be innate.

[6] The (unfortunately chosen) term selfish game refers to the selfishness of the robots' not caring about the effectiveness of the game.

[7] See http://talking-heads.csl.sony.fr

[8] The term conceptual spaces (Gärdenfors, 2000) is used to denote an n-dimensional space in which categories are represented by prototypes. The conceptual space is spanned by n quality dimensions that relate to some (preprocessed) sensorimotor quality. Gärdenfors (2000) has argued that conceptual spaces can form the semantic basis for linguistic categories.

[9] See Loula, Gudwin and Queiroz (2003) for another grounded study on the emergence of alarm calls among vervet monkeys.

[10] Currently, research is carried out to regulate the selection based on the need for energy and use the evolved language to pass on knowledge how to survive in this onvironmont.

[11] New Emerging World Models through Individual, Evolutionary and Social Learning (http://www.new-ties.org).

Chapter VII

Evolutionary Robotics as a Tool to Investigate Spatial Cognition in Artificial and Natural Systems

Michela Ponticorvo, University of Calabria, Italy

Richard Walker, XiWrite s.a.s., Italy

Orazio Miglino, University of Naples "Frederico II", Italy

Abstract

This chapter introduces Evolutionary Robotics as a means of studying spatial cognition in artificial and natural systems. It argues that evolutionary robotics, used to replicate quantitative observations of spatial behavior in laboratory animals, offers a powerful tool to understand the general mechanisms underlying animal orientation. In particular, the authors show that "artificial organisms," with a controller architecture that precludes the presence of "cognitive maps," can accurately replicate the observed behavior of animals in classical experimental set-ups, thus suggesting that spatial orientation may not require abstract spatial representations and that sensory-motor coordination, in the presence of environment constraints, may be enough, on its own, to generate complex spatial behavior.

Introduction

The chapter is divided into four sections: the first section describes examples of spatial behavior in animals, briefly outlines the debate between "cognitivist" versus "action-based" explanations and introduces a number of methodological issues. The second section introduces evolutionary robotics (ER) and discusses its potential role in cognitive research. The third section presents four ER simulations of animal spatial behavior (environmental shape recognition, detour behavior, landmark navigation and spatial learning). The fourth sections concludes, summarizing what has been achieved and outlining the advantages and limitations of ER as a tool in cognitive research.

Spatial Cognition in Animals

Orientation and Navigation

Many animals can "navigate" from one location to another, even when the target location is out of range of their senses. The ability underlying this behavior is "orientation." Animal orientation is extraordinarily effective and is used in many different circumstances; for example, for foraging (the dominant feeding behavior in most species), to visit mating sites and during seasonal migration: whales migrate from the equator to feeding sites in the polar regions; nectar-feeding bats commute between the southern United States and South America according to the seasonal availability of flowers. Many species display impressive "homing" abilities: bees return to the hive after foraging up to 10 km away, Tunisian desert ants use complicated routes to visit areas more than 150 m. from the nest and successfully return as soon as they have found food and many birds and fish have the ability to successfully return to geographical locations (feeding grounds, mating sites, hives, nests and stores of food) they have visited in the past (Healy, 1998; Kamil & Jones, 1997). Captive animals, observed in the laboratory, are also very good at orientation. Rats, for example, have the ability to remember the precise location of food hoards created on previous occasions, to navigate through complex mazes (Tolman, 1930) and to consistently orient towards a target, even when the target is out of view. These behaviors pose interesting questions for researchers: What cues or strategies do animals use? What are the mechanisms underlying spatial orientation?

One basic strategy is *path integration:* animals can calculate their current position by measuring the direction of movement and distances traveled. They can also exploit external cues, as in *beacon homing* or *landmark navigation.* As we will see in Section 3, they also use *geometry.* Finally, animals can learn to navigate using *stimulus-response sequences,* for example by learning to always turn in the same direction when they are exposed to a specific set of stimuli.

Theories of Spatial Cognition

The abilities and the mechanisms described above, which have been observed in the field and replicated in the laboratory, give us an idea of the cues animals use in different circumstances. But one important problem remains: How do they "represent" and process these cues? If we abstract from the capabilities of specific species in specific environments, what can we say about the general mechanisms underlying spatial cognition? Ever since Tolman's work in the 1930s, many psychologists have argued that animals, in particular mammals, use "cognitive maps" of the environment. According to this theory, different cues, such as data from internal compasses, the position of the sun and the arrangement of landmarks, are fused to form a map-like representation of the external world. These maps are enduring, geocentric and comprehensive. Experiments with different species (rats, pigeons, chicks — cf. Cheng, 1986; Vallortigara, Zanforlin, & Pasti, 1990; Kelly, Spetch, & Heth, 1998) suggest that geometrical information (such as the difference between a long and a short wall or left versus right) is coded in a specific module in the brain. In other words, navigation consists of computations in which the input comes from these representations and the output is behavior. Studies with rats provide suggestive evidence for cognitive maps, showing how laboratory animals systematically explore environments they have never experienced before, detect displaced landmarks and choose new, efficient paths between familiar locations (Tolman, 1930; Poucet, 1993).

In the 1970s, the discovery of "place cells" in the rat hippocampus strengthened the argument for "cognitive maps" (O'Keefe & Nadel, 1978). Place cells "fire" when the animal is in a specific location in the environment. This suggests a single cell, neurophysiological mechanism supporting spatial cognition. It seems likely that place cells work together with "head direction cells," which fire when the rat's head faces in a specific direction. Head direction cells have been found in several structures of the limbic system, including the hippocampus. Wang and Spelke (2002) have suggested that, in nature, place and head direction cells act dynamically, using a restricted subset of environmental information, viewed in an egocentric perspective. But regardless of whether they form maps, similar to those created by human geographers, or maintain continuously updated egocentric portrayals, their apparent job is to maintain an "internal picture" of the external world. According to proponents of the "cognitive map" approach, it is this "representation" which provides the underlying mechanisms for spatial cognition.

However, this is not the only way of approaching the issue. An alternative is the action-based, "embodied" perspective that emerged in the late 1980s and early 1990s. This view suggests that many navigational tasks are based on sensory-motor schemes, in which the key input comes not from a complete representation of the geometry of the environment but from local "affordances" which the animal discovers as it moves around. Its intellectual origins can be traced back to Piaget (1971).

Piaget hypothesizes that knowing is an adaptive function, and that all knowledge springs from action. Based on this hypothesis, he proposes a sophisticated model in which human cognition develops through complex mechanisms of self-regulation and negative feedback. According to Piaget, the first stage in children's cognitive development is what he calls the "sensory-motor stage." During this phase, which lasts from birth until about the age of two, children's innate reflexes are gradually substituted by mechanisms allowing them to make more efficient contact with their environment. In Piaget's view, the most elementary units of knowledge are "action-based schemes": non-symbolic structures that originate in children's actions in the external environment and that mediate their future interactions. These motor programs can be generalized to new situations through assimilation and tend to coordinate to form wider and wider behavioral units. In this perspective, cognition is an active, "embodied" process. Changes of perspective deriving from children's movements, the morphology of their bodies and the physics of their sensory organs are just as important as the way in which their brains create and process incoming information.

This view emphasizes the role of coupled interactions between organisms and the environment in the development of cognitive processes, capturing the way mind, body and world interact and influence one another to promote the adaptive success of an organism. As Thelen (2001) puts it:

To say that cognition is embodied means that it arises from bodily interactions with the world. From this point of view, cognition depends on the kinds of experiences that come from having a body with particular perceptual and motor capacities that are inseparably linked and that together form the matrix within which memory, emotion, language, and all other aspects of life are meshed. The contemporary notion of embodied cognition stands in contrast to the prevailing cognitivist stance which sees the mind as a device to manipulate symbols and thus concerned with the formal rules and processes by which the symbols appropriately represent the world.

In other words, the "embodied" perspective is an alternative to the classical, information-processing model of cognition with its focus on internal cognitive processes, abstract representation and computation. But in reality, there may be no need to choose between the cognitivist and the embodied approaches. It is entirely possible that some aspects of animal navigation use "cognitive maps" and that others exploit sensory-motor mechanisms. The precise role of these different mechanisms remains an open scientific issue.

Methodological Issues

Recent field and laboratory research has greatly improved our understanding of the way animals use environmental cues to migrate over long distances or to return to their nests after foraging. Nonetheless, the study of spatial cognition in animal behavior poses a number of methodological issues.

Let us consider, for example, the study of landmark use and cognitive maps in rats. In most experiments, such as those using an eight-arm radial maze (Olton & Samuelson, 1976) or a Morris water maze (Morris, 1981), rats are provided with cues from various sources and involving different sense organs. Often it is difficult to understand the real importance of these cues to the animals. Experimental designs try to solve this problem by testing animals in situations where only a few cues are available or where important information present in the training phase is withdrawn during testing (e.g., by turning off the light or locating the target in an area where cues cannot be perceived). However, it is almost impossible to exclude less evident cues the animals could potentially rely on, such as a rough sense of direction, the noise of an electronic experimental device or an internal compass. A freely moving animal, which the experimenter expects to rely on cues under experimental control, may in reality be exploiting unexpected, uncontrolled cues.

Careful observation and experiments have provided rigorous *descriptions* of specific navigational capabilities. Using these descriptions, psychologists have built *theoretical models* of the general mechanisms underlying spatial cognition. However, these models suffer from at least two critical weaknesses:

1.   Much of the data which would be needed to distinguish between alternative models (e.g., detailed information on neural architecture and on neural patterns of activity) are inaccessible to researchers. Even with very rigorous experimental design, the data from purely behavioral observations and experiments are inadequate to identify underlying mechanisms; the same behavioral data can often be explained by two or more different models.

2.   The majority of models are couched in verbal, and not in quantitative terms. This prevents them from making precise predictions, making them extremely hard to falsify.

So we need new tools to complement classical methods of investigation. One candidate is evolutionary robotics (Nolfi & Floreano, 2000). Evolutionary Robotics has great potential and several limitations. In the following sections we will explore both.

Evolutionary Robotics: A Brief Introduction

Evolutionary Robotics is a new discipline situated within the theoretical framework of artificial life (Langton, 1995). The goal of Evolutionary Robotics is to "evolve" autonomous robots displaying adaptive behavior.

To achieve this goal, ER draws inspiration from the natural evolution of biological organisms, driven by the interaction between populations and the environments they inhabit.

Biological evolution has produced hugely diverse forms of life adapted to a very broad range of ecological conditions. Since Darwin's *The Origin of Species* in 1859, it has been widely accepted that natural evolution is driven by selective reproduction of the fittest. The organisms that survive are those which are most successful in the competition for resources. It is these organisms that reproduce and transmit their genes to their offspring, ensuring that each generation contains an ever increasing proportion of "fit" genes. It is this principle that inspires ER.

ER is inspired by genetic algorithms (Mitchell, 1996). Each experiment begins with a population of robots. The defining characteristics of individual robots (e.g., controller architecture and morphology) are defined in a randomly generated "artificial genome." Each genotype is decoded into its corresponding phenotype. The resulting (physical or simulated) robots are "released" into an artificial environment, where their spontaneous behavior is evaluated in terms of a "fitness function" (pre-determined by the experimenter). The fittest robots reproduce. Reproduction may be either sexual or asexual. In both cases, the genetic algorithm copies the genotypes of the parent robot (asexual reproduction) or robots (sexual reproduction). During the copying process "genetic operators" introduce random variation ("mutations") into the genotypes of the offspring. The offspring of the first generation make up the second generation of robots and the whole cycle begins again, as illustrated in Figure 1.

This process is repeated for many generations, until the robots begin to display the behavior desired by the experimenter. This repeating cycle corresponds to the exploration of a *fitness landscape,* an n-dimensional space in which any combination of n traits (any theoretic individual) can be represented by a point in n-dimensional space, and the fitness of the individual is represented by the altitude of the landscape at that point. At the end of the exploration, the population converges towards mountainous zones, that is, to peaks of high fitness in the landscape.

The role of the experimenter in experiments based on ER is limited to the definition of the "fitness function." Fitness functions summarize and measure robots' ability to perform pre-defined tasks (the equivalent of an animal's ability to find food, to mate and to avoid predators). The results and dynamics of experiments depend closely on the form and content of the fitness function.

Figure 1. Schematic representation of evolutionary robotics methodology

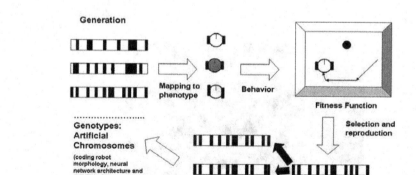

Fitness function in evolutionary robotics consists of many components and constraints. The definition of fitness functions is a non-trivial task. This is particularly true when the goal is not to define desired behavior in advance but only the goal of behavior. This is a form of "reinforcement learning" unsuitable for classical learning algorithms such as Back-propagation (Rumelhart et al., ii, 1986), which require detailed knowledge of what constitutes desirable behavior. By using ER, it becomes possible to discover desirable behaviors — which are often very different from the behaviors expected by the experimenter.

Hardware and Tools

ER uses a range of different technical devices and computational tools. Next we briefly describe the devices and tools used in our own experiments.

Khepera: A Miniature Mobile Robot

Robots for ER have to be mechanically robust. They need a reliable power supply and a control system which is easy to analyze and understand. The experiments reviewed in Chapter III used Khepera, one of several systems that meets these requirements.

Khepera (Mondada et al., 1993) is a miniature robot, designed and built at the Laboratory of Microprocessors and Interfaces of the Swiss Federal Institute of Technology of Lausanne. It is currently supported by K-Team S.A . The robot (see Figure 2) is round with a diameter of 55 mm, a height of 30 mm and a weight of 70 g. The robot has an on-board CPU (a Motorola MC68331 with 128 Kbytes of EEPROM and 256 kbytes of RAM), an A/D converter to process incoming analog signals and an RS232 serial connector used as a power supply and to transmit data to an external computer. Khepera can be connected to a host computer using a serial port. This is very useful in supplying electricity to the

Figure 2. A photo of the Khepera miniature robot

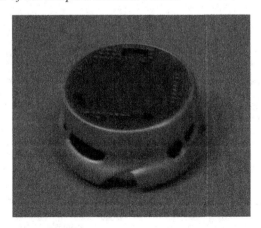

robot during long evolutionary sessions. The serial port can also be used to monitor the robot's activity when it interacts with the physical environment.

Its motor system consists of two wheels (one on each side), supported by two rigid pivots in the front and back. The wheels can rotate in both directions. The sensory system includes eight infrared sensors, six on the front and two on the back of the robot. The sensors can be used either in passive or in active mode. In passive mode, they register infrared light in the environment; in active mode, they emit infrared light and measure the light reflected from nearby surfaces. Active devices can function as proximity sensors, with the ability to detect an obstacle covered with white paper at distances up to about 3 cm. Sensor activation is inversely proportional to the distance to the obstacle, varying between 0 (when the obstacle is out of range) to 1 (when the obstacle is immediately adjacent to the sensor).

This basic apparatus can be easily expanded with additional components. Turrets with their own processors can provide new sensory information. In some of our experiments, we used robot cameras capable of detecting black or white obstacles at a significant distance. Given that the camera is positioned above the robot, and detects distant stimuli, while the infrared sensors are placed along the robot's circumference and detect proximal stimuli, their combined use provides the robot with two quasi-independent sources of information.

Evolving control systems for large populations of physical robots is time consuming and expensive. To resolve this problem, Nolfi (2000) designed and implemented EvoRobot, a realistic simulator of the Khepera robot that makes it possible to run evolutionary experiments in simulation. EvoRobot accurately models the characteristics of Khepera and its interaction with the environment. The robot simulation is based on the *look up table method,* first proposed by Miglino et al. (1995). This is based on the premise that no two physical sensors or actuators ever produce identical behavior. For example, no two cameras ever produce the same responses to color and no two motors generate the same acceleration. The look up table method circumvents this difficultly, by sampling actual sensor and actuator behavior. Samples are taken by placing the robot in different positions and orientations with respect to the wall and other elements of the environment; sensor and actuator responses are found in a *look up table*. During simulations, the simulator "looks up" the position and orientation of the robot and assigns appropriate values to sensors and actuators, in some cases adding noise so as to reproduce the statistical behavior of physical devices.

Control systems evolved with Evorobot can be downloaded to Khepera and validated in a physical test environment. Tests show a close correlation between the behaviors of physical and simulated robots. This implies that Khepera simulators like EvoRobot can be a powerful tool in Evolutionary Robotics experiments. The experiments reported in Section 3 were performed using EvoRobot.

The Robot Brain: A Perceptron

In each of the four experiments presented below, the robot control system (see Figure 3), was modeled by an artificial neural network (ANN). The ANN took the form of a

Figure 3. Schematic representation of robot control system

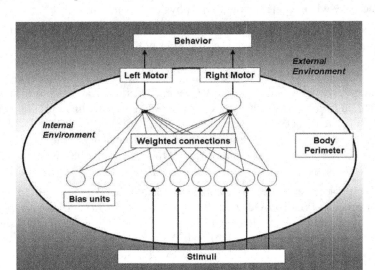

perceptron (Rosenblatt, 1958), in which every input neuron has a direct connection to all the output neurons. Each connection is associated with a weight. At time t_0, when the evolutionary process begins, each of these "weights" is assigned a random value between -1 and 1. During evolution the value of connection weights can vary between $-\infty$ and $+\infty$ (see the following).

Each input unit produces an output with a value between 0 and 1 and unit computes an "activation level" in the range -1 to 1. The activation level is a sigmoid function of the sum of the inputs multiplied by the value of the connections. The function is continuous, monotonic and is defined for all values in the range $-\infty$ to $+\infty$.

As the weighted sum of the input value tends to $+\infty$, activation tends asymptotically to 1. Vice-versa, as the weighted sum tends to $-\infty$, the value of the function tends to -1. The slope of the function is, at maximum, close to the origin and is lower for values further from zero. It thus has strong discriminatory power for values close to zero.

From a functional viewpoint, we use different kinds of input and output units The sensor layer consists of two bias units and of units that receive information from the external world. Bias units are units which are always on (that is, their level of activation is always 1) and which receive no information from the outside environment. These units, as we will see, play a fundamental role in allowing the output units to work in the absence of stimuli from the environment.

The output layer consists of two motor units, whose activation is fed to the wheels. In some of the experiments, we use an additional *decision unit*, which represents the robot's decision whether or not to take a specific action (e.g., digging) in a specific location.

Robot movement is determined by the activation of the output units. The speed of each motor is proportional to the activation of one of the output units. When activation is negative, the motor runs anti-clockwise; when it is positive the motor runs clockwise. For the robot to proceed in a straight line both motors have to run at the same speed in the same direction.

To perform an action, the robot carries out a sequence of operations in which the input units are activated, the signal is transmitted to the output units, and these send their own signal to the motors. The complete cycle lasts roughly 100 milliseconds.

The Genetic Algorithm

Robots are bred using a genetic algorithm (Belew & Mitchell, 1996). Each of the four experiments reported below used the same basic procedure. At the beginning of the breeding process, we generated a first generation of 100 robots. We initialized the robots' control systems with random weights (for details, see previous section). We then tested their ability to perform the experimental task. Performance was measured using a "fitness function." The fitness functions used in individual experiments are described later in the next section. At the end of the testing session, each robot received a "fitness score," measuring its ability on the task. After all robots had been tested, the 80 robots with the lowest fitness scores were eliminated (truncation selection). We then produced five clones of each of the remaining 20 robots (asexual reproduction). During cloning, a certain percentage of connection weights were incremented by random values uniformly distributed in the interval [-1, +1]. The new neural control systems were implanted in 100 robot bodies thereby creating a second generation of robots. This cycle of testing/selection/reproduction was iterated until no further improvements in fitness were observed.

Modeling Spatial Behavior with Evolutionary Robotics

Different Classes of Model: Idea vs. Data Models

Models in ER can be divided in two categories: idea models and data models. Much early work was based on "idea models." In "idea models," evolutionary techniques are used to reproduce very general phenomena in biology such as the role of co-evolution in the emergence of complex behavior, or the effect of interaction between learning and evolution. An example of this approach is Floreano and Nolfi's work (Floreano & Nolfi, 1997, 1999; Nolfi & Floreano, 1998) on the "Red Queen Effect" (Ridley, 1993).

In our own work, we use evolutionary robotics to produce "data models": models in which the robots we evolve accurately reproduce quantitative observations (behavioral indices) of animal behavior in well-defined experimental set-ups. In this section we describe four such experiments.

Modeling Spatial Behavior with ER

The robots generated by evolutionary robotics are the final outcome of an (artificial) evolutionary process of adaptation. Like animals, they are embodied systems that live and act in physical environments. This is very important. Natural cognition does not emerge in an abstract brain, isolated from the body and the environment, but rather through active interaction with the world and active extraction of meaningful information from this interaction.

The fact that robots are physical artifacts means that, at least in theory, they can reproduce the observed behavior of animals in a specific experimental set-up. As "embodied" systems, they can exploit the same physics used by animals, displaying biologically plausible behavior. But in robot experiments, unlike animal experiments, researchers have full control over all key variables. For example, they can evolve robots with little or no "memory" or compare systems governed by different control mechanisms. In the following paragraphs we describe four experiments in which we apply techniques from ER to the study of animal spatial behavior.

Geometric Cognition: Exploiting the Shape of the Environment

Many vertebrates exploit information about the shape of the environment. For example, chimpanzees (Gouteux et al., 2001), pigeons (Kelly et al., 1998), rats (Cheng, 1986; Margules & Gallistel, 1988), human beings (Hermer & Spelke, 1996) and new born chicks (Vallortigara et al., 1990) can all recognize the geometrical relationships between the walls of a room and use this information as the basis for efficient orientation. It seems clear that many species, and not just *homo sapiens,* have a detailed geometrical understanding of the portion of the world they inhabit. Less clear are the neural structures underlying this "spatial cognition." According to Gallistell (1986), the vertebrate brain includes a specialized module providing a "Euclidean" representation of space. This "geometry module" reconstructs an image of space which precisely reproduces the quantitative geometrical relationships between objects. In substance, it produces a metric (cognitive) map. But this view is not universally accepted. Other authors argue that animals do *not* use a complete, explicit representation of space. Rather, they construct their spatial understanding "on the fly," as they move through space, extracting geometrically meaningful information from the stimuli they receive from the environment. In this view, geometrical knowledge emerges from the interaction between a behaving animal, the environment it inhabits and the physical constraints imposed by the environment. In other words, spatial cognition is "situated." If they could view an animal's mental imagery, Gallistel would expect to find a photograph of the environment; the proponents of the "situated" approach would look for a mass of indistinct data which only turns into "knowledge" when the animal uses this information to guide its behavior.

Open field box experiments with rats have provided evidence which appears to support Gallistel's view (Cheng, 1986; Margules & Gallistel, 1988, Gallistel, 1990). The experiments take place in a rectangular arena where cues (patterns of high contrast stripes, the number of lights in the corners, smells and a single long wall painted in a special color) provide information which the animal can use to distinguish individual walls. In an initial training phase, the rat explores the arena, finds highly inviting food and partially eats it. It is then removed from the training arena, disoriented and placed in a testing arena identical to the training arena, except that the food is buried. The task consists of finding the hidden food in the testing arena.

When rats perform this task they make a systematic error. In roughly half of the trials, they dig in the correct location; in the other half they dig in the "rotationally equivalent area" i.e., the area where they should have dug if the arena had been rotated by 180°. This behavior has been interpreted as evidence that the vertebrate brain contains a "geometry module" that encodes geometric features of the environment, such as distance and direction and that rats rely exclusively on this information during navigation. In 2001, however, Miglino and Lund (2001) used techniques from ER to investigate whether robots with no internal representation could produce the same behavior observed in animals. It is this experiment we describe here.

Materials and Methods

The experimental apparatus is represented in Figure 4. The environment consisted of a rectangular wooden box (120*60 cm), containing a circular target area with a radius of 15 cm.

The experiment used the Khepera robot (Mondada et al., 1993), as described earlier. The architecture of the robot's control system was such as to preclude the formation of map-like representations of the external environment. Robots were evolved using the Genetic Algorithm described earlier. At each stage in the evolutionary process, robots were evaluated in eight trials, facing in a different direction on each trial (see Figure 4). The fitness function assigned one point to the robot if, at the end of a trial, it was positioned on the target area. These points were summed over the eight trials to obtain the robot's final fitness score. During cloning, 10% of connection weights were mutated by adding random values between [-1 and 1] to the original value. The test/cloning procedure was iterated 40 times. The results cited below refer to the best performing robot on the last iteration.

Results and Discussion

Table 1 compares the number of correct choices, rotational errors and misses obtained by Khepera with those for rats.

In quantitative terms there was no significant difference between the behavior displayed by the rats and that of Khepera. It is interesting to note that Khepera missed the target less often than the rats.

Figure 4. Experimental apparatus for the rat experiment (Margules & Gallistel, 1988)
as replicated by Miglino and Lund, 2001 (Arrows indicate the eight different starting
positions and orientations used during the test phase)

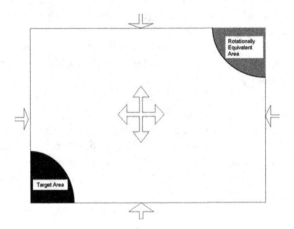

Analyzing the behavior shown in Figure 5, we can describe the robot's strategy as follows: First, the robot identified a long side and moved towards it. On reaching the wall, the robot turned to the right and followed the wall until it came to a corner. This corner was necessarily either the correct corner or its rotational equivalent. The robot could not distinguish the long from the short sides. The only sensors actively available to the robot were the infrared sensors that can only identify obstacles within a distance of 3cm. Therefore, the robot received no information from its sensors until it was very close to a wall. Even when the sensors were active, all they told the robot was that it was near an obstacle. In this way, the robot knew nothing about the length of the wall.

To move towards the long side, the robot evolved different weights for the connections between the bias units and the two output neurons. This led the two motors to run at different speeds, causing the robot to follow a curved trajectory. The radius of this trajectory guaranteed that the robot would automatically hit one of the long sides. In other words the robot adopted a sensory motor scheme that exploited external con-

Table 1. Correct identification of target, rotational errors and misses for rats and for
Khepera robots (Data for rats from Margules and Gallistel (1988); data for Khepera
from Miglino and Lund (2001))

	Correct	Rotational errors	Misses
Rats	35	31	33
Khepera	41	41	18

Figure 5. Khepera trajectories (Results from the "fittest robot" on the last iteration of the evolutionary procedure)

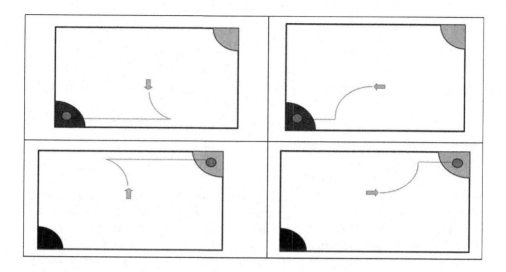

straints (the shape of the environment). It did not need an explicit representation of its environment. Everything it needed to know about its environment was represented implicitly in the connections governing its motor behavior. This suggests that the behavior observed in the rat experiments does not necessarily require a cognitive map of the environment. Perhaps rats too rely on sensory-motor coordination. If this were the case, it would be an example of "situated cognition," independent of any isomorphic representation of the environment inside the rat brain.

Keeping Track of a Disappearing Target "Detour Behavior"

You are walking down the street in a city you scarcely know, heading toward some well-known landmark. Suddenly you come across road work that blocks your route. You are forced to take an indirect route, and you lose sight of the target along the way. Orienting toward a target, when it is not visible, is called "detour behavior." When the target is out of view, there is no stimulus to elicit a response. Consequently, many theorists ascribe this behavior to the presence of an internal representation of the target, which allows the animal to maintain its orientation even when the target is out of sight.

Detour behavior has been observed in many species of animal including chimpanzees (Koehler, 1925), rats (Tolman, 1948) and two-day-old chicks (Regolin et al., 1994). In the experiment described below, Walker and Miglino (1999) replicated Regolin's experiment.

Figure 6. Schematic representation of the experimental set up for Regolin's experiment with new-born chicks (Regolin et al., 1994)

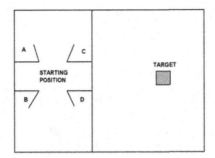

The set-up for the experiment is shown in Figure 6. The chicks were placed in a white cage divided in two by a barrier. The chicks were on one side of the barrier, the target on the other. The chick's side of the cage contained a corridor. At the end of the corridor there was a grill that allowed the chick the see the target. Two openings on the side of the corridor opened onto four compartments, two of which (A and B in Figure 6) faced away from the target while two (C and D) faced towards the target. In the experiment, the chick was placed in the corridor, close to the barrier and allowed to explore its surroundings. Researchers recorded which corners each chick reached and the time they took to reach their target. The results showed that the chicks preferred the compartments facing towards the target. This was taken as evidence that the chicks maintained a mental representation of the target and its position, even when they had lost sight of it along the route.

Walker and Miglino (1999) have replicated this experiment using ER techniques. As in the experiment reported earlier, the architecture of the robot control system precluded the presence of explicit representations of the environment.

Material and Methods

The experiments used a genetic algorithm operating on a population of 100 robots, simulated in software, as described previously, as well as eight infrared proximity sensors. As in the previous experiment, the robot had four sensor units connected to a linear video-camera with a field of vision of 36°. Each of these sensors produced an output of 1 if the center of the target lay within its 9° field of vision. Finally the researchers used 3 "time sensors,", to provide the robot with a sense of "rhythm." Each of these sensors had an initial activation of zero. The activation of the three time sensors increased by 0.01, 0.02 and 0.03 on each cycle of computation. When the activation reached 1 it was reset to zero. All other features of the robot were similar to those reported earlier.

The authors hypothesized that detour behavior might be derived from other, more primitive forms of exploration and food-seeking, namely the ability to move towards a visible target, to negotiate an obstacle and to efficiently search an open space. They therefore designed fitness formulae which rewarded these abilities individually even when they did not lead to successful detours. Fitness was calculated on each cycle of computation, using the following algorithm:

IF ("some infrared sensor" > 0 && old _position >< new_position)

fitness ++

IF ("some infrared sensor" > 0 && old_position = new_posion)

fitness - -

IF (distanceToTarget< 15 cm.)

fitness += 10

The first two components in the fitness formula were designed to encourage obstacle avoidance; the last component rewarded the robot when it approached the target.

To elicit robust behavior, the robots were trained in four different environments, as shown in Figure 7. Each environment consisted of an open field with no external wall. In the first environment, there was no obstacle between the robot and the target. The fitness formula rewarded robots that successfully searched for the target and moved toward it. The second, third and fourth environments selected for detour behavior. In the second environment, the target was placed behind a linear obstacle 80 cm long. In the third environment, Khepera was placed in a 10*80 cm corridor. The fourth environment used a 40*70 cm U-shaped obstacle. In these training sessions, obstacles were 3 cm high and of negligible thickness; the target was 12 cm high. This meant that the robot was always able to perceive the target even when the route to reach it was obstructed.

During training, robots were tested five times in each environment. At the beginning of each test, the robot was placed in a randomly chosen position 90 cm from the target. Each test consisted of 600 cycles of computation.

When all robots had been tested, the 20 robots with the highest overall score were cloned five times. "Mutations" were introduced by flipping bits in the genome with a probability of 0.02 per bit per generation. This process was iterated for 350 generations. Each simulation was repeated six times using a different random number seed on each trial.

Finally, the authors tested the four best robots from the last generation of each simulation in the Regolin et al apparatus (where the robot could not see the target except at the beginning of the experiment). Behavioral indices were computed using the same procedures applied by Regolin et al. (1994), that is by summing the number of robots choosing specific compartments after a pre-determined time (in the robot experiments 600 cycles of computation).

Results and Conclusion

Table 2 compares the performance of robots with those of the chicks in the Regolin et al. experiment.

As can be seen from the table, 1/24 of the robots failed to enter any compartment within the prefixed time (5/25 in the original experiment). Of the remaining 23, 21 chose one of the correct compartments and two chose the wrong compartment (in the Regolin et al., experiment, 20 chicks chose the right compartment and five the wrong one). As is the original experiment, there was no significant difference between the number of robots entering compartment C and the number entering compartment D. In brief, the behavior of the robots successfully replicated that of the chicks.

Figure 7 shows some of the trajectories followed by the robots during the training phase of the experiment. These show robots were able to achieve correct detour behavior here as well as in the Regolin et al. set up.

Table 2. Performance of chicks (Regolin, et al., 1994) and robots (Walker & Miglino, 1999) in the experimental apparatus

	Do not leave the Corridor	Sec.A	Sec.B	Sec.C	Sec.D	Total
Chicks	5	2	3	9	11	25
Robots	1	0	2	10	11	24

Figure 7. Typical trajectories followed by robots in the four training environments

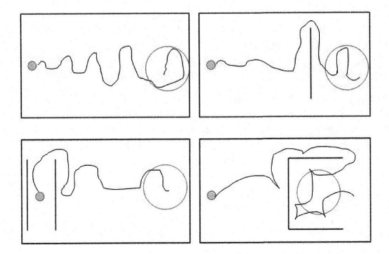

Figure 8. A typical robot trajectory in the experimental apparatus

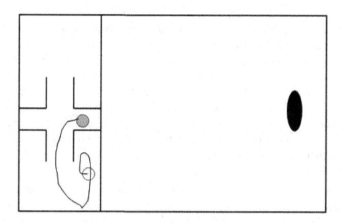

Legend. Small circles: starting points for trajectories. Large circle: target area rewarded by fitness function.

When they were placed in the experimental apparatus, the trajectories followed by robots ending up in compartment C were an approximate mirror image of those leading to compartment D. Figure 8 shows a typical example.

By carefully analyzing the trajectories followed by the robots, Walker and Miglino were able to derive an alternative model of detour behavior which does not require explicit representation of the target position. In this model, detour behavior is built up, step-by-step, from more primitive behaviors, namely:

1.   the ability to move towards a target;

2.   minimization of the time the robot is out of view of the target; and

3.   wall-following.

These abilities emerge in tight interaction with the environment. Detour behavior is structured by the robot's body and the interaction between the robot body and the environment. It is this interaction which allows the robot to discover new adaptive behaviors.

Landmark Navigation

Using landmarks to orient is common in animals. Gallistel (1990) has shown that, at least in rats, navigation mechanisms based on landmarks prevails over other navigation mechanisms based on alternative sources of information. Animals can use their distance from a landmark and its bearing to locate their position. But an interesting experiment by Kamil and Jones (1997) shows that at least one species can do much more than this.

Clark's nutcracker (*Nucifraga columbiana*) is a species of crow with an extraordinary ability to find seeds it has previously hidden. In their experiments, Kamil and Jones demonstrated that in performing this feat, the bird can exploit abstract geometric relationships between landmarks. In their work, wild-caught birds were taught to locate a seed, hidden at the midpoint between two landmarks. In the training phase, the seed was partially buried between green and yellow PVC pipes whose position and distance were changed after each trial. The birds were able to see the seed. In the subsequent, test phase, the seed was completely hidden. In about half the trials, the distance between landmarks was different from the distance in the training phase. This tested the crows' ability to generalize.

The results showed that the animals could locate and dig for the seed with a high degree of accuracy, even in conditions they had not experienced during the training phase. Control experiments confirmed that they were exploiting the abstract geometrical relationship between landmarks and did not rely on their sense of smell or on the size of the landmarks. The crows' observed behavior was consistent with Gallistel's hypothesis that orientation uses a "Euclidean map" of their environment

In the experiment we describe below, Miglino and Walker (2004) replicated these findings, again using a software simulation of the Khepera robot.

Material and Methods

The experimental setting reproduced the setting in which Kamil and Jones had conducted their work. Experiments took place in a 4.4*2.7 m arena. Like Kamil and Jones's observation room, robots entered the arena through a "porthole." The arena contained two landmarks (one grey and one black) emulating the green and yellow landmarks in the original experiment. The landmarks were aligned in parallel to the shorter side, with the grey landmark in the northerly position. At the beginning of each trial, the simulated robot was placed at the mid-point of one of the two short sides of the area (always the same side), facing East. During the experiments, the positions of the landmarks and the distances between them were changed after each trial, following the same procedure as in Kamil and Jones's experiments. The target where the robot was supposed to "dig" was defined as a circular area of radius 2.5 cm.

The robot's sensory input came from a linear camera providing it with a 360° field of vision, a significantly wider field than that of Kamil and Jones's crows. Cameras with a smaller field of vision failed to produce statistically robust behavior. The videocamera's 360° field of vision was divided into twelve 30° segments. Each input unit coded the mean output from one segment. Allowed values were 1.0 (representing a black object), 0.5 (a grey object) and 0.0 (no object).

The output units consisted of the two motor units described earlier plus a *decision unit* which stopped the robot for 5 s, every time its activation was higher than 0.7. This was interpreted as "digging."

During training, each robot was positioned in the arena and tested for its ability to locate the target area. Every time the robot dug in the correct area it received a reward of one point. The robot was tested six times. The final score represented a measure of its ability. In this experiment, 35% of the connections were mutated on each cycle. The testing/ cloning cycle was iterated 130 times.

Results and Discussion

Figures 9 (a)-(b) compare the mean percentage of digs in the target area for robots and for birds. As can be seen, the birds succeeded in digging in the correct area, both in training and "test" trials.

To understand this ability, the authors analyzed the activity of the digging unit, the only unit of the network that was sensitive to the robot's location in the arena. First they measured the activation of the unit when the robot was in one of the positions it had visited during training (i.e., when the robot was allowed to move freely). They then measured the activation of the robot in "imposed positions," i.e., in every possible position within 75 cm of the target. In each position, they measured the activation four times: once when the robot was facing North, once when it was facing West, once when it was facing South and once when it was facing East. Figure 10 shows the results.

In the free movement condition, shown on the left side of Figure, the digger unit displayed highly effective discrimination between target and non-target locations. In the imposed positions, on the other hand, the "digger" unit often fired outside the target area, displaying poor discrimination. This result provides a cue to the mechanism underlying the robot's navigational ability. In the actual experiments, the frequency with which the "digger" unit was activated depended not only on the unit itself but on the robot's overall strategy. If the robot never visited a particular location, the digger unit did not need to

Figure 9. Behavioral indices for robots (a) and for birds (b). Performance is measured by mean percentage of digs in target area; circles represent training trials; triangles represent testing results; robot data from Miglino and Walker (2004); bird data from Kamil and Jones (1997).

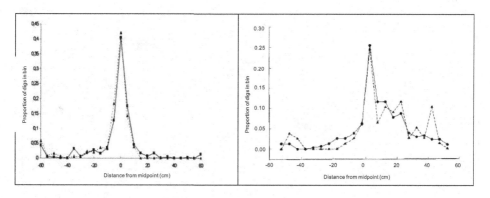

Figure 10. Frequency of above threshold activation of the "digger" unit in an area within 75 cm of the target location: (a) In locations actually visited during experiments (free movement); (b) in all possible locations (imposed positions)

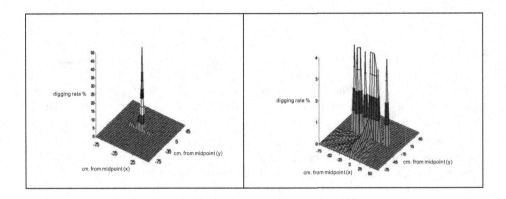

decide whether or not to dig in that location. All it needed was fine discrimination in the areas the robot actually visited. This implies that the robot's ability to exploit geometrical relationships for navigation depends not just on the digging unit but on the two motor units controlling its movement in the environment.

Figure 11 shows two examples of the trajectories followed by robots during experiments. In both cases, the robot starts from positions on the left side of the arena, facing in a perpendicular direction to the landmark line (on the right). Empty circles indicate the position of the landmarks. The filled-in black circle represents the target area. The robot in (a) adopts a near optimal strategy; the robot in (b) follows a sub-optimal trajectory.

The results of the experiment suggest that the ability to exploit geometrical relationship between landmarks depends on a process of active perception, with robot actions playing a fundamental role. Once again we see how spatial behavior emerges from the embodied interaction between a self-organizing system and its environment.

Figure 11. Trajectories for two different robots

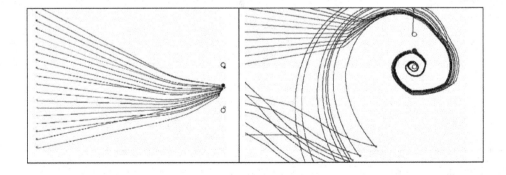

Different Pathways for the Acquisition of Spatial Cognition

Vertebrates exploit different sources of information to orient themselves in the environment. Studies in various species have shown that one kind of commonly used information is shape (for rats see Cheng, 1986; for humans, Hermer & Spelke, 1996). What is not yet entirely clear is the relative importance of different sources of information in different species. Several studies (Margules & Gallistel, 1988) have shown that rats rely completely on shape, ignoring alternative sources of information such as color; children up to a certain age also appear to rely exclusively on shape. Later in their development, however, they begin to exploit other kinds of information as well. These results have been interpreted as evidence for the presence of a geometry module in the vertebrate brain. The presence of this module, it is argued, ensures that geometry prevails over other sources of information. Hermer and Spelke (1996) suggest that humans' ability to use other sources of information may depend on language. But if this is so, it is difficult to explain the results of a recent study showing that *Xenotoca eiseni* (a species of small freshwater fish) can also use non-geometric information (Sovrano et al., 2002).

In the study reviewed here, Ponticorvo and Miglino (2005) used techniques from ER to investigate whether the different behaviors observed in different species could be explained by differences in the kinds of information to which they are exposed during their development. To achieve this goal, the authors recreated the experimental set up used by Sovrano et al. (2002), in their study of *Xenotoca eiseni,* testing the evolutionary pathways followed by populations of robots when researchers manipulated the kinds of information to which they were exposed during different stages in their "development."

Materials and Method

The Sovrano et al. experiments used the so-called "Blue Wall task," a classic experimental paradigm, often used to investigate the integration of geometrical and color information in human children and other animals. In this task, the experimental subject is placed at the center of a rectangular arena, in full view of a reward, which is located in a corner. The subject is removed from the arena and undergoes a disorienting procedure. The reward is hidden and the subject is then returned to the arena. The task is to find the reward.

When no other cue is present, the subject has to rely on the geometry of the arena (the distinction between the long and short walls). But if one long wall is colored blue, the subject can use both color and geometry (Figure 12). In other words, solving the blue wall task requires the merging of two different sources of information: geometry and color.

On the left, we see a rectangular arena presenting no cues except for basic geometry. In these conditions, the subject has no way of distinguishing between the correct and the rotationally equivalent corners. On the right is a rectangular arena in which one wall is painted blue. Here it is always possible to distinguish the correct corner.

The characteristics of the robots were the same as in the previous experiment. Training took place in two different environments. The first was a rectangular arena with four white

Figure 12. Blue Wall task

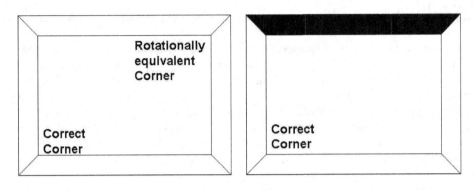

walls, the second had a long black-colored wall. In both arenas, the target area was in a corner of the arena.

At the beginning of each experiment, the researchers tested each robot's ability to locate the target. The robots started from the center 100 times, facing in a different, randomly chosen, direction on each trial. If the robot reached the correct area and recognized it (i.e., if the activation of the decision unit was above a certain threshold), it received a one-point reward. After this test, the best 20 robots were allowed to reproduce following the same procedure used in the experiments reported earlier.

To investigate the effects of exposure to different kinds of spatial information, nine different experiments were performed. Each experiment consisted of 20 simulations. In the first experiment, 10% of the trials were run in the geometric arena and 90% in the colored arena; in each subsequent experiment the percentage of trials in the geometric arena was increased by 10%.

Results and Discussion

A qualitative examination of robot behavior in the two environments shows that in the environment with only geometric cues, robots chose randomly between the two rotationally equivalent corners; in the environment with the additional color cue they were consistently successful in locating the target area.

Taking the single agents with the highest score at the end of each simulation, the authors calculated the percentage of agents with the ability to perform correctly in both environments. Figure 13 shows the results.

The next step was to examine robot halfway through the evolutionary process. To do this the authors tested agents at the midpoint between the start of the simulation and the generation containing the robot with the highest score observed during the simulation.

Figure 13. Percentage of agents' ability to perform correctly in both environments

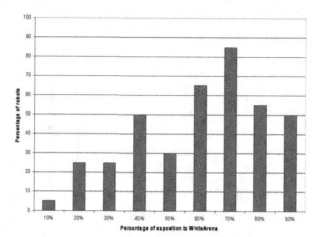

Again they compared robot performance in the two environments. Robots that achieved significantly different scores were classified as specialists in the environment where they obtained the highest score; otherwise they were considered to be "generalists."

Some robots began by learning to perform the task in the white arena and only later learned to perform the task in the black wall arena; others acquired the ability to accomplish the task, first in the black wall arena and only later in the white arena; others achieved correct performance in both arenas at approximately the same time. The sequence in which the robots learned the correct behavior depended entirely on the proportion of trials in the two different arenas. Although the mechanism used by the robots (evolution) was different from the mechanism used by humans (learning), at least some of the robots followed the same *sequence of development* observed in children. The results show that several development sequences are possible and that the sequence organisms actually follow depends on the frequency with which they are exposed to different classes of spatial information. This suggests that the behavior of different species of animal depends on the frequency with which they encounter different classes of cue in their natural environment, in other words, on the ecological adaptation of each species to its own niche.

Evolutionary Robotics and Spatial Cognition: A Scientific and Methodological Perspective

The experiments described in the previous section illustrate how we can use Evolutionary Robotics to produce "artificial organisms" with the ability to replicate quantitative observations of well-designed animal experiments.

Figure 14. Patterns of robot specialization: White area (black), Black wall arena (grey) and Generalists (hatched)

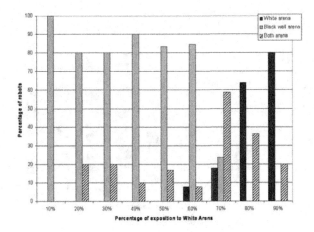

The results suggest that at least in principle, several forms of spatial behavior can be explained without resorting to internal, symbolic and static representations. In all four of the experiments described in the previous section, the robots' ability to perform specific tasks emerged from the interaction between the robot body (including sensor and actuator systems) and the physical environment; robots built up their knowledge of the world by exploiting the constraints imposed by the physical structure of the environment, and the robot's sensor system. This "knowledge" was "stored" in the connections linking the sensors to the motor units. These implement what Piaget called a sensory-motor scheme: "...a direct action co-ordination without representation or thinking" (Piaget, 1971). In our robots, cognition is no longer a property of the brain; it is a *relational property* of the interaction between the agent and the environment.

One possible objection to this view is that the "artificial organisms" used in our experiments are too simple to meaningfully represent natural phenomena. Animals, unlike the robots used in these experiments, produce a rich repertoire of behaviors, adapted to a broad range of environmental conditions. What, a critic could ask, can simple control systems tell us about highly complex animal or human brains?

In judging this criticism the reader should bear in mind the objectives of our research. The goal of our experiments was to reproduce specific quantitative observations ("behavioral indices") of specific behaviors in specific environments. This strategy of simplification — in which a model isolates a specific phenomenon from the broader context — is an essential part of any modeling enterprise. The results are valid within the limits defined by the model. Certainly, ER-based models of animal behavior would be stronger if they could reproduce a broader range of behaviors in a wider set of environmental conditions — a goal to be pursued in future research. They nonetheless retain their validity within the limits defined by the model.

When we apply ER to a specific issue such as spatial behavior the results provide useful insight into the implicit assumptions of biological and ethological research. If new forms of "artificial life" display the same orienting behavior as animals, this suggests new interpretations of the way animals behave. Our work shows that, in many cases, there is more than one mechanism capable of generating a particular set of values for this kind of indicator. The demonstration that it is *possible* to generate a certain behavior using a certain mechanism is by no way a proof that real animals *actually use* the mechanism. What they suggest, therefore, is a need for further research. Deciding which mechanism is used by a specific animal in a specific experimental setting requires additional evidence, such as the careful analysis of trajectories or neuro-physiological recording of brain activity.

Obviously ER has both advantages and limitations. From a methodological point of view, it makes it easy to draw conclusions about the causal effects of independent variables on dependant variables. ER Models have strong "internal validity." Compared to natural experiments, it is easier to link observable variables to theoretical constructs — and there is less need for *ad hoc* assumptions. Since researchers have to "build" their own artificial organisms, they are forced to define these links clearly, thus reducing bias. The possibility of repeating experiments as often as desired and of testing large samples of organisms guarantees the statistical validity of ER models. ER allows us to carry out experiments that would otherwise be impossible for evolutionary, ethical or practical reasons. It allows us to work with organisms that are completely molded by human researchers.

All this suggests that ER can play a complementary role to other research tools in the study of the mechanisms governing spatial cognition. The authors believe that despite the obvious limitations of ER models these advantages far outweigh the disadvantages.

References

Belew, R.K., & Mitchell, M. (Eds.). (1996). *Adaptive individuals in evolving populations: Models and algorithms.* Redwood City, CA: Addison-Wesley.

Cheng, K. (1986). A purely geometric module in the rat's spatial representation. *Cognition, 23,* 149 178.

Darwin, C. (1859). *On the origin of species by means of natural selection or the preservation of favoured races in the struggle of life.* Cambridge, MA: Harvard University Press.

Floreano, D., & Nolfi, S. (1997). God save the red queen! Competition in co-evolutionary robotics. In J.R. Koza, K. Deb, M. Dorigo, D. Foegel, B. Garzon, H. Iba, et al. (Eds.), *Genetic programming 1997: Proceedings of the Second Annual Conference* (pp. 398-406). San Francisco: Morgan Kaufmann.

Floreano D. & Nolfi S. (1999). Adaptive behavior in competing co-evolving species. In P. Husband & I. Harvey (Eds.), *Proceedings of the Fourth Conference on Artificial Life* (pp. 378-387). Cambridge, MA: MIT Press.

Gallistel, C.R. (1990). *The organization of learning*. Cambridge, MA: The MIT Press.

Gouteux, S., Thinus-Blanc, C., & Vauclair, J. (2001). Rhesus monkeys use geometric and nongeometric information during a reorientation task. *Journal of Experimental Psychology: General*, *130*, 505-509.

Healy, S. (Ed.). (1998). *Spatial representation in animals*. Oxford: Oxford University Press.

Hermer, L., & Spelke, E.S. (1996). Modularity and development: The case of spatial reorientation. *Cognition*, *61*, 195-232.

Kamil, A. C., & Jones, J. E. (1997). Clark's nutcrackers learn geometric relationships among landmarks. *Nature, 390*, 276-279.

Kelly, D.M., Spetch, M.L., & Heth, C.D. (1998) Pigeons' encoding of geometric and featural properties of a spatial environment. *Journal of Comparative Psychology, 112*, 259-269.

Koehler, W. (1925). *The mentality of apes*. New York: Harcout Brace.

Langton, C. G. (Ed.). (1995). *Artificial life: An overview*. Cambridge, MA: The MIT Press/ A Bradford Book.

Margules, J., & Gallistel, C.R. (1988). Heading in the rat: Determination by environmental shape. *Animal Learning and Behavior*, *16*, 404-410.

Miglino, O., Lund, H.H., & Nolfi, S. (1995). Evolving mobile robots in simulated and real environments. *Artificial Life*, *2*(4), 417-434.

Miglino, O., & Lund H.H. (2001). Do rats need Euclidean cognitive maps of the environmental shape? *Cognitive Processing, 4*, 1-9.

Miglino, O., & Walker, R. (2004). An action-based mechanism for the interpretation of geometrical clues during animal navigation. *Connection Science, 16*(4), 267-281.

Miglino, O., Nafasi, K., & Taylor, C. (1994). *Selection for wandering behavior in a small robot*. Technical Reports. UCLA-CRSP-94-01. Department of Cognitive Science, University of California, Los Angeles.

Mitchell, M. (1996). *An introduction to genetic algorithms*. Cambridge, MA: MIT Press.

Mondada, F., Franzi, E., & Ienne, P. (1993). Mobile robot miniaturization: A tool for investigation in control algorithms. In T. Yoshikawa & F. Miyazaki (Eds.), *Proceedings of the 3rd International Symposium on Experimental Robotics* (pp. 501-513). Kyoto, Japan. Springer Verlag.

Morris, R.G.M. (1981). Spatial localization does not require the presence of local cues. *Learning and Motivation, 12*, 239-60.

Nolfi, S., & Floreano, D. (1999). Co-evolving predator and prey robots: Do 'arm races' arise in artificial evolution? *Artificial Life*, *4*(4), 311-335.

Nolfi, S., & Floreano, D. (2000) *Evolutionary robotics: The biology, intelligence, and technology of self-organizing machines (intelligent robotics and autonomous agents)*. Boston: MIT Press.

Nolfi, S., Floreano, D., Miglino, O., & Mondada, F. (1994). How to evolve autonomous robots: Different approaches in evolutionary robotics. In R. Brooks & P. Maes

(Eds.), *Proceedings of the International Conference on Artificial Life IV* (pp.190-197). Cambridge, MA: MIT Press.

O'Keefe, J., & Nadel, L. (1978). *The hippocampus as a cognitive map*. Oxford: Clarendon.

Olton, D.S., & Samuelson, R.J. (1976). Remembrances of places passed: Spatial memory in rats. *Journal of Experimental Psychology: Animal Behavior Processes, 2*, 97-116.

Piaget, J. (1971). *Biology and knowledge: An essay on the relations between organic regulations and cognitive processes*. Chicago: Chicago University Press.

Ponticorvo, M., & Miglino, O. (2005). Is language necessary to merge geometric and non-geometric spatial cues? The case of "blue-wall task." *Proceedings of the Ninth Neural Computation and Psychology Workshop—Modeling Language, Cognition, and Action* (pp. 202-207). World Scientific.

Poucet, B. (1993). Spatial cognitive maps in animals: New hypotheses on their structure and neural mechanisms. *Psychological Review, 100*, 163-182.

Regolin, L., Vallortigara, G., & Zanforlin, M. (1994). Object and spatial representations in detour problems by chicks. *Animal Behavior, 48*, 1-5.

Ridley, M. (1993). *The red queen: Sex and the evolution of human nature*. New York: Penguin Books.

Rosenblatt, F. (1958). The perceptron: A probabilistic model for information storage and organization in the brain. *Psychological Review, 65*, 386-408.

Sovrano, V.A., Bisazza, A., & Vallortigara, G. (2002). Modularity and spatial reorientation in a simple mind: Encoding of geometric and non-geometric properties of a spatial environment by fish. *Cognition, 8*, 51-59.

Thelen, E., Schoner, G., Scheir, C., & Smith, L.B. (2001). The dynamics of embodiment: A field theory of infant preservative reaching. *Behavioral and Brain Sciences, 24*, 1-86.

Tolman, A.C. (1930). Insight in rats. *Psychology, 4*, 215-32.

Tolman, E. C. (1948). Cognitive maps in rats and men. *Psychological Review, 36*, 13-24.

Walker, R., & Miglino, O. (1999). Replicating experiments in "detour behavior" with evolved robots: An A-life approach to comparative psychology. In *European Conference on Artificial Life (ECAL '99)* (pp. 205-214). MIT Press.

Chapter VIII

The Meaningful Body:
On the Difference Between Artificial and Organic Creatures

Willem Haselager, Raboud University, The Netherlands

Maria Eunice Q. Gonzalez, UNESP, Brazil

Abstract

The question as to how sign processes can be meaningful to artificial agents has been a fundamental one for cognitive science throughout its history, from Turing's (1950) argument from consciousness, to Searle's (1980) Chinese room and Harnad's (1990) symbol grounding problem. Currently, the question is even more pressing in the light of recent developments in AI robotics, specifically in the area of reactive and evolutionary approaches. One would perhaps expect that given the embodied and embedded nature of these systems, meaningful sign processes would emerge from the interactions between these robots and their environment. So far, however, robots seem to lack any sensitivity to the significance of signs. In this chapter we will suggest that the artificiality of the body of current robots precludes the emergence of meaning. In fact, one may question whether the label "embodied" genuinely applies to current robots.

It may be more truthful to speak of robots being "physicalized," given that the types of matter used in creating robots bears more similarity to machines like cars or airplanes than to organisms. Thus, we are driven to an investigation of how body and meaning relate. We suggest that meaning is closely related to the strengths and weaknesses of organic bodies of cognitive systems in relation to their struggle for survival. Specifically, as long as four essential characteristics of organic bodies (autopoiesis, metabolism, centrifugal development and self-organization) are lacking in artificial systems, there will be little possibility of the emergence of meaningful sign processes.

Introduction: The Problem of Meaning

According to an anecdote, told by Daniel Hillis in a BBC documentary (1991), he once fed an expert system on skin diseases a description of his old car, including its age, the color of specific spots on the skin (reddish-brown: rust), etc. The expert system came up with a perfect diagnosis: the car had measles. The system did not know the difference between cars and people. MYCIN, the most famous medical expert system in the history of AI, was great in diagnosing specific illnesses on the basis of descriptions of symptoms it received. On several tests it scored better than medical students, teachers and practicing doctors. In its early days of development, MYCIN was known to ask every time, before it decided on the kind and amount of drugs to be prescribed, whether the patient was pregnant. MYCIN didn't know the difference between men and women. In fact, MYCIN didn't understand the meaning of "disease," or even what the difference is between life and death. These little details about the performances of expert systems illustrate the difference between artificially signaling something and knowing what the signals mean.

The question as to how sign processes can be meaningful to artificial agents has been a fundamental and much debated one for cognitive science throughout its history, as is evident from Turing's (1950) discussion of the argument from consciousness, to Searle's (1980) Chinese room and Harnad's (1990) symbol grounding problem.

Turing (1950) discussed the position of Prof. Jefferson who claimed that:

No mechanism could feel (and not merely artificially signal, an easy contrivance) pleasure at its successes, grief when its valves fuse, be warmed by flattery, be made miserable by its mistakes, be charmed by sex, be angry or depressed when it cannot get what it wants.... Not until a machine can write a sonnet or compose a concerto because of the thoughts and emotions felt, not by the chance fall of symbols, could we agree that machine equals brain — that is, not only write it but know that it had written it. (p. 42)

Turing responded by saying that in its most extreme form it leads to solipsism, and that "instead of arguing continually over this point it is usual to have the polite convention that everyone thinks." For Turing, then, convincing verbal behavior combined with politeness is enough to warrant the ascription of meaning. In all fairness, one has to note that "convincing verbal behavior" is not an easy criterion, e.g., MYCIN (and, so far, *every* AI system) would definitely fail for the Turing test.

Searle (1980) made clear in an intuitive way that symbol processing on the basis of syntax alone will not lead to any appreciation of the meaning involved. Instead, he argued, there is something about the brain that allows our awareness of meaning. Unfortunately, he left completely unspecified what the "special causal features" of the brain were, or how they could be discovered.

Harnad (1990) formulated the basic question as follows:

How can the semantic interpretation of a formal symbol system be made intrinsic to the system, rather than just parasitic on the meanings in our heads?. . . The problem is analogous to trying to learn Chinese from a Chinese/Chinese dictionary alone. (p. 335)

He suggests that representations must be grounded in iconic (analogs of proximal sensory projections of distal objects and events) and categorical (invariant features of objects and events) representations. Both iconic and categorical representations are, though to a different degree, causally connected to the sensory information that gave rise to them, but they still need to be interpreted (Harnad, 1990). Harnad goes on to suggest that meaning will arise from stringing together iconic and categorical representations into propositions that can enter into systematic relationships with other propositions.

Without wishing to deny the merits of these three influential papers, we feel that more is needed than convincing behavior combined with polite convention (Turing), special causal features of the brain (Searle) or grounding in iconic and categorical representations supplemented by systematicity (Harnad). Connecting representations to the world in the right way is crucial, but, as cognitive science has found out, rather problematic. We suggest that meaning originates from incorporated patterns of interaction with the world and that any representations that are to be found within a system derive their meaning from bodily interactions with the environment. In other words, if meaning is related to the connection between mind and world, we better investigate the properties of that which connects and for the sake of which the mind is operating: the body.

Embodied Embedded Cognition and the Promise of Robotics

Given this position, it is reasonable to look with some expectation at recent developments in AI robotics, specifically in the areas of reactive and evolutionary approaches. One would perhaps imagine that given the embodied and embedded nature of these systems, meaningful sign processes would emerge.

Robots interact through their bodies with their environment, and their embeddedness *in the world* shapes their behavior and cognitive processes. Especially in relation to this latter aspect, much of the behavior of robots has been designated to be not predetermined but, on the contrary, emergent. The behavior of the robot is not directly controlled or programmed for in a straightforward way (Clark, 2001, 114), but arises out of the interactions between a limited number of components that can be substantially different in their properties and action possibilities. The origins of the robot's behavior are causally spread out over its control system, features of its body and aspects of its environment. Causal spread is defined by Wheeler and Clark (1999, 106) as follows: "The phenomenon of interest turns out to depend, in unexpected ways, on causal factors external to the system."

In all, in order to understand the behavior of robots it is necessary to take into account diverse and varying aspects of their body and their environment and the way these aspects interact and self-organize. Thus, one could argue that the bodily interaction with the environment adds an essential element to the "Chinese-Chinese dictionary": it relates the robot's internal processes to what it is capable of achieving in the world outside, to what it can perceive and perform. Moreover, it is possible to provide robots with the capacity to learn (ontogenetically) and to adapt (phylogenetically) by equipping them with neural networks and letting them develop over generations through artificial evolution (e.g., Nolfi, 1998; Nolfi & Floreano, 2000). Thus, the internal processes are not just grounded in the interactive processes momentarily taking place between a system and its world, but also in the history of such interactions.

Surely, one might think, such robots would have, or at least develop, an inkling of the meaning of their interactions with the environment? However, no evidence for any such development in robots is forthcoming, as can be derived from robots' general incapacity to deal with relevance. To see this, imagine that one would train a robot to deal in the wrong way (e.g., relative to its own existence) with particular stimuli. That is, its neural net would receive positive feedback on making decisions that would be detrimental to its own physical integrity (e.g., by driving fast into a brick wall, or by riding off a cliff, etc.). These robots would learn, and have no problem in learning, to be completely self-destructive. Because of the lack of any bodily constraints related to self-preservation, *any* type of behavioral control can be learned. Robots are *indifferent* to both self-preserving and self-destructive goals. Indeed, they can be programmed either way with the same amount of ease or difficulty. As a more mundane example, there is no problem in setting up a chess program either aiming to win or to lose. Winning or losing doesn't genuinely *matter* to computational systems. They don't *care*. This is in strong contrast with organic systems in general that tend to be strongly disposed towards learning self-preserving behavior. Similarly, and equally perverse, there is no problem in setting up an artificial evolutionary process that would favor self-mutilating robots. A fitness-function that would favor the reproduction of clumsy robots would result in the type of robots that make the English comic character Mr. Bean look like the prototype of efficiency. In short, robots can be made to display whatever type of behavior possible, regardless of its meaning for their own existence. Like MYCIN, they have no idea about even the most basic distinctions, such as life and death. But even single-cell creatures already "know" how crucial this difference is. Organisms do care, intrinsically, about their survival. It is this intrinsic capacity for caring about survival that allows things in the world to become *significant*. This grounds meaning, and it finds its origin in the bodily inclination towards self-preservation.

We suggest that the *artificiality of the body* of current robots precludes the emergence of meaning. In fact, one may question whether the label "embodied" genuinely applies to current robots. In part, this is due to the ambiguity of the concept of embodiment itself. Ziemke (2003) distinguishes between six types of embodiment:

1. Embodiment as *structural coupling* refers to the existence of perturbatory channels between a system and its environment. Simply put, a system is embodied in this sense if it can affect and be affected by its surroundings. Ziemke notes that the exact difference between perturbatory channels and sensors and motors is rather difficult to make.

2. The notion of *historical* embodiment emphasizes the temporal aspects of the coupling between system and environment. This includes changes occurring in nonliving systems such as mountains (e.g., due to weather and gravity), as well as evolutionary and developmental changes taking place in organisms.

3. *Physical* embodiment applies to anything existing in space and time, and thus includes everything from quarks to chairs, elephants and planets.

4. *Organismoid* embodiment is more restrictive than in that it applies to bodies that have forms and sensorimotor capacities at least roughly similar to organisms. There is considerable room for discussion here as Ziemke, for instance, grants Khepera robots that placed two microphones at the same distance that separates the two "ears" of crickets this type of organismoid embodiment. For us, it is hard to see how Kheperas (small circular shaped robots on wheels) could be seen as organismoid. However, robots developed in computational ethology, such as robots that are based on the kinematics of the cockroach *Blaberus discoidalis,* do qualify for this type of embodiment (e.g., Beer, Quinn, Chiel, & Ritzmann, 1997; Kingsley, Quinn, & Ritzmann, 2003).

5. *Organismic* embodiment covers living bodies, which for Ziemke means that these bodies are autonomous and autopoietic instead of heteronomous and allopoietic (Ziemke & Sharkey, 2001): Living organisms are acting plans aimed at maintaining their own organization. Finally, and as Ziemke notices, orthogonal to the previous kinds of embodiment, the notion of ...

6. ... *social* embodiment points to the central role that the body in social information exchange and processing. One could think here of the robot Kismet who responds to prosody and movements by facial expressions of basic emotions such as happiness and sadness and accompanying sounds.

Given this taxonomy, it seems that robots at best could be said to qualify as being "physical" or "organismoid" because the types of matter used in creating robots bear more similarity to machines like cars or airplanes than to organisms. In relation to the issue of meaning, one would not, intuitively speaking, expect any appreciation of meaning in physical structures of various degrees of complexity (e.g., ranging from piles of sand via elaborate buildings (houses and castles) to airplanes and space ships). We propose to investigate this difference between robots and organisms in a bit more detail next.

Organic Meaning

Meaning is a vexing topic. In dictionaries one can find phrases such as "something that is conveyed or signified, sense or significance, an interpreted goal, intent, or end, the gist of a specific action or situation,", etc. In this chapter we will specifically focus on the significance or gist that specific objects, situations or actions can have for organisms. How does this significance arise? In virtue of what do organisms have the capacity not just to be the subject of forces, but also to be concerned, if only in a dim, non-conceptual way, of what the forces are about? One particularly promising approach, in our view, attempts to relate the meaning of a particular situation for a specific animal to the coordinated set of actions that are available to it (Glenberg & Robertson, 2000):

When affordances, experiences, and goals are successfully meshed, they form a coherent, doable, and envisionable set of actions: the individual's meaningful construal of the situation. (p. 383)

Although we are in full agreement with this suggestion as a point of departure for the analysis of meaning, we feel that one aspect bears further emphasis and analysis. We suggest that meaning, understood as involving significance, value, purpose and action (Bohm, 1989) is, at its most fundamental level, closely related to the strengths and weaknesses of organic *bodies*. It is the struggle for continuing existence of the body that ultimately grounds meaning or, to put the same point differently, that makes semantic interpretation an intrinsic (and not derived) capacity of the system. Basically, the suggestion is that in the attempt to survive, certain aspects of the environment become significant in the sense of being either good or bad for the continued existence of the organism. As Damasio (1999) suggests, there is a continuous monitoring of the effects of the body's interaction with objects and events in the environment relative to its own well-being. Bodily self-preservation is, so to speak, the "ultimate marker" in relation to which objects in the world become labeled as positive or negative. In our view, this provides the foundation of meaning. In passing, one may note that even though individual behaviors (as can be observed, e.g., in the immune system) might sometimes appear to be contrary to self-preservation of the individual elements, the proper meaningfulness of these actions can only be established by placing them in the larger context of the overall system and its relations to the environment. That is, the self-destructive behavior may be part of a larger set of behaviors to preserve a more encompassing complex unity.

The body need not be of comparatively high complexity. Emmeche (2001, 18), for instance, suggests that though unicellular eukaryotic cells (protozoa) lack a nervous system, they do have "a simpler 'autokinetic or self-moving circle' by which they enter into semiotic interactions with the exterior milieu." In a similar vein, Damasio (1999) says that:

A simple organism made up of one single cell, say, an amoeba, is not just alive but bent on staying alive. Being a brainless and mindless creature, an amoeba does not know of its own organism's intentions in the sense that we know of our equivalent intentions. But the form of an intention is there, nonetheless, expressed by the manner in which the little creature manages to keep the chemical profile of its internal milieu in balance while around it, in the environment external to it, all hell may be breaking loose. (p. 136)

As far as we can see, there are four issues that are particularly relevant for understanding how an organism is able to keep the internal milieu in balance in relation with events in the environment: autopoiesis, metabolism, centrifugal development and self-organization. We will examine them next.

Autopoiesis

The notion of autopoiesis (Maturana, 1970; Maturana & Varela, 1987) refers to the ability of living systems to maintain their structure and organization by means of the self-creation and self-maintenance of their basic constituents. All systems have an organization, not just living systems. Maturana and Varela (1987) indicate that:

What is distinctive about them [living beings], however, is that their organization is such that their only product is themselves, with no separation between producer and product. The being and doing of an autopoietic unity are inseparable, and this is their specific mode of organization. (pp. 48-49)

This orientation towards self-creation and self-maintenance that forms the driving force behind the interactions between the system and its environment is a crucial factor in the origination of meaning. It immediately gives a *value* to every interaction event: whether it is good or bad in relation to self-preservation. It is not a sufficient condition though; organizations (social groups, political parties, multinationals, states, etc.) have a similar kind of drive towards self-perpetuation, but do not constitute meaningful systems from our perspective because they do not fulfill the other three conditions discussed further below.

Maturana and Varela (1987) point towards a very important point regarding the material constitution of autopoietic systems:

Like any organization, autopoietic organization can be attained by many different types of components. We have to realize, however, that as regards the molecular origin of terrestrial living beings, only certain molecular species probably possessed the characteristics required for autopoietic unities, thus initiating the structural history to which we ourselves belong. For instance, it was necessary to have molecules capable of forming membranes sufficiently stable and plastic to be, in turn, effective barriers, and to have changing properties for the diffusion of molecules and ions over long periods of time with respect to molecular speeds. Molecules from silicon layers, for instance, are too rigid for them to participate in dynamic unities (cells) in an ongoing and fast molecular interchange with the medium. (p. 49)

It is the small range in-between stability and plasticity that seems important in allowing both sufficient resilience towards disturbances from outside and enough flexibility in order to interact in a dynamic way with the environment. Importantly, "environment" here can refer either to the outside world and/or to other elements of the system itself, i.e., other cells for instance. In both cases, the material constitution of meaning-grounded systems needs to fulfill this requirement being stable-yet-plastic, solid-yet-permeable.

Metabolism

A second aspect that differentiates organic from artificial bodies is metabolism, i.e., the chemical processes in which some substances are broken down to yield energy for vital processes and/or synthesize useful substances. Metabolism constitutes one of the ways in which self-maintenance and self-creation are made possible (other ways include sufficient uptake of oxygen, regulating the reception of enough but not too much sunlight and various other homeostasis related aspects). The difference between the intricate processes involved in the energy uptake in living organisms and the straight-forward electricity consumption in robots is large. In our view, metabolism plays an important role in the development of meaningful interactions between a creature and its environment. As Maturana and Varela (1987) say in relation to autopoietic systems:

First, the molecular components of a cellular autopoietic unity must be dynamically related in a network of ongoing interactions. Today we know many of the specific chemical transformations this network, and the biochemist collectively terms them "cell metabolism." ...This cell metabolism produces components which make up the network of transformations that produced them. (pp. 43-44)

The cell membrane, for instance, plays a role in the biochemical dynamics (e.g., letting certain molecules pass through and keeping others either inside or out) that are constitutive for its very own existence.

Kauffman (2000) indicates that metabolism:

... solves the thermodynamic problem of driving the rapid synthesis of molecular species above their equilibrium concentrations by linking such synthesis to the release of energy by the breakdown of other chemical species. (p. 47)

The process of metabolism constitutes the necessary combination of exonergic (release of energy) and endonergic (uptake of energy) processes to be able to complete a so-called work cycle, i.e., to return to the initial high energy state necessary to accomplish mechanical work necessary for self-maintenance and self-reproduction. As Kauffman (2000) indicates:

... the linking of exergonic and endergonic reactions appears to be essential to the definition of an "autonomous agent", that mysterious concatenation of matter, energy, information, and something more that we call life. (p. 47)

The uptake and transformation of external ingredients for one's own continuing existence is a further specification of the "good" and "bad" that originates with autopoiesis. In the case of autopoiesis, the good and bad is related exclusively to the existence of the system itself. It is because of metabolism specifically that certain objects in the world start to get labeled as good or bad food. Importantly, it is the ongoing existence of the organism that provides the origin for the values to be distributed among things and events in the environment. Of course, the labeling is not a result of some explicit decision or labeling mechanism within, but results from the functional organization of the whole system aimed at "getting by" in the world.

Most currently existing robots rely on externally provided energy sources, such as batteries, in order to function and are far removed from anything remotely similar to this uptake and chemical transformation of matter in order to engage in the energetic processes necessary for autopoiesis. We would like to discuss one project here that seems to be one of the most relevant around because of its explicit attempt to "imitate metabolism" in "biologically inspired robots" (Ieropoulos, Greenman, & Melhuish, 2003; see also http://www.ias.uwe.ac.uk/Energy-Autonomy-New/New%20Scientist%20-%20Detailed%20EcoBot%20project.htm). The project aims to develop a robot that can convert a chemical substrate by means of an artificial digestion system into energy required for behavior and cognition. A microbial fuel cell (MFC) forms the core of the project. It uses bacteria to convert the sugars derived from raw substrate into energy that can be used by a robot, EcoBot I, for photo-taxis (light following behavior). Basically, inside the cell, bacteria metabolize sugar molecules producing electrons that are "harvested" and passed on to an electrode, ultimately resulting in an electric current. Ieropoulos et al. (2003) claim that EcoBot I is "the first robot in the world to be directly and entirely powered from bacterial reducing power and the second to be running on sugar."

There are a few things to note about such robots that are interesting for our purposes here. In EcoBot I, the conversion of raw materials into sugars has not been implemented, the robot is fed directly with sugars, and thus does not implement a full metabolic process. However, a follow up robot, EcoBot II, is capable of transforming raw food (rotten fruit and dead flies) into useable energy. One could argue, therefore, that metabolism is taking place in the full sense of the word in EcoBot II. We resist this conclusion, however, for the following reason. The microbial fuel cell is a module that can exist on its own. It can be removed from a system and put back or inserted in a totally different energy consuming system and function as if nothing had happened. In this sense it is different from the metabolic systems of organisms for which such a separation is completely impossible. Microbial fuel cells are as much comparable to metabolic systems as batteries. They merely provide energy and are far from providing the origin of value that forms the basis for labeling things in the world. A second aspect of metabolism that is lacking in the robots just considered is that matter is not just transformed into energy but also into new matter: biological tissue. Organisms do more than regulate their energetic processes, they also, literally, (re)build themselves. This brings us to a third point: the centrifugal development of organisms.

Centrifugal Principles

The bodies of current robots are constructed from sets of components that are put together from the "outside in," by connecting prearranged parts (like a robot-arm or an optical censor) to a central frame. The development of organisms, however, follows what von Uexküll (1982) called "centrifugal" principles: They develop from the inside out. The construction, or rather development, of an animal always starts centrifugally from a single cell. This contrast between robots and organisms is directly related, in our view, to the issue of metabolism and the notion of autopoiesis. As quoted above, Maturana and Varela stress that the organization of an organism is such that *its product is itself*, with no separation between producer and product. This obviously also applies to metabolic processes in organisms, which operate from within the system and are an integral part of it. In the case of the EcoBots discussed in the previous section, however, the "metabolic system" is "transplantable." As a result, the interaction between internal parts of modularly constructed systems falls far short of the codependence that exists between the elements of centrifugally developed systems.

We suggested above that metabolism is relevant to the origins of meaning because things in the world get labeled due to the functional organization of the system as a whole, as good or bad for the survival of the system. For organisms, there is no such thing as "surviving in part" (at least for the vital parts and under natural conditions, before the advent of biotechnology). Rather, they survive or perish as a whole. If we are correct in our suggestion that the origin of meaning lies in distinguishing the significance of objects as being good or bad for survival of the organism, our suspicion appears to be reasonable. Put differently (and in the terminology used earlier in the chapter) why would a module "care" about the survival of the organism if it could be transplanted without any problem, as is the case in current robotics? For organisms, the consequences of the system's actions for its own continuing existence "reverberate" within itself (intuitively, one may think of how strongly significant events are not just intellectually recognized but are felt as such throughout the body, e.g., in the stomach). Centrifugal development is an important factor in creating the inseparability between producer and product.

Self-Organization

Self-organizing systems are characterized by a collective interaction between the components of a system such that a higher-level pattern, called the order parameter or the collective variable, emerges from the dynamic relations established amongst the elements at a lower level, which, in turn, causally constrains the behavior of the low-level components. Incidentally, one might argue that the term "parameter" is ill-chosen, since it actually refers to a collective or overarching variable. However, one may argue that according to the theory of self-organization, the collective variable can be seen as a parameter, due to its downward causality, modifying the interaction between the lower-level components of the system. For better or for worse, this terminology is used widely in the literature. In self-organizing systems, the behavior of all the elements helps to shape the behavior of all other elements through upward and downward causative influences. Self-organization is essential to the topic of meaning since it seems to be one of the very few ways (in fact, the only one we can think of) in which meaning can arise without being presupposed as being infused from the outside. It is in the unsupervised interaction between aspects of the body (such as the ones outlined above) and the world that objects, events, goals and actions become meaningful. Furthermore, it is important to realize that higher levels of meaning are not built up in a pre-established hierarchic bottom-up fashion, but develop out of the dynamic co-dependent interaction between bodily aspects of the organism and the environment. This emphasis on the importance of self-organization for the creation and expansion of meaning can also be found in Emmeche (2001), who says:

If such a material device as a robot could have that special organic flexibility of an animal that allows it to instantiate anything like the law of mind, that is, the tendency to let signs influence or affiliate with other signs in a self-organizing manner, it is difficult to see why such devices should not be able to realize genuine signs (including qualisigns). (p. 21)

We especially value his conditional "if" in the quote above. It appears that the interaction between the components of a robot precisely lacks the complexity of the co-dependent (autopoietic), self-organizing and systemic functioning of an organism. Kheperas, LEGO-bots and other plastic and metal based robots miss any genuine form of bodily self-organization because the type of matter out of which they are made does not provide the required interactive plasticity to support this (see also Haselager, 2003). The problem is that there are no robots like organisms in which, as Goodwin (1994, p.183) puts it: "...the parts exist for as well as by means of one another."

Conclusion

In this chapter we examined the thesis that robotic bodies are lacking four characteristics of organic bodies, namely autopoiesis, metabolism, centrifugal development and self-organization. All these characteristics are important to the issue of meaning because they are involved in grounding an organic body in its environment, allowing it to respond to the significance of an object or event for its own survival. Meaning, then, develops out of the bodily struggle for self-creation and -preservation. Research in robotics has, perhaps paradoxically, illustrated the enormous significance of being genuinely embodied. For future research, therefore, it would be important to inquire more deeply into the corporeal aspects of the behavioral interaction with the world. Moreover, the systemic unity of the bodily organism-environment interaction from which meaning arises could be more thoroughly appreciated. From this perspective, organisms still provide the most sophisticated examples of meaningful cognitive behavior. In the fragility of our bodies and their complete interdependence with the world lies the foundation of meaning. Merleau-Ponty (1962) phrased it beautifully, quoting the biologist von Uexküll:

Every organism' said Uexküll, 'is a melody that sings itself.' This is not to say that it knows this melody and attempts to realize this; it is only to say that it is a whole which [has] significance.

It is this "significance as a whole" that organisms have and current computational systems and robots lack. Without it, how could signs become meaningful?

Note

We would like to thank an anonymous reviewer, Marian Broens and the editors of this book for their many constructive comments, the NICI institute at the Radboud University in Nijmegen, the Netherlands and UNESP, Marilia, Brazil, as well as FAPESP and CNPq for the logistic and financial support during the preparation and writing of this chapter.

References

BBC (1991). *The thinking machine.* TV-documentary. London. Retrieved October 11, 2005 from, http://ei.cs.vt.edu/~history/TMTCTW.html#ThinkingMachine

Beer, R.D., Quinn, R.D., Chiel, H.J., & Ritzmann, R.E. (1997). Biologically inspired approaches to robotics. *Communications of the ACM,* 30-38.

Bohm, D. (1989). *Exploration into the meaning of the word "meaning".* Retrieved October 11, 2005, from http://www.ratical.org/many_worlds/K/meaning.html

Chiel, H.J., & Beer, R.D. (1997). The brain has a body: Adaptive behavior emerges from interactions of nervous system, body and environment. *Trends In Neurociences, 20*(12), 553-557.

Clark, A. (2001). *Mindware: An introduction to the philosophy of cognitive science.* Oxford: Oxford University Press.

Damasio, A. (1999). *The feeling of what happens.* New York: Harcourt Brace & Co.

Emmeche, C. (2001). Does a robot have an umwelt? Reflections on the qualitative biosemiotics of Jakob von Uexküll. *Semiotica, 134* (1), 653-693.

Glenberg, A.M., & Robertson, D.A. (2000). Symbol grounding and meaning: A comparison of high-dimensional and embodied theories of meaning. *Journal of Memory and Language, 43*, 379-401.

Goodwin, B. (1994). *How the leopard changed its spots: The evolution of complexity.* New York: Charles Scribner's Sons.

Haselager, W.F.G. (2003). Form, function and the matter of experience. *SEED, 3*(3), 100-111.

Harnad, S. (1990). The symbol grounding problem. *Physica D, 42*, 335-346.

Ieropoulos, I., Greenman, J., & Melhuish, C. (2003). Imitating metabolism: Energy autonomy in biologically inspired robotics. In *Proceedings of the AISB 2003, Second International Symposium on Imitation in Animals and Artifacts* (pp. 191-194). Aberystwyth, Wales.

Kauffman, S. (2000). *Investigations.* Oxford: Oxford University Press.

Kingsley, D. A., Quinn, R. D., & Ritzmann, R. E. (2003). A cockroach inspired robot with artificial muscles. *International Symposium on Adaptive Motion of Animals and Machines,* Kyoto, Japan.

Maturana, H.R. (1970/1980). Biology of cognition. Biological Computer Laboratory Research Report BCL 9.0. Urbana: University of Illinois. (Reprinted from *Autopoiesis and cognition: The realization of the living*, pp. 5-58). (http://www.enolagaia.com/M70-80BoC.html). Dordecht, The Netherlands: D. Reidel Publishing.

Maturana, H.R. & Varela, F.J. (1987). *The tree of knowledge: The biological roots of human understanding.* Boston: Shambhala.

Merleau-Ponty, M. (1962). *The structure of behavior.* London: Routledge.

Nolfi, S. (1998). Evolutionary robotics: Exploiting the full power of self-organization. *Connection Science, 10*(3-4), 167-184.

Nolfi, S., & Floreano, D. (2000). *Evolutionary robotics: The biology, intelligence and technology of self-organizing machines.* Cambridge, MA: The MIT Press.

Searle, J. (1980). Minds, brains, and programs. *Behavioral and Brain Sciences, 3*(3), 417-457.

Turing, A. (1950). Computing machinery and intelligence. *Mind, 59*, 433-460.

Uexküll, J. von (1982). The theory of meaning. *Semiotica, 42*(1), 25-82.

Wheeler, M., & Clark, A. (1999). Genic representation: Reconciling content and causal complexity. *British Journal for the Philosophy of Science, 50*(1), 103-135.

Ziemke, T. (2003) What's that thing called embodiment. *Proceedings of the 25th AMCSS.*

Ziemke, T., & Sharkey, N.E. (2001). A stroll through the worlds of robots and animals: Applying Jakob van Uexküll's theory of meaning to adaptive robots and artificial life. *Semiotica, 134*(1/4), 701-746.

Section IV

Cognition in Virtual Agents

Chapter IX

Making Meaning in Computers:
Synthetic Ethology Revisited

Bruce MacLennan, University of Tennessee, USA

Abstract

This chapter describes synthetic ethology, a scientific methodology in which we construct synthetic worlds in which synthetic agents evolve and become coupled to their environment. First we review the motivations for synthetic ethology as an experimental methodology and explain how it can be used to investigate intentionality and meaning, and the mechanisms from which they emerge, with a special emphasis on communication and language. Second, we present several examples of such experiments, in which genuine (i.e., not simulated) meaningful communication evolved in a population of simple agents. Finally, we discuss the extension of the synthetic ethology paradigm to the problems of structured communications and mental states, complex environments and embodied intelligence, and suggest one way in which this extension could be accomplished. Indeed, synthetic ethology offers a new tool in a comprehensive research program investigating the neuro-evolutionary basis of cognitive processes.

Introduction

Synthetic ethology was developed as a methodology for constructing experiments in which artificial agents could exhibit real (i.e., not simulated) intentionality and other mental phenomena. Our first experiments using this methodology demonstrated the evolution of communication in a population of simple machines and illustrated ways of relating the emergence of meaning to underlying mechanisms (MacLennan, 1990, 1992, 2001, 2002; MacLennan & Burghardt, 1993). In these experiments, as I will explain, the communications were meaningful to the artificial agents themselves, but they were only secondarily and partly meaningful to the experimenters.

This chapter has two purposes. The first is to review the motivations for synthetic ethology as an experimental methodology and to explain how it can be used to investigate intentionality and meaning, and the mechanisms from which they emerge, with an especial emphasis on communication and language. The second purpose is to reconsider these issues with the hindsight of fifteen years, and discuss new approaches to the use of synthetic worlds in the scientific investigation of problems in epistemology and cognitive science.

Background

Definition of Synthetic Ethology

Synthetic ethology can be defined as an experimental methodology in which the mechanisms underlying cognitive and intentional phenomena are investigated by constructing synthetic agents and observing them in their *environment of evolutionary adaptedness* (EEA, the environment in which they have evolved), which is also synthetic. These synthetic worlds are commonly constructed inside a computer. I will briefly summarize the most important considerations motivating the synthetic ethology paradigm (a fuller discussion can be found in MacLennan, 1992).

In discussing his research program in *synthetic psychology*, which was a direct inspiration for synthetic ethology, Braitenberg (1984, 20) distinguished "uphill analysis and downhill invention." By this he meant to distinguish the enormous difficulty of analyzing natural systems, as opposed to the comparative simplicity of synthesizing systems exhibiting a behavior of interest. His intention was to advocate the synthesis of neural networks and robots exhibiting intelligent behavior as an important adjunct to the analysis of intelligent agents in nature. Synthetic ethology extends this approach to phenomena for which populations and their evolution are relevant, such as communication.

The synthetic approach is especially valuable for investigating phenomena that depend essentially on the evolutionary history of the agents. Our ability to test evolutionary hypotheses about natural species is limited; we cannot go back into the past and restart the evolution of a species with different initial or boundary conditions, but we can do this with synthetic populations. That is, in synthetic ethology we can make systematic investigations of the effects of various parameters on the evolutionary outcome. Synthetic-ethology experiments are also facilitated by the rapid pace of evolution in synthetic worlds.

The ability to rerun evolution is just one example of the greater experimental control afforded by synthetic ethology over ordinary ethology. Because synthetic ethology constructs the world in which the experiments take place, every variable is under control, and we can intervene in the experiment whenever it is advantageous to do so. Some examples of useful control include the abilities to determine the genotypes in the population to allow genetically identical initial populations to evolve under different conditions, and to inspect, control or alter the behavioral mechanism (e.g., neural network) of an agent. Furthermore, since the entire synthetic world is contained in the computer, any mechanism underlying intentional or meaningful behavior is potentially open for inspection. This characteristic is critical, because it allows connecting the behavioral mechanisms (corresponding in natural organisms to neuron-level structures and processes) to the social-evolutionary level (that is, the evolution of a population over many generations). When meaningful behavior is observed in the population, there need be no "ghost in the machine"; the underlying mechanism is completely accessible.

Intrinsic Intentionality and Meaning

Even in a philosophical context, *intentionality* has several (interrelated) meanings. For instance, Searle (1983, 1) says, "Intentionality is that property of many mental states and events by which they are directed at or about or of objects and states of affairs in the world." For my purposes, intentionality may be defined informally as the property of a physical state or process when it is *about* something else (e.g., Blackburn, 1994, 196; Gregory, 1987, 383; Gutenplan, 1994, 379). For example, states in our brains may instantiate propositional attitudes about real or imaginary objects, such as beliefs, doubts, desires, hopes, fears, memories, anticipations and so forth. However, our linguistic expressions are also generally about something (their semantics), and therefore potentially meaningful to us (if we understand the expression). Thus, we are led to another ambiguous term: "meaning." One of its senses, and the one that I will use in this paper, is to refer to the intentional aspect of signals, linguistic expressions and similar meaning-bearing physical states and processes (e.g., Gutenplan, 1994, 386; Searle, 1983, 26-9). Thus, we may refer to the *meanings* of a vervet's alarm call, a peacock's mating display or a human utterance or gesture.

Many physical states and processes are meaningful, and therefore intentional, in this broad sense. For example, the states of a computer memory are almost always *about* something — for example, a student's academic record is *about* that student — but no one claims that the information is meaningful to the computer in the same sense that it is meaningful to us. Therefore, philosophers (e.g., Dennett, 1987, 288-9; Haugeland, 1997, 7-8) distinguish *derived* intentionality from *intrinsic* (or original, authentic, etc.) intentionality. *Our* intentional states and processes (e.g., brain states and communicative activities) normally have *intrinsic intentionality* because they are meaningful to us (the bearers, producers or consumers of the states and processes). In contrast, information in a computer memory or database has *derived intentionality*, because it is not intrinsically meaningful to the computer and derives its intentionality only from its meaningfulness to us, the users of the computer.

Intrinsic intentionality is a fundamental (even defining) property of mental states, cognition, communication and many related phenomena and processes. We can judge the intrinsic intentionality of our own internal states by introspection (the basis of the Chinese room argument), but this approach cannot be applied to artificial agents or even to most animals; this complicates the scientific investigation of intrinsic intentionality's physical basis. One of the principal motivations of synthetic ethology is the creation of systems that exhibit intrinsic intentionality, but are simple enough to permit complete explication of the underlying mechanisms. To accomplish this, we must identify non-introspective criteria of intrinsic intentionality.

How can we determine if physical states are intrinsically meaningful to agents, natural or artificial? For the purposes of this article, the argument must be abbreviated and restricted to a particular manifestation of intentionality, namely communication (see MacLennan, 1992, for a fuller discussion). We may begin with Grice's (1957) analysis of the *meaning* of a communication act as the speaker's intention to affect the audience by means of the audience's understanding of that intention. More generally, we may say that in a *communication act* one agent behaves with the *intention* (purpose) of eliciting a response (external or internal) in other agents that perceive the behavior or its result. Here, of course, "intention" refers to a certain goal-directed or purposeful behavioral disposition or state of mind (e.g., Blackburn, 1994, 196; Gutenplan, 1994, 375-379). (Therefore, an intention is an instance of intentionality by virtue of its being *about* its goal or purpose. Thus an internal state may be "intentional" both in the narrower sense of being an intention and in the wider sense of having intentionality.)

Determination of intention or purpose is problematic, of course, especially in the context of non-human agents, such as the artificial agents used in synthetic ethology, but we can learn from the ways that ethologists make these determinations about non-human animals. In general, ethologists explain the purpose of an innate behavior in terms of its selective advantage in the species' EEA. In particular, questions of whether genuine communication is taking place are answered by looking at its effect on the inclusive fitness of a group of animals in their EEA (Burghardt, 1970). In broad terms, we may say that an animal's behavior is purposeful if it has, or has had, the probability of being relevant to the survival of that animal or its group. We can apply a similar criterion in synthetic ethology, indeed more rigorously than it is applied in natural ethology; for we can test directly whether particular behaviors or internal states of the agents contribute to their survival in the environments in which they have evolved. Such experiments can also reveal the meaning of these states or behaviors to the agents, that is, their specific relevance to the agents' inclusive fitness. Certainly, this is not the only approach to determining purpose, but it has the advantage of being applicable to very simple artificial agents.

Ecological Validity and Pragmatic Context

Ecological validity refers to the fact that many behaviors are adaptively meaningful only in a species' EEA, that is, only in the environment that has conditioned the species' adaptations. When agents are placed in conditions that are too different from their EEA, they behave in abnormal ways, from which it may be difficult to draw valid conclusions about normal behavior (Neisser, 1976, 2, 7-8). Indeed, this is the motivation for ordinary (natural) ethological methods, which relate behavior to its EEA, as opposed to behaviorist methods, which typically study behavior in unnatural laboratory settings. Internal ("mental") states and external signals acquire meaning through their functional role in the life of the agents, and so they can be understood best in relation to their EEA. Therefore synthetic ethology strives for ecological validity by studying behaviors and cognitive phenomena in their synthetic EEA.

A related issue is the *pragmatic context* of a behavior. In particular, when we are dealing with communication, and especially when we are concerned with non-human communication, we must recognize that communication is rarely purely semantic, that is, serving the purpose of transmitting a proposition (truth-bearing signal). Indeed, communication may be deceptive, among humans as well as other animals, and often serves non-propositional purposes. This is well known from studies of animal communication as well as from philosophical investigations of ordinary language use (e.g., Austin 1975; Wittgenstein, 1958, sec. 19). Now, *pragmatics* refers to the purpose served by a communication or other behavior, and, as for intentionality, this purpose can be derived or intrinsic, that is, derived from the designer of an artificial agent, or intrinsic to the agent itself. Therefore, in order to investigate behaviors with an intrinsic pragmatic context, those behaviors must be fulfilling some purpose intrinsic to the agents, considered either individually or as a population. Synthetic ethology addresses these issues by investigating agents in an environment in which their behaviors matter *to them*. This is so because an agent's behaviors affect its inclusive fitness, that is, the reproductive fitness of itself or related agents (it is not necessary, of course, that the agents be *aware* that the behavior matters to them).

In summary, we may say that a communication act is *meaningful* to an agent if within a pragmatic context it serves a purpose, which is understood as the likelihood of increasing the selective advantage of the agent or its group in its EEA (thus maintaining ecological validity). In broad terms, the *meaning* of the communication act may be identified with this purpose (this is the sense with which "meaning" and "meaningfulness" are used in this chapter).

Synthetic Worlds are Physically Real

Since most synthetic ethology experiments take place on general-purpose digital computers, there is a danger of confusing them with simulations. The distinction is important because, as has been remarked often, no one gets wet when a meteorologist simulates a hurricane on a computer. If we are using simulated agents to investigate intentional phenomena, then the objection may be made that although the agents may *simulate* understanding (for example), they do not *really* understand anything, since nothing real is taking place in the computer; it is all simulated. For example, it may be claimed, there is no true meaningful communication, only simulated communication; any apparent intentionality is either derived or simulated (i.e., illusory).

Putting aside, for a moment, the topic of simulation, it is important to stress that synthetic ethology depends crucially on the fact that a computer is a physical device (made of silicon, etc.), and therefore that the states and program-controlled state-changes within the computer are (real) physical states and state-changes (involving the movement of electrons, etc.).[1] In effect, the program determines the way in which physical law operates within the confines of the computer. Of course, in contrast to *simulated* physical processes, the *real* physical processes in a computer cannot disobey physical law, but these (real) physical processes can be controlled by the program (itself a physical configuration in the computer). In particular, a computer is a non-equilibrium thermodynamic system, and so a program controlling the computer can deploy physical law in such a way that synthetic agents are also (literal, physical) non-equilibrium structures, which must behave (physically) in a specified manner in order to maintain their structure. Thus the behavioral and cognitive processes in the synthetic agents have real relevance to their continued existence ("survival") as real, physical non-equilibrium systems.

It is on this basis that we can claim that agents in synthetic ethology experiments exhibit intrinsic and not just derived intentionality. That is, within the synthetic world constructed in the computer (which is physically real, despite being synthetic), the internal states and behaviors of the agents will have a real influence on their persistence as definite physical structures (particular arrangements of matter and energy in the computer). Therefore these states and behaviors are meaningful *to them*. By observing the relevance of these states and behaviors to the agents, we, as outside observers, may *infer* (more or less correctly and more or less precisely) the meaning of the states and behaviors for the agents, much as if we were observing another animal species. The meaning *we* attribute to the states and behaviors will be *derived* from their meaning to the agents. For us, the states and behaviors have only derived intentionality, but for the agents they have intrinsic intentionality.

Synthetic Ethology Experiments vs. Ethological Simulations

I must say a little more about the difference between synthetic ethology and ordinary ethological simulations, since the two are easy to confuse. First, recall that a scientific *model* is a representation of some system of interest, such a representation being chosen because it is easier to investigate in some way than the system being modeled (e.g., Bynum, Brown, & Porter, 1981, 272-4). Thus a model always has reference to some other *subject system* (which is the primary system of interest and justifies the existence of the model), and so we are concerned with the relation of the model to this subject system, such as its accuracy, range of applicability, etc. There are, of course, many kinds of models: mathematical models, mechanical models, computer models and so on. A (computer) *simulation* is a particular kind of model in which a computer is programmed to be a model of some other subject system of interest. It is worth noting that in a running simulation we have one physical system (the programmed computer) being used as a model of another (the simulated subject system). In this way a computer model is like a mechanical model, in which one physical system serves as a model for another.

To understand the difference between experiments in synthetic ethology and ordinary ethological simulations, we can look at an analogous distinction in the physical sciences. First consider a scientific investigation using an ordinary computer simulation of a hurricane. Here one physical system (the programmed computer) is used as a model of another (the earth's atmosphere), and the usefulness of the model (in a particular context of questions) will depend on the relation between the two systems. Next consider a different scientific investigation, in which we attempt to discover and validate gas laws (e.g., Boyle's and Charles') by placing various gasses in a cylinder in which their pressure, volume and temperature may be controlled and measured. In this case we have created a specialized physical system designed in such a way that we can control the relevant variables and investigate their interaction. However, this physical system is not a model of anything else; its purpose is not to facilitate the investigation of some *other* system, but to facilitate the investigation of *its own* properties in order to discover or validate general laws. Certainly an improved understanding of the gas laws will help us to understand atmospheric hydrodynamics, but our gas cylinder is not intended as a model of anything in the atmosphere.

Similarly, although synthetic ethology makes no attempt to simulate specific natural systems, it may produce scientific results that are relevant to a wide variety of natural systems. This is because it is directed toward basic science, for synthetic ethology is based on the observation that fundamental, general scientific laws have usually been discovered and confirmed by means of experiments in which there are relatively few variables, which can be controlled precisely. Behaviorist experiments have the control but lack ecological validity. Ethological field studies have ecological validity, but the number of variables is enormous and difficult to control. Synthetic ethology maintains both control and ecological validity by having the agents evolve in a complete but simple synthetic world. Furthermore, because the mechanisms of behavior are transparent, synthetic ethology may facilitate the discovery of causal laws, whereas the nervous-system complexity of animals defeats a detailed causal account of behavior (at least with current technology). The goal of synthetic ethology, therefore, is to discover fundamental scientific laws of great generality underlying intentional phenomena in natural and synthetic systems. Once discovered, their applicability to particular natural systems could be confirmed through ordinary ethological investigations and simulations.

It remains to consider one more issue concerning the difference between synthetic ethology and ordinary ethological simulations, for it is relevant in assessing the relevance to synthetic ethology of simulation studies of language evolution, animal behavior and related topics. A system that is designed as a model of some other subject system may be found to exemplify properties of much wider interest. For example, Lorenz's computer simulation of weather patterns turned out to be more interesting as an example of chaotic dynamics (Gleick, 1987, Ch. 1). That is, we may shift attention from the simulating system as a model of something else to a system interesting in its own right; this is a change in the *goal* of the scientist using the system, not in the nature of the system. Therefore it is quite possible that an ethological simulation of some interesting natural process (e.g., the evolution of vervet alarm calls) might turn out to be interesting in its own right as a physical system exemplifying general scientific principles, and thus be usable in synthetic ethology. As in the case of Lorenz's simulations, we might use the system to investigate principles that are much more widely applicable than just to vervet alarm calls. Thus, we may find particular ethological simulations that can be reinterpreted and used as synthetic ethology experiments.

Review of Early Results

In this section I will review, very briefly, our experiments demonstrating the evolution of intrinsically meaningful communication in a population of simple machines (MacLennan, 1990, 1992, 2001, 2002; MacLennan & Burghardt, 1993). I will also mention some related experiments by other investigators, but I will not attempt a comprehensive literature review.

One-Symbol Communication

Method

In our first experiments we wanted to determine if it was even possible for genuine communication to evolve in an artificial system (for additional detail, see MacLennan, 1990, 1992, 2001, 2002; MacLennan & Burghardt, 1993). Therefore, in order to put selective pressure on the evolution of communication, we decided to select for behavior that would be aided by communication, but could be accomplished less effectively without it. That is, there should be something relevant to the agents for them to communicate about. Therefore, we decided to select for a simple kind of cooperation that would be more likely if one agent had information about another agent that was not directly accessible to the first agent.

This requirement was satisfied by placing each agent in a *local environment*, the state of which was directly accessible only to that agent. In accord with our goal of keeping the experiments as simple as possible, each local environment was defined to be in one of a small number L of discrete states; in this first series of experiments, $L = 8$. Each agent could sense the state of its local environment, but not alter it. The states of the local environments were randomized periodically so that there would be no way to predict them.

In addition to the local environments associated with each agent, there was a single *global environment* to which all the agents had access. It could be sensed by all the agents, but also modified by them. Thus, the global environment provided a potential medium for communication, but of course there was no built-in requirement that the agents use it for this or any other purpose. For simplicity, the global environment was restricted to a small number G of discrete states; in these experiments, $G = 8$. See Figure 1 for a schematic diagram of the relation of the agents and environments.

Figure 1. Schematic of environment structure: Outer ovals are local environments, the central circle is a global environment and spheres are agents; this diagram shows only eight agents and their local environments.

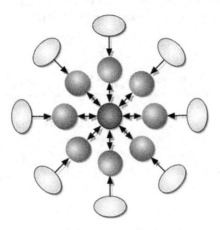

Our agents were capable of only two kinds of behavior: They could *emit* (that is, change, the global environment) or they could *act* (attempt cooperation). In these experiments cooperation took a very simple form, namely, an agent A attempted to cooperate by trying to match the local-environment state of a specific other agent B. Since there were L possible local-state values, in any given situation there were L different possible actions A might take, denoted **act** (m), for each local-state value m; such an action was an attempt to match m against B's local environment. If B's local environment was indeed in state m, then a match occurred and the agents were deemed to have cooperated; if they did not match, the attempted cooperation failed.

Since B's local-environment state was unpredictable, in the absence of some form of communication the chances of a successful match were $1/L$. The target of the attempted match B was required to be the last emitter, that is, the last agent to have changed the global environment. Restricting the attempted match to pertain to a specific agent made random actions less likely to succeed than if a match to any other agent were allowed.

Although this matching process was simple, it was genuine cooperation, for it contributed to the continued existence of the cooperating agents. Specifically, when an agent succeeded in matching the local environment of the last emitter, both agents received a point of credit. If it failed, then neither agent was credited. (We also investigated variants in which there was penalty for failed matching attempts, differential rewards, etc.) As will be explained in more detail later, these credits were used to determine which agents were more likely to "survive" (persist as organized structures in the population) and to reproduce. Therefore, successful cooperations (by chance or any other means) enhanced the fitness (probability of survival and reproduction) of the cooperating agents.

These rules for cooperation may seem somewhat abstract and arbitrary. They were chosen for their simplicity, since synthetic ethology does not require us to simulate any particular natural system. Nevertheless, there is a sort of story we can tell that may make them more comprehensible. When an agent A emits, it can be thought of as a call that it needs help in dealing with something in its local environment. Another agent B may respond by acting, but it will succeed in cooperating only if it acts in a way appropriate the agent A's local environment (i.e., if its action matches A's local environment). Be that as it may, in synthetic ethology we are free to define the "laws of nature" in our synthetic world in whatever way required for our experiments.

Our agents require some behavioral control mechanism, which allows them to sense the state of the global environment and of their own local environment, and then to behave in either of two ways: change the global environment to a particular value or act in a particular way. We use the notation **emit** (g) to denote the action of changing the global environment to state g, and **act** (l) for the action of attempting to match state l in the last emitter's local environment. In addition, it is useful if an agent's actions depend on its own internal state, which can be thought of as the contents of its short-term memory. (In this first series of experiments, the agents did not have any memory, however.)

We have used two behavioral control mechanisms in our experiments, finite-state machines (FSMs) and artificial neural networks (ANNs). In this first series of experiments we used FSMs. They get their name from the fact that they have a finite number I of internal or memory states. Therefore, a FSM can be defined by a table, called a *state transition table*, that describes the machine's behavior for each possible combination of inputs and internal state. For our machines, the inputs are the shared global state and the machine's own local-environment state. Thus there are $I{\times}G{\times}L$ possible conditions to which the machine must respond, and therefore $I{\times}G{\times}L$ entries in its state transition table. Such a FSM's transition table can be visualized as follows:

old int. state	global state	loc. env. state	new int. state	response
⋮	⋮	⋮	⋮	⋮
3	7	2	5	**emit** (1)
⋮	⋮	⋮	⋮	⋮
4	0	1	4	**act** (4)
⋮	⋮	⋮	⋮	⋮

To the right of the double line, the table lists a new internal state and a response for each possible combination of old internal state, global-environment state and local-environment state, as enumerated to the left of the double line. For example, this table says that if the machine is in internal (memory) state 3, and the shared global state is 7, and the machine's own local-environment state is 2, then the machine will change its internal state to 5 and respond with **emit** (1), which changes the global-environment state to 1. Similarly, if its internal state is 4, the global state is 0 and its local-environment state is 1, then it will stay in internal state 4 and respond with **act** (4), which attempts to match 4 against the local-environment state of the last emitter.

In each of these conditions the table must determine a new internal state (I possibilities) and either emit (G possibilities) or act (L possibilities). So there are $I(G+L)$ different ways the machines can respond to each condition. Since in this first series of experiments $I = 1$ (no memory), there are GL table entries and $G + L$ possible responses. In particular, since $G = 8 = L$, there are 64 entries, each defining one of 16 responses (henceforth we will assume $I = 1$ unless otherwise stated).

It is worth observing that although the FSM is a simple behavioral control mechanism, it has some subtlety in this application. This is because the behavior of an agent is always determined by the combination of global, local and internal state. Therefore, for example, the signal emitted for a particular local-environment state depends also on the global state and the internal state; that is, the signal emission is context-dependent. In addition, the way an agent responds to a signal in the global environment depends on its own internal state (as we would expect), but also on its own local environment, another kind of context-dependence. An agent's response to each particular combination of circumstances is potentially unique; there is no built-in ability to generalize over similar situations. Therefore, if agents have evolved that are able to signal their local-environment state in a context-free way, that is, independently of the global environment and their internal state, it is because they have adapted to do this in every combination of global and internal state with this local state. Likewise, to respond to a signal independent of context, the agents must have this response for every combination of local and internal state. So the evolutionary problem that the population has to solve is actually quite difficult (as will be discussed later, we have also investigated behavioral control mechanisms, such as ANNs, which do have some ability to generalize).

We also experimented with a simple form of single-case learning, which could be enabled or disabled as an experimental control. When learning was enabled, it operated in the following way: Suppose in global-environment state g and local-environment state l the table for an agent B defined the response **act** (m), that is, the attempt to cooperate with action m. Further, suppose that this was the incorrect action, because local-environment state of the last emitter (A) was n. In this case the table for agent B will be changed to **act** (n) under conditions (g, l). In other words, it is changed to *what would have been* the correct action in the current conditions. This is actually a very weak form of learning, since there is no guarantee that action n will be correct the next time the global environment is g and this agent's local-environment state is l.

Our goal was to investigate communication in its environment of evolutionary adaptedness, and therefore it was necessary for our population of agents to evolve. The behavioral table of an FSM is represented simply by a "genetic string" of GL genes (representing the possible conditions), each of which has $G + L$ alleles (representing possible responses to those conditions). This was coded simply as a string of GL numbers in the range 0 to $G + L - 1$. This string defines the *genotype* of an agent, which is used to initialize its behavioral table when it is "born" (see below). The behavioral table, representing the agent's *phenotype,* is constant throughout the agent's "life" if learning is disabled, but if learning is enabled, the behavioral table (phenotype) may change according to the learning rule.

Our goal was to select for cooperative activity, therefore we counted the number of successful cooperations for each agent over a specified interval of time. Specifically, each agent was given several opportunities (five, in these experiments) to respond to a given configuration of (randomly determined) local-environment states. Then the local environments were re-randomized and the agents were tested again; this was repeated several times (10, in these experiments). The *fitness* of an agent was defined to be the number of successful cooperations in this interval of simulated time, and thus reflects the rate of cooperation.

The preceding events are called a *breeding cycle* because at the end of them two agents are chosen to "breed," producing a single "offspring," and one agent is chosen to "die" and be replaced by that offspring. Thus, the population size is constant (100 in these experiments). The probability of choosing an agent to breed was made proportional to its fitness (rate of cooperation), and the probability of dying was inversely related to its fitness. Preliminary experiments showed that always choosing the most fit to breed and the least fit to die led to premature convergence in the population. After replacement of the "dead" agent by the parents' offspring, a new breeding cycle began, and the run continued for a specified number of breeding cycles (5,000 in most experiments). The initial populations had randomized genomes.

Genetic algorithms (GAs) typically replace the entire population after breeding, thus defining non-overlapping generations (e.g., Goldberg, 1989). We decided to use incremental replacement — one individual at a time — to allow a simple form of "cultural transmission" of learning, which we thought might be important when learning was enabled.

It remains to say how the genotype of the offspring was determined. The genetic operators were similar to those used in GAs, but with minor differences. First, a genetic string for the offspring was determined by *two-point crossover* of the parents' genotypes. That is, two uniformly random numbers k, l were chosen in the range 1 to GL. The offspring's genes in the range k to l were taken from one parent, and those in the range 1 to $k - 1$ and $l + 1$ to GL from the other. Finally, with low probability (typically 0.01) a random gene was mutated by replacing it with a randomly chosen allele in the range 0 to $G + L - 1$. The resulting genetic string became the genome of the offspring and determined its phenotype (initial behavioral table).

During these experiments we gathered several kinds of data in order to assess whether communication had evolved in the population. According to Burghardt's (1970) definition of communication, if genuine communication is taking place then it ought to have a demonstrable positive effect on the inclusive fitness of the population. Therefore the most fundamental information we gathered was *degree of coordination*, defined as the average number of cooperations per breeding cycle. We computed both the maximum and average for the population. The time series of these quantities (smoothed by a moving average) allowed us to track any progressive changes in the rate of cooperation in the population and its best representative.

In order to be able to investigate any communication that might evolve, we also compiled a *co-occurrence table* during each experiment. This was a $G \times L$ matrix in which the (g, l) entry reflected the frequency with which global-environment state g and local-environment state l co-occurred in a successful cooperation (that is, the correct action l was performed). If no communication were to take place, then one would expect all (g, l) pairs to be equally likely. On the other hand, if systematic communication were to take place, in which certain global states g ("symbols") are used to denote certain local-environment states l ("situations"), then one would expect a non-uniform distribution.

Furthermore, if communication were evolving in the population, then one would expect to see a change in the co-occurrence matrix over time, from a uniform distribution at the beginning of the experiment and becoming progressively more structured as communication emerged. Therefore, we computed the co-occurrence table over the recent history of the simulation (50 breeding cycles), so that it would reflect the behavior of the population at a particular time. To quantify the degree of structure in the matrix we used several measures, including entropy, coefficient of variation and chi-square. By plotting these quantities as a function of time, we were able to see changes in degree of structure as evolution progressed.

Symbols and Communication

In anticipation of discussing the results of these experiments, it is worth observing that although the preceding use of "symbols" to refer to global-environment states might be considered metaphorical, it is in fact consistent with the technical use of this term in semiotics (e.g., Colapietro, 1993, 190), deriving from Peirce (1955, 102-3 = CP^2 2.243-52). To explain this, it is necessary for me to reiterate several characteristics of these synthetic ethology experiments. The global and local states are both physical states in the synthetic world external to the agents; they correspond to physical conditions in the vicinity of an animal. Global-environment states are analogous to physical sound waves in the air; local-environment states are analogous to conditions nearby an animal, such as the physical presence of a food source, but these are just analogies. Global-state values and local-state values come from conceptually distinct alphabets, although for programming convenience in these experiments they were both represented by nonnegative integers (i.e., the global-state values are in $\{0, ..., G\text{-}1\}$ and the local-states are in $\{0, ..., L\text{-}1\}$). As will be seen when we discuss the results of these experiments, statistical regularities in the co-occurrence tables (e.g., Tables 2 and 3) show that global-state values are used systematically by the agents to denote local-state values. Therefore, certain physical conditions (global states) are used to *denote* other physical conditions (local states). Thus, the global states are *referential*, which qualifies them as *signs* in the usage of semiotics (Colapietro, 1993, 179-80).

Furthermore, the relationship between the global-state values and local-states values (between the *signs* and their *referents*) is arbitrary and conventional. In different experiments (i.e., with different random initial populations) we get different correspondences between the signs and their referents. Indeed, the correspondence must be arbitrary, for the global- and local-state values are drawn from different alphabets and the machines have no mechanisms for comparing the elements of these different spaces. (They can, in effect, compare local states to local states and global states to global states, but not local states to global states; this is implicit in the structure of the FSMs. Also, the agents have no access to the fact that in the computer, both global-state values and local-state values are represented by nonnegative integers, that is, by bit strings.) Therefore, the correlation between the sign vehicle (global-state value) and its object (local-state value) is not based on any similarity or physical connection, and so, in Peirce's terms, these signs are neither *icons* nor *indices*, but *symbols* (Colapietro, 1993, 190; Peirce, 1955, p 102-4 = CP 2.243-52, 2.304). The initially random correspondences are amplified by evolution and (in some experiments) learning; that is, they are conventional.

While on the topic of semiotic issues, it will be worthwhile to mention several other characteristics of these symbols and the agents' use of them. First, these symbols are context sensitive, for an agent's behavior is always determined by a combination of the global-environment state and its local-environment state. As it turns out, this context dependence is of no use to the agents in these experiments (and indeed interferes with the straight-forward use of the global environment for communication), and so the agents have to adapt (through evolution and perhaps learning) to ignore their local-environment state when attempting to respond to signals in the global environment (conversely, they need to adapt to ignore the global environment when attempting to signal the state of their local environment).

Second, we normally expect an external sign to correspond to some internal representation, its *sense (Sinn)*, which is distinct from its *referent (Bedeutung)*. As I have remarked elsewhere, the agents in these experiments are so simple that they can hardly be said to have psychological states. Nevertheless, if we look closely we can see a rudimentary internal representation of external conditions. For when an agent responds to its environment, the computer implementing the FSM must copy the global- and local-environment states from their physical locations in the computer's memory, and use them to compute an index into the FSM's transition table. Thus, these two physical conditions external to the agent are copied to different physical locations and integrated to determine the agent's behavioral response (had we not used nonnegative integers to represent the global-state values, a less trivial transformation to the internal representation would have been required). We find similarly rudimentary internal representations in simple organisms such as bacteria.

Third, we can understand a symbol as a triadic relation between a sign, its referent, and the *receiver* or *interpreter*, and we can observe this triadic relation in our synthetic ethology experiments. For example, the co-occurrence matrices (e.g., Tables 2 and 3) show how the symbols (global-environment states) are interpreted by the population at a given point in time. A substantially different population (either in a different experiment, or in the same experiment at a substantially different point in time) may interpret the symbols differently. Furthermore, as will be discussed later, we can sometimes discern two or more subpopulations that interpret one or more symbols differently. Finally, we can look at individual agents and determine what a symbol means to *it* (i.e., how it responds to the symbol) in any particular context.

Indeed, one of our FSM's behavioral rules (i.e., rows in its transition table) can be understood directly in terms of the five-place relation that, according to Morris (1964, 2), characterizes a *sign process* or *semiosis*. For, suppose that under conditions (g, m) the FSM R responds **act** (n) and that the last emitter's local environment is in state n. Then, in this semiosis, (1) global state g is the *sign*, (2) R is the *interpreter*, (3) **act** (n) is the *interpretant* (the effect of the sign qua sign), (4) local-state n is the *signification* (or *referent*) and (5) m is the *context* of the sign.

Finally, before discussing the experimental results, it is worth observing that synthetic ethology affords much easier experimental control than natural ethology, and we made use of this control in these experiments. The fundamental control addressed Burghardt's

(1970) definition of communication: For genuine communication to be taking place we would have to show that it was contributing to the inclusive fitness of the population. Therefore, we wanted to be able to compare the evolution of the population under conditions in which it was possible for communication to evolve with those under which it was impossible. Thus, we designed the experiments so they could be run with communication, suppressed or not. To suppress communication, we randomized the global-environment state at every opportunity, in effect raising the noise level so high that the only potential medium of communication was unusable. This allowed us to run parallel experiments with genetically identical (random) initial populations differing only in whether communication was suppressed or not. The second major control that we used in this series of experiments was to enable or disable the simple learning rule described above. This allowed us to do some preliminary investigations of whether learning facilitated the evolution of communication or not.

Results

We ran over one hundred experiments with the parameters as described above. In most cases we made three parallel runs with the same random initial populations: (1) communication suppressed, (2) communication not suppressed and learning disabled and (3) communication not suppressed and learning enabled. This allowed us to investigate the effects of communication and learning independently of the initial population. Although there was considerable quantitative difference from experiment to experiment, due to the random initial populations and the many other random factors, nevertheless the qualitative results were quite predictable. Therefore, in the following I will discuss a typical experiment.

Figure 2. Degree of coordination: Communication suppressed

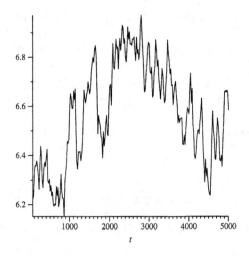

Figure 3. Degree of coordination: Communication permitted with learning disabled

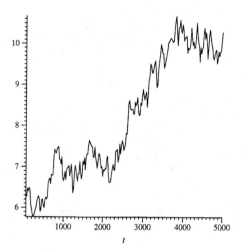

Analysis (MacLennan, 1990) shows that in the absence of communication agents can be expected to exhibit a degree of coordination of 6.25 cooperations per unit time (one breeding cycle, in this case). Indeed, when communication is suppressed we find that the average degree of coordination begins at this value and stays very close to it. Nevertheless, linear regression shows a slight upward trend, 3.67×10^{-5} coop. / unit time / unit time, a somewhat surprising result discussed later. The degree of coordination was up to 6.6 coop. / unit time after 5,000 breeding cycles, and had been as high as 6.95 (see Figure 2).

When communication was not suppressed (but learning was still disabled), the degree of coordination began at the chance level, but increased at a rate of 9.72×10^{-4} coop. / unit time / unit time, a rate 26 times as great as when communication was suppressed. After 5,000 breeding cycles, the degree of coordination was up to 10.28 coop. / unit time, which is 60% higher than when communication was suppressed, and had been as high as 10.6 (see Figure 3). This significant difference shows that the population is using the global environment for genuine communication, since it has increased the agents' inclusive fitness.

When communication was not suppressed and learning was enabled, the degree of coordination began at about 45 coop. / unit time, which is much higher than the 6.25 expected with neither communication nor learning. This high level of coordination, achieved before communication has evolved, is a consequence of the fact that an agent has several opportunities to respond to a local-environment configuration before the local environments are re-randomized. So, there is a baseline advantage to learning even in the absence of communication. Over the 5,000 breeding cycles, the degree of coordination increased at a rate of 3.71×10^{-3} coop. / unit time / unit time, which is 3.82 times the rate when learning was disabled and approximately 100 times the rate when communication was suppressed. By the end of the experiment, the degree of coordination had

Figure 4. Degree of coordination: Communication permitted with learning enabled

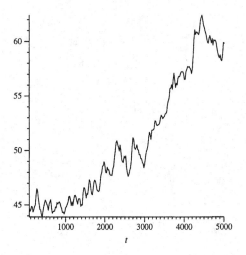

reached 59.84 coop. / unit time, which is 857% above that achieved when communication was suppressed (see Figure 4). Therefore learning reinforces the selective benefits of communication.

Finally, we must consider why there is a very slow increase in the degree of coordination even when communication is suppressed. This results from the population evolving to exploit a loophole in the fitness determination rule by means of *partial cooperation*. Recall that a cooperation is judged to have taken place only if the action of an agent matches the local environment of the *last emitter*; to allow it to match any local environment would increase the probability of chance cooperation too much, decreasing the selective pressure. Therefore, the population can increase the probability of cooperation by co-evolving so that agents emit only in a small subset of local-environment states and only act in ways appropriate to this same subset. As a further consequence, we observed that in long experiments with communication suppressed, the uniform co-occurrence matrix would become slightly structured due to attempted cooperations being attempted in only a subset of the local-environment states. This explanation was confirmed by Noble and Cliff (1996). It is worth emphasizing that these simple agents found a way to improve their performance that was not anticipated when we designed the experiment, and that required some investigation in order to explain.

We can get more information about the agents' evolved ability to communicate by inspecting the co-occurrence tables. As previously mentioned, we quantified the structure of the tables by several measures, including entropy. For $G = 8 = L$, the maximum entropy, which occurs with a uniform distribution, is $H_{max} = 6$ bits. For comparison, we can compute the entropy for an ideal code, in which there is a one-to-one correspondence between global- and local-environment states; it is $H_{ideal} = 3$ bits.

Table 1. Co-occurrence matrix: Communication suppressed

loc.→ glob.↓	0	1	2	3	4	5	6	7
0	94	130	133	34	166	0	150	682
1	16	105	279	228	261	307	0	118
2	0	199	229	12	0	0	161	274
3	95	19	93	283	669	89	0	201
4	1	97	212	200	112	0	0	0
5	28	135	84	8	600	215	0	351
6	0	0	0	118	59	70	0	690
7	0	33	41	0	371	0	0	0

When communication was suppressed, the entropy started at approximately 6 bits, but by the end of 5,000 breeding cycles, had decreased to 4.95. This resulted from partial cooperation, as already discussed. An inspection of the co-occurrence matrix at the end of the experiment, and therefore reflecting the last 50 breeding cycles (Table 1), showed that there was little or no cooperation in a subset of the local-environment states (e.g., 0 and 6).

When communication was not suppressed (but learning was disabled) the entropy decreased to 3.87 bits, which is much closer to $H_{ideal} = 3$ bits (see Figure 5). Visual inspection of the final co-occurrence matrix (Table 2) reveals much more systematic use of the global environment as a communication medium. Sometimes a global-environment state denotes a single local-environment state almost exclusively, and vice versa. We

Figure 5. Entropy: Communication permitted with learning disabled

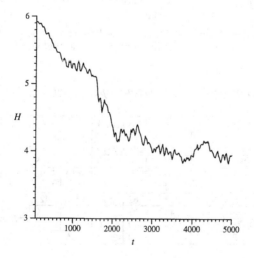

Table 2. Co-occurrence matrix: Communication permitted with learning disabled

loc. → glob. ↓	0	1	2	3	4	5	6	7
0	0	0	2825	0	500	20	0	0
1	206	0	0	505	999	231	2	0
2	1	0	0	277	39	4935	1	2394
3	385	1	1	94	0	0	1483	1
4	0	292	0	0	19	555	0	0
5	0	0	1291	0	0	144	0	0
6	494	279	0	403	0	1133	2222	0
7	140	2659	0	202	962	0	0	0

also find examples of *ambiguity*, in which a global state denotes primarily two local states, and *synonymy*, in which two global states denote the same local state. Other complexities, typical of natural communication, also appear. The occurrence of ambiguity and synonymy in the population's communication could result from competing "dialects" in the population or from inconsistent signal use by individual agents (or by both in combination). Experiments by Noble and Cliff (1996) seem to have ruled out the dialect explanation. Rather, their research supports ambiguous signal use by individual agents, that is, the same symbol is emitted for two different local-environment states.

When communication was not suppressed and learning was enabled, then the entropy achieved in this experiment was 3.91 bits, about the same as in the non-learning case (see Table 3). This is typical; sometimes it is a little greater than the non-learning entropy, sometimes a little less. Table 4 summarizes the entropy and coefficient of variation under the three experimental conditions.

It is worth stepping back from these experiments to stress an important point. The symbols used by the population, as recorded in the co-occurrence matrices, are meaningful *to the agents themselves*, because they are relevant to the inclusive fitness, indeed to the continued existence, of the agents. That is, the symbols exhibit intrinsic intentionality, not a derivative intentionality coming from us as designers or observers of the system. Indeed, we cannot know the meaning of the individual symbols except through

Table 3. Co-occurrence matrix: Communication permitted with learning enabled

loc. → glob. ↓	0	1	2	3	4	5	6	7
0	3908	29172	1287	12281	2719	1132	93	3836
1	191	634	107	1039	0	0	2078	0
2	4675	1306	0	37960	85	410	7306	26611
3	0	410	0	0	0	126	1306	304
4	0	0	353	62	575	1268	420	519
5	36	0	46	469	0	0	0	26
6	1075	156	0	0	0	951	0	1086
7	0	73	54	0	2764	135	461	102

Table 4. Summary of order measures

Measurement	Random	Communication/Learning			Ideal
		N/N	Y/N	Y/Y	
Coefficient of Variation, V	0	1.27	2.13	2.39	2.65
Entropy, H (bits)	6	4.95	3.87	3.91	3

empirical investigation. Thus, we may study their use as reflected, for example, in a co-occurrence matrix, and compile a "dictionary" based on observation, or we may "dissect" the agents, as described later, to see how they interpret the symbols (see MacLennan, 1990, for examples). Indeed, any meaning the symbols have for us is derived from the intrinsic meaning of the symbols to the synthetic agents.

Now, certainly these agents are very simple, and they do not have any awareness of the meaning of the symbols; their response is purely mechanical. But conscious awareness is not necessary for intrinsic intentionality and meaningful communication, which can be found in microorganisms with no (or very little) awareness. For example, bacteria communicate meaningfully (e.g., Dunny & Winans, 1999) and fitness-enhancing chemotaxis shows they have intentional internal states, for example, internal representations of external chemical gradients (Dretske, 1985, 29), but bacteria are not conscious. Thus synthetic ethology provides a means of investigating intrinsic intentionality in its barest, simplest form, which is exactly where experimental investigations should begin.

Neuroethology seeks to understand the neural basis of a species' behavior in an evolutionary context, but neuroethological investigations are difficult because of the complexity of nervous systems, the slow pace of evolution and the difficulty of doing controlled experiments. On the other hand, in synthetic ethology we are dealing with simpler agents and their behavioral control mechanisms are completely transparent for investigation. If some interesting behavior evolves in a population, then we can "dissect" the members of the population and determine their entire behavioral control system (see MacLennan, 1990, for examples). In particular, if, as in these experiments, the agents evolve to exhibit intrinsic intentionality, then we can completely explicate the mechanism underlying that intentionality; there can be no "ghost in the machine." Thus synthetic ethology provides a means of bridging the gap between inherently mental phenomena, such as intentionality, and the physical processes supporting them.

Other Experiments

I'll briefly review some of our other early experiments in synthetic ethology. One simple extension to the preceding experiments was to test the population's evolution of the ability to communicate by emitting and recognizing sequences of two signals (MacLennan, 2001). To create selective pressure toward this result, we reduced the number of global-environment states to $G = 4$ while keeping the local-environment states at $L = 8$; thus, there were not enough global-environment states to uniquely denote the local-environment states. Of course, using sequential signals requires that the agents be able to remember the signals they have already generated as well as those they have already recognized. Therefore, we increased the number of internal (memory) states to $I = 4$. As a consequence, the agents' genomes contained 128 genes with 48 alleles each. In other respects the setup was the same as our previous experiments.

Two-symbol communication was comparatively slow to evolve and never reached the same degree of organization as we observed for single-symbol communication. For example, the final co-occurrence matrix (Table 5) shows that, for the most part, the meaning is conveyed by the second (i.e., most recently received) symbol. Thus, the local-environment state 5 is denoted primarily by signals 0/1, 1/1, 2/1, and 3/1. On the other hand, there are some cases in which both symbols have meaning: although 0/0, 1/0, and 3/0 denote primarily state 4, 2/0 denotes primarily state 0. Furthermore, order is significant, because 0/2 denotes primarily state 3.

Although we ran experiments considerably longer than the 5,000 breeding cycles used in the preceding experiments, two-symbol communication never seemed to evolve much beyond the level of organization shown in Table 5. This is displayed clearly in Figure 6, which shows the entropy of the co-occurrence matrix. Over 5,000 breeding cycles it decreases from $H_{max} = 7$ bits to about $H = 4.5$ bits, at which point it stalls, still well above $H_{ideal} = 3$ bits. Changes to the fitness calculation formula and other experimental parameters (such as population size) did not seem to have much effect on the qualitative result, nor did enabling learning.

In retrospect it is not surprising that these agents did not do better (indeed, it is somewhat remarkable they did as well as they did), for they were being asked to solve a very hard problem. Consider the problem of an agent trying to transmit its local-environment state by a two-symbol signal. Since every emission depends on the combination of local, global

Table 5. Co-occurrence matrix: Communication permitted with learning disabled (Two symbols)

loc.→ glob.↓	0	1	2	3	4	5	6	7
0/0	31	22	42	0	144	0	0	0
1/0	26	15	62	0	175	0	0	0
2/0	119	23	44	0	47	0	0	0
3/0	8	9	18	0	31	0	0	0
0/1	0	54	106	2	74	59	516	0
1/1	0	33	174	3	423	227	1979	0
2/1	0	23	65	17	139	74	125	0
3/1	0	1	24	0	48	96	51	0
0/2	50	4	4	366	7	0	8	42
1/2	35	9	0	32	1	0	6	44
2/2	52	76	0	112	7	0	13	135
3/2	52	6	1	215	2	0	2	78
0/3	0	2	13	17	0	3	0	0
1/3	0	66	19	6	0	4	0	0
2/3	0	33	61	27	0	2	0	0
3/3	0	39	38	8	0	0	0	0

Figure 6. Entropy: Two-symbol communication

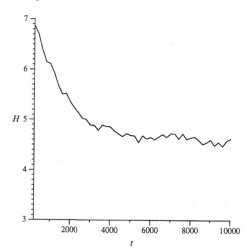

and internal state, any change by another agent to the global environment will probably disrupt the first agent's emission of the second symbol. Also observe that there is no global-environment state that represents the absence of a symbol; therefore there is no way to determine the beginning or ending of a transmission, which means that it is difficult for the population to make use of the distinction between, for example, 2/0 and 0/2. Finally, since every agent must act or emit on every cycle (there is no "do nothing" operation), the only way an agent can avoid a premature attempt at cooperation after receiving the first symbol is by emitting a symbol, which will probably change the global environment and prevent any other agents from receiving the first symbol. Clearly, the experiments could be designed differently to avoid these difficulties, and so we explored several alternatives.

For example, Crumpton (1994) studied a system in which (1) in each time slice the agents cycled twice, thus giving them the opportunity to emit or recognize two symbols without interference from other agents, and (2) agents could "do nothing" in addition to acting or emitting; other parameters were the same. In these experiments he observed a significantly higher use of non-repeating symbol pairs than in the preceding experiments, but the entropy level attained was about the same.

As previously mentioned, we considered alternative behavioral control mechanisms to FSMs. For example, my students Stroud and Jerke conducted preliminary experiments using artificial neural networks (ANNs) as the control mechanism (MacLennan, Jerke, Stroud, & VanHeyningen, 1990, sec. 2; MacLennan, 2001). Aside from the greater biological verisimilitude of ANNs, these experiments were motivated by two other considerations. First, in the experiments already described both the global and local environments were associated with discrete state spaces, and so the agents were not faced with the problem of dividing a continuum of states into discrete categories, which is a significant problem faced by biological agents (e.g., Wiley, 1983, 163-4; MacLennan, 1992; Steels, 1997a, 1997b). Second, the behavioral mechanism used in our earlier experiments did not facilitate generalization. Therefore, for example, to attach a unique response to a global-environment state, an agent would have to acquire (through evolution or learning) that response in the context of every possible state of its local environment. Similarly, to emit a unique signal whenever its local environment was in a particular state, an agent would have to acquire that response in every possible prior global-environment state. In brief, the FSM's rules are inherently context-dependent, but the optimal signaling system, for this problem, is context-free.

To explore these issues, both the global and local environments were allowed to take real-valued states in the range [0, 1]. Thus, each agent had two real-valued inputs: the state of the global environment and the state of its own local environment. Each agent also had two real-valued output neurons. One, with values in [-1, 1], indicated whether the agent was emitting or acting (as indicated by the sign of the output value). The other output, with values in [0, 1], was the value to be put into the global state in the case of an emission, or the value to be matched against the last emitter's local state in the case of an action (attempted cooperation). The match was deemed successful if the action value was within a certain distance e of the last emitter's local-state value; to simplify comparison with the earlier experiments, they set $\varepsilon = 0.125$. There were six hidden layer neurons and the network was trained by back-propagation.

The experiments were similar in structure to the FSM-based experiments. The genetic strings determined the signs of the connections between the neurons, but not their weights, which adapted through back-propagation. That is, the genetic strings defined the initial pattern of excitatory and inhibitory connections, but back-propagation learning adapted the connection strengths.

In order to capture signaling patterns in a way comparable to the co-occurrence matrices, Jerke and Stroud divided the global and local-state spaces into ten bins of size 0.1 and kept track of the correlation of global- and local-environment states whenever a successful cooperation occurred. Non-random signal use, similar to that in the FSM experiments, was observed, but it was partial cooperation (as described) resulting from the agents communicating about only a subset of the state spaces. See MacLennan et al. (1990, sec. 2) and MacLennan (2001) for more information about these experiments.

Related Work

As previously noted, Noble and Cliff (1996) replicated our earliest experiments on the evolution of communication (Maclennan, 1990, 1992; MacLennan & Burghardt, 1993) and extended them in several informative ways. In addition to investigating partial cooperation and ambiguous and synonymous symbol use, as already mentioned, they investigated the effect of the order in which agents were serviced in the experiments.

Werner and Dyer (1992) also demonstrated the evolution of communication by synthetic ethology. They used ANN-controlled agents of two kinds, "male" and "female," which had to find each other in order to mate. The females were immobile, but could determine the location of the males, who were blind but mobile. In their experiments, the population evolved so that the females signaled the males how to find them.

The use of computers to study the origins and evolution of communication and language has developed into a rich and diverse research area. Cangelosi and Parisi (2001) is a good sampling of progress up to that time, and Wagner, Reggia, Uriagereka, and Wilkinson (2003) is a useful review of recent progress. Unfortunately, Wagner et al. incorrectly classify our experiments as an investigation of *nonsituated* communication. In situated experiments, "agents are evaluated based on their performance on a task instead of being directly evaluated on their communication abilities" (Wagner et al., 2003). Although the task performed by our agents is simple, it is distinct from any communication that might or might not be taking place (indeed, it can be accomplished to a limited degree when communication is impossible, as already explained). Agents are evaluated according to whether their actions are appropriate for other agents' local environments, which are out of the agents' control; the local-environment states are determined by the environmental physics of the synthetic world. Thus, they exemplify a rudimentary degree of *symbol grounding* (Harnad, 1990), for the signals (global-state values) refer to conditions in the agents' local environments, which are external to them. Agents are causally responsive to their local environments and interact causally with the global environment. Certainly, however, the topology of the synthetic world in our experiments was too simple to permit the exploration of spatial factors, as in the experiments of Werner and Dyer (1992), Cangelosi and Parisi (1998) and Reggia, Schulz, Wilkinson, and Uriagereka (2001), for example.

Reconsideration and New Directions

In this section I will address some lessons that we learned from our synthetic ethology experiments and consider some important new directions.

Making Real Worlds Inside a Computer

In the spirit of keeping the experiments as simple as possible while still exhibiting the phenomena of interest, most of our synthetic ethology experiments have made use of a very simple world, in which the states about which the agents communicated were simple and unstructured. The communication system that they evolved was similarly simple, as were the agents' "psychological states" (internal representations). More structured representations and systems of communication would be expected to evolve in order to cope with a more structured environment. For example, we would not expect to observe the evolution of a language including nouns, adjectives and verbs unless the synthetic world included objects, properties and actions of various kinds. Nor, in the absence of these, would we expect the evolution of propositional mental states. We could, of course, build a more structured synthetic world, but there is a pitfall we must avoid in order to investigate these more complex phenomena through synthetic ethology.

As mentioned, the obvious approach to studying more complex communication, psychological states, etc., is to populate the synthetic world with various sorts of macroscopic objects (including other agents) with various sorts of properties. However, no matter how many objects and properties we build into such a system, it will still be unrealistically simple compared to any natural environment. The sum-total of things that can occur in such a world will be limited to the combinations of built-in objects and properties. This is not a problem for some investigations, but if we are trying to understand how animals parse the complexity of the natural world into meaningful categories, then by constructing our synthetic world in this way we will be begging the question, since we will have built the categories into the basic structure of the world. For example, if we build into our system two kinds of agents (which we think of as predator and prey), and we build in a behavior (which we think of as the predator killing the prey), then it is not such a surprise if our agents discover categories corresponding to **predator**, **prey** and **predator-kills-prey**. In the natural world, in contrast, there is not such a simple relationship between the structure of the world and the categories used by humans and other animals. Even simple sensory categories are radically underdetermined (Steels, 1997a, 1997b). Therefore, if we want to use synthetic ethology to study the emergence of categories, we must be careful not to build them in from the beginning.

Certainly, the synthetic ethology experiments described in this chapter are not immune to this objection. Most of these experiments made use of unstructured discrete state spaces and the relevant categories were small finite sets (e.g., a specific value from one space paired with all possible values from the other). Even our ANN-based experiments, which use continuous state spaces, did not require significant category construction. Therefore, I believe that future experiments should address the emergence of categories meaningful to the agents, as opposed to those meaningful to the experimenters.

If we don't build objects and properties into our synthetic world, how will they get there? Here we may take a hint from the natural world, in which objects and properties are emergent phenomena arising from the interaction of fundamental particles. Thus, in physical terms, when we say, "the fox sees the hare," we are giving a high-level, approximate description of a situation in which the particles constituting the hare are interacting with the particles of the fox through the intermediary of photons. From a physical perspective, only the particles and their interactions are real in a primary sense; the fox, hare and act of seeing have only derivative reality, as high-level descriptions of fundamental physical reality (i.e., the perspective of the *intentional stance,* Dennett, 1987). Nevertheless, the hare is meaningful to the fox (for it is relevant to its continued existence as an organized physical system). Therefore, if we want to study the *emergence* of meaning, we cannot begin with macroscopic objects and relations (e.g., **fox**, **hare** and **sees**), for then we have simply encoded *our* meanings (*our* context of relevance) into the synthetic world. Rather, we must allow meaning to emerge from underlying, fundamentally meaningless processes (i.e., processes explainable from the physical stance but not from the intentional stance), as it does in the natural world.

How can this be accomplished? One way would be to simulate the real world at the level of elementary particles (or strings) and allow meaning to emerge in macroscopic objects, just as it does in the natural world. However, aside from the computational impossibility of doing such a simulation, the shear complexity of the system (comparable to nature itself) would limit our ability to understand it. The goal of synthetic ethology is to investigate experimentally systems that are as simple as possible while still exhibiting the phenomena of interest (in this case, the emergence of meaning).

We do not want (and cannot have) the complexity of the natural world in our synthetic worlds, but we can use a simpler version of the same separation of levels. By a judicious choice of microscopic objects and interactions to build into our world, we can have emergent macroscopic objects and interactions with a rich and unpredictable structure. The agents, which are macroscopic objects whose fundamental interactions with the environment are at the microscopic level, will have to construct whatever macroscopic categories they need. In this way we will not "rig the game" by building them in from the beginning, although of course they are implicit in the microscopic objects and interactions.

It may seem implausible that we could design a synthetic world that is, on the one hand, complex enough to exhibit emergent objects, properties and interactions, and is, on the other hand, simple enough to be computationally tractable and transparent to investigation. At present, this is a topic for investigation, but I can offer one example of a possible approach.

It is well known that cellular automata (CAs), such as Conway's "Game of Life" (Gardner, 1970), can exhibit rich emergent behavior. Although the individual cells interact with their neighbors in a simple way, in "Life" we can observe the emergence of moderately-sized macroscopic objects that are able to maintain their shape, move through space, and interact with other macroscopic objects. This emergent behavior is especially characteristic of CAs whose transition rules have been designed to place them at the "edge of chaos," Wolfram's class IV (Langton, 1991; Wolfram, 1984).

Therefore, we can imagine designing a synthetic world based on CAs in which agents interact with the emergent objects in terms of cell-level interactions. The agents themselves need not be modeled by CAs (although I will consider that possibility below), but their sense organs and effectors must operate at the cell level, for that is the only level of the environment that is real (in the synthetic physics). Higher-level interactions are emergent from these lower level ones, presumably through adaptive processes such as evolution and learning. Just as, according to our interests, we may categorize macroscopic "Life" configurations (e.g., as "gliders") and their group behavior (e.g., as "translation"), so we can expect synthetic agents to develop categories of objects, relations and actions that are relevant *to them*. The behavior of the agents may be controlled by non-cellular processes, such as production rules, FSMs or ANNs. We may construct the physics of our synthetic world so that agents must interact with the environment (or with other agents via the environment) in certain ways (defined in terms of elementary cell properties) in order to survive and reproduce.

It might be argued that CAs are not much like the physics of the natural world (although Wolfram has argued the contrary), but that is not important. Again, our goal in synthetic ethology is not to simulate any specific natural system. So, for studying the emergence of meaning, it does not matter that the CA does not model the fundamental physical processes of our world, or that the emergent objects do not correspond with macroscopic objects in our world. In the synthetic world within the computer, the CA is a physical environment, in which synthetic agents may behave and evolve.

Artificial Embodiment

A similar limitation of conventional simulations arises in connection with embodiment. We understand better now the essential role played by embodied interaction with an environment as a foundation for genuine intelligence (see below). Also, the fundamental test of an agent's intelligence is how well it can cope with the natural world (especially its EEA), and it is arguable whether a truly intelligent system can exist in the absence of embodiment. This had led some researchers to conclude that artificial intelligence research should be conducted in the context of autonomous robots operating in the natural world (e.g., Brooks, 1986, 1997; Steels, 1997a, 1997b; Ziemke & Sharkey, 2001). I'll briefly consider the issues.

We agree that autonomous robotics provides the fundamental benchmark of genuine intelligence, but it is a complex and difficult approach, because the building of robots may be slowed by problems of mechanical and electrical engineering and of physical construction that have no direct relevance to artificial intelligence. On the other hand, decades of AI research have shown that investigation of simulated agents in simulated worlds (micro-worlds) is inadequate to address the fundamental issues of embodied intelligence; simulated worlds do not have the complexity, unpredictability, uncertainty, openness and genuine novelty of the natural world (Dreyfus, 1997).

For example, in a micro-world, if an agent is told **move-to** (23, 488), it can be expected to move to that location; if it tests **ahead** (**rock**) it can be expected to determine reliably whether there is an object of type **rock** in front of it; and if it executes **grasp** (**rock**) it can be expected to be in the state **holding** (**rock**). However, for an autonomous robot moving in a natural environment, all these assumptions are problematic. In attempting to move to a location, it may encounter an obstruction, get stuck or topple over; it may be difficult to determine if there is an object ahead of it, and if it is a rock; and the attempt to grasp the rock may fail, or the rock may slip out of its grip later. These are among the myriad problems faced by real autonomous robots (and by insects crawling through the undergrowth), which are left out of micro-world simulations. Of course, we can build such hazards into the simulation: randomly distribute some simulated **obstacles**, introduce noise or a probability of misclassification, allow an object to be dropped with some probability, etc. However, the problems that occur will be just those we have built into the simulation; genuine surprises cannot arise, because the modes of failure are predefined, just like the objects, properties and actions.

In the foregoing I have focused on the problems that are faced by autonomous robots, but that are missing from micro-world simulations. However, autonomous robots may have some advantages compared to their disembodied counterparts. There is a great deal of information that every animal knows implicitly just by virtue of having a physical body.

In both biology and situated, embodied robotics (Brooks, 1997), higher-level faculties are built upon lower-level faculties, and intelligence emerges from the interaction of less intelligent components. The foundation of this pyramid consists of low-level sensory and motor modules in direct, dynamic physical interaction with the real world. As a consequence, such intelligence is always grounded in the real world. Further, low-level sensory-motor competencies, such as the ability to perceive structure in visual and auditory inputs and the ability to sequence and coordinate motor activities, provide a neurological basis for higher faculties such as language, propositional thought and planning (see also Moravec, 1984).

Another advantage of embodiment is that by being situated in the real world, a robot can often avoid having a complex internal model of the world; the external world provides the only model necessary (Brooks, 1997). This is one of the ways that simple animals, such as insects, are able to accomplish complex tasks without elaborate mental models (a principle called *stigmergy*; see Camazine, Deneubourg, Franks, Sneyd, Theraulaz, and Bonabeau, 2001, 56-59, ch. 19). As Simon (1969) and others have observed, complex behavior may emerge from a simple agent interacting with a complex environment, and so complex intelligent behavior may arise as much from the interaction of the agent with its environments as from the agent itself (insects, especially social insects, are again an example). Furthermore, as explained in "Background," genuine semiosis may occur in very simple agents with correspondingly simple internal representations.

As a consequence of the foregoing considerations, we are faced with a research dilemma. On the one hand, we realize the inadequacy of micro-world approaches and the necessity of studying intelligence in the context of embodied agents situated in a complex, unpredictable environment. On the other, autonomous robotics research is difficult and expensive, and plagued by many engineering problems only peripherally related to the scientific study of intelligence. Therefore, we would like is to bring the relative simplicity of micro-worlds to the investigation of embodied, situated intelligence.

We believe that synthetic ethology may provide such a compromise. The goal is a real but synthetic world (inside the computer) that is simpler than the natural world, but is unpredictable and open, and so can serve as an environment in which genuine intelligence may function. As before, the approach is to construct the synthetic world at the micro level, so relevant objects and behaviors emerge at the macro level; in this way we may expect genuine novelty, open-endedness, unpredictability, and uncertainty. However these objects must include the agents themselves, so that the microscopic physics of the synthetic world is sufficient for everything that takes place in it, agent behavior as well as environmental processes. The result will be a synthetic real world, simple but complete, in which we can investigate the evolution and adaptive functioning of (genuinely) intelligent agents.

It seems likely the CA model previously described could be extended to incorporate the agents. An agent would correspond to a macroscopic configuration of CA cells, which would define the agent's behavior. It is well known that the "Life" CA can be configured to compute (e.g., implementing logic gates or simulating a Turing machine), but we have not decided the best approach to use for synthetic ethology. We do not necessarily need computational universality, and the approach should be as simple as possible, for the sake of experimental control as well as computational efficiency. Further, to ensure that the agents become coupled with their environment, the synthetic world must support the evolution of the population in some form.

Conclusion

We have described synthetic ethology, a scientific methodology in which we construct synthetic worlds in which synthetic agents evolve and become coupled to their environment. Such a world is complete — in that it defines all the conditions for the survival and reproduction of the agents — but it is simple, which permits greater experimental control than does the natural world. As a result, we can perform experiments relating the mechanisms of behavior to social phenomena in an evolutionary context. We presented several examples of such experiments, in which genuine (i.e., not simulated) meaningful communication evolved in a population of simple agents. The communication was intrinsically meaningful to the agents, but only indirectly meaningful to us, as observers. These experiments demonstrate intrinsic intentionality arising from a transparent mechanism. Finally, we discussed the extension of the synthetic ethology paradigm to the problems of structured communications and mental states, complex environments and embodied intelligence, and suggested one way in which this extension could be accomplished. Indeed, synthetic ethology offers a new tool in a comprehensive research program investigating the neuro-evolutionary basis of cognitive processes.

Acknowledgements

The development of synthetic ethology was furthered by the intellectual climate of the Institute for Advanced Studies of the Collegium Budapest, where the author was a Fellow in the summer of 1997. He is especially grateful for stimulating discussions there with Eörs Szathmáry, Jim Hurford, Simon Kirby, Mike Oliphant, Luc Steels and Terrence Deacon.

References

Austin, J. L. (1975). *How to do things with words* (2nd ed., J. O. Urmson, & M. Sbisà, Eds.). Cambridge: Harvard University Press.

Blackburn, S. (1994). *The Oxford dictionary of philosophy*. Oxford: Oxford University Press.

Braitenberg, V. (1984). *Vehicles: Experiments in synthetic psychology*. Cambridge: The MIT Press.

Brooks, R. (1986). A robust layered control system for a mobile robot. *IEEE Journal of Robotics and Automation, RA-2*, 14-23.

Brooks, R. (1997). Intelligence without representation. In J. Haugeland (Ed.), *Mind design II: Philosophy, psychology, artificial intelligence* (rev. & enlarged ed.) (pp. 395-420). Cambridge, MA: The MIT Press.

Burghardt, G. M. (1970). Defining 'communication.' In J. W. Johnston Jr., D. G. Moulton, & A. Turk (Eds.), *Communication by chemical signals* (pp. 5-18). New York: Appleton-Century-Crofts.

Bynum, W. F., Browne, E. J., & Porter, R. (Eds.). (1981). *Dictionary of the history of science*. Princeton: Princeton University Press.

Camazine, S., Deneubourg, J. L., Franks, N. R., Sneyd, J., Theraulaz, G., et al. (2001). *Self-organization in biological systems*. Princeton: Princeton University Press.

Cangelosi, A., & Parisi, D. (1998). The emergence of a "language" in an evolving population of neural networks. *Connection Science, 10*, 83-97.

Cangelosi, A., & Parisi, D. (Eds.). (2001). *Simulating the evolution of language*. London: Springer.

Colapietro, V. M. (1993). *Glossary of semiotics*. New York: Paragon House.

Crumpton, J. J. (1994). *Evolution of two-symbol signals by simulated organisms*. Master's thesis. Dept. of Computer Science, University of Tennessee, Knoxville.

Dennett, D. (1987). *The intentional stance*. Cambridge, MA: The MIT Press.

Dretske, F. (1985). Machines and the mental. In *Proceedings and Addresses of the American Philosophical Association, 59* (pp. 23-33).

Dreyfus, H. L. (1997). From micro-worlds to knowledge representation: AI at an impasse. In J. Haugeland (Ed.), *Mind design II: Philosophy, psychology, artificial intelligence* (rev. & enlarged ed.) (pp. 143-182). Cambridge, MA: The MIT Press.

Dunny, G. M., & Winans, S. C. (Eds.). (1999). *Cell-cell signaling in bacteria*. Washington, DC: ASM Press.

Gardner, M. (1970). Mathematical games: The fantastic combinations of John Conway's new solitaire game "Life." *Scientific American, 223*(4), 120-3.

Gleick, J. (1987). *Chaos: Making a new science*. New York: Viking.

Goldberg, D. E. (1989). *Genetic algorithms in search, optimization, and machine learning*. Reading, MA: Addison-Wesley.

Gregory, R. L. (Ed.). (1987). *The Oxford companion to the mind*. Oxford: Oxford University Press.

Grice, H. P. (1957). Meaning. *Philosophical Review, 66*, 377-88.

Gutenplan, S. (Ed.). (1994). *A companion to the philosophy of the mind*. Oxford: Blackwell.

Harnad, S. (1990). The symbol grounding problem. *Physica D, 42*, 335-346.

Haugeland, J. (Ed.). (1997). *Mind design II: Philosophy, psychology, artificial intelligence*. Cambridge, MA: The MIT Press.

Langton, C. G. (1991). Life at the edge of chaos. In C. G. Langton, C. Taylor, J. D. Farmer, & S. Rasmussen (Eds.), *Artificial life II: The second workshop on the synthesis and simulation of living systems* (pp. 41-91). Redwood City, CA: MIT Press.

MacLennan, B. J. (1990). *Evolution of cooperation in a population of simple machines*. Tech. Rep. CS-90-99. Dept. of Computer Science, University of Tennessee, Knoxville.

MacLennan, B. J. (1992). Synthetic ethology: An approach to the study of communication. In C. G. Langton, C. Taylor, J. D. Farmer, & S. Rasmussen (Eds.), *Artificial Life II: The Second Workshop on the Synthesis and Simulation of Living Systems* (pp. 631-658). Redwood City, CA: The MIT Press.

MacLennan, B. J. (2001). The emergence of communication through synthetic evolution. In V. Honavar, M. Patel, & K. Balakrishnan (Eds.), *Advances in evolutionary synthesis of neural systems* (pp. 65-90). Cambridge, MA: The MIT Press.

MacLennan, B. J. (2002). Synthetic ethology: A new tool for investigating animal cognition. In M. Bekoff, C. Allen, & G. M. Burghardt (Eds.), *The cognitive animal: Empirical and theoretical perspectives on animal cognition* (pp. 151-6). Cambridge, MA: The MIT Press.

MacLennan, B. J., & Burghardt, G. M. (1993). Synthetic ethology and the evolution of cooperative communication. *Adaptive Behavior, 2,* 161-188.

MacLennan, B. J., Jerke, N., Stroud, R., & VanHeyningen, M. D. (1990). *Neural network models of cognitive processes: 1990 progress report.* Tech. Rep. CS-90-125. Dept. of Computer Science, University of Tennessee, Knoxville.

Moravec, H. P. (1984). Locomotion, vision and intelligence. In M. Brady & R. Paul (Eds.), *Robotics research: The first international symposium* (pp. 215-224). Cambridge, MA: MIT Press.

Morris, C. (1964). *Signification and significance: A study of the relations of signs and values.* Cambridge, MA: MIT Press.

Neisser, U. (1976). *Cognition and reality: Principles and implications of cognitive psychology.* San Francisco: W. H. Freeman.

Noble, J., & Cliff, D. (1996). On simulating the evolution of communication. In P. Maes, M. Mataric, J. A. Meyer, J. Pollack, & S. W. Wilson (Eds.), *From Animals to Animats: Proceedings of the Fourth International Conference on Simulation of Adaptive Behavior* (pp. 608-617). Cambridge, MA: The MIT Press.

Peirce, C. S. (1931/1935). *Collected papers of Charles Sanders Peirce* (Vols. 1-6). C. Hartshorne, & P. Weiss (Eds.). Cambridge, MA: Harvard University Press.

Peirce, C. S. (1955). *Philosophical writings of Peirce.* J. Buchler (Ed.). New York: Dover.

Reggia, J. A., Schulz, R., Wilkinson, G. S., & Uriagereka, J. (2001). Conditions enabling the emergence of inter-agent signalling in an artificial world. *Artificial Life, 7*(1), 3-32.

Searle, J. (1983). *Intentionality: An essay in the philosophy of mind.* Cambridge, MA: Cambridge University Press.

Simon, H. A. (1969). *The sciences of the artificial.* Cambridge, MA: The MIT Press.

Steels, L. (1997a). Constructing and sharing perceptual distinctions. In M. van Someran & G. Widmer (Eds.), *Proceedings of the European Conference on Machine Learning* (pp. 4-13). Berlin: Springer-Verlag.

Steels, L. (1997b). The synthetic modeling of language origins. *Evolution of Communication, 1,* 1-34.

Wagner, K., Reggia, J. A., Uriagereka, J., & Wilkinson, G. S. (2003). Progress in the simulation of emergent communication and language. *Adaptive Behavior*, *11*(1), 37-69.

Werner, G. M., & Dyer, M. G. (1992). Evolution of communication in artificial organisms. In C. G. Langton, C. Taylor, J. D. Farmer, & S. Rasmussen (Eds.), *Artificial Life II: The Second Workshop on the Synthesis and Simulation of Living Systems* (pp. 659-687). Redwood City, CA: The MIT Press.

Wiley, R. H. (1983). The evolution of communication: Information and manipulation. In T. R. Halliday & P. J. B. Slater (Eds.), *Animal behavior volume 2: Communication* (pp. 156-89). New York: W. H. Freeman.

Wittgenstein, L. (1958). *Philosophical investigations* (3rd ed.). New York: Macmillan.

Wolfram, S. (1984). Universality and complexity in cellular automata. *Physica D*, *10*, 1-35.

Ziemke, T., & Sharkey, N. E. (2001). A stroll through the worlds of robots and animals: Applying Jakob von Uexküll's theory of meaning to adaptive robots and artificial life. *Semiotica*, *134*, 701-46.

Endnotes

[1]   I hope I may be excused for belaboring the obvious fact that a computer is a physical object and that its computation is a physical process. It is a common source of confusion due, no doubt, to our habit of treating programs and computers as abstractions (e.g., Turing machines).

[2]   "CP" refers to Peirce's Collected Papers (1931-1935).

Chapter X

Environmental Variability and the Emergence of Meaning:
Simulational Studies Across Imitation, Genetic Algorithms, and Neural Networks

Patrick Grim, State University of New York at Stony Brook, USA

Trina Kokalis, State University of New York at Stony Brook, USA

Abstract

A crucial question for artificial cognition systems is what meaning is and how it arises. In pursuit of that question, this paper extends earlier work in which we show the emergence of simple signaling in biologically inspired models using arrays of locally interactive agents. Communities of "communicators" develop in an environment of wandering food sources and predators using any of a variety of mechanisms: imitation of successful neighbors, localized genetic algorithms and partial neural net training on successful neighbors. Here we focus on environmental variability, comparing results for environments with (a) constant resources, (b) random resources, and (c) cycles of "boom and bust." In both simple and complex models across all three mechanisms of strategy change, the emergence of communication is strongly favored by cycles of "boom and bust." These results are particularly intriguing given the importance of environmental variability in fields as diverse as psychology, ecology and cultural anthropology.

Introduction

Meaning is crucial to cognitive systems. It can be expected to be as crucial for artificial cognitive systems as it is for the ones we find occurring naturally around us, or indeed for the cognitive systems that we ourselves are. A crucial question for artificial cognition, then, is what meaning is and how it arises.

This paper is a development of earlier work in which we study the emergence of simple signaling in simulations involving communities of interacting individuals. Crucial to the model is an environment of wandering food sources and predators; our agents are "embodied" in an artificial environment and subject to its spatial and temporal contingencies. Crucial to the model is also the fact that it is not a single individual but a community of potentially interacting individuals that are embedded in such an environment. Our individuals develop coordinated behavioral strategies in which they make and respond to "sounds" in their immediate neighborhoods. Crucial to variations of the model explored here are different updating mechanisms of strategy change, all of which key to the behavior of most successful neighbors.

What our earlier work has shown, using any of various updating mechanisms in such a model, is the consistent emergence of communities of communicators using simple patterns of signaling. In an environment in which food sources and predators wander in a random walk, communities of individuals emerge that make a particular sound on successfully feeding, and respond to that same sound from neighbors by positioning themselves to feed. They make a different sound when hit by a predator, and respond to *that* sound from immediate neighbors by "hiding." Our models are biologically inspired in emphasizing strategy changes across a community of individuals embodied in a common environment. What consistently emerges are coordinated strategies of behavior that look a lot like simple signaling, and thus offer at least one clue to one kind of meaning.

What we introduce in this paper is a further characteristic of environments: variability. Our essential question is what role environmental variability — and environmental variability of what type — may play in the emergence of simple communication. Our inspiration comes from the role that environmental variability seems to play in a range of apparently disparate phenomena, from species diversity to individual learning.

In behavioral psychology, environmental variability has long been established as an important factor in operant conditioning. Intermittent schedules of reinforcement prove far more effective than constant reinforcement; variable-ratio schedules of reinforcement generally produce the highest number of responses per time period, establishing behavior most resistant to extinction (Reynolds, 1975; Honig & Staddon, 1977). "A pigeon may peck the key 50 to 100 times after reinforcement has been cut off if it previously was on a schedule of continuous reinforcement. After some types of intermittent reinforcement, the bird will peck from 4,000 to 10,000 times before responding extinguishes" (Nye, 1992, p. 31).

In ecology and evolution, rates of environmental fluctuation have been proposed as a major factor in inter-species dynamics. A number of different mechanisms have been proposed linking environmental fluctuation to increased species diversity (Hutchinson, 1961; Harris, 1986; Huston, 1979; Hubbell & Foster, 1986; Chesson & Huntly, 1989, 1997). It has recently been proposed that Pleistocene climatic fluctuations are responsible for the evolution of larger brained mammals in general and higher primates in particular, with suggested links to social learning (Potts, 1996; Opdyke, 1995; Odling-Smee, Laland, & Feldman, 2000; Boyd & Richerson, 1985, 1989, 2000).

In cultural anthropology, variable environments appear to play a major role in the transition from foraging cultures to incipient agriculture. In a comprehensive computer model for archaeological data from the Guilá Naquitz cave site, R. G. Reynolds characterizes climate in terms of wet and dry years. Wet years show a wider range of food-acquisition behaviors with more new strategies, while dry years show a concentration on competitive and efficient strategies, with more critical pressure on strategy choice. Reynolds explains the role that environmental variability may play in the emergence of agriculture:

The selective pressure placed on the group can vary unpredictably, and it is this variation that may be an important factor in determining the rate of change within the system. If, for example, the group was exposed only to a sequence of dry years that constantly put selective pressure on the group, the wet-year strategies that introduce most of the variation into the system would disappear or never be used. The resource scheduling system as a whole would be extremely conservative... On the other hand, an overbalance of wet years would introduce a good deal of variability into the system, but the group would seldom have an opportunity to test the worth of these adaptations in a more strenuous environment. (Reynolds, 1986, p. 499)[1]

What our results here show is that environmental variability of a very specific sort plays a positive role in the simulational emergence of communication as well. Within spatialized models of self-serving individuals in an environment of wandering food items and predators, where each individual can hear and react to arbitrary sounds from immediate neighbors, a sine-wave variable environment with cycles of "boom and bust" promotes the development of communication. This effect appears regardless of important differences in how strategies are updated: Variable environments promote communication whether strategy change is by imitation of most successful neighbor, by genetic algorithm recombination with strategies of locally successful neighbors or by neural net training on successful neighbors.

Our previous work relied on biologically-inspired factors of environmental embodiment, emphasis on a community of individuals and development of coordinated behavior over time. What the results outlined in this paper indicate is that environmental variability of a particular kind may be a further factor of importance in the development of meaning crucial to cognition systems.

More tentatively, we also want to offer a more speculative suggestion. It is tempting to think that the appeals to environmental variability across disciplines may have something in common. Perhaps there is some central mechanism of variability and selection which, in different forms, is responsible for aspects of individual learning, of species diversity in ecological communities and of the development of cultures.[2] That speculative suggestion is one that we will not pursue further here. It is an additional point in its favor, however, that environmental variability of a particular kind turns out to be of importance even in simulations of the emergence of simple patterns of meaning.

The Basic Model

We work throughout with a 64×64 two-dimensional cellular automata array of 4,096 individuals, each of which follows a particular strategy. Initially these are chosen at random from our sample space of strategies (Figure 1). All action and reproduction are local within this spatialized array: Individuals interact only with their eight immediate neighbors, the cells that touch them at each side and at their corners. The array as a whole forms a torus, "wrapping around" so that individuals on the bottom edge have neighbors at the top edge and those at the left have neighbors on the right.

Individuals in the array alter their behavior in terms of what is happening immediately around them, but they do not move. In our simplest models, what move are food sources, which migrate in a random walk across the array. In our more complicated models we use both wandering food sources and wandering predators.

If a food source lands on an individual with its mouth open, that individual "feeds" and gains points. Individuals feed from food sources, but the sources are not consumed and don't disappear. Like a cloud of plankton or a school of fish, perhaps, they continue their random walk across the array. In more complicated models, we include wandering predators and an appropriately more complicated repertoire of behaviors; individuals can open their mouths, "hide" or coast in neutral. An individual is "hurt" by losing a point if a predator lands on it when it isn't hiding. In "neutral," an individual fails to gain points from food sources but is still hurt if hit by a predator.

On any given round, an individual's strategy may dictate that it opens its mouth or does not, where mouth-opening carries a particular cost in energy. In our more complex models, the strategy also dictates whether the individual hides or not, where "hiding" carries an energy cost as well. In all models, individual cells are capable of making sounds heard by their immediate neighbors. Sound-making, like mouth-opening and hiding, exacts an energy cost, but sounds come without any hard-wired significance: Nothing is built into the model in order to make a particular sound take on a particular meaning, or indeed to take on any meaning at all.

For even these simple individuals in this simple environment, there are behavioral strategies that seem to qualify as elementary forms of signaling or communication.

Figure 1. Initially randomized 64×64 array of 16 strategies

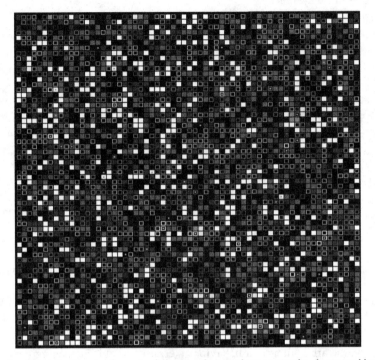

Strategies for different cells are shown in different colors, with open mouths shown as black central squares and migrating food sources as small white dots.

Imagine a spatially contiguous community of individuals that share the following strategy:

- They make a sound when they are successfully fed.
- They react to hearing a sound from their neighbors by opening their mouths.

When an individual in such a community feeds, it makes a sound. Its immediate neighbors, which share the same strategy, open their mouths in response. Since the food source continues its random walk, it will then fall on an open mouth on the next round. *That* individual, feeding successfully, will in turn make a sound and *its* neighbors will open their mouths in response. The result, in a community sharing such a strategy, is a chain reaction in which the food source is successfully exploited on each round (Figure 2). We term individuals with such a strategy "Communicators."

In our more complex models the environment contains both food sources and predators, and individuals can open their mouths, hide or coast in neutral on each round. In these

Figure 2. Migration of a single food source in a random walk across a hypothetical array of Communicators

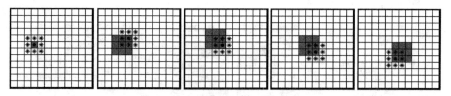

In the left frame, a food source dot lands on an open mouth, indicated by gray shading. That central individual makes a sound * heard by its immediate neighbors, which in the second frame open their mouths in response. One of them feeds successfully, making a sound heard by its immediate neighbors, which are shown opening their mouths in the third frame. The result in a community of Communicators is a chain reaction of efficient feeding.

models our agents have two sounds at their disposal, and a more complex form of communication is possible. Our "Perfect Communicators" are those that follow the following strategy:

They make sound 1 when they are fed.

They react to hearing sound 1 by opening their mouths.

They make sound 2 when they are hurt.

They react to sound 2 by hiding.

In previous work we have shown that these simple forms of communication can emerge from initially randomized arrays using any of several mechanisms for strategy change. In our earliest studies we used strategy change by simple imitation. At each "generation" — each 100 rounds of gain and loss from food capture and predation — each cell surveyed its immediate neighbors in order to see if any had garnered a higher score. If so, it changed to the strategy of its most successful neighbor (Grim, Kokalis, Tafti, & Kilb, 2000). In later studies we used strategy change by local genetic algorithm. Here the strategy of a less successful cell was replaced with a hybrid formed from its strategy and that of its most successful neighbor (Grim, Kokalis, Tafti, & Kilb, 2001). Most recently, we have instantiated strategies in the weights of simple neural nets, and have used strategy change by partial training on the behavior of more successful neighbors (Grim, St. Denis, & Kokalis 2002). Using any of these mechanisms in a wide variety of environments, we have been able to show that communities of Communicators will emerge and grow.[3] Figure 3, for example, shows a typical emergence of two forms of Communicators in an array of randomized neural nets over 300 generations. One of these Perfect Communicators uses sound 1 for food and sound 2 for predators; the other uses sound 2 for food and sound 1 for predators. Figure 4 plots the same results in terms of percentages of particular strategies within the population as a whole (Grim, Kokalis, Alai-Tafti, Kilb, & St. Denis, 2004).

Figure 3. Emergence of two dialects of Perfect Communicators, shown in solid black and white, in a randomized array of simple neural nets with partial training on successful neighbors

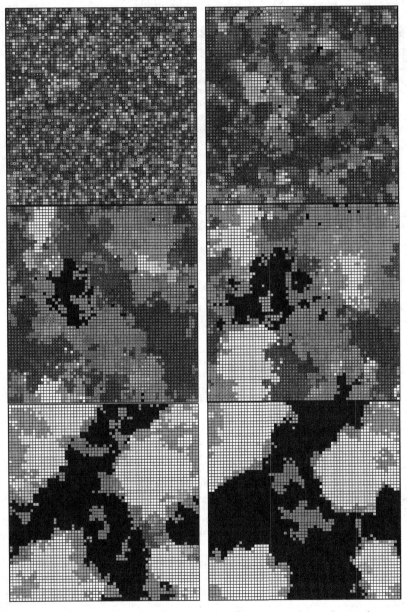

Initially each of the 4,096 individuals in the array is randomly assigned one of seven discrete weights between -3.5 and + 3.5 for each of its 12 weights and biases. Cells are coded for different behaviors using background and dot color, with no visual representation for food sources, predators or reactions of opening mouths or hiding. Generations 1, 10, 50, 100, 200 and 300 are shown.

Figure 4. Emergence of communication in a randomized array of simple neural nets with partial training on successful neighbors

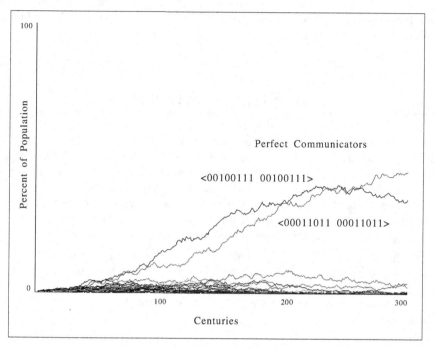

Percentages of population graphed over 300 generations.

In all of our earlier studies, however, we considered sample spaces of strategies that came most easily with the strategy updating mechanism at issue. As a result we ended up with data on imitation runs, localized genetic algorithms and neural nets for quite different sample spaces of behaviors in a way that made it impossible to compare them side by side. In the current work we have deliberately structured our coded strategies and neural nets so as to produce the same range of possible strategies, allowing for a more direct comparison.[4]

In previous studies, we also used a constant environment of food sources and predators: Although each of these migrates in a random walk across the array, the total number of food sources and predators remains constant from generation to generation. Here, we focus instead on the role of a *variable* environment. Is change in the environment a factor of importance in the emergence of communication? Does the pattern of change matter, and does it perhaps have a different impact when different mechanisms of strategy change — imitation, localized genetic algorithms and spatialized neural nets — are in play?

The results that follow indicate that a variable environment does indeed have a major impact on the emergence of communication. The pattern of variability is crucial: Sine-wave variation in resources, with waves of boom and bust, has an effect that entirely random changes in resources with the same mean do not. In our studies that effect holds regardless of whether the basic mechanism of strategy change at issue is one of imitation, genetic recombination or neural net learning, and holds in similar ways in both simpler and more complex environments.

The Simple Studies

Our initial studies use an environment with wandering food sources but without predators. The behavioral repertoire of our individuals is similarly limited: They can open their mouths or not, and can make a single sound heard by their immediate neighbors or remain silent. Individuals know only whether they have been successfully fed — whether a food source has landed on them when their mouth was open — and whether they or an immediate neighbor has made a sound on the previous round. Mouth opening carries an energy cost of .95 points, with an energy cost of .05 points for sounding.[5]

We code the behavior of these simple individuals in terms of four-tuples $<f, \sim f, s, \sim s>$. Variable f dictates whether an individual makes a sound or not when it is fed, $\sim f$ whether it makes a sound when it is not fed, s dictates whether it opens its mouth when it hears a sound from itself or an immediate neighbor and $\sim s$ whether it opens its mouth when it hears no such sound.

This gives us only sixteen possible strategies, coded in binary as follows:

<0,0,0,0>	Never makes a sound, never opens its mouth
<0,0,0,1>	Never makes a sound, opens its mouth only when it hears no sound
<0,0,1,0>	Never makes a sound, opens its mouth only when it hears a sound
<0,0,1,1>	Never makes a sound, mouth always open
<0,1,0,0>	Makes a sound when not fed, never opens its mouth
<0,1,0,1>	Makes a sound when not fed, opens its mouth only when it hears no sound
<0,1,1,0>	Makes a sound when not fed, opens its mouth only when it hears a sound
<0,1,1,1>	Makes a sound when not fed, mouth always open
<1,0,0,0>	Makes a sound when fed, never opens its mouth
<1,0,0,1>	Makes a sound when fed, opens its mouth only when it hears no sound
<1,0,1,0>	Makes a sound when fed, opens its mouth only when it hears a sound
<1,0,1,1>	Makes a sound when fed, mouth always open

<1,1,0,0>	Always sounds, never opens its mouth
<1,1,0,1>	Always sounds, opens its mouth only when it hears no sound
<1,1,1,0>	Always sounds, opens its mouth only when it hears a sound
<1,1,1,1>	Always sounds, mouth always open

Those cells that carry strategy <1,0,1,0> are our "Communicators." They make a sound when fed, and open their mouths when they hear a sound. A hypothetical community of Communicators will therefore behave as illustrated in Figure 2. We should also note that we use "imperfect" worlds throughout. All cells follow their programmed strategies subject to a 5% measure of error. In 5% of those cases in which the strategy specifies mouth opening, the mouth fails to open; in 5% of cases where it is specified as opening, it stays shut. Nowak and Sigmund (Nowak & Sigmund, 1990, 1992) have argued that a measure of stochastic "noise" makes for a more realistic model of cooperation. In previous work we have outlined its importance for the emergence of communication as well (Grim, Kokalis, Tafti, & Kilb, 2000).

This sample space of behaviors remains the same across our simple studies. These behaviors are instantiated in different ways in different cases, however — as coded behaviors or as operating neural nets. This allows us to compare different mechanisms for strategy change side by side: strategy change by imitation, by localized genetic algorithm and by localized training of neural nets.

In one series of runs our individuals carry behaviors coded as series of binary digits and follow an imitation algorithm for strategy change. After 100 rounds of food gathering, point gain and energy loss, each cell surveys its immediate neighbors and sees if any has garnered a higher score. If so, it adopts the strategy of its highest-scoring neighbor in place of its own.

In a second series of runs, we use the same coding for behaviors but employ a localized genetic algorithm for strategy change. After 100 rounds, each cell surveys its immediate neighbors to see if any has garnered a higher score. If not, it retains its current strategy. If it has a more successful neighbor, however, that cell's strategy is replaced with a genetic algorithm hybrid formed from its current strategy and that of its most successful neighbor. We use two-point crossover, choosing one of the offspring at random to replace the parent (Figure 5).

Genetic algorithms are usually applied globally to a population, breeding from only a small number of those strategies that perform most successfully on some uniform fitness function. Ours in contrast is a *localized* genetic algorithm. All genetic recombination is local: Cells with locally successful neighbors change their strategies to local hybrid recombinations. Unlike global genetic algorithms, localized genetic algorithms seem promising here not merely as a sampling device — the sample space in our simple studies is only 16 strategies — but as a means of facilitating strategy similarity and thus the possibility of behavioral coordination between neighbors.

In a third series of runs we generate the same sample space of behaviors using very simple neural nets (Figure 6). On each round, an individual has either heard a sound from one of its immediate neighbors or it has not, coded as a bipolar input of +1 or -1. It has also

Figure 5. Genetic recombination of simple strategies

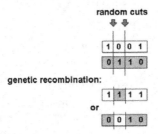

successfully fed on that round or not, again coded as a bipolar +1 or -1. Our neural structure involves just two weights and two biases, each of which carries a value between -3.5 and +3.5, "chunked" at one-unit intervals. A bipolar input at "hear sound," for example, is multiplied by weight w1. To that product is added the bias value, which might equivalently be thought of as a weight on an input of +1. The two values are summed at the output node. If the result is greater than a threshold of 0, the output is treated as +1; the individual opens its mouth, for example. If it is less than or equal to 0, the output is treated as -1 and the individual keeps its mouth closed.

These simple nets generate the same range of behaviors as their coded counterparts, but they allow for a different mechanism of strategy change. For our neural nets, strategy change is by partial training on successful neighbors. After 100 rounds, each cell surveys its immediate neighbors to see if any has garnered a higher score. If so, it does a partial training on the behavior of its most successful neighbor. A single training consists of a random pair of inputs for both the "trainee" cell and its more successful neighbor. If the two nets give the same output, no change is made in the trainee's weights. If the outputs are not the same, the trainee's weights are nudged a single unit toward what would have given its neighbor's response on that run. Biases are shifted in the same way. With bipolar coding and within the limits of our value scale, using "target" for the

Figure 6. Simple neural nets

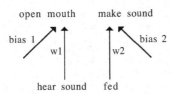

Simple neural nets with bipolar inputs of +1 or -1 at "hear sound" and "fed," multiplied by weights w1 and w2 "chunked" at one-unit intervals between -3.5 and +3.5. Biases carry similar weights. If the total at the output node > 0, the output is treated as +1 and the individual opens its mouth, for example. If the total output is ≤ 0, the output is treated as -1 and the individual keeps its mouth closed.

neighbor's output, we can calculate the delta rule as simply $w_{new} = w_{old} + (\text{target} \times \text{input})$ and $\text{bias}_{new} = \text{bias}_{old} + \text{target}$.

Our aim was to compare these three different mechanisms — imitation, localized genetic algorithm and neural net training — across a range of different environments. In one series of runs, we used environments constant with regard to food resources: Exactly 50 food sources migrated across the array each generation. In a second case, we used randomly variable environments. Here the average was again 50 food sources each generation, but the specific number of food sources at any given generation was a random number between 0 and 100. In a third form of variability, we assigned food sources by sampling at regular intervals along a sine wave oscillating between 0 and 100. This again gave us an average of 50 food sources each generation, but in waves of increasing and decreasing resources each generation.

The core question was whether these differences in environmental variability would make a difference in the emergence of communication. We also wanted to know whether any such difference would depend on a particular mechanism of strategy change.

Environmental Variability and the Emergence of Communication

Constant Environment

Our constant environments contained exactly 50 food items each time. We used the gain allotted for successful feeding as an independent variable: Tests were run with gains from 1 to 140 points for each successful feeding. What we wanted to plot was what strategy an array would evolve to for particular gains — to Communicators or otherwise — and in what number of generations. We could then compare results across mechanisms of imitation, localized genetic algorithms and neural nets.

Figure 7 shows results across different gains for the imitation algorithm, in which strategies simply switch to those of their most successful neighbors. Starting from the left of the graph, we sample gains of 1 through 9, shown in narrow bars. From that point we switch to sampling gains at 10-point spreads, with the wider bars representing gains from 10 through 140. Runs are to 1,500 generations; the height of each bar indicates how many generations were required for fixation on a single strategy across the entire array. Should no single strategy occupy the entire array by 1,500 generations, the bar tops out. For bars below 1,500, then, color indicates the strategy in total occupation of the array. For bars that reach 1,500, color indicates the dominant strategy across the array at that point. Dominant strategies at each gain are also indicated by their codes in the list at the left. In a constant environment, the initial winner at most gains below 9 is the null strategy <0,0,0,0>, which neither sounds nor opens its mouth. Strategy <0,0,1,0>, a "free rider" which responds to sound by opening its mouth but reciprocates with no sound in return, makes a brief appearance at gains of 6 and 8 points. Starting at a gain of 7, however, and

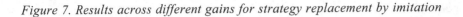

Figure 7. Results across different gains for strategy replacement by imitation

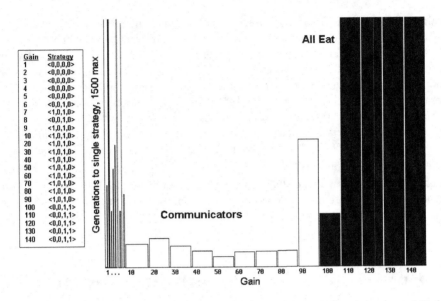

Strategy replacement by imitation of most successful neighbor in a constant environment of 50 food sources, showing runs up to 1,500 generations with gains from 1 to 140 points for each successful feeding. Columns below 1,500 generations show total conquest by strategy; those at 1,500 show dominant strategy at that point. All Eat conquers or proves dominant at gains of 100 and above.

then from gains of 9 through 90, it is our Communicators <1,0,1,0> to which the array converges.[6]

It is immediately obvious from the graph, and somewhat surprising, how large the window for communication is. Communicators dominate the array from the point at which each successful feeding is worth 10 points to the point at which it is worth 9 times as much. But it is also clear that communication has an upper terminus: Above a gain of 100 points it is a strategy of All Eat proves dominant. Beyond this point all arrays are dominated by <0,0,1,1>, which doesn't bother to communicate at all: It sits with a constant open mouth, ready to catch passing food sources, but never making a sound.

Strategy change by localized genetic algorithm in the same constant environment and for the same set of gains gives us the results shown in Figure 8. For genetic algorithm recombination, as for imitation, there is a clearly circumscribed window for communication. Here the window is somewhat smaller, extending only from gains of 20 to gains of 80. Below that dominance goes to the null strategy <0,0,0,0> or the "free rider" <0,0,1,0>. At gains of 90 and above dominance again goes to the incommunicative All Eat.

Though the overall pattern is similar, the genetic algorithm runs take several times longer. This is perhaps not too surprising. In an imitation model, a successful strategy is imitated

Figure 8. Strategy replacement by localized genetic algorithm

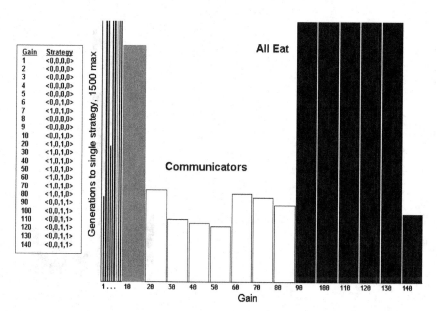

Gain	Strategy
1	<0,0,0,0>
2	<0,0,0,0>
3	<0,0,0,0>
4	<0,0,0,0>
5	<0,0,0,0>
6	<0,0,1,0>
7	<1,0,1,0>
8	<0,0,0,0>
9	<0,0,0,0>
10	<0,0,1,0>
20	<1,0,1,0>
30	<1,0,1,0>
40	<1,0,1,0>
50	<1,0,1,0>
60	<1,0,1,0>
70	<1,0,1,0>
80	<1,0,1,0>
90	<0,0,1,1>
100	<0,0,1,1>
110	<0,0,1,1>
120	<0,0,1,1>
130	<0,0,1,1>
140	<0,0,1,1>

Strategy replacement in an environment by localized genetic algorithm combination with most successful neighbor in a constant environment of 50 food sources, showing runs up to 1,500 generations with gains from 1 to 140 points for each successful feeding. Columns below 1,500 generations show total conquest by strategy; those at 1,500 show dominant strategy at that point. All Eat conquers or proves dominant at gains of 90 and above.

immediately by its neighbor. In a localized genetic algorithm, complete cloning to a successful neighbor may take a significant number of hybrid recombinations. Where a large number of possible strategies is at issue, one advantage to genetic algorithm recombination is that it can explore a larger portion of the strategy space: Strategies will be produced which don't exist in either parent. Where we are dealing with a sample space of only 16 strategies, that general advantage doesn't show to effect.

The window for communication in an array of neural nets with constant environment is closely comparable to arrays updating strategy by imitation and localized genetic algorithm. Here the null strategy <0,0,0,0> dominates at gains of 8 and below for each successful feed. Communicators dominant for gains between 9 and 80, but All Eat proves dominant at gains of 90 and above.

Despite greater complexity and partial training, our neural nets reach fixation in this simple environment at about the same rate as mere imitators where Communicators dominate, and much faster where dominance is by All Eat.[7] It should be noted, however, that speed is comparable only when measured in numbers of generations; actual computer time for each run was significantly longer in the case of neural nets.

Figure 9. Strategy replacement by partial neural net training

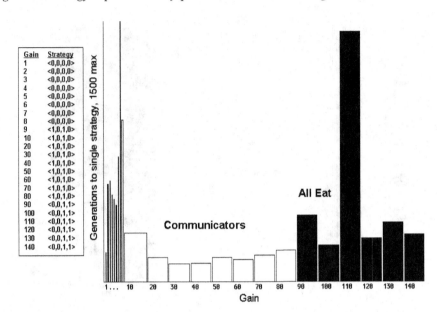

Strategy replacement by partial neural net training on most successful neighbor in a constant environment of 50 food sources, showing runs up to 1,500 generations with gains from 1 to 140 points for each successful feeding. Columns below 1,500 generations show total conquest by strategy; those at 1,500 show dominant strategy at that point. All Eat conquers or proves dominant at gains of 90 and above.

Random Environment

What if, instead of a constant environment of 50 food sources, we use a changing environment? In a second series of studies we assigned a random number of food sources between 0 and 100 each generation. The average number of food sources remained at 50, but the particular number of food sources on any generation might be anywhere between 0 and 100. The amount of gain allotted for successful feeding was again our independent variable: Tests were run with gains for each successful feeding from 1 to 140 points for each successful feeding. Figure 10 shows results in a random environment for strategy change by imitation, localized genetic algorithm and neural nets.

With any of our mechanisms of strategy change, it turns out, results in a randomized environment show at most a slight increase in the upper limit for Communicators. With constant food sources, we found an upper limit of 90, 80 and 80 as the gains at which Communicators proved dominant for strategy change by imitation, localized genetic algorithm and neural nets respectively. With a randomized number of food sources that lifts slightly to upper limits of 100, 90 and 90 for the three cases. In both constant and randomized environments, however, the window for Communicators closes at a gain of 90 or 100 and All Eat proves dominant from that point on.

Figure 10. Strategy replacement in an environment of randomized food sources

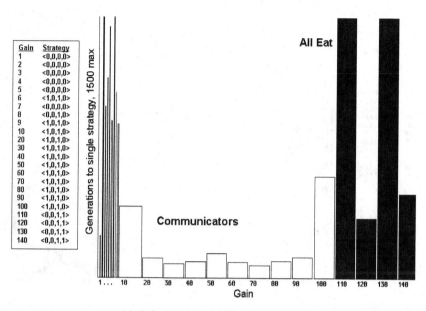

(a) Imitation in a random environment

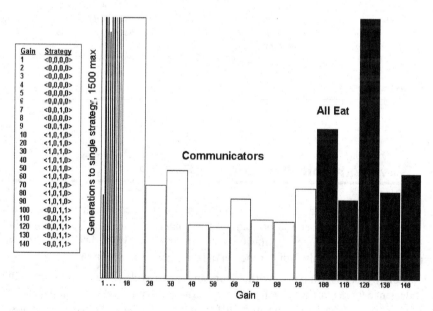

(b) Localized genetic algorithm in a random environment

Figure 10. continued

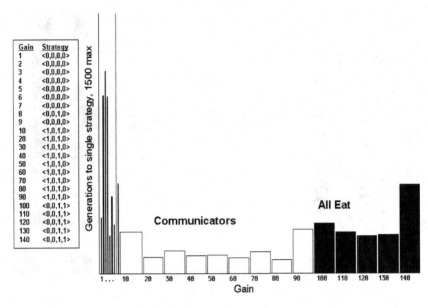

(c) Neural nets in a random environment

Strategy replacement in an environment of randomized food sources with a mean of 50 by (a) imitation of most successful neighbor, (b) localized genetic algorithm combination with most successful neighbor and (c) partial neural net training on most successful neighbor. Runs are shown up to 1,500 generations with gains from 1 to 140 points for each successful feeding. Columns below 1,500 generations show total conquest by strategy; those at 1,500 show dominant strategy at that point. All Eat conquers or proves dominant at gains of 100 or 110 and above in each case.

Sine-Wave Variable Environment

An environment with a random number of food sources produces much the same effects as one with a constant number of food sources. But what if we use an environment which, though variable, shows greater regularity? What if there is a cycle of "boom and bust," for example — will this make a difference in the emergence of communication?

The decision to test environments with "boom and bust" cycles still leaves a great deal of latitude, since there may be very different patterns qualifying as "boom and bust." We conceived of different patterns in terms of different intervals marked out on a regular sine wave oscillating between 0 and 100. With values of that wave taken at intervals of 1, we get one pattern of numbers for our food sources. With values taken at intervals of 2, we get a different series.

Figure 11. Different patterns of variation in the number of food sources in the environment over time

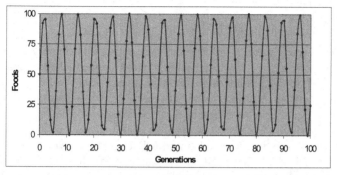

(a) Sin+1 variability

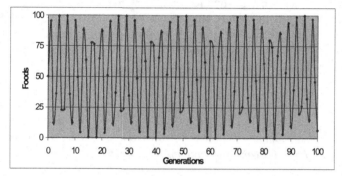

(b) Sin+2 variability

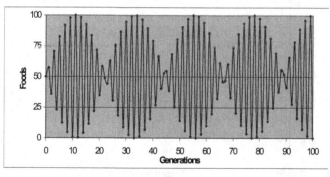

(c) Sin+3 variability

Each data point in each graph, representing number of food sources in the array at that generation, is given by [sin(x) + 1] * 50 *food sources for a series* x_0, x_1, ... x_n. *In each series* $x_{n+1} = x_n + c$ *for a specific c. In* (a), $x_{n+1} = x_n + 1$. *In* (b), $x_{n+1} = x_n + 2$. *In* (c), $x_{n+1} = x_n + 3$.

More formally, our number of food sources each time was dictated by a regular series x_0, x_1, ... x_n, where each x_n adds some constant c to its predecessor x_{n-1}. We take our number of food sources as $[\sin(x)+1] * 50$ for this series, giving us some number of food sources between 0 and 100 for each generation. The distance c we choose between elements of our series then dictates the particular form of "boom and bust."

Figure 11 shows different patterns of variation. Each data point in the first graph is $[\sin(x)+1] * 50$ for a series $x_0, x_1, ... x_n$ that increments by units of one. In the first graph, in other words, $x_{n+1} = x_n + 1$. In the second graph our series increments by units of two: $x_{n+1} = x_n + 2$. In the third graph we increment by units of three: $x_{n+1} = x_n + 3$. Although we average 50 food sources in each case, the differences in boom and bust patterns are clear. A sine value for a series which changes by increments of + 1 gives a fairly gradual change between boom and bust, with one or two intermediate points between a high and a low. Sine value for a series which changes by increments of two show a more polarized boom and bust, with a midpoint present in only half of the transitions from top to bottom. Sine values for a series which changes by increments of three swing instantaneously from boom to bust without any midpoints, though the interval distance between boom and bust progressively enlarges and narrows in cycles over time. Because of their more dramatic shifts, we used the second and third patterns of variation as our samples, referring to these patterns simply as sin+2 and sin+3.

Figure 12. Triumph of Communicators at all gains above 10 in an environment of food sources between 0 and 100 varying in the pattern of sin+2

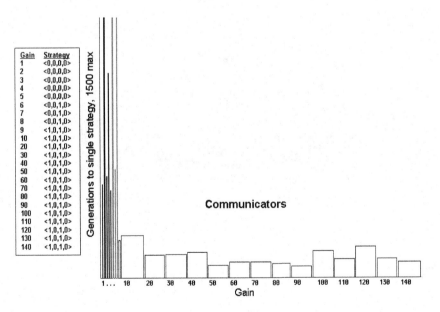

(a) Imitation in a Sin+2 environment

Figure 12. continued

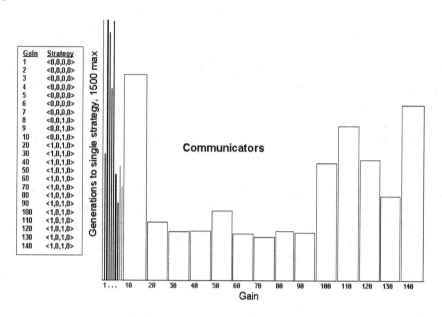

(b) Localized genetic algorithms in a Sin+2 environment

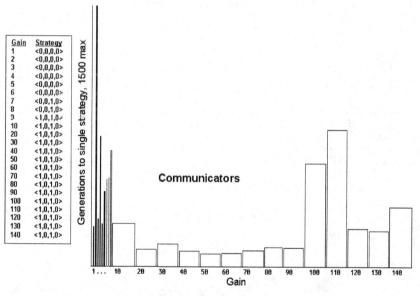

(c) Neural nets in a Sin+2 environment

Strategy replacement is by (a) *imitation of most successful neighbor,* (b) *localized genetic algorithm combination with most successful neighbor and* (c) *partial neural nets training on most successful neighbor.*

What impact does a sine-wave variable environment have on the emergence of communication? Figure 12 shows emergence of communication in an environment changing on the pattern of sin+2 for each of our three mechanisms of strategy change. The surprising result is that a variable environment allows conquest by Communicators all the way up. Unlike constant and random environments, increased gains in a variable environment on the pattern of sin+2 do not favor All Eat at any point within the scope of the graph. We have sampled larger gains, beyond the scope of the graph; up to gains of 500 and 1,000 it is still the Communicators that succeed.

The result is sensitive to patterns of variability — the more gradual changes of a sin+1 pattern do not show as dramatic a result. The effect on communication is by no means confined to the pattern of sin+2, however. Similar results for resources following the pattern of sin+3 are shown in Figure 13.

Across all of our modes of strategy change, sine-wave variable environments of these patterns show a dramatic widening of the window of gain values in which Communicators appear and flourish. Although the average number of food sources remains the same as in our constant and randomly variable environments, cycles of "boom and bust" strongly favor the emergence of communication.[8]

Figure 13. Triumph of Communicators at all gains above 10 in an environment of food sources between 0 and 100 varying in the pattern of sin+3

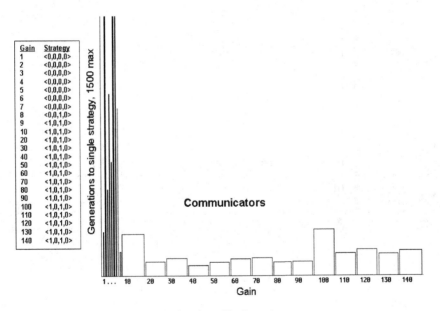

(a) Imitation in a Sin+3 environment

Figure 13. continued

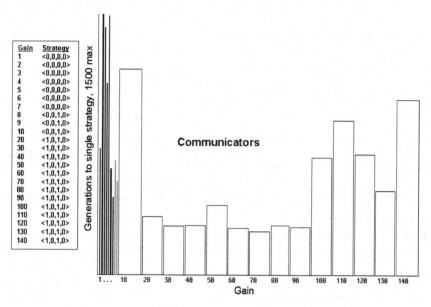

(b) Localized genetic algorithms in a Sin+3 environment

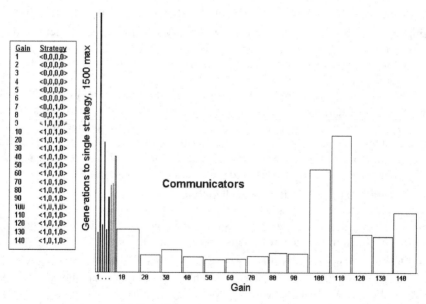

(c) Neural nets in a Sin+3 environment

Strategy replacement is by (a) imitation of most successful neighbor, (b) localized genetic algorithm combination with most successful neighbor and (c) and partial neural nets training on most successful neighbor.

The Complex Studies

We extend the model into a range of more complex studies in which environments contain not only food sources but predators. Here we use 75 food sources and 150 predators, each of which wanders in a random walk across the array.[9]

In this second series of studies, our individuals have a larger behavioral repertoire. On any given round they can open their mouths, hide or coast in neutral. An individual is awarded a particular gain if it "feeds" — if its mouth is open when a food source lands on it, but also loses a point when "harmed" — when it is hit by a predator and is not hiding. Mouth-opening and hiding each carry an energy cost of .05 points.[10] Coasting in neutral carries no energy cost, but when in neutral an individual can neither benefit by feeding nor avoid predation by hiding. Here our individuals also have two arbitrary sounds at their disposal rather than one. Sound-making, like mouth-opening and hiding, carries an energy cost of .05 points.

We again compare three mechanisms of strategy change: imitation, localized genetic algorithm and partial training of neural nets. In the case of imitation and genetic algorithm, we encode our strategies as ternary six-tuples $<ø, f, h, s1, s2, sø>$. The first three variables specify what sound an individual makes when neither fed nor hurt $ø$ (no sound, sound 1 or sound 2), what sound it makes when fed f (the same three options) and what sound it makes when hurt h (the same three options). The second three variables specify what action an individual takes when it hears sound 1 (coast in neutral, open its mouth or hide), when it hears sound 2 and when it hears no sound $sø$ (the same three options in each case).

For simplicity, we allow our individuals to respond only to being fed, hurt or neither; there is no provision for responding to being both fed or hurt. We also have our individuals respond to only one sound or neither, again with no provision for both. If an individual is both fed and hurt, or hears both sounds 1 and 2, we randomize which input it responds to. We structure individuals so that they can make only one sound at a time and can engage in only one action — mouth-opening or hiding. With these restrictions we can keep our specifications to six-tuples $<ø, f, h, s1, s2, sø>$, with a sample space of 729 possible strategies. Here, as before, we should also mention that an element of "noise" is built in: An individual will open its mouth in a random 5% of cases even if its code specifies otherwise, and will similarly hide in a random 5% of cases.

Where strategy change is by imitation, each individual looks around to see if a neighbor has acquired a higher score after 100 rounds of point gain and loss. If so, it adopts the strategy of its most successful neighbor. Should there be more than one neighbor with equal higher scores, the strategy of one is chosen randomly.

Using a localized genetic algorithm, here as before, we hybridize the strategy of an individual with that of its highest scoring neighbor, should any neighbor prove more successful. We use two-point crossover on our ternary six-tuples, choosing one of the offspring at random (Figure 14).

Our neural nets are structured as the simple perceptrons shown in Figure 15. This two-lobe structure for communication has been re-invented or re-discovered repeatedly in the history of the literature. Since De Saussure (1916), many have noted an intrinsic distinction between (1) making sounds or sending signals, and (2) responding to sounds

Figure 14. Genetic recombination applied to strategies of six variables

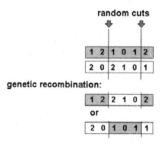

or signals received. It seems natural to embody that distinction in the neural architecture of the individuals modeled.[11] Here we use eight weights with four biases, each of which carries a value between -3.5 and +3.5, "chunked" at one-unit intervals. We use a bipolar coding for inputs, so that "hear sound 1" takes a value of +1 if the individual hears sound 1 from an immediate neighbor on the previous round, for example, and takes a value of -1 if it does not. Each input is multiplied by the weight shown on arrows from it, and the weighted inputs are then summed with the weight of the bias at the output node. Were we operating these nets "pure," their inputs at "hear sound 1" and "hear sound 2," for example, could both be +1. Their outputs at "open mouth" and "hide" could also both be +1. In order to allow comparison with our coded behaviors in imitation and genetic algorithm runs, we constrain inputs and outputs. In operation, we "cripple" our nets. We program our simulation so that only one sound or neither can be fed into a net as input on any given round, with a similar constraint on "fed" and "hurt" inputs. Where there are two sounds in the environment, or a cell is both fed or hurt, one input is chosen at random much as in the imitation and genetic algorithm models. Even with these input limitations, however, it would be possible for nets with particular patterns of weights to give a positive output for both "make sound 1" and "make sound 2," for example, or for both "open mouth" and "hide." Here we change our threshold for outputs. Should neither output give a weighted sum >0, both are treated as outputting -1, with the result that no sound is made, for example. Should only one output give a sum >0, that output is treated as the sole output of +1. Should both outputs give a sum >0, we treat that with the greater sum as +1 and the other as -1; when both are >0 and equal, we pick one at random. Here, as in the other cases, we also build in an element of "noise"; in a random 5% of cases individuals will open their mouths regardless of weights and inputs, hiding in a random 5% of cases as well.

We must admit that these constraints on our neural nets are in some way "unnatural"; without those constraints they would show a greater range of behaviors in a greater variety of input situations. We also speculate that these constraints contributed to the slowness with which our nets operated and the slowness with which large arrays of such nets evolved.[12]

In our neural net runs, as in the others, our individuals total their points over the course of 100 generations. If any of their eight immediate neighbors has garnered a higher score,

Figure 15. Neural nets in the more complex model, using eight weights and four biases for each individual

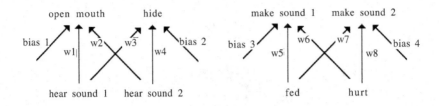

Bipolar inputs of +1 or -1 are taken at "hear sound 1," "hear sound2," "fed" and "hurt," and are multiplied by the weights on arrows from them. Biases carry similar weights. "Open mouth," "hide," "make sound 1" and "make sound 2" are the output nodes. If the total at an output node > 0, the output is treated as +1 and the individual "opens its mouth" or "makes sound 2," for example. If the total output is ≤ 0, the output is treated as -1 and the individual keeps its mouth closed or does not make sound 2.

the cell's highest-scoring neighbor is taken as its "target." For a set of four random inputs, with no provision against duplication, the cell then compares its outputs with those of its target. At any point at which outputs differ, each weight and bias in the "trainee" is nudged a single unit toward what would have given its neighbor's response on that run. With bipolar coding, we can calculate changes in weights and biases as $w_{new} = w_{old} + (target \times input)$ and $bias_{new} = bias_{old} + target$. Any such training will clearly be partial. Only four sets of inputs are sampled, rather than the full 16 possible, and indeed the same set may be sampled repeatedly. The delta rule is applied using each set of inputs only once, moreover, leaving no guarantee that each weight will be shifted enough to match the target behavior. The idea of partial training is deliberately built into the model in order to allow behavioral strategies to emerge that might not have existed in either trainee or target.

In each form of strategy change we are now dealing with the same 729 behaviors, representable in ternary notation as six-tuples $<\emptyset, f, h, s1, s2, s\emptyset>$. Of these, there are only two that qualify as "Perfect Communicators." $<0,1,2,1,2,0>$ makes no sound when neither fed nor hurt, makes sound 1 when fed and makes sound 2 when hurt. It correspondingly responds to hearing sound 1 by opening its mouth, and responds to hearing sound 2 by hiding. $<0,2,1,2,1,0>$, on the other hand, uses sound 2 when fed and sound 1 when hurt, responding to sound 2 by opening its mouth and to sound 1 by hiding.

In this more complicated environment, however, with a significantly wider range of possible behaviors, a number of broader categories of behavior turned out to be important:

- *All Eat:* A total of 27 of our coded behavioral strategies fell in this category: Any with a string of three 1s on the right-hand side of the code. These strategies vary in the sounds they produce when they are fed or hurt. But they don't vary in the action they take in response to any sound pattern; regardless of whether they hear sound 1, sound 2 or neither, they sit with open mouths. Our All Eat strategies therefore include:

```
000111  100111  200111
001111  101111  201111
002111  102111  202111
010111  110111  210111
011111  111111  211111
012111  112111  212111
020111  120111  220111
021111  121111  221111
022111  122111  222111
```

- *All Hide:* These 27 strategies differ in that their final three digits are 2s rather than 1s:

```
000222  100222  200222
001222  101222  201222
002222  102222  202222
010222  110222  210222
011222  111222  211222
012222  112222  212222
020222  120222  220222
021222  121222  221222
022222  122222  222222
```

- *Eat Default Communicators:* These eight strategies have some signal operating as a predator warning — sending sound 1 when hurt and responding to sound 1 by hiding, for example — but only against a background default to "open mouth" in the absence of any signals. They therefore have a "1" in the furthest column to the right. This category includes communicators that use and respond to symbols for both food and predators, but only against an "open mouth" default.

```
001201  001211
001221  002021
002121  002221
012121  021211
```

- *Hide Default Communicators:* Here it is "hiding" that is the default, with at least communication signals for the presence of food.

      010102 010112
      010122 012122
      020012 010112
      020212 021202

- *Food Communicators:* These six strategies communicate perfectly with each other, including a no-action "neutral" in the absence of signals, but communicate only about the presence of food. Their code may specify a response to a signal that is "idle" in the sense that they don't send it, but there is no signal sent in the absence of feeding and no default action in the absence of signals.

      010100 010110
      010120 020010
      020110 020210

- *Predator Communicators:* These six strategies communicate perfectly, but only about the presence of predators.

      001200 001210
      001220 002020
      002120 002220

- *Perfect Communicators:* Two strategies send and receive signals about both food and predators, coasting in neutral in the absence of any signals.

      012120 021210

In our simple studies, we used the gain allotted for successful feeding as the independent variable with which to measure the "window" for communication in different environments. We use the same measure in our more complex studies, keeping "loss" for predation constant at 1 point but varying the "gain" for successful feeding from 0 to 150.

In a first series of runs, across all modes of strategy change, we used a constant environment of precisely 75 wandering food sources and 150 wandering predators. In a second series, we used an environment with the same averages for food sources and predators, but with the number of food sources picked as a random number between 1 and 150 each generation and the number of predators picked at random between 1 and

300. In a third series, we used an environment with the same average for each but with coordinated sine-wave variation for numbers of food sources and predators. Here, as before, the question was whether these differences in environment would make a difference in the emergence of communication.

Constant Environment

Gain for feeding is again our independent variable, but is sampled at larger intervals than before: here at 1, 5, 10, 25, 50, and 150 points for each successful feeding. Because of the complexities of a larger sample space of strategies, we concentrated not on particular strategies but on which category of strategies proved dominant at each gain. Results for strategy change by simple imitation in a constant environment are shown in Figure 16.

With a gain of 1, Perfect Communicators occupy the entire array of 4,096 cells in 375 generations. For gains of 10, 25, 50, 100, and 150, however, the array goes to fixation with all cells playing All Eat. The fact that our bar goes to the top of the graph for a gain of 5 indicates that no single strategy category occupied the entire array by our limit of 1,500 generations. In this case the color of the bar indicates only the category dominant in the array at that point: In this case, for example, Eat Default Communicators occupied 3,842 cells of the 4,096. All Eat occupied 254 cells. A graph of the particular dynamics in that case is shown in Figure 17.

For strategy change by imitation, then, a constant environment favors All Eat for all gains over 5. All Eat also proves dominant when strategy change is by localized genetic algorithm (Figure 18).

Figure 16. Dominance by All Eat with strategy change by imitation

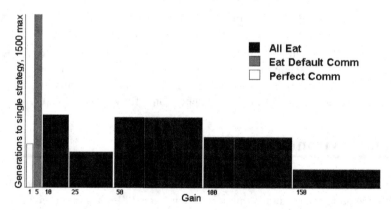

Dominance by All Eat with strategy change by imitation of most successful neighbor in a constant environment of food sources and predators. Generations to conquest by a single strategy category shown for different gains, 1,500 generations maximum.

Figure 17. Competition between All Eat and Eat Default Communicators for a gain of 5; 1,500 generations of strategy change by imitation in a constant environment

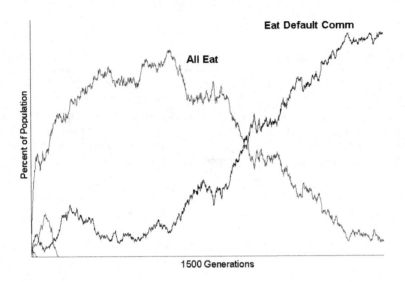

What of neural nets? Throughout our trials, arrays of the more complex but constrained neural nets took significantly longer to come to fixation. For none of our gain settings did we arrive at a single strategy category within 1,500 generations. Figure 19 is thus remarkably dull, showing merely that All Eat was the dominant category at 1,500 generations for all gains greater than 1. Here, another way of graphing results proves more informative. Figure 20 shows relative populations for different categories established by generation 1,500 at each gain. Bars don't extend to the end, it should be noted, because of an assortment of strategies that don't fall into any of our listed categories.

Despite the slowness of our nets, this too appears to be a relative victory for All Eat. At 1,500 generations, and for gains of 5 and above, All Eat is the only one of our behavioral categories that has established itself in a significant proportion of the population. Perfect Communicators and Food Communicators appear only for very small gains.

Random Environment

For the random runs, we set food sources at a random number between 1 and 150 each time, with predators at a random number between 1 and 300. These averaged to 75 food sources and 150 predators over the course of a run, but of course varied unpredictably from generation to generation. Results for each mode of strategy change are shown in Figure 21.

Figure 18. Dominance by All Eat with strategy change by localized genetic algorithm

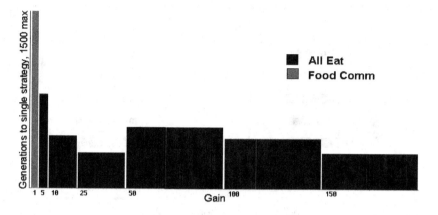

Dominance by All Eat with strategy change by localized genetic algorithm combination with most successful neighbor in a constant environment of food sources and predators.

Figure 19. Dominance by All Eat with strategy change by localized neural net training

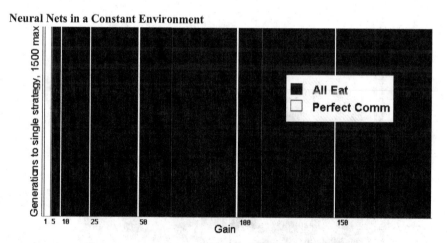

Dominance by All Eat with strategy change by localized neural net training on most successful neighbor in a constant environment of food sources and predators. Colors of bars at 1,500 indicate strategy dominance but not necessarily full conquest.

Figure 20. Domination by All Eat: Populations of strategy categories

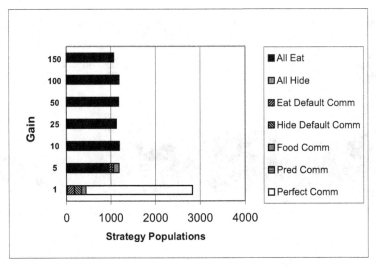

Domination by All Eat: Populations of strategy categories at different gains for partial neural net training on most successful neighbor in constant environment of food sources and predators.

Figure 21. Categories dominant in an environment of randomized numbers of food courses and predators

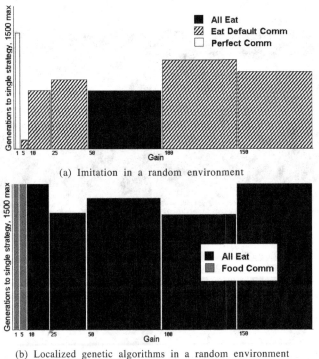

(a) Imitation in a random environment

(b) Localized genetic algorithms in a random environment

Figure 21. continued

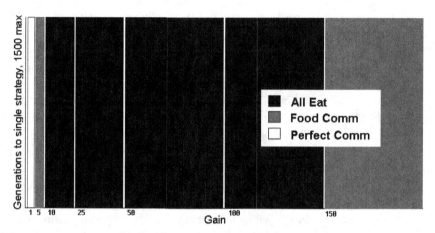

(c) Neural nets in a random environment

Categories dominant in an environment of randomized numbers of food sources and predators. Strategy replacement by (a) imitation of most successful neighbor, (b) localized genetic algorithm combination with most successful neighbor and (c) partial neural nets training on most successful neighbor. Colors of bars at 1,500 indicate strategy dominance but not necessarily full conquest.

Figure 22. Populations of strategies in major categories at different gains for partial neural net training in an environment with random numbers of food sources and predators

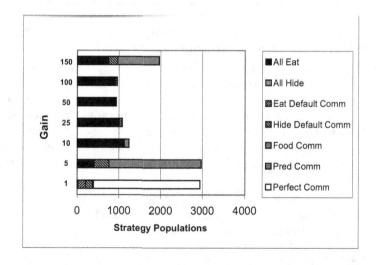

In the imitation runs, Perfect Communicators take over with a gain of 1, but at greater gains the general winners are Eat Default Communicators. This is a family of strategies that qualify as "Communicators" because of reciprocal signaling regarding predators. Like All Eat, however, the winner at a gain of 50, they maintain an open mouth in the absence of any signal.

In the genetic algorithm runs, Food Communicators prove dominant with gains of 1 and 5, though they don't completely occupy the array within 1,500 generations. Food Communicators resemble Perfect Communicators in that they send no signal when neither fed nor hurt, and take no action when no signal is received. But their communication is limited to the presence of food. Beyond a gain of 5 it is All Eat that takes over.

Populations of strategies in major categories at different gains for partial neural net training in an environment with random numbers of food sources and predators.

In no case did our neural nets reach fixation on a single strategy category within 1,500 generations. Here again results for neural nets are clearer in Figure 22. Perfect Communicators are dominant at a gain of 1, with Food Communicators at a gain of 5. Beyond that, the dominant category is All Eat, with the peculiar exception of close competition between Food Communicators and All Eat at a gain of 150.

In an environment of randomized numbers of food sources and predators, there do seem to be important differences in the outcomes of our models depending on whether we use imitation, localized genetic algorithm or partial training of neural nets. In the case of imitation, in particular, Eat Default Communicators make a significant showing that doesn't appear with either of our other modes of strategy change. In neural nets and genetic algorithms, Food Communicators also make a more significant showing than they did in a constant environment. All Eat, however, is still the most significant category for gain levels above 5 in both neural nets and genetic algorithms.

Sine-Wave Variable Environment

In our simple studies, communication was strongly favored in sine-wave variable environments. Will the same hold for the more complex model?

With one major qualification, the answer is "yes": Here again, cycles of "boom and bust" strongly favor the emergence of communication. The major qualification has to do with the precise form of communication that is favored. Our more complex models include both food sources and predators, with the possibility of communicative strategies regarding either or both. Numbers of both food sources and predators vary together in cycles of "boom and bust."[13] The variable we use to test the "window" for communication, however — level of gain for successful feeding — is clearly relevant only to communication regarding food.

Communication regarding food, it turns out, *is* strongly favored in sine-wave variable environments: Food Communicators dominate, unthreatened by All Eat, at very high levels of gain. Because loss for predation remains constant at one penalty point across our runs, on the other hand, communication regarding predation does not appear. With up to 150 points to be gained by successful feeding, the one point that might be lost by predation proves insufficient to produce either Pred Communicators or fully Perfect Communicators.

Here, as before, we explored two patterns of sine-wave variability, shown in Figure 23. In this case, data points represent both numbers of food sources between 1 and 150 and predators between 0 and 300. In the sin+2 graph, our food sources are plotted as $[sin(x) + 1] * 75$ for a series x_0, x_1, ... x_n which increments by units of two; predators are plotted as $[sin(x) + 1] * 150$ for the same series. In the second series, our increments are by units of three. Although we compiled full data for both forms of variation, the final results prove nearly identical. We therefore exhibit only the results for the sin+2 series as representative of both.[14]

Because almost all runs failed to reach fixation by 1,500 generations, results appear in a less informative form in Figure 24. What these graphs do make clear is the complete dominance by Food Communicators for all modes of strategy change and all gains greater than one. Proportions of populations in each case are shown in Figure 25.

Figure 23. Patterns of variation for food sources and predators

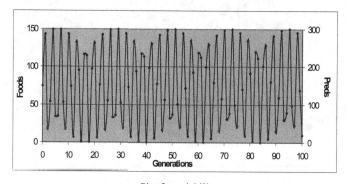

Sin+2 variability

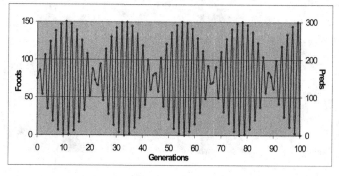

Sin+3 variability

$[sin(x) + 1] * 75$ for food sources and $[sin(x) + 1] * 150$ for predators with different incremental series x_0, x_1, ... x_n. In the top series, $x_{n+1} = x_n + 2$. In the second series, $x_{n+1} = x_n + 3$.

Figure 24. Full dominance by Food Communicators across all modes of strategy change in a sine-wave variable environment

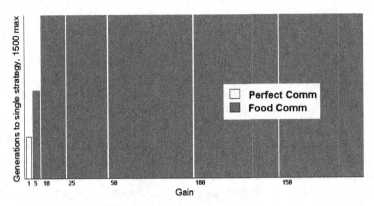

(a) Imitation in a Sin+2 environment

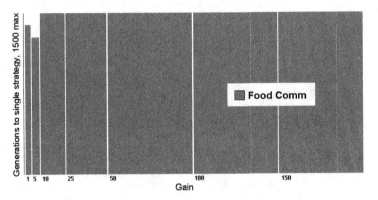

(b) Localized genetic algorithm in a Sin+2 environment

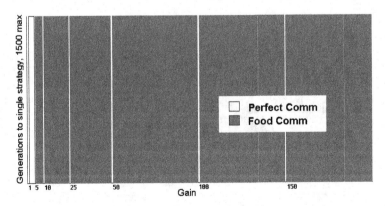

(c) Neural nets in a Sin+2 environment

Results shown are for sin+2. Sin+3 results are nearly identical.

Figure 25. Full dominance by Food Communicators across all modes of strategy change in a sin+2 variable environment

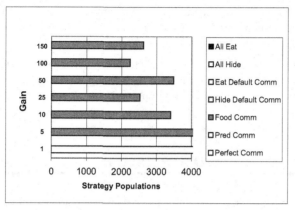

(a) Imitation in a Sin+2 environment

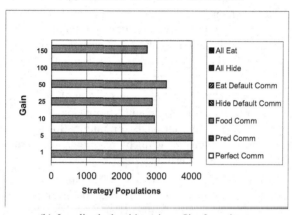

(b) Localized algorithms in a Sin+2 environment

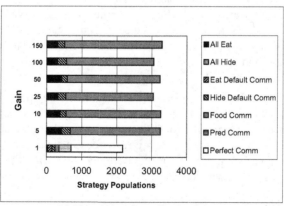

(c) Neural nets in a Sin+2 environment

Populations of strategies at 1,500 generations. Sin+3 results are nearly identical.

We take these results as clear evidence that sine-wave variable environments of at least the "boom and bust" form of sin+2 and sin+3 strongly favor the emergence of communication. In constant and random environments dominance at gains above 5 goes to either All Eat or Eat Default Communicators. Food communicators play a subsidiary role. With a variable environment of the forms explored here, on the other hand, dominance is by Food communicators for gains from 5 to 150.

Our more complex simulations therefore underscore the lesson of the simpler models above. Across a range of modes of strategy change, sine-wave variable environments can play a major role in the emergence of communication.

Conclusion

In earlier studies we found that communities of Communicators can emerge from an initially randomized array of strategies in an environment of wandering food sources and predators. Communication can emerge, moreover, using any of three different mechanisms of strategy change: imitation of successful neighbors, combination by localized genetic algorithm with most successful neighbors and partial neural net training on the behavior of most successful neighbors (Grim, Kokalis, Tafti, & Kilb, 2000, 2001; Grim, St. Denis, & Kokalis, 2002).

In our earlier studies, however, we used environments with a constant number of wandering food sources and predators. Here our attempt has been to expand those studies to questions of environmental variation: Is communication about resources more favored in an environment in which the level of resources are variable than in an environment in which resources are constant?

For an environment with randomly variable resources, the answer is "no." In both our simpler and more complex simulations, random variation in resources showed much the same effect as constant resources with the same average. In an environment with sine-wave variable resources, on the other hand — an environment of "boom and bust" resource cycles — the answer is clearly "yes." It is thus not merely variability but the particular pattern of variability that is of importance; communicative strategies are much more strongly favored in sine-wave variable environments. That effect holds whether the mechanism of strategy change at issue is one of imitation, localized genetic algorithm or partial training on neural nets.

The advantage to communication in a variable environment, we speculate, is that the behavior of a community of Communicators can be environmentally sensitive. Unlike many of their competitors, communities of Communicators can take effective advantage of "boom" cycles and yet harbor their energy resources in times of "bust." A more thorough understanding of the mechanisms of environmental variability in this kind of simulation, however, as well as a wider exploration of different patterns of variation, will require further work.

Meaning is crucial to cognitive systems, whether artificial or natural. Our earlier work suggests that a key to understanding meaning may lie in understanding the development of behavioral coordination in communities of agents embodied in an environment. The current results suggest that environmental variability may also play an important role in the emergence of meaning. In terms of natural cognition systems, these results offer hints of a deeper understanding of some of the mechanisms of meaning. They may also offer hints toward richer development of meaning in artificial cognition.

It is intriguing that environmental variability has been appealed to as an important explanatory factor in a range of different disciplines. In ecology, environmental fluctuation has been seen as playing an important role in species diversity (Hutchinson, 1961; Harris, 1986; Huston, 1979; Hubbell & Foster, 1986; Chesson & Huntly, 1989, 1997). In cultural anthropology, cycles of boom and bust have been linked to the growth of agriculture (Reynolds, 1986). Pleistocene climatic fluctuations have recently been proposed as instrumental in the evolution of larger brained mammals in general and higher primates in particular, with speculative links to social learning and culture (Potts, 1996; Opdyke, 1995; Odling-Smee, Laland, & Feldman, 2000; Boyd & Richerson, 1985, 1989, 2000). The study of particular patterns of environmental variability and their impact is perhaps most developed in decades of careful work on schedules of reinforcement and operant conditioning (Reynolds, 1975; Honig, & Staddon, 1977; Nye, 1992). It is tempting to speculate that these appeals to environmental variability across disciplines may have some central mechanism in common. We take it as a suggestive fact, worthy of further investigation, that environmental variability turns out to be important even in the simple simulational studies of communication and meaning we have outlined here.

References

Boyd, R., & Richerson, P. J. (1985). *Culture and the evolutionary process.* Chicago: Chicago University Press.

Boyd, R., & Richerson, P. J. (1989). Social learning as an adaptation. *Lectures on mathematics in the Life Sciences, 20,* 1-26.

Boyd, R., & Richerson, P. J. (2000). Built for speed: Pleistocene climate variation and the origin of human culture. In F. Tonneau & N. S. Thompson (Eds.), *Perspectives in ethology, Vol. 13: Evolution, culture, and behavior* (pp. 1-45). New York: Kluwer Academic/Plenum.

Cangelosi, A., & Parisi, D. (1998). The emergence of a 'language' in an evolving population of neural networks. *Connection Science 10,* 83-97.

Chesson, P. L., & Huntly, N. (1989). Short-term instabilities and long-term community dynamics. *Trends in Ecology and Evolution, 4,* 293-298.

Chesson, P. L., & Huntly, N. (1997). The roles of harsh and fluctuating conditions in the dynamics of ecological communities. *American Naturalist, 150,* 519-553.

De Saussure, F. (1916). *Cours de linguistique generale.* R. Harris (Trans. 1983). *Course in general linguistics.* London: Duckworth.

Flannery, K. V. (1986). Adaptation, evolution, and archaeological phases: Some implications of Reynolds' simulation. In K. V. Flannery (Ed.), *Guilá naquitz: Archaic foraging and early agriculture in Oaxaca, Mexico* (pp. 501-507). New York: Academic Press.

Grim, P. (1995). Greater generosity in the spatialized Prisoner's Dilemma. *Journal of Theoretical Biology, 173,* 353-359.

Grim, P. (1996). Spatialization and greater generosity in the stochastic Prisoner's Dilemma. *Biosystems, 37,* 3-17.

Grim, P., Kokalis, T., Alai-Tafti, A., Kilb, N., & St. Denis, P. (2004). Making meaning happen. *Journal of Experimental and Theoretical Artificial Intelligence, 16,* 209-243.

Grim, P., Kokalis, T., Tafti, A., & Kilb, N. (2000). Evolution of communication in perfect and imperfect worlds. *World Futures: The Journal of General Evolution, 56,* 179-197.

Grim, P., Kokalis, T., Tafti, A., & Kilb, N. (2001). Evolution of communication with a spatialized genetic algorithm. *Evolution of Communication, 3,* 105-134.

Grim, P., Mar, G., & St. Denis, P. (1998). *The philosophical computer.* Cambridge, MA: The MIT Press.

Grim, P., St. Denis, P., & Kokalis, T. (2002). Learning to communicate: The emergence of signaling in spatialized arrays of neural nets. *Adaptive Behavior, 10,* 45-70.

Harris, G. P. (1986). *Phytoplankton ecology, structure, function, and fluctuation.* London: Chapman & Hall.

Honig, W. K., & Staddon, J. E. R. (Eds.). (1977). *Handbook of operant behavior.* Englewood Cliffs, NJ: Prentice Hall.

Hubbell, S. P., & Foster, R. B. (1986). Biology, chance, history and the structure of tropical rainforest communities. In J. Diamond & T. J. Case (Eds.), *Community ecology* (pp. 314-329). New York: Harper and Row.

Huston, M. (1979). A general hypothesis of species diversity. *American Naturalist, 113,* 81-101.

Hutchinson, G. E. (1961). The paradox of the plankton. *American Naturalist, 95,* 145-159.

MacLennan, B. J. (1991). Synthetic ethology: An approach to the study of communication. In C. G. Langton, C. Taylor, J. D. Farmer, & S. Rasmussen (Eds.), *Artificial Life II, SFI Studies in the Sciences of Complexity* (Vol. X, pp. 631-655). Redwood City, CA: Addison-Wesley.

Nowak, M. A., Plotkin, J. B., & Jansen, V. A. A. (2000). The evolution of syntactic communication. *Nature, 404,* 495-498.

Nowak, M. A., Plotkin, J. B., & Krakauer, D. C. (1999). The evolutionary language game. *Journal of Theoretical Biology, 200,* 147-162.

Nowak, M., & Sigmund, K. (1990). The evolution of stochastic strategies in the prisoner's dilemma. *Acta Applicandae Mathematicae, 20,* 247-265.

Nowak, M., & Sigmund, K. (1992). Tit for tat in heterogeneous populations. *Nature, 355,* 250-252.

Nyc, R. D. (1992). *The legacy of B. F. Skinner: Concepts and perspectives, controversies and misunderstandings.* Pacific Grove, CA: Brooks/Cole.

Odling-Smee, F. J., Laland, K. N., & Feldman, M. W. (2000). Niche construction and gene-culture coevolution: An evolutionary basis for the human sciences. In F. Tonneau & N. S. Thompson (Eds.), *Perspectives in ethology: Vol. 13. Evolution, culture, and behavior* (pp. 89-111). New York: Kluwer Academic/Plenum.

Oliphant, M., & Batali, J. (1997). Learning and the emergence of coordinated communication. *Center for Research on Language Newsletter, 11*(1).

Opdyke, N. (1995). Mammalian migration and climate over the past seven million years. In E. S. Vrba, G. H. Denton, T. C. Partridge, & L. H. Burckle (Eds.), *Paleoclimate and evolution with emphasis on human origins* (pp. 8-23). New Haven, CT: Yale University Press.

Potts, R. (1996). *Humanity's descent: The consequences of ecological instability.* New York: William Morrow.

Reynolds, G. S. (1975). *A primer of operant conditioning.* Glenview, IL: Scott, Foresman & Company.

Reynolds, R. G. (1986). An adaptive computer model for the evolution of plant collecting and early agriculture in the eastern valley of Oaxaca. In K. V. Flannery (Ed.), *Guilá naquitz: Archaic foraging and early agriculture in Oaxaca, Mexico* (pp. 439-500). New York: Academic Press.

Seth, A. K. (1998). The evolution of complexity and the value of variability. In C. Adami, R. Belew, H. Kitano, & C. Taylor (Eds.), *Artificial Life VI: Proceedings of the Sixth International Conference on the Simulation and Synthesis of Living Systems.* Cambridge, MA: The MIT Press.

Werner, G., & Dyer, M. (1991). Evolution of communication in artificial organisms. In C. G. Langton, C. Taylor, J. D. Farmer, & S. Rasmussen (Eds.), *Artificial Life II, SFI Studies in the Sciences of Complexity* (Vol. X, pp. 659-687). Redwood City, CA: Addison-Wesley.

Endnotes

[1]   See also Flannery (1986).

[2]   Questions of environmental variability are applied to robotics and the evolution of complexity in Seth (1998).

[3]   For earlier work with a similar model regarding cooperation rather than communication (see Grim, 1995, 1996, and Grim, Mar, & St. Denis, 1998).

[4]   Although we haven't pursued it here, we take direct comparison of different computational structures to be of both practical and theoretical importance. In terms of practical implications, new program optimization algorithms are constantly being proposed, including new variations on some of those used here. It is to be expected that some of these will prove more successful in the optimization of some kinds of programs, under some conditions, while others prove more successful for other kinds of programs or under other conditions. Only rarely, however, has there

been any attempt to "bench test" optimization algorithms side by side. With regard to theoretical implications, it is clear that animal behavior can be shaped by different mechanisms, including, for example, genetics and individual learning. Will one form of mechanism prove optimal for a particular range of behaviors, for a particular batch of organisms or in a particular set of conditions, while another mechanism turns out to be optimal for other behaviors or organisms in other conditions? Here a number of theoretical questions seem ripe for simulational studies using direct comparisons between different mechanisms.

[5]   These energy costs were carried over from earlier studies that did not address environmental variability but in which they proved auspicious for the development of communication at low gains. Results across different costs are detailed in Grim, Kokalis, Tafti, and Kilb (2000, 2001), and Grim, St. Denis, and Kokalis (2002).

[6]   Because of limited computer resources and the extensive computing time required for some runs across ranges of gains, particularly those involving neural net training, graphs throughout represent results of single runs at each gain. In a more comprehensive study, it would clearly be desirable to average multiple runs at each point. Consistency of results across ranges of gains, however, offers similar assurance of reliability — the fact Communicators triumph consistently at gains from 10 through 90 in Figure 7, for example.

[7]   We do not have a tidy explanation for the quicker convergence to All Eat using neural nets.

[8]   A speculation as to why this result holds is offered in the conclusion.

[9]   The reason for using twice as many predators as food sources is detailed in Grim, Kokalis, Tafti, and Kilb (2000). A bit of reflection on the dynamics of feeding and predation built into the model shows an important difference between the two. In an array composed entirely of Communicators, as illustrated in Figure 2, a chain reaction can be expected in terms of food signals and successful feedings. The dynamics of a "hurt" alarm are very different. Among even Perfect Communicators, a cell signals an alarm only when it is hurt — that is, when a predator is on it and it isn't hiding. If successful, that "alarm" will alert a cell's neighbors to hide, and thus the predator will find no victim on the next round. Precisely because the predator then finds no victim, there will be no alarm sounded, and thus on the following round even a fellow "communicator" may be hit by a predator. Here one sees not a chain reaction of successful feeding on every round, but an alternating pattern of successful avoidance of predation every second round. An important difference between the dynamics of feeding and the dynamics of predation is thus built into the model. With equal numbers of food sources and predators, that difference in dynamics would strongly favor communication regarding food over communication regarding predators. One way to compensate for that difference is simply to proportion food sources and predators accordingly, as we have done here.

[10]   The .05 "tax" for mouth-opening is significantly less than the .95 tax in the simpler studies because there is an additional down-side to mouth-opening in this richer environment. When its mouth is open, an individual cannot be hiding and so is vulnerable to predators.

[11]   This maps precisely onto the distinction between "emissions" and "actions" in MacLennan (1991) and between "transmission behavior" and "reception behavior" in Oliphant and Batali (1997). These two functions are separated between two different sexes in Werner and Dyer (1991), and between two separate sets of connection weights in the neural nets of Cangelosi and Parisi (1998). Martin Nowak notes that an active matrix for signal-sending and a passive matrix for signal-reading can be treated as completely independent in Nowak, Plotkin, and Krakauer (1999) and in Nowak, Plotkin, and Jansen (2000).

[12]   Results below were often compiled using multiple computers running sub-sets of gains over a period of weeks and months.

[13]   The possibility of varying food sources and predators independently, and at different rates, remains an open question. The initial and limited explorations we made in this direction gave no clear or decisive results.

[14]   Full data for both series are of course available on request.

Section V

Theoretical and
Philosophical Issues

Chapter XI

Mimetic Minds:
Meaning Formation through Epistemic Mediators and External Representations

Lorenzo Magnani, University of Pavia, Italy

Abstract

The imitation game between man and machine, proposed by Turing in 1950, is a game between a discrete and a continuous system. In the framework of the recent studies about embodied and distributed cognition, Turing's "discrete-state machine" can be seen as an external cognitive mediator that constitutively integrates human cognitive behavior. Through the description of a subclass of these cognitive mediators I call "mimetic minds," the chapter deals with some of their cognitive and epistemological aspects and with the cognitive role played by the manipulations of the environment that includes them. The illustrated topics directly affect the problem of meaning formation in the light of both human and artificial reasoning, taking advantage of a study on the role of external representations and of what I call "epistemic mediators."

Introduction

More than a hundred years ago, the American philosopher C.S. Peirce suggested the idea of *pragmatism* (or *pragmaticism*, in his own words) as a logical criterion to analyze what words and concepts express through their practical meaning. Many words have been spent on creative processes and *meaning formation*, especially in the case of scientific practices. In fact, philosophers have usually offered a number of ways of construing hypothesis generation, but all aim at demonstrating that the activity of generating hypotheses is paradoxical, illusory or obscure, and thus not analyzable. Consequently, the common views associate unusual and mysterious qualities to creativity and meaning formation.

This conclusion has also been supported by many philosophers of science who studied conceptual change in science during the second half of the last century. Some of them claimed that a logic of discovery (and a rational model of discovery) could not exist: Scientific conceptual change is cataclysmic and sometimes irrational, dramatic, incomprehensible and discontinuous. I maintain we can overcome many of the difficulties of creativity and meaning formation studies, developing a theory of abduction, in the light of Charles Sanders Peirce's first insights.

The "computational turn" and the creation of "artificial cognition systems" gave us new ways to understand cognitive processes in a strictly pragmatic sense. The creation of new meanings through creative processes is no longer seen as a mysterious irrational process but, thanks to constructive accounts, as a complex relationship among different inferential steps that can be clearly analyzed and identified. Artificial intelligence and cognitive science tools allow us to test concepts and ideas previously conceived in abstract terms. It is in the perspective of these *actual models* that we find the central role of *abduction* in the explanation of meaning formation. What I call *theoretical abduction* (sentential and model-based) certainly illustrates much of what is important in abductive reasoning, especially the objective of selecting and creating a set of hypotheses to furnish good (preferred) explanations of data, but fails to account for many cases of explanation occurring in science or in everyday reasoning when the exploitation of the environment is crucial.

The first part of the paper illustrates that at the roots of the creation of new meanings there is a process of *disembodiment of mind* that exhibits a new cognitive perspective on the mechanisms underling the emergence of meaning processes. I will take advantage of Turing's comparison between "unorganized" brains and "logical" and "practical machines," and of some paleoanthropological results on the birth of material culture, that provide an evolutionary perspective on the origin of some meaningful behaviors. Then I will illustrate the centrality to meaning formation of the disembodiment of mind from the point of view of the cognitive interplay between internal and external representations that will be divided in *mimetic* and *creative* . I consider this interplay critical in analyzing the relation between meaningful behavior and dynamical interactions with the environment.

I also think the disembodiment of mind can nicely account for low-level cognitive processes of meaning creation, bringing up the question of how higher-level processes could be comprised and how they would interact with lower-level ones. To the aim of explaining these higher-level mechanisms, I provide the computational philosophy analysis of *model-based* and *manipulative* abduction, and of *external representations* and *epistemic mediators*. The concept of *manipulative abduction* is devoted to capturing the role of action in many interesting situations: action provides otherwise unavailable information that enables the agent to solve problems by starting and performing a grounded, meaningful abductive process of generation or selection of hypotheses. Many external things, usually inert from the epistemological point of view, can be transformed into what I call "epistemic mediators." I believe it is important not only to delineate the actual practice of abduction, but also to further enhance the development of artificial cognition systems computationally adequate to reproduce meaningful creative scientific behaviors, for example, in rediscovering, or discovering for the first time, scientific hypotheses or mathematical theorems.

In the last part of the paper, the concept of *mimetic mind* is introduced to shed new cognitive and philosophical light on the role of computational modeling and on the decline of the so-called Cartesian computationalism. The concept also emphasizes the possible impact of the construction of new types of universal "practical" machines, available over there, in the environment, as new tools underlying the emergence of meaning processes.

Pragmatism as a Rule for Clarity

Charles Sanders Peirce suggested the idea of *pragmatism* as a logical criterion to analyze what words and concepts express through their practical meaning. In "The fixation of belief" (1877) Peirce enumerates four main methods by means of which it is possible to fix belief: the method of tenacity, the method of authority, the *a priori* method and, finally, the method of science, by means of which, thanks to rigorous research, "we can ascertain by reasoning how things really and truly are; and any man, if he has sufficient experience and he reasons enough about it, will be led to the one True conclusion" (Peirce, 1986, p. 255). Only the scientific method leads to identifying what is "real," that is, true.

Peirce will more clearly explain the public notion of truth here exposed, and the interpretation of reality as the final purpose of the human inquiry, in his subsequent paper "How to make our ideas clear" (1878). Here Peirce addresses attention on the notions of "clear idea" and "belief": "Whoever has looked into a modern treatise on logic of the common sort, will doubtlessly remember the two distinctions between *clear* and *obscure* conceptions, and between *distinct* and *confused* conceptions" he writes (Peirce, 1986, p. 257).

A clear idea is defined as one which is apprehended so that it will be recognized wherever it is met, and so that no other will be mistaken for it. If it fails to be clear, it is said to be obscure. On the other hand, a distinct idea is defined as one which contains nothing which is not clear. In this paper Peirce is clearly opposing traditional philosophical positions, such as those by Descartes and Leibniz, who consider clarity and distinction of ideas only from a merely psychological and analytical perspective: "It is easy to show that the doctrine that familiar use and abstract distinctness make the perfection of apprehension has its only true place in philosophies which have long been extinct; and it is now time to formulate the method of attaining to a more perfect clearness of thought, such as we see and admire in the thinkers of our own time" (Peirce, 1986, p. 258).

Where do we have, then, to look for a criterion of clarity, if philosophy has become too obscure, irrational and confusing, if "for an individual, however, there can be no question that a few clear ideas are worth more than many confused ones" (Peirce, 1986, p. 260).

"The action of thought is excited by the irritation of doubt, and ceases when belief is attained; so that the production of belief is the sole function of thought" (Peirce, 1986, 261). And belief "is something that we are aware of [...] it appeases the irritation of doubt; and, third, it involves the establishment in our nature of a rule of action, or, say for short, a habit" (Peirce, 1986, 263). Hence, the whole function of thought is to produce habits of action. This leads directly to the *methodological* pragmatic theory of meaning, a procedure to determine the meaning of propositions, according to Peirce (1986):

To develop its meaning, we have, therefore, simply to determine what habits it produces, for what a thing means is simply what habits it involves. Now, the identity of a habit depends on how it might lead us to act, not merely under such circumstances as are likely to arise, but under such as might possibly occur, no matter how improbable they may be. Thus, we come down to what is tangible and conceivably practical, as the root of every real distinction of thought, no matter how subtle it may be; and there is no distinction of meaning so fine as to consist in anything but a possible difference of practice. (pp. 265-266)

In this way Peirce creates the equivalence among idea, belief and habit, and can define the rule by which we can reach the highest grade of intellectual clearness, pointing out that is impossible to have an idea in our minds which relates to anything but conceived sensible effects of things. Our idea of something is our idea of its sensible effects: "Consider what effects, that might conceivably have practical bearings, we conceive the object of our conception to have. Then, our conception of these effects is the whole of our conception of the object" (Peirce, 1986, 266). This rule founds the pragmatic procedure thanks to which it is possible to fix our ideas.

Computational Modeling and the Enigmatic Concept of Meaning

Peirce's conception of clarity contains the idea that to define the meaning of words and concepts we have to "test," to "subject to" them: The whole conception of some quality lies in its conceivable effects. As he reminds us by the example of the concept of *hardness,* "there is absolutely no difference between a hard thing and a soft thing so long as they are not brought to the test" (Peirce, 1986). Hence, we can define the "hardness" by looking at those predictable events that occur every time we think of testing some thing.

This methodological criterion can be useful to solve the problem of *creative* reasoning and to describe, in rational terms, some aspects of the delicate question of a meaning formation: What do we mean by "creative," and how can a "creative meaning process" be described? I see *meaning formation* — I am mainly interested here in the formation of "new" meanings from the point of view of conceptual change, and so in the perspective of creative reasoning — as considering concepts either cognitively, like mental structures analogous to data structures in computers, or, epistemologically, like abstractions or representations that presuppose questions of justification. Belief revision is able to represent cases of conceptual change such as adding a new instance, adding a new weak rule or adding a new strong rule (Thagard, 1992), that is, cases of addition and deletion of beliefs, but fails to take into account cases such as adding a new part-relation, a new kind-relation, a new concept, collapsing part of a kind-hierarchy and reorganizing hierarchies by branch jumping and tree switching, in which there are reorganizations of concepts or redefinitions of the nature of a hierarchy.

Let us consider concepts as composite structures akin to frames of the following sort:

CONCEPT:

A kind of:

Subkinds:

A part of:

Parts:

Synonyms:

Antonyms:

Rules:

Instances:

It is important to emphasize (1) kind and part-whole relations that institute hierarchies, and (2) rules that express factual information more complex than simple slots. To understand the cases of conceptual revolutions that involve meaning change we need to illustrate how concepts can fit together into conceptual systems and what is involved in the replacement of such systems. Conceptual systems can be viewed as ordered into kind-hierarchies and linked to each other by rules.

Adding new part-relations occurs when in the part-hierarchy new parts are discovered: An example is given by the introduction of new molecules, atoms and subatomic particles. Thomson's discovery that the "indi-visible" atom contains electrons was sensational.

Adding new kind-relations occurs when a new superordinate kind is added that combines two or more things previously taken to be distinct. In the nineteenth century scientists recognized that electricity and magnetism were the same and constructed the new concept of electromagnetism. Another case is shown by differentiation, that is the making of a new distinction that generates two kinds of things (heat and temperature were considered the same until the Black's intervention).

The last three types of formation of new meanings can be illustrated by the following examples. The Newtonian abandon of the Aristotelian distinction between natural and unnatural motion exemplifies the collapse of part of the kind-hierarchy. Branch jumping occurred when the Copernican revolution involved the recategorization of the earth as a kind of planet, when previously it had been considered special, but also when Darwin reclassified humans as a kind of animal. Finally, we have to say that Darwin not only reclassified humans as animals, he modified the meaning of the classification itself. To Thagard (1992), this is a case of hierarchical tree redefinition:

Whereas before Darwin kind was a notion primarily of similarity, his theory made it a historical notion: being of common descent becomes at least as important to being in the same kind as surface similarity. Einstein's theory of relativity changed the nature of part-relations, by substituting ideas of space-time for everyday notions of space and time. (p. 36)

These last cases are the most evident changes occurring in many kinds of creation of new meanings in science, when adopting a new conceptual system is more complex than mere belief revision. Related to some of these types of scientific conceptual change are different varieties of *model-based abductions* I will describe below in Section 10. In these cases, the hypotheses "transcend" the vocabulary of the evidence language, as opposed to the cases of simple inductive generalizations: The most interesting case of creative abduction is called by Hendricks and Faye (1999) trans-paradigmatic abduction. This is the case where the fundamental ontological principles given by the background knowledge are violated, and the new discovered hypothesis transcends the immediate empirical agreement between the two paradigms, like, for example, in the well-known case of the abductive discovery of totally new physical concepts during the transition from classical to quantum mechanics.

Much has been said on the problem of *creativity* and hypothesis generation. In the history of philosophy there are at least three important ways for designing the role of hypothesis generation, considered in the perspective of problem solving performances. But all aim at demonstrating that the activity of generating hypotheses is paradoxical, either illusory or obscure, implicit and not analyzable.

Plato's doctrine of *reminiscence* can be looked at from the point of view of an epistemological argument about the paradoxical concept of "problem-solving": In order to solve a problem one must in some sense already know the answer, there is no real generation of hypotheses, only recollection of them. The activity of Kantian *schematism* is implicit too, resulting from imagination and completely unknowable as regards its ways of working, empty and devoid of any possibility of being rationally analyzed. It is an activity of tacit knowledge, "an art concealed in the depths of the human soul, whose real modes of activity nature is hardly likely ever to allow us to discover, and to have open to our gaze" (Kant, 1929, A141-B181: 183). In his turn, Polanyi thinks that if all knowledge is explicit and capable of being clearly stated, then we cannot know a problem or look for its solution; if problems nevertheless exist, and discoveries can be made by solving them, we can know things that we cannot express: Consequently, the role of so-called *tacit knowledge,* "the intimation of something hidden, which we may yet discover" is central (Polanyi, 1966).

On the other hand, philosophers of science in the twentieth century, following the *revolutionary* theory developed by Kuhn (1970),[1] have traditionally distinguished between the logic of discovery and the logic of justification. Most have concluded that no logic of discovery exists and, moreover, that a "rational" model of discovery is impossible. In short, scientific creative reasoning should be non rational or irrational and there is no reasoning to hypotheses. Consequently, the emergence of new meaning processes is obscure and the Kuhnian idea that there is a kind of radical "meaning variance" in different scientific theories is certainly related to this point of view.

In all these descriptions, the problem is that the definition of concepts like "creativity" and "discovery" is *a priori*. Following Peirce, the definitions of concepts of this sort have not usually rested upon any observed facts, at least not in any great degree; even if sometimes these beliefs are in harmony with natural causes. They have been chiefly adopted because their fundamental propositions seemed "agreeable to reason," that is, we find ourselves inclined to believe them.

Usually this frame leads to a proliferating verbosity, in which theories are often incomprehensible and bring to some foresight just by intuition. But a theory which needs intuition to determine what it predicts has poor explanatory power. It just "makes of inquiry something similar to the development of taste" (Peirce, 1986, p. 254).

A suggestion that can help to solve the enigma of discovery and creativity of new meanings comes from the "computational turn" developed in the last years. Recent computational philosophy research in the field of cognitive science makes use of tools able to give up those puzzling speculative problems, or, at least, to redefine them in a strict pragmatical sense. In fact, taking advantage of modern tools of logic, artificial intelligence and other cognitive sciences, computational philosophy permits one to construct actual models of studied processes. It is an interesting constructive rational alternative that, disregarding the most abstract level of philosophical analysis, can offer clear and testable architectures of creative processes and meaning formation.

Inside the computational philosophy framework, a new paradigm, aimed at unifying the different perspectives and providing some design insights for future ones, rises by emphasizing the significance of the concept of *abduction*, in order to illustrate the problem-solving process and to propose a unified and rational epistemological model of scientific discovery, diagnostic reasoning and other kinds of creative reasoning (Magnani, 2001a). The concept of abduction nicely ties together both issues related to the dynamics of information and its systematic embodiment in segments of various types of knowledge.

In AI research, however, since Simon, two characteristics seem to be associated to creativity: the *novelty* of the product and the *unconventionality* of the process that leads to the new product. Hence, in a strictly *pragmatic* sense, when we can clarify what behavior we are looking for, we could implement it in a machine: A methodological criterion enables us to define and consider just those practical effects we conceive to be associated with novelty and unconventionality (Buchanan, 2001).

I maintain we can overcome many of the difficulties of the concept of meaning and of the creation of new meanings developing a theory of abduction, in the light of Charles Sanders Peirce's first insights.

The Centrality of Abduction

If we decide to adopt this kind of methodology, it is necessary to develop a cognitive model of creativity able to represent not only "novelty" and "unconventionality," but also some features commonly referred to as the entire creative process, such as the expert use of background knowledge and ontology (defining new concepts and their new meanings and searching heuristically among the old ones) and the modeling activity developed in the so called "incubation time" (generating and testing, transformations in the space of the hypotheses). The philosophical concept of *abduction* may be a candidate to solve this problem, and offers an approach to model creative processes of meaning generation in a completely explicit and formal way, which can fruitfully integrate the narrowness proper of a merely psychological approach, too experimentally human-oriented.

A hundred years ago, C. S. Peirce (*CP*, 1931-1958) coined the concept of abduction in order to illustrate that the process of scientific discovery is not irrational and that a methodology of discovery is possible. Peirce interpreted abduction essentially as an "inferential" *creative process* of generating a new hypothesis. Abduction has a logical form (fallacious, if we model abduction by using classical logic) distinct from deduction and induction. Reasoning which starts from reasons and looks for consequences is called *deduction*; that which starts from consequences and looks for reasons is called *abduction*.

Abduction — a distinct form of reasoning — is the process of *inferring* certain facts and/ or laws and hypotheses that render some sentences plausible, that *explain* or *discover* some (eventually new) phenomenon or observation; it is the process of reasoning in which explanatory hypotheses are formed and evaluated. There are two main epistemological meanings of the word abduction (Magnani, 2001a): (1) abduction that only generates "plausible" hypotheses ("selective" or "creative") and (2) abduction considered as inference "to the best explanation," which also evaluates hypotheses. An illustration from the field of medical knowledge is represented by the discovery of a new disease and the manifestations it causes which can be considered as the result of a creative abductive inference. Therefore, "creative" abduction deals with the whole field of the growth of scientific knowledge. This is irrelevant in medical *diagnosis* where instead the task is to "select" from an encyclopedia of pre-stored diagnostic entities. We can call both inferences ampliative, selective and creative, because in both cases the reasoning involved amplifies, or goes beyond, the information incorporated in the premises (Magnani, 1992).

Theoretical abduction[2] certainly illustrates much of what is important in creative abductive reasoning, in humans and in computational programs, but fails to account for many cases of explanations occurring in science when the exploitation of environment is crucial. It fails to account for those cases in which there is a kind of "discovering through doing," cases in which new and still unexpressed information is codified by means of manipulations of some external objects (*epistemic mediators*). The concept of *manipulative abduction*[3] captures a large part of scientific thinking where the role of action is central, and where the features of this action are implicit and hard to be elicited: Action can provide otherwise unavailable information that enables the agent to solve problems by starting and by performing a suitable abductive process of generation or selection of hypotheses.

In the following section I will describe how manipulative abduction can nicely account for the relationship between meaningful behavior and dynamical interactions with the environment. The following sections illustrate that at the roots of the creation of new meanings there is a process of *disembodiment of mind* that exhibits a new cognitive description of the mechanisms underlying the emergence of meaning processes.

Turing Unorganized Machines

Logical, Practical, Unorganized and Paper Machines

Aiming at building intelligent machines, Turing first of all provides an analogy between human brains and computational machines. In "Intelligent Machinery," written in 1948 (Turing, 1969) he maintains that "the potentialities of human intelligence can only be realized if suitable education is provided" (p. 3). The concept of an *unorganized machine* is then introduced, and it is maintained that the infant human cortex is of this nature. The argumentation is indeed related to showing how such machines can be educated by means of "rewards and punishments."

Unorganized machines are listed among different kinds of existent machineries:

- *(Universal) logical computing machines (LCMs)*. A LCM is a kind of discrete machine Turing introduced in 1937, that, according to Turing (1992a), has:

[...] an infinite memory capacity obtained in the form of an infinite tape marked out into squares on each of which a symbol could be printed. At any moment there is one symbol in the machine; it is called the scanned symbol. The machine can alter the scanned symbol and its behavior is in part described by that symbol, but the symbols on the tape elsewhere do not affect the behavior of the machine. However, the tape can be moved back and forth through the machine, this being one of the elementary operations of the machine. Any symbol on the tape may therefore eventually have innings. (p. 6)

This machine is called universal if it is "such that if the standard description of some other LCM is imposed on the otherwise blank tape from outside, and the (universal) machine is then set going it will carry out the operations of the particular machine whose description is given" (p. 7). The importance of this machine refers to the fact that we do not need to have an infinity of different machines doing different jobs. A single one suffices: It is only necessary "to program" the universal machine to do these jobs.

- *(Universal) practical computing machines (PCMs)*. PCMs are machines that put their stored information in a form very different from the tape form. Given the fact that in LCMs the number of steps involved tends to be enormous because of the arrangement of the memory along the tape, in the case of PCMs "by means of a system that is reminiscent of a telephone exchange it is made possible to obtain a piece of information almost immediately by 'dialing' the position of this information in the store" (Turing, 1992a, p. 8). Turing adds that "nearly" all the PCMs under construction have the fundamental properties of the universal logical computing machines: "[G]iven any job which could have be done on an LCM one can also do it on one of these digital computers" *(Ibid);* so we can speak of universal practical computing machines.

- *Unorganized machines*. Machines that are largely random in their constructions are called "unorganized machines": "So far we have been considering machines which are designed for a definite purpose (though the universal machines are in a sense an exception). We might instead consider what happens when we make up a machine in a comparatively unsystematic way from some kind of standard components. [...] Machines which are largely random in their construction in this way will be called 'unorganized machines.' This does not pretend to be an accurate term. It is conceivable that the same machine might be regarded by one man as organized and by another as unorganized" (Turing, 1992a, p. 9). They are machines made up from a large number of similar units. Each unit is endowed with two input terminals and has output terminals that can be connected to the input terminals of 0 or more of other units. An example of the so-called unorganized A-type machine with all units connected to a synchronizing unit from which synchronizing pulses are emitted at more or less equal intervals of times is given in Figure 1 (the times when the pulses arrive are called moments and each unit is capable of having two states at each moment). The so-called A-type unorganized machines are considered very interesting because they are the simplest model of a nervous system with a *random arrangement of neurons* (cf. the following section "Brains as Unorganized Machines").

- *Paper machines*. "It is possible to produce the effect of a computing machine by writing down a set of rules of procedure and asking a man to carry them out. [...]

Figure 1. (In Turing, 1969)

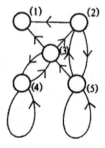

A man provided with paper, pencil and rubber, and subject to strict discipline, is in effect a universal machine" (Turing, 1992a, p. 9). Turing calls this kind of machine "Paper Machine."

Continuous, Discrete, and Active Machines

The machines described above are all *discrete* machines because it is possible to describe their possible states as a discrete set, with the motion of the machines occurring by jumping from one state to another. Turing remarks that all machinery can be regarded as continuous (where the states form a continuous manifold and the behavior of the machine is described by a curve on this manifold) but "when it is possible to regard it as discrete it is usually best to do so. Moreover machinery is called "controlling" if it only deals with information, and "active" if it aims at producing some definite physical effect. A bulldozer will be a continuous and active machine, a telephone continuous and controlling. But also brains can be considered machines and they are — Turing says "probably" — continuous and controlling but "very similar to much discrete machinery" (Turing, 1992a, p. 5). To Turing:

Brains very nearly fall into this class [discrete controlling machinery — when it is natural to describe its possible states as a discrete set] and there seems every reason to believe that they could have been made to fall genuinely into it without any change in their essential properties. However, the property of being "discrete" is only an advantage for the theoretical investigator, and serves no evolutionary purpose, so we could not expect Nature to assist us by producing truly "discrete brains". (p. 6)

Brains can be treated as machines but they can also be considered discrete machines. The epistemological reason is clear: This is just an advantage for the "theoretical investigator" that aims at knowing what are intelligent machines, but certainly it would not be an evolutionary advantage. "Real" human brains are of course continuous systems, only "theoretically" they can be treated as discrete.

Following Turing's perspective, we have derived two new achievements about machines and intelligence: Brains can be considered machines and the simplest nervous systems with a random arrangement of neurons can be considered unorganized machines, in both cases with the property of being "discrete."

Mimicking Human Education

Turing (1992a) also says:

The types of machine that we have considered so far are mainly ones that are allowed to continue in their own way for indefinite periods without interference from outside. The universal machines were an exception to this, in that from time to time one might change the description of the machine which is being imitated. We shall now consider machines in which such interference is the rule rather than the exception (p. 11).

Screwdriver interference is when parts of the machine are removed and replaced with others, giving rise to completely new machines. *Paper* interference is when mere communication of information to the machine modifies its behavior. It is clear that in the case of the universal machine, paper interference can be as useful as screwdriver interference: We are interested in this kind of interference. We can say that each time an interference occurs, the machine is probably changed. It has to be noted that paper interference provides information that is both external and material (further consideration on the status of this information is given later in the chapter).

Turing thought that the fact that human beings have already made machinery able to imitate any small part of a man was positive in order to believe in the possibility of building thinking machinery: Trivial examples are the microphone for the ear, and the television camera for the eye. What about the nervous system? We can copy the behavior of nerves with suitable electrical models and the electrical circuits which are used in electronic computing machinery seem to have essential properties of nerves because they are able to transmit information and to store it.

Education in human beings can model "education of machinery." "Mimicking education, we should hope to modify the machine until it could be relied on to produce definite reactions to certain commands" (Turing, 1992a, p. 14). A graduate has had interactions with other human beings for twenty years or more and at the end of this period "a large number of standard routines will have been superimposed on the original pattern of his brain" (p. 14).

Turing maintains that:

1. in human beings the interaction is mainly with other men and the receiving of visual and other stimuli constitutes the main forms of interference;

2. it is only when a man is "concentrating" that he approximates a machine without interference; and

3. even when a man is concentrating, his behavior is mainly conditioned by previous interference.

Brains as Unorganized Machines

The Infant Cortex as an Unorganized Machine

In many unorganized machines, when a configuration[4] is reached and possible interference suitably constrained, the machine behaves as one organized (and even universal) machine for a definite purpose. Turing provides the example of a B-type unorganized machine with sufficient units where we can find particular initial conditions able to make it a universal machine also endowed with a given storage capacity. The set up of these initial conditions is called "organizing the machine," that indeed is seen as a kind of "modification" of a preexisting unorganized machine through external interference.

The infant brain can be considered an unorganized machine. Given the analogy previously established (see the earlier section, "Logical, Practical, Unorganized, and Paper Machines), what are the events that modify it into an organized universal brain/machine? "The cortex of an infant is an unorganized machinery, which can be organized by suitable interference training. The organization might result in the modification of the machine into a universal machine or something like it. [...] This picture of the cortex as an unorganized machinery is very satisfactory from the point of view of evolution and genetics" (p. 16). The presence of human cortex is not meaningful in itself: "[...] the possession of a human cortex (say) would be virtually useless if no attempt was made to organize it. Thus if a wolf by a mutation acquired a human cortex there is little reason to believe that he would have any selective advantage" (*Ibid.*). Indeed, the exploitation of a big cortex (that is its possible organization) requires a suitable environment: "If however the mutation occurred in a milieu where speech had developed (parrot-like wolves), and if the mutation by chance had well permeated a small community, then some selective advantage might be felt. It would then be possible to pass information on from generation to generation" (*Ibid.*).

Hence, organizing human brains into universal machines strongly relates to the presence of:

1. *speech* (even if only at the level of rudimentary but meaningful parrot-like wolves); and

2. a *social setting* where some "techniques" are learnt ("the isolated man does not develop any intellectual power. It is necessary for him to be immersed in an environment of other men, whose techniques he absorbs during the first twenty years of his life. He may then perhaps do a little research of his own and make a very few discoveries which are passed on to other men. From this point of view the search for new techniques must be regarded as carried out by human community as a whole, rather than by individuals" (p. 23).

This means that a big cortex can provide an evolutionary advantage only in the presence of that massive storage of meaningful information and knowledge on external supports that only an already developed small community can possess. Turing himself considered this picture rather speculative but evidence from paleoanthropology can support it, as I will describe in the following section.

Moreover, the training of a human child depends on a system of rewards and punishments that suggests that organization can occur only through two inputs. The example of an unorganized P-type machine that can be regarded as a LCM without a tape, and largely incompletely described, is given. Through suitable stimuli of pleasure and pain (and the provision of an external memory), the P-type machine can become a universal machine (p. 20).

When the infant brain is transformed into an intelligent one, both discipline and initiative are acquired: "to convert a brain or machine into a universal machine is the extremest form of discipline. [...] But discipline is certainly not enough in itself to produce intelligence. That which is required in addition we call initiative. [...] Our task is to discover the nature of this residue as it occurs in man, and try and copy it in machines" (p. 21).

Examples of problems requiring initiative are the following: "Find a number n such that..." and "See if you can find a way of calculating the function which will enable us to obtain the values for arguments...." The problem is equivalent to that of finding a program to put on the machine in question.

We have seen how a brain can be "organized," but how can that brain be creative enough to account for the emergence of interesting meaning processes?

From the Prehistoric Brains to the Universal Machines

I have said that a big cortex can provide an evolutionary advantage only in presence of a massive storage of meaningful information and knowledge on external supports that only an already developed small community of human beings can possess. Evidence from paleoanthropology seems to support this perspective. Some research in cognitive paleoanthropology teaches us that high level and reflective consciousness in terms of thoughts about our own thoughts and feelings (that is consciousness not merely considered as raw sensation) is intertwined with the development of *modern language* (speech) and *material culture*. About 250,000 years ago, several hominid species had brains as large as ours today, but their behavior lacked any sign of art or symbolic behavior. If we consider high-level consciousness as related to a high-level organization — in Turing's sense — of human cortex, its origins can be related to the active role of environmental, social, linguistic and cultural aspects.

Handaxes were made by early humans and firstly appeared 1.4 million years ago and were still made by some of the Neanderthals in Europe just 50,000 years ago. The making of handaxes is strictly intertwined with the development of consciousness. Many needed conscious capabilities constitute a part of an evolved psychology that appeared long

Figure 2. Human psychology and making handaxes (In Mithen, 1999)

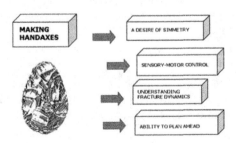

before the first handaxes were manufactured. It seems humans were pre-adapted for some components required to make handaxes (Mithen, 1996, 1999) (Figure 2).

1. Imposition of *symmetry* (already evolved through predators' escape and social interaction). Symmetry has been an unintentional byproduct of the bifacial knapping technique but also deliberately imposed in other cases. It is also well-known that the attention to symmetry may have developed through social interaction and predator escape, as it may allow one to recognize that one is being directly stared at (Dennett, 1991). It also seems that "Hominid handaxe makers may have been keying into this attraction to symmetry when producing tools to attract the attention of other hominids, especially those of the opposite sex" (Mithen, 1999, p. 287).

2. Understanding *fracture dynamics* (for example, evident from Oldowan tools and from nut cracking by chimpanzees today).

3. Ability to *plan* ahead (modifying plans and reacting to contingencies, such as unexpected flaws in the material and miss-hits), still evident in the minds of Oldowan tool makers and in chimpanzees.

4. High degree of *sensory-motor control*: "Nodules, pre-forms, and near finished artefacts must be struck at precisely the right angle with precisely the right degree of force if the desired flake is to be detached" (Mithen, 1999, 285).

The origin of this capability is usually tracked back to encephalization – the increased number of nerve tracts and of the integration between them allowing for the firing of smaller muscle groups — and bipedalism, that requires a more complexly integrated and highly fractionated nervous system, which in turn presupposes a larger brain.

The combination of these four resources produced the birth of what Mithen calls *technical intelligence* of the early human mind, consequently related to the construction of handaxes. Indeed, the resources indicate high intelligence and good health. They cannot be compared to the artefacts made by animals, like honeycomb or spider web, deriving from the iteration of fixed actions which do not require consciousness and intelligence.

Private Speech and Fleeting Consciousness

Two central factors play a fundamental role in the combination of the four resources above:

*   The exploitation of *private speech* (speaking to oneself) to trail between planning, fracture dynamic, motor control and symmetry (also in children there is a kind of private muttering which makes explicit what is implicit in the various abilities); and

*   A good degree of *fleeting consciousness* (thoughts about thoughts).

In the meantime, these two aspects played a fundamental role in the development of consciousness and thought:

So my argument is that when our ancestors made handaxes there were private mutterings accompanying the crack of stone against stone. Those private mutterings were instrumental in pulling the knowledge required for handaxe manufacture into an emergent consciousness. But what type of consciousness? I think probably one that was a fleeting one: one that existed during the act of manufacture and that did not the [endeavor]endure. One quite unlike the consciousness about one's emotions, feelings, and desires that were associated with the social world and that probably were part of a completely separated cognitive domain, that of social intelligence, in the early human mind (Mithen, 1998, p. 288).

This use of private speech can be certainly considered a "tool" for organizing brains and so for manipulating, expanding and exploring minds, a tool that probably evolved with another: talking to each other.[5] Both private and public language act as tools for thought and play a fundamental role in the evolution of "opening up our minds to ourselves" and so in the emergence of new meaning processes.

Material Culture

Another tool appeared in the latter stages of human evolution that played a great role in the evolutions of primitive minds, and that is in the organization of human brains. Handaxes also are at the birth of *material culture*, and so, as new cognitive chances, can co-evolve:

- The mind of some early humans, like the Neanderthals, was constituted by relatively isolated cognitive domains that Mithen calls *different intelligences*, probably endowed with different degrees of consciousness about the thoughts and knowledge within each domain (natural history intelligence, technical intelligence and social intelligence). These isolated cognitive domains became integrated also, taking advantage of the role of public language.

- *Degrees of high level consciousness* appear, human beings need thoughts about thoughts.

- *Social intelligence* and *public language* arise.

According to Mithen (1998), it is extremely important to stress that *material culture* is not just the product of this massive cognitive chance but also cause of it. "The clever trick that humans learnt was to *disembody* their minds into the material world around them: a linguistic utterance might be considered as a disembodied thought. But such utterances last just for a few seconds. Material culture endures" (p. 291).

In this perspective we acknowledge that material artefacts are tools for thoughts as is language: tools for exploring, expanding and manipulating our own minds. In this regard the evolution of culture is inextricably linked with the evolution of consciousness and thought.

Early human brains become a kind of universal "intelligent" machine, extremely flexible so that we no longer need different "separated" intelligent machines doing different jobs. A single one will suffice. As the engineering problem of producing various machines for various jobs is replaced by the office work of "programming" the universal machine to do these jobs, so the different intelligences become integrated in a new universal device endowed with a high-level type of consciousness.[6]

From this perspective the expansion of the minds is, in the meantime, a continuous process of *disembodiment* of the minds themselves into the *material world* around them. In this regard, the evolution of the mind is inextricably linked with the evolution of large, integrated and material cognitive systems. In the following sections I will illustrate this extraordinary interplay between human brains and the cognitive systems they make.

Disembodiment of Mind

A wonderful example of meaning creation through disembodiment of mind is the carving of what most likely is the mythical being from the last ice age, 30,000 years ago, of a half human/half lion figure carved from mammoth ivory found at Hohlenstein Stadel, Germany.

An evolved mind is unlikely to have a *natural home* for this being, as such entities do not exist in the natural world. Whereas evolved minds could think about humans by exploiting modules shaped by natural selection, and about lions by deploying content rich mental modules moulded by natural selection and about other lions by using other content-rich modules from the natural history cognitive domain, how could one think about entities that were part human and part animal? According to Mithen (1999), such entities had no home in the mind (p. 291).

A mind consisting of different separated intelligences cannot come up with such an entity (Figure 3). The only way is *to extend* the mind into the *material word*, exploiting

Figure 3. Modern human and early human minds (In Mithen, 1999)

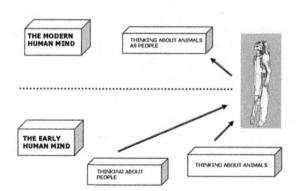

rocks, blackboards, paper or ivory and writing, painting and carving: "artefacts such as this figure play the role of anchors for ideas and have no *natural home* within the mind; for ideas that take us beyond those that natural selection could enable us to possess" (p. 291).

In the case of our figure, we are faced with an anthropomorphic thinking created by the material representation serving to anchor the cognitive representation of a supernatural being. In this case, the material culture disembodies thoughts that otherwise will soon disappear, without being transmitted to other human beings. The early human mind possessed two separated intelligences for thinking about animals and people. Through the mediation of the material culture, the modern human mind can arrive at a stage where it *internally* thinks about the new concept of animal and person at the same time. But the new meaning occurred in the external material world where the mind picked up it.

Artefacts as *external objects* allowed humans to loosen and cut those chains on our unorganized brains imposed by our evolutionary past, chains that always limited the brains of other human beings, such as the Neanderthals. Loosing chains and securing ideas to external objects was also a way to creatively reorganize brains as universal machines for thinking.

Mimetic and Creative Representations

External and Internal Representations

We have said that through the mediation of the material culture the modern human mind can arrive at a place *internally* to think the new meaning of animals and people in the same time. We can account for this process of disembodiment from an impressive cognitive point of view.

I maintain that representations are external and internal. We can say that:

- *External representations* are formed by external materials that express (through reification) concepts and problems that do not have a *natural home* in the brain.
- *Internalized representations* are internal re-projections, a kind of recapitulation (learning) of external representations in terms of neural patterns of activation in the brain. They can sometimes be "internally" manipulated like external objects and can originate new internally reconstructed representations through the neural activity of *transformation* and *integration*.

This process explains why human beings seem to perform both computations of a *connectionist* type, such as the ones involving representations as:

- (I Level) *patterns of neural activation* that arise as the result of the interaction between body and environment (and suitably shaped by the evolution and the individual history): pattern completion or image recognition, and computations that use representations as,

- (II Level) *derived combinatorial syntax and semantics* dynamically shaped by the various external representations and reasoning devices found or constructed in the environment (for example, geometrical diagrams); they are neurologically represented contingently as pattern of neural activations that "sometimes" tend to become stabilized structures and to fix, and so *to permanently belong to,* the I Level above.

The I Level originates those *sensations* (they constitute a kind of "face" we think the world has), that provide room for the II Level to reflect the structure of the environment, and, most important, that can follow the computations suggested by these external structures. It is clear we can now conclude that the growth of the brain, and especially synaptic and dendritic growth, are profoundly determined by the environment.

When the fixation is reached, the patterns of neural activation no longer need a direct stimulus from the environment for their construction. In a certain sense they can be viewed as *fixed internal records* of *external structures* that *can exist* also in the absence of such external structures. These patterns of neural activation that constitute the I Level Representations always keep record of the experience that generated them, and, thus always carry the II Level Representation associated to them, even if in a different form, the form of *memory* and not the form of a vivid sensorial experience. Now the human agent, via neural mechanisms, can retrieve these II Level Representations and use them as *internal* representations or use parts of them to construct new internal representations very different from the ones stored in memory (cf. also Gatti & Magnani, 2005).

Human beings delegate cognitive features to external representations because in many problem-solving situations, the internal computation would be impossible or it would involve a very great effort because of the human mind's limited capacity. First, a kind of alienation is performed, second, a recapitulation is accomplished at the neuronal level by re-representing internally that which was "discovered" outside. Consequently, only later on do we perform cognitive operations on the structure of data that synaptic patterns have "picked up" in an analogical way from the environment. We can maintain that internal representations used in cognitive processes, like many events of *meaning creation,* have a deep origin in the experience lived in the environment.

I think there are two kinds of artefacts that play the role of *external objects* (representations) active in this process of disembodiment of the mind: *creative* and *mimetic.* Mimetic external representations mirror concepts and problems that are already represented in the brain and need to be enhanced, solved, further complicated, etc. so they sometimes can creatively give rise to new concepts and meanings.

Following my perspective, it is at this point evident that the "mind" transcends the boundary of the individual and includes parts of that individual's environment.

Constructing Meaning through Mimetic and Creative External Objects

Model-Based Abduction

What exactly is model-based abduction from a philosophical point of view? Peirce stated that all thinking is in signs, and signs can be icons, indices or symbols. Moreover, all *inference* is a form of sign activity, where the word sign includes "feeling, image, conception, and other representation" (*CP*, 5.283), and, in Kantian words, all synthetic forms of cognition. That is, a considerable part of the creative meaning processes is *model-based*. Moreover, a considerable part of meaningful behaviour (not only in science) occurs in the middle of a relationship between brains and external objects and tools that have received cognitive and/or epistemological delegations (cf. the following subsection).

Of course model-based reasoning acquires its peculiar creative relevance when embedded in abductive processes. Let me show some examples of model-based inferences. It is well known the importance Peirce ascribed to diagrammatic thinking, as shown by his discovery of the powerful system of predicate logic based on diagrams or "existential graphs." As we have already stressed, Peirce considers inferential any cognitive activity whatever, not only conscious abstract thought; he also includes perceptual knowledge and subconscious cognitive activity in this category. For instance, in subconscious mental activities, visual representations play an immediate role.

We should remember, as Peirce noted, that abduction plays a role even in relatively simple visual phenomena. *Visual abduction*, a special form of nonverbal abduction, occurs when hypotheses are instantly derived from a stored series of previous similar experiences. It covers a mental procedure that tapers into a non-inferential one, and falls into the category called "perception." Philosophically, *perception* is viewed by Peirce as a fast and uncontrolled knowledge-production procedure. Perception, in fact, is a vehicle for the instantaneous retrieval of knowledge that was previously structured in our mind through inferential processes. Peirce says: "Abductive inference shades into perceptual judgment without any sharp line of demarcation between them" (Peirce 1955, 304). By perception, knowledge constructions are so instantly reorganized that they become habitual and diffuse and do not need any further testing: "[...] a fully accepted, simple, and interesting inference tends to obliterate all recognition of the uninteresting and complex premises from which it was derived" (*CP* 7.37). Many visual stimuli — that can be considered the "premises" of the involved abduction — are ambiguous, yet people are adept at imposing order on them: "We readily form such hypotheses as that an obscurely seen face belongs to a friend of ours, because we can thereby explain what has been observed" (Thagard, 1988, 53). This kind of image-based hypothesis formation can be considered as a form of *visual* (or *iconic*) *abduction*. Of course, such subconscious visual abductions of everyday cognitive behavior are not of particular importance but we know that in science they may be very significant and lead to interesting new discoveries (Shelley, 1996). If perceptions are abductions, they are withdrawable, just like the scientific hypotheses abductively found. They are "hypotheses" about data we can accept (sometimes this happens spontaneously) or carefully evaluate.

Peirce gives an interesting example of model-based abduction (Magnani, 2001a) related to sense activity: "A man can distinguish different textures of cloth by feeling: but not immediately, for he requires to move fingers over the cloth, which shows that he is obliged to compare sensations of one instant with those of another" (*CP*, 5.221); this idea surely suggests that abductive movements also have interesting *extra-theoretical* characteristics and that there is a role in abductive reasoning for various kinds of manipulations of external objects (cf. the following section on "action-based, manipulative abduction"). One more example is given by the fact that the perception of tone arises from the activity of the mind only after having noted the rapidity of the vibrations of the sound waves, but the possibility of individuating a tone happens only after having heard several of the sound impulses and after having judged their frequency. Consequently, the sensation of pitch is made possible by previous experiences and cognitions stored in memory, so that one oscillation of the air would not produce a tone.

To conclude, all knowing is *inferring* and inferring is not instantaneous, it happens in a process that needs an activity of comparisons involving many kinds of models in a more or less considerable lapse of time. All sensations or perceptions participate in the nature of a unifying hypothesis, that is, in abduction, in the case of emotions too: "Thus the various sounds made by the instruments of the orchestra strike upon the ear, and the result is a peculiar musical emotion, quite distinct from the sounds themselves. This emotion is essentially the same thing as a hypothetic inference, and every hypothetic inference involved the formation of such an emotion" (*CP*, 2.643).

What happens when the abductive reasoning in science is strongly related to extra-theoretical actions and manipulations of "external" objects? When abduction is "action-based" on *external models*? When thinking is "through doing" as illustrated in the simple case above of distinguishing the simple textures of cloth by feeling? To answer these questions I will delineate the features of what I call *manipulative abduction* by showing how we can find in scientific and everyday reasoning methods of constructivity based on external models and actions.

Constructing Meaning through Manipulative Abduction

We can cognitively account for the process of disembodiment of mind we have seen in the perspective of paleoanthropology taking advantage of the concept pf *manipulative* abduction. It happens when we are thinking *through* doing and not only, in a pragmatic sense, about doing. For instance, when we are creating geometry, constructing and manipulating a triangle and are looking for new meaningful features of it, as in the case given by Kant in the "Transcendental Doctrine of Method" (cf. Magnani, 2001b; cf. also the following subsection). It refers to an extra-theoretical behavior that aims at creating communicable accounts of new experiences to integrate them into previously existing systems of experimental and linguistic (semantic) practices.

Gooding (1990) refers to this kind of concrete manipulative reasoning when he illustrates the role in science of the so-called "construals" that embody tacit inferences in procedures that are often apparatus- and machine based. The embodiment is, of course, an expert manipulation of meaningful objects in a highly constrained experimental environment, and is directed by abductive movements that imply the strategic application of old and new *templates* of behavior mainly connected with extra-rational components, for instance emotional, esthetical, ethical and economic.

The hypothetical character of construals is clear: They can be developed to examine or discard further chances, they are provisional creative organization of experience and some of them become in their turn hypothetical *interpretations* of experience, that is, more theory-oriented, their reference/meaning is gradually stabilized in terms of established observational practices. Step-by-step the new interpretation — that at the beginning is completely "practice-laden" — relates to more "theoretical" modes of understanding (narrative, visual, diagrammatic, symbolic, conceptual and simulative), closer to the constructive effects of theoretical abduction. When the reference/meaning is stabilized, the effects of incommensurability with other established observations can become evident. But it is just the construal of certain phenomena that can be shared by the sustainers of rival theories. Gooding (1990) shows how Davy and Faraday could see the same attractive and repulsive actions at work in the phenomena they respectively produced; their discourse and practice as to the role of their construals of phenomena clearly demonstrate they did not inhabit different, incommensurable worlds in some cases. Moreover, the experience is constructed, reconstructed and distributed across a social network of negotiations among the different scientists by means of construals.

It is difficult to establish a list of invariant behaviors that are able to describe manipulative abduction in science. As illustrated above, certainly the expert manipulation of objects in a highly constrained experimental environment implies the application of old and new *templates* of behavior that exhibit some regularities. The activity of building construals is highly conjectural and not immediately explanatory: These templates are hypotheses of behavior (creative or already cognitively present in the scientist's mind-body system, and sometimes already applied) that abductively enable a kind of epistemic "doing." Hence, some templates of action and manipulation can be *selected* in the set of the ones available and pre-stored, others have to be *created* for the first time to perform the most interesting creative cognitive accomplishments of manipulative abduction.

Moreover, I think that a better understanding of manipulative abduction at the level of scientific experiment could improve our knowledge of induction, and its distinction from abduction: Manipulative abduction could be considered as a kind of basis for further meaningful inductive generalizations. Different generated construals can give rise to different inductive generalizations.

Some common features of these tacit templates that enable us to manipulate things and experiments in science to favour meaning formation are related to:

1. Sensibility towards the aspects of the phenomenon which can be regarded as *curious* or *anomalous*; manipulations have to be able to introduce potential inconsistencies in the received knowledge (Oersted's report of his well-known experiment about electromagnetism is devoted to describing some anomalous aspects that did not depend on any particular theory of the nature of electricity and magnetism; Ampère's construal of experiment on electromagnetism — exploiting an artifactual apparatus to produce a static equilibrium of a suspended helix that clearly shows the role of the "unexpected").

2.   Preliminary sensibility towards the *dynamical* character of the phenomenon, and not to entities and their properties, the common aim of manipulations is to practically reorder the dynamic sequence of events in a static spatial one that should promote a subsequent bird's-eye view (narrative or visual-diagrammatic).

3.   Referral to experimental manipulations that exploit *artificial apparatus* to free, new and possibly stable and repeatable sources of information about hidden knowledge and constraints (Davy's well-known set-up in terms of an artifactual tower of needles showed that magnetization was related to orientation and does not require physical contact). Of course this information is not artificially made by us: The fact that phenomena are made and manipulated does not render them to be idealistically and subjectively determined.

4.   Various contingent ways of epistemic acting: *looking* from different perspectives, *checking* the different information available, *comparing* subsequent events, *choosing*, *discarding*, *imaging* further manipulations, *re-ordering* and *changing relationships* in the world by implicitly *evaluating* the usefulness of a new order (for instance, to help memory).

From the general point of view of everyday situations, manipulative abductive reasoning exhibits other very interesting templates:

5.   Action elaborates a *simplification* of the reasoning task and a redistribution of effort across time when we "need to manipulate concrete things in order to understand structures which are otherwise too abstract" (Piaget 1974), or when we are in the presence of *redundant* and unmanageable information.

6.   Action can be useful in the presence of *incomplete* or *inconsistent* information — not only from the "perceptual" point of view — or of a diminished capacity to act upon the world: It is used to get more data to restore coherence and to improve deficient knowledge.

7.   Action as a *control of sense data* illustrates how we can change the position of our body (and/or of the external objects) and how to exploit various kinds of prostheses (Galileo's telescope, technological instruments and interfaces) to get various new kinds of stimulation: Action provides some tactile and visual information (e. g., in surgery), otherwise unavailable; 8. action enables us to build *external artifactual models* of task mechanisms instead of the corresponding internal ones, that are adequate to adapt the environment to the agent's needs: Experimental manipulations exploit *artificial apparatus* to free new possible stable and repeatable sources of information about hidden knowledge and constraints.[7]

The whole activity of manipulation is devoted to building various external *epistemic mediators*[8] that function as an enormous new source of information and knowledge. Therefore, manipulative abduction represents a kind of redistribution of the epistemic and cognitive effort to manage objects and information that cannot be immediately represented or found internally (for example, exploiting the resources of visual imagery).[9]

If we see scientific discovery like a kind of opportunistic ability of integrating information from many kinds of simultaneous constraints to produce explanatory hypotheses that account for them all, then manipulative abduction will play the role of eliciting possible hidden constraints by building external suitable experimental structures.

Manipulating Meanings

If the structures of the environment play such an important role in shaping our representations and, hence, our cognitive processes, we can expect that physical manipulations of the environment receive a cognitive relevance.

Several authors have pointed out the role that physical actions can have at a cognitive level. In this sense, Kirsh and Maglio (1994) distinguish actions into two categories, namely *pragmatic actions* and *epistemic actions*. Pragmatic actions are the actions that an agent performs in the environment in order to bring itself physically closer to a goal. In this case, the action modifies the environment so that the latter acquires a configuration that helps the agent to reach a goal which is understood as physical, that is, as a desired state of affairs. Epistemic actions are the actions that an agent performs in the environment in order to discharge the mind of a cognitive load or to extract information that is hidden or that would be very hard to obtain only by internal computation.

In this section I want to focus specifically on the relationship that can exist between manipulations of the environment and representations. In particular, I want to examine whether external manipulations can be considered as a means to construct external representations.

If a manipulative action performed upon the environment is devoted to create a configuration of elements that carries relevant information, that action will well be able to be considered as a cognitive process and the configuration of elements it creates will well be able to be considered an external representation. In this case, we can really speak of an embodied cognitive process in which an action constructs an external representation by means of manipulation. We define *cognitive manipulating* as any manipulation of the environment devoted to construct external configurations that can count as representations.

An example of cognitive manipulating is the diagrammatic demonstration illustrated in Figure 4, taken from the field of geometry. In this case, a simple manipulation of the

Figure 4. Diagrammatic demonstration that the sum of the internal angles of any triangle is 180°: (a) Triangle, (b) diagrammatic manipulations

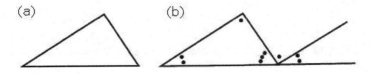

triangle in Figure 4 (a) gives rise to an external configuration — Figure 4 (b) — that carries relevant information about the internal angles of a triangle.

The entire process through which an agent arrives at a physical action that can count as cognitive manipulating can be understood by means of the concept of manipulative abduction (Magnani, 2001a). Manipulative abduction is a specific case of cognitive manipulating in which an agent, when faced with an external situation from which it is hard or impossible to extract new meaningful features of an object, selects or creates an action that structures the environment in such a way that it gives information which would be otherwise unavailable and which is used specifically to infer explanatory hypotheses.

Mimetic Minds

It is well-known that there are external representations that are representations of other external representations. In some cases they carry new scientific knowledge. To take an example, Hilbert's *Grundlagen der Geometrie* is a "formal" representation of geometrical problem-solving through diagrams: In Hilbertian systems, solutions of problems become proofs of theorems in terms of an axiomatic model. In turn, a calculator is able to re-represent (through an artifact, and to perform) those geometrical proofs with diagrams already performed by human beings with pencil and paper. In this case we have representations that *mimic* particular cognitive performances that we usually attribute to our *minds*.

We have seen that our brains delegate cognitive (and epistemic) roles to externalities and then tend to "adopt" and recapitulate what they have checked occurring outside, over there, after having manipulated — often with creative results — the external invented structured model. A simple example: It is relatively neurologically easy to perform an addition of numbers by depicting in our *mind* thanks to that brain device that is called a visual buffer — the images of that addition *thought* as it occurs concretely, with paper and pencil, taking advantage of external materials. We have said that mind representations are also over there, in the environment, where mind has objectified itself in various structures that *mimic* and *enhance* its internal representations.

Turing adds a new structure to this list of external objectified devices. an abstract tool (LCM) endowed with powerful mimetic properties. We have concluded Section 9 remarking that the creative "mind" is in itself extended and, so to say, both internal and external: The mind transcends the boundary of the individual and includes parts of that individual's environment. Turing's LCM, which is an externalized device, is able to mimic human cognitive operations that occur in that interplay between the internal mind and the external one. Indeed, Turing already in 1950 maintains that, taking advantage of the existence of the LCM, "Digital computers [...] can be constructed, and indeed have been constructed, and [...] they can in fact mimic the actions of a human computer very closely"(Turing, 1950).

In the light of my perspective, both (universal) logical computing machine (LCM) (the theoretical artifact) and (universal) practical computing machine (PCM) (the practical artifact) are *mimetic minds* because they are able to mimic the mind in a kind of universal way (wonderfully continuing the activity of disembodiment of minds our ancestors rudimentary started). LCM and PCM are able to re-represent and perform in a very powerful way plenty of human cognitive skills.

Universal turing machines are discrete-state machines, DMS, "with a Laplacian behavior" (Longo, 2002; Lassègue, 1998, 2002): "it is always possible to predict all future states") and they are equivalent to all formalisms for computability (what is thinkable is calculable and mechanizable), and because universal they are able to simulate — that is to *mimic* — any human cognitive function, what is usually called mind.

Universal turing machines are just a further extremely fruitful step of the *disembodiment* of the mind I have described above. A natural consequence of this perspective is that they do not represent (against classical AI and modern cognitivist computationalism) a "knowledge" of the mind and of human intelligence. Turing is perfectly aware of the fact that the brain is not a DSM, but as he says, a "continuous" system, where instead a mathematical modeling can guarantee a satisfactory scientific intelligibility (cf. his studies on morphogenesis).

We have seen that our brains delegate meaningful cognitive (and epistemic) roles to externalities and then tend to "adopt" what they have checked occurring outside, over there, in the external invented structured model. And a large part of meaning formation takes advantage of the exploitation of external representations and mediators.

Our view about the disembodiment of mind certainly involves that the mind/body dualist perspective is less credible as well as Cartesian computationalism. Also the view that mind is computational independently of the physical (functionalism) is jeopardized. In my perspective on human cognition in terms of mimetic minds, we no longer need Descartes dualism: We only have brains that make up large, integrated, material cognitive systems like, for example, LCMs and PCMs. The only problem seems, "How meat knows": We can reverse the Cartesian motto and say "sum ergo cogito." In this perspective, what we usually call mind simply consists in the union of both the changing neural configurations of brains together with those large, integrated, and material cognitive systems the brains themselves are continuously building.

Conclusion

The main thesis of this paper is that the disembodiment of mind is a significant cognitive perspective able to unveil some basic features of creative thinking and its computational problems. Its fertility in explaining the interplay between internal and external levels of cognition is evident. I maintain that various aspects of creative meaning formation could take advantage of the research on this interplay: For instance, study on external mediators can provide a better understanding of the processes of explanation and discovery in science and in some areas of artificial intelligence related to mechanizing discovery processes. [10]

From the paleoanthropological perspective we have learnt that an evolved mind is unlikely to have a *natural home* for new concepts and meanings, as such concepts and meanings do not exist in the already known artificial and natural world: The cognitive referral to the central role of the relation between meaningful behaviour and dynamical interactions with the environment becomes critical to the problem of meaning formation. I think that the issue could further suggest research on the role played by language in the perspective of its emergence and evolution. The research in this area is open and even controversial but promises new insightful results especially if we will be able to link the role of *sensorial epistemic actions* and *eliciting epistemic actions* to the emergence of language.

Finally, I think the cognitive role of what I call "mimetic minds" can be further studied by also taking advantage of the research on ipercomputation. The imminent construction of new types of universal "abstract" and "practical" machines will constitute important and interesting new "mimetic minds" externalized and available over there, in the environment, as sources of mechanisms underlying the emergence of new meaning processes. They will provide new tools for creating meaning formation in classical areas like analogical, visual and spatial inferences, both in science and everyday situations, so that this can extend the epistemological and the psychological theory.

The perspectives above, resorting to the exploitation of a very interdisciplinary interplay, will further shed light on how concrete manipulations of external objects influence the generation of hypotheses and so on, the characters of what I call manipulative abduction showing how we can find methods of constructivity — and their computational counterparts — in scientific and everyday reasoning based on external models and "epistemic mediators" (Magnani, 2004).

Some results in specific domains of calculus presented in Magnani and Dossena (2005) were diagrams which play an *optical* role — microscopes and "microscopes within microscopes," telescopes, windows, a *mirror* role (to externalize rough mental models) and an *unveiling* role (to help create new and interesting mathematical concepts, theories and structures) are studied. They play the role of epistemic mediators able to perform the explanatory abductive task of endowing with new "intuitive" meanings difficult mathematical concepts and of providing a better understanding of the calculus through a nonstandard model of analysis. I maintain they can be used in many other different epistemological and cognitive situations. Another interesting application is given in the area of chance discovery (see Magnani, Piazza, & Dossena, 2002): Concrete manipulations of the external world constitute a fundamental passage in chance discovery; by a process of manipulative abduction it is possible to build prostheses that furnish a kind of embodied and unexpressed knowledge that holds a key role not only in the subsequent processes of scientific comprehension and discovery but also in ethical thinking and in moral deliberation. For example, I have viewed moral reasoning as a form of "possible worlds" anticipation, a way of getting chances to shape the human world and act in it (Magnani, 2003). It could be of help to prefigure risks, possibilities and effects of human acting, and to promote or prevent a broad variety of guidelines. Creating ethics means creating the world and its directions when facing different (real or abstract) situations and problems. In this way events and situations can be reinvented either as an opportunity or as a risk for new moral directions. I have also described some "templates" of manipulative behavior which account for the most common cognitive and moral acting related to chance discovery and chance production. I maintain this kind of research could be furthermore specifically addressed to the analysis of the construction of new meaning processes by chance.

References

Agre, P., & Chapman, D. (1990). What are plans for? In P. Maes (Ed.), *Designing autonomous agents* (pp. 17-34). Cambridge, MA: The MIT Press.

Anderson, M.L. (2003). Embodied cognition: A field guide. *Artificial Intelligence 149*(1), 91-130.

Brooks, R., & Stein, L. (1994). Building brains for bodies. *Autonomous Robots, 1*, 7-25.

Buchanan, B.G. (2001). Creativity at the metalevel: AAAI-2000 presidential address. *AI Magazine*, Fall, 13-28.

Carruthers, P. (2002). The cognitive function of language. *Behavioral and Brain Sciences, 25*(6), 657-74.

Clancey, W.J. (2002). Simulating activities: Relating motives, deliberation, and attentive coordination. *Cognitive Systems Research, 3*(1-4), 471-500.

Clark, A. (1998). Magic words. In P. Carruthers & J. Boucher (Eds.), *Language and thought: Interdisciplinary themes* (pp. 162-183). Oxford University Press: Oxford.

Clark, A. (2003). *Natural-born cyborgs: Minds, technologies, and the future of human intelligence*. Oxford: Oxford University Press.

Clark, A. (2005). Material symbols: From translation to co-ordination in the constitution of thought and reason. In B. Bara, L. Barsalou, & M. Bucciarelli (Eds.), *CogSci 2005, XXVII Annual Conference of the Cognitive Science Society*, CD. Stresa, Italy.

Clowes, R. W., & Morse, A. (2005). *Scaffolding cognition with words*. Accepted draft for the 5th International Workshop on Epigenetic Robotics.

Dennett, D. (1991). *Consciousness explained*. New York: Little, Brown, and Company.

Dennett, D. (2003). *Freedom evolves*. New York: Viking.

Donald, M. (1998). Hominid enculturation and cognitive evolution. In C. Renfrew, P. Mellars, & C. Scarre (Eds.), *Cognition and material culture: The archaeology of external symbolic storage* (pp. 7-17). Cambridge: The McDonald Institute for Archaeological Research.

Donald, M. (2001). *A mind so rare. The evolution of human consciousness*. New York: W.W. Norton & Company.

Gatti, A., & Magnani, L. (2005). On the representational role of the environment and on the cognitive nature of manipulations. In L. Magnani (Ed.), *Computing, philosophy, and cognition. Proceedings of the European Conference of Computing and Philosophy*, Pavia, Italy, June 3-4, 2004 (forthcoming).

Gooding, D. (1990). *Experiment and the making of meaning*. Dordrecht: Kluwer.

Hameroff, A.R., Kaszniak, A.W., & Chalmers, D.J. (Eds.). (1999). *Toward a science of consciousness III: The third Tucson discussions and debates*. Cambridge, MA: The MIT Press.

Hendricks, F.V., & Faye, J. (1999). Abducting explanation. In L. Magnani, N.J. Nersessian, & P. Thagard (Eds.) (pp.271-294).

Hutchins, E. (1995). *Cognition in the wild*. Cambridge, MA: The MIT Press.

Hutchins, E. (1999). Cognitive artifacts. In R.A.Wilson & F.C. Keil (Eds.), *Encyclopedia of the cognitive sciences* (pp. 126-7). Cambridge, MA: The MIT Press.

Kant, I. (1929/1998). *Critique of pure reason*. N. Kemp Smith (Trans.). London: MacMillan. Originally published 1787.

Kirsh, D., & Maglio, P. (1994). On distinguishing epistemic from pragmatic action. *Cognitive Science, 18*, 513-549.

Kuhn, T.S. (1962/1970). *The structure of scientific revolutions* (2nd ed.). Chicago: University of Chicago Press.

Lassègue, J. (1998). *Turing*. Paris: Les Belles Lettres.

Lassègue, J. (2002). Turing entre formel et forme; remarque sur la convergence des perspectives morphologiques. *Intellectica, 35*(2), 185-198.

Longo, G. (2002). Laplace, Turing, et la géométrie impossible du "jeu de l'imitation": aléas, determinisme e programmes dans le test de Turing. *Intellectica, 35*(2), 131-161.

Magnani, L. (1992). Abductive reasoning: Philosophical and educational perspectives in medicine. In D.A. Evans & V.L. Patel (Eds.), *Advanced models of cognition for medical training and practice* (pp. 21-41). Berlin: Springer.

Magnani, L. (2001a). *Abduction, reason, and science: Processes of discovery and explanation*. New York: Kluwer Academic/Plenum Publishers.

Magnani, L. (2001b). *Philosophy and geometry: Theoretical and historical issues*. Dordrecht: Kluwer Academic.

Magnani, L. (2002). Epistemic mediators and model-based discovery in science. In L. Magnani & N.J. Nersessian (Eds.) (pp. 325-329). New York: Kluwer Academic/Plenum Publishers.

Magnani, L. (2003). Moral mediators: Prefiguring ethical chances in a human world. In H. Shoji & Y. Matsuo (Eds.), *Proceedings of the 3rd International Workshop on Chance Discovery*, HCI International Conference, Greece (pp. 1-20).

Magnani, L. (2004). Conjectures and manipulations: Computational modeling and the extra-theoretical dimension of scientific discovery. *Minds and Machines, 14*, 507-537.

Magnani, L. (2005). *Knowledge as a duty: Distributed morality in a technological world* (forthcoming).

Magnani, L. & Dossena, R. (2003). Perceiving the infinite and the infinitesimal world: Unveiling and optical diagrams and the construction of mathematical concepts. In *Proceedings of CogSci2003*. Boston: CD-ROM produced by X-CD Technologies.

Magnani, L., Nersessian, N.J., & Pizzi, C. (2002). *Logical and computational aspects of model-based reasoning*. Dordrecht: Kluwer Academic.

Magnani, L., Nersessian, N.J., & Thagard, P. (Eds.). (1999). *Model-based reasoning in scientific discovery*. New York: Kluwer Academic/Plenum Publishers.

Magnani, L., Piazza, M., & Dossena, R. (2002). Epistemic mediators and chance morphodynamics. In A. Abe (Ed.), *Proceedings of PRICAI-02 Conference, Working Notes of the 2nd International Workshop on Chance Discovery* (pp. 38-46). Tokyo.

Mithen, S. (1996). *The prehistory of the mind: A search for the origins of art, religion, and science*. London: Thames and Hudson.

Mithen, S. (1999). Handaxes and ice age carvings: Hard evidence for the evolution of consciousness. In Hameroff et al. (Eds.) (pp. 281-296).

Norman, D.A. (1993). *Things that make us smart: Defending human attributes in the age of the machine*. Reading. MA: Addison-Wesley.

Peirce, C.S. (1931-1958). *Collected Papers*, 8 vols. C. Hartshorne & P. Weiss (Eds.) (Vols. I-VI) & A.W. Burks (Ed.) (Vols. VII-VIII). Cambridge, MA: Harvard University Press.

Peirce, C.S. (1955). Abduction and induction. In C.S. Peirce, *Philosophical writings of Peirce* (pp. 150-156) & J. Buchler (Ed.). New York: Dover.

Peirce, C.S. (1986). *Writings of Charles Sanders Peirce: A chronological edition* (vol. 3, pp. 1872-1878). Bloomington: Indiana University Press.

Piaget, J. (1974). *Adaptation and intelligence*. Chicago: University of Chicago Press.

Polanyi, M. (1966). *The tacit dimension*. London: Routledge and Kegan Paul.

Popper, K.R. (1959). *The logic of scientific discovery*. London; New Nork: Hutchinson.

Reichenbach, H. (1938). *Experience and prediction*. Chicago: University of Chicago Press.

Shelley, C. (1996). Visual abductive reasoning in archaeology. *Philosophy of Science, 63*(2), 278-301.

Thagard, P. (1988). *Computational philosophy of science*. Cambridge, MA: The MIT Press.

Thagard, P. (1992). *Conceptual revolutions*. Princeton: Princeton University Press.

Turing, A.M. (1937). On computable numbers with an application to the Entscheidungsproblem. *Proceedings of the London Mathematical Society, 42*, 230-265.

Turing, A.M. (1948/1969). Intelligent machinery. In B. Meltzer, & D. Michie (Eds.), *Machine Intelligence 5*, 3-23. Also in A.M. Turing (1992a) (pp. 3-23).

Turing, A.M. (1950). Computing machinery and intelligence. *Mind, 49*, 433-460. Also in A.M. Turing (1992a) (pp. 133-160).

Turing, A.M. (1992a). *Collected works of Alan Turing, mechanical intelligence.* DC Inc (Ed.). Amsterdam: Elsevier.

Turing, A.M. (1992b). *Collected works of Alan Turing, morphogenesis.* P.T. Saunders (Ed.). Amsterdam: Elsevier.

Endnotes

[1]   A perspective established by Reichenbach (1938) and Popper (1959).

[2]   Magnani (2001, 2002) introduces the concept of theoretical abduction. He maintains that there are two kinds of theoretical abduction, "sentential," related to logic and to verbal/symbolic inferences, and "model-based," related to the exploitation of internalized models of diagrams, pictures, etc.

[3]   Manipulative abduction and epistemic mediators are introduced and illustrated in Magnani (2001).

[4]   A configuration is a state of discrete machinery.

[5]   On languages as cognitive artefacts, cf. Carruthers (2002), Clark (1998, 2003, 2004, 2005), Norman (1993), and Clowes and Morse (2005).

[6]   On the relationship between material culture and the evolution of consciousness, cf. (Donnald, 1998, 2001; Dennett, 2003).

[7]   The problem of manipulative abduction and of its tacit features is strongly related to the whole area of recent research on embodied reasoning (Anderson, 2002), but also relates to studies on external representations and situated robotics (Clancey, 2002; Agree & Chapman, 1990; Brooks & Stein, 1994).

[8]   I derive this expression from the cognitive anthropologist Hutchins, that coins the expression "mediating structure" to refer to various external tools that can be built to cognitively help the activity of navigating in modern but also in "primitive" settings (Hutchins, 1995).

[9]   It is difficult to preserve precise spatial relationships using mental imagery, especially when one set of them has to be moved relative to another.

[10] On the recent achievements in the area of the machine discovery simulations of model-based creative tasks, cf. (Magnani, Nersessian, & Pizzi, 2002).

Chapter XII

First Steps in Experimental Phenomenology

Roberto Poli, University of Trento, Italy

Abstract

The main thesis defended by this chapter is the thesis of the autonomy — i.e., non-reducibility — of the phenomenic level of analysis of the psyche. The thesis will be defended by exploiting four main ideas: (1) the theory of levels of reality, (2) the distinction between act and object of presentation, (3) the structure of internal time, and (4) the distinction between egological and non egological acts. I shall present these theses from the point of view of the experiments conducted by Meinong and his pupils, notably Benussi, first at Graz and then at Padua. I may therefore claim that I am here adopting the point of view of what has been called experimental phenomenology, meaning the experimental study of phenomenic or first-person experiences.

Background

In this chapter I shall use some of the ideas developed by early phenomenologists in order to sketch fragments of a new architecture for both natural and artificial minds. In Europe, the sixty years from 1870 to 1930 have seen the elaboration of an enourmous amount of new scientific and philosophical ideas. Some of the ideas are collectively referred to as Central-European philosophy and science. The main figures behind that label are Franz Brentano and his pupils, notably Edmund Husserl, Alexius Meinong, Kazimierz Twardowski, Carl Stumpf, Christian von Ehrenfels and Anton Marty.[1] None of them play a major role in contemporary mainstream science and philosophy any longer.[2] Moreover, when their ideas are occasionally referred to, references are often generic and based on highly questionable, if not wrong, interpretations.[3] The only partial exception to this depressing picture is provided by the case of Husserl, substantially better known than any of the other mentioned thinkers. However, even in the case of Husserl, the scientific relevance of his contributions is obstructed by a converging set of impeding factors. In fact, the idea that phenomenology was a throughly scientific-oriented philosophy has been buried under, (1) widely held misunderstandings about its development and its basic theses;[4] (2) Husserl's writing style, and in particular his adoption of an overtly complex terminology, one that most contemporary scholars take as not worth penetrating; and (3) the success encountered by the ascientific philosophy of Martin Heidegger, possibly the best known pupil of Husserl. Heidegger's fame throws a sinister light on the scientific suitability of Husserl's phenomenology. It is worth noticing that the sad fate encountered by phenomenology has been at least partly shared by strict scientific theories, the clearest case being provided by the psychology of Gestalt.[5]

My task here is to show that at least some of the ideas developed by Central-European thinkers are still fruitfully exploitable for the scientific advancement of our understading of the world and our experience of it. The main thesis defended by this chapter is the thesis of the autonomy — i.e., non-reducibility — of the phenomenic level of analysis of the psyche. The thesis will be defended by exploiting four main ideas: (1) the theory of levels of reality, (2) the distinction between act and object of presentation, (3) the structure of internal time, and (4) the distinction between egological and non-egological acts. With a bit of simplification, it can be fairly stated that behind each of those ideas stands a major figure: Nicolai Hartmann for the theory of levels of reality, Franz Brentano for the distinction between acts and objects of presentation, Edmund Husserl for the structure of internal time and Edith Stein for the distinction between egological and non-egological acts.[6] I shall present all the above theses from the point of view of the experiments conducted by Meinong and his pupils, notably Benussi, first at Graz and then at Padua.[7] I may therefore claim that I am here adopting the point of view of what has been called *experimental phenomenology*, meaning the experimental study of phenomenic, or first-person, experiences.

The expression "experimental phenomenology" comes from Thinès and has been used by various psychologists and philosophers, notably by Michotte, Kanizsa and Albertazzi.[8] I shall use it in a more inclusive sense, incorporating all the ideas and categorial framework above mentioned. Furthermore, I shall twist its meaning from an epistemologically-oriented reading to an ontologically-oriented one.

Levels of Reality

The ontological theory of levels runs against a number of deeply entrenched presuppositions of mainstream science and philosophy. It is therefore advisable to lay down with some care its main claims. Three aspects are relevant. Let us consider them in the form of dichotomies, as follows:

- levels of reality vs. levels of interpretation;
- descriptive vs. genetic; and
- categorial vs. individual.

For each dichotomy, the first option is the reference one. Although confusion between *levels of reality* and *levels of interpretation*[9] is not infrequent, trading one for the other is to blur or confound ontological dimensions with epistemological ones. In short, only some of the many possible levels of interpretation can be properly taken as levels of reality, namely those that are grounded on ontological categories. Further information will shortly be provided.[10]

As far as levels of interpretation are concerned, the choice about the granularity of the scene under description — the *windowing of attention*[11] — depends only on the observer and his or her purpose. On the other hand, levels of reality are grounded on the object, on its intrinsic nature.[12] Even if it is not the task of this chapter to argue in favor of this apparently old-fashioned vision, two basic remarks are appropriate. First, what is at stake here is one of the guiding ideas of the phenomenological attitude, namely the assumption that what appears — the phenomenon — is always the appearance of some underlyining reality. Otherwise stated, phenomena show in their own way aspects, sides and components of what they are phenomena of. This means that — through phenomena — we access the nature of reality.[13] Second, the concept of *essence* or *nature* of something is again one of the basic features of the phenomenological attitude. As a first, and only partial, approximation, the nature of an object is given by the object's structure as shown by the web of internal and external causes that make explicit the object's behavior. I shall come back on the problem of causation and the web of causes towards the end of this section.

Atoms, molecules and organisms distinguish levels of reality because of the causal links that govern their behavior, both horizontally (atom-atom, molecule-molecule and organism-organism) and vertically (atom-molecule-organism). This is the first intuition of the theory of levels. Even if the further development of the theory will require imposing a number of qualifications to this initial intuition, the idea of a series of entities organized on different levels of complexity will prove correct. Shortly, the difference between levels of reality and levels of interpretation requires acknowledging that the *items* composing levels of reality are endowed with their own form of *agency*.[14] From the point of view of the theory of levels of reality, the two requirements of agency and presence of a causal web are equivalent. The former goes from above, the latter from below. A fully-developed theory of levels requires both a properly generalized concept of causation, able to consider not only material causes but psychological and social causes as well, and a correspondingly generalized idea of *agency*, able to explain not only psychological and social dynamics but material dynamics as well.

With a grain of salt, the difference between levels of reality and levels of interpretation amounts to the thesis that the former constrains the items of the universe as to which types of causation and agency are admissible. A level of reality can therefore be taken as a level of interpretation endowed with an appropriate web of causes or an appropriate type of agency.

Developing the theory of causation (or the theory of agency, for that matter) requires passing to a new framework. This is where the opposition between description and genesis enters the scene. The distinction between a descriptive framework and a genetic one goes back to Brentano, where it was presented as the difference between descriptive and genetic psychology. The idea is that before studying the causes that structure and connect the phenomena under observation, one should know them. Otherwise stated, the first step in any scientific effort concerns the accurate *description* of the relevant data. If we are able enough, we may succeed in connecting data within an appropriate web of causal dependences. Such a web is termed *genetic* in the sense that it explains why some items derive from other items. In this sense, *genetic* therefore means *dynamical*. It may well be — and more often than not this is precisely the case — that only a fraction of the relevant phenomena are so explicable. Different sciences have been developed in order to efficaciously segment the whole of reality into classes of more or less uniformly connected phenomena. The guiding idea being that phenomena occurring within each class should be more causally homogeneous than phenomena pertaining to other classes, and therefore the task of explaining their behavior should be more easily achieved.

This *dividi et impera* (divide and rule) strategy has proved immensely successful, at least for some regions of reality. Other regions have proved to be more refractory, for a number of serious reasons. A first reason is that different regions may require different types of causation, some of which are still unknown or only partially known.[15] A second reason is that for some regions of reality, the analytic strategy of breaking items into pieces does not work appropriately. A third, and somewhat connected reason, is the lack of a synthetic methodology.

The complexity of reality requires adopting the analytic strategy of segmentation into *categorially* homogeneous regions. This first move is not questioned. However, some regions contain only items that can be further analytically segmented into pieces. These items are entirely governed by their parts (from below, so to speak). Other regions contain items following different patterns: they are governed by both their parts and the whole that results from them. Our understanding of these more complex items is still defective. Unfortunately, this is not the end of the story. Something more is required: Sooner or later the products arising from the segmentation into categorially homogeneous regions should be synthesised. As a matter of fact, we all live in *one* world, and not in two or twenty-five worlds.[16] This second synthetic move has proved much more troublesome than the original analytic move.

The ontology of the world cannot rest on the analytic decomposition into different scientific frameworks. Sooner or later we should arrive at their reunification. Reductionism is the desperate answer provided by those thinking that a synthetic picture will never be achieved.[17]

There is no denying that we are still lacking many answers. However, the theory of levels of reality is a needed step toward the elaboration of a fully developed synthetic strategy.

Most details of the links connecting together the various levels of reality are still unknown. This should not come as a surprise. The various sciences had mainly been working on causal links *internal* to their regional phenomena. More often than not, the nature of inter-regional links is still unknown. The lack of a theory of levels of reality has been the major obstruction to the development of the needed theories. For this reason, the first and most needed, task is to elaborate the *descriptive* framework of the theory of levels. Proposals concerning the architecture of levels and their basic connections will improve our understanding of the world and its many types of dependence.[18] Later on we will see that the theory of levels helps asking a number of new scientific questions.

The last opposition concerns the difference between the individual and the categorial. Let us assume that the differences have been accepted between levels of reality and levels of interpretation from one side and between descriptive and genetic frameworks on the other side. Suppose then that a descriptive theory of levels is accepted.

The remaining problem is then: How to describe levels? Apparently, the choice is between descriptions based on individuals and descriptions based on categories. However, it is straightforward to realize that descriptions based on individuals do not work. The easiest way to see it goes as follows. Assume that the distinction is accepted among the physical, the biological and the social levels.[19] The decision should now be taken about whether each level contains its own group of individuals. If this were true, we should hypothesize three different groups of individuals, one for each level. However, it may well be that the physical individuum, the biological individuum and the social individuum are the only one individuum existing in the real world. Any of us is a good exemplification of such a situation. The given exemplification may be easily made as sophisticated as wished by distinguishing theory-based (or model based) individuals from real, transcendent individuals. Be that as it may be, what interests us is the world. It is always the same individuum that may be eventually subjected to physical, biological and social scrutiny. If we decide that each level of reality is composed by its own group of individuals, a number of demanding and possibly unsolvable problems immediately arise. My claim is that there is no principled reason for going that way. Even if that strategy may occasionally prove helpful, on the long run it is deemed to systematically reify categorial distinctions. The opposite strategy is based on categories, not on individuals. According to a categorially-based strategy, levels of reality are defined by their categories.

Some brief specifications will be helpful.

- *Apparently, the choice between (transcendent) individuals and categories does not rule out theory-based individuals.* A moment's reflexion proves that the latter are fictions, because the strategy based on theory-based individuals is isomorphic to the category-based strategy.

- *Nobody denies that the same phenomenon (or group of phenomena) can be categorized in many different ways.* Correct. However, it shouldn't be forgotten that we are conducting ontology. Only ontological categories are relevant to our task.

- *Even in such a case, there can be different ontologies.* Well, perhaps. I am inclined to deny such a possibility. Furthermore, none of the great ontologists was an ontological relativist.

- *Suppose that we are willing to accept the via difficilior (more difficult road) of a unique ontology. Even so, the ontology can be presented in different ways, based on different groups of categories, mutually isomorphic but not identical one another.* I accept this claim. However, it is ontologically immaterial because it concerns the formal architecture of the theory more than its ontological content. For what we are here interested in, we may select any of those categorial groups and deem canonical its categories.[20]

Summing up what we have so far seen, our main conclusion is the choice to adopt a categorial viewpoint. In short, a level of reality is represented by a group of (ontological) categories.

The next step is to distinguish *universal* categories, those that pertain to the whole of reality, from *level* categories, those that pertain to one or more levels, but not to all of them.

As far as universal categories are concerned, the old Aristotelian list of categories is still helpful. Whatever the items under analysis, they may present qualitative and quantitative determinations, temporal and spatial locations, relations to other *items* and they may exhert influence on other items and undergo influence from other items. It goes without mentioning that each of these categories requires developments going well beyond Aristotle. However, his main intuitions, as far as determinations are concerned, are still worth considering.

Substance and determination are then the first two universal categories we have met. The analysis of substance requires the development of a number of new theories. One of them is the theory of particulars, i.e., the systematic analysis of categories like thing, process, stuff and state of affairs. A second required theory is the theory of wholes and their parts. These basic references help understanding that substance is the heading for a complex net of topics. Determinations as well present a demanding complexity, mainly organized around the difference between extensive and intensive determinations.[21]

In its turn, the theory of levels of reality articulates the dichotomy between substance and determination. This distinction requires subsequent specifications: certain families of determinations may inherit to specific families of substances. On the other hand, families of substances admit only corresponding families of determinations. Having a given length is a determination that can only inherit to a material substance;[22] the determination of an irrepressible joy can only inherit to a psychological substance; the determination of the fulfilment of some legal requirements through revocation can only inherit to a social substance.[23] The theory of the levels of reality provides the categorial framework for systematically articulating all these differences.

Distinction is widespread among three basic realms or regions (or strata, as I will call them) of reality. Even if the boundaries between them are differently placed, the distinction among the three realms of material, mental and social phenomena is essentially accepted by most thinkers and scientists. A major source of discussion is whether inanimate and animate beings should be placed in two different realms (which means that there are in fact four, not three, realms) or within the same realm. The latter option defends the thesis that a phase transition or something similar connects inanimate and animate items.

From a categorial point of view, the problem of how many strata there are can be easily solved. Leaving apart universal categories, two main categorial situations can be distinguished: (a) Types (items) A and B are categorially different because the canonical description of one of them requires categories that are not needed by the canonical description of the other; (b) Types (items) A and B are categorially different because their canonical description requires two entirely different groups of categories. Following Hartmann, I term the two relations as respectively relations of over-forming (*Überformung*) and building-above (*Überbauung*).[24]

Strata or realms of reality are connected by building-above relations. That is to say, the main reason for distinguishing as clearly as possible the different strata of reality is that any of them is characterized by the birth of a *new* categorial *series*. The group of categories that are needed to analyze the phenomena of the psychological stratum is essentially different from the group of categories needed to analyze the social one, which in its turn requires a group of categories different from the one needed to analyze the material stratum of reality.

The two following situations exemplify the difference between over-forming and building-above. Consider first the relationships between say chemistry and physics. Let us assume that we possess a categorially adequate analysis of physics.[25] Shortly, $j = \{C_{p_1},...,C_{p_n}\}$. Let us further suppose to possess a categorially adequate analysis of chemistry, say $c = \{C_{c_1},...,C_{c_n}\}$. The following question can now be asked: Which type of relation connects physical and chemical reality? The answer is straightforward: Chemistry is based on physics, but says something more. Chemical phenomena go beyond (purely) physical phenomena, i.e., chemistry is a creative extension of physics. Trying to categorize chemical phenomena resorting to physical categories only, does not produce false results but proves useless because it dissolves what is characteristic of chemical phenomena. Categorially speaking, the just sketched situation can be summarized by saying that the set of chemical categories extends the set of physical categories. Passing from the physical to the chemical level means adding *new* categories.[26] This is the situation we have baptized *over-forming*.

Let us now discuss a different case, e.g., the one concerning the connections between physics and psychology. As for the previous example, we assume that adequate categorizations are available, in the form of, say, $p = \{C_{p_1},...,C_{p_m}\}$ and $y = \{C_{y_1},...,C_{y_m}\}$. However, everybody sees that the new situation is substantially different from the previous one. We cannot claim — as it was for the previous case — that the categories of psychology *extend* the categories of physics and that the group of psychological categories is obtained by adding new categories to the categories of physics. What we must eventually claim is that psychological categories are orthogonal to physical categories. However, something more is needed, namely the claim that psychical

Figure 1. Two configurations of levels of reality

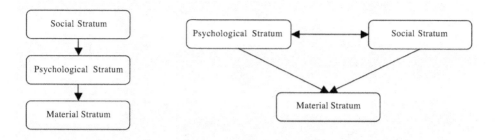

phenomena require physical bearers.[27] Psychological phenomena are difficult to categorize because they are *categorially independent* and *existentially dependent* from their bearers. Relations between levels characterized by both categorial independence and existential dependence will be termed *building-above* relations.

Some terminological conventions will help the further development of the theory of levels. In the following, levels connected by building-above relations will be called *strata*, levels connected by over-forming relations will be called *layers*. I shall eventually use the expressions "sub-layer" and "sub-stratum" when analysis requires them. The term *level* will be used as generic between strata and layers.

The question now arises as to how the material, psychological and social strata are connected together. The most obvious answer is that they have a linear structure like the one illustrated by the left side of Figure 1. On this view, the social stratum is founded on the psychological stratum, which in its turn is founded on the material one. Likewise, the material stratum is the bearer of the psychological stratum, which in its turn is the bearer of the social one. However, I shall defend a different option, illustrated by the right side of Figure 1.

Material phenomena act as bearers of *both* psychological *and* social phenomena. In their turn, psychological and social phenomena determine each other reciprocally. Psychological and social systems are formed through co-evolution, meaning that the one is the environmental prerequisite for the other.[28] Both present a double existential dependence: firstly they both depend on their material bearer; secondly, each depends on the twin stratum: Psyches require societies and societies require psyches.

The next step is to articulate the internal organization of each stratum. The material stratum has a basically linear structure (Figure 2; for a slightly more precise analysis see Poli, 2001b).

Shown on the left in Figure 2 are the three main layers of the material stratum. To show that the articulation can be further developed, the biological layer is "exploded" into its main sub-layers (right).

Each of the three strata of reality has its specific structure. The case of the material stratum is the best known and the least problematic. Suffice it to consider the series atom-molecule-cell-organism (which can be extended at each of its two extremes to include sub-

Figure 2. Three main layers of the material stratum and the biological sub-layers

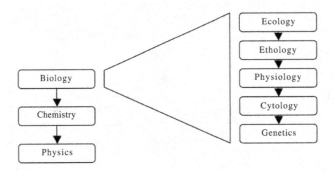

atomic particles and ecological communities, and also internally, as needed). In this case we have a clear example of a series that proceeds by levels of granularity. The basic distinction of the realm (stratum) into physical, chemical and biological components can be considerably refined (e.g., by distinguishing biology into genetics, cytology, physiology, ethology and ecology — a slightly more articulated picture is provided by Poli, 2001a,b). Compared to the material realm, the psychological and social ones are characterized by an interruption in the material categorial series and by the onset of new ones (relative to the psychological and social items). More complex types of over-forming are instantiated by them. Later on I shall consider some of the intricacies of the psychological stratum.

Before passing to the next topics, it is worth mentioning that the theory of levels of reality is the natural setting for elaboration of an articulated theory of the forms of causal dependence. In fact, it smoothly grounds the hypothesis that any ontologically different level has its own form of causality (or family of forms of causality). Material, psychological and social forms of causality can therefore be distinguished (and compared) in principled manner.

Beside the usual kinds of basic causality between phenomena of the same nature, the theory of levels enables us to single out upward forms of causality (from the lower level to the upper one). But this is not all. A theory of levels also enables us to address the problem of *downward* forms of causality (from the upper to the lower level). The point was first made by Donald Campbell some years ago (1974,1990); Andersen et al. (2000) also collects a series of studies on the theme.

The connection between the theory of levels and causality entails recognition that every level of reality may trigger its own causal chain. This may even be taken as a definition of level of reality: A level of reality is distinguished by its specific form of causality. As a consequence, we thus have a criterion with which to distinguish among levels of reality and levels of description.

This acknowledgement also enables us to develop a theory able to accommodate different senses of causality (distinguishing at least among material, mental and social causality). However, if the downward option is also available, the direct or elementary forms of causality should have corresponding non-elementary forms. I tend to adopt the expression *theory of unfoldings* as a convenient label for the many different types of causation linking items within and among themselves, and among their corresponding levels.

The theory of levels of reality comes equipped with a further framework, which I baptize the theory of chronotopoids. The expression refers to a generalized form of the relational theory of time and space. During the 20th century, a number of philosophers, biologists, psychologists and sociologists have tried to defend the idea that there are biological, psychological and social forms of time and space. More often than not, those talks have been metaphorical and allusive, methodologically unclear and uncertain about the exact nature of their claims. As for the previous case of the theory of unfoldings, most talks about varieties of time and space failed for the lack of a theory of levels of reality. A source of confusion must immediately be dispelled. Chrono-topoids do not question the utility, relevance and necessity of the usual understanding of temporal and spatial reference-frames. Calendars, maps, landmarks and traffic lights are accepted, welcome and re-spected as everything else. They are not under discussion. The problem I am trying to address is substantially different from the discussion of clocks and maps.

The easiest way to mark the difference between the two cases is possibly to oppose as clearly as possibile absolute and relational theories of time and space. Topoids and chronoids, as said, are relational. They consider their items "as seen from the inside," something like the intrinsic geometry of a surface. On the other hand, customary time and space see their items "from the outside." This is why they can be taken as containers. Material, psychological and social topoids and chronoids may behave differently from absolute time and space. This is not to deny that they are "in" absolute space and time as well, but they should *not* be taken as *reducible* to instances of absolute time and space only. Customary time and space can be understood as external semantics of the ontologically-based chronoids and topoids, whereas the latter are to be taken as (part of) the internal semantics of items.

First Intermezzo:
Levels as the Guiding Idea

The above introduction to the theory of levels of reality paves the way for developing a categorially crisper analysis of the psychological phenomena. The framework of levels immediately offers a number of guiding theses. Let me sketch at least some of them explicitly:

1. Psychological phenomena present a double type of causal dependence, from appropriate material bearers (mainly in the form of biological bearers) and from social bearers. The latter are, in their turn, supported by psychological bearers too, so that the causal dependence between psychological and social phenomena runs both ways. In such a case I shall speak of a mutual, or bilateral, type of dependence.

2.   On the other hand, psychological phenomena are categorially independent from both material and social phenomena.

3.   Furthermore, psychological phenomena are endowed with their specific type of causes and with their specific types of times and spaces. This general thesis must be supported by appropriate evidence grounded on specific, detailed analyses of relevant phenomena.

4.   There is no reason for assuming that the internal organization of the psychological stratum is in any respect similar to the internal organization of either the material or the social stratum. No internal uniformity among strata is either required, assumed or hypothesized.

5.   The enormous amount of psychological knowledge accumulated during the past decades has substantially deepened our understanding of many psychological phenomena and their internal links. However, the understanding of the connections linking material and psychological phenomena is still rather cursory and fragmentary. Lacking the framework of the theory of level, the temptation is permanently active for absorbing (reducing) psychological phenomena within biological ones. A quick survey of the literature shows how astonishingly often mind and brain are in any relevant aspect identified.

Psychological Acts and their Correlates

I shall now start considering the nature and structure of psychological phenomena. The first requirement when addressing the problem of the structure of the psychological stratum is to realize the twofold nature of the psyche: As far as mental activities are concerned, it is a process; on the other hand, mental processes are so structured to present correlated contents. The traditional way to present the thesis of the processualistic nature of the psyche is to claim that psychological phenomena are temporal phenomena. I shall consider the thesis of the processual nature of the psyche in the version of it developed by Brentano:

Main ontological thesis on psychological phenomena: (Brentano's thesis): Psychological phenomena have two sides, one independent, the other dependent. The indepen-

Figure 3. Main ontological thesis on psychological phenomena

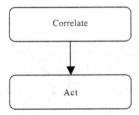

dent side is a process, termed "act"; the dependent side is an object, termed "correlate," of the act (Figure 3).

Correlates are sometimes termed "internal accusatives." The easiest way to show the connection between act and correlate is by examples, as follows: For every seeing there is something that is seen; for every thinking there is something that is thought; for every feeling there is something that is felt, etc. Correlates depend on their acts as their ontological bearers. But something more is at stake, because the dependence connection between correlate and act is of a more intimate nature than the usual bearer-borne relation. In fact, borne correlates are dependent on their bearer acts not only existentially but *materially* as well. *Material* here should be taken in the Husserlian sense, where it is opposed to *formal*.

We shall distinguish two main families of acts, which Stein baptized "egological" and "non-egological." The latter family is further subdivided into "perceptive presentations" and "mental presentations."[29]

Presentations form what is usually called stream of consciousness, specious present or moment now. They regard the basic temporal structure of our conscious life. Mental presentations, in particular, deal with what is nowadays usually ascribed to propositional knowledge. However, we shall see that the difference between non-propositional and propositional knowledge does not fit well with the difference between perceptive and mental presentations. Egological acts deal with the so-called emotional components of the psyche. I shall come back on them later in this chapter.

Three major problems characterize the theory of psychological acts, namely the problems of (1) the structure of the act, (2) the interaction among different acts and (3) the production of an act on the basis of previous acts. A number of correlated but different problems concern the act's correlates. The latter can be simple or complex (or higher-order), and complex correlates are grounded on simple (or less complex) ones. Furthermore, correlates are partially dependent on their acts, in the sense that *modifications* of the acts result in *corresponding modifications* of the correlates. Distinguishing the aspects of the correlate that depend on the corresponding act from those that are independent of it is not always straightforward. The next sections will address some of these problems.

Presentations

Acts of presentations, as said, constitute the specious present, the basic temporal flow of intentionality. The present is the multiplicity of what is actually given to the mind. However, the present is not only simultaneous perception; it is also *unification* of the given multiplicity. In short, the present "is that feature of the psychic change which is apprehended as unity and which is the object of a single mental act of apprehension."[30]

According to Husserl, intentional phenomena are complex realities requiring a number of different structures dealing with (1) the act's internal structure (a component sometimes called "latitudinal" intentionality) and (2) the ordering of the acts, i.e., the past-present-future rhythm of the succession of acts ("longitudinal" intentionality). The former heading comprises (a) the phases of the intentional act, (b) the forms of self-organization of the act's correlate (contrast, fusion, grouping, figure/background and pairing) and the time required by such self-organizations, (c) the modalization of the act (through attention or alertness, or their lack, and through emotional attitudes) and (d) the modalization of the act's correlate (its profiling or saliencing). The latter heading comprises the many complications arising from series of acts, ranging from the sinking of past acts into memory to the anticipation of the future in the form of projects. In this chapter I shall consider only *some* of the intricacies that characterize a single act of presentation.

The first questions to be asked are: How long does the specious present last? And, how can we determine its length? One possible way is to present two objects in succession and to measure the duration of the interval necessary for their perceptions not to interfere with each other. The idea being that if the two presentations are below the threshold, their objects mingle into the correlate of a single act of perception. It results that the minimum duration required for perception to take place without interference is ca. 700 ms.[31]

If two different visual presentations follow one another at a quicker pace, the resulting perception is composed by elements coming from both of the original presentations. Suppose that two groups of six different objects each are presented one after the other. What is seen is a group of six objects composed by some of objects from the first sextet and the remaining from the second sextet. This shows that a single act of apprehension requires a specific amount of time and that the complexity of its correlate is constrained.

One of the major points of disagreement between the mainstream theory of Gestalt (the Berlin fraction) and the minority version developed by Meinong, Ameseder and Benussi (the Graz fraction) is whether acts of presentations come in one blow or are structured in successive phases.[32] Berliners defended the idea that perceptions do not come in phases. On the other hand, the Grazers substantiated both conceptually and experimentally the opposite thesis, according to which perception is organized in phases. The latter thesis does not imply that the different phases are perceptively separated. Perceptors are not aware of them. Perceptors apprehend only the final result of an act of presentation.

Benussi succeeded in finding phenomena that can be better explained by accepting the thesis of the phases of the presentation. The most interesting is possibly the case of temporal inversions. Consider the following sequence of sounds: Lah (100ms) — white noise (35ms) — Soh (100ms). What happens is that a positive temporal reorganization occurs so that what is heard is either the succession Lah — Soh — white noise, or white noise — Lah — Soh. That is to say that a perceptive reordering occurred.[33]

The thesis of the phases of presentation is flanked by a twin thesis according to which the formation of percepts requires some time. In a sense, nobody denies it. However, the difference is between those that defend the thesis according to which the formation of the percept occurs at a purely neurophysiological level and those that defend the different thesis according to which the formation of the percept occurs within the act of presentation. The difference is substantial. The former thesis claims that all the operations producing percepts are neurophysiological while the latter thesis claims that they are phenomenic. If the phases of the act are phenomenic, some ways for making them appear should be imaginable. Benussi thought that hypnosis could be used to slow dawn the usual speed of presentation in order to better describe its various phases.

Benussi distinguished three phases: (a) critical phase, (b) the phase of consecutive impression and (c) the mnestic phase. The three phases are now described for the case of acoustic perceptions.[34]

The critical phase is characterized by *perceptive presentness*, in a sequential order, of its elements. The phase of consecutive impression requires immediate memory. Three transformations govern this second phase: (1) the elements constituting the critical phase are unified into a *whole*; (2) the original elements are no more perceptively present, but they are experienced as *still present* in the form of a *simultaneous mental contemporaneity*; and (3) the elements experienced as mentally simultaneous are different from the original elements in that they now have the character of an *order of succession*. In short, the phase of consecutive impression is based on a mental whole, whose parts have the content of being organized in some given order. The third and final phase, the mnestic phase, is such that the simultaneous mental whole obtained in the second phase splits into constitutive parts according to some pattern. It is remarkable that the elements so obtained are usually *different* from the one constituting the critical phase.[35] Temporal inversions provide a confirmation of the claim.

In short, the three phases may perhaps be synoptically summarized as *hearing some sounds*, *sounds heard* and *melody*.

Albertazzi notes that "the theory of the three phases is important for two reasons: (1) it raises the problem of the decomposing, or slowing down, of real psychic processes in order to see their internal articulation, and (2) it establishes a difference between perceptive presence and mental presence."[36] Having already shortly considered (1), I now pass to (2), the problem of the difference between perceptive and mental presence.

Properly speaking, three different types of *presence* have been distinguished:

1. *Modal* presence
2. *Amodal* presence
3. *Mental* presence of representations

Both modal and amodal presence are forms of *perceptive* presence. The data of consciousness endowed with perceptive presence constitute the concept of *empirical reality*. Those with mental presence constitute representations or representative states.

The main structural difference between mental and perceptive items is that the former are associative, whereas the latter are assimilative. Associativity means here that new features may always be added to the relevant items. It may also be said that mental items are analytic. On the other hand, assimilative items are integral wholes. Assimilation is fusion, integration, synthesis. This means that they arrive at some fixed point, in the sense of a best configuration that does not admit further improvements.

Assimilative objects can be *enriched* with perceptive elements without the correspond-ing adequate external conditions.[37] An important case is the segmentation of the perceptive field into figure and ground, where the ground behind the figure is (amodally) completed. The figure has a rear which is not visible but phenomenally present. Objects experienced as three-dimensional present an interior, which is encountered and not solely thought.

Figure 4. Amodal perception

Coming back to the difference between modal and amodal presence, Kanizsa specifies the latter as follows: "By 'amodal presence' is meant that type of perceptive presence (not only imagined but 'enountered' as Metzger says) which does not occur in any sensory modality."[38] The triangle that bears his name is a well-known case of amodal perception (Figure 4).

Benussi distinguishes assimilative processes from associative processes as follows:[39]

1. Associative processes develop according to an additive pattern; assimilative processes alter the perceptive element from which they start (and therefore become one with it). I see an English word and I associate the corresponding Italian word with it: associative process. I see a word spelled incorrectly and I read it in its correct form: assimilative process.

2. The additive pattern of associative processes is unlimited; assimilative processes tend towards a limit.[40]

3. Assimilative elements are perceptively experienced in the object in which they are presented; associative elements are presented in representative or mnestic situations.

4. Assimilative processes are activated before, and independently of, mnestic factors.[41]

Amodal presence is a case of phenomenal presence added to a modal base which, although not given in any sensory modality, is perceived (experienced) as if it were effectively given, and not just mentally represented.[42] On the basis of phenomena of this type, Kanizsa claims that visual phenomena are "a domain of 'emergent' reality not reducible to other domains of reality and therefore to be studied using the methods of experimental phenomenology adequate to handle its specificity."[43]

Furthermore: "The organization is not contained in the stimulation ... the brain goes beyond the information given in the primary process ... in the primary process, as well as in the secondary one, we have phenomena of totalization, of completion, of integration, of gap-filling; we can, that is to say, observe the 'presentification of the absent'".[44]

Summing up and integrating with experimental data what we have so far seen, the following are some of the basic features of presentations:

1. Presentations last from 200ms to 3000ms ca. On average, they last approximately 700ms.

2. The duration of presentations depends on a variety of factors, ranging from the subject's mood feelings (they are shorter when the subject is excited and longer when s/he is relaxed) to the cognitive state of the subject (attention shortens presentation), to the content of what is presented, etc.

3. Presentations come with an inner organization, on various dimensions. Of these, the most important are: (a) the distinction between focus and periphery, (b) the presence of internal laws of organization and (c) the elaboration of their content in subsequent stages. Point (a) entails that there are upper limits to the complexity of the correlate in the focus. Point (b) yields possibly most surprising results, namely the laws of temporal and spatial inversion.[45] Point (c) claims that presentations themselves have a temporal structure. This last point is highly significant in that it marks the difference between the Berlin and Graz schools of Gestalt psychology.

4. Presentations come in a (temporal) series, often called stream of consciousness.

Second Intermezzo:
Forms of Reality Construction

This is the chapter's only section dealing with correlates of the acts. The only point I would like to take into consideration is the apparently surprising fact that occasionally acts are driven by their correlates. I have already presented Benussi's distinction between perceptive and mental acts, i.e., between assimilative and additive acts. Assimilation and addition can be taken as two of the basic procedures providing experience of external and internal reality.

In the 1920s, Musatti — the main pupil of Benussi — singled out four forms of construction of both external and internal reality.

The forms concerning the construction of external reality are as follows:

*   *First form of external reality construction.* Given two simultaneous discordant phenomenal givens, relative to two distinct sensory fields, we assume that one corresponds to reality and that the other is apparent (example of the stick half immersed in water). The discordance between the two phenomena is removed if one is used to give account of the other. We can describe this situation as the

assumption, between discordant perceptive givens of one datum as real and the other as apparent.

- *Second form of external reality construction.* This proceeds by assuming reality to be the imaginary phenomenal datum of a practically impossible, but rationally thinkable, experience, for example the molecular structure of organisms. Atomic structure is real for science although none of our immediate impressions correspond to it. But we can imagine ourselves as able enormously to expand our perceptive capacities until we are putatively able to "go and see." By using the concept of "extended perceptive apparatus," we can unite these first two forms of reality construction.

- *Third form of external reality construction.* This proceeds by assuming as real the imaginary phenomenal datum of an experience which is not only practically impossible but also rationally absurd, and only thinkable if we ignore the condition that defines the problem. Think of the world as it was before the appearance of the human species. By definition, we cannot describe it. Moreover, this is an assumption that enables one to account for otherwise incomprehensible phenomena (geology, etc.).

- *Fourth form of external reality construction.* This is a reality determined outside the terms of our phenomenal experience. A better formulation would be that reality is indirectly determined only in relation to those given phenomena that it serves to organize. All cases of physical energy, physical or chemical properties or conditions of bodies are cases of this form of reality construction.[46]

The following are the corresponding forms for inner reality. It is worth noting that these forms of construction are more on the side of acts:

- *First form of internal reality construction.* In situations of close concentration we realize the real complexity of phenomena which on other occasions we may have perceived in less complex terms. It is in regard to the latter, therefore, that we speak of the illusory or apparent poverty of data.

- *Second form of internal reality construction.* Consider the onset phases of a process introspectively experienced as immediate. It appears immediate to us although we know that it is constituted by a sequence of phases. What appears to us as a single and immediate perceptive event is in fact only the final event in that process. We explain the appearance by assuming that the phases are too brief to be grasped.

- *Third form of internal reality construction.* The unconscious is an example of the third form of inner reality construction. The reality of unconscious processes is constructed by means of a fiction which ignores the condition that they cannot be raised to the level of consciousness.

- *Fourth form of internal reality construction.* Examples are: capacities and dispositional attitudes (intelligence, memory and discernment). Properly speaking, memory, intelligence and so on, are not psychic facts; they are not introspectively graspable states or processes.[47]

In short, the four forms of reality construction understand reality as:

- effectively given experience;
- practically impossible but rationally thinkable experience;
- practically impossible and rationally absurd experience; and
- a reality determined independently of phenomenal experience.

The chief interest of Musatti's analysis of the mechanisms used to construct empirical reality resides in its ability to show that it is possible to proceed from actually given experiences to those which though practically impossible are nevertheless rationally thinkable, to those that are rationally absurd, and finally to those that lie entirely beyond our capacity for phenomenal experience.

Mental Acts

Beside perceptive presence, the other type of presence is mental presence. We shall refer to the corresponding acts indifferently as mental acts, cognitive acts or non-egological acts. These acts concern imagery, phantasy, reasoning and (reactualized) memory.

Here I shall not consider them in any detail. The dialectic between "seeing" and "thinking" is awfully complex and will be eventually dealt with on other occasions.[48] In this chapter I shall instead address the case of egological, or emotional, acts.

Emotional Acts

Emotional, or egological, acts are structured in levels of depth, ranging from acts conveying more superficial information to those conveying more intimate information.[49] Three different layers can be distinguished.

The most external (superficial) layer concerns information about how we sense our body. *Feeling cold*, *warm* or just *okay* are some of the most typical cases. Let us call them *sensorial feelings*.

The next layer comprises information about our moods. *Feeling bored, excited, relaxed, angry* and *exhausted* make up only a tiny section of the rich and highly articulated field of moods. Feelings pertaining to this second group are typically twofold: They have a more bodily-oriented side and a more psychologically-oriented one. By default they merge, but they may diverge and their manifestation may follow different routes according to a variety of conditioning factors, from social to individual. Let us call this second group of feelings *mood feelings*.

Figure 5. Different layers of emotional acts

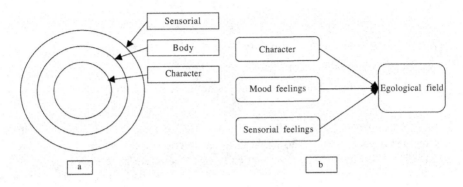

The third and deepest-lying layer is our personal style, the way in which we react to what happens to us. Suppose that something hurts you. You may *resist* the pain, *tolerate* it, *combat* it, *accept* it or even *enjoy* it. Let us denote this third group of feelings with the term *character*.[50]

The General Architecture

From what we have so far seen, presentations are determined by at least three different types of acts: perceptive, mental and emotional. Details of their interaction are still

Figure 6. Interaction of perceptive, mental and emotional acts

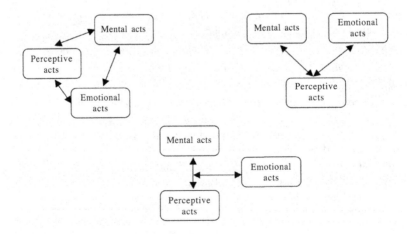

waiting to be spelled out in all the needed detail. A major unsolved problem concerns their place within the overall architecture of the specious present. A number of different hypotheses can be advanced (Figure 6)

The architecture on the top left of Figure 6 says that perceptive, mental and emotional acts interact with one another. The architecture on the top right says that perceptive acts are the basis upon which both mental and emotional acts are built (which may or may not influence each other). The architecture on the bottom says that the organization of the specious present is multileveled and presents two different types of dependence. A first dependence is held between mental and perceptive acts. A second dependence is between emotional acts and those constituted by both perceptive and mental acts.

All the arrows are double headed. This means that all the dependences are bilateral (i.e., they come in the form of *interactions*). Formally speaking, I take this picture as essentially correct. However, it hides the fact that the *force* of the two directions may be different, e.g., it may well be that the influence exerted by perceptive acts is greater than the influence exerted by mental acts on perceptive acts. As a matter of fact, the thesis is assumed that interactions are always asymmetrical, in the sense that one of the two directions prevails over the other.

With this proviso, which of the three architectures is likely to better approximate the real architecture of the specious present? And, secondly, should the arrows connecting them be interpreted as cases of over-forming or as cases of building-above?

As to the first question, I am not aware of any experimental result able to unquestionably provide a definite answer. I cannot therefore offer solid arguments in defence of one of the architectures against all the others. My personal guess is that the third architecture (the one on the bottom) may be closer to the truth. The idea is embedded in the structure of the third architecture that emotional acts may facilitate or hamper the *interactions* between perceptions and cognitions. This is something lacking from the other two architectures.

The second question is as demanding as the first one. Neither of the first two architectures provides definite answers about whether the dependences among their components are of the over-forming or building-above types. Both options are possible. However, this is likely untrue for the third architecture. Apparently, the arrow between perceptive and mental presentations is of an over-forming type, whereas the arrow between egological and non-egological acts is of a building-above type. As to the *direction* of the building-above relation connecting the egological and non-egological sub-strata, the most likely hypothesis is that non-egological acts build-above egological acts.[51] The reason for choosing the said direction is that the egological sub-stratum can apparently exist without the non-egological one, but not the other way round. Providing that this interpretation will prove correct, it follows that the egological field *existentially* depends from the non-egological field as its bearer. Otherwise stated, a purely emotional psyche without perceptions and cognitions is imaginable, but not the other way round.[52]

Figure 7. Double trancendence

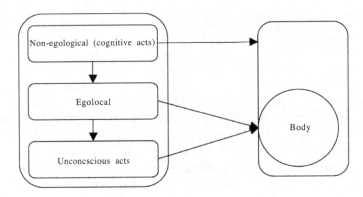

The Double Trancendence of our Internal Life

The psychological stratum emerges from the material stratum as a type of reality characterized by a new series of categories. This means that the psychological stratum requires the material one as its existential bearer. In the meantime, we have realized that there is more than one building-above relation connecting the material to the psychological stratum. In order to keep things as simple as possible, let us explicitly distinguish between the *family* of building-above relations concerning presentation and the *family* of building-above relations concerning (sensorial and mood) feelings. There is nothing to rule out the existence of a third *family* of building-above relations connected to unconscious acts. Figure 7 shows the case.

Presentations make reference to some transcendent reality. The exact meaning of "transcendent" is far from being clear. In one sense, whichever meaning is given to the term "transcendent," it should include the thesis that the connection between "external" reality and its "internal" presentation is far from being simple or direct (e.g., as a one-to-one connection between suitably chosen elements). Perception, and visual perception in particular, offers an enormous range of illuminating exemplifications. Among them, consider the well known phenomena whereby we see "things" that are not there and do not see "things" that are there.[53]

As far as non-egological acts are concerned, the relation of transcendence between the act's referent and its correlate is an instance of the building-above type of relation between the material and the psychological strata. Egological acts have the same structure as far as sensorial feelings are concerned: They are based on the same type of transcendent connection that we have just seen in the case of presentations. The situation of mood feelings and character is more complex. The component we have called character has a transcendent connection with "something" that can be taken as its source. Unfortunately, the deep-lying nature of this "something" is obscure and very difficult to pin down. Experience shows that something of the kind exists, but no evidence about its intrinsic nature and collocation is descriptively available. The most likely hypothesis is that the transcendent source of character is somehow buried in the unconscious layer of the psychological stratum. One of the merits of this hypothesis is its ability to explain why the "unconscious" is unconscious: because it is transcendent with respect to our awareness. However, this is only a very preliminary step and much work remains to be done.

For the time being, let us assume that things stand as described above. If so, the conclusion we are forced to draw is that both the most external or superficial types and the most internal or deep types of egological acts are transcendent. The intermediate type of mood feelings is connected with both the external and internal types of sensory feelings and character. Not by chance this intermediate layer has a mixed nature supported by two different forms of energy. Besides the *biological* energy sustaining our body and its functioning, a *psychological* type of energy exists as well. The former depends on interaction with the environment (e.g., for food), the latter on interaction with other persons. Here lies one of the deepest links between the psychological and the social strata of reality.

Something more should be added, before closing this section. According to Metzger, the phenomena composing the specious present are the borderzone where phenomena occur whose physical and psychic properties are closely connected, in the sense of "physical states with psychic consequences and psychic states with physical consequences."[54] The framework provided by the theory of levels helps in reformulating the thesis in a slightly more precise form according to which the specious present is a borderzone within the *material* and the *psychological* strata, more precisely, between the biological and the psychological. In an even more correct fashion, the thesis is that the specious present offers a borderzone between physiological and psychological acts, either in the form of egological or non-egological acts.

Representational attitudes determine mental forms of presence. These are causally inefficient. However, mental presence can succeed in activating perceptive presence, and this is causally efficient in the sense of possibly activating a new causal series. Representations can therefore become "realizers or transformers of reality ... and ... causal multipliers of reality."[55]

Benussi studied these phenomena through *real psychic analysis*, understood as the decomposition, isolation, immobilization and increase of psychic states obtained by means of hypnosis. By its means, Benussi was able to uncouple emotional functions from intellective ones. He succeeded in inducing pure emotional states (terror, pleasure, happiness, etc.) and pure intellective or pseudo-intellective states (evidence, assent, denial, etc.) *independently* of each other.

Hypnotic suggestion was used as a means for transforming the mental presence of an object (through comprehension of a sign or of a word) into its corresponding perceptive presence. In so doing Benussi investigated the dependence between emotional states and behavioral patterns. He discovered that a specific respiratory pattern corresponds to each type of emotion. Living an emotion facilitates the adoption of the corresponding respiratory pattern. Adopting a given respiratory pattern facilitates the activation of the corresponding emotion.

Scientifically speaking, hypnosis has nowadays fallen into disrepute, for good reasons. I am not asking for its rehabilitation. However, there is no need to throw away the baby with the bath water. Benussi is known for having been a thoroughly scrupulous experimentalist. Lack of more developed tools forced him to adopt hypnosis as the only available procedure. Nobody has ever questioned the rigour of his methodology and the seriousness of his data. The studies he conducted in the Twenties[56] should therefore be reproduced and verified or discomfirmed and, if verified, integrated with the other results acquired in the meantime. If proved, something like the dawn of a new vision can be in sight.

Conclusion

In this conjectural chapter I have combined experimental data on the structure of the specious present with categorial analyses driven by the framework of the theory of levels of reality and a few bold speculations on the general structure of the psyche. Many aspects have been touched on only briefly (e.g., the structure of the acts' correlates[57]) or not considered at all.

A question to be further considered is whether the architecture I have so far discussed has any role to play in the actual efforts for arriving at an artificial cognition system. Leaving aside many details, to be eventually considered elsewhere, the main issue is whether the introduction of a specious present module may improve (and in what sense) the functioning of an artificial cognition system. In order to properly start addressing this question, the main features of the specious present module should be spelled out as precisely as possible. The following list presents some *prima facie* features of the module:

1.   All inputs from the external world should arrive at the specious present module — please note that it is not required that all the external inputs arrive *only* at the specious present module; some or all of them may duplicate and enter other modules as well.

2.   The specious present module has its own architecture, which may conveniently be organized in two sections, respectively dealing with inner and outer determinations.

   a.   Outer determinations govern the temporal size of the specious present module. Its temporal variations may depend also upon the activity (and needs) of other modules. For the time being one may adopt the overly simplified assumption that the specious present module has a fixed duration (say, one second). This assumption will obviously eliminate some of the modules' inter dependencies.

   b.   Inner determinations spell out the rules for input manipulation. By default, these rules are proprietary to the specious present module. This means that they do not suffer variation from the interplay with other modules. Inner determinations manipulate inputs' trains and the outcomes resulting from their application are sent to higher-order modules (those dealing with representations) and long-term memory. Subjects are aware only of the final results of acts of presentation (intermediate outcomes are below the threshold of awareness).

The manipulation of input trains may result in outcomes in which some of the inputs are dropped, some are stressed, some are merged or blurred and others are so heavily transformed to be unrecognizable. This chapter has shown that at least some of the inner determinations have a holistic or Gestaltic nature. I may even venture to claim that most of them are of that type. However, this is immaterial to my claim that the main merit of the architecture I have sketched is to provide a filter to input trains. Boldly speaking, the idea is that nothing arrives at higher-order modules dealing with representations without suffering appropriate transformations by the specious present.

Only the most apparent surface of a series of enormously complex problems has been scratched. Further studies will have to complete this sketch with the many results obtained by cognitive science and verify whether the framework suggested is able to smoothly accept and incorporate them. Time will tell. At any rate, the chapter's main thesis should be clear enough, namely the idea that the guiding structure of the psyche is provided by the specious present, its organization and its parameterization.

Acknowledgment

Thanks to Liliana Albertazzi.

References

Albertazzi, L. (1994). The psychological whole: 1. The temporal parts of presentation. *Axiomathes, 5*(1), 145-175.

Albertazzi, L. (2001a). Vittorio Benussi (1878-1927). In L. Albertazzi, D. Jacquette, & R. Poli (Eds.), *The school of Alexius Meinong* (pp. 95-129). Aldershot: Ashgate.

Albertazzi, L. (2001b). The legacy of the Graz psychologists. In L. Albertazzi, D. Jacquette, & R. Poli (Eds.), *The school of Alexius Meinong* (pp. 315-339). Aldershot: Ashgate.

Albertazzi, L. (Ed.). (2001c). *Early European contributors to cognitive science*. Dordrecht: Kluwer.

Albertazzi, L. (2001d). Presentational primitives: Parts, wholes and psychophysics. In L. Albertazzi (Ed.), *Early European contributors to cognitive science* (pp. 29-60). Dordrecht: Kluwer.

Albertazzi, L. (2003). From Kanizsa back to Benussi: Varieties of intentional reference. *Axiomathes*, *13*(3-4), 239-259.

Albertazzi, L. (2004). Stereokinetic shapes and their shadows. *Perception*, *33*, 1437-1452.

Albertazzi, L. (2006). *Immanent realism: Introduction to Franz Brentano*. Dordrecht: Springer.

Albertazzi, L., Jacquette, D., & Poli, R. (Eds.). (2001). *The school of Alexius Meinong*. Aldershot: Ashgate.

Albertazzi, L., Libardi, M., & Poli, R. (Eds.). (1996). *The school of Franz Brentano*. Dordrecht: Kluwer.

Andersen, P.B., Emmeche, C., Finnemann, N.O., & Christiansen, P.V. (Eds.). (2000). *Downward causation: Minds, bodies and matter*. Aarhus: Aarhus University Press.

Benussi, V. (1913). *Psychologie der Zeitauffassung*. Heidelberg: Winter.

Benussi, V. (1927). *La suggestione e l'ipnosi come mezzi di analisi psichica reale*. Bologna: Zanichelli.

Blitz, D. (1992). *Emergent evolution*. Dordrecht: Kluwer.

Campbell, D.T. (1974). Downward causation in hierarchically organised biological systems. In F.J. Ayala & T. Dobzhansky (Eds.), *Studies in the philosophy of biology* (pp. 179-186). London: Macmillan.

Campbell, D.T. (1990). Levels of organization, downward causation, and the selection-theory approach to evolutionary epistemology. In G. Greenberg & E. Tobach (Eds.), *Theories of the evolution of knowing* (pp. 1-17). Erlbaum.

De Monticelli, R. (2000). *La persona: Apparenza e realtà. testiFenomenologici 1911-1933*. Milano: Raffaello Cortina Editore.

Gnoli, C., & Poli, R. (2004). Levels of reality and levels of representation. *Knowledge Organization*, *31*(3), 151-160.

Hartmann, N. (1935). *Zur grundlegung der ontologie*. Berlin: W. de Gruyter.

Hartmann, N. (1952). *The new ways of ontology*. Chicago.

Herre, H., & Poli, R. (in preparation). *Formal ontology of levels of reality*.

Hill, C.O., & Rosado Haddock, G. (2000). *Husserl or Frege? Meaning, objectivity and mathematics*. Chicago; La Salle: Open Court.

Kanizsa, G. (1979). *Organization in vision*. New York: Praeger.

Kanizsa, G. (1991). *Vedere e pensare*. Bologna, Italy: Il Mulino.

Luhmann, N. (1995). *Social systems*. Stanford, CA: Stanford University Press.

Metzger, W. (1966). *Allgemeine psychologie* (2 vols.). Göttingen: Verlag für Psychologie.

Musatti, C. (1964). *Condizioni dell'esperienza e fondazione della psicologia*. Firenze, Italy: Editrice Universitaria.

Pattee, H.H. (1973). *Hierarchy theory*. New York: Braziller.

Poli, R. (1996). Ontology for knowledge organization. In R. Green (Ed.), *Knowledge organization and change* (pp. 313-319). Frankfurt: Indeks.

Poli, R. (Ed.). (1997). *In itinere: European cities and the birth of modern scientific philosophy*. Amsterdam: Rodopi (Special issue of the *Poznan Studies in the Philosophy of the Sciences and the Humanities*).

Poli, R. (Ed.). (1998a). *The Brentano puzzle*. Aldershot: Ashgate.

Poli, R. (1998b). Levels. *Axiomathes*, 9(1-2), 197-211.

Poli, R. (1999). The concept of empirical reality between logics and psychology: The proposals of the young Musatti. *Axiomathes*, 10(1-3), 126-162.

Poli, R. (2001a). The basic problem of the theory of levels of reality. *Axiomathes, 12*(3-4), 261-283.

Poli, R. (2001b). *ALWIS: Ontology for knowledge engineers*. Ph.D. Thesis, Utrecht.

Poli, R. (2001c). Foreword. *Axiomathes, 12*(1-2), 5-9.

Poli, R. (2003). Descriptive, formal and formalized ontologies. In D. Fisette (Ed.), *Husserl's logical investigations reconsidered* (pp. 193-210). Dordrecht: Kluwer.

Poli, R., (2006). Levels of reality and the psychological stratum. *Revue Internationale de Philosophie* (special issue on ontology), 165-182.

Rosen, R. (1985). *Anticipatory systems: Philosophical, mathematical and methodological foundations*. Pergamon Press.

Smith, B.C. (1996). *On the origin of objects*. Cambridge, MA: MIT Press.

Spiegelberg, H. (1984). *The phenomenological movement* (3rd revised and enlarged ed.). The Hague: Nijhoff.

Talmy, L. (2003). The windowing of attention in language. In L. Talmy (Ed.), *Toward a cognitive semantics* (vol. 1, 257-309). Cambridge MA: The MIT Press.

Thinès, G. (1977). *Phenomenology and the science of behaviour: An historical and epistemological approach*. London: Allen and Unwin.

Werkmeister, W. (1990). *Nicolai Hartmann's new ontology*. Tallahassee: Florida State University.

Endnotes

[1]   Albertazzi, Libardi, and Poli (1996), Poli (1997, 1998), Albertazzi, Jacquette, and Poli (2001), and Albertazzi (2006).

[2]   However, see Albertazzi, 2001c and 2004.

[3]   Chisholm's possibly being the main source of confusion.

[4]   One of the widest accepted falsities — particularly widespread within analytic philosophers — concerns the Husserl-Frege connections. See Hill and Rosado Haddock (2000).

5   Two aspects are worth mentioning. First, the apparently unbelievable fact that a number of experimental results have been forgotten, among others those concerning the structure of the specious present. Secondly, the dim awareness of the dialectic internal to the school. Most contemporary psychologists are poorly, if at all, aware of the differences distinguishing the Berlin (Köhler, Koffka, Wertheimer) from the Graz (Meinong, Benussi, Ameseder) versions of Gestaltism. Furthermore, a proper reconstruction of the richness of the period should take into consideration a number of other partially close but nevertheless different schools, notably the *Ganzheitpsychologie* of Sander, Volkelt, and Krüger, the *Denkpsychologie* of Külpe and Bühler, and the *produktive Denken* psychology of Selz. Only tiny fragments of this overwhelming richness are available to English reading scholars.

6   Hartmann wasn't a pupil of Brentano; therefore, he pertains more to the phenomenological movement at large than to the School of Brentano. See Spiegelberg (1984, Ch. VI). On Hartmann, see Werkmeister (1990).

7   See Albertazzi (2001)a for a well documented reconstruction of Benussi's work and results.

8   Thinès (1977).

9   Often termed *levels of description*. In order to avoid overlapping with the concept of *description* occurring in the second dichotomy, the expression *levels of interpretation* will be interpreted as referring to the epistemological interpretation of level, as opposed to their ontological interpretation.

10   For an outline of my views on the relationship between epistemology and ontology, see Poli (2001c); for a general presentation of my views on levels, see Poli (1998, 2001a, 2001b, 2003, 2006), Gnoli and Poli (2004), Herre and Poli (in preparation).

11   Talmy (2003).

12   Dimensions of reality grounded on the interaction between subject and object or between subjects require a more sophisticated framework. The chapters on the psychological and the social strata provide required details.

13   Two further specifications deserve to be added. First, besides real being, ideal being too should be taken into account. Second, "object" is taken as the most general term for bearers of properties. So understood, the category of object comprises things, processes, stuffs, states of affairs and any other particular required by analysis of real and ideal items.

14   Providing that *agency* is properly neutralized.

15   This shows that a properly generalized theory of causation is still being awaited.

16   Smith (1996).

17   The belief is usually buried under the apparently neutral move of taking synthesis as the inverse of analysis, the idea being that ASx = SAx. See Rosen (1985).

18   It may be worth noting that the theory of levels may provide guidance to the teaching of sciences and their interrelationships.

19   The psychological level offers special problems, which we will shortly address. We will as well see that there are reasons for adopting a distinction among levels

different from the common-sense one given in the text. However, the difference is immaterial for the point under discussion.

[20]   Different choices may result that are more or less suitable from a modeling perspective.

[21]   A determination can be extensive or intensive in either time or space. Nothing prevents determinations being, say, extensive in space and intensive in time, or vice versa (see Poli, 2001b, chap. 6).

[22]   *Material* as used in this sentence should be taken, not as opposed to formal but to psychological and social, according to a distinction I will shortly provide.

[23]   Examples show that the relation of inheritance is rather complex and may be tuned by various structures. Aristotle glimpsed the problem through his theory of the *propria*.

[24]   Cf. Hartmann (1935). The simplified version presented in Hartmann (1952) is worth reading as well. For an introduction to Hartmann, cf. Werkmeister (1990) and the essays collected in the special issue of *Axiomathes* (2001, *12*(3-4)). Even if my vision is substantially different from Hartmann's, his contribution is an obligatory starting point for anybody interested in the problem of levels of reality.

[25]   It should go without saying that such categorial analysis must be produced by physicists, not by philosophers.

[26]   This is only the simplest feature. A less cursory description would require discussing a number of other features, notably the possibility that not all the lower level categories should be lifted to the higher order level and that in the two contexts the same category may play a different role because it interacts with different groups of level categories.

[27]   It would be better to say *biological*. However, we will shortly see that from a categorial viewpoint, the connection holds between the psychological and the material strata of reality, biology being included in the latter.

[28]   Luhmann (1984). I have defended the latter scheme in a number of papers, notably in Poli (2001b).

[29]   The two last terms are not Stein's.

[30]   Albertazzi (2001a, 110-111).

[31]   Albertazzi (2001a, 111).

[32]   On the School of Meinong see the essays collected in Albertazzi, Jacquette and Poli (2001).

[33]   Albertazzi (1994, 161).

[34]   Visual perceptions require a slightly different wording. See Albertazzi (2003).

[35]   Albertazzi (2001a, 115).

[36]   Albertazzi (2001a, 116).

[37]   Musatti (1964, 37).

[38]   Kanizsa (1979).

[39]   Benussi (1925, 30 and 32).

40   Musatti (1964, 38).

41   Musatti (1964, 39).

42   Albertazzi (2001b, 327).

43   Kanizsa (1991, 19).

44   Kanizsa (1979).

45   Benussi (1913).

46   Musatti (1964, 16-19).

47   Musatti (1964, 99-102). For a wider analysis see Poli (1999).

48   For a relevant analysis see Albertazzi (2003).

49   Poli (2006).

50   De Monticelli (2000).

51   It amounts to saying that egological and non egological acts are to be understood as sub-strata of the psychological stratum. According to our definition of complexity provided in Poli (2006), the psychological stratum has at least a Type[1,1] form of complexity and therefore is more complex than the material stratum.

52   The distinction between the two cases looks like the difference between prokaryotes and eukaryotes. The main difference between them is that the genome of the latter is embedded within the cell's nucleous. The evolution of complex organisms depends precisely on this particular constraint. Similarly, the evolution of complex minds depends on constraining psychological activitiy within the structure of the specious present.

53   The Kanizsa's triangle given in Figure 4 is a perfect exemplification of the former claim; any case of masking fits well with the latter case.

54   Metzger (1966, 70).

55   Albertazzi (2001a, 119).

56   Benussi (1927).

57   It is worth mentioning that the School of Graz that flourished around Meinong developed two interrelated categorial and experimental frameworks called the theory of production and the theory of objects. The former analysed psychic acts, the latter objects, interpreted as act correlates. In this paper I have sketched only a tiny fragment of the theory of production and said almost nothing of the theory of objects. For a first reconstruction of the School of Meinong, see Albertazzi, Jacquette, and Poli (2001).

About the Authors

Angelo Loula is an assistant professor in informatics with the Department of Exact Sciences (DEXA), State University of Feira de Santana (UEFS) and a PhD student in the Department of Computer Engineering and Industrial Automation (DCA), School of Electrical and Computer Engineering (FEEC), State University of Campinas (UNICAMP). He earned his MSc in electrical engineering from FEEC, his BSc in electrical engineering from the Federal University of Bahia, and a technologist degree in computing from Ruy Barbosa Faculty. He is the leader of the Group for Basic and Applied Research in Intelligent Systems at UEFS. He is also a member of the Computational Semiotics Group and research coordinator of the Group for Research on Artificial Cognition, both at UNICAMP. His research interests include artificial cognition, semiotic and meaning processes, communication, language evolution and acquisition, artificial life, embodied and situated cognition.

Ricardo Gudwin is an associate professor with the Department of Computer Engineering and Industrial Automation (DCA), Faculty of Electrical and Computer Engineering (FEEC), State University of Campinas (UNICAMP). He earned a BS in 1989, an MS in 1992 and a PhD in 1996, all of them in electrical engineering from the FEEC-UNICAMP. His current research interests include cognitive science, artificial cognition, artificial thinking, the study of intelligence and intelligent systems, intelligent agents, semiotics and computational semiotics. He is the head of the Computational Semiotics Group (http://www.dca.fee.unicamp.br/projects/semiotics) and a scientific member / director of the Group for Research on Artificial Cognition (http://www.dca.fee.unicamp.br/projects/artcog) both at DCA-FEEC-UNICAMP. He is also a member of the board of governors of SEE - Semiotics-Evolution-Energy Virtual Institute in Toronto, Canada, and member of the editorial board of the *On Line Journal for Semiotics, Evolution, Energy Development* (SEE Virtual Institute). Besides that, he is the editor-in-chief of the journal *Controle & Automação* (Brazilian Society for Automatics (SBA)).

João Queiroz (PhD, communication and semiotics) is currently a post-doc researcher with the Department of Computer Engineering and Industrial Automation (UNICAMP) (supported by State of São Paulo Research Foundation), where he directs the Group for Research on Artificial Cognition (http://www.dca.fee.unicamp.br/projects/artcog/). e is an invited researcher at Federal University of Bahia (UFBA, Graduate Studies Program in History, Philosophy, and Science Teaching; Graduate Studies Program in Ecology and Biomonitoring). He is a member of the Cognitive Science Society and of the International Association for Semiotic Studies. He was a visiting scholar (November 1997-June 1998) at the Research Center for Language and Semiotic Studies (Bloomington, Indiana University), a visiting researcher (October-December 1999) at the Peirce Edition Project (Indianapolis, IUPUI), and at the Institut de Recherche en Sémiotique, Communication et Education (March-August 2001) (Perpignan, Universite de Perpignan). He was distinguished with the '2000 Mouton de Gruyter d'Or Award' for the article *Notes for a dynamic diagram of Charles Peirce's classifications of signs*. Semiotica 131-1/2, 19-44. His interests include C.S.Peirce's philosophy, biosemiotics and cognitive science.

* * *

Guilherme Bittencourt was born in Porto Alegre, Brazil. His undergraduate studies were in electronic engineering and physics at the Universidade Federal do Rio Grande do Sul (Brazil) and he earned his PhD in computer science at Karlsruhe University (Germany) in 1990. From 1982 to 1995, he worked at Instituto Nacional de Pesquisas Espaciais in São José dos Campos (Brazil). Since 1995 he has been a professor in the Department of Automation and Systems (DAS) of Universidade Federal de Santa Catarina. His research interests include knowledge representation, cognitive modeling and multi-agent systems.

Gerd Doeben-Henisch has been a professor of computer science at the University of Applied Sciences in Frankfurt a.M. (Germany) since March 2002. From 1968 until 1990 he was member of the Jesuit Order working in the realms of theology, philosophy as well as theory of science. During the period between 1990 and 1998 he worked as a scientist at the Ludwig Maximilian University in Munich (Germany) as well as the Institute for New Media in Frankfurt a.M. His specialty topics throughout these years have been cognition, language and computation. He is responsible for the Intelligent Systems Master of the University, is the executive officer for E-Learning and is active in the PlanetEarthSimulator project.

James H. Fetzer, McKnight Professor of Philosophy at the University of Minnesota, Duluth, has published more than 20 books on the philosophy of science and the theoretical foundations of computer science, artificial intelligence and cognitive science.

Among his important contributions to this field are: *Artificial Intelligence: Its Scope and Limits* (1990), *Philosophy and Cognitive Science* (1991; 2nd edition 1996; Portuguese translation 2000) and *Computers and Cognition: why Minds are not Machines* (2001). His latest book is, *The Evolution of Intelligence: Are Humans the only Animals with Minds* (2005).

Maria Eunice Q. Gonzalez received her bachelor's degree in physics and her master's degree in logics and philosophy of science. Her PhD thesis dealt with aspects of the theory of information and the main premises of the theory of self-organization applied to neural networks. Since 1991, she has been one of the coordinators of the research group on cognitive studies at UNESP. In 1995 she founded the Brazilian Society for Cognitive Science and started the first interdisciplinary post-graduation course (master's degree and PhD) in Brazil in the area of philosophy of cognitive science and philosophy of mind.

Patrick Grim is distinguished teaching professor of philosophy at the State University of New York at Stony Brook. He is author of *The Incomplete Universe: Totality, Knowledge, and Truth* (MIT, 1991), co-author of *The Philosophical Computer: Exploratory Essays in Philosophical Computer Modeling* (MIT, 1998) and founding co-editor of over 20 volumes of the *Philosopher's Annual*. Grim's work in philosophical logic and contemporary metaphysics appears in standard philosophical journals; his work in computational modeling has also appeared in scholarly journals in theoretical biology, computer science, linguistics and decision theory.

Willem Haselager has master's degrees in philosophy and psychology and a PhD in the philosophy of psychology. He is an assistant professor in the Department of Artificial Intelligence / Cognitive Science (NICI) at Radboud University, Nijmegen, The Netherlands. For the last five years, he has also been working part-time at the Philosophy Department of UNESP, Marília, SP, Brazil. He is particularly interested in the integration of empirical work (i.e., psychological experiments, computational modeling and robotics) with philosophical issues regarding knowledge and intelligent behavior. His recent research focuses on the embodied embeddedness of cognition (EEC) in relation to the theory of self-organization.

Trina Kokalis has published in *Adaptive Behavior*, *Journal for Experimental and Theoretical Artificial Intelligence*, *Evolution of Communication*, *Minds and Machines* and *World Futures: The Journal of General Evolution*. Her work has been presented in conference papers for the Cognitive Science Society, American Philosophical Association, International Association for Computers and Philosophy, Society for Machines and Mentality and Artificial Life.

Bruce MacLennan has a BS in mathematics (Honors, 1972) from Florida State University and an MS (1974) and PhD (1975) in computer science from Purdue University. He joined

Intel Corporation in 1975 as a senior software engineer, but in 1979 he returned to academia, joining the computer science faculty of the Naval Postgraduate School, Monterey, CA, where he investigated massively parallel computing and artificial intelligence. Since 1987, he has been a member of the computer science faculty of the University of Tennessee, Knoxville. For the last two decades MacLennan's research has focused on novel models of computation intended to better exploit physical processes for computation, and provide new concepts of information representation and processing in natural and artificial systems.

Lorenzo Magnani, Philosopher and Cognitive Scientist, is a professor at the University of Pavia, Italy, and the director of its Computational Philosophy Laboratory. He has taught at the Georgia Institute of Technology and The City University of New York and currently directs international research programs between the EU, USA and China. His book, *Abduction, Reason, and Science* (New York, 2001) has become a well-respected work in the field of human cognition. In 1998, he started a series of international conferences on model-based reasoning (MBR).

Jerusa Marchi was born in São Miguel do Oeste, Brazil. Her undergraduate studies were in computer science at the Universidade Estadual do Oeste do Paraná - UNIOESTE (Brazil). She obtained her master's degree in electrical engineering from the Universidade Federal de Santa Catarina—UFSC (Brazil) in 2001 and her PhD in both electrical engineering from UFSC and computer science from Université Toulouse I, France, in 2006, in the context of a research cooperation agreement between Brazil and France. Her research interests include cognitive robotics, knowledge representation, belief change and planning.

Alexander Mehler studied computational linguistics at Trier University, Germany. From 1994 to 1998 he was head of a research and development department in industry. In 2000 he received his PhD in computational linguistics. From 1998 to 2004 he worked as a scientific assistant in computational linguistics at Trier University. In the winter term 2003/2004 he was Visiting Professor at Karl-Franzens-Universität Graz, Austria. Since April 2004 he has been an assistant professor (Juniorprofessor) at Bielefeld University, Germany. Alexander Mehler is member of several scientific associations. Since 2004 he has been the editor of the *Journal for Computational Linguistics and Language Technology*. His research interests include agent-based simulations of language evolution and cognitive systems, machine learning, text and web mining as well as formal, numerical semantics.

Orazio Miglino is full professor at the University of Naples "Federico II" and holds a research charge at the Institute of Sciences and Technology of Cognition (previously Institute of Psychology) of the National Council of Research of Rome. His research activity is mainly concentrated on cognitive science and artificial life. In particular, his interest is oriented toward construction of formal models based on neural networks and mobile robots that simulate cognitive and adaptive processes of natural beings, such as orientation and spatial navigation.

Leonid Perlovsky is principal research physicist and technical advisor at the Air Force Research Laboratory. Previously, from 1985 to 1999, he served as chief scientist at Nichols Research, a $.5 b high-tech organization, leading corporate research in information science, intelligent systems, neural networks, optimization, sensor fusion and algorithm development. In the past, he has served as professor at Novosibirsk University and New York University. He has participated as a principal in commercial startups developing tools for text understanding, biotechnology and financial predictions. He has published about 50 papers in refereed scientific journals and about 230 papers in conferences, delivered invited keynote plenary talks, tutorial courses and authored a book, *Neural Networks and Intellect: Model-based Concepts* (Oxford University Press, 2001) (currently in the third printing). Dr. Perlovsky received several best paper awards and the IEEE Award of "Distinguished Member." He organizes IEEE conferences, serves as chair for the IEEE Boston Computational Intelligence Chapter, as editor-at-large for *Natural Computations* and as editor-in-chief for *Physics of Life Reviews*.

Roberto Poli (BA, Honors, sociology; PhD, philosophy, Utrecht) teaches philosophy at the University of Trento (Italy). His research interests include ontology, in both its traditional philosophical understanding and the new, computer-oriented understanding, and the so-called Central-European philosophy — interpreted as a repository of conceptual tools for the advancement of contemporary science. He is currently working on the elaboration of the general categorical framework for an ontology both philosophically robust and well suited for applications in the field of information sciences. Poli is editor-in-chief of *Axiomathes* (Springer), a peer-reviewed academic journal devoted to the study of ontology and cognitive systems, and member of the board of directors of the Mitteleuropa Foundation (www.mitteleuropafoundation.it), a research centre in ontology and cognitive analysis.

Michela Ponticorvo studied psychology at the Second University of Naples (graduation (2002), Habilitation (2004)). She is currently a PhD student in the psychology of programming and artificial intelligence at the University of Calabria. Her research interest is mainly in the interdisciplinary study of brain, behaviour and evolution through computational models ranging from artificial intelligence (artificial life, evolutionary robotics, artificial neural networks and genetic algorithms) to sychology: sensory-motor co-ordination and spatial orientation.

Alexander Riegler obtained a PhD in artificial intelligence and cognitive science in 1995 from the Vienna University of Technology on the basis of a dissertation about constructivist artificial life. His research interests include cognitive science, philosophy of science and biological and cognitive complexity. His previous affiliations include the Departments of theoretical biology (University of Vienna) and computer science (University of Zurich). Since 1998, he has been a research fellow at the interdisciplinary center Leo Apostel at the Free University in Brussels.

Paul Vogt received an MSc in cognitive science and engineering (currently artificial intelligence) in 1997 from the University of Groningen (NL). For this degree, he did his thesis work at the AI Lab of the Vrije Universiteit Brussel in Belgium, where he also received his PhD on the thesis *Lexicon Grounding in Mobile Robots*. He was a Marie Curie research fellow at the Language Evolution and Computation research unit at the University of Edinburgh (UK), until early 2006, where he is still affiliated as a visiting researcher. Currently, Vogt is a research fellow at the Induction of Linguistic Knowledge group at Tilburg University (NL). His research focuses on computational models of language evolution and acquisition, particularly on those aspects related to symbol grounding and cultural transmission.

Richard Walker has been active for many years in *Artificial Intelligence* and *Artificial Life*. In 2005 he was visiting professor at the Joint Cultural Research Centre on "Media and Cultural Communication," managed by the Universities of Aachen, Bonn, Cologne and Bochum. He is a member of the editorial board of *Cognitive Processing*. From 1999 to 2003 he was a lecturer on the faculty of psychology at Università di Napoli II, teaching artificial intelligence. In 2000 he founded Xiwrite (www.xiwrite.com), a research consultancy firm which provides support services and consultancies to companies and universities engaged in international collaborative research.

Index

A

abduction 328, 334
abductive reasoning 328
absence of embodiment 278
absolute and relational theories of time 367
abstract propositional symbol 33
abstract propositions 33
act 260, 261, 359
active machine 337
active mental model 151
actual model 328
adaptation 112
adaptation of life 110
aesthetic emotions 73, 92
aesthetics 84
agency 360
AI robotics 240
Akaike information criterion 77
alignment in communication 143, 153
ambiguity 270
ambiguous 274
Amodal 371
anthropomorphic 11
anthropomorphic ascription 16
anthropomorphizations 6
anticipate 9

anticipate sequences 9
anticipatory 8
apparatus 14
Aristotelian logic 108
artificial agent 141
artificial agent community 141
artificial apparatus 349
artificial cognition model 12
artificial cognition system 328
artificial embodiment 278
artificial intelligence 67, 73, 84, 109, 141, 328
artificial neural network (ANN) 261
artificial organic creatures 238
artificial organism 233
artificiality of the body 242
assimilative 371
assimilative element 372
associative process 372
attention 200
automatic translation 108
autonomous agent 110
autonomous robotics 278, 279
autopoiesis 31, 244
autopoiesis theory 28
autopoietic activity 37
axiomatized models (A-models) 112

S

S(N)R-model 129
schematic knowledge 151
schematism 332
schematization 150
scientific framework 111
second intermezzo 373
selected aphorisms 30
self 90
self-organization 140, 157, 187, 247
self-regulation 140
semantic diversification 164
semantic similarity 148
semantic Web topology 18
semantically blind 6
semantics 12, 142, 254, 345
semiosis process 128
semiotic preference order 164
semiotic symbol 180, 183, 196, 199
semiotic triangle 180
sensation 345
sense relations 147
sensory-motor control 341
set theoretical language 112
sharing semiotic symbols 186
sign family 120
sign process 265
sign processing 141, 143
sign systems 141
sign vehicle 120
signal subset 85
signals 275
signification 265
signs 118, 264
simple learning rule 266
simple robot 35
simulated data 160
simulation 108, 141, 257
simulation model 140, 156
simulation validity 140
simultaneous mental contemporaneity 371
single agent 147
single processing layer 76
situated experiments 275
situation concepts 198
situational systems 4

small world 155
smile 80
SNPR 113, 120
SNR-domain 113
SNR-model 113
social network 143, 155, 157
social setting 339
soft constraint 144
somatic marker 34
space 31
spatial cognition 210, 233
species 113
specious present 369
speech 339
speech community 157, 164
SPR-model 113
SR-domain 113
SR-model 113
start object 119
state transition table 261
statistical moment 160
steady state 146
stigmergy 279
still present 371
stim maps 115
stimulus 118
stimulus object 119
stimulus-response 4, 211
stratification 143
stratified constraint network 146
stratified constraint satisfaction network 140
stream of consciousness 369
strong learning 114
structural meaning 147
structure 31, 33
structure modelling 160
structure of the mind 69
subjective phenomenal consciousness 129
subjective states 117
sublime 83, 93
substance 363
suppressed communication 266
symbol 265
symbol grounding 177, 179, 201, 275
symbolic AI 109